Text smart

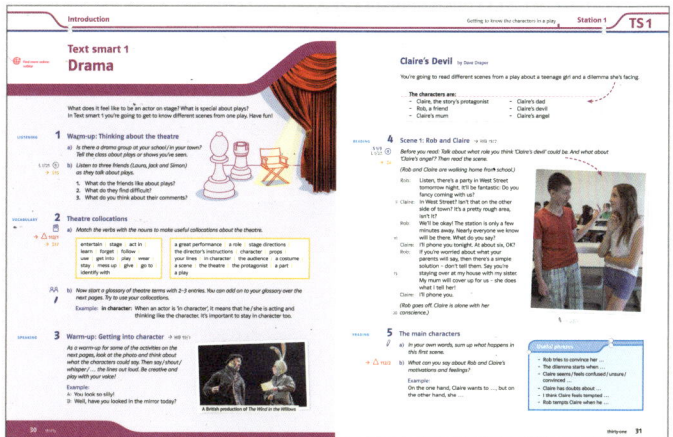

Auf den *Text smart*-Seiten lernst du, wie du mit authentischen Texten (z. B. Sachtexten, Werbetexten) umgehst und sie im Anschluss für deine eigenen Arbeiten nutzen kannst.

Across cultures

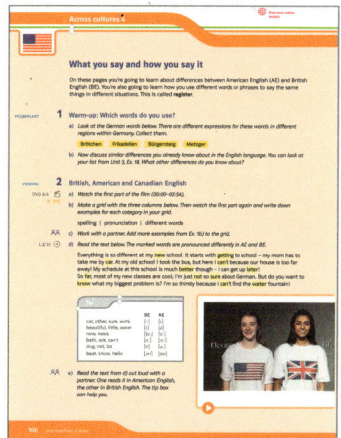

Vergleiche auf diesen Seiten deinen Alltag mit der Alltagskultur Großbritanniens und der USA und lerne, mit verschiedenen Begegnungssituationen umzugehen.

Diff pool

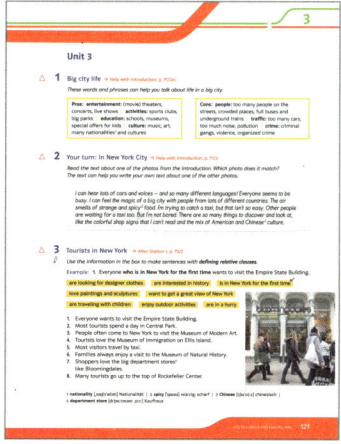

Skills

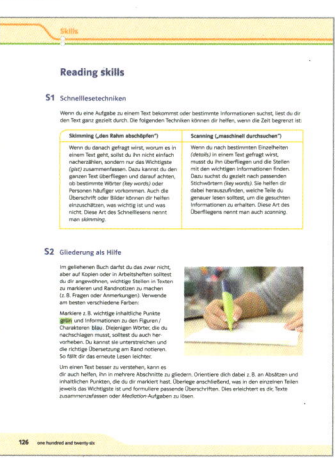

Grammar, Vocabulary

Im hinteren Buchteil stehen dir hilfreiche Anhänge zur Verfügung. Achte auf die Verweise in den Units, die dir sagen, in welchem Anhang du nachschlagen kannst.

Symbole

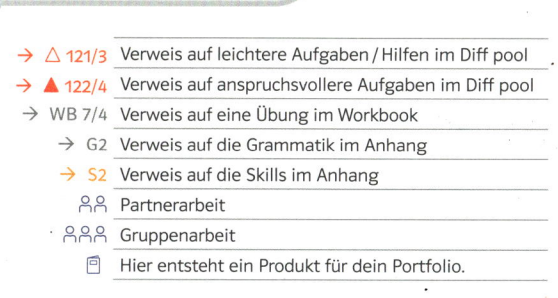

→ △ 121/3 Verweis auf leichtere Aufgaben / Hilfen im Diff pool
→ ▲ 122/4 Verweis auf anspruchsvollere Aufgaben im Diff pool
→ WB 7/4 Verweis auf eine Übung im Workbook
→ G2 Verweis auf die Grammatik im Anhang
→ S2 Verweis auf die Skills im Anhang
👥 Partnerarbeit
👥👥 Gruppenarbeit
📖 Hier entsteht ein Produkt für dein Portfolio.

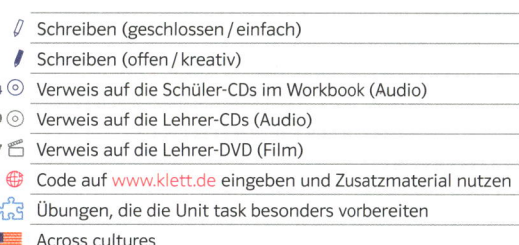

✏ Schreiben (geschlossen / einfach)
✏ Schreiben (offen / kreativ)
S1/14 ◉ Verweis auf die Schüler-CDs im Workbook (Audio)
L1/19 ◉ Verweis auf die Lehrer-CDs (Audio)
DVD 3/7 🎞 Verweis auf die Lehrer-DVD (Film)
🌐 Code auf www.klett.de eingeben und Zusatzmaterial nutzen
🧩 Übungen, die die Unit task besonders vorbereiten
🇬🇧🇺🇸 Across cultures

Green Line 4 G9 für Klasse 8 an Gymnasien

Herausgeber: Prof. Harald Weisshaar, Bisingen

Autorinnen und Autoren: Jennifer Baer-Engel, Göppingen; Carolyn Jones, Beckenham; Jon Marks, Ventnor; Harald Weisshaar, Bisingen; Alison Wooder, Ventnor sowie Cornelia Kaminski, Fulda; Elise Köhler-Davidson, Exeter; Katja Krey, Reutlingen; Bernd Wick, Neckartenzlingen

Beratung: Paul Dennis, Lahnstein; Cornelia Kaminski, Fulda; Nilgül Karabulut, Aachen; Hartmut Klose, Seevetal; Antje Körber, Merseburg; Jörg Nieswand, Berlin; Jörg Schulze, Dresden

---

Zusätzliche Informationen in der Lehrerfassung:

Produktiver Lernwortschatz   **Rezeptiver Wortschatz**   **Neue Grammatik**

△ → ▲ → **Help with/Instead of/After . . .:** Verweis auf unterstützende/alternative/weiterführende Aufgaben im Diff pool des Schülerbuchs für leistungsschwächere bzw. -stärkere Schüler/innen.

HA: Vorschlag zur Hausaufgabe

Transfer: Einbeziehung der Lebenswelt der Schüler/innen

Folie 1: Hier können Sie Folie 1 des Folienordners einsetzen.

WB 4/1: Hier können Sie im Workbook Seite 4, Aufgabe 1 einsetzen.

KV 1: Hier können Sie Kopiervorlage 1 des Lehrerbands einsetzen.

Voc.: Hier sind Verweise auf Wortschatzhilfen im Schülerbuch und Workbook (WB) angegeben.

Lösung: Hier finden Sie Lösungen zu den geschlossenen Aufgaben.

---

1. Auflage   1 6 5 4 3 2 | 2023 22 21 20 19

Alle Drucke dieser Auflage sind unverändert und können im Unterricht nebeneinander verwendet werden.
Die letzte Zahl bezeichnet das Jahr des Druckes.

Redaktion: Michael Mattison; Anette Mohamud; Martina Reckart; Lektorat editoria: Cornelia Schaller, Fellbach sowie für die Lehrerfassung: Juliane Rebstock; Gaby Bauer-Negenborn, Weßling
Herstellung: Anita Bauch; Anne Leibbrand; Cristina Dunu

Gestaltung: Petra Michel, Essen
Umschlaggestaltung: know idea, Freiburg; Koma Amok, Stuttgart
Illustrationen: Peer Kramer, Düsseldorf; jani lunablau, Barcelona sowie Christian Dekelver, Weinstadt *(Karten)*; Denise Drews, Zürich *(Time line)*
Satz: Satzkiste GmbH, Stuttgart, Fotosatz Kaufmann, Stuttgart
Reproduktion: Schwaben-Repro, Stuttgart
Druck: Mohn Media Mohndruck GmbH, Gütersloh

Printed in Germany
ISBN 978-3-12-854242-3

Green Line 4 G9

Lehrerausgabe

von
Jennifer Baer-Engel
Carolyn Jones
Jon Marks
Harald Weisshaar
Alison Wooder
Cornelia Kaminski
Elise Köhler-Davidson
Katja Krey
Bernd Wick

herausgegeben von
Harald Weisshaar

Ernst Klett Verlag
Stuttgart · Leipzig

Inhalt

Inhalt

Inhalt

Legende

🧩 Kompetenzaufgabe
🇬🇧 *Across cultures*
🇺🇸 *Across cultures*
‹ › fakultativ

Die in diesem Band aufbereiteten Inhalte stellen ein Angebot dar; sie sind nicht obligatorisch durchzunehmen. Maßgeblich für die Auswahl der Texte und Übungen ist der Lehrplan Ihres Bundeslandes bzw. Ihr schulinternes Curriculum.

Find more online:
8ak7n4

Unit 1
On the move

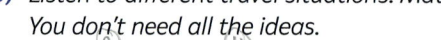

Folie 3/22: Bildbeschreibung, Reaktivierung von Vorwissen
WB 2/1 Vocabulary (travelling)

SPEAKING

1 **Reasons for travelling** → WB 2/1

Voc.: Holiday accommodation, WB (Word bank), p. 10

a) *Look at the photos above. What are the people doing? What might they be thinking?*

b) *Why do you think these people are travelling? Share your ideas in class. The words and phrases in the box can help you.*

c) *Collect more reasons for travelling.*

> **Word bank**
>
> class trip | family holiday | have fun | escape from hard life | get to know other cultures | hope for a better future | visit family | learn a <u>foreign</u> language | have a break | meet exchange partners

---

LISTENING **2** **Travel situations** KV 1: Travel situations

a) *What can happen when you're travelling to another country? Share your ideas in class.*

L 1/1–5 ◉

🖉

→ S15

S15 Hörverstehen üben

b) *Listen to different travel situations. Match the speakers with the problems they're talking about. You don't need all the ideas.*

feel <u>seasick</u> | get lost | have too much <u>luggage</u> | have communication problems

be <u>afraid of</u> flying | lose money | forget tickets | miss train / <u>plane</u>

B

C

D

In Unit 1 you learn

… how to talk about travel experiences and reasons for <u>travelling</u>. You learn:

- how to <u>report</u> what people have said
- how to report questions, <u>commands</u> and <u>requests</u>
- words and phrases for talking about travel

WB 2/2 Vocabulary (crossword)
WB 2/3 Vocabulary (word pairs)

VOCABULARY **3** Travel words → WB 2/2–3

→ S17

S17 Vokabeln ordnen und strukturieren

a) *Make a grid and sort the words into the following categories:*

transport | places | people | things you need

b) *Can you think of more travel words? Add them to the grid.*

Transfer HA

c) *Your turn: Choose five of the words from your grid and use them to write a short text about your last holiday or trip.*

Example: Sometimes we go by car to another town to visit my grandparents. During our last holiday we went by plane to … We left for the airport very early in the morning …

departure lounge | by bike / car / bus | passport | boarding card | check-in desk | on foot | visa | passenger | flight attendant | train station | by train / plane | customs | suitcase | public transport | tickets | guide | airport | by boat / ferry / ship | tourist | passport control | arrivals hall | luggage | foreign currency | duty-free shop

SPEAKING **4** Your turn: Your travel plan

KV 13: Working with vocabulary (Wortschatz Unit 1)

Transfer
→ △ 108/1

What type of travelling would you like to do when you're older? Where would you like to go? Get into groups of three and share your ideas. Then tell the class how your plans are similar or different.

108/1 Your turn: Your travel plans
△ → Instead of …

L 1/6 ◉ **You told us there was free wifi!**

My first trip away from home was really exciting, and I tried to enjoy every minute of it. But my best friend Steve is completely different. I'll tell you why.

5   On the way to France with our <u>athletics</u> team, Steve and I were out on the top deck of the ferry. It was a nice, quiet moment. Then Steve's phone rang.

"YEAH?" he said, in his big loud special 10 telephone voice. "No, sorry, I didn't have time. Uh huh … Uh huh … WHAAAT?! Ha ha ha! OK, see you!"

"Who was that?" I asked.

"It was my friend Eddie," Steve answered. 15 "He said he was at the leisure centre with Amarjit. He told me they were having crisps and drinks from the <u>vending machine</u>."

"Wow," I said. "That's so much more interesting than a ferry trip to another country. 20 Why did you go 'WHAAAT'?"

"Er … oh yeah. Eddie said Amarjit had just spilt his drink over his crisps."

"Amarjit's crisps or Eddie's crisps?"

"Oh, I've forgotten. Hang on, I'll send them 25 a message to ask."

It's only an hour from Dover to the French <u>coast</u>, and we could already see the houses of Calais. French houses often have <u>shutters</u> at the windows. British houses never have 30 shutters. I love things that remind me I'm in a different country.

Ms Woodruff, the coach, came out of a door and onto the deck.

"It's time to get back on the coach," she said. Then she saw that Steve was still busy 35 with his phone.

"I promised your parents I wouldn't let you use your phone in France!" she said. "You know it's really expensive to use it <u>abroad</u>!"

"But we aren't in France yet," said Steve. 40 "We're still on the ferry."

"Where do you think the signal is coming from?" she said.

With a big <u>groan</u> Steve gave her his phone.

"Can I have it back when we arrive? You told 45 us there was free wifi at the <u>hostel</u>. My parents said I could use my phone over wifi. They did. Honest!"

"Really? They told *me* you were an <u>addict</u>, and they thought you needed a break from 50 your smartphone. You can have your phone for half an hour in the evenings, OK?"

"This is going to be an awful trip," <u>muttered</u> Steve.

"This is going to be a great trip," I thought. 55

WB 3/4 Listening (French hostel)

READING   **1**   **Understanding the text** → WB 3/4

→ S1–3

S1 Schnelllesetechniken
S2 Gliederung als Hilfe
S3 Umgang mit neuen
     Wörtern

Transfer

a) *What do the narrator and Steve like / not like about the trip? Make a grid and write down what the text tells you about the two characters.*

b) *What does the coach decide about Steve's smartphone? Do you agree with her decision? Explain why or why not.*

c) *Your turn: Can you identify more with Steve or with the narrator? Say what's important for you when you travel.*

KV 2: Working with language
WB 3/5 Language (indirect speech)

LANGUAGE **2** From direct to **indirect speech** → WB 3/5 → G1

→ △ 108/2
→ ▲ 109/3

a) *The following sentences are in the text, but in* indirect *speech. Copy the grid. Write down the sentences in* direct speech. *Then add the sentences in indirect speech from the text. Underline the words that change from direct to indirect speech.*

/2 Eating on board
  ferry
→ After …

/3 Trips without parents
→ After …

Direct speech	Indirect speech
1. Eddie: **I'm** at the leisure centre with Amarjit.	Eddie said **he was** at the leisure centre with Amarjit.

ung: c) 1. *Steve said he*
n't had time. 2. *Steve said*
had forgotten. He would
d them a message
sk. 3. *Ms Woodruff said it*
s time to get back on the
ch. 4. *Steve said they*
ren't in France yet. They
re still on the ferry. 5. *The*
ch said Steve could have
phone for half an hour in
evenings.

2. "We're having crisps and drinks from the vending machine."   3. "Amarjit has just spilled his drink over my crisps."   4. "I won't let Steve use his phone in France."   5. "There's free wifi at the hostel."   6. "You can use your phone over wifi."   7. "Steve is an addict. He needs a break from his smartphone."

b) *How do tenses change when you report what someone has said? Look at the sentences from a) and write down the verb forms.*

He told me they were … /
said … / I promised … /
told us … / They thought

Example: I'm → he was   simple present → simple past

c) *Read these sentences from the text. Report what the people say. Use* **indirect speech**.

1. Steve: I didn't have time.   2. Steve: I've forgotten. I'll send them a message to ask.
3. Ms Woodruff: It's time to get back on the coach.   4. Steve: We aren't in France yet. We're still on the ferry.   5. Coach: You can have your phone for half an hour in the evenings.

re verbs: *shout, underline,*
te, report, guess, suppose,
sper, add, …

d) *Which verbs are used to* underline *indirect speech in the text? Can you think of more verbs? Make a list.*

Example: He **told** me they were ….

KV 3: Reporting what people have said
WB 3/6 Language (post)
WB 4/7 Language (verb forms)
WB 4/8 Vocabulary (French food)

LANGUAGE **3** Steve's latest post → WB 3/6, 4/7–8 → G2

You're a friend of Steve's. While he was in France with his athletics team, he wrote this post. A few days later, you tell a friend about it. Look at the sentences with the words in green. *Report them to your friend. Change the words in* green *to the words below. Then explain why you need to do this.*

ung: *… That day they*
d gone into a little town.
ve thought that it had all
n fantastic there – apart
m the food! He said the
y before they had had
nd of soup with lots of
bs and garlic in it. That
ning they had had a
rger au cheval'. The next
y there was an event, he
te.

You need to change
se words when you report
mething on a different day
(in a different place) than
en (or where) it was said.

Start like this: Steve wrote a post a few days ago. He said that **he was having** a really good time **there**. …

that   there (2x)   that day   the next day   the day before

Just a quick post. (I'm only allowed half an hour on my phone!) 😣 You won't believe it. I'm having a really good time here. Today we went into a cute little town. I thought it was a holiday because all the shops were closed. Then I found out that French shops close for lunch! I think lunch is a big deal in France. Anyway, it's all been *fantastique* here. Well, apart from the food! Yesterday we had a kind of soup with lots of herbs and garlic in it. Ugh! But I guess that's typical of French cooking.
This evening we had 'burger au cheval'. I thought that meant 'burger in the style of a town called Cheval' but then I realised that it was MADE OF HORSE! Some people just ate the chips and salad, but I thought, "Well, why not finish it?" To be fair, it tasted OK. Got to go and get some sleep now. The event starts tomorrow. *A bientôt!*

SPEAKING **4** **Role play: Around the world**

→ △ 109/4
→ S11

109/4 What did she say?
△ → Instead of …
S11 Gespräche führen

a) A: *You're a film star. For your latest film, you act in some amazing places around the world. First make notes about where you are now, what you did last week, and what you're going to do next.*
B: *You're a magazine reporter who wants to interview the film star. You're going to call him / her and ask about his / her journey. First make notes about the questions you're going to ask. After the role play, report to the class what A told you. Just report the most important information!*

Start like this: I interviewed … He / she said he / she was ….

b) *Now change roles: B is the film star and A is the reporter.*

WRITING **5** **What happened?** → WB 5/9–10, 6/11

WB 5/9 Writing (travel blog)
WB 5/10 Mediation (hostel problems)
WB 6/11 Speaking (conversation)

→ △ 109/5

109/5 What happened?
△ → Help with …

a) *The Jones family had some problems during their holiday. Now their friends want to know about everything that went wrong. Look at the pictures and write down what they tell their friends.*

→ △ 109/6

Transfer
109/6 Travel situations
△ → Help with …

b) *Your turn: Think of a funny, scary or embarrassing situation which you experienced during your last holiday or on a trip. Tell your partner about it. Try to make it as interesting as possible.*

LISTENING **6** ⟨ **A song: Island in the sun** ⟩ Weezer

KV 4: ⟨A song: Island in the sun⟩

L 1/8 ◉
→ S15

S15 Hörverstehen üben

When you're on a holiday
You can't find the words to say
All the things that come to you
And I wanna feel it too

On an island in the sun
We'll be playing and having fun
And it makes me feel so fine
I can't control my brain

When you're on a golden sea
You don't need no memory
Just a place to call your own
As we drift into the zone

On an island in the sun
…

We'll run away together
We'll spend some time forever
We'll never feel bad any more

a) *Listen to the song. Which words / phrases tell you how the main character feels?*

b) *Write an extra verse for the song. Think of words that rhyme first.*

Start like this: When you're on a lonely beach … / When you're feeling really cool …

L 1/9 ◉ **Idiot nephew?**

Rafiq: Did I tell you about my trip to
Bangladesh last month?

Anya: No, you didn't. How was it?

Rafiq: Not bad, thanks, <u>although</u> it
5   didn't start very well.

Anya: What happened?

Rafiq: At passport control, <u>the man</u>
<u>asked me what the purpose</u>
<u>of my visit was.</u> I was really
10   ⟨surprised⟩, and I just couldn't
think of an answer. <u>So I said I</u>
<u>didn't know.</u>

Anya: Ha! That wasn't very clever.

nervous

Rafiq: I know. I think he thought I
15   ⟨was some kind of idiot. But it
was my parents' idea for me to
visit my family in Bangladesh.⟩
<u>Next the man asked me if I was</u>
<u>travelling with my parents.</u>

c.: At the airport, p. 164

*annoyed
bored*

20 Anya: What did you say?

Rafiq: <u>I told him I was travelling alone.</u> <u>So then</u>
<u>he asked me how old I was.</u>

Anya: And you said you were fourteen, right?

Rafiq: I was really ⟨tired.⟩ I forgot about my
25   last birthday, and I said I was thirteen.
Then he looked at the <u>date of birth</u>
on my passport, and it didn't match.
I think that's when he started to get
<u>suspicious.</u> <u>He told me not to lie to him.</u>

worried →

30 Anya: Oh dear. What happened then?

*scared
alone*

Rafiq: <u>He told me to ⟨go into a side room⟩ to</u>
<u>answer some more questions.</u> I was
⟨lucky I⟩ had the address and phone
number of my uncle and aunt with me.
35   <u>The airport <u>security</u> people called them,</u>
<u>and asked if they knew who I was.</u>

Anya: And they said, "No, we don't have an
idiot nephew who can't even remember
how old he is."

Rafiq: Very funny. <u>Anyway, my uncle said my</u>
40   <u>aunt was waiting for me at the airport,</u>

*em-
barrassed
stupid*

and gave them her mobile number. <u>They</u>
<u>called her, and asked her to come to the</u>
<u>immigration office in the arrivals hall.</u>

relieved

Then a security guard took me there to
45   meet her. When we got there, <u>he asked</u>
<u>her if I really was her nephew.</u>

Anya: Did the security guy believe her?

Rafiq: Yeah. I think he knew she was telling
the <u>⟨truth⟩</u> because she didn't seem
50   worried.

happy

WB 6/12 Listening (passport control)

READING **7** **At passport control** → WB 6/12

→ S1   **a)** *Explain Rafiq's problem when he arrives in Bangladesh.*

Schnelllesetechniken

   b) *How do you think Rafiq felt during his conversation with the man at passport control?*
And how do you think he felt when he left the airport?

     Start like this: Rafiq feels **embarrassed** because the man at passport control thinks that he's
lying to him. He's **worried** …

→ S11

   c) *Role play: Act out the scene between Rafiq and the man at passport control.*

Gespräche führen

LANGUAGE **8** **Find the rule: Indirect questions** → G3

KV 5: Working with language

a) *Look at the following sentences. What do you need to make indirect questions?*
Write down the rules for questions with and without question words.

"What's the purpose of your visit?" → The man **asked me what** the purpose of my visit **was**.
"Are you travelling with your parents?" → He **asked me if** I **was travelling** with my parents.

b) *Find more examples of indirect questions in the text on p. 13. Write them down in your grid from Station 1, Ex. 2, and add the direct questions that go with them.*

LANGUAGE **9** **Rafiq's questions** → WB 6/13

KV 6: Reporting questions, commands and requests
WB 6/13 Language (visa problems)

→ △ 110/7
→ ▲ 110/8

*Before the trip to Bangladesh, Rafiq had a lot of questions for his parents. Turn them into **indirect questions.***

Start like this: Rafiq asked his parents if they ....

110/7 A curious aunt
△ → After ...
110/8 What did he ask?
▲ → After ...

1. "Did you give Aunt Sadia my flight details?"
2. "Do I need a large suitcase for the trip?"
3. "Does the flight take long?"
4. "Don't you want to come too?"
5. "What can I bring them as a present?"
6. "Where will I meet them at the airport?"
7. "Where have you put my passport?"
8. "Why do I have to go at all?"

LANGUAGE **10** **Getting around in Dhaka and London** → WB 7/14 → G4

WB 7/14 Language (security check)

→ △ 110/9
→ ▲ 111/10

a) *Find the sentences that report these commands and requests in the text on p. 13. Write them down in your grid. What do you need to make indirect commands and requests?*

110/9 I told you
to call!
△ → After ...
111/10 Everyone
orders me about ...
▲ → After ...

1. Man at passport control: Don't lie to me!
2. Man at passport control: Go into this side room to answer some more questions.
3. Airport security people: Please come to the immigration office in the arrivals hall.

b) *Rafiq is talking to Masud, his cousin from Dhaka, the capital of Bangladesh. What do they tell each other to do? Use **indirect commands and requests.***

Start like this: Masud tells Rafiq to visit ....

Masud: You must visit the old centre of Dhaka. It's quite small, but it's very interesting.
Rafiq: OK, I will. What's the best way to get there?
Masud: Walk. The traffic here is *very* slow. It's usually quicker to walk.
Rafiq: But it's so hot! I don't want to walk.
Masud: Then take a taxi. They're very cheap, but only if you agree on the price first.
Rafiq: OK, I'll remember that. When you go to London next month, use buses or the Tube. They're *much* cheaper than taxis.
Masud: Thanks for telling me. Send me a transport map when you are back in London. I want to study it before I travel.
Rafiq: You can download one from the internet. Just search for 'Transport for London'. Their website has all the information you need.
Masud: Yes, OK. I'll do that.

Lösung: b) *Masud tells Rafiq to visit the old centre of Dhaka. Masud tells Rafiq to walk because it's quicker. Masud tells Rafiq to take a taxi if he doesn't want to walk. He tells him to agree on the price before he gets in. Rafiq tells Masud to use buses or the Tube in London because they are cheaper than taxis. Masud asks Rafiq to send him a transport map when he is back in London. Rafiq tells Masud to download it from the internet. He tells him to search for 'Transport in London'.*

WB 7/15 Vocabulary (travel words)

LANGUAGE **11** A travel joke → WB 7/15

a) *Read what happened to Jenny, a young business traveller, while she was waiting for her flight to Seattle.*

In the departure lounge, Jenny sat down next to an old man who was looking very nervous.

"Sorry to bother you," he said. "Could I ask your advice about something?"

Jenny took off her headphones. "I'm sorry," she said. "Could you repeat that?"

"I'm going to meet my daughter in Seattle," the old man told her. "I'm worried about the flight because air travel always makes my ears hurt. Can you suggest anything to help?"

"Don't worry. Use chewing gum during take-off and landing. It always helps me."

Seven hours later, the plane landed in Seattle. When Jenny was waiting for her luggage, she saw the old man.

"How was your flight? Did my advice help?"

"Sorry, I didn't catch that," he said. Jenny repeated her question.

"The chewing gum worked very well, thank you," replied the old man, "but … can you tell me how to get it out of my ears?"

b) *At the airport in Seattle, Jenny tells a friend what happened between her and the old man. Write down what she says.*

c) *Make a grid with the following headings:* **asking for information, asking for advice, asking for clarification / repetition** *and* **apologising**. *Find examples for these categories in the text. Can you think of more examples? Write them down in the grid.*

MEDIATION **12** Airport announcements → WB 8/16

KV 7: Airport announcements
WB 8/16 Listening (London Heathrow)

L 1/11

→ S 13, 15

S13 Bearbeitung von *Mediation*-Aufgaben
S15 Hörverstehen üben

...sung: a) Important: 2, 3, 5.
...s about safety regulations
...r all passengers.
...s about the flight's delayed
...arding (at 9:35 instead
...9:15). 5 tells you that
...arding begins and that
...ur flight leaves from Gate
...(instead of Gate 40).

a) *After a holiday in Great Britain, you're waiting with your family at London Heathrow for your flight back to Berlin. You're taking British Airways flight BA0982 at 9:15. While you're waiting, you hear several announcements. First read the skills box. Then listen to the announcements. Which of them are important for you? Take notes. The key words in the box can help you.*

b) *Your parents were busy when the announcements were made. Report the most important points to them in German.*

Mediation skills

Announcements at airports or train stations often contain new words, and background sounds make them difficult to understand. It can help you to focus on important words, e.g. names of people or places, numbers or times, nouns and verbs as key words.

| flight number | boarding time | gate |
| delay / why? | luggage |

SPEAKING **13** Your turn: Travel plans → WB 8/17–18

WB 8/17 Writing (competition)
WB 8/18 Speaking (phone call)

Transfer

→ 111/11

111/11 Your turn: Travel plans
△ → Help with …

Choose a foreign capital you'd like to visit. Use websites in English to find out how to get there by plane. Which airport will you use? How long will the flight take? What would you like to do there? Take turns to tell each other about your plans. Then report to the class what your partner told you.

Passwort AnswerGarden

S1/4–7
L1/13–16 ◉

Where I belong

Folie 3/23: Sicherung des Hör-/Leseverstehens, Förderung interkultureller Kompetenz
KV 8: Questioning the text

SPEAKING

1 Before you read

🧑‍🤝‍🧑 *With your partner, talk about reasons why people might want to leave their country.*

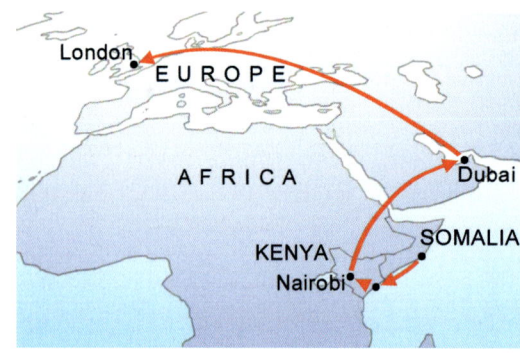

A My father grabbed my arms and looked down at me. "Listen," he said. "You can't do anything here. It's getting harder and harder for people like us who travel around with our
5 animals. Soon we'll have nothing left. If you go to England, you'll be able to help the whole family. And maybe, one day, you can come back and help Somalia too."

A week ago, I'd been nothing but a girl
10 who would lead the same kind of life as her mother. I thought I would have a husband one day, and children to look after and teach. But now, suddenly, I was responsible for my whole family – and the future of my country too.
15 For a moment I was too scared to answer my father. But I knew he wouldn't change his mind. He had chosen me for this task and I had to accept it. "Yes," I said. "Yes, I will."

There was no time for anything else. My
20 father jumped back into his car, turned round quickly and drove off, his face like a mask. I walked down the road to join the man who was taking me away.

> ○ **Stop and think:** ○
> What do you think the narrator's journey will be like?

B The smuggler first took me to Kenya in a boat.
25 Those journeys are very dangerous because the boats are always overloaded and the sea

is full of sharks. Many people have died while they were trying to do what I was doing. But I didn't know that until much later. While we were at sea, I had other things to worry about. 30

It was a little boat, and I was crushed between men I had never seen before. It was the first time I had ever been in a boat, and Uncle didn't tell me that it would rock so badly as the waves smashed against it. I was scared, 35 and I thought every moment that I was going to be sick.

I closed my eyes and repeated the things that Uncle had told me to learn.

My name is Khadija Ahmed Mussa. I'm 40 *thirteen years old. I'm going to England to join my mother and my brother and sisters. My sisters' names are Fowsia, Maryan and Sabra. Fowsia is eleven, Maryan is seven and Sabra is four. And my brother Abdi is fourteen.* 45 I didn't try to imagine their faces or what they were like. They weren't people at all, just words that I had to learn. *My name is Khadija …*

Those hours in the boat were the worst hours of my life. I survived by closing myself 50 away from what was happening, and when we landed in Kenya, I felt like a different person.

C What happened to me is called piggyback. Uncle was giving me a 'piggyback' to England. That was his business, and he did exactly what 55 my father had paid for. Nothing else.

After we had left the boat, we travelled by road and then by plane, and every time we went through a checkpoint Uncle smiled at me. That was part of his routine. When we 60 were through, the smile was put away together with my passport and he ignored me again, even when we were sitting next to each other.

I could have run away when we changed planes in Dubai. He showed me a seat in the 65 airport and told me to sit there until he came back. But where would I have run to? I didn't know anything about that place and I had no

responsible

passport <u>except</u> the one in Uncle's pocket. My
70 <u>father had paid for me to go to England and
that was where I had to go.</u>

I felt cold in the <u>air-conditioning</u>, and I
<u>concentrated</u> on repeating the same words
inside my head. *My name is Khadija …*

> **Stop and think:**
>
> How do you think Britain will
> be different for the narrator?

*desperate
indifferent*

D When we landed in England, the sky was grey,
and it was raining. Not clean, heavy <u>rain</u>, like
the *gu*, but a <u>steady, depressing drizzle</u>. I didn't
see how it was going to make anything grow
because everywhere I looked the <u>ground</u> was
80 <u>covered</u> with <u>concrete</u>. <u>I felt hard and cold</u>,
like that concrete ground. If I hadn't, maybe
everything would have happened differently
and the <u>officials</u> would have sent me home.
But they didn't. They looked at my face and
85 then at my passport and let me into the
country.

On the train, there were people from all
over the world – they were all taking care
not to look at each other. Was the whole city
90 like that? Thousands of people who were all
<u>pretending</u> that nobody else was there?

We travelled through streets of tall, yellow-
grey buildings, and all the time the <u>useless</u>
rain went on falling. When I looked up at the
95 sky, I couldn't see any sign of the sun. Was it
always <u>invisible</u> here?

I thought Uncle would take me to my new
family's house. But when we got off the train,
he took some coins out of his pocket and gave
100 them to me. "Can you use a telephone?" he said.

I looked at him. "Of course I can!"

"You see the phone there?" He pointed
down the road. "Call the number I give you.
Then stay in the <u>phone box</u>. The person who
answers the phone will come and <u>fetch</u> you." 105

I was too surprised to do anything except
stare at him. "Don't waste time," he said.
"People will notice you. Go!" The piggyback
was over and suddenly I was on my own,
walking down this strange road. 110

The phone was different from the phones
I had used before, but it was easy to see how
to use it. I pressed the <u>buttons</u> very carefully:
I had no more money to put in if I made a
mistake the first time. 115

"Hello," said a boy's voice. He spoke
<u>Somali</u>, but his accent was very strange. "Are
you in the phone box?"

"Yes," I said. "But I don't know where –"
"Just wait," he said. "I'm coming." 120

I knew it was him as soon as he came
round the corner. A tall Somali boy who came
<u>straight</u> towards me. He opened the door and
stared at me.

"I'm Abdi," he said. When I hesitated, he 125
said his full name this time. "I'm Abdirahman
Ahmed Mussa."

He was much older than my brother
Mahmoud, and tall too, but he was – more
of a boy. That was when I really understood 130
how far I had travelled. I was far away from
Somalia, and far from myself, in a place where
the people were going to be different. And I
had to learn how to live there.

I stared straight back at Abdi. "And I'm 135
Khadija Ahmed Mussa," I said.

From: *Where I belong* by Gillian Cross

SPEAKING

2 **Your reaction**

a) *Do you like the story? Explain why or why not.*

b) *Have you heard or read about people who try to come to Europe as <u>refugees</u>? How are these stories similar to the narrator's experience? The ideas from the introduction pages can help you.*

> WB 9/19 Reading (headings)
> WB 9/20 Reading (writing style)

READING

3 **Understanding the story** → WB 9/19–20

→ S1–4

S1–4 Reading skills HA

a) *Explain why the narrator must leave her country.*

b) *Look at the map on p. 16 and the text again. How does the narrator get from Somalia to England? Copy the grid and fill in the first line.*

	Part A	Part B	Part C	Part D
How?	by boat, overloaded			
Feelings?	I was scared … (l. 35)			

c) *How does the narrator feel during her journey? Find lines in the text that tell you about her feelings. Add them to your grid from b).*

 d) *Imagine you'd have to go on a journey like the narrator in the story. What would be the scariest part for you? Share your ideas with a partner.*

READING

4 **Reading between the lines**

→ △ 111/12

111/12 Reading between the lines △ → After …

First read the skills box. Then find information in the text that answers these questions.

1. What's the situation of the narrator's family?
2. What do you think the relationship is between the narrator and her father?
3. What kind of person is Uncle, the smuggler who takes the narrator to England?

> **Reading skills**
>
> Sometimes important information is not mentioned directly in a text. You need to **read between the lines** to get ideas about the characters and their relationships.
>
> **Example:** When the narrator's father drives away, his face is like a mask. (l. 21) That might tell us that he tries to hide his feelings.

> WB 9/21 Writing (options)

WRITING

5 **More thoughts about the story** → WB 9/21

a) *After she was picked up by Abdi at the phone box, the narrator meets her 'new' family. What do you think will happen? What might be new for the narrator compared with her old life? Make notes. The ideas in the box can help you.*

> **Word bank**
>
> different culture | new gadgets | modern house | different <u>climate</u> | no friends | <u>be homesick</u> | go to school | new rules

 b) *Get into groups of 3–4. Together write a plan of how you think the story might <u>continue</u>. Present your ideas to the class.*

The <u>guitar</u> lesson → S16

S16 Wichtige filmische Mittel

SPEAKING

1 Warm-up

What do you think of when you hear the words "<u>I go wherever the wind takes me</u>"?

VIEWING

2 Ciara and Hayley → WB 10/22

Folie 3/24: Sicherung des Hörsehverstehens, Vermutungen zum Handlungsablauf
KV 9: Every picture tells a story
WB 10/22 Writing (travel blog)

DVD 3/7

a) *Watch the film and collect information about Ciara and Hayley. Think of the topics below. Then compare the two women.*

<mark>future plans / dreams</mark>

<mark>origin</mark>   <mark>work</mark>

<mark>travel destinations (past and future)</mark>

b) *What do you think of Ciara and Hayley? Would you like to meet them? Say why / why not.*

> **Word bank**
>
> friendly | <u>outgoing</u> | interesting | nice |
> boring | cool | sad | <u>easy-going</u> |
> strange | silly | rude | funny | happy |
> quiet | clever | crazy | odd

VIEWING

3 Film genres

KV 10: Talking about film genres

a) *Read the skills box. What elements match the film 'The guitar lesson'?*

HA

b) *Make a list with the genres from the box and add two films you've already seen (or heard of) for each genre.*

Lösung: a) *romance: adventure (Hayley); relationship between two characters (Marley and Alicia); love / happy ending (We don't know!)*

> **Film skills**
>
> There are many different **kinds of films**, or 'film genres'. Films from one genre usually have similar **main elements**. Here are some examples:
>
> **Science fiction**: inventions in science / technology; often <u>set in</u> the future; time travel; aliens; <u>unreal</u> atmosphere
>
> **Romance**: relationship between two characters; love; adventure; happy ending
>
> **Historical**: set in <u>specific</u> historical <u>era</u>; often about real historical person / event; often <u>lavish</u> costumes / props
>
> **Fantasy**: story about <u>magic</u> or <u>supernatural</u> <u>forces</u>; set in <u>mythical</u> time; often tells the story of a hero / heroine

WRITING

4 A film poster

Design a film poster for your favourite film from Ex. 3b).

How to tell a travel story

1   Listening: One travel story – two versions

L 1/17–18 ⊙
→ S15

S15 Hörverstehen üben

a) *Listen to a young man's travel story and say if you find it interesting or not. Give reasons for your opinion.*

b) *Listen to another version of the same travel story. Compare the two versions.*

c) *Note down which phrases from the box you can hear in the story.*

> **Useful phrases**
>
> Did I tell you about …? | As I've already told you, … | … and then I realised / remembered that … | The next thing I knew … | A few seconds later … | The weirdest / funniest / scariest thing happened to me <u>the other day</u>. | After a while … | Anyway, <u>it turned out that</u> … | In the end, I decided to …

WB 11/24 Skills (phrases)

2   What makes a good travel story? → WB 11/24

a) *Talk about what makes a travel story a **good** travel story. List your points.*

→ S4

S4 Wichtige Merkmale von literarischen Texten

b) *Read this travel story. Find examples of the points you listed in a).*

Voc.: Nouns and verbs with the same form, p. 163

The weirdest thing happened to me last year. I was on holiday in Italy. We visited a really nice little hill town, and then we decided to have a picnic. We walked out of the town into a small forest. It seemed like the perfect place to stop for a picnic. The next thing I knew, I started to have a really strange feeling. There was something about the place I just didn't like, and I *really* wanted to leave. I told my parents. At first they thought I was joking, but after a while they realised I was serious. I think they were disappointed I didn't want to stay, but they're cool (well, when it isn't about the music I like!) and they agreed. We left the forest area and found another place to have a picnic. Anyway, a few days later, I looked up the town on the internet. I found that a lot of people had died there in a <u>war</u> in the 16th century. Some soldiers had killed almost all the people in the town – women, children, old men. And guess where it had happened? In that forest! I don't believe in ghosts, but something weird definitely happened to me while I was there!

3   Write a travel story

KV 11: Summer camps in the USA
WB 11/25 People/Logic/Word smart

a) *This travel story is very short and it wouldn't be very interesting to listen to. Rewrite it as you'd tell it to a friend. Use the phrases from Ex. 1 and your ideas from Ex. 2 for help.*

→ S7–9

S7–9 Writing skills

> *I was on holiday in Egypt. I made a mistake when I ate with my left hand. My brother and I met some <u>Egyptian</u> guys about our age in a café. They invited us to play <u>dominoes</u> with them. Then they <u>ordered</u> some food to share with us. My brother and I started eating with our left hands. Then we realised that was a mistake. In Egypt and other <u>Arab</u> countries you should only eat with your right hand because people think the left hand isn't clean.*

b) *Take turns to tell your travel story and give each other feedback.*

True or not true?

You're going to have a storytelling competition in two teams! Your task is to think of travel stories which you must present to the other team. The other team then has to guess if your team's stories are true or not.

Step 1

WB 12/26 True/False sentences

Plan your travel story → WB 12/26

Divide your class up into two teams. In each team there are five groups of 2–3 students. Each group thinks of two travel stories – one true and one not. In your groups, first collect ideas for your travel stories. These questions can help you:

- Where did you go?
- Why did you go there?
- What happened?
- What was funny / scary / embarrassing about it?

If your story isn't true, try to make it sound as <u>convincing</u> as possible. If it's true, it's important to make the other team believe that you've invented it. So be creative!

Step 2

HA

WB 12/27 Key words

Write a prompt card → WB 12/27

Write a prompt card for each travel story. Remember not to write whole sentences, but just key words with the most important points. Don't forget to include useful phrases that will make your story more interesting or exciting. → indirect speech (pp. 10–12, pp. 13–15) → How to tell a travel story (p. 20)

Step 3

WB 13/28 Travel story

Practise telling your stories → WB13/28

Decide who will present your group's travel stories to the other team. Then practise your presentation. The other group member(s) should make suggestions about how you could improve each story. → How to tell a travel story (p. 20)

Step 4

Start your competition

Get into the two teams and take turns to tell the different groups' stories. When the other team guesses correctly, they get a point. The team with the most points wins.

Step 5

KV 12: Peer evaluation: True or not true?
WB 13/29 Feedback

Give your feedback → WB 13/29

After the competition, think of the travel stories you've heard. What did you find good / not so good about them? Explain why.

Find more online:
9s82pk

Dos and don'ts

Folie 3/20: Bildbeschreibung, Reaktivierung von Allgemeinwissen
WB 15 Listening/Speaking (dialogues)

SPEAKING

1 Good or bad behaviour? → WB 15/1

S11

S11 Gespräche führen

a) *Work with a partner. Look at the situations in the pictures. Then look at the dos and don'ts below which are typical for English-speaking countries (and for others too). Which ones can you use to describe each situation? Explain why.*

A

B

C

D

Say thank you.   Don't stare.   Don't point.   Be polite.   Don't stand in the way.

Hold the door open for others.   Don't jump the queue.   Don't talk with your mouth full.

Smile.   Say hello back.   Don't litter.   Don't stand too close to others.

b) *What counts as good or bad behaviour in your family / your school / among your friends? You can look at the dos and don'ts in a) for help.*

WB 15/2 Language (logical order)

SPEAKING

2 Your turn: Your experiences → WB 15/2

Transfer

Can you remember a situation in which someone behaved differently to what you'd normally expect (in Germany or in another country)? Tell your partner about what happened. How did you feel about it? How did you react?

Useful phrases

Just imagine what happened to me when … | I saw something really funny / strange / odd when … | I was really surprised. | I couldn't believe my eyes / ears. | I didn't understand what was going on. | Well, I guess every country has its own customs. | For me, it looked like good / bad behaviour, but then I realised …

VIEWING

3 Aliens in London!

Folie 3/21: Vorentlastung/Sicherung des Hörsehverstehens, Bildbeschreibung
KV 14: The aliens are here!

DVD 3/6

Just imagine: Aliens have landed in central London. It's a strange experience for everyone. Find out more!

→ S16

a) *Watch the film. What did the aliens do wrong from a British point of view? Take notes.*

b) *Look at the stills. What's the situation and what goes wrong? Work with your notes from a).*

» Wichtige filmische Mittel

A

B

WRITING

4 Role play: Breaking the ice

KV 15: Breaking the ice

→ S11

Gespräche führen

a) *You're at a train station and your train is late. Another person is waiting for the train too. The person looks friendly and smiles at you. Write down a conversation you could have with him / her. Look at the <u>icebreakers</u> in the box for ideas.*

Useful phrases

Icebreakers
I hope the train will arrive soon. | How long do you think we'll have to wait for …?! | How long have you been …? | I'm <u>glad</u> it isn't so <u>crowded</u> / busy / hot / cold here today. Yesterday it was so … | Cool T-shirt! You must be a … fan. | I've heard the film / show / band / … is really good. | Have you seen the <u>latest</u> film with …?

b) *Act out your conversation in class.*

KV 14: The aliens are here!
WB 15/3 Language (error spotting)

WRITING

5 Tips for aliens → WB 15/3

→ S7–9

9 Writing skills

Work in groups of 3–4. Write a <u>leaflet</u> for aliens who have come to visit earth. Give them tips about how to behave.

Tips for aliens

It's good / bad <u>manners</u> to …
You should always …
You shouldn't ever …
People here (don't) usually … when …
It's a good / bad idea to … because …
People (don't) like it when you …

LISTENING

1 Do as I say, not as I do

L 1/20 ⊙ **a)** *Listen to the first part of a conversation between Ricky and his parents. Where are they going? Why is Ricky not happy? Then listen to the second part. What happens at the train station?*

b) *Listen to both parts again. What do Ricky's parents tell him not to do? Which of those things do his parents do? Make notes.*

c) *Why is the title 'Do as I say, not as I do?'*

d) *Role play: Partner A: You are queueing at a station ticket office. Your train leaves in ten minutes. It's your turn next, but somebody jumps the queue and goes to the ticket office window in front of you. What are you going to say? Partner B: You are at a station ticket office. Your train leaves in two minutes, and you don't have time to queue for a ticket. Jump the queue.*

VOCABULARY

2 Airport talk

a) *Match the sentence halves.*

1. Collect your luggage	a. at passport control.
2. Get a visa and some foreign currency	b. at the check-in desk.
3. You can take public transport	c. before you travel.
4. Show your boarding card	d. in the arrivals hall.
5. Show your passport and visa	e. in the departure lounge.
6. Show your ticket	f. to the flight attendant.
7. Wait for your flight	g. to your hotel.

b) *Number the sentences in the most logical order. Compare with your partner.*

c) *Think about a journey you took recently by plane or any other type of public transport. Write at least six numbered sentences to describe your journey.*

Example: 1. I went to the train station by bus. **2.** I bought a ticket from the ticket office ... etc.
Lösung: a) *1d, 3c, 3g, 4f, 5a, 6b, 7e;* **b)** *2, 6, 5, 7, 4, 1, 3*

WRITING

3 An awful journey

 a) *Write a travel story based on the pictures. Use these words:*

| ferry | traffic | queue | seasick | passports | official |

b) *Think of three other things that could go wrong on a journey. Write a short travel story which tells what happened.*

4 Messages from a ferry

*Use the words given to complete the text messages with the **present perfect simple** (I have done …) or the **present perfect progressive** (I have been doing …). Add **for/since** where necessary.*

I'm bored already! I **…** (sit on this ferry | an hour).

… (you | ever | go on a ferry | before?)

This is my first time, but there's nothing to do. I **…** (already | see all the ferry).

… (you | see the outside deck | yet ?)

No. It **…** (rain | we got on the ferry). I hope the weather will be better when we get to France.

I **…** (just check | the weather forecast online). It said it was going to be nice for the rest of the week.

Great! I **…** (look forward | to this holiday | a long time). I don't want bad weather to ruin it!

5 A post from Austria

a) *Read the blog post from a British teenager, who is staying at an activity centre in Austria. Your friend is going to spend the next two weeks at the same activity centre. Tell him/her about the rules and activities he/she will find there. Use **will/won't + be allowed to/have to**.*

I've finally arrived at the activity centre in Austria. There are kids from lots of other countries here, which is great. The first thing I learned is that we mustn't only hang out with kids from our own country. I think that's a good rule, but I'm not sure about some of the others. For example, getting up time is 7 am. Ouch! If you're 14 or older, you may leave the centre in a group, but if you're under 14 you must stay in the centre. I'm 13 and 11 months! There are lots of great activities to choose from. It's not necessary to do any particular activity, but we must choose something each morning and afternoon. We can't just do nothing, but that's not going to be a problem. I want to do almost all of the activities, starting with climbing!

b) *Read the next entry from the blogger in exercise above. Write the dialogue as it must have happened.*

It was about 8.30, and I was relaxing after dinner, chatting with my new friends. I told them I'd had a really nice first day, and one girl said they'd all enjoyed meeting me. Then she stood up and said it was nearly time for bed. I laughed and said she was joking, but then she told me that everybody had to be in bed by 9 o'clock. I couldn't believe it! One of the 'instructors' (that's what they call the adults who work here) was there too. I told him that I couldn't go to bed when it was still light outside. He told me that everybody else would be in bed – even the instructors – so I'd be alone. I said that was fine, but then he told me that it was the rule, and I had to follow it. I said it was like being in prison, but he just told me that I'd get used to it. So now I'm in my bed typing this on my phone. It's dark outside now, so perhaps I'll be able to go to sleep soon.

WB 17/2 Language (indirect speech)

6 About the weather → WB 17/2

LANGUAGE

a) *Tell the story of what happened on a school trip to the mountains. Use **indirect speech** to report the things the teacher, the students and the driver said.*

Teacher: The weather forecast is good. We'll have a really nice trip.

Later, on the coach in the mountains:

Student A: The sky is getting darker. I think it's going to rain.

Student B: That isn't clouds. It's fog[1].

Student A: Fog is a cloud down on the ground.

The fog gets worse.

Driver: I've never seen such bad fog.

The fog gets even worse.

Driver: I can't drive any further because it's too dangerous. We'll have to stop and wait until the fog clears.

Teacher: Everything's going to be OK. We'll just be a little late getting home.

They don't get home until midnight.

VOCABULARY

b) *Use the words to complete the text.*

sun   climate   cloudy   windy   drizzle   raining   hot   clear

Britain is famous for having a cool, wet **1** . Every year, millions of Britons escape the **2** skies and **3** of a typical British summer, and fly south for some Mediterranean[2] **4** . But before you book a flight, remember the south of Europe does not always have **5** , blue skies. The Mediterranean coast can be **6** at all times of the year, which may be good for windsurfing but it's not so good for swimming. The sun can also be too **7** for people who are not used to it. Perhaps a traditional cold, wet holiday in Cornwall isn't so bad after all. It may be **8** , but at least you won't get sunburnt[3].

Lösung: b) 1. climate, 2. cloudy, 3. drizzle, 4. sun, 5. clear, 6. windy, 7. hot, 8. raining

LANGUAGE

7 Airport worries

Lösung: 2. I thought I'd lost my plane ticket but … 3. I thought they wouldn't give me anything to eat or drink on the plane but … 4. I thought my flight was going to arrive late but … 5. I thought there was going to be a big queue at passport control but … 6. I thought it would be difficult to get from the airport to the city centre, but …

What did Dawn think when she was at the airport?
What really happened? Write the complete sentences.

Example: I thought I was in the wrong part of the airport, but it was the right part.

> I'm in the wrong part of the airport. ✔ | I've lost my plane ticket. | They won't give me anything to eat or drink on the plane. | My flight is going to arrive late. | There's going to a big queue at passport control. | It will be difficult to get from the airport to the city centre.

1. … but it was the right part. ✔   2. … but then I found it in my jacket pocket.   3. … but a flight attendant gave me a delicious meal and a nice drink.   4. … but it really arrived a few minutes early.   5. … but I only had to wait for a few minutes.   6. … but in the end it was really easy. There were buses every ten minutes.

1 fog [fɒg] Nebel | **2 Mediterranean** [ˌmedɪtrˈeɪniən] Mittelmeer- | **3 to get sunburnt** [ˌget ˈsʌnbɜːnt] einen Sonnenbrand bekommen

8 A cancelled[1] flight

You are waiting for an evening flight at a British airport when you hear a conversation at a help desk. The passenger is German and doesn't speak English, and the help desk assistant doesn't speak German. Help them and mediate the German into English and the English into German.

Passenger: *Als ich am Check-in war, sagte man mir, dass mein Flug gerade gestrichen wurde.*
You: He says that the people at the check-in desk told him …
Assistant: Are you on the flight to Frankfurt?
You: …
Passenger: *Ja. Warum können wir nicht fliegen? Am Check-in wusste es niemand.*
Assistant: I don't know for sure, but somebody told me there was a problem with the plane.
Passenger: *Man sagte mir, ich könnte ein Ticket für einen Flug morgen bekommen. Bin ich hier an der richtigen Stelle dafür?*
Assistant: Yes it is. I can give you a ticket now.
Passenger: *Man sagte mir auch, dass die Fluglinie mir für heute Nacht ein Hotelzimmer bezahlt.*
Assistant: That's right. They told me a few minutes ago that they would organise a bus to take you and the other passengers to the hotel. They said it would be here soon.

 HA 9 Bad news, good news

Match the bad news on the left with the good news on the right. Then write the sentences.

Example: 1. There was a lot of traffic on the road to the airport,
but my flight was delayed so I didn't miss it.

1. a lot of traffic / road to airport
2. flight / took off / late
3. hungry / at the station
4. train / very crowded
5. left suitcase / bus to airport
6. mobile phone / not work / abroad

a. got / last seat / not have to stand
b. lots of / phone boxes / could call home
c. landed on time / not late for meeting[2]
d. ticket and passport / in pocket / took the flight anyway
e. flight / delayed / not miss it
f. vending machine / snacks

Lösung: 2c. My flight took off late, but it landed on time so I wasn't late for my meeting. 3f. I was hungry at the station, but there was a vending machine with snacks. 4a. The train was very crowded, but I got the last seat so I didn't have to stand. 5d. I left my suitcase on the bus to the airport but my ticket and my passport were in my pocket so I took the flight anyway. 6b. My mobile phone didn't work abroad but there were lots of phone boxes so I could call home.

 10 How was your journey? (Student A)

Look at the pictures and plan a travel story. Then talk to your partner about the experiences you each had.

Start like this: How was your journey?

Flight AC4102 to Madrid is now boarding at Gate 17

1 **cancelled** [ˈkænsld] gestrichen | 2 **meeting** [ˈmiːtɪŋ] Besprechung

SPEAKING

11 How was your journey? (Student B)

Look at the pictures and plan a travel story. Then talk to your partner about the experiences you each had.

Start like this: How was your journey?

LANGUAGE
HA

12 Lost in New Delhi

Write the dialogue with the taxi driver and with the people at the shopping centre.

Start like this: Tourists: Can you take us the India Gate, please?

Lösung: *Father: Can you take us to the India Gate, please? Driver: Do you want to do some shopping? Narrator: Yes, we do. Driver: Here we are. Man + woman: Are you lost? Father: Where are we? Man + woman: You're several miles away from the city centre. Woman: Don't worry. We live in the centre. Would you like to go there with us in our car? Narrator: Yes, we'd like that very much.*

I was in New Delhi with my dad. It's a really big city, and it's not easy to get around it. We got into a taxi, and asked the driver to take us to the India Gate. It's a big historic monument in the middle of the city. The driver asked us if we wanted to do some shopping. We wanted to buy some souvenirs, so I said we did. After a while, the driver said that we were there and stopped. We got out of the taxi and looked for the India Gate but all we could see was a big shopping centre.

Then we saw the sign: India Gate Shopping Centre. A man and a woman came up to us and asked us if we were lost. We asked them where we were. They said we were several miles away from the city centre. The woman told us not to worry. She told us they lived in the centre, and asked us if we'd like to go there with them in their car. I said we'd like that very much.

LANGUAGE
HA

WB 18/4 Language (indirect speech)

13 We're just about to close → WB 18/4

The narrator from the exercise above is now at a museum near the India Gate.
*Rewrite the dialogue as a travel story. Use only **indirect speech** to report what was said.*
*You will need to use **asked him / us if** … and **asked / told us to** … .*

Attendant:	I'm sorry, we're just about to close.
Father:	Oh dear. Can we come in anyway, just for a few minutes? This is our last day in New Delhi.
Attendant:	I'm sorry. I really can't let you in.
Father:	Never mind. Thank you anyway.
Attendant:	Where are you from?
Narrator:	We're from Birmingham.
Attendant:	Really? My brother lives in Birmingham. He has restaurant there. It's called the Delhi Kitchen. Do you know it?
Narrator:	Yes, we do. We've been there several times. We like it very much.
Attendant:	OK, come in, but don't tell anybody I let you in. You can stay for about half an hour.

OCABULARY

14 Fiesta!

*Complete the travel story
with the words in the box.*

| afraid of | air-conditioning | although | coast |
| crowded | energy | garlic | leaflet | outgoing | steady |

I was on holiday with my family on the east ⬛1 of Spain. Some other tourists told us to go to a
city called Alicante, and gave us a tourist ⬛2 about it. It looked interesting, so we decided to visit.
When we arrived, we found that they were having a big festival with bonfires and fireworks. We
all thought it was amazing, ⬛3 my sister is a bit ⬛4 fireworks. There was lots of fantastic street
food too. I had some mushrooms with more ⬛5 than I'd ever tasted before. It was all great!
It was lucky we had booked a hotel, as the city was really ⬛6 . When we were tired, we went back to
the hotel, and tried to sleep, but it was impossible. There was some loud music playing in the street
just outside the hotel – a ⬛7 *Thud! Thud! Thud! Thud!* It was also really hot in the room, and the ⬛8
wasn't working. So we put on our clothes, and went back to join the party. It went on until about
5 a.m.! The local people we spoke to were all so cool – really friendly, ⬛9 and full of ⬛10 . It was a
wonderful experience.

Lösung: 1. coast, 2. leaflet, 3. although, 4. afraid of, 5. garlic, 6. crowded, 7. steady, 8. air-conditioning, 9. outgoing, 10. energy

OCABULARY

15 Personality adjectives

ung: a) *positive: calm,
y-going, gentle, kind, out-
ng,...; negative: annoying,
npy, odd, rude, silly, ...*

a) *Put these personality adjectives into two lists (positive – negative).
Then think of more words to add to the lists.*

| annoying | calm | easy-going | gentle | grumpy | kind | odd outgoing | rude | silly |

b) *Have you ever been grumpy, silly or annoying? (Be honest!) Have you ever met anybody who was
especially outgoing, calm, gentle or easy-going? Tell your partner about it.*

WRITING

16 Holiday photos

ung: *Pete: Why were they
ring Christmas hats?
e: That guy was taking a
e while you were taking
oto! Pete: What was that
carrying? Artie: It was an
suitcase. He found it in
sea, and he was bringing
to the beach. Pete: Why
e you having a bonfire?
e you having a barbecue?
e: I wasn't playing it. I was
holding it for the photo.*

*Use the words in brackets with the **past progressive** to complete the dialogue.*

Artie: Here, these are some of my holiday
 photos. Those people are some friends I
 made at the activity centre.

Pete: ⬛ (why | they | wear) Christmas hats?

Artie: I was in Australia, remember. Christmas
 is in the middle of summer there.

Pete: ⬛ (That guy | take) a selfie while
 ⬛ (you | take) the photo!

Artie: He took about 200 selfies every day.

Pete: ⬛ (What | that boy | carry)?

Artie: It was an old suitcase. He found it in
 the sea, and ⬛ (he | bring) it onto the
 beach.

Pete: ⬛ (why | you | have) a bonfire?
 ⬛ (you | have) a barbecue?

Artie: No, it was just for fun. That's me, with
 the guitar. A friend took the photo.

Pete: I didn't know you could play the guitar.

Artie: ⬛ (I | not play) it. ⬛ (I | just hold it)
 it for the photo.

Text smart 1
Drama

 Find more online:
xa56yr

What does it feel like to be an actor on stage? What is special about plays?
In Text smart 1 you're going to get to know different scenes from one play. Have fun!

LISTENING

1 Warm-up: Thinking about the theatre

a) *Is there a drama group at your school / in your town? Tell the class about plays or shows you've seen.*

L 1/21 ⊙
→ S15

b) *Listen to three friends (Laura, Jack and Simon) as they talk about plays.*

S15 Hörverstehen üben

1. What do the friends like about plays?
2. What do they find difficult?
3. What do you think about their comments?

VOCABULARY

2 Theatre collocations

→ △ 112/1
→ S17

a) *Match the verbs with the nouns to make useful collocations about the theatre.*

112/1 Theatre collocations
△ → Instead of …
S17 Vokabeln ordnen und
strukturieren

entertain | stage | act in | learn | forget | follow | use | get into | play | wear | stay | mess up | give | go to | identify with

a great performance | a role | stage directions | the director's instructions | character | props | your lines | in character | the audience | a costume | a scene | the theatre | the protagonist | a part | a play

b) *Now start a glossary of theatre terms with 2–3 entries. You can add on to your glossary over the next pages. Try to use your collocations.*

Example: **in character:** When an actor is 'in character', it means that he / she is acting and thinking like the character. It's important to stay in character too.

WB **19/1** Writing/Speaking (scenes)

SPEAKING

3 Warm-up: Getting into character → WB 19/1

As a warm-up for some of the activities on the next pages, look at the photo and think about what the characters could say. Then say / shout / whisper / … the lines out loud. Be creative and play with your voice!

Example:
A: You look so silly!
B: Well, have *you* looked in the mirror today?

A British production of *The Wind in the Willows*

Claire's Devil   by Dave Draper

You're going to read different scenes from a play about a <u>teenage</u> girl and a <u>dilemma</u> she's <u>facing</u>.

The characters are:
- Claire, the story's protagonist
- Rob, a friend
- Claire's mum
- Claire's dad
- Claire's devil
- Claire's <u>angel</u>

WB 19/2 Reading (character profiles)

READING

S 1/9
L 1/22 ◎

→ S4

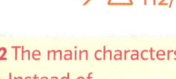Wichtige Merkmale literarischen Texten ennen

4 **Scene 1: Rob and Claire** → WB 19/2

Before you read: Talk about what role you think 'Claire's devil' could be. And what about 'Claire's angel'? Then read the scene.

(Rob and Claire are walking home from school.)

Rob: Listen, there's a party in West Street tomorrow night. It'll be fantastic: Do you fancy coming with us?

5 Claire: In West Street? Isn't that on the other side of town? It's a pretty rough area, isn't it?

Rob: We'll be okay! The station is only a few minutes away. Nearly everyone we know
10   will be there. What do you say?

Claire: I'll <u>phone</u> you <u>tonight</u>. At about six, OK?

Rob: If you're worried about what your parents will say, then there's a simple solution – don't tell them. Say you're
15   staying over at my house with my sister. My mum will cover up for us – she does what I tell her!

Claire: I'll phone you.

*(Rob goes off. Claire is alone with her
20 <u>conscience</u>.)*

READING

5 **The main characters**

🖉 a) *In your own words, sum up what happens in this first scene.*

→ △ 112/2

2 The main characters
► Instead of …

b) *What can you say about Rob and Claire's <u>motivations</u> and feelings?*

Example:
On the one hand, Claire wants to …, but on the other hand, she …

Useful phrases

- Rob tries to convince her …
- The dilemma starts when …
- Claire seems/feels confused/<u>unsure</u>/<u>convinced</u> …
- Claire has doubts about …
- I think Claire feels <u>tempted</u> …
- Rob <u>tempts</u> Claire when he …

READING

S1/10–11
L 1/23–24

6   **Scene 2: The angel and the devil** → WB 19/3

WB 19/3 Writing (statements)

a) *In Scene 2, Claire's 'angel' and 'devil' speak for the first time. Before you read the scene, read the skills box.*

b) *Now read how the angel and the devil try to tell Claire what to do.*

Drama skills

Most stories feature characters in **typical roles.** There might be a hero / heroine on the one side and a villain on the other ('good guy' / 'bad guy'). These characters have good or bad <u>motives</u>. What characters from plays / films / books do you know in typical 'good' or 'bad' roles?

Devil:

Angel:

The trouble with you is that you never <u>take risks</u>. You always worry about what your parents tell you. What's the matter with you? Just have a little fun!

5 How boring can you get?! Do you want to lose *all* your friends? They'll all be there, and you'll be at home in front of the TV, like a good little girl.

<u>Let's face it</u> – you're scared! You always back
10 down from things.

All kids lie to their parents. And it would only be a small lie, a <u>white lie</u>. Say you're going to stay with Rob's sister; that's partly true: You can sleep at their house after the party.

What if something bad happened? What if   15
there's a fight? And you're not old enough to go. They'll see that you're not old enough; you'll end up embarrassed and miserable in front of Rob. Tell him you're sorry but you can't go.

Rob is <u>exaggerating</u> as usual. Most of your   20
school friends won't be allowed to go because their parents are as <u>sensible</u> as yours.

It wouldn't be right to lie to your parents. You know they love you, and only want what's best for you. If they found out you had lied they'd   25
never trust you again.

READING

7 Understanding Scene 2

→ S1-3

Schnelllesetechniken
Gliederung als Hilfe
Umgang mit neuen
-tern

a) *What makes the devil and angel 'typical roles'? Read what these three students say about it. Say why you agree or disagree. (You can also look back at the skills box on p. 32.)*

   Example:
   A: That's easy! The devil is <u>mean</u>. He's a bad guy.
   B: I agree that he's a typical bad guy, but I don't agree that a bad guy is always mean. This devil is <u>pushy</u>, but not mean. But what about the angel?
   C: The angel sounds so scared. Is that typical for an angel? Maybe it is …

b) *Sum up the <u>arguments</u> of the devil and angel. Say which arguments you find the most convincing, and why.*

   Example:
   The devil says, "Just have a little fun!" Well, I think he's right.
   How can you beat *that* argument?

c) *How would you decide if you were Claire?*

SPEAKING

8 White lies

→ △ 113/3

/3 Telling lies
Help with …

      Transfer

a) *Go back to Scene 2 and read the devil's suggestion for a 'white lie' in lines 11–14. Explain what a white lie is, and if there's a difference between a white lie and a normal one.*

b) *Your turn: Have you ever told a white lie? What was it, and why did you tell it? Tell a partner.*

WB 20/4 Listening/Speaking (feelings and voices)

SPEAKING

9 Getting into character: Reading a scene out loud → WB 20/4

→ S11

S11 Gespräche führen

ung: a) angel: helpful,
et, nice, quiet, fearful,
ndly; devil: helpful,
et, nice, loud, tempting,
ry, scary, fast, pushy,
ndly; both: helpful,
et, nice, quiet, angry,
, friendly

a) *Think – pair – share: Read the skills box. Then look at the words below the box. Which ones describe how a 'devil' voice or an 'angel' voice should sound? Which words match **both** voices? Write down your ideas and exchange them with your partner. Then tell the class what you've both agreed on.*

> **Drama skills**
>
> When you read the lines of a play, think about how they'll sound on stage. **Play with your voice** so you can get into character. A voice on stage can be many things: angry, happy, loud, quiet, …

b) *Warm-up: Take turns with your partner to read lines 1–14 in a devil voice and lines 15–26 in an angel voice.*

c) *Reading <u>in chorus</u>: Half your class reads the devil's lines out loud together, the other half reads the angel's lines together. Think about which key lines need more 'angel' or 'devil' feeling than the others.*

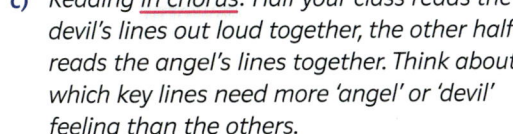

helpful   sweet   nice   quiet   fearful
loud   <u>tempting</u>   angry   scary   fast
pushy   friendly

d) *In groups of four, practise **the whole scene**. The angel and devil use their voices, but Claire never speaks: She only uses her face and <u>gestures</u> to show her dilemma. And one of you is the director; you give the others feedback. Then swap roles and find out which part each of you can read best. When you're ready, read your version of the scene to the class.*

→ △ 113/4

/4 Getting into
racter
Help with …

WB 20/4 Listening/Speaking (feelings and voices)

READING **10** **Scene 3: Claire and her parents** → WB 20/4

S1/13–15
L1/26–28 ⊙

*Before you read: In the next scene, Claire makes her decision. How do you think she'll decide:
Has she listened to her angel or her devil? Explain why you think so.*

(Later at Claire's house. Claire is talking to her mum and dad.)

Claire: Mum, is it okay if I stay over at Jenny's house on Saturday night?

5 Mum: I didn't know you two were friendly.

Claire: Well, I like her a lot.

Mum: I hope you're not getting involved with that brother of hers. Rob isn't the sort of boy you should be mixing with.

10 Claire: Rob isn't as bad as people think.

Mum: From what I've heard, he's heading for trouble. So be <u>warned</u>!

Claire: Rob has his own circle of friends – we <u>hardly</u> ever speak to each other. Is it

15 okay then, Mum?

Mum: All right. But check with your dad first.

(Claire's mother goes out. Claire is alone with her conscience.)

Angel: See! So many lies already. She'll be
20 terribly hurt if she finds out you've been so <u>dishonest</u>. She trusts you, Claire!

Devil: She'll sleep easy and you can have a great time. Now, you need a good story to convince your dad.

(Later, Claire is with her dad.) 25

Claire: Dad, Mum says it's okay for me to stay at Jenny Costello's on Saturday, as long as you agree too.

Dad: As long as her parents don't mind, then, that's fine! Have I met her? 30

Claire: No, she's new in my class. We're working on a design project and I need money for materials.

Dad: What sort of design work is it?

Claire: Er … it's a dress design project. Could I 35 have £25?

Dad: That's a lot! What's this dress going to be made out of? Silk?

Claire: Of course not. But we'd like to <u>do</u> really <u>well</u> on the project so we're buying a 40 couple of books to help us.

Dad: Well, I don't mind paying out if it's to help with <u>schoolwork</u>. Here you are.

(He gives Claire £25 and leaves.)

READING

11 Understanding Scene 3

a) *Compare your answer from Ex. 10 with Claire's decision. Explain why Claire makes this decision.*

b) *Now answer these questions:*

1. Are Claire's parents worried about her? If yes, what do they say to express it?

   Example: Well, when the mother says, "I didn't know you two were friendly," that shows that she is surprised and unsure about who her daughter's friends are.

2. What lies does Claire tell in Scene 3?

c) *Discuss with your partner why you think Claire's decision was right or wrong.*

> **WB 20/5** Reading (stage)
> **WB 20/6** Reading/Writing (script)

SPEAKING

12 Acting out Scene 3 → WB 20/5–6

In Ex. 9, you had the chance to practise 'getting into character' with different roles, and how it feels to read them out loud. Here, you'll take a step further: It's your turn to act out a whole scene.

→ △ 113/5
→ S11

/5 Acting out a scene
→ Help with …
  Gespräche führen

a) *First, read the skills box. Then read out and **act** out Scene 3. Focus on your voice, your face and your gestures. (Decide if the five roles are enough, or if you need a director again too.)*

b) *Do you think it helps to understand the characters more when you act out a scene like this?*

Example:
A: When I was playing the angel, I almost felt like I needed to help Claire. I think I was 'in character' as an angel, as someone who helps.
B: Yeah, when I played Claire, I really had to fake an 'extra friendly' face when I was lying to my parents. I felt a bit <u>fake</u> myself!

> **Drama skills**
>
> Think about these ideas before you act out a scene:
> - Decide **who is going to play which role**.
> - First **read out your role**, but look up from the page again and again to learn your part, <u>bit by bit</u>.
> - Try out **different voices**.
> - **Get into character**: Sometimes it helps to think of a person you know who is similar to the person you're playing.
> - On stage, your **face** and **gestures** are almost as important as your lines. Make sure your face matches your lines, and make sure that you sit, stand or move in the right way too.

READING   **13**   **Scene 4: Farewell**

S 1/16
L 1/29 ◎

Before you read: Look at these lines from the next scene. Which characters from the play do you think will say each line? Explain why.

You've got to make the most of your <u>youth</u> while you still have it!

You'll have to live with that on your conscience.   You've been dishonest.

One lie nearly always leads to another.   Stop preaching!

Devil: Easy, wasn't it? Now everyone's happy: Your parents think you're a really keen student and that they're <u>supporting</u> you. What could be better?

5 **Angel:** But you've been dishonest and you'll have to live with that on your conscience. Once you start being dishonest it is hard to stop. One lie nearly always leads to another.

10 **Devil:** It's their own fault. If they were a bit more <u>tolerant</u> and easy-going then <u>there'd be no need to</u> lie to them.

Angel: Wouldn't you feel safer if your parents knew where you were and what time to 15 <u>expect</u> you?

Devil: Safer? Where's the danger? A lively night out with a group of friends: Sounds safe enough to me. You've got to make the most of your youth while 20 you still have it! Enjoy yourself while you've got the chance.

Claire: 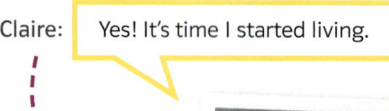 Yes! It's time I started living.

(On Saturday evening at Claire's house, with her dad and mum.)

Claire: Bye, then. I'll see you tomorrow lunchtime.   25

Mum: Have a good time. Why not bring Jenny round here next weekend? It would be nice to meet your new friend. Perhaps I should <u>ring</u> Jenny's mother later this 30 evening. Just to check it's still okay for you to stop the night. It'll give me the chance to thank her.

Claire: There's no need. Anyway, you can't. Their phone is <u>out of order</u>.   35

Mum: But I thought Jenny rang you a little while ago. You did say it was Jenny, didn't you?

Claire: Er … Yes, it was. She had to ring from somewhere else. Bye, now.   40

Angel: See? What did I tell you? Lies lead to more lies. It never stops.

Devil: Stop preaching! It was an excellent piece of quick thinking. Well done, Claire! Now for a night out on the town! 45 Let's go!

READING **14** **Understanding Scene 4**

a) *Were you right about who said the different key lines in Ex. 13? Were there any surprises at all? Tell the class.*

b) *Explain Claire's sentence "It's time I started living". Why is it a key line in the play?*

c) *Imagine you're acting the play for your school's Drama Club and you're practising the scene when Claire leaves the house for her night out ("Bye, now", line 40). In groups of six, show the* **freeze frame** *of* **Claire**, **her parents** *– and her* **angel** *and* **devil** *too! One of you is the* **director**: *He / She takes a photo and makes sure you're all in character. Before you do your freeze frame, make a grid with important words to help you to get into character for this scene. The word bank can help you. (Some words fit more than one role.)*

→ △ 113/6

6 Staying in character
Help with …

> **Word bank**
>
> shocked | happy | confused | fearful | guilty | angry | fantastic | worried

Claire	Mum	Dad	Devil	Angel
…	confused …	…	…	fearful …

WB 21/7 Writing (ending)

LISTENING **15** **A happy ending?** → WB 21/7

a) *Now think about the whole story. For each of the four scenes, write a short summary of 2–3 lines.*

b) *With a partner, think about an ending for the play: a happy / sad / surprising / strange ending? Then present your ideas to the class.*

L 1/30 ◉ c) *Listen to the original ending of the play* Claire's Devil. *What happens?*

d) *Now that you know the whole story, do you feel the story has a message? If yes, a message for whom? Write about it in 5–6 lines.*

KV 16: Evaluate your group work
KV 17: An invitation
KV 18: An article for your school magazine
WB 21/8 Vocabulary (photo story)

16 **Options: Bring the story to life** → WB 21/8

Choose one of these options and bring Claire's Devil *to life!*

→ △ 114/7

7 Bringing the story fe
Help with …

Option A: Stage the play	Option B: Write a photo story
You've practised reading and acting different roles and one scene. Now you can stage the whole play. Look back at the tips on these pages for help, and you'll find helpful tips in your Workbook too. Think about:	*In different groups, take photos of the key parts of each scene with yourselves as the actors. Your 'freeze frame' skills can help you. When you have the photos you need, do the following:*
– casting – costumes and props – where to stage your play – learning your lines by heart – playing with your voice	– Write speech bubbles for the characters. – Write short texts to explain more background information from the plot / action that isn't in the bubbles.

Find more online:
bf599t

The USA: Country of contrasts

Folie 4/1: Umgang mit Karten; Erweiterung des Orientierungswisse

How many contrasts can a country have? If you're talking about the United States of America (or 'the US'), the answer is: Lots! Find out for yourself on these pages and in the rest of this book.

A In New York City, the 'city that never sleeps', there are more than 13,600 taxis. But outside the big urban centers, in the endless, sparsely populated rural areas of the US, you can drive for hours and hours and not see a single car. (Well, maybe a tractor.)

B In Arizona the summers are hot – and the winters too. In the desert Southwest, temperatures often climb to 110°F or more. No problem for a cactus! But if you fly about two hours to the northwest, you'll be in a much cooler climate zone: The Pacific Northwest has green forests and huge mountains, like Mt. Rainier in Washington State.

C The country which started as a British colony and later became the United States was built on immigration. In the 19th and 20th centuries, immigrants were usually Europeans and arrived by boat at Ellis Island in New York. Today, most immigrants come from Asia and Latin America. Together, all the immigrants have created a country rich in cultural contrasts.

D The biggest, the best, the fastest: You can find lots of superlatives in the US!

For example, the world's tallest trees are found in California, like this huge redwood here. They can be 250 ft., 300 ft. tall or even taller!

In the early 20th century, Chicago and New York gave the world the first really tall skyscrapers. In 1931, the Empire State Building in New York became the world's tallest building at 1,454 ft. It isn't the tallest anymore, but it's probably still the world's most *famous* skyscraper.

E You can see American flags all over the country – at sports events, at schools, in front of homes, in big cities and in small towns. Each state also has its own flag.

People fly flags to show who or what they identify with. For some first-time visitors to the US, all the flags are a contrast to their own countries, where you don't see as many.

F Lifestyles can be hugely different in the US. More than 45 million Americans are poor: This means a family of four has only about $24,000 a year. At the same time, there are about 10 million millionaires in America – that's more than the population of Austria or Sweden. And billionaires? There are more of them in the US than in all of China, India and Russia together.

SPEAKING

Folie 4/1: Umgang mit Karten; Erweiterung des Orientierungswissens
WB 24/1 Vocabulary (word puzzle)

1 Getting to know the US → WB 24/1

a) *Describe the scenery or the situation in each photo on pages 38–39. What can you see? These words and phrases can help:*

> ### Word bank
> crowded | sparsely / densely populated | urban | rural | out in the country | landscape | region | scenery | distances | open spaces | dry | wet | hot | cool | to rain | water | climate | desert | mountainous | flat | tall | high | low | gigantic | tiny | rich | wealthy | poor | wasteful | luxury | lifestyle | to love your country | to leave your old life behind | to start a new / better life | refugee | immigrant

> ### Tip
> Americans usually call their country 'the United States', 'the US' or simply 'America'. They don't often say 'the USA'.

> ### Useful phrases
> – The picture on the left shows … while the picture on the right is an example of …
> – The picture of … shows / represents / symbolizes …
> – The picture is a way to say that people in America …

b) *Now describe how the four photo pairs (A, B, D, F) show contrast in the US.*

c) *Write a heading for the four photo pairs and for the two single photos.*

d) *If **you** had chosen the photos to show the US as a 'country of contrasts', would you have chosen other ones? Which? Based on what information? Explain your reasons.*

VOCABULARY

WB 24/2 Writing (holiday photos)

2 Word-building: Adjective + noun collocations → WB 24/2

→ S17

S17 Vokabeln ordnen und strukturieren

a) *Lots of the words that you see on these pages are used in typical **adjective** + **noun** collocations: **rural area**, **hot climate**, etc. These collocations are useful for describing people and places. With your partner, make as many collocations as you can with the words below.*

> **Adjectives:**
> high | low | dry | wet | hot | cool | harsh | mountainous | flat | extreme | open | crowded | sparsely / densely populated | rural | urban | cultural | wealthy | healthy | beautiful | interesting

> **Nouns:**
> region | landscape | climate | climate zone | area | scenery | lifestyle | standard of living | temperature | space

b) *Once you have your collocations, arrange them in **categories** that interest you (climates, landscapes, regions). As you learn more information and vocabulary about the US in this book, add on to your list / lists to make a mini-dictionary.*

Example: **Rural areas:** sparsely populated; open spaces; beautiful scenery; …

WRITING

Transfer

HA

3 Your turn: Contrasts in your country

What photos would you choose to show contrasts in Germany? Choose one topic (nature, food, buildings, etc.) and find two photos for that topic which represent it well. Write a short text (4–5 sentences) for your topic and photos. Share your results with the class.

READING

4 Do you know how big everything is here?!

L 2/1 ⊙

KV 19: Working with vocabulary

Tristan and Callum's families became friends on vacation in Cornwall some years ago. Tristan lives in San Diego; Callum in London. Right now they're chatting online.

Dude, our summer vacation starts on June 10. When will you get to San Diego?

We're going to leave London on 12 June and stay in America for 5 (!) weeks.

5 weeks of surfing. AWESOME!

Sorry, first NYC and a Broadway play for Mum. Then surfing.

So 2–3 days in NYC and then a 6-hour flight to SD. CU you on the 15th?

Wait, how many US states are there?

50. Why?

My mum and dad want to see half. Do you think we can see that many?

Hey, your mom and dad have no clue! Do you know how big everything is here?!

It isn't like it would take YEARS to see it all. And hey, we've got 5 whole weeks.

Not enough. My route planner says NYC to SD is 2,800 miles! 41 hours by car!!! And that's just time in the car. NO STOPS.

Wow, that's 4,500 km. That IS far. So besides SD, what should we see? Boston?

Brits in Boston? Ever heard of the Boston Tea Party? American colonists who threw all the British tea into the harbour?

Oh, sounds like history. Don't tell my dad, he'll want to go. What about the South?

Callum, wrong direction! California is out WEST. Hello!

There are lots of states in the middle there. What could we see in the Midwest?

Endless corn and wheat fields. Some mountains too. The Rockies.

Sounds like lots of open space. Cool! Not like England. Good for riding horses?

Maybe, but not for riding WAVES. Get to Cali, man. Surfing! Fun in the sun!

Mum says we'll be in SD on 4th July. Isn't that the day with all the fireworks?

Epic, that's Independence Day! HUGE beach party on the 4th of July every year.

Massive! But wait: I'm going to celebrate how you guys became independent from us Brits?! I don't know about that …

Chill out. That was a long time ago. JUST GET HERE!

a) *Look at the map of the US at the back of your book and find all the places that are mentioned in the chat. Which place would you be most interested in? Explain why.*

b) *Understanding the text:*
   1. <u>Point out</u> the moments in which Tristan could have given Callum more or better information about his country, for a more complete picture of the US.
   2. Explain why you think Tristan *doesn't* offer more information. Isn't he interested?

Transfer

HA

c) *Your turn: Which places could you visit 2,800 miles from where you live? Do some internet research on one place 2,800 miles from home. In a short text (8–10 lines) with photos, describe how you could travel there and what you could do and see when you get there.*

Unit 2
Kids in America

Find more online:
8n27xv

A

B

VOCABULARY

1 Teen life in the US: First impressions

Folie 4/2: Bildbeschreibung und Erweiterung des Orientierungswissens

a) *Describe what you see in each picture. You can look at the word bank on the next page for ideas.*

b) *If you wanted to find out more about the topic 'Kids in America' on the internet, which words from the word bank (or other words) would you use as key words for search engines? Which of the photos give you ideas for your research? Explain why.*

SPEAKING

2 Preparing to live in America

On p. 43, you'll hear about a group of European teenagers who have just arrived in America for a year. Their families have moved to the US for work reasons.

Think – pair – share: What aspects of the three topics on the right would you want to know about if you moved to the US? On your own, think of 1–2 questions you might have. Exchange ideas with your partner before you both share your ideas with the class.

family life

school life

free time activities

In Unit 2 you learn

… how to talk and write about everyday life in the United States. You learn:

- about school life, family life and free time
- how to describe and analyze pictures
- what goes into a school yearbook
- how to use gerund and infinitive constructions to express your ideas

KV 32: Working with vocabulary (Unit 2)
WB 25/1 Vocabulary (urban vs. rural)
WB 25/2 Vocabulary/Speaking (orientation

LISTENING **3** **Orientation weekend: Welcome to America!** → WB 25/1–2

L 2/2-3

→ △ 115/1
→ S15

√1 Welcome to erica!
→ Help with …
Hörverstehen
n
.: Urban vs. rural,
73

a) *Josh, an American teenager, is giving a talk for European teenagers at an orientation weekend in New York. What information does he start with? Listen to the first part and then sum it up. The word bank can help here too.*

b) *Listen to the rest of Josh's talk. Take notes and sum up what he says about* **neighborhood / family life**, **school life** *and* **free time activities**.

c) *Which of your questions from Ex. 2 does Josh answer? What else would you have asked him about?*

Transfer

d) *Your turn: Talk about what you find surprising / interesting / strange / different about life in America. Think of what you know from Across cultures 1 and from these pages.*

Word bank

urban / city life | rural / country life | suburb | suburban | lots of / not enough space | long / short distances | apartment | front yard | backyard | swimming pool | lifestyle | shopping mall | rich | poor | quiet | noisy | safe | dangerous | middle school | high school | hallway | hall pass | dress code | restroom | locker | have fun | make friends | be the new boy / girl

L 2/4 ◎ **Living here isn't bad**

Matt (from Cambridge) and Lena (a German-American from Hamburg) are two of the teenagers from the New York orientation weekend.

Hi Matt! I can't believe it's only been a week since we met in New York. So much has happened! Living here in rural Pennsylvania isn't bad – but it sure isn't like in the movies. Our house is huge – I love having a big bedroom. You should see my huge walk-in closet! There are a few young people around and I like hanging out with Madison, the girl down the road. They have a swimming pool in their backyard! But there isn't much to do here where the suburbs end and the country begins. Madison has talked about organizing a party for Thanksgiving, but that's not until NOVEMBER! There's a huge shopping mall with 400 stores on the other side of Pittsburgh, but getting there is difficult; it's a long drive. Madison's 16-year-old brother has a car (!), but he doesn't always want his little sister and her friends along for the ride. 😠😠😠 And all the families around here have strict curfews for their kids – Madison has to be home very early each night. 😠😠😠 Same in your neighborhood? – Anyway, I'm homesick for Germany! I miss seeing my old friends and I'm scared of changing too much so they won't like me anymore when I go back. I enjoyed meeting you in New York; how about meeting up in Pittsburgh soon?
Lena

Hey Lena. Sounds like our experiences here are quite different. I don't miss my life in England at all! Being in a city is cool – Pittsburgh is big and we live in an apartment close to downtown. I'm still getting used to living on the 22nd floor – the elevator is a BIG part of my life! Can you imagine walking up 22 floors if it stopped working? I miss having a garden (= yard!) so I go out a lot. I take the bus everywhere; the buses are cheap. And luckily we've got shops, cafés, parks and cinemas (or 'movie theaters', as the Americans say) super close to where we live. I'm looking forward to starting school and making new friends next week. I'm good at swimming and football (= soccer!); maybe that will help at Birchview Middle School. But stop worrying about losing your old friends or your identity – just jump in and enjoy the experience. – Hey, I'm afraid I'm very busy right now; meeting up isn't easy. Do you remember Sophie from orientation? She's going to move to Pittsburgh soon – it'll be cool to see her again! Well, keep in touch. CU! 🙂 Matt (PS: I keep forgetting your dad is American; no wonder your English is so good!)

KV 20: Writing (Lena and Matt)
WB 26/3 Vocabulary (BE and AE)

READING

1 **Two different experiences in America** → WB 26/3

→ S1

S1 Schnelllesetechniken

HA ✎

a) *Sum up Lena's and Matt's situation in America. Whose situation sounds better to you? Say why.*

b) *Compare how Lena and Matt have been experiencing the US. What's the same, what's different?*

c) *Write another message from Matt to Lena to cheer her up with advice.*

Folie 4/3: Bildbeschreibung und Vorentlastung des Leseverstehens
KV 21: Speaking (Talking about holidays)
WB 26/4 Listening (Thanksgiving)

READING **2** **Thanksgiving: A very American holiday** → WB 26/4

a) *Lena mentioned an important American holiday: Thanksgiving. Read the box and talk to your partner about festivals and holidays that are celebrated in Germany.*

> **Across cultures**
>
> **Thanksgiving** is one of the most important national holidays in the United States – and a very important day for families too. On the fourth Thursday in November each year, families all over the country get together for a big, wonderful meal. The meal is a symbol of everything one should be thankful for. This tradition started nearly 400 years ago …
>
> In late 1620, the Pilgrims left England for America so they could practice their religion freely. The first American winter was very hard; the Pilgrims had to build houses and they had to find food. By spring more than half of them had died. The survivors then asked the Native Americans for help with planting food. With that help, the harvest in 1621 was a success. The colonists gave thanks with a big meal which they enjoyed together with the Indians. **What was on the menu?** Roast turkey, cranberry sauce, sweet potatoes and pumpkin pie – the same dishes you'll still find on lots of Thanksgiving tables today.

The first Thanksgiving, 1621

A typical Thanksgiving meal

b) *Your turn: What do you have to be very thankful for? Write about it in 5–6 sentences.*

c) *Why do you think Lena can't wait for Thanksgiving?*

LANGUAGE **3** **Different categories of gerunds** → G5

KV 22: Working with language

*Each of the underlined left-hand sentences below features a **noun**. To the right of each sentence you see a sentence which is almost the same, but with a **gerund** instead of a 'normal' noun. This shows you how gerunds are really verbs which work as nouns:*

1. **Homework** isn't bad.	→ **Living** here isn't bad.
2. I like **burgers**.	→ I like **hanging out** with Madison.
3. I'm good at **football**.	→ I'm good at **swimming**.
4. I'm looking forward to **our trip** to New York.	→ I'm looking forward to **starting** school.

a) *The sentences above are examples of the four gerund categories you see on the right. Match each category to one of the four gerund sentences above.*

a) gerund after adjective + preposition
b) gerund after verb + preposition
c) gerund as sentence subject
d) gerund as sentence object

b) *Go back to Lena's and Matt's messages. Find four different gerund examples which work in the same way as the four examples above. Make a grid.*

Lösung: a) *1c), 2d), 3a), 4b)*

→ 115/2

/2 Different categories gerunds
→ Help with …

LANGUAGE

→ △ 116/3

116/3 Do you like talking to your partner?
△ → After …

4 [Gerunds as subject or object] → WB 27/5

WB 27/5 Language (US population)

*Sophie was another girl at orientation in New York. She has posted her first thoughts about the US on a <u>social media</u> page for the others who were there. Use the words on the right to <u>complete</u> her post with gerunds as **subject** or **object**.*

travel | move ✔
live | hang out | be
share | cycle (2x) | have

Help! I didn't <u>mind</u> **moving** from Germany to America, but I never imagined **1** in the middle of nowhere! Luckily, we're only staying here with my aunt and uncle until our apartment in Pittsburgh is ready. **2** a bedroom with my messy cousin really gets on my nerves! I just can't get used to **3** such a messy room. Anyway, Dad always says how beautiful it is out here in the country, but where's the *action*?! **4** bored is no fun! I miss **5** with my friends. And, can you believe this? **6** to the next mall takes TWO HOURS by car! My cousin has just suggested **7** somewhere this afternoon – but I don't feel like **8** anywhere. I mean, where to anyway? We're <u>in the middle of nowhere</u>!

Lösung: 1. *living*, 2. *Sharing*, 3. *having*, 4. *Being*, 5. *hanging out*, 6. *Traveling*, 7. *cycling*, 8. *cycling*

LANGUAGE

5 Gerunds in phrases

*Now read Matt's reply to Sophie's post. Put in the missing **verb + preposition** or **adjective + preposition** to make complete gerund phrases.*

Don't **1** feeling bored. When you get to Pittsburgh, you'll soon have to **2** being busy all the time! It's a great place, with lots to do. I'll never be **3** living here! I'm already very **4** <u>finding my way around</u> the city and I'm not at all **5** getting lost. I'm **6** going to my first baseball match soon. Do you **7** meeting up and going together? I'm **8** seeing you when you get here. Can't wait!

looking forward to
worry about | feel like
thinking of | tired of
good at | scared of
get used to

Lösung: 1. *worry about*, 2. *get used to*, 3. *tired of*, 4. *good at*, 5. *scared of*, 6. *thinking of*, 7. *feel like*, 8. *looking forward to*

SPEAKING

6 Gerunds to talk about likes and dislikes → WB 27/6

WB 27/6 Language (New York City)

→ △ 116/4

116/4 Gerunds to talk about likes and dislikes
△ → Instead of …

*Gerunds are often helpful when you want to talk about <u>likes</u> and <u>dislikes</u>. Here, Lena is talking to her new friend, Madison. Rewrite their sentences with the phrases on the right and with **gerunds**. Don't change the meaning!*

keep | look forward to
start | don't mind ✔ | stop
think of | be interested in | love

Lena
1. I'm a bit shy when I meet new people, but it's OK.
   → I **don't mind meeting** new people.
2. Maybe I'll go to the mall; I'm not sure yet.
3. Mom tells me to <u>unpack</u> every day!
4. There's a dress code so I don't wear crazy T-shirts to school anymore.

Madison
5. My brother learned to drive when he was 16.
6. Would you like to meet some more people in the area?
7. I can't wait to plan our Thanksgiving party!
8. I listen to music all the time!

Lösung: 2. *I'm thinking of going to the mall, but …* 3. *Mom keeps telling me to …* 4. *I've stopped wearing crazy T-shirts to school because …* 5. *My brother started driving when …* 6. *Are you interested in meeting …?* 7. *I'm looking forward to planning our …* 8. *I love listening to …*

SPEAKING **7** **Your turn: Likes and dislikes**

a) *With the words on the right, tell your partner about things you like and dislike. (Tip: It* might *help to write out some of your ideas first. Also, the vocabulary box on p. 175 can help.)*

→ 116/5

6/5 I like/I hate
→ Help with …
c.: Likes and dislikes,
175

Transfer

Example:

A: I'm never crazy about being the 'new person'.
It always makes me feel so insecure. What about you?

B: For me, trying new things is great! You'll never know you're good at something until you try.

love	hate	enjoy
dislike	dream of
be tired of	be interested in
be scared of	be worried about
be good at	be crazy about

b) *Go back to p. 43 and 'climb into' photo C. Imagine* **you** *are there in the hallway on your first day at school. In 5–6 sentences, describe what's going through your mind.*

SPEAKING **8** **How to: Describe pictures** → WB 28/7–9

Folie 4/4: Reaktivierung von Vorwissen und Bildbeschreibung
KV 23: How to: Describe pictures
WB 28/7 Speaking (American regions); **WB 28/8** Writing (American lifestyle)
WB 28/9 Mediation (dress code)

→ S5

Fotos beschreiben
d analysieren
c.: Describing people
d animals/Describing
ngs, Word bank (WB),
. 14–17

What does America look / feel like for teens in rural areas? And in the city? After you read the skills box, work with a partner and answer the questions below. He / She chooses one of the pictures; you choose the other. The useful phrases box can help you too.

1. Describe your picture. Who's in it? What's happening?
2. Do you think your picture is a good example for showing what America might look like for Americans the same age as you? Why do you think so? Explain your ideas.

Speaking skills

When you talk about pictures (photos, cartoons), do it in steps:

1. First, **describe** what is happening. For this, you use the **present progressive**. It's also important to talk about what you can see in the foreground, middle and background.

2. After that, you can **analyze** a picture: You can give your opinion about it or explain what you think it means. For this you use the **simple present**.

Look at the phrases box below for examples.

A

Useful phrases

Describing pictures:
- In picture X, a person is talking / running / having fun with … / asking … | Somebody else is laughing / shouting / …
- In the foreground, there's a/an … / there's some …
- In the background, you see a/an … / lots of …

Analyzing pictures:
- In my opinion, the picture is a typical example of … because it shows …
- The picture represents … / shows …
- The picture tries to show … but I think a picture with … instead of … would work better because …

B

L 2/6 ◎   # That's the worst thing to do!

Matt is on Birchview's yearbook committee. They decide what goes into the yearbook – and what doesn't. Matt is sitting with two of the most popular 8th-graders, Scott and Eva.

"Yeah, I mean, who wants to be around people whose idea of fun is to go to the mall and shout at the shoppers?"   20

Matt was confused. "I don't understand."

"They keep on talking about changing the world. So whenever there's a protest against child labor and sweatshops, the geeks are   25 always the first to shout at the people who buy cheap sweatshop clothes."

"I mean, I agree: Child labor is awful," Eva went on. "But now the geeks want us to write about it in the yearbook. That isn't what it's for.   30 A yearbook should be for fun things, for the highlights of our year!"

Another girl in the room had a different opinion: "Sorry Eva, but demonstrating for children's rights *is* a highlight of the year!"   35

Matt agreed. But all he could say was, "Well, I guess it isn't so easy to decide what goes into the yearbook!" He was smiling, but inside he didn't know what to think. "Do Scott and Eva expect me to drop my new friends   40 just because they're different? I was looking forward to hanging out with them again," he thought. "Should I go to lunch with the in-crowd?" He didn't know. Yesterday had been his first day at this school, with two surprises: The   45 day started with the Pledge of Allegiance – very different to the UK! And then in the cafeteria came another surprise: He was looking for a place to sit when two boys invited him to their table. They seemed a bit different and at first   50 they talked a lot about their protests, but then they went on to talk about other things too. Matt liked them. Did he really need to choose between them and the others?

Scott, Eva and Matt were looking at different layouts in second period when Scott stopped to say something in Matt's direction. "Hey, let's go for lunch together."

   5   "Yeah, with us this time, Matt. You don't want to sit with Henry and Tyler again, do you?" Eva added with a funny look on her face. "Stop talking to them. They're geeks."

"If you want to be popular, that's the worst 10 thing to do!" Scott agreed.

Matt went on looking at the different layouts in front of him; he needed time to think – what a dilemma! "So, they want me to be friends with them," he thought to himself. 15 "But why are they so mean about the boys I had lunch with yesterday, the 'geeks'?"

"The geeks are no fun to hang out with because they never *have* fun."

anhalte (annotation)

aufhören (annotation)

fortsetze (annotation)

→ anschließend mache (annotation)

WB 29/10 Vocabulary (prepositions)

READING   **9**   **Matt's dilemma**   → WB 29/10

a) *Eva and Scott are part of the popular in-crowd, and they talk about Henry and Tyler as 'the geeks'. What do you think of cliques like this at school?*

Transfer

HA

b) *What is Matt's dilemma? Describe it in your own words.*

c) *How would you react in Matt's situation? Write him an e-mail with your advice.*

→ ▲ 117/6   117/6 Role play: Matt, his angel and his devil
▲ → After …

WB 29/11 Pronunciation (British/American accents)

READING 🧩 **10** **Everyday life in American schools** → WB 29/11

L 2/7 ⊙

Across cultures

Most American students take the **Pledge of Allegiance** every morning. They stand, face the American flag, put their right hand over their heart and say:

"I pledge allegiance to the Flag of the United States of America, and to the Republic for which it stands, one Nation under God, indivisible, with liberty and justice for all."

a) *What do you think of the Pledge of Allegiance?*

b) *With your partner, talk about other ways people show that they belong to a country / group / school / club / …*

KV 24: Working with language

LANGUAGE **11** **Find the rule: Infinitives with question words** → G6

→ △ 117/7–8
→ ▲ 118/9

7 Infinitives with
stion words
→ Help with …
8 Do you know how
elp a friend?
→ After …
9 New at our school
→ After …
.: Phrases with
stion words, p. 176

a) *When you talk about what people ask themselves, you often use **infinitive constructions**. Look at these examples. Make a rule for questions with and without question words.*

Matt asked himself, "What should I think?"   → Matt didn't know **what to think**.
He thought, "Should I go for lunch with   → He wasn't sure **whether to go** for lunch
the in-crowd?"   with the in-crowd.

Lösung: a) *with: question word + infinitive construction; without: whether + infinitive construction*

b) *Matt had a lot of questions during his first days at school. Make sentences about him.*

Start: He wanted to know **where to go** for a drink of water.

– Where can I go for a drink of water? ✔
– Should I use my own laptop? *whether to use*
– Should I buy lunch or bring my own? *whether to buy*
– How much money must I bring for lunch? *how much money to bring*
– When can I use my locker? *when to use*
– What do I have to wear for PE? *what to wear*

Lösung: b) *… whether to use his own laptop. … whether to buy lunch or bring his own. … how much money to bring for lunch. … when to use his locker. … what to wear for PE.*

LANGUAGE 🧩 **12** **Infinitives after superlatives**

.: Phrases with super-
/es, p. 176

Superlative phrases with **infinitives** are easy to use. Look at the example below. Then use the words on the right to complete what some students in the school café are saying to each other.

1. You eat so quickly. You're always **the first to finish**!
2. You take so long to choose your food! You're always …
3. You're having salads?! I want a burger! Am I …?
4. We shouldn't eat too much before swimming. That's …
5. The pizza here is fantastic. I always think it's …
6. If you don't have much money, soup is …
7. I like having lunch with you guys. You're …

the only one / eat meat
the cheapest thing / have
the first / finish ✔
the funniest people / sit with
the worst thing / do
the last / sit down and eat
the best thing / order

Lösung: 2. *You're always the last to sit down and eat.* 3. *Am I the only one to eat meat?* 4. *That's the worst thing to do.*
5. *I always think it's the best thing to order.* 6. *…, soup is the cheapest thing to have.* 7. *You're the funniest people to sit with.*

LANGUAGE **13** **Object + infinitive: Expressing wishes and expectations**

 a) *Change the sentences below into German. Then compare the German and English constructions:*

Lösung: a) *Scott:* Komm Matt. Setz dich heute an unseren Tisch. → Scott will, dass Matt sich heute an ihren Tisch setzt. *(In German you use 'dass'.)*

1. Scott: Come on, Matt. Sit at our table today!
   ↓
2. Scott wants Matt to sit at their table today.

→ △ 131/10
→ ▲ 131/11

131/10 I want you to write back!
△ → After …
131/11 What I'd like others to do
▲ → After …

Lösung: b) 1. *Eva would prefer him to sit with … 2. They don't want me to be friends with … 3. We'd like people to think we're … 4. We'd like them to start thinking about … 5. The teachers don't want us to work on … 6. Scott and Eva expect everybody to agree with …*

b) *What do these people want or expect others to do? Look at the example and rewrite the other sentences in the same way. The yellow grid below can help too:*

Example: Scott: Don't sit with Henry and Tyler, Matt.
→ Scott doesn't **want Matt** to sit with Henry and Tyler.

1. Eva: No, sit with us instead. → Eva **would prefer** *him to sit*
2. Matt to himself: They don't think that I should be friends with Henry and Tyler.
   → They **don't want** …
3. Tyler: We're happy when people think we're different. → We**'d like** …
4. Henry: We hope they'll start thinking about where their clothes are made.
5. Tyler to Matt: The teachers say we can't work on our protest events during class.
6. Matt to himself: Scott and Eva always think that everybody should agree with them.

want / would like would prefer would expect	object (noun or <u>pronoun</u>)	infinitive with *to*
I (don't) want I expect I'd like I'd prefer	**+** me you him / her / it us them	**+** to …

Tip
Be careful! It's a typical mistake not to use an **infinitive with *to*** in sentences with *want you to …* or *expect you to …* because the sentence structure is different in German.

LANGUAGE **14** **Infinitives with and without *to*** → WB 30/12

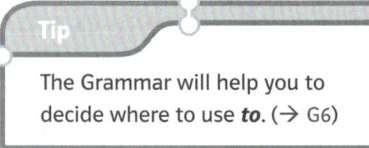
WB 30/12 Language (conversation)

*Read this e-mail from Sophie to Matt. Complete it with the verbs below. Use the infinitive form, with or without **to**.*

get   meet up   take   come   have   keep

do (2x)   control   calm down

Tip
The Grammar will help you to decide where to use *to*. (→ G6)

Hi Matt – You know we wanted [1] in Pittsburgh next week? Well, sorry but I can't. My parents have been worried about me all the time since we moved to the big city and they don't let me [2] anything. They're crazy! They've decided [3] everything I do! Today, I had planned [4] a coffee with friends after school but they made me [5] straight home. I think it's probably better just [6] as they say – but soon I'll make my escape! They should [7] and relax – but it <u>might</u> [8] a while! I promise [9] in touch – let's [10] together soon. xo 😊 Sophie

Lösung: 1. *to meet up,* 2. *do,* 3. *to control,* 4. *to have,* 5. *come,* 6. *to do,* 7. *calm down,* 8. *take,* 9. *to keep,* 10. *get*

KV 25: Working with language
WB 30/13 Language (leaflet)

LANGUAGE **15** Gerund or infinitive: It depends on the meaning → G7 → WB 30/13

a) *Some verbs (begin, like, prefer etc.) can be followed by an infinitive or a gerund with no difference in meaning. But with a few verbs, the meaning changes. It's important to learn by heart when you need a gerund and when you need an infinitive. First, write these two sentences in German to find out how the meaning of* **remember** *changes:*

1. He **remembered** <u>saying</u> goodbye to his friends back home; it made him feel sad. *→ sich erinnern*
2. She **remembered** <u>to tell</u> her parents what time she was coming home. *→ daran denken, etw. zu tun*

→ △ 119/12
/12 Infinitive or gerund?
→ Help with ...

b) *In the text on page 18, the verbs* **go on** *and* **stop** *are each used with an infinitive and with a gerund. Talk about how the meaning changes for each verb. Then write the sentences in German; this will help you to see the difference more clearly.*

c) *Read these sentences from an argument Sophie had with her mother and complete them with a* **gerund** *or an* **infinitive**.

Sophie:	I'll never forget **1** (hear) that you were taking me away from all my friends in Germany! *→ vergesse wie man etwas getan hat*
Mom:	Don't forget **2** (call) me when you arrive at your friend's house! *→ vergesse etw. zu tun*
Sophie:	Please stop **3** (give) me rules and curfews all the time!
Mom:	Can't you stop **4** (have) some lunch? I'm tired of <u>arguing</u> with you!
Sophie:	Try **5** (listen) to me sometimes. I just want to make friends and fit in! Why don't you try **6** (understand) how I feel?
Mom:	Playing sport is a good way to meet friends.
Sophie:	Sure, but it means **7** (stay) after school – and you won't let me!
Mom:	I don't mean **8** (upset) you. But America is new for all of us and I worry.

Methode probieren
Handlung probieren

bedeuten
wollen / beabsichtige

Lösung: c) 1. *hearing*, 2. *to call*, 3. *giving*, 4. *to have*, 5. *listening*, 6. *to understand*, 7. *staying*, 8. *to upset*

WB 31/14 Speaking (role play activity)
WB 31/15 Writing (demonstration)

MEDIATION **16** Clean out your attics for the <u>clothing drive</u>! → WB 31/14–15

→ △ 119/13
→ S13
/13 Useful phrases for
a's video chat
→ Help with ...
Bearbeitung von
diation-Aufgaben

Birchview Middle School is having a clothing drive for a <u>homeless shelter</u>. The committee for the project has written a flyer for it. On video chat, Lena wants to tell some students at her old school in Hamburg about it. One of you plays Lena and describes the main ideas in the flyer; 2–3 others play students who ask Lena questions about it.

HELP THE <u>HOMELESS</u>!
Birchview Middle School Clothing Drive

Are you tired of looking at all the old clothes in your closet? Worried about what your next new outfit will be? Well, some people <u>wish</u> they had problems like that. The Lakeview Homeless Shelter needs our help, and Birchview has ALWAYS been good at helping.
So ... **Donate as many old clothes as you can!**
(We'll accept clothing for kids and adults, and also shoes, belts, toys and bikes.) **The <u>benefits</u>:** Our school will get 15 cents a <u>pound</u> for all of the <u>items</u> we donate. And YOU'LL get a great feeling of knowing you helped homeless people, your school *and* your parents! (Remember, cleaning out the attic and garage is something they really expect you to do!) 😊 THANK YOU!

(Clothing <u>drop-offs</u>: Mo–Fr this week in the cafeteria, before or after school)

S 1/19–26
L 2/9–16 ⊙

Nightmare at the mall!

SPEAKING

1 Before you read

What teen films have you seen that felt believable at first, but then went in a direction that didn't seem believable at all? What was that moment? Use the words and phrases below to help you explain your ideas.

exaggerated actions / feelings / …   unrealistic situation / language / coincidence

actions which didn't match the character / the role

A Lena was excited. Madison's mom was finally driving them to the big mall on the other side of Pittsburgh. It was a long drive through lots of suburbs. After three weeks of waiting far
5 outside the city, where the suburbs end, she was going to see the *real* America and have an afternoon away from her boring life. She could still hear her own mom's voice in her ears: "If you lose your friends, call me – and don't do
10 anything silly!"

In the car, Madison's older brother Josh explained to Lena what was happening at the mall that day. "We're going to see a really famous baseball player, Wayne Larson," he
15 explained. "He's going to <u>open</u> a new sports store, so expect big crowds. He might even <u>sign</u> a T-shirt for you!"

B When they finally arrived, Lena was <u>amazed</u>. So many stores, so many people, so much noise! For a moment she felt <u>scared</u> – but only 20 for a moment. "This will be fun!" she thought. "Mom will come back later," said Madison. "If we lose each other, we need to meet here at these benches at 5 o'clock."

"Don't worry. I'm going to stay <u>right</u> next to 25 you!" said Lena. But exactly at that moment, there was a huge <u>cheer</u> and she was suddenly pushed into a big crowd of hundreds of people; everyone was trying to get a look at Wayne Larson. Lena tried to grab Madison's 30 arm, but the crowd was moving too fast and she soon realized that she had lost her friends – after only five minutes at the mall!

C Lena tried to turn around as the crowd pressed against her but she couldn't move at all. She 35 started to feel sick and <u>dizzy</u>. The voices all around her were getting louder, then some voices became even louder than the rest …

"<u>Down</u> with child labor!" …
"What if they were YOUR children?!" 40

What was going on? Wayne Larson was looking very worried as his bodyguards helped him to <u>escape from</u> the crowd. Who were the <u>protesters</u>? Lena was just able to see a group of young people who were all carrying signs 45 and shouting. Then the crowd started pushing again. This time, her feet didn't <u>touch</u> the ground and she flew through the air. She landed very close to the protesters. Then she felt a very strong pair of hands which then 50 took her away.

D "I've got one of the <u>troublemakers</u> right here!" a man shouted. "So what do you have to say for yourself, young lady?"

55 Lena couldn't believe it! Now the police were arresting her! She tried to speak but nothing came out. "I …, I …,"

"Well, you'd better think of some good answers to our questions quickly or you'll find 60 yourself in big trouble!" said the police officer. Lena could easily imagine spending a night in prison and she was starting to panic when a voice shouted from behind her. "<u>LEAVE HER ALONE</u>!" Who was that?

E "She isn't doing anything wrong! She isn't from here. Let her go!" the voice continued. She tried again to speak "I …, I …"

"Sshh," whispered the voice. Pretend you don't speak English!"

70 She turned around and came face to face with … Matt?! From the New York weekend?! "What are YOU doing here?!" she asked.

"Er, rescuing you!" he answered. "Now, don't say anything else. I'll get you out of 75 here." Lena waited while Matt spoke to the police officer and soon she was free to go.

F "What are you really doing here?" she asked Matt as they pushed through the crowds. "Oh, I've come to support the protesters – 80 they're my friends, from my new school in Pittsburgh."

Lena wanted to ask more questions, but then she remembered. What was she thinking? Matt had clearly told her that he didn't want to 85 meet up with her – while he had made it very <u>obvious</u> that he wanted to meet *Sophie!* Lena

found a small gap in the crowd and hurried away from Matt.

G What a nightmare! Lena wasn't enjoying her afternoon at the mall at all. Where were 90 Madison and the others in this sea of people? Lena was going up and down escalator after escalator; she looked everywhere and just couldn't find them. She needed to call her mom and felt silly about it – surely she was old 95 enough to look after herself better than this? But Lena accepted that it was time to give up and call her mom, so she opened her bag to get her phone and – it wasn't there.

H As Lena moved down *another* escalator, still 100 looking all around her for Madison, she was trying so hard not to cry that she almost didn't notice the boy in front of her – Josh!

"Lena!" he shouted when he saw her. "We couldn't find you! Madison has already gone 105 home with Mom – but don't worry. My friend, Nick, has a car. Come on!"

Lena didn't think <u>twice</u>: "Yeah, sure!"

"Cool, I'll drive you!" smiled Nick. But then Lena knew she really shouldn't go. She didn't 110 know Nick and she didn't like his smile. And, her mom would go crazy … But really, she was too tired to care. She was just walking along slowly with the boys when from behind her she suddenly heard a voice she knew. "Lena! 115 Here you are. I lost you! Look, here's your phone. You dropped it!" Matt was all smiles.

"He's just saved my life – for the *second* time today!" Lena thought. "I can't forgive him yet for liking Sophie more than me …" But 120 then she said: "Let's have a coffee before I call my mom." They both smiled.

KV 26: How does the story continue?
KV 27: Mediation: Child labor in sweatshops
WB 32/16 Reading (section summaries)

READING

2   Understanding the story → WB 32/16

a) *Match one of these headings to each of the eight parts of the story.*

1. Next stop: Prison?!
2. I can't be his friend
3. Alone already?!
4. Too old to be in this <u>mess</u>

5. Rescued again!
6. Escaping from home – finally!
7. Protests and shopping don't <u>mix</u>!
8. A friend to the rescue

b) *The title of the story is 'Nightmare at the mall'. Can you think of a title which would work better? Write it down and tell the class why you chose it.*
Lösung: a) *A: 6, B: 3, C: 7, D: 1, E: 8, F: 2, G: 4, H: 5*

READING

3   Believe it or not?

Which of these events in the story did you find believable – or not? Explain your reasons.

1. Lena lost her friends at the mall.
2. Matt was at the same mall as Lena.
3. Lena was stopped by the police.
4. Matt found Lena's phone.

5. Lena agreed to get into Nick's car.
6. Matt found Lena twice.
7. Lena invited Matt for a coffee.
8. The mall was so crowded.

WRITING

WB 32/17 Speaking/Writing/Mediation (options)

4   An exaggerated <u>storyline</u>: Make it more realistic → WB 32/17

→ S7–9
S7–9 Writing skills

Writing skills

Storylines are often exaggerated for more action and excitement. Examples:

- **coincidence:** *She turned around and came face to face with Matt.* (lines 70–71)

- **exaggerated language:** *He's just saved my life!* (line 118); *What a nightmare!* (line 89)

- **unrealistic situation:** *She felt a very strong pair of hands which then took her away.* (lines 49–51)

- **extreme action:** *Her feet didn't touch the ground; she flew through the air.* (lines 47–48)

- **extreme reaction:** *Pretend you don't speak English!* (lines 68–69)

- <u>**out-of-character**</u> **actions:** *Lena didn't think twice.* (line 108)

a) *Collect all the coincidences and unrealistic situations in the story.*

b) *Decide which situations in a) you would have <u>left out</u> of the story. Explain why.*

→ △ 119/14
119/14 What really happened at the mall
△ → Help with …

c) *Creative writing: Choose one part of the story to rewrite <u>so that</u> it's more believable.*

SPEAKING

5   ⟨ Your turn: Are you telling the truth? ⟩

Transfer

a) *What **true stories** can you think of which are exaggerated and almost impossible to believe? Which stories can you think of which would be fun to tell but **didn't really happen**? Make notes about a story you can tell in b).*

b) *Play a game: Now tell your stories to the class. Everyone can show if they believe your story or not: A **green** card means "I believe it" and a **red** card means "No way, I don't believe it!" Each person needs to explain his/her green or red card.*

Go on, text her! → S16

S16 Wichtige filmische Mittel

SPEAKING

WB 33/18 Vocabulary (matching)

1 Warm-up: What do you look for in others? → WB 33/18

*Share your ideas in your group about what you find <u>attractive</u> in others.
The words / phrases in the boxes can help you.*

> **Useful phrases**
>
> – I look for … in a friend / <u>boyfriend</u> /
>   girlfriend.
> – The person should have / be …
> – The most important thing to me is …
> – It's attractive if the person is / has …

> **nouns:**
> positive <u>attitude</u> | nice smile | good looks |
> sense of humor | sense of style |
> good listener | lots of the same interests

> **adjectives:**
> honest | fair | funny | attractive | smart |
> popular | outgoing | laid-back

VIEWING

2 The characters   KV 28: A character network

DVD 4/1

a) *Watch the two scenes with Wesley and Jessica (till 04:09). Then describe each character in the story so far: Wesley, Jessica and also Leanne. What are their roles in the storyline?*

b) *Now watch again and answer these questions:*

1. Describe what Jessica means at these moments with her advice for Wesley:

   Don't you think that's <u>overdoing</u> it? It's not really you.   Just relax and be yourself.

   Remember not to eat anything with garlic.   Clothes aren't everything.

2. Explain why it's good advice – or not.   3. What advice would you give Wesley?

VIEWING

3 The <u>date</u>

Folie 4/5: Bildbeschreibung und Vorentlastung des Hörsehverstehens
KV 29: Speaking (Talking about Wesley)

a) *How does Wesley change between the scene on the left (03:34) and the scene on the right (05:25)? Describe what happens (in 5–6 sentences) and how these two stills show the difference. Think of how Wesley acts, talks and looks.*

b) *Do you think Wesley and Leanne have a chance together? Go back to Ex. 1. Think of what Wesley and Leanne might find attractive and interesting in each other.*

WB 33/19 Across cultures

How to write in the appropriate style

This page can help you to find the right style and <u>tone</u> when you write different kinds of texts.

1   Listening: Students on the yearbook committee

L 2/17 ⊙

a) *Listen to two students who are discussing yearbook pages. Take notes about these points:*

the three main sections in yearbooks | typical <u>content</u> for each section | the appropriate language for each section

→ S15

S15 Hörverstehen üben

b) *Listen again. Which of these photos and texts are good and which ones need to be changed? What changes do the students suggest?*

OMG, how cute is Austin Ford's smile?! No surprise that he won 'Boy with the Best Smile'! (What <u>toothpaste</u> does he use?)

((Dear yearbook team – we still need a text here!))

Why does Janie ALWAYS have to be in the middle of EVERY photo? Here she is again! She'll never learn, will she?

WB 34/20 Skills (yearbook or newspaper)

2   Find the right writing style   → WB 34/20

In pairs, make a grid with three columns for **Student Superlatives**, **Highlights of the Year** *and* **Clubs and Sports**. *What language tone do you need for each category? What style of photos? What phrases are typical? Fill in your grid with ideas and phrases from the boxes below.*

3   Write a short yearbook text

Now go back to Ex. 1b). Write the text for photo 2 and improve the text for photo 3. Peer-edit each other's texts. Are the tone and the language appropriate?

→ S9

S9 Tipps für einen guten Schreibstil

HA

Word bank

Language tone:
funny | serious | <u>ironic</u> | simple | <u>informative</u>

Style of photos:
silly | <u>natural</u> | serious | <u>individual</u> / group | a silly / serious / … <u>pose</u>

Useful phrases

The swim / soccer / … team had their best <u>season</u> ever. | Being in / Participating in the Drama Club / the Yearbook Committee was … special / different / interesting this year because … | The Art Club started the year with … | Wasn't the Spring Dance / the <u>championship</u> basketball game the best ever? | We'll always remember the day when … | Here he / she is again with … | He / She will never learn! | We wanted you to see THIS! | How could we ever forget …?

An American-style yearbook

Here you get the chance to create some typical double pages in English for an American-style yearbook about your own school.

...: Important ...erences, p. 179

Step 1

Form groups

*Divide up into six groups. There should be **two groups** for each of the **three categories** of typical yearbook content you see on the right.*

Student Superlatives

Highlights of the Year

Clubs and Sports

Step 2

KV 30: Role cards (for group work)
WB 35/21 Skills (texts and photos)

Think about typical content for your pages → WB 35/21

*Each group is going to plan **a model double page** for its category. First you need to think about what kind of content is typical for your category. Think about these points as you <u>brainstorm</u> your ideas:*

- What kind of **texts** will you need: short / long; factual / funny?
- What kind of **photos**: individual / group; serious / funny; several / few / just one?
- What kind of a **design** would look best for your pages?
- What **examples** of school and free time activities from this unit can give you ideas for your own pages? What funny / strange / interesting things are there to report?
- What **vocabulary** and **language** from the unit could help you?

> **Tip**
>
> For the category 'Highlights of the Year', many yearbook commitees feature **free time** activities and events too (e.g. something that happened at the mall / a <u>concert</u> / at a party / …)

→ Vocabulary about teenage life (Introduction) → Likes / dislikes (Station 1) → Describing pictures (p. 47) → Questions and superlative phrases (Station 2) → Using the appropriate style and tone / Yearbook phrases (p. 56)

Step 3

WB 35/22 Poster checklist

Make a poster for your plan → WB 35/22

On a poster, make a plan that shows what your double page could look like. Then trade posters with the other group that has your category. Make sure you aren't doing the same things!

Step 4

Create your pages

Now divide up the work in your group: Collect photos, write texts, peer-edit each other's work. Also, somebody will need to present your pages to the class.

Step 5

Present your pages   **KV 31:** Self-evaluation (yearbook)

Present your pages to the class. Explain why the topics, photos and texts are good examples. Other groups will say which parts of your pages they liked best, and give their reasons.

LISTENING

1 **Moving** 🔴 KV 33–36: Test yourself

L 2/18 ◎ **a)** *Listen to the conversation between Kim and her best friend Tina. What is Kim's problem? What does Tina tell her?*

🖊 **b)** *Listen again and find examples of exaggerated language and extreme reaction. How does this match the turning point in the girls' conversation?*

👥 **c)** *Partner A: You're going to move to another town / country with your family and you're really sad to leave your friends. Partner B: One of your best friends is going to move to another town / country. What do you tell him / her to make him / her feel better? Collect ideas and act out your conversations first together and then for the class.*

VOCABULARY

🔴 WB 38/2 Language (forum post)

2 **Urban vs. rural** → WB 38/2

🖊 **a)** *Replace¹ the words and phrases in **bold** with the adjectives below to make the text more interesting. Sometimes you have to add the verb **be**.*

awesome   wealthy   dizzy   endless   flat   amazed   insecure   natural

gigantic   homeless

When I first saw New York City, I was **very surprised** by all the lights in the city. They seemed to be everywhere and to be on 24 hours a day! Sometimes when I looked up, I felt **like everything was spinning²** because all the buildings were **very, very big**. New York is a city of contrasts too. I saw people who were **very rich** and people who **didn't have a home**.

After three days in New York, I was ready to leave the city, but out in the country I felt small too because the landscape **had no mountains** and the sky **never stopped**. Everywhere I went people were **really, really great**. At first I **didn't feel very sure of myself**, but the Americans I met were all so friendly that soon it was **completely normal** for me to speak English with everybody!

HA 🖊 **b)** *Use five of the adjectives from a) to write your own sentences.*

Lösung: a) *amazed, dizzy, gigantic, wealthy, were homeless, was flat, was endless, awesome, was insecure, natural*

LANGUAGE

3 **I'm looking forward to …**

🖊 *Use the words and phrases to rewrite the conversation with **gerunds**.*

Start like this: A: **I'm looking forward to seeing** you on Friday!

be good at | keep | look forward to ✔ | stop | be used to | be worried about

Lösung: B: … *I keep counting the days.* A: *I'm worried about taking the train.* B: *Stop worrying!* … A: … *You're used to taking the train.* B: … *I'm not good at running like you are.*

A: I can't wait to see you on Friday! ✔
B: Me too! I'm counting the days.
A: I'm not so sure if I should take the train.
B: Don't worry! It's easy to use the train.

A: Yeah, for you it's easy. You take the train all the time.
B: Yes, I do. But when I'm late, I have a problem. I can't run like you can!

1 to replace (by/with) [rɪ'pleɪs] ersetzen (durch) | **2 to spin** [spɪn] sich drehen

LANGUAGE

WB 38/3 Speaking/Language (photo competition)

4 Sophie's bedroom → WB 38/3

a) *What do the things in Sophie's bedroom and her telephone conversation say about her? Use the words and phrases to make sentences with **gerunds**.*

Example: Sophie **loves buying** new shoes.

> decide against | dream of | be crazy about | be excited about | be good at | love ✔

> dance | watch | go | listen | travel | buy ✔

> I want to buy new shoes …

(margin notes, partially visible:)
ing: a) *She's good at ...cing. She's crazy about ...ning to 'The 4'. She dreams ...raveling around the world ...en she's 22). She's decided ...inst going on a student ...hange to Mexico. She's ...ted about watching a movie ...h Josh on Friday.*

HA

b) *Think about things in your room. What do they say about you? Write three sentences with **gerunds**.*

WRITING

5 America is different

a) *Imagine you've spent some time in America. Think of three things that are different there. Write down tips for someone who is visiting America for the first time.*

Start like this:
If you have to use the toilet in America, don't ask where the 'toilet' is. Instead …

Transfer

b) *Your turn: What is different in Germany? Work with a partner and write down three tips for people who are visiting Germany for the first time.*

LANGUAGE

6 Too many rules

*Put the words in the right order to make sentences with **gerunds as subject or object**.*

1. the rules | isn't | following | cool
2. what everyone else | I | don't like | does | doing
3. with my parents | arguing | is awful | about my curfew
4. isn't | with a troublemaker | a good idea | being friends
5. don't mind | with the popular kids | I | hanging out
6. but | having | I | my own ideas | love

(margin notes, partially visible:)
ing: 1. *Following the ...s isn't cool.* 2. *I don't like ...g what everyone else ...s.* 3. *Arguing with my ...nts about my curfew is ...ul.* 4. *Being friends with a ...blemaker isn't a good idea. ...don't mind hanging out ... the popular kids.* 6. *But I ... having my own ideas.*

LANGUAGE

7 Celebrating Thanksgiving

a) *Use the verbs to complete the text with **gerunds as subject or object**.*

be   bother   celebrate   eat (2x)   play   talk   wait   watch

1 Thanksgiving is good and bad. I don't mind **2** turkey every year because my mom makes the best turkey ever. **3** polite and **4** my grandma's potatoes although I don't like them is hard. One of the worst parts is **5** with my annoying little cousins. They never know when to stop **6** me. **7** for dessert is probably the worst part. The adults spend so much time **8** before we get our pie. There's another big Thanksgiving tradition. I love **9** football on TV with all my uncles.

Lösung: a) 1. *Celebrating*, 2. *eating*, 3. *Being*, 4. *eating*, 5. *playing*, 6. *bothering*, 7. *Waiting*, 8. *talking*, 9. *watching*

b) *What do you like / don't you like about holidays with your family? Make sentences with **gerunds** and share them with your partner. These ideas can help you:*

Transfer

Celebrating holidays with my family is … | On holidays I really like / don't like … | … is the best part of holidays. | I always look forward to …

MEDIATION

WB 37/1 Reading/Speaking (child labor)

8 Fair for everyone → WB 37/1

Lena is showing Matt a website about a fair trade group in Germany. Answer Matt's questions.

1. Why are they showing the picture of a clothes store?   2. What do they say about being fair?
3. The children in the picture are wearing school uniforms. What is said about this in the text?

FAIR FÜR ALLE – Wir setzen uns ein, damit alle fair handeln können.

Immer mehr Leute wollen Produkte kaufen, die „fair" hergestellt wurden, egal ob es sich um Lebensmittel oder Kleidung handelt. Oft wissen sie aber nicht, welche Produkte sie kaufen sollen und was „fair" genau bedeutet. Unser Ziel ist es, dass mehr Menschen sich für das Thema „fairer Handel" interessieren.

Und „fair" hat viele verschiedene Aspekte. Einer davon ist die Kinderarbeit, denn in manchen Ländern müssen die Kinder arbeiten, um zum Familienunterhalt beizutragen. Wir sind der Meinung, dass etwas dagegen getan werden muss. Alle Kinder sollten die Chance haben, eine Schule zu besuchen.

LANGUAGE

9 In the yearbook office

🖋 Use **infinitive constructions** to rewrite the sentences.

HA

Example: 1. Tom loves the yearbook. He is always **the first to arrive** at the office.

1. Tom loves the yearbook. He is always the first person who arrives at the office. ✔
2. Julie has a good camera. So she is the only one who takes pictures.
3. Sue is very careful. She is always the first person who finds mistakes in the captions.
4. David is responsible. He is the last person who looks at the yearbook.
5. The last yearbook was amazing. It was the only one that won a prize.

Lösung: 2. ... *the only one to take pictures.* 3. ... *the first person to find mistakes in the captions.*
4. ... *the last person to look at the yearbook.* 5. ... *the only one to win a prize.*

SPEAKING

10 Student superlatives

In some yearbooks students are asked to vote in different categories, e.g. 'Most likely¹ to succeed', 'Most likely to become president²'.

a) *Describe the cartoon. If you need help, go back to the skills box on p. 47.*

b) *Explain the message of the cartoon. The useful phrases in the box can help you.*

> **Useful phrases**
>
> In my opinion, the cartoon's message is ... |
> I think the cartoon wants to show / tell
> us that ... | The cartoonist wants us to
> think about ... / wants to make fun of ³ ...

Talk about Snooty. She was listed as 'most likely to be googled' in the class yearbook.

LANGUAGE

11 Pocket money

🖋 a) *Use the prompts to make sentences with **object + infinitive**.*

Example: 1. Jill doesn't have any money. She **wants her father to lend** her some.

1. Jill doesn't have any money. her father | lend her some | she | want ✔
2. Her father thinks Jill is lazy. get an after-school job | he | her | would like
3. Jill says she doesn't have enough time. give her more pocket money | her parents | expect | she
4. Jill's father believes there is an easy solution. tell | he | her | to get a calendar
5. Jill gets angry. her father | her | to be polite | warn
6. Suddenly Jill is very sweet again. her father | remind | she | to give her her pocket money. Today is the first of the month!

ng: a) 2. ... *He would like to get an after-school job. She expects her parents to give her more pocket money. He tells her to get a calendar.* 5. ... *Her father warns her to be polite.* 6. ... *reminds her father to give her pocket money.* ...

Transfer

🖉 b) *What do your parents like or expect you to do? And what do you like or expect your parents to do? Make a list and share your ideas in class.*

1 likely [ˈlaɪkli] wahrscheinlich | **2 president** [ˈprezɪdnt] Präsident/-in | **3 to make fun of** [ˌmeɪk ˈfʌn̩ əv] sich lustig machen über

VOCABULARY

12 English in Britain and America

a) *Look at these words in American English. Find British English words which have the same meaning.*

vacation   yard   restroom   movie   downtown   elevator   movie theater

soccer   apartment   period   store

b) *Answer the following questions about American English.*

1. What do the Americans mean when they talk about a 'holiday'?   2. Where's the first floor in America?   3. Why do the Americans use the word 'soccer'?   4. Why is the temperature in America always so high?

LANGUAGE

13 At the shopping mall

Change the infinitive constructions back into **questions**.

Example: There were so many entrances to the mall. Lena didn't know which to use.
→ Lena: Which entrance should I use?

1. She wanted to know where to buy a new winter jacket.
2. She didn't know which store to go to first.
3. She wasn't sure whether to buy a jacket now or wait.
4. She asked herself what to do.
5. She didn't know who to ask about a restroom.
6. She wasn't sure when to take the bus home.

WB 39/4 Language (poster)
WB 39/5 Language (speech)

LANGUAGE

14 How to get around → WB 39/4–5

a) *Change the verbs into* **gerunds** *or* **infinitives**.

I'd always dreamed of [1] (travel) across America, but I wasn't sure how [2] (do) it. By bus? By train? By plane? I decided [3] (use) all different kinds of <u>transportation</u>[1]. I don't really like [4] (fly) so I did that first and flew to New York City. The next morning I went to the train station and was the first one [5] (buy) a ticket. My mother wants me [6] (take) lots of pictures on my trip so my first photos were of the train that arrived at the station. [7] (ride) on the train to Florida was nice, but I was tired of just [8] (sit) so next I rented a car and drove myself all the way to Chicago. [9] (drive) in America is easy because the roads are flat and wide and I'm good at [10] (concentrate). In Chicago I was really excited about [11] (get) a motorcycle, but I took the bus to the Grand Canyon instead. That's where I got a horse. At first I was worried about [12] (fall) off, but [13] (ride) it was so great that I rode it all the way to California!

Transfer

b) *Think of places you'd like to visit in the US. Share your ideas with a partner. Tell him / her why you'd like to go there. Then present your partner's ideas in class.*

1 transportation (*AE*) [trænspɔːˈteɪʃn] Verkehrsmittel; Transport

SPEAKING

15 Who do you want to help?

a) *Look at the pictures. Say what the people are doing. Can you think of more ways to help other people? Collect ideas and share them in class.*

b) *Which of the three people or groups would you like to help? Explain why. Discuss your ideas with a partner.*

VOCABULARY

16 Across the USA

Complete the text with the words in the box.

> attitude | colonists | European | harvest | populated | population | rights | rural | symbolizes | temperatures | tractors | vacation | wealthiest | attractive | demonstrated | skyscrapers | religion | urban | shopping malls

ing: 1. *vacation,*
uropean, 3. *colonists,*
opulated, 5. *skyscrapers,*
ral, 7. *temperatures,*
opulation, 9. *religion,*
emonstrated, 11. *rights,*
ractors, 13. *harvest,*
hopping malls, 15. *urban,*
ymbolizes, 17. *attitude,*
ttractive, 19. *wealthiest*

If you want to spend your ⬛1 in the United States, there are many different destinations to choose from. Let's start on the East Coast. Many people say that this is the most ⬛2 region in America; maybe because that's where most of the ⬛3 in the 1600s were from. The East Coast is also densely ⬛4 and has many big cities such as Boston, Washington, D.C., New York and Philadelphia. If you want to see ⬛5 , you should start in New York City. In contrast, the rest of New York State is quite ⬛6 .

States in the South are known for their warm ⬛7 . That's one of the reasons these states have an older ⬛8 . In the South many

people practice a ⬛9 so there are a lot of churches, and this is also where, in the past, many people ⬛10 so that black and white people could have the same ⬛11 .

In the middle of the US there are a lot of farms. People here enjoy living in the country and far away from cities. It's normal here for teenagers to drive ⬛12 and to help with the ⬛13 . But they also enjoy spending time at ⬛14 just like ⬛15 teens.

For some people the West Coast ⬛16 an easy-going lifestyle and a relaxed[1] ⬛17 . But the West Coast is more than Hollywood and beaches. It is also a very ⬛18 location for the computer industry and some of the ⬛19 Americans have started their companies here.

1 **relaxed** [rɪˈlækst] entspannt; locker

Text smart 2
Advertisements

Find more online:
n6sx2g

SALE !

$4.99

Buy one,
get one
FREE

You can see advertisements for <u>products</u> <u>just about anywhere</u> you look. How and why do <u>advertisers</u> try to <u>win</u> customers <u>over</u>? What are key features of most print ads? Find out here!

VOCABULARY

→ S17

S17 Vokabeln ordnen und strukturieren
Voc.: You, one, they, p. 180

1 Warm-up: Are you a dream customer?

a) *Describe what you think of when you hear the word 'advertisement'. Explain why you think that way.*

b) *Are you an advertiser's dream customer? Take the test and find out!*   Yes ↓   No ↓

Start here

On the radio, they mention a big sale at a clothes store in the mall. They're offering two T-shirts for the price of one. And it's your favorite brand!

If you can avoid it, you don't pay attention to ads on the radio, on TV or anywhere.	You decide to go to the mall immediately to look for the T-shirts from the radio ad.	You're going to go to the mall anyway, so you'll have a look at them while you're there.
At the mall, they don't have any T-shirts in your favorite color. But you love a bargain, so you decide to buy two anyway.	You don't need one new T-shirt, so why would you need *two*? Forget it!	You don't like the T-shirts in the sale. But you see another T-shirt that looks really great. Maybe you'll buy it.
They're <u>giving away</u> free <u>samples</u> of a new <u>chocolate bar</u>, but you walk away; you'd feel guilty about not buying one.	They're giving away free samples of a new chocolate bar. You take one. Mmm, good! Then you decide to buy one.	They're giving away free samples of a new chocolate bar. You take one but won't buy one later. You never <u>fall for</u> *that* trick!
You see your favorite movie star on a new shampoo. You buy it because he/she has *perfect* hair.	You see your favorite movie star on a new shampoo. You aren't really happy with the product you're using now. Maybe you'll try this one; maybe not.	You never buy products that are advertised by celebrities. They earn enough money already.
You seem to be an advertiser's dream customer! You're <u>receptive</u> to ads and interested in buying new products.	You're interested in new things but you don't react immediately to every new <u>temptation</u> the advertisers try to sell you.	You seem to be <u>sceptical</u> about <u>advertising</u> and having new things. Ad people won't have an easy time with you!

c) 1. Say why you agree or disagree with your test results.
   2. Give a short definition of what you think an advertiser's dream customer is.
   3. Explain which *one* situation above comes closest to describing how *you* typically react.

Transfer

d) *Your turn: Give an example of how an ad has succeeded in making you buy something.*

Did you see that new ad?

Folie 4/6: Bildbeschreibung und -analyse

So everyone and their dog has more style than you?

<u>Spice up</u> your style with the extra-cool and <u>highly</u> individual looks at *Retro 4ever*. <u>Brand-new</u> collection <u>available</u> in stores now!

From the past, for the future.

<u>Glamorous</u> girls   Cool dudes   Funny friends   <u>Lovely</u> ladies   Nice <u>nerds</u>

Locations in Boston – Manhattan – Brooklyn – Philadelphia – Washington, D.C.

WB 40/1 Vocabulary (new ad)
WB 40/2 Vocabulary (products)

READING

2 The features of print ads → WB 40/1–2

→ S7

Textsorten und ihre Besonderheiten

a) *Study the ad above.*

1. Describe what product the advertisers are trying to sell to their customers.
2. Say who you think the <u>target</u> group of customers is.

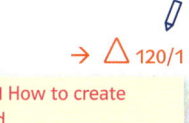

→ △ 120/1

/1 How to create ad
→ Help with …

b) *How is the ad above put together to sell the product? Point out the different features. (The skills box can help you.)*

c) *Now think about the language of the ad. Give examples of how these features work in the ad copy:*

humor   adjectives

> **Reading skills**
>
> With print advertisements, <u>be aware of</u> the **typical building blocks** that work together to sell the product:
>
> - an **eye-catcher** (a <u>visual</u> and / or a text)
> - a **slogan**
> - the **ad copy** (the text parts of an ad)
> - one or more **images** of the product
> - **contact** and **location** information

Transfer

d) *Your turn: If you were the customer and saw the ad above in a magazine, on a poster or on a <u>billboard</u>, would you be interested? Explain your opinion.*

SPEAKING

3   Slogans: A closer look

a) *'From the past, for the future'* is the slogan for the **Retro 4ever** ad. In your group of 4–6, discuss reasons why you think it fits – or doesn't fit – the product.

b) Go back to the Retro 4ever ad. Together, <u>think up</u> a better slogan for the product. Why is it better? Compare your slogan with another group's.

Folie 4/7: Bildbeschreibung und -analyse
WB 41/3 Vocabulary (adjectives)

READING

4   Print ads: Similar product, different approach   → WB 41/3

→ △ 120/2

120/2 Talking about a target group
△ → Help with …

a) *Study the ad below and answer these questions:*

1. Describe what product the advertisers are trying to sell.
2. Say who you think the target group is.

b) *Point out which features of print ads you can find in this ad and describe them.*

c) *Give your opinion on the quality of the ad:*

1. Explain how <u>effective</u> it is for the target group the advertisers are trying to <u>attract</u>.
2. Explain what '<u>fabulous</u>' means here.

WRITING   **5** **Comparing the two ads**

a) *Think – pair – share: Use the headings below to make a grid for each ad. On your own, write down key words for your opinion of the different features. Then talk about your ideas with a partner from your group in Ex. 3. In a classroom discussion, point out the differences and <u>similarities</u> between the two ads.*

visuals | slogan / ad copy | humor | product | target group | effectiveness

→ △ 120/3

/3 Improving an ad
→ Help with ...

b) *With your partner, use your ideas from a) to improve the two ads. You choose ad 1, your partner chooses ad 2. Make changes that you feel would be <u>improvements</u>. Then <u>swap</u> ads. <u>Afterwards</u>, explain to each other why you made your changes.*

> **KV 37:** Crosswords: Advertising
> **KV 38:** Create your own ad
> **KV 39:** It's all about money
> **WB 41/4** Writing (an ad)

WRITING   **6** **Options: Create your own ads**   → WB 41/4

Option A: <u>Trash</u> to treasure

→ S7–9

S7–9 Writing skills

a) *Each of you finds an object at home you think is useless / <u>ugly</u> / awful / too old. It should be something you think nobody would buy!*

b) *Now <u>slip into</u> the role of the advertiser: What kind of an ad could make one of your objects sound like a great product? Together, write and design an ad for it.*

c) *Present your product to the class. How many classmates think your ad is convincing?*

Option B: Create an ad around the visual

→ S7–9

S7–9 Writing skills

a) *Choose one of the photos below. What kind of a product could a print ad be about with a photo like that? Think of how you could <u>combine</u> the typical features of print ads to make your product sound wonderful for your target group! Together, write and design your ad.*

b) *Present your product to the class. How many classmates would buy your product?*

WB 42 <Reading corner> (two ads)

Find more online:
2px5br

School life – dos and don'ts

SPEAKING

Transfer

1 Your turn

Talk about rules at your school. Look at the different situations below and the phrases on the right.

corridor | cafeteria |
gym | laboratory |
classroom | computer
room | library | outside

Useful phrases

We can / can't | are / aren't allowed to | have to / don't have to
be late | eat / drink water | use our cell phones | shout | wear
a uniform | be there without a teacher | skip classes | cheat |
leave bags on the floor | …
If we break the rules / get caught …
– we have to stay after school | do extra work | stand outside |
see the principal | …
– we are suspended | sent home
– we get detention
– our parents get a letter / phone call

VIEWING

2 A look at a US school   KV 40: Viewing (US school)

a) *Look at the film still. What do you think the problem is?*

DVD 4/2
→ S16

S16 Wichtige
filmische Mittel

b) *Watch the film. Describe the situation. What's the problem with Ruby?*

Tip

If you break a rule in a US school, your teacher might give you **detention**.
This means that you have to stay in the classroom with a teacher in your free time – at lunchtime or after school. The teacher will give you some work to do and you have to do it in silence. You must complete all the work before you can leave the room.

c) *Watch the film again. What are the consequences for Ruby? The phrases in the box can help you.*

d) *Give your opinion: What do you think about the way Ruby is acting? Does she deserve the consequences? Why / Why not?*

Useful phrases

– If she …, she'll …
– If she doesn't …, her teacher might …
– She shouldn't … because …
– It's a bad idea for her to … because …
– If I were Ruby, I'd …
– Otherwise, she'll …

WB 43/1 Vocabulary/Speaking (democratic school)

VOCABULARY

3 **A further look at rules** → WB 43/1

a) *Match the verbs with the phrases. Then write down the correct rule (positive or negative!).*

Example: Don't bring stuff into the classroom!

get   use   bring ✔   skip   stand in line (*AE*)   be (2x)   stand

1. stuff into the classroom ✔
2. late
3. in the hallway
4. for lunch
5. in the corridor without a hall pass
6. classes
7. detention
8. your cell phones

b) *Look at what the teacher is saying to her students. What do you think the student has or hasn't done in each situation?*

1. The class started 10 minutes ago!
2. Please put your bag into the locker!
3. Where were you this morning?
4. <u>Switch</u> it <u>off</u> right now, please!
5. You call this 'homework'?!

WRITING

4 **Reasons behind the rules**

Look at the rules from Ex. 3 again. Take turns to write a rule and to explain the reasons behind that rule.

Example:
A: 'No texting friends during class' means that they want students to listen to the teacher and focus on their work.

SPEAKING

5 **Role play**

→ S11

S11 Gespräche führen

a) *Your friend doesn't agree with a school rule and <u>is about to</u> break it. You don't want your friend to <u>get into trouble</u> <u>so</u> you try to persuade him/her not to break the rule. Choose from one of the situations below and write the conversation. The phrases in the box can help you.*

fake hall pass so that he/she can skip classes

cheat in a test/use a cheat sheet

b) *Act out your conversation in class.*

Useful phrases

Persuading someone to change their behavior
– You're going to get into so much trouble!
– You're so going to get detention!
– You'll be suspended if you …
– They have that rule because …
– I see your point but …
– You might be right but …
– <u>You'd better</u> …/You should…/Why don't you …?
– <u>If I were you</u>, I'd …

Expressing an attitude
– <u>No risk, no fun!</u>
– They want me to …
– They make me so <u>mad</u>!
– Why can't I …?
– They can't stop me …!
– <u>I can't see the point of</u> …
– It's a <u>waste</u> of time telling him/her …
– I don't understand why …

Lösung: a) 2. Don't be late! 3. Don't stand in the hallway! 4. Stand in line for lunch! 5. Don't be in the corridor without a hall pass! 6. Don't skip classes! 7. Don't get detention! 8. Don't use your cell phones!

Find more online:
dr3h3e

Unit 3
City of dreams: New York

A   Times Square – New York's busiest intersection and home to its theater district

> **Folie 4/8:** Bildbeschreibung und Erweiterung des Orientierungswissens
> **KV 41:** Listening (Alicia Keys)

LISTENING   **1**   **A song: Empire State of Mind (Part II)**   Alicia Keys

 a) *In small groups, describe the photos to each other. Can you think of more photos that represent New York City for you?*

L 2/19 ⊙   **b)** *Listen to the song and say how it makes you feel. Does it give you a positive or negative image of New York?*
→ S15

S15 Hörverstehen üben   **c)** *Look at the photos again and read the lines from the song. Which of the photos do these lines match? Explain why.*

the streets are mean   I got a pocketful of dreams   I'm gonna make it by any means

big lights will inspire you   such a melting pot   all looking pretty   make you feel brand-new

concrete jungle where dreams are made of

Transfer   **d)** *There are more songs about New York City than most places in the world. Can you think of reasons why? Do you know a song about a German city or town? If you do, say what it is about.*

In Unit 3 you learn

… about different aspects of New York City. You learn:

* how to talk about personal experiences, hopes and dreams
* how to give extra information
* useful phrases for <u>conducting</u> an interview

B   The Chrysler Building in Midtown Manhattan

C   Central Park – New York's big green lung

D   In Chinatown

E   Homeless people in the streets

LISTENING   **2**   Big city life   **KV 52:** Working with vocabulary (Unit 3)

→ △ 121/1

*1 Big city life
> Help with …*

a) *Think – pair – share: Imagine you lived in a big city like New York with your family. What do you think you'd enjoy most? What wouldn't be so great about it? Exchange ideas with a partner before you both share your ideas in class. Here are some topics to start with:*

people | entertainment | activities | education | culture | traffic | crime

L 2/20 ⊙

b) *Listen to the interview with David, a teenager from New York. What does he or doesn't he like about life in the city? Take notes.*

→ S15

15 Hörverstehen üben

c) *Compare your ideas from a) with David's answers. What's the same, what's different?*

WB 44/1 Vocabulary (New York)
WB 44/2 Vocabulary (songs)

WRITING   **3**   Your turn: In New York City   → WB 44/1–2

→ △ 121/2

*2 Your turn: In New
< City
> Help with …*

Look at the photos again. Which photo could you imagine yourself in? Write a short text about what you're doing in the photo and what you can feel (see, hear, smell, taste).

Transfer

HA

L 2/21 ⊙

Saving the best for last

"Hey, Diego! Come here, please!" Diego's boss called to him. "These two young ladies need help getting around New York. I told them that nobody knows this city better than you. Take
5 the rest of the day off and show them the best places." Diego was more than happy to leave his after-school job at the diner early. Rylee, who was 17 and from Alabama, and her cousin Lea, who was from Berlin, had a day to spend
10 in New York while Rylee's parents were at a conference.

"Where are we going first?" Rylee asked. "The Empire State Building?"

"No," Diego said, "I'll show you sides of New
15 York you'll never read about in a guidebook."

As they entered a big office building, the girls gasped. Classical music filled their ears. "These are students from the Juilliard School, which is a famous music school,"
20 Diego explained. While they were listening, he thought about his parents. They'd like him to work in an office building like this, for a bank maybe. A nice safe job. Something better than they had. But he wanted excitement.
25 After they'd had a look at the Astor Place Cube, an outdoor sculpture, they went to Times Square, which was always crowded with tourists. Diego loved being part of the crowds of New York although his parents hated it.
30 Since he knew 'The Naked Cowboy', who was really only *almost* naked, the girls could take a picture with him for free. Diego's idea of New York on a shoestring was working well so far! He had two more free places to show them
35 before the big surprise. He had to time it just right.

First they walked to the Alvin Ailey Dance Studio, which is just a couple of blocks from Central Park, and watched the dance
40 class through the tall windows. "Diego, this is absolutely wonderful," Rylee said full of enthusiasm. "We'd never have found this without you!" They made it to the 5th floor of the Metropolitan Museum of Art just in time
45 for the sunset over Central Park.

"This is the best, Diego," Lea said. "Thanks for a really great day."

He looked at them and smiled. "An entertainer always saves the best for last. So let's go!"   50

Diego led them to 30 Rockefeller Center, which is one of the tallest skyscrapers in New York, but they didn't use the front entrance. Instead they snuck into a service entrance and then into an elevator. "We're going to the top,"   55
he told the girls, "to the Top of the Rock."

Both girls looked at him. "To the top of Rockefeller Center? But every tourist knows how expensive tickets are!"

"Leave that to me," he told them.   60

When the elevator stopped and the doors opened, they entered a dark hallway. Just then a bright light shone in Diego's eyes and a loud voice with a strong accent shouted, "Stop! Who's there?"   65

With his hands covering his eyes, Diego said, "It's me. It's just me, dad."

"Diego?" the voice asked. *¿Qué estás haciendo aquí?*

"We just wanted to enjoy the view," Diego   70
said quietly.

READING

→ S1

Schnelllesetechniken

1 Diego's New York

Folie 4/9: Sicherung des Leseverstehens und Erweiterung des Orientierungswissens

a) *Sum up which places Diego showed to the girls. Why didn't he take them to the typical New York sights?*

b) *What would you have done in the girls' shoes – gone with Diego or followed your guidebook? Explain why.*

LANGUAGE

→ △ 121/3
→ ▲ 122/4

3 Tourists in New York
→ After …

4 A stopover in New York
→ After …

WB 45/3 Language (The Big Apple)

2 Revision: Defining relative clauses → G8 → WB 45/3

a) *Look at these sentences. Explain when you use the relative pronoun* **who**, **which** *or* **that**.

1. Most of the people **who** live in New York weren't born there.
2. The restaurants **which** we went to weren't expensive.
3. The musicians **that** play in the office building don't get any money.
4. We followed the plan **that** Diego gave us.

ung: a) 'who' is used for
ple; 'which' for things or
nals; 'that' is used for
ple, animals or things.
y can be used either as
ect or object.
. who / that he worked
3. – / which / that Diego
wed us, 4. which / that
n't in every guidebook,
/ which / that everyone
to see, 6. which / that
ws people the real New
k

b) *Read Rylee's message to one of her friends. Use the phrases to complete the text with* **defining relative clauses**. *Decide where you can leave out the relative pronoun.*

Example: 1. This guy **(who/that) we met at lunch** said he'd show us the city.

aren't in every guidebook   everyone has to see   Diego showed us   he worked for

we met at lunch ✔   shows people the real New York

Dear Ashley,

You won't believe what happened to us in New York! This guy **1** said he'd show us the city. First we weren't sure if we should go with him, but the man **2** told us he was okay. The things **3** were amazing. They were all places **4** . Well, except for Times Square. But Diego said that's a place **5** . It was amazing! And you know what happened at the end of our tour: We got caught by Diego's father! He's a security man at Rockefeller Center and he found us after we'd snuck into a service entrance. That was a bit embarrassing, but we still had a wonderful day. Diego could start a tour company **6** .

Miss you! xoxo – Rylee

KV 42: Working with language

LANGUAGE

3 Find the rule: Non-defining relative clauses → G8

a) *Explain the difference between these two sentences.*

1. The Juilliard School, which is located in Manhattan, is known around the world.
2. My cousin goes to a music school which is known around the world.

b) *Find at least five more examples of* **non-defining relative clauses** *in the text.*

> **Tip**
>
> In non-defining relative clauses …
> – you use 'who' for people and 'which' for things. You never use 'that'.
> – you always need a **comma** to separate the main clause from the relative clause.

LANGUAGE

4 What happened before

*Read what happened before Rylee and Lea met Diego. Decide if the sentences have **defining** or **non-defining relative clauses**. Put in commas where you need them.*

Lösung: *... who had never been to NY before, ... that was home to only 10,000 people, ... who never got lost. ... which suggested a walking tour through Chinatown. ... which is where they'd started.*

After the girls had said goodbye to Rylee's parents, Rylee who had never been to New York before decided to give her cousin a tour of the city. Rylee lived in a city that was home to only 10,000 people, but she wasn't worried at all. She told herself that she was a person who never got lost. The two girls took the subway to Lower Manhattan. Rylee planned to follow their guidebook which suggested a walking tour through Chinatown. 20 minutes later, the two girls were back at Wall Street Subway Station which is where they'd started. "So that's what you call an amazing tour," Lea groaned.

LANGUAGE

5 Flying to New York

*Combine the two sentences into one. Use **non-defining relative clauses**.*

Lösung: *2. ..., which is one of the busiest airports in the US. 3. ..., who works in the Empire State Building. 4. ..., who gives tours of the building, speaks six languages. 5. ..., which has 102 floors, was built in 1931. 6. ..., which only takes one minute to get to the 80th floor, is really fast.*

Example: 1. Our plane is going to leave from Stuttgart Airport, which is close to our house.

1. Our plane is going to leave from Stuttgart Airport. This is close to our house. ✔
2. We're going to fly to JFK International. This is one of the busiest airports in the US.
3. We're going to visit my Aunt Nancy. She works in the Empire State Building.
4. Aunt Nancy speaks six languages. She gives tours of the building.
5. The Empire State Building was built in 1931. It has 102 floors.
6. The elevator is really fast. It only takes one minute to get to the 80th floor.

LANGUAGE

6 Make the text more interesting → WB 45/4

WB 45/4 Language (The Empire State Building)

→ △ 122/5

122/5 Defining or non-defining?
△ → After ...

Lösung: *1. ..., which stands in New York harbor, 2. ..., which has become so important for American culture, 3. ... who based his figure on the Roman Goddess of Liberty, 4. ..., which took nine years to build, 5. ..., which is now known as 'Liberty Island'. 6. ..., which stands for 'enlightenment', 7. ..., which is the date of America's Independence from Britain. 8. ..., which is visited by millions of people each year.*

*Use **non-defining relative clauses** to add the extra information below.*

The Statue of Liberty is one of New York's most famous sights. But did you know that this symbol of freedom was a present from France? It was designed by the French artist Auguste Bartholdi. The statue was completed in France in 1884 and then brought to America. There it was rebuilt on Bedloe Island. In her right hand, 'Lady Liberty' is holding a torch, and in her left, a tablet with the date July 4th, 1776. The seven spikes on her crown stand for the seven seas and the seven continents of the world. Today the Statue of Liberty is a popular tourist attraction. You can even go up to the Statue's crown!

1. The Statue of Liberty stands in New York harbor.
2. This symbol of freedom has become so important for American culture.
3. Bartholdi based his figure on the Roman Goddess of Liberty.
4. The statue took nine years to build.
5. Bedloe Island is now known as 'Liberty Island'.
6. The torch stands for 'enlightenment'.
7. July 4th, 1776 is the date of America's independence from Britain.
8. The Statue of Liberty is visited by millions of people each year.

SPEAKING

7 Your turn: Give extra information

Transfer

*Get into two teams. One team gives the main clause and the other team has to add a **non-defining relative clause**. Take turns.*

Example: My friend Ben has a dog. → My friend Ben, who is sitting next to me, has a dog.

READING

8 Food in New York City   KV 43: Create your own New York style food

Read the box about different food in New York. Then talk to your partner about food and places to eat where you live.

Across cultures

Life in New York City has been strongly influenced by its millions of immigrants from all over the world. You can best experience this when you start looking for New York **ethnic** food. From the outside, some restaurants look like just a hole in the wall, but inside you can find delicious Indian food like samosa, which is a fried pastry with a vegetarian filling. Another famous New York dish is bagel and lox – typical Jewish food.

Walking down the street is a great way to find delicious food too. New York has hundreds of **food trucks and carts** around the city which sell everything from hot dogs – New York's most famous snack – to schnitzel or tacos. New Yorkers are still combining flavors and specialities to create new dishes, e.g. the cronut – a combination of croissant and doughnut.

MEDIATION

WB 46/5 Vocabulary (a special tour of NY)

9 What do you eat? → WB 46/5

→ △ 122/6
→ S13

On their tour of New York City, Lea told Diego about some typical German food. A few days later, Diego sends her an e-mail and asks about more typical food from her region. Lea finds this article on the internet. In their next video chat she tells Diego about it.

*Say what Lea tells Diego. Use **non-defining relative clauses** to give extra information.*

Ein weiteres beliebtes Gericht aus der Mitte Deutschlands ist „Himmel und Erde". Hinter dem Wort „Himmel" versteckt sich der Apfel, der am Baum in den Himmel ragt. „Erde" bezieht sich auf die Kartoffel, die bekanntlich in der Erde wächst. Das sind die Hauptzutaten für dieses vegetarische Gericht. In manchen Regionen werden die gekochten, zerkleinerten Äpfel und Kartoffeln vermischt und mit Brot serviert. Häufig isst man dazu auch Blutwurst, Speck oder Leberwurst. Und bitte die Röstzwiebeln nicht vergessen …

KV 30: Role cards for your group work

WB 46/6 Listening (sights in NY)
WB 47/7 Mediation/Speaking (in a NY diner)
WB 47/8 Speaking (a new burger)
WB 47/9 Writing (food tester)

WRITING  **10 Your turn: Your city on a shoestring** → WB 46/6, 47/7–9

a) *You're helping to write a guidebook about your hometown or region. In small groups, choose 3–4 interesting facts you want to include. These ideas can help you:*

the best view | the best thing for free | the best lunch under €10 | the highest spot | …

Transfer

HA

b) *Write short texts for each of the points you chose in a). Remember to give extra information.*

Example: The highest spot in our town, which is in a castle, is easy to get to. It's …

L 2/23 ⊙ # Life is a trip

Diego's father, Emilio, had been waiting in his taxi for just 20 minutes before his first passenger came. He lifted the young man's big suitcase into the trunk and then asked him
5 where he wanted to go. "To the airport," the man groaned, "I'm done with this city." He'd come to New York when he was 19 and had been hoping for his big break for five years. All this time he'd gone to hundreds of
10 auditions and had sung thousands of songs, but nobody had wanted him. He'd been thinking about his decision for quite some time and that morning, when he got another rejection e-mail, he'd decided the time had
15 come. Now he was going home to Wisconsin, where he had an offer to teach music at a high school. "My dream just didn't come true here," he explained. "At least as a teacher I can make music every day."
20   Emilio wished the young man good luck and thought of his own dreams. They hadn't been as big when he'd come to America, but he still understood what it meant to get disappointed.
25   When Emilio got back in his car, another passenger was waiting on the sidewalk. Emilio knew the type – successful businessman but not necessarily happy. The man gave Emilio an address on Wall Street. And then something
30 surprising happened. The man started talking to him, asking him questions. Emilio told him

about his son, Diego, and how he and his wife had such big hopes for him. They'd been saving for his education since he was born, working two jobs each and now Diego said he   35 wanted to be an entertainer. Emilio was sure this rich businessman would understand how disappointed Emilio felt. However, when they arrived in Manhattan, the man said something completely different. "Let your son follow his   40 dreams. It's better to have a son with dreams you aren't happy about than not to have your son at all." He pressed a large bill into Emilio's hand and quickly got out of the taxi without his change.   45
    Emilio's taxi wasn't empty for long. Two teenage girls and about 20 shopping bags got in. The girls didn't say hello; they just gave him an address on Park Avenue. Emilio listened to them as they talked about a life so   50 different from his and yet so typical of New York. They'd been walking around Manhattan since 10 o'clock and now they were tired after all the shopping. They complained that today it was hard to find any good clothes in New   55 York. Obviously they'd been shopping at the same stores for hours when they realized that London might be the better place to shop. Needless to say, they didn't give Emilio a tip. And needless to say, they didn't give the   60 homeless woman on the sidewalk a single look as they got out of the taxi.

KV 44: An interview with Emilio's passengers
KV 45: How does the story continue?
WB 48/10 Vocabulary (homeless people in NY)

READING   **11**   **A day in the life of Emilio** → WB 48/10

→ S1

1 Schnelllesetechniken

a) *Collect information about Emilio's passengers. Think of what is said about them in the text, but also about what they say or how they act. Make a mind map.*

b) *Use your mind map from a) to compare the different passengers.*

c) *Role play: Choose one of Emilio's passengers – the musician, the businessman or one of the rich girls. With your partner, write down five questions you'd like to ask this person and the answers this person might give. Then act out the dialogue.*

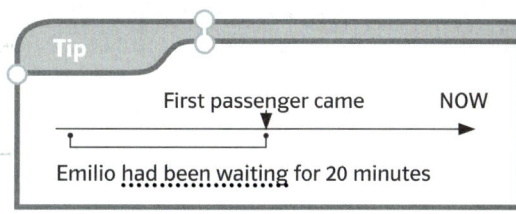

LANGUAGE   **12**   **Revision: Present perfect progressive**

→ △ 122/7

/7 Since or for?
→ After …

*Remember: You can use the present perfect progressive for activities which began in the past and have been going on until now. Use the prompts to make sentences with the **present perfect progressive** and **since** or **for**.*

Example: 1. It's already 10 o'clock. We'**ve been waiting** for our taxi since 9:30.

sung: 2. We've been ening … 3. We've been king … 4. They haven't building … 5. I've been aming … 6. He's been g …

1. It's already 10 o'clock. We | wait for our taxi | 9:30. ✔
2. Can we leave? We | listen to the piano player | one hour.
3. We'll never get to the show on time. We | walk | hours.

4. Look how tall the skyscraper is already. They | not build | long.
5. I got a part in a play! I | dream about this | I arrived in New York.
6. It's so sad. He | live on the streets | he was 16.

KV 46: Working with language
WB 48/11 Language (homelessness in NY)

LANGUAGE   **13**   **Find the rule: Past perfect progressive** → G9 → WB 48/11

ung: a) 'had been' + present ticiple (verb + -ing)

a) *Look at these two sentences. Say which verb forms you need to form the **past perfect progressive**.*

1. Emilio **had been waiting** for 20 minutes.
2. They **had been walking** around Manhattan since 10 o'clock.

b) *Find more examples of the **past perfect progressive** in the text.*

c) *Look at the tip box and the sentences from a) and b). Write down the rule of how the **past perfect progressive** is used. Compare it to the use of **present perfect progressive**.*

Tip

First passenger came   NOW

Emilio had been waiting for 20 minutes

LANGUAGE   **14**   **What had Meredith been doing?**

*Complete the sentences with the **past perfect progressive**.*

ung: 1. *Meredith had n talking,* 2. *She'd been nning,* 3. *she hadn't n living,* 4. *she'd been cticing,* 5. *She'd been ting,* 6. *she'd been king,* 7. *she'd been hoping*

1. Meredith (talk) about becoming an actor even before she saw her first Broadway play.
2. She (plan) to move to New York for eight years before she finally arrived there.
3. When she went to her first audition, she (not live) in New York for very long.
4. She was very tired that day because she (practice) all night long.

5. She (wait) for two hours when they told her that they didn't need any more people.
6. Her friends didn't know how long she (walk) around the city before she came home at midnight.
7. They knew she (hope) for a part in the play, but they told her that tomorrow was another day!

Folie 4/10: Bildbeschreibung und Vertiefung des *past perfect progressive*
WB 49/12 Language (dialogue in a cab)

LANGUAGE   **15**   **Why were they tired when Emilio's taxi arrived?** → WB 49/12

→ △ 123/8
→ ▲ 123/9

*When Emilio arrived in Central Park at 11 o'clock yesterday, he saw different people who needed a taxi. Why were they tired? Make sentences with the **past perfect progressive** and **since** or **for**.*

123/8 Present perfect progressive or past perfect progressive?
△ → After …
123/9 Mixed bag: Different tenses
▲ → After …

Example: **1.** The young girl **had been running** for one hour / **since** 10 o'clock.

LANGUAGE   **16**   **What had been happening before?**

→ △ 123/10

*Complete these sentences with your own ideas. Use the **past perfect progressive** and an **expression of time** (since / for …, all morning / day / week / night / year etc.).*

123/10 What had been happening before?
△ → Instead of …

Example: When I looked out of the window this morning, the ground was all wet.
          It **had been raining all night**.

1. I was very tired when I got home after school because I'd been …
2. Dave got the best <u>grade</u> on the test because he …
3. We … when there was a heavy storm and we had to go back.
4. When Kelly arrived at the café, her friends …
5. Our dog was very dirty. He …
6. Lisa thought her friend would never call. She …
7. Mary's eyes were very red. She …

SPEAKING   **17**   **Your turn: Your experiences in a new place**

Transfer

Do you remember the last time you were in a foreign city / a new place? What kind of people did you meet? What did you experience, see, hear, feel, smell? Tell your partner about it and ask each other about your experiences.

WB 49/13 Listening (phone calls)

LISTENING **18** **Differences between British and American English** → WB 49/13

L 2/24 ⊙
→ S15

 Hörverstehen üben

a) *Listen to a conversation between a British and an American student. What are they talking about? What differences do you notice in the way they speak?*

b) *Listen to the conversation again. Then look at these sentences. Change the British words to American and the American words to British.*

1. Buskers perform on the street to make a living.
2. It is easiest to take the subway when you want to explore the city.
3. Traffic is so slow here, let's use the freeway instead.
4. If you want to transport something that is big and heavy, you'll need a lorry.

HA

c) *Can you think of more words that are different between British and American English? Start a list.*

Folie 4/11: Bildbeschreibung
WB 50/14 Speaking (interview with homeless person)
WB 50/15 Writing (a day in the life …)

READING **19** **Living in New York City** → WB 50/14–15

a) *In her song about New York Alicia Keys sings: "If I can make it here, I can make it anywhere." What does this tell us about how people see New York?*

b) *Read the box about life in New York. Have you seen huge contrasts like this where you live?*

> **Across cultures** 🇺🇸
>
> As a city of superlatives, New York attracts people from all different social backgrounds – rich and poor, young and old, from the US and from abroad. They all come to New York with their **hopes and dreams**. A lot of them live their own 'rags to riches' success story, but others fail to make their living.
>
> Today New York is one of the cities with the widest **gap between rich and poor** in the US. There are one-bedroom apartments for $5 million, and in New York's most expensive apartment building a penthouse was sold for $100 million. On the other hand, there are almost 60,000 homeless people who live on the streets or in poor conditions.

c) *Imagine you're either very rich or homeless. What would be different compared to your real life? Share your ideas with a partner.*

SPEAKING **20** **Before you read**

a) *You're going to read a graphic novel which is set in New York City. Read the quotation below from OG, one of the main characters in the story. Think about what he could mean.*

"Here is where you are. There is where you want to be. But you can't get there from here." (Harrison Blanchard aka OG)

b) *What might the graphic novel be about? Keep in mind what you've read in the Across cultures box.*

Asphalt Tribe by Stefani Kampmann

SPEAKING

1 Your reaction

What do you think of the graphic novel? With a partner, agree on three aspects you like or don't like about it. Explain why.

READING

2 Understanding the story → WB 51/16

WB 51/16 Reading (graphic novel)

a) *Divide the underlined excerpt from the graphic novel into scenes. Sum up each scene in 2–3 sentences.*

b) *Compare your summaries with a partner's. Explain how you found out about what is happening in each scene.*

READING

3 How a graphic novel works

Folie 4/12–14: Bildbeschreibung und Sicherung des Leseverstehens

a) *Look at the first panel of the graphic novel (p. 50). Describe the picture and the atmosphere. Why do you think the artist used this picture as a lead-in to her story?*

b) *Now have a closer look at pages 54 and 58. What are the differences between them? Make a grid and fill in the information for both pages. Use these headings:*

content | sizes and shapes of panels | sequence of panels | shots

> **Reading skills**
>
> Graphic novels are divided into **panels** (the individual pictures) which can be different sizes and shapes. Some of the panels have **speech** or **thought bubbles** and / or **captions**. The short caption texts tell part of the story from the perspective of a first- or third-person narrator.
>
> The **sequence** (or order) of the panels can play an important role. Sometimes panels are not arranged consecutively, but they overlap. This means that some smaller panels are laid over a larger one.
>
> Just like in films, graphic novels make use of different kinds of **shots**. There can be long or medium shots (the camera is at a great or medium distance from the object that is being filmed) and **close-ups** (the camera is very close to the object).

→ △ 124/11
11 Stylistic elements graphic novel
► Help with …

c) *Look at your grid from b) and the two pages from the graphic novel again. Describe the effects the stylistic elements have. How does that match the content? The useful phrases in the box can help you.*

d) *Explain how the choice of black and white matches the story. Do you know any other graphic novels? If you do, does the artist's choice / style of visuals match the story?*

> **Useful phrases**
>
> create suspense / a quiet atmosphere | make the reader live through / experience the story | show reactions / feelings of characters | introduce fast action / speed | create a distance

WRITING
HA

4 What happens next?

What do you think happens when the kids run away from the police? Make a plan for the next two pages of the graphic novel. Think of content, sizes and shapes of panels, sequence of panels and shots. If you like being creative, you can even draw the panels.

READING

5 ‹ Comparing the genres › → WB 51/17

WB 51/17 Writing (options)

a) *The graphic novel* Asphalt Tribe *is based on the novel* Can't Get There from Here *by Todd Strasser. Read this short excerpt. Think about how the artist might convert the scene into panels.*

Chapter One: New Year's Eve

It was one of those nights when there wasn't much traffic on the streets of New York. Most people were done with their stupid New Year's celebrations and back in the four-walled
5 cells they called apartments. Prisoners of the system, Maggot said. Out here in the cold where we weren't walled in, we were free to go where we wanted to.

"Guess the cops have the night off,"
10 Maggot said, his brown dreadlocks stringy from the mist.

"The rest of the world too," muttered 2Moro. She was wearing a red-and-orange patchwork jacket, a tight black skirt, and high
15 black boots. The piercings in her ears and eyebrow and nose glinted in the streetlight. Tattooed around her neck was a circle of black barbed wire.

I drank cold coffee from a paper cup. At
20 night we drank coffee to stay awake. It was safer to sleep during the day.

A man and a woman came around the corner wearing raincoats and sharing a red umbrella. They slowed down when they saw
25 us. The woman slid her arm through the man's and said something in his ear. Probably wanted him to turn around and go another way. But the man shook his head.

When they got near, the woman wrinkled
30 her nose like something smelled bad.

"Have fun tonight?" Maggot asked, kind of menacing.

The couple stopped. "Yes, we did," the man answered.

"No work tomorrow, huh?" Maggot said. 35

"That's right."

"Day after that it's back to the old nine-to-five routine," Maggot said.

"You could say that," answered the man.

"Happy New Year," said 2Moro, not in a 40
friendly way.

"Same to you," said the man. He and the woman hurried past. She kept glancing over her shoulder at us until they reached the next corner. 45

"Robots," Maggot said. "Just following the rules. Work till they die. Then new robots replace them."

Handwritten margin notes:
- attitude towards "normal" people
- behaviour on the street

b) *Give a summary of the excerpt in 2–3 sentences.*

c) *With your partner, make a list of the differences between a graphic novel and a novel. How are they effective in different ways?*

d) *What would you prefer to read – the graphic novel or the novel? Give reasons for your choice.*

WRITING

6 ‹ Writing the novel version of a scene ›

KV 47: Peer evaluation (writing)

a) *Look back at the scenes you were working with in Ex. 2a). Divide up the scenes among the class. Then write a short novel text for your scene. Keep in mind the differences between a graphic novel and a novel which you collected in Ex. 5c).*

→ △ 124/12
124/12 Write the story!
△ → Help with …
HA

b) *With a partner, peer-edit each other's texts.*

New Yorkers don't do things like that!

S16 Wichtige filmische Mittel
→ S16

SPEAKING

WB 52/18 Speaking (embarrassing situations)

1 Warm-up: Embarrassing situations → WB 52/18

a) *In the film, one of the characters says this to another character: "Stop it, it's embarrassing! I'm a New Yorker and New Yorkers don't do things like that!" What do you think this could mean?*

b) *Describe the kind of embarrassing behavior that makes you cringe.*

KV 48: Viewing (focus on interaction)
WB 52/19 Writing (two dialogues)

VIEWING

2 Out and about in Manhattan → WB 52/19

DVD 4/3

a) *Watch the film till 00:50. Then think about your ideas from Ex. 1 again. What does Christine mean when she tells Sarah that "New Yorkers don't do things like that"?*

b) *Now watch till 04:00 and sum up the action. Include these points about Christine, Sarah and Lawrence:*

characters and their personalities | what happens

c) *Watch the rest of the film. Describe the unexpected ending and the reactions to it.*

VIEWING

3 How music and film work together

Folie 4/15: Bildbeschreibung und Sicherung des Hörsehverstehens
KV 31: Talking about music and film

a) *Watch the film again and note down the moments with music. Describe which scene or person has music and what kind of music it is.*

b) *Explain how you think the music helps to tell the story in A (04:01–04:52) and B (06:01–06:17):*

c) *Read the skills box. Then watch 04:01–04:52 again. Explain why you think this part of the film is featured as a montage.*

d) *If you could choose a theme song or theme music for one of the characters, what would you choose? Give your reasons.*

Film skills

A **montage** is a popular film technique to show a lot of action in very little time. To make a montage, scenes are cut up into very short 'pieces' and then combined, usually with **music**.

WB 52/20 Across cultures (helping tourists)

How to <u>conduct</u> a podcast interview

For the unit task you're going to do podcast interviews about different people in New York City. This page will give you some useful phrases and a model for your interview.

WB 53/21 Skills (biographical profile)

1 Before the interview: A short biographical profile → WB 53/21

a) *In a podcast interview, the <u>interviewer</u> often gives his / her listeners a short profile of the person he / she is going to interview. With a partner, think of <u>general</u> kinds of biographical information that listeners might like to know before the <u>actual</u> interview. Make a list.*

b) *Read the biographical profile about Rita Moreno, an immigrant from Cuba who lives in New York. Compare the information with your list from a).*

Rita Moreno came to New York from Cuba when she was 16 years old. Her aunt and uncle, who had already been living there for three years, gave Rita a bedroom, but she had to work hard for everything else. Her dream was to become a dancer. In Cuba she'd already been going to a dance school for ten years, but she and her family saw no future for her there; the country was just too poor. Rita's <u>path</u> to success was very long and hard. She cleaned offices, sold tickets in a theater and always went to auditions. It took her almost three years before she got her first dancing job. Today she makes her living by dancing on stages around New York and the world, but she also helps young dancers who have their own hopes and dreams.

HA **c)** *You want to find out more about what Rita likes or doesn't like about her life in New York. Write down five questions you'd ask her in an interview.*

2 Conducting an interview: Daniel's Do-it-yourself Diner

KV 50: Role cards for an interview

L 2/29 ⊙
→ S15
S15 Hörverstehen üben

a) *Listen to the interview. Then sum up what you've found out about Daniel and his New York City dreams. Why is his diner called 'Do-it-yourself'?*

b) *Listen to the interview again. Note down which phrases from the box you hear in the interview.*

c) *What's important for a good interview? Make a list of criteria with your partner.*

> **Useful phrases**
>
> **Small talk:** This is a beautiful office / area / room. | How long have you been living / working here? | Where did you grow up?
>
> **Follow-up:** Can you tell me more about …? | That's interesting. Tell me a little more about that. | But don't you think that …? | Can you explain that to me? | Sorry, I didn't catch that.
>
> **Getting specific:** How long have you …? | How many …? | When did you …? | How often …? | How long had you been … (+-ing) before you became … / went … / found …
>
> **Open questions:** What are your feelings about …? | What do you think about …? | What are your goals?
>
> **At the end:** Thanks, I enjoyed talking to you. | Thank you very much for this interesting <u>talk</u>.

HA **d)** *Write a short biographical profile about Daniel. Keep in mind the points you collected in Ex. 1.*

A pocketful of New York City dreams

You're going to make a series of podcast interviews with different people in New York City who talk about their hopes and dreams. You can use information you learned in Unit 3 and do some internet research too.

: Important
rences, p. 187

Step 1

WB 53/22 Skills (collect ideas)

Get into groups, choose characters → WB 53/22

Get into groups of 4–5. Each group chooses a different person who lives in New York City or who is visiting. Here are some ideas:

tourist | tourist guide | rich boy / girl | successful businessman / -woman | taxi driver | young student who has just moved to New York | homeless person

Step 2

WB 54/23 Language (add information)

Write a biographical profile → WB 54/23

In your groups, write a short biographical profile of the person you've chosen. Try to make your listeners interested, but don't give away too much information.

→ Introduction (pp. 70–71) → Giving extra information (pp. 72–75) → Talking about personal experiences (pp. 76–78) → Writing a biographical profile (p. 92)

Step 3

WB 54/24 Skills (prepare questions)

Prepare your interviews → WB 54/24

Prepare questions you're going to ask about the person's hopes and dreams. Think of answers you're going to give.

→ Conducting an interview (p. 92)

Step 4

Practise your interviews

Decide who is going to take the role of the interviewer and the interviewee. Then practise the interview. Don't forget that the interviewer should give the short biographical profile first.

Step 5

KV 51: Peer evaluation: Podcast interviews

Present your interviews

Record your podcast interviews or present them directly to the class. After the presentations, discuss the interviews in class. Give feedback about which person or which interview was the most convincing. Explain why.

LISTENING

1 **I ♥ NYC**   **KV 53–56:** Test yourself

L 2/30 ◎

a) *Listen to Makenna as she talks about her hometown New York. What does she say about these topics? Take notes.*

Stuyvesant High School | crime | people in New York | activities

Transfer
HA

b) *Make notes about your school and your hometown. Use your ideas to write a short text like Makenna's.*

MEDIATION

WB 56/1 Reading/Writing (factual texts)

2 **Getting around in New York** → WB 56/1

You're spending a year as an exchange student in New York and your parents are visiting you for five days. They want to do some sightseeing on their own and ask you which subway ticket you think is best for them. You find this information about the MetroCard on a website. Tell them about the different options. Then say which ticket you think is best and why. Use a dictionary to look up new words.

To find out about the different ticket options, press 'Start', then 'MetroCard' and next 'Get new card'. Now you have to decide between an 'unlimited' and a 'regular' card. An unlimited MetroCard for seven days costs $31. This card is good if you want to use the subway a lot – even if you're going to be in New York for less than seven days. It's the best deal if you're going to use the subway at least 12 times, or do six round trips. Then each ride costs $2.38. The more you ride, the cheaper each ride is! If you ride 25 times, it's only $1.24 per ride. But remember – only one person can use the card! If you don't want to use the subway that often, you can buy a pay-per-ride or regular MetroCard. Up to four people can share the same card. You choose the amount that you want to put onto your card. The more you put on it, the more you save because you get an 11% bonus for every $5.50 you purchase. You can pay at the machines with cash, an ATM card or a credit card. If you pay in cash, your change will be all in coins.

LANGUAGE

3 **Who is who?**

You're new in New York and you don't know the people who live next door – Mr. Singh, Mr. Masengi and Mr. Nelson – very well, but you need a ride to the airport. Find out who the taxi driver is. Read the clues and make a grid in your exercise book.
Lösung: *Mr. Singh is the taxi driver. He lives in the blue house.*

| The neighbor who lives in the yellow house doesn't drive a taxi. | Mr. Masengi, who is a security man, doesn't like the color red. | The actor, who doesn't live in a yellow house, is Mr. Nelson. | The house that Mr. Singh has been living in for five years isn't red. |

WB 57/2 Reading (factual or personal)

LANGUAGE

4 More facts about New York → WB 57/2

*Write 2–3 sentences about each topic below. Use **non-defining relative clauses** where possible.*

Example: New York, **which is the largest city in the US**, is located on the East Coast.

New York

- largest city in the US
- located on the East Coast
- about 8 million live here; 1.6 million on island of Manhattan
- Manhattan: most famous of NY's five boroughs[1]

New York taxis

- bright yellow in color
- can be seen all around the city
- many of the taxi drivers born outside the US
- transport about 241 million passengers each year

The Brooklyn Bridge

- connects[2] Manhattan and Brooklyn
- designed by John A. Roebling in 1869
- completed after Roebling's death by his son
- one of NY's top tourist attractions
- cost $15 million to build

The Staten Island Ferry

- in service[3] since 1817
- operates[4] 24 hours a day, 7 days a week
- transports about 21 million passengers each year
- free of charge[5]

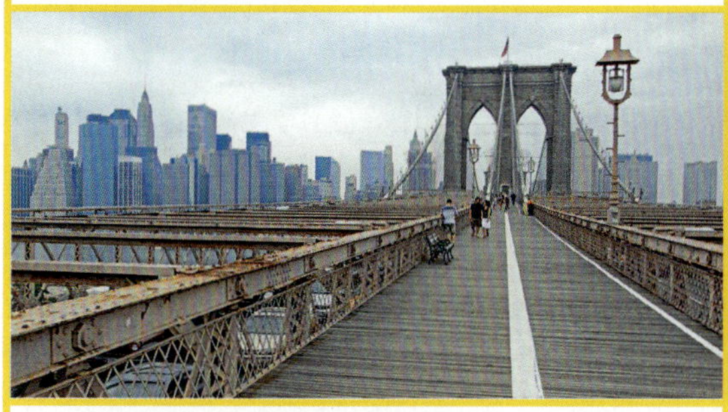

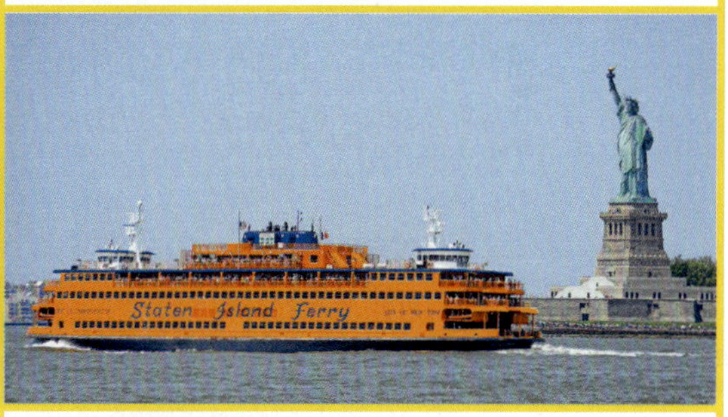

LANGUAGE

5 Moving to NYC

ng: 1. Moving, 2. to leave, ting, 4. trying, 5. to leave, stay, 7. surprising, lowing

a) *Put in a **gerund** or an **infinitive with to**.*

1. ___ (move) to New York City was the best decision I've ever made!
2. I was the first one in my family ___ (leave) our town.
3. At first my parents were afraid of ___ (let) me go on my own.
4. But I've always been crazy about ___ (try) new things.
5. I decided ___ (leave) as soon as I was done with high school.
6. My family didn't expect me ___ (stay) in New York for more than a year.
7. But I keep ___ (surprise) them with new dreams and ideas.
8. Now my brother is thinking of ___ (follow) me to NYC!

Transfer

b) *What's the best decision that you've ever made? What happened because of this decision? Tell your partner about it.*

1 **borough** ['bʌrə] Stadtteil | 2 **to connect** [kə'nekt] verbinden | 3 **to be in service** [ɪn 'sɜːvɪs] in Betrieb sein | 4 **to operate** ['ɒpreɪt] in Betrieb sein | 5 **free of charge** [ˌfriː əv 'tʃɑːdʒ] kostenlos

READING

6 New York in a poem

Untitled by Jasbel
In this city
full of buildings
big, small, brown, orange
tiny windows
1 out of 1000
small and black
but still you and I
look outside
see the bridge
or the trees
mostly cars
and yellow taxis
cheese buses
and MTA buses
But where am I
If I go downtown alone
no one knows me
If I go to Brooklyn
no one knows me
alone in the middle of the big apple
places unexplored unknown to me
clueless¹, lost
In the middle of this jungle

a) *Read the poem. Find lines that show how Jasbel feels about New York City.*

b) *Discuss if this poem gives a good description of New York in your opinion. Explain why, why not.*

LANGUAGE

WB 57/3 Language (netiquette)

7 Defining or non-defining? → WB 57/3

*Decide if these sentences have **defining** or **non-defining relative clauses**. Put in commas where you need them.*

1. Diego who we met at a diner showed us some fantastic sights.
2. Some of the sights that Diego showed us were fantastic.
3. Rockefeller Center which is located in the heart of Manhattan is a huge shopping and entertainment center.
4. Rockefeller Center is a huge shopping and entertainment center that is located in the heart of Manhattan.
5. The Chinese dumplings² which we bought for lunch from a food truck on 14th Street tasted delicious.
6. The best restaurant for falafels is in Greenwich Village which is on the west side of Lower Manhattan.
7. In Times Square we saw the Naked Cowboy who is a famous street artist.
8. In Times Square we saw a street artist who was almost completely naked.

Lösung: *defining relative clauses: 2, 4, 5, 8; non-defining relative clauses: 1, 3, 6, 7*

LANGUAGE

WB 58/4 Language (reported speech)
WB 58/5 Language/Speaking (for or since)

8 New in New York → WB 58/4–5

*Put the verbs into the **past perfect progressive**. Use **since** or **for** where it is needed.*

Lösung: 1. had been saving, 2. since, 3. had already been traveling, 4. for, 5. had been hoping, 6. hadn't been expecting, 7. had been looking, 8. for, 9. had been helping, 10. since

In August, Tyler and Missy finally left for New York City. They ▮1▮ (save) their money for the trip ever ▮2▮ they finished high school. They took the bus from Idaho to New York, and when they finally arrived in Manhattan, they ▮3▮ (already travel) ▮4▮ 24 hours. They ▮5▮ (hope) to stay with Missy's sister, but when they called, nobody answered the phone.

Missy's sister ▮6▮ (not expect) them until the week after, and now they didn't know where to go! They ▮7▮ (look) at their map ▮8▮ a long time when a man asked if they needed help. He told them it was their lucky day. He ▮9▮ (help) people to find rooms in New York ▮10▮ 2005. That's when he had first arrived in New York without a room and someone had helped him!

1 **clueless** [ˈkluːləs] ahnungslos | 2 **dumpling** [ˈdʌmplɪŋ] Kloß

SPEAKING

9 New York's nicknames[1]

a) *There are many different names for New York. Which one do you think describes the city best? Exchange ideas with your partner.*

The melting pot   The center of the universe[2]

The city that never sleeps   The Big Apple

The city so nice they named it twice

Transfer

b) *Think of nicknames for your hometown. They can be realistic or funny.*

LANGUAGE

10 What had people been doing?

a) *Use the prompts to write sentences with the **past perfect progressive**.*

Example: **1.** Meredith came home late for dinner. She **had been shopping** since 10 o'clock.

1. Meredith came home late for dinner. She | shop | 10 o'clock.
2. Sam was feeling very tired. He | wait to get into the Empire State Building | two hours.
3. When Maisie came back to the hotel, she looked very red from the sun. She | walk | in the sun | all day.
4. Alex didn't know which subway station was next. He | sleep | 15 minutes.
5. Joe left the diner at 8 o'clock. He was very upset with his friends. He | wait | for them | 7 o'clock.
6. When Julie's mom arrived home at 10 p.m., the TV was still on. Julie | watch videos | all evening.

ung: 2. He had been ~~~ing, 3. She had been ~~king, 4. He had been ~~ping for, 5. He had been ~~ting for, 6. Julie had been ~~ching

Transfer

b) *Your turn: Partner A asks a question, Partner B answers. Use the **past perfect progressive**.*

Example: **A:** Why were you so tired last night?
B: I**'d been playing** football with my friends for three hours.

OCABULARY

11 Avoiding mistakes

a) *Look at these three words. Explain their different meanings.*

my cousins | my cousin's | my cousins'

b) *Complete the sentences with the correct form of the nouns.*

1. When I first came to New York, I lived in my ▮ (sister) apartment.
2. She had crazy ▮ (ideas) and we had lots of fun together.
3. One day we went to a party at her ▮ (friends) place.
4. They lived in one of ▮ (New York) tallest skyscrapers.
5. It was amazing to see the ▮ (city) lights from up there.
6. And guess what? My best ▮ (friend) brother came to the party.
7. He and his sister lived near my ▮ (grandparents) house when we were kids.
8. He is one of the most attractive ▮ (guys) I've ever met!

ung: b) 1. *sister's,* *eas, 3. friends', 4. New 's, 5. city's, 6. friend's, andparents', 8. guys*

1 **nickname** ['nɪkneɪm] Spitzname | 2 **universe** ['juːnɪvɜːs] Universum

LANGUAGE

12 An interview with Colin

a) *A reporter from TeenMusicMag interviewed Colin, a young musician who plays his piano in Washington Square Park. Complete the interview. Decide if you need the* **present perfect progressive** *or* **past perfect progressive**.

Lösung: 1. *have been living,* 2. *had been dreaming,* 3. *had been working,* 4. *hadn't been looking,* 5. *hadn't been expecting,* 6. *have you been performing,* 7. *have been doing,* 8. *had been playing,* 9. *had been listening,* 10. *have you been playing,* 11. *have been taking*

TMM: Were you born in New York, Colin?
Colin: No, I'm originally from Tennessee, but I ⬛1 (live) here for five years.
TMM: And why did you come here?
Colin: I ⬛2 (dream) about it forever! And then one day I was finally brave enough to do it.
TMM: Colin, why did you decide to play your piano outside?
Colin: Well, I ⬛3 (work) in a bar as a musician for two years, but I didn't like working every night.
TMM: Did you look for a new job then?
Colin: Yes, but I ⬛4 (not look) for long when I decided to play in the park.
TMM: And do you make enough money with that?
Colin: I ⬛5 (not expect) that before I started, but I do make enough.

TMM: How long ⬛6 (perform) in Washington Square Park?
Colin: I ⬛7 (do) it for two years now.
TMM: What do you do if the weather is bad?
Colin: I stay home! But one day I ⬛8 (play) for only half an hour when it suddenly started to rain.
TMM: What did you do? Your poor piano!
Colin: The people who ⬛9 (listen) helped me to cover it and then I quickly pushed it home.
TMM: And how long ⬛10 (play) the piano altogether[1]?
Colin: I ⬛11 (take) lessons since I was five.
TMM: Are you still taking lessons?
Colin: Well, not at the moment. My audience is my teacher!

b) *Write down questions you'd like to ask your partner. Then take turns to interview each other. Use the* **present perfect progressive** *and* **past perfect progressive**.

Example: A: How long **had you been playing** basketball before you joined our team?
      B: I**'d been playing** basketball for one year.
      A: And how long **have you been playing** basketball altogether?
      B: I**'ve been playing** basketball since I was 12.

VOCABULARY

13 New York collocations

a) *Combine the words from the two boxes to make collocations you've learned in Unit 3.*

Lösung: *classical music, melting pot, brand new, follow a dream, social background, make a living, ethnic food, food cart, city life, office building, concrete jungle*

classical	melting	brand
follow	social	make	ethnic
food	city	office	concrete

a living	background	building
jungle	life	music	new	pot
a dream	cart	food

b) *Write a sentence for each of the phrases from a), but leave a gap where the phrase should go. Then exchange sentences. Your partner needs to find out which phrase goes in which sentence. Take turns.*

---

1 **altogether** [ˌɔːltəˈɡeðə] insgesamt

WRITING **14** **I want to go to New York!**

If you want to go on a student exchange, you usually have to fill out an online application¹ form. Answer the following questions about yourself in full sentences.

1. Which foreign languages have you studied, and for how many years?
2. What are your favorite school subjects?
3. Are you active in sports? If yes, which sports?
4. Which (if any) foreign countries have you visited?
5. What are your favorite hobbies, interests etc.?
6. Use one adjective to describe yourself. Explain why you have chosen it.

LANGUAGE **15** **9/11 – New York had to rebuild**

a) *As you've already learned, you can only use the modal verbs in the simple present. With other tenses, you use their substitute forms: **be allowed to**, **be able to** and **have to**. Rewrite these sentences in the simple past. Use the right substitute form.*

1. I can't call us a taxi because my phone is broken. We must take the subway.
2. We needn't buy tickets for the museum. Our class can go in for free.

b) *Complete the text with the verbs and the right substitute form: **be allowed to**, **be able to** or **have to**.*

On September 11, 2001, several terrorists ⬛1 (hijack²) two planes and fly them into the twin towers of the World Trade Center in New York. At first nobody knew what had happened. One survivor said, "All I knew was that I ⬛2 (get) out of the building." Of course the people in the World Trade Center ⬛3 (not use) the elevators because of the fires. Firefighters³ from all over New York came to help, but they ⬛4 (not rescue) a lot of the people and at some point they

⬛5 (leave) the scene because the buildings collapsed⁴. More than 3,000 people died. Until several months later, people who had lived near the World Trade Center ⬛6 (not move) back into their apartments. Soon after 9/11, however, New Yorkers decided that they ⬛7 (find) hope again. In 2014, One World Trade Center was opened as a new office building. At the place where the twin towers once stood there is now a memorial⁵ and a museum, which tells the story of 9/11.

1 **application** [ˌæplɪˈkeɪʃn] Bewerbung | 2 **to hijack** [ˈhaɪdʒæk] entführen | 3 **firefighter** [ˈfaɪəˌfaɪtə] Feuerwehrmann/-frau | 4 **to collapse** [kəˈlæps] einstürzen | 5 **memorial** [məˈmɔːriəl] Denkmal

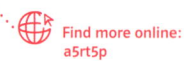
Find more online:
a5rt5p

Text smart 3
Internet texts

In Text smart 3 you're going to take a look at typical kinds of online texts. Who writes them, what are their typical features, how <u>reliable</u> is the information you get online?

VOCABULARY

1 Warm-up: The internet in everyday life

a) *How would you finish this sentence: "If I had to spend a whole Saturday without my smartphone / my tablet, it would be so <u>inconvenient</u> because …"*

L 2/31–32
→ S15
S15 Hörverstehen üben

1) forgot his phone
doesn't know the
exact location-
where he has
to pick st. up
2) quick information-
social media
movie theatre
school stuff

b) *Part 1: Tim and Marlon meet each other on the bus.*

   1. Describe what Tim's problem is and how Marlon can help.
   2. Then sum up what both boys say about the internet. The words below can help you.

> **Word bank**
>
> get quick information with apps | stay <u>up-to-date</u> on social media | watch <u>tutorials</u> | do research for school projects | follow / read blogs | follow social media profiles | post an opinion / comment on blogs / social media websites / …

 c) *Now listen to part 2.*

   1. Describe the problems Tim and Marlon mention.
   2. Discuss how you feel about those problems.

1) unreliable information on
the internet; reduced content
trust on the internet; "friends"
you don't even know

SPEAKING

2 Your turn: Your reasons for using the internet

Transfer

What were your main reasons for using the internet during the last 2–3 days? Compare your experiences with your partner's.

SPEAKING

3 America and the moon landing

On the following pages, you're going to work with internet texts about the first moon landing.

Read the box. Then say what other great moments or inventions in <u>science</u> and technology you can think of. Describe one for your partner.

> **Across cultures**
>
> On July 20, 1969, NASA <u>astronaut</u> Neil Armstrong became the first <u>human</u> on the moon. The **moon landing** <u>is considered</u> one of the greatest moments in the history of science and technology.

An online wiki text

The moon landing

The first moon landing took place on July 20, 1969, as the climax of NASA's Apollo 11 mission. Hundreds of millions of TV viewers watched on live TV as the landing module Eagle touched down on the moon's surface. Astronaut and Apollo 11 commander Neil Armstrong announced to mission control in Houston: "The Eagle has landed," words which soon became famous. More famous words followed six hours later when Armstrong stepped out of the Eagle and onto the moon: "That's one small step for (a) man, one giant leap for mankind." Armstrong was then joined by astronaut Buzz Aldrin. Together they took pictures to document the historic event and collected 46 pounds of moon rocks. After 21 hours, Armstrong and Aldrin returned to the command module Columbia, where astronaut Michael Collins had been waiting in orbit.

Years before, in 1961, the moon landing had become one of President John F. Kennedy's top priorities. He challenged the engineers and scientists at NASA to put a man on the moon by the end of 1969. It was clear to all that this would be the biggest challenge ever. It was also clear that it would be very political: During the Cold War, a triumph like the first moon landing was a prize that both the US and the Soviet Union wanted very much.

READING

→ S1–3

S1–3 Reading skills

WB 59/1 Reading (moon landing)

4 Understanding the text → WB 59/1

a) *Read the wiki text above. Sum up what happened in your own words.*

b) *Find phrases in the text that make the style factual and convincing. This box can help you:*

Reading skills

- A **factual text** should concentrate on **facts**. Opinions don't belong here.
- Factual texts about history focus on **times**, **dates**, **places** and **people**. Information like this can be easily checked at other text sources.

Tip

- **Wiki texts** are written to give information in the style of an encyclopedia. But wiki texts can be written or changed by any reader.
- Wikis try to be as **factual** as possible. But with so many authors, the regulators of wiki websites can't always keep their content completely free of opinions. So it is important to always look for **other reliable sources of information**. Don't rely only on wiki texts.

A blog post

READING

→ △ 125/1

125/1 Reasons
△ → Help with …

5 Hoaxes and conspiracy theories

Across cultures

In the English-speaking world, there have been some famous hoaxes and conspiracy theories. The internet is full of such stories.

- When somebody stages a **hoax**, the person is playing a trick on the public. A typical hoax often features realistic photos that show something unbelievable like a UFO, or a monster.
- A **conspiracy theory** often involves an event or situation that a group of people would like to keep secret in a cover-up. The conspiracy theorists often see governments at the center of cover-ups. A famous example: Is the US government trying to keep real aliens a secret at the Area 51 air-force base?

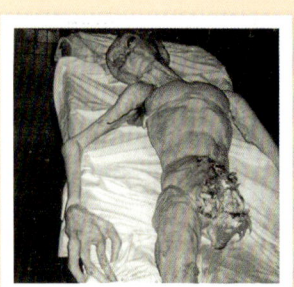

Read the box. Then talk about these questions in class:

1. Think of reasons why people would want to stage a hoax.
2. Explain why people often believe in conspiracy theories.

READING

6 A blog post on the moon landing: Was it all just a hoax?!

a) *Pre-reading: Some conspiracy theorists say the moon landing was just a hoax!*
But who could stage something so big? Share your ideas. The phrases below can help you.

b) *Now read the blog post. Point out the main argument the blogger uses to claim that the moon landing never happened.*

c) *Give your opinion about the blogger's argument.*

Was it all just a hoax?! YES!

If this was possible then (with all that ANCIENT technology) why is nobody flying to the moon TODAY?!
The way I see it, this argument is still one of the strongest. It makes sense. I mean, my smartphone has more computing power than the Eagle had, and that was the height of engineering at the time. So a small computer would be enough to run all the software you'd need to control the landing module.

If that is correct (and it IS correct), why haven't we been there since 1972? NASA doesn't want to go? Of course they want to go! Did our tech improve? Of course it improved! Do we know more about the moon today than we did 40 years ago? Of course we do! So WHY, WHY, WHY?! It must have been a conspiracy. There's NO WAY we could have been there in 1969.

POSTED BY MR_WISEGUY ON NOV. 7 AT 8:43 PM

Useful phrases

You can't believe everything you read / see / … | With enough money / power, you can stage / fake / … | I bet a powerful company / the government / Hollywood could … | Something that big / complicated would be easy / impossible / … to fake.

Tip

A **blog** is a website which the blogger uses as a platform for his / her **blog posts** on a personal-interest subject. There are blogs for just about any topic. The word 'blog' is made up from the words *web* + *logbook*.

WRITING

7 Characteristics of a blog post

a) *Read the skills box. What key points would you add; what would you leave out?*

b) *Go back to the blog post in Ex. 6. Which key points from the list can you find there? Write down as many examples as you can find.*

> ### Writing skills
>
> **Blog posts** are written for others, not just for the blogger. These are **key points** many bloggers follow:
>
> 1. **Opinions** can be strong, but they should be fair too.
> 2. A blogger who is **honest** with his / her readers will probably enjoy the most <u>respect</u>.
> 3. **Clear**, **simple writing** and **short** <u>paragraphs</u> are easier to read.
> 4. **Spelling** is important online too, not just on paper.
> 5. Bloggers often have their own special **writing style**.
> 6. Readers will probably leave more **comments** if the blogger asks questions in his / her posts.
> 7. Headings and visuals **grab the reader's attention**.
> 8. People like **entertaining** posts, not boring ones.

WB 59/2 Reading (wiki or blog)

READING

8 Comparing wiki and blog texts → WB 59/2

a) *Have a closer look at the wiki text and the blog post. Compare them in the three categories below. Then discuss them in class.*

<u>function</u> | language | reader interest

b) *Which of the two texts seems more reliable to you? Explain your choice. The words in the box can help you.*

> ### Word bank
>
> lie | fake sth | play a <u>trick</u> on sb / trick sb | stage a hoax | claim | be based on facts | <u>estimate</u> | make sth sound convincing | <u>question</u> somebody's motivations | think <u>critically</u> | informative | reliable | believable

WRITING

9 Your turn: Write your own blog <u>response</u>

→ △ 125/2
→ S7–9

*2 Your turn: Write own blog response
Help with …
9 Writing skills*

Transfer

HA

Would you support the writer's conspiracy theory in Ex. 6 or would you argue against it? Write your own blog response.

Start like this:

– This is a comment on the … / on what you said about … | I'd like to comment on …
– I agree / disagree with you about … / with the idea that …
– In my opinion … | The way I see it, you …
– You might be right about …, but I don't think you're right about …

> ### Tip
>
> When you write a response, make sure you make it clear **what you're <u>referring to</u>**:
>
> – the whole blog post?
> – just one part of it?

Online ratings

SPEAKING

10 **Reasons for rating things**

Give reasons why so many people go online to <u>rate</u> things, e.g. films or restaurants.

READING

11 **Films about <u>space</u>: Two film summaries**

Read the two summaries below. Talk about them with a partner to make sure you both understand the plots. You need this information to deal with online ratings in Ex. 12.

Capricorn One (1978)

Imagine that the greatest moment in space exploration never happened! The NASA engineers on the Mars <u>space program</u> are unable to land their astronauts on the red planet. So they decide to fake the first Mars landing before the US government ends the expensive Mars program. Will NASA be able to stage the greatest hoax of all time?

The Martian (2015)

What do you do all alone on Mars, millions and millions of miles from home? After a voyage to Mars goes terribly wrong, astronaut Mark Watney (Matt Damon) is left alone to die on the red planet. Can he find a way to survive? What options are there in such a hostile environment? Will NASA even try to rescue Watney?

READING

12 **Ratings on a website for film fans**

a) *Read the two ratings. Describe how positive or negative each one is for its film.*

A Overall, this is a pretty good film. The plot and the acting are convincing, in my opinion. There's <u>well-written</u> dialogue too. But to be honest, it's a bit <u>disappointing</u>. I think I would have enjoyed the movie much more if I'd seen it when it was new. Back then, there weren't that many movies about space or conspiracy theories. But now there are so many great space movies. ★ ★ ★

B This is about as good as a film can get, if you ask me! As if the <u>breathtaking</u> visuals weren't already enough, Matt Damon has given one of his very best performances. Best of all: It's a strong, believable plot; a perfect combination of science, suspense, the power of friendship and BIG emotions. You really feel how lost and lonely a person can be. Excellent! ★ ★ ★ ★ ★

b) *Explain which rating motivates you more to watch the film. Give reasons.*

c) *Can you trust ratings? Give and explain your opinion about how reliable they are or aren't.*

READING

13 **‹ Internet research ›** KV 57: Your own film about space

→ S18

S18 Im Internet recherchieren

Find out as much as you can about the film above that interests you the most. Write down possible search terms before you start your search.

WB 60/3 Vocabulary (opposites)
WB 60/4 Reading (a rating)

WRITING **14 Characteristics of ratings** → WB 60/3–4

Writing skills

When you rate a film (or book), think about these points:

1. Structure your rating in **categories**. This helps you to concentrate on **what is important**, e.g. the acting | the plot | the special effects.
2. You don't need to write a summary for the film's plot; this is almost always included on the rating website already. Concentrate on **your opinion**.
3. Explain what you like or don't like, but **always be fair**. It isn't necessary to use bad language or make rude comments.
4. **Words and phrases** from other people's ratings can be very useful to help you to express your ideas. Examples from Ex. 12: *breathtaking visuals; well-written dialogue*.
5. Use the **simple present** to describe action and scenes (*When the story begins …; The main character never knows … etc.*).

→ ⚠ 125/3
/3 A film rating gone
ng
> After …

a) *Read the points in the skills box above. Then go back to the two ratings in Ex. 12. Find examples of points 1–4 and put them in a grid. (For point 4, you might find phrases in the box on the right to add to your grid.)*

Transfer
HA

b) *Your turn: In a group of 3–4, choose a film that three of you have recently seen. You each write a short rating (6–8 sentences) for it. Then peer-edit each other's texts. Say whose rating you like best and why!*

Useful phrases

well-developed / undeveloped / convincing characters | well-written / badly-written dialogue | a good performance / one of his / her very best performances | great / disappointing actors / acting | silly / weak / creative / believable / … plot | In my opinion … | If you ask me …

WRITING **15 Options: Create wall displays** KV 58: A crossword: Electronic media

→ S7–9

9 Writing skills
.: How words can start
nd, p. 189

Option A:

Internet research for your own wiki text

Some people believe that aliens have really landed on Earth, e.g. in Roswell, New Mexico!

a) *As a group, find one example of a UFO sighting and do research on different websites about it. Which are the most helpful and reliable?*

b) *In your group, write your own wiki text about your subject. Decide what sections your wiki text will need and divide the work up so that everyone has the same amount of work.*

c) *Arrange your wiki text as a wall display for your classroom.*

Option B:

Watch a film together and rate it

You've talked about the films on p. 104, now it's time to watch one together and then rate it.

a) *Form a group of classmates who would like to watch one of the movies you read about on p. 104.*

b) *Find the film on DVD or online.*

c) *After you've watched it, each person in your group will write a rating of the film. Don't forget to give each rating a number of stars from 1 to 5! Then peer-edit each other's texts.*

d) *When the ratings are finished, arrange them as a wall display for your classroom.*

WB 61 <Reading corner> (space events)

What you say and how you say it

On these pages you're going to learn about differences between American English (AE) and British English (BE). You're also going to learn how you use different words or phrases to say the same things in different situations. This is called **register**.

VOCABULARY

1 Warm-up: Which words do you use?

a) *Look at the German words below. There are different expressions for these words in different regions <u>within</u> Germany. Collect them.*

Brötchen   Frikadellen   Bürgersteig   Metzger

b) *Now discuss similar differences you already know about in the English language. You can look at your list from Unit 3, Ex. 18. What other differences do you know about?*

VIEWING

2 British, American and <u>Canadian</u> English   KV 59: Spot the difference: AE or BE?

DVD 4/4
→ S16

S16 Wichtige filmische Mittel

a) *Watch the first part of the film (00:00–02:54).*

b) *Make a grid with the three columns below. Then watch the first part again and write down examples for each category in your grid.*

spelling | pronunciation | different words

c) *Work with a partner. Add more examples from Ex. 1b) to the grid.*

L 2/33

d) *Read the text below. The <u>marked</u> words are <u>pronounced</u> differently in AE and BE.*

Everything is so different at my new school. It starts with getting to school – my mom has to take me by car. At my old school I took the bus, but here I can't because our house is too far away! My schedule at this school is much better though – I can get up later!
So far, most of my new classes are cool; I'm just not so sure about German. But do you want to know what my biggest problem is? I'm so thirsty because I can't find the water fountain!

Tip		
	BE	AE
car, other, sure, work	[–]	[r]
beautiful, little, water	[t]	[d]
new, news	[juː]	[uː]
bath, ask, can't	[ɑː]	[æː]
dog, not, lot	[ɒ]	[ɑː]
boat, know, hello	[əʊ]	[oʊ]

e) *Read the text from d) out loud with a partner. One reads it in American English, the other in British English. The tip box can help you.*

Elevator

VIEWING

3 Register differences

a) *Watch the second part of the film (02:55 – end). What happens in the two scenes?*

b) *Describe how register plays a role in the scenes. Explain why it is important to speak in different registers.*

c) *Your turn: In what situations do you change the way you talk? Say why and how you change it.*

Transfer

WB 62/1 Vocabulary (informal conversation)
WB 62/2 Vocabulary (formal to informal)

VOCABULARY

4 Changing register → WB 62/1–2

a) *Match the words and phrases to the correct category:*

formal register **|** informal register

Hey! **|** How are you? **|** anymore **|** I really don't like it much. **|** child **|** Nope. **|** It really sucks. **|** Sorry, but I don't think so. **|** It's, like, so wild to … **|** I ain't … **|** I'm, like, … **|** Hello. **|** Totally! **|** Whatever! **|** kid **|** What's up? **|** No, I'm not. **|** How nice to … **|** no more **|** It's really boring. **|** I'm sorry. **|** Yes, I have. **|** Not in a million years! **|** I'm not … **|** It's totally not my thing.

b) *Change the register of this conversation between Brodie and his aunt June to make Brodie's words more formal and polite.*

Brodie:	Whoa, sorry dude! Didn't mean to … – Oh! Hey, Auntie June! It's you! What's up?
June:	Brodie! How nice to see you again. Happy Thanksgiving!
Brodie:	Thanks! Same to you. It's, like, so wild to see you again.
June:	How are you? You look like you've really grown in the last year.
Brodie:	Totally! I'm, like, 6 feet tall now. I ain't no little kid no more!
June:	How's school? Are you enjoying it?
Brodie:	Nope. It's, like, so totally not my thing.
June:	Well, I guess I didn't always enjoy school either.
Brodie:	No. It really sucks!
June:	I'm sorry you feel that way. But please mind your language!
Brodie:	Whatever! The only parts I like are lunch and the final bell.
June:	Maybe you can talk to one of your teachers.
Brodie:	Not in a million years!

Legende

Diese Symbole und Erklärungen zeigen dir, wie du mit den Hilfen, Aufgaben und Aktivitäten auf den *Diff pool*-Seiten arbeiten kannst.

△ Hilfe zur Unit-Aufgabe | oder eine leichtere Variante der Unit-Aufgabe | oder eine zusätzliche Aufgabe

▲ eine zusätzliche Herausforderung

Unit 1

△ **1** **Your turn: Your travel plans** → Instead of Introduction, p. 9/4

Where would you like to spend your holiday? Choose one of these places. Find two other people who have chosen a different place. Use the phrases below to tell each other about your holiday plans.

enjoy nature | see wild animals / flowers | breathe fresh air | go for long walks / climbing | good food | …

go swimming / on a sailing trip / surfing | relax in the sun | build a sand castle | eat seafood[1] | …

go sightseeing / shopping | visit museums | travel on hop-on hop-off bus | eat international food | …

△ **2** **Eating on board the ferry** → After Station 1, p. 11/2

*Some friends from the athletics team are talking about the different breakfasts on board the ferry. Read their conversation and answer the questions. Use **indirect speech**.*

Fiona: I don't want to eat a French breakfast here. I've heard it's terrible.

Andrew: I tried it on my trip to France last year and it was really good.

Sally: Kevin and I are having the full English breakfast. We're really hungry because we didn't have breakfast this morning.

Andrew: Oh, I think that's too expensive. My parents only gave me € 150 for the whole trip.

1. Why didn't Fiona want to have a French breakfast?   2. Why did Andrew want to eat the French breakfast?   3. Why were Kevin and Sally hungry?   4. Why couldn't Andrew afford the full Englisch breakfast?

Start like this: 1. Fiona said she … That's why she didn't want to have a French breakfast.

1 **seafood** ['si:fu:d] Meeresfrüchte

▲ **3 Trips without parents** → After Station 1, p. 11/2

Most parents are very worried when their children travel alone. Would you tell your parents about everything that went wrong? Look at these problems Steve had on the trip and think of more. Then say what he told his parents and what he didn't.

1. was ten minutes late for the coach 2. paid too much for the breakfast and didn't ask for the change 3. had to borrow some money from other team members 4. had trouble with his host family because he took photos of the food 5. …

△ **4 What did she say?** → Instead of Station 1, p. 12/4

Before their trip to France, Ms Woodruff told the team everything about the trip. Here's what she said – but what did the narrator tell his parents?

"I have some important information about our trip to France for you. Our coach will leave at 5 a.m., and it can't wait for people who are late – we need to catch the ferry in Dover at 8:40 a.m. We'll arrive in Calais at 9:10 a.m. There's a food court[1] on board the ferry where we can enjoy our first French breakfast. The last time I was on board a P&O ferry they also had free wifi. Some people spent most of the trip playing video games. But I hope nobody on our team wants to stare at a video screen[2] when they can enjoy the sea instead. Oh, I forgot to give you this form. All parents must sign it before we leave."

Start like this: "Ms Woodruff said she had … She told us our coach …"

△ **5 What happened?** → Help with Station 1, p. 12/5a)

These words and phrases can help you to talk about the experiences of the Jones family:

Picture 1:
in Italy – go swimming – leave everything on the beach – come back – all things gone – see thief – can't catch – too far away

Picture 2:
very hot – wear shorts and tops – visit old city – go into church – want to take photos – priest[3] – tell us to leave – no shorts / tops and camera

Picture 3:
camp – long day – tired – sleep in tent[4] – suddenly hear noise – tent start to shake[5] – open – cow looking at us

△ **6 Travel situations** → Help with Station 1, p. 12/5b)

These phrases can help you to talk about your travel experiences:

When I was in … last year … | During the holidays, I … | I felt very stupid / embarrassed / terrible / scared when … | Everyone / Someone was staring / looking at me / trying to explain something to me. | I was confused / upset / angry because … | I wanted to …, but I couldn't … | Next time, I'll use my mobile / ask someone about … / remember to …

ung: *Rafiq's aunt wanted know … 1. what had pened at passport control. hy the man had become picious. 3. who had told to go into the side room. hat the security people said. 5. if they'd scared 6. if he really had forgot- his birthday. 7. where his gage was. 8. if he needed with his suitcase. 9. if he'd his parents about this.*

1 food court [fuːd kɔːt] Gastronomiebereich | **2 screen** [skriːn] Bildschirm | **3 priest** [priːst] Priester | **4 tent** [tent] Zelt | **5 to shake** [ʃeɪk] wackeln

7 A curious[1] aunt → After Station 2, p. 14/9

*At the airport, Rafiq's aunt wants to know exactly what happened. Turn her questions into **indirect speech**.*

1. "What happened at passport control?" **2.** "Why did the man become suspicious?" **3.** "Who told you to go to the side room?" **4.** "What did the security people say?" **5.** "Did they scare you?" **6.** "Have you really forgotten your birthday?" **7.** "Where's your luggage?" **8.** "Do you need help with the suitcase?" **9.** "Will you tell your parents about this?"

8 What did he ask? → After Station 2, p. 14/9

*Write down **five questions** you could ask your classmates. Then get into groups of three (Student A, B and C).*

Student A whispers the first question on his list into the ear of Student B. Student C asks Student B: "What did he / she ask?" and Student B reports the question in **indirect speech**. Student C gives an answer, then Student B whispers a question into his ear – and Student A asks: "What did he / she say?" Take turns until you've answered all the questions on your lists.

9 I told you to call! → After Station 2, p. 14/10

When Rafiq comes back from Bangladesh, his mother is happy to see him again – but she's angry too. What did she tell him to do before he left? Complete her sentences.

Example: Did you take photos out of the plane? – I **asked you to take** photos out of the plane.

1. You didn't call when you arrived. Why not? I told you …
2. I don't think you said 'hello' to your aunt and uncle from us. But I …
3. Masud didn't take you to the old centre, did he? I know I …
4. Did you go there all alone? That's so dangerous! I …
5. I hope your aunt and uncle showed you my village. I …
6. Did Aunt Sadia cook black rice[2] for you? I …
7. I haven't got a postcard yet – did you write one? I …
8. Where is the saree[3] for me? Did you buy one? I …
9. Someone stole your money? You didn't take it to the old centre, did you? I …
10. I hope your aunt and uncle will visit us next year. Did you invite them? I …

1 curious [ˈkjʊəriəs] neugierig | **2 rice** [raɪs] Reis | **3 saree** [ˈsɑːri] Sari

Lösung: 1. *I told you to call.* 2. *I told you to say 'hello'.* 3. *I know I told him to take you there.* 4. *I told you not to go alone.* 5. *I asked them to show it to you.* 6. *I asked her to cook it for you.* 7. *I asked you to write a postcard.* 8. *I asked you to buy me a saree.* 9. *I told you not to take it to the old centre.* 10. *I told you to invite them.*

▲ **10 Everyone orders me about[1] ...** → After Station 2, p. 14/10

Young people hear commands from lots of different people in their lives. What commands do you get from these people? Complete the list. Then tell the class what they tell you to do. Use **indirect speech**.

Teachers	Parents	Coach
Do your homework! ...	Tidy up your room! ...	Be on time for training! ...

△ **11 Your turn: Travel plans** → Help with Station 2, p. 15/13

You can choose from these European cities to find ideas for your plans:

	Barcelona	Dublin	Vienna
Flights from Frankfurt / Munich	1h 55 / 2h 5	2h 5 / 2h 35	1 h 20 / 1 h 5
Places of interest / Things to do	La Sagrada Familia church | Las Ramblas street | Magic Fountain[2] show | Camp Nou football stadium | beach	Ha'penny Bridge | O'Connell Street | The Book of Kells | Dublin Ghost Bus Tour | National Aquatic Centre	opera[3] house | Schönbrunn Zoo | Imperial Palace | National History Museum | Prater fun park

△ **12 Reading between the lines** → After Story, p. 18/4

Read these short texts. Then decide which important information can be found between the lines.

 sung: 1b), 2c), 3a), 4c)

1. It was wet outside. Very wet. Ryan looked at the kitchen clock: football training was at 4 p.m., and now it was already 3:50. He picked up his shoes and jacket, and with a sigh[4] walked out into the rain.
   a) Ryan lives close to the football stadium.
   b) Ryan hates playing football in the rain.
   c) The kitchen clock doesn't show the right time.

2. Kimberly ran all the way home, her Maths test still in her hand and a big smile on her face. "Mum!" she shouted. "You won't believe this!"
   a) Kimberly hurries home to help her mum in the kitchen.
   b) Kimberly is a very good student, especially[5] in Maths.
   c) She has a good mark in a Maths test, which is a surprise for her.

---

1 to order sb about [ˈɔːdə əˈbaʊt] jmdn. herumkommandieren | **2 fountain** [ˈfaʊntɪn] Brunnen | **3 opera** [ˈɒprə] Oper
4 sigh [saɪ] Seufzer | **5 especially** [ɪˈspeʃli] besonders

3. Mrs Lynch looked at the students who were playing outside the school building. Laura was standing all by herself under what looked like 'her' tree now. She was staring down at her feet, as usual.
   a) Laura is unhappy because the other students don't talk to her.
   b) Mrs Lynch likes trees and students.
   c) The weather is great, so everyone can play outside.

4. Ethan checked his mobile for the tenth time – still no message. He played with the empty glass in front of him and asked himself if he should ask for another drink or give up and go home.
   a) Ethan likes drinks in restaurants and cafés.
   b) Ethan doesn't know what to do when he is alone in a restaurant.
   c) Ethan is waiting for someone, but that person doesn't come.

Text smart 1

△ **1** **Theatre collocations** → Instead of Introduction, p. 30/2a)

Read the following conversation between two actors and note down the theatre collocations they use.

Lösung: *forget your lines, give a great performance, learn the lines, mess up the play, get into character, identify with your character, follow the director's instructions, stage a play, play a part, stay in character, follow the stage directions, play the scene, use the props, learn your role*

Alex: Ian! You've forgotten your lines again! We can't give a great performance if you don't learn the lines! If you go on like that, you'll mess up the whole play.

Ian: Sorry, I just can't get into my character today. He's such a sad guy, and I'm just too happy right now.

Alex: Well, if you can't identify with your character, just try following the director's instructions, OK? They help you to understand your role. We've staged the play before – if you don't feel you can do it, Sam can play your part.

Ian: Sam? You can't be serious. He never stays in character – one moment he's a super hero, and the next a sad old man.

Alex: At least he knows how to follow the stage directions and play the scene right.

Ian: Are you sure? Remember how he forgets to use the props – he was supposed to give me the magic book in our last play but he forgot it backstage! I looked like a fool!

Alex: I don't think the audience noticed. Now just learn your role well and let's get on with our rehearsal.

△ **2** **The main characters** → Instead of Station 1, p. 31/5b)

Try to get into Claire's head and say what might happen.

Start like this: If I ask my parents, they'll say no. If they say no, I can't … If I can't …, Rob will … If I tell my parents that I want to spend the night at Rob's house, …

△ **3 Telling lies** → Help with Station 2, p. 33/8

*In which of the following situations are people telling a white lie? Discuss if it's OK to tell these white lies, or if it's **never** OK!*

1. Your friend has bought a new dress and looks terrible in it. She asks you if you like it and you say "It's just great!"
2. You forgot to do your homework yesterday, so you tell the teacher that you didn't understand it.
3. A friend calls, but you don't feel like talking to him and don't answer. When he asks you later why you didn't answer the phone, you say you didn't hear it.
4. You lost your mum's sunglasses, and you hadn't asked her if you could borrow them before. She asks you if you know where they are – you just tell her to take better care of her things.

△ **4 Getting into character** → Help with Station 2, p. 33/9d)

Get into groups of three. One student stands in the middle. Now one of you doesn't want this student to do something, but he/she can only say "Don't!" Your partner wants the student to do it, but he/she can only say "Come on!" Keep repeating your words in as many different ways as possible to convince the student in the middle. Who is more convincing? How does the student in the middle show that?

△ **5 Acting out a scene** → Help with Station 3, p. 35/12a)

Work together with another group of five. Decide who is going to play which role. Now go through the following steps together:

1. Work together with the person in the second group who has the same role as you.
2. One of you reads out the lines (reader), the other acts them (actor). If you're the reader, make sure that you read slowly and pay a lot of attention to your voice; if you're the actor, make sure that you listen carefully to the lines and pay a lot of attention to facial expressions and gestures[1].
3. Change roles and practise again.
4. Now one group acts out the scene while the other watches. Take turns. What ideas do you have to improve the scene? Try them out.

△ **6 Staying in character** → Help with Station 4, p. 37/14c)

Copy these adjectives onto little pieces of paper and put them face down on the desk. Take turns to pick up a piece of paper, and use facial expressions and gestures to demonstrate[2] the feeling on your piece of paper. Don't speak! Your partner must guess which feeling you're trying to express.

angry   worried   afraid   scared   nervous   guilty   ashamed[3]   sad   shocked

disappointed   happy   confused   like an idiot   tired   fantastic

---

1 gesture [ˈdʒestʃə] Geste; Handbewegung | **2 to demonstrate** [ˈdemənstreɪt] zeigen |
3 ashamed [əˈʃeɪmd] beschämt

△ **7   Bringing the story to life** → Help with Options, p. 37/16

These ideas can help you with your options:

Option A:
When you act each scene, ask the students who aren't playing in that scene to watch. Pay attention to these points:

Where does each of you stand? | When do you move, and where do you go? | Who do you look at when you speak? | Make sure you don't turn your back on the audience!

Take notes for each scene and repeat the scenes with these notes in mind.

Option B:
This is what you should think about before you start:

What scenes do you want to take a photo of? | What effects can the camera angle and field size have? | What lighting do you want? | Do you need props?

When you edit the photos, these tips can be helpful:

Add the text which is necessary to understand what the scene is about (key information, dialogue, thoughts, and exclamations). | Write short texts that link the photos so that someone who doesn't know the play can understand it too.

Unit 2

△ **1 Welcome to America!** → Help with Introduction, p. 43/3

*Read the questions below **before** you listen. They can help you to sum things up in Ex. 3 on p. 43.*

– Why are the European teens in America?	– What can you do in your free time if you live in the suburbs?
– Why is Josh the right person to talk to them?	– Where will the Europeans go to school?
– What is he going to talk about?	– What does Josh say about lockers?
– Where does Josh live?	– Where else do students meet?
– What does he say about American apartment buildings?	– Do American students have to work hard?
– Where does he meet his friends?	– What does Josh say about other activities at school?
– What does he say about city life?	– What do Americans do in their free time?
– What is good about life in the suburbs?	– What else does Josh think is important?
– How are suburbs different from cities?	

△ **2 Different categories of gerunds** → Help with Station 1, p. 45/3b)

✎ *Copy the grid into your exercise books. Complete it with the gerund phrases below.*

Gerund after adjective + preposition	Gerund after verb + preposition	Gerund as sentence subject	Gerund as sentence object
I'm scared of changing		Living here isn't bad	

I miss seeing my old friends | Getting there is difficult | I like hanging out with … | We talked about organizing a party | Living here isn't bad ✔ | I miss having a garden | I'm looking forward to starting school | I enjoyed meeting you | Being in a city is cool | I love having a big bedroom | Can you imagine walking up 22 floors? | I'm scared of changing ✔ | I'm looking forward to making friends | I'm good at swimming | How about meeting up? | Stop worrying about losing your old friends | Meeting up isn't easy | I keep forgetting your dad is American | I'm getting used to living on the 22nd floor

3 Do you like talking to your partner? → After Station 1, p. 46/4

Work with a partner to create little dialogues about things you like and don't like.
You can use these phrases to start with. Can you think of more?

Do you like skiing? / Do you …? Are you good at playing chess? Do you feel like reading a book? Do you enjoy going for long walks? Are you crazy about texting your friends? Is dancing good for you?	✔	Yes, … is great / fantastic / fun. Yes, I love … / like … / always enjoy …
	✘	No, … takes too much time / makes me sick / is boring / isn't interesting at all. No, I hate … / don't like … at all / find … boring.

Example: Do you feel like going swimming? – No, I hate swimming.

4 Gerunds to talk about likes and dislikes → Instead of Station 1, p. 46/6

Gerunds are often helpful when you want to talk about likes and dislikes. Here, Lena is talking to her new friend, Madison. Finish the sentences below with **gerund phrases**. Each sentence with a gerund phrase should have the same meaning as the original sentence with the same number.

Lösung: 1. … *new people.* 2. … *going to the mall, but …* 3. … *telling me to unpack.* 4. … *wearing crazy T-shirts to school because …* 5. … *driving when he was 16.* 6. … *meeting some more people in the area?* 7. … *planning our Thanksgiving party!* 8. … *listening to music!*

Lena
1. I'm a bit shy when I meet new people, but it's OK.
2. Maybe I'll go to the mall; I'm not sure yet.
3. Mom tells me to unpack every day!
4. There's a dress code so I don't wear crazy T-shirts to school anymore.

Madison
5. My brother learned to drive when he was 16.
6. Would you like to meet some more people in the area?
7. I can't wait to plan our Thanksgiving party!
8. I listen to music all the time!

Lena
1. I don't mind meeting …
2. I'm thinking of …
3. Mom keeps …
4. I've stopped …

Madison
5. My brother started …
6. Are you interested in …
7. I'm looking forward to …
8. I love …

5 I like / I hate → Help with Station 1, p. 47/7

What do you like or hate? The words and phrases on the right can help you with sentences.
Write your ideas down first before you talk to your partner.

Examples:
- I love chilling out on the sofa, but I hate washing the dishes.
- I'm really interested in …, but I'm scared of …

take tests | chill out with friends | travel around the world | discover new countries | go hiking | see / find dangerous animals | chill out on the sofa | text my friends | play games on my phone | watch TV | clean the kitchen | listen to music | tidy my room / the kitchen

▲ 6 Role play: Matt, his angel and his devil → After Station 2, p. 48/9

In groups of three, write a short role play for Matt, his angel and his devil:

- – Matt talks out loud about his dilemma;
- – his angel and his devil try to tell him what to do from their different points of view.

The ideas below can help you to write your role play. Then act it out for the class.

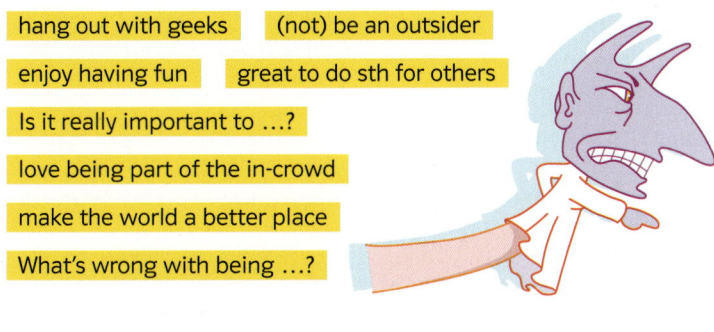

hang out with geeks   (not) be an outsider

enjoy having fun   great to do sth for others

Is it really important to …?

love being part of the in-crowd

make the world a better place

What's wrong with being …?

△ 7 Infinitives with question words → Help with Station 2, p. 49/11a

Compare A and B: Which words are left out in B? What is used instead? What else is different? This can help you to do Ex. 11a) on p. 49.

 ung: *with question word: stion word + infinitive struction; without stion word: 'whether' + nitive construction*

A

Matt asks himself a lot of questions at lunchtime:

How do I pay for my lunch?   →
Where do I sit?   →
What can I say to the other students? →
Should I talk about the lessons?   →

B

He told his parents about it when he came home. He didn't know …

… how to pay for his lunch.
… where to sit.
… what to say to the other students.
… whether to talk about the lessons.

△ 8 Do you know how to help a friend? → After Station 2, p. 49/11

A group of kids from Matt's school is hiking in the hills of Pennsylvania. Suddenly Scott stumbles[1], falls down and doesn't get up again. Everyone is worried and asking questions. Turn their questions into **infinitive sentences**. *Use words like these:*

wonder | ask themselves | not know |
have no idea | not sure

Example: How can we help him? → They're wondering **how to help** him.

 ung: *1. whether, hether, 3. whether, hether, 5. whether, hether, 7. … who to 8. where to find*

1. Should we feel his pulse[2]?
2. Do we have to check his breathing[3]?
3. Do we have to put up his legs?
4. Should we stay here?
5. Should we cover him with our jackets?
6. Shouldn't we try to find some adults?
7. Who can we call?
8. Where can we find some water for him?

1 to stumble [ˈstʌmbl] stolpern | **2 pulse** [pʌls] Puls | **3 breathing** [ˈbriːðɪŋ] Atmung

▲ **9** **New at our school** → After Station 2, p. 49/11

a) *What kinds of things do new students want to know about their new school?*
Work with a partner to finish the sentences on the left with information on the right.

1. Students who are new at our school
   want to know where to …
2. They wonder whether …
3. Some ask themselves how …
4. They would like to know who …
5. They don't know when …

> find the cafeteria / the computer room |
> use the computers | borrow books | say
> hello to the teachers | ask for the computer
> passwords | bring books back to the library

b) *Work with a partner to write down questions a new student at your school might have.*

△ **10** **I want you to write back!** → After Station 2, p. 50/13b)

a) *Lena has told her grandma back in Germany what she is worrying about.*
First, read the tips and advice that her grandma wrote back.

> Liebe Lena,
> ich möchte, dass du dich in Amerika zu Hause fühlst. 🙂🙂🙂 Und ich möchte natürlich nicht, dass
> du traurig bist! 😰😰😰 Das tut mir so leid! Ich hätte gern, dass du Matt schreibst und ihm sagst,
> wie du dich fühlst. Natürlich würde ich es vorziehen, dass ER dir zuerst schreibt, aber er scheint
> sehr beschäftigt zu sein. Deshalb kannst du auch nicht erwarten, dass er dir sofort antwortet. Aber
> wenn du möchtest, dass er sich mit dir trifft, musst DU etwas tun.
> Jetzt hätte ich gern, dass du mir bald antwortest! --Oma 😍🙂😍

But Lena isn't so sure about her grandma's advice and wants Madison's opinion.
Write what Lena could tell Madison about it.

Start like this: Grandma wants me to feel at home in America, and she doesn't …
            She's really sorry for me. She'd like me to …

b) *Lots of people tell Matt what to do too. Write sentences about him:*

Eva and Scott would like Matt to …

    spend the lunch break with them   go to the mall with them   not hang out with the geeks

Here's what Matt's parents expect from him:

    always do his homework right after school   find new friends quickly   do what they say

And here's what Matt would prefer his friends to do:

    everyone like each other   not talk bad about others   all his friends have lunch together

▲ **11** **What I'd like others to do** → After Station 2, p. 50/13b)

Think of all your teachers (or classmates / parents / friends): What do they do, what don't they do?
What do you like about it, what don't you like? Make a list of things you'd like them to do or not
*to do! Use **infinitive constructions**. Be creative!*

Examples: I'd like my English teacher to give us less homework. | I'd prefer the Math teacher to
        stop writing silly numbers on the board. | I expect …

◻ **12** Infinitive or gerund? → Help with Station 2, p. 51/15b)

Copy the grid into your exercise books. Then read the text below. Complete the grid with the verbs in yellow and decide: How do you write them when they're used with a **gerund**? And how do you write them with an **infinitive**? Write the German translation of the verbs into your grid.

Verb	⊕ Gerund	⊕ Infinitive
remember	sich erinnern, etwas getan zu haben	…
…	…	…

Matt's mom remembers her last trip from England to the US: "I'll never forget losing my passport last year. I had forgotten to put it into my suitcase. I remember holding it in my hand and thinking that I shouldn't put it into my purse[1], and then I tried to open the suitcase – but the zipper[2] got stuck[3]. I tried using soap[4] on the zipper after someone had told me it helps, but it didn't. Then the doorbell rang, and I stopped to answer it. Well, once I stop doing something, I don't always remember to finish it, and that's what happened. I stopped thinking about the passport and put it into my purse. But my purse was stolen on my way to the airport! So I missed the flight *and* lost my passport!"

◻ **13** Useful phrases for Lena's video chat → Help with Station 2, p. 51/16

Altkleidersammlung | keine Lust mehr haben, … zu tun | sich fragen wie … sein wird | Obdachlosenunterkunft | Kleider spenden | gut darin sein zu … / das gute Gefühl haben, … | Vorteile | von etwas profitieren | entrümpeln | etwas von jemandem erwarten

◻ **14** What *really* happened at the mall → Help with Story, p. 54/4c)

These pictures and phrases can help you to write your own version of the story:

A

B

C

Lena sees group of young people with big signs | no Madison | the crowd pushes; Lena falls, loses her phone | sees her phone | grabs it before somebody steals it

tells officer that phone was stolen | Lena not worried; she knows she'll see the others at 5:00 | officer looks worried; tells her she might not see her phone again

Matt calls Lena's phone, Madison answers | phone was in Madison's bag the whole time | Lena waits at bench at 5:00 | Matt and Madison walk towards her

1 purse [pɜːs] Handtasche | **2 zipper** [ˈzɪpə] Reißverschluss | **3 get stuck** [stʌk] sich verhaken | **4 soap** [səʊp] Seife

Text smart 2

△ **1 How to create an ad** → Help with Station, p. 65/2b)

These words and phrases can help you to describe the ad on p. 65:

Useful phrases

- The ad for … is a typical …
- There's a large / small / funny / interesting eye-catcher on the left / right side …
- The eye-catcher shows … / is a photo of …
- It works as an eye-catcher because …

- Several photos show …
- The ad also gives / presents information on …
- The slogan is the part that says "…"
- The slogan focuses on …
- The ad copy tells the reader about …

△ **2 Talking about a target group** → Help with Station, p. 66/4a)

Look at the different target groups in the first box below. Which ones would find the Fa$hion Fabulou$ ad attractive? And the Retro 4ever ad?

Lösung: 1. *The advertisers want to sell (cheap) clothes/ fashion.* 2. *Target group: girls, young people, families*

large families | fashion models | husbands who need a present for their wife's birthday | teachers | students | people with lots of / with little money | fashion addicts | tourists | hipsters | people who need an outfit for a wedding / for a party | skaters

These words might be able to help you to give more information about the target group:

people who want everyday / sporty[1] / cheap / nice / trendy[2] / … clothes | people who want to spend / save money | people who want …

△ **3 Improving an ad** → Help with Station, p. 67/5b)

These questions might help you to find ideas for improving the ads on pages 65–66:

Visuals: Is there a link between the eye-catcher and the product? | Does the eye-catcher make the customer curious[3]? | Do the visuals cause positive / negative feelings? | Do the visuals present the product in the best possible way?

Slogan / ad copy: Does the slogan match the product? | Is the slogan catchy? | Does it tell the customer what the product is good for? | Does the ad copy tell the reader clearly where he / she can buy the product? | Does the ad copy clearly speak to a special target group?

Humor: Does the humor of the ad work for everyone? | Does it hurt anybody's feelings? | Are there ways it could be funnier?

Product: Does the ad feature enough information about the product?

Target group: Is it clear who the target group is? | Is there more than one target group? Could the target group be bigger if you changed the ad?

Effectiveness: Would you buy the product? | Do you know anybody who would buy it?

1 **sporty** ['spɔːti] sportlich | 2 **trendy** ['trendi] trendig | 3 **curious** ['kjʊəriəs] neugierig

Unit 3

△ 1 Big city life → Help with Introduction, p. 71/2a)

These words and phrases can help you to talk about life in a big city:

Pros: entertainment: (movie) theaters, concerts, live shows | **activities:** sports clubs, big parks | **education:** schools, museums, special offers for kids | **culture:** music, art, many nationalities[1] and cultures

Cons: people: too many people on the streets, crowded places, full buses and underground trains | **traffic:** too many cars, too much noise, pollution | **crime:** criminal gangs, violence, organized crime

△ 2 Your turn: In New York City → Help with Introduction, p. 71/3

Read the text about one of the photos from the Introduction. Which photo does it match?
The text can help you to write your own text about one of the other photos.

I can hear lots of cars and voices — and so many different languages! Everyone seems to be busy. I can feel the magic of a big city with people from lots of different countries. The air smells of strange and spicy[2] food. I'm trying to catch a taxi, but that isn't so easy. Other people are waiting for a taxi too. But I'm not bored: There are so many things to discover and look at, like the colorful shop signs that I can't read and the mix of American and Chinese[3] culture.

△ 3 Tourists in New York → After Station 1, p. 73/2

*Use the phrases below to make sentences with **defining relative clauses**.*

Example: 1. Everyone **who is in New York for the first time** wants to visit the Empire State Building.

are looking for designer clothes | are interested in history | is in New York for the first time ✔

love paintings and sculptures | want to get a great view of New York

are traveling with children | enjoy outdoor activities | don't have time

1. Everyone wants to visit the Empire State Building.
2. Most tourists spend a day in Central Park.
3. People often come to New York to visit the Museum of Modern Art.
4. Tourists love the Museum of Immigration on Ellis Island.
5. Most visitors travel by taxi.
6. Families always enjoy a visit to the Museum of Natural History.
7. Shoppers love the big department stores[4] like Bloomingdales.
8. Many tourists go up to the top of Rockefeller Center.

[left margin solutions:]
...ung: 2. ... who enjoy ...door activities ... ...eople who love paintings ... sculptures ... 4. Tourists ... are interested in history ... Most visitors who don't ...e time ... 6. Families ... are traveling with ...dren ... 7. Shoppers who ...ooking for designer ...hes ... 8. Many tourists ... want to get a great ...w of New York ...

---

1 nationality [ˌnæʃnˈæləti] Nationalität | **2 spicy** [ˈspaɪsi] würzig; scharf | **3 Chinese** [tʃaɪˈniːz] chinesisch |
4 department store [dɪˈpɑːtmənt ˌstɔː] Kaufhaus

4 A stopover[1] in New York → After Station 1, p. 73/2

Imagine you have a two-hour stopover in Manhattan. What would you like to see and do?
Write a short text. Give reasons for your choice of activities and places.

5 Defining or non-defining? → After Station 1, p. 74/6

Use the phrases to make sentences about Rylee and Lea in New York City.
*Decide if you need **defining** or **non-defining relative clauses**.*

Example: 1. Lea and Rylee, **who are in New York for the first time**, only have one day to spend in the city.

Diego shows the girls | Diego thinks of | is only a few blocks from Central Park

are in New York for the first time ✓ | catches Diego and the girls at the top of Rockefeller Center

calls himself 'The Naked Cowboy' | Diego and the girls visit | works in a diner

1. Lea and Rylee only have one day to spend in the city.
2. Diego takes the girls on a sightseeing tour of New York.
3. The places are for free.
4. The first place is a famous music school.
5. The man is a popular tourist attraction.
6. At the Alvin Ailey Dance Studio people take dance classes.
7. The big surprise is the view from Rockefeller Center.
8. The security man is Diego's father.

Lösung: 2. *Diego, who works in a diner, … 3. The places (which/that) Diego and the girls visit … 4. The first place (which/that) Diego shows the girls … 5. The man, who calls himself 'The Naked Cowboy', … 6. At the Alvin Ailey Dance Studio, which is only a few blocks from Central Park, … 7. The big surprise (which/that) Diego thinks of … 8. The security man, who catches Diego and the girls at the top of Rockefeller Center, …*

6 Typical German food → Help with Station 1, p. 75/9

Match the English phrases on the left with the German expressions on the right.
The English words can help you with Ex. 9 on p. 75.

black pudding | liver sausage | grow in the earth | serve with | vegetarian | point to the sky | chopped apples | the main ingredients | a popular dish

Leberwurst | die Hauptzutaten | in den Himmel ragen | ein beliebtes Gericht | Blutwurst | in der Erde wachsen | mit … servieren | vegetarisch | zerkleinerte Äpfel

7 *Since* or *for*? → After Station 2, p. 77/12

*Complete the sentences with **since** or **for**.*

1. People have been calling New York 'The Big Apple' ▮ a very long time.
2. A large Christmas tree has decorated Rockefeller Center every year ▮ Christmas 1933.
3. Carnegie Hall has been one of the world's most famous concert halls ▮ it was opened in 1891.
4. New Amsterdam has been called New York ▮ Peter Stuyvesant had to give the city to the English in 1664.
5. Yellow taxis have been driving around New York ▮ more than a hundred years.
6. New York has been important in foreign trade[2] ▮ the opening of the Erie Canal in 1825.

Lösung: 1. *for,* 2. *since,* 3. *since,* 4. *since,* 5. *for,* 6. *since*

1 stopover [ˈstɒpˌəʊvə] Zwischenstopp | **2 foreign trade** [ˈfɒrɪn ˈtreɪd] Außenhandel

8 Present perfect progressive or past perfect progressive? → After Station 2, p. 78/15

*Complete the text with the right verb forms and **since** or **for**.*

Lisa checked the time. She `1` (wait) `2` half an hour now, and still the airport bus wasn't in sight. Others were waiting with her. She noticed a woman who `3` (talk) to someone on her phone `4` 20 minutes. "I `5` (live) here `6` May last year, and you haven't been here to see me once!" She'd heard her say. How could anyone not want to visit a friend in New York? Lisa `7` (dream) of coming to New York `8` she was a teenager. One day her boss had told her: "We `9` (look) for someone to take over our office in New York `10` last summer, and it seems that you're the best person for the job!" Lisa, who `11` (think of) moving to New York `12` several months, had accepted at once. "This is the chance I `13` (wait) for `14` I started working for this company," she'd told her husband. But now, after the first week in New York, she missed her husband and her kids. If only the airport bus would come …

9 Mixed bag: Different tenses → After Station 2, p. 78/15

*As a taxi driver in New York, Emilio meets lots of interesting people. Here's a story he told his son Diego. Use the right tense for the verbs in brackets: **simple past**, **past progressive**, **present perfect**, **past perfect** or **past perfect progressive**.*

I `1` (drive) around for a while when I `2` (pass[1]) the airport bus stop at Grand Central Station. There `3` (be) an accident on Lexington Avenue and traffic `4` (be) very slow. I `5` (notice) a family with a little boy and a teenage girl who `6` (point) at my taxi, so I `7` (stop). The man `8` (tell) me that they `9` (wait) for the airport bus for more than an hour. The family and another woman with a big suitcase `10` (get) into the taxi. They `11` (agree) to share a taxi and pay for it together. When we `12` (arrive) at the airport, the man `13` (say) he'd put it on his credit card[2]. But my credit card machine `14` (not work), so I `15` (ask) them to pay in cash[3]. Well, guess what – the family `16` (spend) all their cash and so they `17` (not be able to) pay. "Don't worry, I'll pay," the other woman `18` (say). "They can give it back to me later." She `19` (give) them her address in New York and `20` (pay): nearly $90! Isn't that cool? I `21` (never meet) such a generous person before.

10 What had been happening before? → Instead of Station 2, p. 78/16

*Complete the sentences with the ideas below. Use the **past perfect progressive**.*

study hard for weeks   walk around Central Park for half an hour

look for rabbits in a muddy field for hours   chill out and talk for two hours

cry all morning   work hard all day   wait for him to call since 10 o'clock

1. I was very tired when I got home after school because I'd been …
2. Dave got the best grade on the test because he …
3. We … when there was a heavy storm and we had to go back.
4. When Kelly arrived at the café, her friends …
5. Our dog was very dirty. He …
6. Lisa thought her friend would never call. She …
7. Mary's eyes were very red. She …

1 to pass [pɑːs] vorbeikommen an | **2 credit card** [ˈkredɪt ˌkɑːd] Kreditkarte | **3 cash** [kæʃ] Bargeld

△ **11 Stylistic elements in a graphic novel** → Help with Story, p. 89/3c)

Which of these stylistic elements can you find in the story? Use the prompts to talk about the effect they have in Asphalt Tribe.

large panel	several small panels	overlapping panels

set the scene | introduce the setting | create a distance / a quiet atmosphere	show action in the story | show reactions / feelings of characters	introduce fast action / speed | create suspense | make the reader live through the story

long shot

medium shot

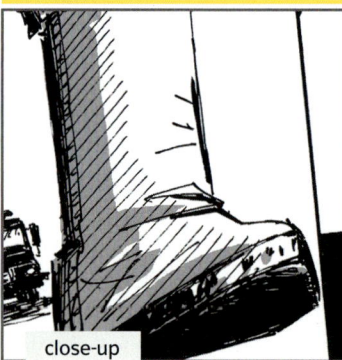

close-up

△ **12 Write the story!** → Help with Story, p. 90/6

a) *Look at these beginnings of different parts of the story. What scene do they match?*

A: These streets, so busy and hectic during the day, but so dark and scary at night, were our home.

B: I ran away as fast as I could, but when I turned around, I saw that Maybe wasn't following me.

C: After a hard day in the streets we enjoyed our food – even if it was from the dumpster.

b) *Choose one of the opening sentences from a) and use the information and phrases below to continue the story.*

A: sleep under bridges | no family, only gang members | fight to survive | lonely | hard life | depressing | often hungry | invent new names	B: shout at Maybe | run at top speed | stupid rich ladies | no chance to catch us in their designer shoes | hope that handbag full of money	C: relax for a moment | glad to be with friends, not so lonely | suddenly hear police car | scared to death | drop everything and run away into the dark

Text smart 3

△ 1 Reasons → Help with Station 1, p. 102/5

There are different reasons why people would want to stage a hoax or why they believe in conspiracy theories. Maybe some of the statements below can help you with Ex. 5:

You could make a lot of money with it!

Governments or companies will do anything to look good or to cover up bad news!

When something is hard to explain, it's easy to say it was a government trick or a cover-up.

A boring person becomes interesting with a good story.

Some people will do anything for attention!

It's fun to trick people, and some will people believe anything!

△ 2 Your turn: Write your own blog response → Help with Station 1, p. 103/9

These ideas and arguments can help you to write your answer to the blog entry on the moon landing. Which ones support the blog writer? Which ones don't?

- moon landing not important → being better than the Soviet Union important
- then and now, good entertainment important → fake or real, only the show counts
- faking it → a good idea; good way to save money for a *real* trip to the moon
- flying to the moon → no benefits; too expensive
- reasons for not going anymore → other problems / challenges in world now; one successful mission enough
- clear facts → astronauts brought back stones, took photos

△ 3 A film rating gone wrong → After Station 2, p. 105/14a)

Look back at the skills box on p. 105. Then read the rating below. Talk to your partner about what's wrong here and how you could improve the text. Then write a new version.

Star Wars Episode 7: How bad can a film get?!
The film tells the story of a group of heroes who fight the dark powers and try find Luke Skywalker. On some websites people give this movie a rating of 9 or even 10 stars. Are they crazy?! Stupid?! Or both?! Were we watching the same movie?! THIS IS THE WORST STAR WARS FILM EVER! Let's start with the awful actors: Harrison Ford and Carrie Fisher are both too old and ugly to play their parts. I wish they had costumes like Chewbacca's so we wouldn't have to see their faces! Another joke: There are so many badly-done special effects! Han Solo's spaceship, the Millennium Falcon, was used in so many battles for the Rebel Alliance, especially in episodes 4 to 6, that it just looks like a silly old toy now. And can we talk about Rey, the new female[1] hero? As a girl, let me just say that it wasn't convincing for her to win a fight against Kylo Ren, Han Solo's son! Seriously! A woman who is good at mechanics[2], engineering[3] AND fighting?! Completely unbelievable!!! I wish I could give NO stars, but I have to give at least one, so here it is. ★
POSTED BY SCARY_CHICK ON DEC. 14 AT 10:08 PM

1 **female** ['fiːmeɪl] weiblich | 2 **mechanics** [mɪˈkænɪks] Technik | 3 **engineering** [ˌendʒɪˈnɪərɪŋ] Maschinenbau

Reading skills

S1 Schnelllesetechniken

Wenn du eine Aufgabe zu einem Text bekommst oder bestimmte Informationen suchst, liest du dir den Text ganz gezielt durch. Die folgenden Techniken können dir helfen, wenn die Zeit begrenzt ist:

Skimming („den Rahm abschöpfen")	Scanning („maschinell durchsuchen")
Wenn du danach gefragt wirst, worum es in einem Text geht, sollst du ihn nicht einfach nacherzählen, sondern nur das Wichtigste *(gist)* zusammenfassen. Dazu kannst du den ganzen Text überfliegen und darauf achten, ob bestimmte Wörter *(key words)* oder Personen häufiger vorkommen. Auch die Überschrift oder Bilder können dir helfen einzuschätzen, was wichtig ist und was nicht. Diese Art des Schnelllesens nennt man *skimming*.	Wenn du nach bestimmten Einzelheiten *(details)* in einem Text gefragt wirst, musst du ihn überfliegen und die Stellen mit den wichtigen Informationen finden. Dazu suchst du gezielt nach passenden Stichwörtern *(key words)*. Sie helfen dir dabei herauszufinden, welche Teile du genauer lesen solltest, um die gesuchten Informationen zu erhalten. Diese Art des Überfliegens nennt man auch *scanning*.

S2 Gliederung als Hilfe

Im geliehenen Buch darfst du das zwar nicht, aber auf Kopien oder in Arbeitsheften solltest du dir angewöhnen, wichtige Stellen in Texten zu markieren und Randnotizen zu machen (z. B. Fragen oder Anmerkungen). Verwende am besten verschiedene Farben:

Markiere z. B. wichtige inhaltliche Punkte grün und Informationen zu den Figuren / Charakteren blau. Diejenigen Wörter, die du nachschlagen musst, solltest du auch hervorheben. Du kannst sie unterstreichen und die richtige Übersetzung am Rand notieren. So fällt dir das erneute Lesen leichter.

Um einen Text besser zu verstehen, kann es dir auch helfen, ihn in mehrere Abschnitte zu gliedern. Orientiere dich dabei z. B. an Absätzen und inhaltlichen Punkten, die du dir markiert hast. Überlege anschließend, was in den einzelnen Teilen jeweils das Wichtigste ist und formuliere passende Überschriften. Dies erleichtert es dir, Texte zusammenzufassen oder *Mediation*-Aufgaben zu lösen.

S3 Umgang mit neuen Wörtern

Viele Wörter in einem Text kannst du verstehen, obwohl du sie noch nicht gelernt hast.
Die folgenden Tipps können dir dabei helfen:

Ähnlichkeit mit Wörtern, die du schon kennst

Oft haben verwandte Wörter den gleichen Stamm, aber andere Präfixe oder Suffixe. Wenn du z. B. *usual* schon kennst, wirst du *unusual* sicher verstehen. Und wenn du das Wort *guide* als Nomen kennst, kannst du dir bestimmt denken, was das Verb *to guide* oder die Zusammensetzung *travel guide* bedeutet.

Ähnlichkeit mit Wörtern, die du aus einer anderen Sprache kennst

Viele englische Wörter gibt es genauso oder ähnlich auch im Deutschen, z. B. *computer* oder *hobby*. Manchmal hilft dir auch ein Wort, das du aus einer anderen Sprache kennst, ein englisches Wort zu verstehen, z. B. weil es ähnlich geschrieben wird oder ähnlich klingt.

Verstehen der Wörter im Zusammenhang

Manchmal kannst du dir anhand eines Bildes oder einer Überschrift denken, was ein Wort in einem Text bedeutet. Und wenn du alle Wörter in einem Satz verstehst außer einem, kann dieses oft nur eine bestimmte Bedeutung haben. Was bedeutet z. B. *ridiculous* in folgendem Satz: *That's the silliest thing I've ever heard. It's **ridiculous**!*

Auf den Zusammenhang musst du auch achten, wenn du Wörter im Wörterbuch nachschlägst, denn dort findest du meist mehrere Bedeutungen für ein Wort. Schau dir die folgenden Beispiele an:

*Take the second street on the **right**. That's the **right** way for the station.*
*I haven't got **time** to sit and chat today. We can chat when I come next **time**.*
*This is a very small **room**. There's **room** for only one bed.*

S4 Wichtige Merkmale von literarischen Texten erkennen

Story

Wenn du eine Geschichte genauer liest oder analysierst, solltest du nicht nur über die Handlung *(plot)* selbst nachdenken, sondern auch darüber, wie die Geschichte erzählt wird. Zu den wichtigsten Erzähltechniken *(narrative techniques)* gehören:

Atmosphere / Mood	Bestimmte Wörter und Beschreibungen schaffen in einer Geschichte eine gewisse Stimmung *(atmosphere* oder *mood)*. Stimmung entsteht z. B. dadurch, dass die fünf Sinne *(five senses)* angesprochen werden: Wenn man liest, was die Figuren sehen, hören, riechen, schmecken und fühlen, ist es leichter, sich in sie hineinzuversetzen.
Climax	Der Höhepunkt *(climax)* ist der Hauptwendepunkt in einer Geschichte. Die Spannung ist hier am höchsten. Die Hauptfigur befindet sich oft in einer schwierigen Situation und macht Veränderungen durch, sie wird z. B. stärker oder selbstbewusster. Siehe auch *turning point.*

Flashback	Eine Rückblende *(flashback)* erzählt Ereignisse, die vor einem bestimmten Zeitpunkt in der Geschichte stattgefunden haben. So wird z. B. die Erinnerung einer Figur an etwas Vergangenes beschrieben.
Narrative perspective	Die Wirkung, die eine Geschichte auf den Leser hat, wird stark von der Erzählperspektive *(narrative perspective)* beeinflusst. Wer ist der Erzähler und wie ist seine Einstellung zu den Figuren der Geschichte? Was erzählt er und wann? Die häufigsten Erzählperspektiven sind: **Ich-Erzähler *(first-person narrator)*** Der Ich-Erzähler erzählt aus seiner eigenen Perspektive und oft (aber nicht immer) ist er die Hauptfigur der Geschichte. Der Leser und der Ich-Erzähler erleben die Geschichte sozusagen „gemeinsam". **Er- / Sie-Erzähler *(third-person narrator)*** Dieser Erzähler erzählt die Geschichte „von außen". Die Perspektive ist nicht die der Hauptfigur.
Suspense	Spannung *(suspense)* ist eine wichtige Erzähltechnik, um den Leser in die Geschichte hineinzuziehen. Spannung kann direkt in den ersten Zeilen oder aber langsam im Verlauf der Geschichte aufgebaut werden. Sie wird z. B. durch starke, dramatische Sprache oder durch das Zurückhalten von Informationen erzeugt.
Turning point	Ein Wendepunkt *(turning point)* ist der Teil einer Geschichte, in dem eine Figur eine wichtige Entscheidung treffen muss. Diese Entscheidung beeinflusst den weiteren Verlauf der Geschichte. Sie kann für die Hauptfigur und die anderen Figuren gut oder schlecht sein. Siehe auch *climax*.

Graphic novel

In Comicromanen *(graphic novel)* wird eine Geschichte nicht nur mit Worten, sondern vor allem mit Bildern erzählt. Es ist deshalb wichtig, dass du nicht nur auf die Sprechblasen *(speech bubbles)* und die Bildtexte *(captions)* achtest, sondern auch auf die Gestaltung und Anordnung der einzelnen Bilder *(panels)*.

Poetry

Ein Gedicht ist wie eine Zeichnung oder ein Gemälde, das mit Wörtern „gemalt" wurde, daher ist bei der Interpretation jedes einzelne Wort wichtig. Denke daran: Beim Verständnis von Gedichten geht es nicht darum, die „richtige" Bedeutung zu finden – das gleiche Gedicht kann von verschiedenen Menschen ganz unterschiedlich verstanden werden. Wichtig ist aber, dass du deine Interpretation am Text belegen kannst. Dazu ist es hilfreich, auch formale Merkmale zu untersuchen und mit dem Inhalt in Verbindung zu bringen. Zu den wichtigsten Merkmalen von Gedichten gehören:

Rhyme scheme	Gedichte, die sich reimen, folgen immer einem bestimmten Reimschema *(rhyme scheme)*. Typische Reimschemata sind: **AABB** und **ABAB** sowie **ABCB**. Es gibt aber auch Gedichte, die sich nicht reimen, sogenannte *free verse poems*.
Rhythm / Stress	Ein Gedicht funktioniert nur mit dem richtigen Rhythmus *(rhythm)*. Er bestimmt, welche Stelle in jeder Zeile betont wird. Die Betonung *(stress)* liegt dann immer an der gleichen Stelle. Bei Gedichten, die sich nicht reimen, ist es wichtig, dass du selbst entscheidest, wo die Betonung liegt oder wo eine Pause gemacht werden sollte.
Symbol / Simile / Metaphor	In Gedichten spielen Symbole eine wichtige Rolle. Ein **Symbol** *(symbol)* steht stellvertretend für etwas anderes, z. B. für ein Gefühl, eine Idee oder eine Handlung. So ist das Herz ein Symbol für die Liebe. Bei einem **Vergleich** *(simile)* werden Dinge oder Personen mit etwas anderem verglichen, um auszudrücken, dass sie die gleichen Eigenschaften besitzen. Dabei wird *like* oder *as* verwendet, z. B. *Happy as a rainbow*. Eine **Metapher** *(metaphor)* ist ein verkürzter Vergleich ohne *like* oder *as*, z. B. *I'll be the light to guide you*.

Drama

Theaterstücke sind in Akte *(act)* und Szenen *(scene)* unterteilt. Sie sind dafür gedacht, von Schauspielern auf der Bühne aufgeführt zu werden. Es gibt in der Regel keinen Erzähler, der die Figuren genauer beschreibt. Stattdessen wird die Handlung direkt durch die gesprochene Sprache und durch die Darstellung der Figuren vermittelt. Deshalb ist es bei der Interpretation von Theaterstücken besonders wichtig, neben dem Text auch auf die Sprechweise, Gestik und Mimik zu achten. So kannst du Rückschlüsse auf Charaktereigenschaften, Gedanken und Gefühle der Figuren ziehen.

Characters	Die Figuren *(characters)* stellen oft klassische Typen oder Rollen dar. Auf der einen Seite gibt es einen Helden *(good guy)*, dem ein Bösewicht *(bad guy)* gegenübersteht.
Language	In Theaterstücken wird die Handlung durch gesprochene Sprache vermittelt. Die Figuren sprechen in Dialogen miteinander.
Stage directions	Alles, was nicht durch gesprochene Sprache vermittelt werden kann, wird in Regieanweisungen *(stage directions)* vorgegeben. Diese Anweisungen beschreiben, wie die Schauspieler ihre Rolle spielen und wie sie sprechen sollen. Hier werden auch Angaben zu Requisiten *(props)*, Bühnenbild und Licht gemacht. Wenn man ein Theaterstück liest, können die Regieanweisungen wichtige Hinweise z. B. auf die Stimmung der Szene und die Gefühle der Figuren geben. Sieht man das Theaterstück auf der Bühne, wird die Handlung und Stimmung des Stückes durch Körpersprache, Bewegungen, Bühnenbild, Licht, usw. getragen.

Dealing with visuals

S5 Fotos beschreiben und analysieren

Wenn du ein Foto beschreiben und analysieren sollst, kannst du in folgenden Schritten vorgehen:

1. Beschreibe, was auf dem Foto zu sehen ist. Dafür verwendest du das *simple present*. Konzentriere dich zunächst auf Personen oder Dinge, die im Vordergrund zu sehen sind, aber vergiss nicht, auch Personen oder Dinge im Hintergrund zu beschreiben. Wenn du ausdrücken willst, was auf dem Foto passiert, verwendest du das *present progressive*.

2. Nachdem du das Foto beschrieben hast, kannst du deine Meinung dazu äußern oder du kannst erklären, was es deiner Meinung nach ausdrücken möchte. Für die Analyse des Fotos verwendest du das *simple present*.

> **Useful phrases**
>
> **Describing photos:**
> – At the top / bottom you can see …
> – In the foreground / background / middle …
> – On the left / right there is / are …
> – The people in the photo are talking / having fun / celebrating / fighting / …
>
> **Analysing photos:**
> – I like / don't like the photo because …
> – The photo is interesting / boring / exciting / … because …
> – The photo shows … / represents …
> – The photo tries to show … but I think a photo with … instead of … would work better because …

S6 Statistiken auswerten

Mit Diagrammen lässt sich eine Vielzahl von Informationen auf sehr kleinem Raum zusammenfassen. Häufig findest du die folgenden Diagramme, die jeweils einen anderen Schwerpunkt in der Darstellung haben:

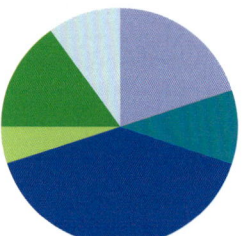 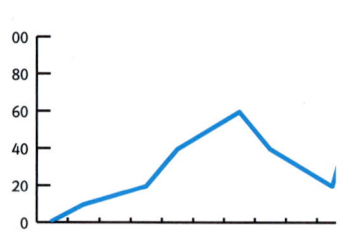 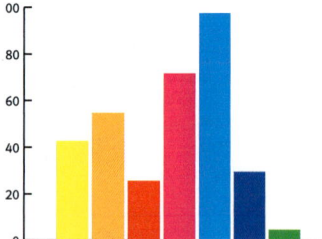

Mit einem Kuchendiagramm (*pie chart*) lassen sich Prozentzahlen darstellen, ausgehend vom gesamten Kreis (= 100 %).

Ein Kurvendiagramm (*line graph*) verwendest du, um eine Entwicklung über einen längeren Zeitraum hinweg darzustellen.

Ein Säulen- oder Balkendiagramm (*bar graph*) nutzt du, um Zahlen direkt miteinander zu vergleichen.

Wenn du deine Auswertung eines Diagramms präsentieren sollst, hilft es dir, schrittweise vorzugehen:

1. Sage zunächst, um welche Art von Diagramm es sich handelt und was es darstellt. Vergiss nicht, die Quelle und das Jahr der Veröffentlichung zu nennen.
2. Beschreibe, was du aus dem Diagramm ablesen kannst.
3. Fasse die wichtigsten Aussagen des Diagramms in 1–2 Sätzen zusammen.

> **Useful phrases**
>
> – The table / bar graph / line graph / pie chart / … was published by … in …
> – It's about … / deals with … / …
> – The (next) largest group of … | The majority / minority of … | Half of … | Most of … | 30 percent of the people …
> – The number of … goes up / grows by … / drops / goes down / doesn't change.
> – The numbers / figures show / suggest that …
> – We can draw the conclusion that …

Writing skills

S7 Textsorten und ihre Besonderheiten

Du kennst schon einige wichtige Textsorten und ihre Haupteigenschaften:

Print ads	Werbeanzeigen in Zeitungen, Zeitschriften oder auf Plakaten versuchen, den Leser davon zu überzeugen, ein bestimmtes Produkt zu kaufen. Hierzu sprechen sie den Leser direkt an und verwenden emotionale Sprache. Wichtige Elemente sind ein *eye-catcher* (ein Bild und / oder ein Text), ein ansprechender Slogan, weitere Textelemente *(ad copy)*, 1–2 Fotos des Produkts sowie Kontaktinformationen bzw. Angaben, wo das Geschäft oder die Firma zu finden ist.
Blog post	Ein Blog ist eine Art Online-Tagebuch, in dem regelmäßig Beiträge veröffentlicht werden. Es gibt unterschiedliche Arten von Blogs, z. B. Reiseblogs, Nachrichtenblogs oder Musikblogs. Meist sind Blog-Einträge aus der Ich-Perspektive geschrieben und drücken den persönlichen Standpunkt des Bloggers aus.
Dialogue / Film script	Wenn du einen Dialog schreibst, z. B. für eine Filmszene, denke daran, dass du ihn kurz hältst und echte mündliche Sprache verwendest, also z. B. *short forms*, *question tags*, verstärkende Ausdrücke, usw. Achte bei den *stage directions* für ein Film- oder Theaterskript darauf, dass du nur das angibst, was man auch sehen oder darstellen kann. Gedanken kann man nicht sehen, aber du kannst in den *stage directions* Hinweise auf die Gefühle einer Person geben, z. B. durch Anweisungen für Gesichtsausdrücke und Körpersprache.
Diary entry	Ein Tagebucheintrag erzählt und kommentiert vergangene und erwartete Ereignisse aus der ganz persönlichen Sicht einer Person und ist normalerweise nicht für andere Leser bestimmt. Verwende ausdrucksstarke Adjektive und Adverbien, um die Gedanken und Gefühle dieser Person zu beschreiben.

E-mail / Letter / Postcard / Invitation	Achte auf die richtige Anrede für den Adressaten, z. B. *Dear ...*, Gruß-formeln am Schluss, z. B. *Yours / Love / Best wishes*, und beachte die Höflichkeitsregeln. Bei formellen E-Mails oder Briefen verwendet man eher die Langformen, z. B. *I am* statt *I'm*. Denke bei einem Brief an die Angabe der Empfänger- und Absenderadresse und an das Datum.
Flyer	Ein Flyer sollte gut lesbar sein (Schriftart- und größe) und alle wichtigen Informationen enthalten: *Who? What? When? Where? Why?* Formuliere außerdem einen ansprechenden Slogan.
Instructions	Anweisungen sind meist in mehrere, klare Schritte gegliedert. Diese Schritte können von Überschriften eingeleitet werden. Sprachlich werden vor allem Imperative und *phrases* wie *Make sure ...*, *You / It must ...* oder *Never ...* verwendet.
News report	Konzentriere dich bei einem Tatsachenbericht auf die Fakten und spare deine persönliche Meinung aus. Achte außerdem auf eine sachliche Sprache und vermeide emotionale Ausdrücke. Die Schlagzeile *(headline)* sollte direkt auf das Thema des Artikels hinweisen und außerdem das Interesse des Lesers wecken. Beachte, dass in Zeitungsberichten häufig Passivformen verwendet werden.
Prompt cards	Wenn du dich auf eine Präsentation vorbereitest, notiere dir auf Karteikarten nur Stichwörter, die dich an die einzelnen Punkte des Vortrags erinnern. Schreibe z. B. wichtige Namen, Ereignisse, Orte und Daten auf.
Report	Bei einem Bericht ist die Vollständigkeit und Verständlichkeit der sachlichen Informationen das Wichtigste. Er wird im *simple past* geschrieben.
Review / Online rating	Eine Rezension bzw. Kritik hilft dem Leser zu entscheiden, ob es sich lohnt, einen bestimmten Film anzuschauen oder ein bestimmtes Buch zu lesen. Zuerst beschreibst du kurz die wichtigsten Details, dann folgt deine Bewertung, die du mit guten Argumenten belegen solltest.
Story	Wenn du deine eigene Geschichte schreibst, schmücke sie aus und gestalte sie sprachlich abwechslungsreich. Meistens sind Geschichten im *simple past* geschrieben. Wenn du eine Geschichte vervollständigen sollst, muss dein Teil zum vorgegebenen Text passen. Vermeide also inhaltliche Widersprüche. Außerdem sollten sich die Erzählperspektive und die Erzählzeit im Verlauf der Geschichte nicht ändern.
Wiki text	Ein Wiki-Eintrag hat zum Ziel, ähnlich wie ein Lexikonartikel Informationen zu vermitteln. Da jede beliebige Person die Texte schreiben bzw. ergänzen oder abändern kann, ist es wichtig, dass du auch nach anderen zuverlässigen Informationsquellen suchst und dich nicht nur auf die Informationen in dem Wiki verlässt.

S8 Einen eigenen Text schreiben

Es ist wichtig, dass du deine Texte gut planst und zuerst einen Entwurf schreibst, den du dann überarbeitest. So wird es für den Leser einfacher, deinen Gedanken zu folgen und deinen Text flüssig zu lesen.

1. Die Planung deines Textes

Nimm dir für diese Phase ausreichend Zeit. Lies die Aufgabenstellung genau durch und über-lege, für wen dein Text bestimmt ist (Adressat) und welche Textsorte verlangt wird (Bericht, Zusammenfassung, Kommentar, usw.). Vor dem Schreiben machst du dir am besten einen Plan: Notiere in Stichwörtern, was in der Einleitung, dem Hauptteil und dem Schluss deines Textes stehen soll. So vergisst du nichts Wichtiges und findest auch leichter eine interessante Einleitung und einen passenden Schluss.

Ein guter Text besteht normalerweise aus den folgenden drei Teilen:

Einleitung (*introduction*): Hier erfährt der Leser, worum es in deinem Text geht. Du kannst auch eine Fragestellung einführen, die in deinem Text erörtert werden soll.

Hauptteil (*main part*): Der Hauptteil ist in mehrere Abschnitte gegliedert und beinhaltet die Details (Fakten, Argumente, Beispiele, usw.) zu deinem Thema.

Schluss (*conclusion*): Deinen Text solltest du mit einem geeigneten Schlussteil beenden. Dies kann eine Zusammenfassung von dem sein, was du im Hauptteil geschrieben hast, oder eine persönliche Äußerung.

2. Der erste Entwurf

Auf der Grundlage deiner Planung kannst du einen ersten Entwurf schreiben. Denke daran, dass du für jede neue Idee einen eigenen Abschnitt beginnst. Tipps für einen guten Schreibstil findest du im folgenden Kapitel (→ S9).

3. Die Überarbeitung

Nachdem du den ersten Entwurf erstellt hast, ist es wichtig, dass du oder einer deiner Mitschüler den Text noch einmal kritisch durchliest. Am hilfreichsten ist es, wenn du den Text mehrmals liest, jedes Mal mit einem anderen Schwerpunkt. Dabei kann dir eine Checkliste helfen (siehe rechts).

Überarbeite anschließend die kritischen Stellen. Wenn du Feedback von einem Mitschüler bekommen hast, sieh es dir genau an und entscheide, was davon du für deinen Text übernehmen möchtest. Wenn du von einem Mitschüler gebeten wirst, seinen Text zu lesen, achte darauf, dass du bei deiner Kritik fair bleibst.

Inhalt:
- Sind alle wesentlichen Punkte enthalten?
- Gibt es keine inhaltlichen Fehler?
- Ist der Text logisch aufgebaut und hat eine klare Struktur?

Rechtschreibung:
- Sind die Wörter richtig geschrieben?
- Stimmt die Zeichensetzung?
- Ist der Text einheitlich im *British* oder *American English* geschrieben?

Grammatik:
- Stimmen die Zeitformen?
- Ist die Formenbildung richtig (z. B. Adjektive, Adverbien, usw.)?

S9 Tipps für einen guten Schreibstil

Je größer dein Wortschatz wird, desto mehr Möglichkeiten eröffnen sich dir beim Schreiben deiner eignene Texte. Lies die folgenden Tipps aufmerksam durch, bevor du mit dem Schreiben beginnst:

Adjektive und Adverbien

Du kannst deine Sätze interessanter gestalten, indem du z. B. Nomen durch Adjektive näher beschreibst. Verben kannst du durch Adverbien oder adverbiale Bestimmungen ergänzen. Vergleiche die folgenden beiden Sätze:

A *I went to the shop.*
B *I went to the big pet shop with my sister last Saturday.*

Achte darauf, dass du Adjektive wie *good*, *bad*, *nice* und *big* nicht zu häufig verwendest. In der Tabelle findest du Beispiele für Adjektive, die du stattdessen verwenden kannst:

good	*amazing, awesome, beautiful, brilliant, exciting, fantastic, fascinating, great, interesting, spectacular, wonderful*
bad	*awful, boring, terrible*
nice	*amazing, beautiful, fascinating, interesting, lovely, pretty, wonderful*
big	*gigantic, great, huge, large, wide*

Konjunktionen *(linking words)*

Ein Text liest sich leichter, wenn die Sätze darin miteinander verknüpft sind. Mit Hilfe von Konjunktionen werden logische Zusammenhänge hergestellt. Vergleiche die beiden folgenden Textausschnitte. Der erste wirkt durch die unverbundenen Hauptsätze abgehackt. Der zweite liest sich durch Satzgefüge aus Haupt- und Nebensätzen und durch Konjunktionen flüssiger. Außerdem geben die vielen Adjektive und Adverbien genauere Informationen und machen den Text interessanter.

A *I went to the shop. I wanted a guinea pig. We looked at all the guinea pigs. I didn't like them. We wanted to leave. A girl came in with a box. She brought back a guinea pig. It was cute! I bought it. I'm happy.*
B *I went to the big pet shop with my sister last Saturday because I wanted to buy a nice guinea pig. We looked at all the guinea pigs, but I didn't like them. Just when I wanted to leave, a girl came in with a box. She brought back a guinea pig which was really cute. So I bought it and I'm very happy now.*

Relativsätze *(defining and non-defining relative clauses)*

Mit Relativsätzen kannst du Sätze verbinden oder zusätzliche Informationen zu einer Person oder Sache einführen:

- *This is the food cart which sells the best hot dogs in New York. (defining relative clause)*
- *The food cart with the city's best hot dogs, which I'd never even heard about until last week, is really worth a visit. (non-defining relative clause)*

Zeitangaben *(time markers)*

Adverbiale Bestimmungen der Zeit können dem Leser helfen, sich in einem Text oder einer Geschichte zeitlich zurechtzufinden. Du kannst *time markers* auf unterschiedliche Weise einsetzen:

- um die Ereignisse zeitlich einzuordnen: *two years ago*, *last summer*, *when I came home yesterday*, …
- um zu zeigen, in welcher Reihenfolge sie passieren: *at first*, *next*, *finally*, …
- um zu verdeutlichen, wie viel Zeit zwischen den Ereignissen vergeht: *for two hours*, *just five minutes later*, …

- um auszudrücken, wie schnell oder langsam etwas passiert: *immediately*, *quickly*, *it took hours*, …
- um zu sagen, dass mehrere Ereignisse zeitgleich passieren: *while I was waiting*, *during lunch*, …

S10 Eine Zusammenfassung schreiben

Die folgenden Schritte können dir helfen, einen Text schriftlich zusammenzufassen:

1. Lies dir den Ausgangstext einmal komplett durch, damit du weißt, um was es geht. Achte dabei auch auf die Überschrift, denn sie verrät meist schon viel über den Inhalt des Textes.
2. Dann lies den Text noch einmal durch, um weitere Details zu verstehen. Erst wenn du den Text im Detail verstanden hast, kannst du entscheiden, welche Aspekte du in deiner Zusammenfassung *(summary)* erwähnen solltest und welche nicht. Du kannst dir Notizen dazu machen oder wichtige Stellen im Text markieren (wenn er nicht in deinem Englischbuch steht). Beim Verständnis des Textes können dir auch die *wh*-Fragen helfen *(Who? What? Where? When? Why?)*.
3. Entscheide, welche Informationen du in deine Zusammenfassung übernehmen möchtest. Beispiele, Zahlen, direkte Rede, Wertungen oder Interpretationen gehören nicht in eine Zusammenfassung.
4. Schreibe einen ersten Entwurf deiner Zusammenfassung. Beginne mit einer Einleitung, die wichtige Informationen wie z. B. Titel, Autor, Thema und Hauptaussage des Textes beinhaltet. Wenn du einen Zeitungsartikel zusammenfasst, solltest du hier auch die Quelle nennen. Verwende für deine Zusammenfassung das *simple present* und achte darauf, dass du nicht einfach nur den Text abschreibst, sondern deine eigenen Worte findest.

Tip

Denke daran, dass du die Personen in deiner Zusammenfassung ändern musst. Ist der Ausgangstext aus der Perspektive der 1. Person geschrieben („ich", „wir"), musst du für deine Zusammenfassung die 3. Person verwenden („er", „sie").

5. Lies deine Zusammenfassung am Ende noch einmal sorgfältig durch und vergleiche sie mit dem Ausgangstext. Hast du alle wichtigen Aspekte genannt und unwichtige Details weggelassen? Ist dein Text durchgängig im *simple present* geschrieben? Achte auch auf Rechtschreibung und grammatische Stolpersteine.

Speaking skills

S11 Gespräche führen

Es ist nicht immer leicht, sich mit Menschen zu unterhalten, die man noch nicht so lange kennt oder gerade erst kennengelernt hat. Mach dir vor dem Gespräch klar, mit wem du redest. Wenn du dich mit einem gleichaltrigen Jugendlichen unterhältst, kannst du viel informeller sprechen als wenn du mit jemand Älterem sprichst. Überlege auch, ob es kulturelle Unterschiede gibt, und passe deine Sprache entsprechend an.

Die folgenden Schritte können dir helfen, ein Gespräch zu beginnen und aufrecht zu erhalten:

1. Beginne freundlich, z. B. mit etwas, was euch beide verbindet (der Ort, die Situation, usw.).
2. Halte die Unterhaltung am Laufen. Es ist wichtig, deinem Dialogpartner immer das Gefühl zu geben, dass er einbezogen wird. Dazu dienen *feedback phrases*, Nachfragen und *question tags*, wie du anhand des folgenden Beispiels sehen kannst:

   Then we went to the new shoe shop in town, you know. And there were these amazing trainers – I showed you a photo, didn't I? Guess what Linda said when she saw them!

   Wenn du etwas nicht verstehst, frage höflich nach *(What was that you mentioned about …? Sorry, I didn't catch what you just said about …)*. Wenn du etwas nicht sagen kannst, weil dir der nötige Wortschatz fehlt, versuche es zu umschreiben oder bitte deinen Gesprächspartner um Hilfe.
3. Beende das Gespräch so freundlich, wie du es angefangen hast, und verabschiede dich. Vergiss nicht, dich zu bedanken, wenn du um Hilfe gebeten hast.

In vielen Situationen des täglichen Lebens – im Klassenzimmer, mit Freunden, in der Familie – hast du es in Diskussionen mit unterschiedlichen Meinungen zu tun. Umso wichtiger ist es, Kompromisse zu finden. Die *useful phrases* können dir helfen, typische Diskussionssituationen zu meistern.

> **Tip**
>
> Lass dich nicht verunsichern, wenn du beim Sprechen ins Stocken gerätst. In der gesprochenen Sprache ist es normal, dass Pausen, unvollständige Sätze, Wiederholungen oder Füllwörter vorkommen: *Well, I – I really don't know. It's – er, maybe you want to …?*

> **Useful phrases**
>
> **Asking for an opinion:** How do you feel about …? | What do you think about …?
> **Making a suggestion:** Why don't we …? | I've got an idea. Can we …? | If we did it this way, we could …
> **Agreeing:** Yes, we should do that. | No, I don't mind doing that.
> **Disagreeing:** You've got a point but … | I don't think that's a good idea. It would be better to …
> **Finding a compromise:** Can we meet halfway? | If we did it this way, we could …

S12 Eine Präsentation vorbereiten und halten

Ob in der Schule oder später im Beruf, die Fähigkeit, eine gut vorbereitete und klar strukturierte Präsentation zu halten, spielt eine wichtige Rolle. Die folgenden Schritte können dir bei der Vorbereitung und Durchführung deiner Präsentation helfen:

1. Recherchiere Informationen zu deinem Thema und strukturiere sie, indem du z. B. eine Gliederung anlegst.
2. Überlege dir, mit welchem Material du deine Präsentation unterstützen willst. Gestalte dein Poster / deine Folie / dein Handout.
3. Bereite deine Präsentation vor, indem du nummerierte Karteikarten *(prompt cards)* anlegst, auf denen du dir die wichtigsten Punkte in Stichworten notierst.
4. Übe deine Präsentation zu Hause vor dem Spiegel oder vor einem kleinen Publikum (Eltern, Großeltern, Freunde). Stoppe die Zeit, die du brauchst, damit du bei deiner Präsentation nicht in Zeitnot gerätst.
5. Wenn du deine Präsentation hältst, achte darauf, dass du die Aufmerksamkeit aller Zuhörer hast. Dann erkläre kurz, worüber du sprechen wirst und wie deine Präsentation aufgebaut ist. Sprich langsam und möglichst frei. Verwende deine *prompt cards* nur als Hilfestellung. Beende deine Präsentation mit einer kurzen Zusammenfassung der wichtigsten Punkte. Bedanke dich fürs Zuhören und frage nach, ob deine Zuhörer Fragen haben.

Useful phrases

– My presentation is about … | Today I'll talk about … | First I'd like to talk about … Then …
– Here's a new word. It's … in German.
– On my poster you can see … | The mind map shows … | I've prepared a handout for you.
– That's the end of my presentation. Do you have any questions?
– Thanks for listening.

Mediation skills

S13 Bearbeitung von *Mediation*-Aufgaben

Mediation ist die Übertragung wichtiger Informationen aus einem gesprochenen oder geschriebenen Text in eine andere Sprache, z. B. aus dem Englischen ins Deutsche oder umgekehrt. Das machst du, wenn du einen Text für jemanden zusammenfassen sollst, der die Sprache des Ausgangstextes nicht versteht. Gelegentlich kann es auch sein, dass du dolmetschen musst, also zwischen Gesprächspartnern vermittelst, die nicht dieselbe Sprache sprechen. Ganz wichtig: Es geht bei der *mediation* niemals um eine wörtliche Übersetzung *(translation)*!

Lies dir die *Mediation*-Aufgabe gut durch und beachte besonders folgende Dinge:

Adressat:
Für wen ist die Information bestimmt?

--→ Je nachdem, wer die Person ist und wie viel sie schon weiß, sprichst du sie unterschiedlich an.

Ausgangstext

Zweck:
Wozu benötigt die Person die Information?

--→ Du musst nur die Informationen wiedergeben, die für den Adressaten in der jeweiligen Situation wichtig sind. Alles andere kannst du weglassen. Es kann aber auch vorkommen, dass du Dinge zusätzlich erklären musst.

wichtige Info

Beispiel: Dein Ausgangstext ist die Infobroschüre eines Museums. Wenn dein Gegenüber dich fragt, ob das Museum heute geöffnet ist, musst du nicht unbedingt alle anderen Öffnungszeiten nennen. Will die Person den Eintrittspreis wissen, kommt es auf ihr Alter an und darauf, ob sie allein oder mit einer Gruppe unterwegs ist.

Einen schriftlichen Ausgangstext kannst du in Ruhe durchlesen und die wichtigsten Informationen auswählen. Dabei helfen dir die Lesetechniken, die unter *Reading skills* beschrieben werden (→ S1). Formuliere die entsprechenden Inhalte so, dass der Adressat sie gut verstehen kann.

Tip

Achte bei einer schriftlichen *mediation* darauf, dass dein Text nicht länger als ca. 35–40 % des Ausgangstextes ist, ähnlich wie bei einer Zusammenfassung (→ S10).

Bei einer Dolmetschaufgabe wird eine echte mündliche Gesprächssituation simuliert. Deshalb musst du schneller reagieren, um möglichst viel von dem sinngemäß wiederzugeben, was die Gesprächspartner zueinander sagen. Nicht ganz einfach ist es, wenn du Durchsagen am Flughafen oder am Bahnhof aus dem Englischen ins Deutsche übertragen sollst, da sie oft unbekannte Wörter enthalten und durch die Hintergrundgeräusche schwer zu verstehen sind. Hier kann es dir helfen, dich auf die Namen von Personen oder Orten, Zahlen, Zeitangaben oder auf andere wichtige Schlüsselwörter *(key words)* zu konzentrieren.

S14 Paraphrasieren

Wenn du wichtige Informationen aus einer Sprache in die andere übertragen willst, kann es vorkommen, dass dir ein Wort nicht einfällt, besonders in Gesprächssituationen, wenn alles sehr schnell gehen muss. Bleibe ganz ruhig und versuche, das Wort zu umschreiben *(paraphrasing)*.

Useful phrases

- It's somebody / a person who …
- It's something that you use to …
- It's a place that / where …
- It's the same as … | It's the opposite of …

Wenn du Zeit brauchst, um das richtige Wort oder eine Umschreibung dafür zu finden, kannst du dir mit folgenden *phrases* behelfen: *Just a second …* | *Let me think …*

Listening skills

S15 Hörverstehen üben

Es ist immer sinnvoll, viele authentische englische Texte anzuhören, z. B. Nachrichten in Radio und Fernsehen oder Hörbücher. Dabei ist es nicht schlimm, wenn du nicht jedes Wort verstehst. Dir wird außerdem auffallen, wie unterschiedlich die Aussprache des Englischen je nach Herkunft des Sprechers sein kann. So gibt es neben Unterschieden zwischen britischem und amerikanischem Englisch auch innerhalb Großbritanniens verschiedene Dialekte oder regionale Akzente. Auch dann ist es nicht schlimm, wenn du nicht alles verstehst. Selbst ein Engländer aus London könnte Schwierigkeiten haben, einen Schotten aus Glasgow auf Anhieb zu verstehen.

Manchmal hilft dir beim Hörverstehen auch die Kenntnis von typischen Textsorten und Situationen. Wenn du die Textsorte des Hörtextes kennst, überlege dir, worauf es beim Telefonieren, beim Dolmetschen, bei Präsentationen, Durchsagen, Radio- oder Fernsehsendungen ankommt und welche Themen jeweils zu erwarten sind. Gelegentlich geben dir auch Bilder Hinweise zur entsprechenden Situation: Wenn z. B. bestimmte Personen oder Orte dargestellt sind, kannst du leichter einschätzen, worum es in dem Hörtext geht. Achte beim Hören auf Geräusche sowie Stimme und Tonfall des Sprechers. In echten Gesprächssituationen oder Filmen können dir Gestik und Mimik das Verständnis erleichtern.

Analog zum Lesen (→ S1) helfen dir beim Hörverstehen die folgenden Techniken:

Listening for gist	Listening for detail
Versuche, das Wichtigste (gist) in einem Hörtext zu erkennen und zusammenzufassen. Achte dabei besonders auf Wörter und Themen, die mehrmals vorkommen und vermutlich eine wichtige Rolle spielen.	Versuche gezielt, dem Text bestimmte Einzelinformationen (details) zu entnehmen. Achte dabei besonders auf Wörter, die du in der Antwort erwartest, und die Informationen dazu.

Viewing skills

S16 Wichtige filmische Mittel

Genre
Es gibt viele unterschiedliche Arten von Filmen, man nennt sie auch Genres. Du erkennst Filme eines Genres normalerweise daran, dass sie ähnliche Hauptmerkmale aufweisen.

Crime

Fantasy

Hier sind einige Beispiele:

Action	In Actionfilmen geht es meist um einen Helden oder eine Heldin im Kampf gegen das Böse. Dabei kommen häufig spektakuläre Stunts, Verfolgungsjagden und Gewaltszenen vor.
Crime	Im Mittelpunkt eines Kriminalfilms steht ein Verbrechen, das meist im Laufe des Films aufgeklärt wird. Dabei gibt es viele spannende Szenen und überraschende Wendungen.
Comedy	Komödien haben eine humorvolle Handlung, die zum Lachen anregt. Häufig werden die Charaktere übertrieben dargestellt und Sprachwitz spielt eine wichtige Rolle.
Fantasy	Fantasyfilme handeln von magischen oder übernatürlichen Kräften. Häufig steht ein Held oder eine Heldin im Mittelpunkt der Handlung.
Historical	Historienfilme spielen in einer bestimmten geschichtlichen Epoche. Häufig basieren sie auf wahren Begebenheiten. Die Kostüme und Requisiten sind meist aufwendig gestaltet.
Romance	In Liebesfilmen steht die Beziehung zwischen zwei Figuren im Mittelpunkt. Das Ende dieser Filme fällt meist positiv aus.
Science Fiction	Science-Fiction-Filme handeln z. B. von Erfindungen in Wissenschaft und Technik, von Zeitreisen oder Außerirdischen. Sie spielen häufig in der Zukunft und wirken unrealistisch.

Story
Wenn du einen Film anschaust, achte darauf, wo und wann der Film spielt *(setting)*, auf die Besetzung der Rollen *(cast)*, auf den Schauplatz *(location)* und die Handlung *(plot)*.

Audio-visual effects
Ein Film erzählt eine Geschichte mit Worten, aber auch mit Bildern, Geräuschen, Licht, Farben und Musik. Diese audiovisuellen Effekte *(audio-visual effects)* schaffen eine ganz bestimmte Atmosphäre *(atmosphere)* und verstärken damit die Wirkung des Gesehenen. So wird z. B. eine Actionszene meist mit schneller, lauter Musik unterlegt, eine romantische Szene eher mit ruhiger, leiser Musik.

Camera
Die Kameraeinstellung *(shot)* beeinflusst, wie wir Szenen wahrnehmen, ob z. B. Personen oder Objekte als Nahaufnahme *(close-up)*, aus der mittleren Distanz *(medium shot)* oder als Totale *(long shot)* aufgenommen sind.

Long shot

Medium shot

Close-up

Study skills

S17 Vokabeln ordnen und strukturieren

Wörter sind die Bausteine der Sprache. Du musst sie natürlich lernen und jedes für sich verstehen. Zur Beherrschung einer Sprache gehört aber auch zu wissen, welche Kombinationen dieser Bausteine möglich sind. Schreibe deshalb Wörter möglichst immer in typischen Zusammenhängen auf:

–   Lerne bei Verben passende Ergänzungen mit *(collocations)*, z. B. *a dry / wet / hot / cool climate | to read a book / a magazine / a comic | to write a letter / an e-mail / a blog | to go swimming / shopping / home / to the cinema.*
–   Schreibe dir auf, welche grammatischen Formen auf bestimmte Wörter folgen, z. B. *I would like to swim / to read / to go shopping. | I like swimming / reading / going shopping.*
–   Notiere dir Beispiele bei Wörtern mit Präpositionen, z. B. *The party is on Friday / at seven. | My house is in Dover Street. | We're on the road to London. | London is on the Thames.*

Deinen Wortschatz kannst du auch erweitern, indem du die Wörter eines Wortfeldes *(word field)* lernst, da thematisch zusammenhängende Vokabeln leichter zu merken sind. Oder du kannst dir Wörter aus derselben Wortfamilie *(word family)* notieren und die Liste mit Hilfe deines Wörterbuchs ergänzen:

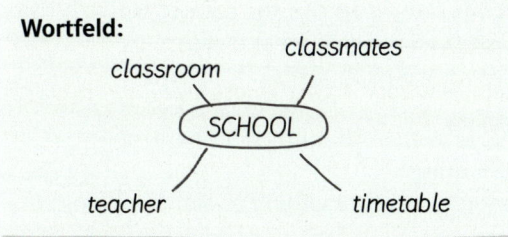

Wortfamilie:
shop – to shop – shopper – shopping
music – musician – musical
immigration – to immigrate – immigrant
colony – to colonize – colonist
information – to inform – informative

Achte beim Lesen unterschiedlicher Textsorten auf hilfreiche Formulierungen *(useful phrases)*. Diese kannst du später in eigenen Texten immer wieder verwenden.

S18 Im Internet recherchieren

Das Internet bietet eine Fülle von Informationen, die in der Regel frei zugänglich sind. Die folgenden Tipps können dir dabei helfen, genau die Informationen zu finden, die du für eine Präsentation oder für die Erstellung eines Textes brauchst:

1.   Überlege dir gute Stichwörter, die du in eine Suchmaschine eingeben kannst. Wenn du z. B. eine Übersicht über das amerikanische Schulsystem suchst, kannst du als Stichwort *US school system* eingeben. Je mehr Stichwörter du eingibst, desto genauer sind deine Ergebnisse.
2.   Wenn du eine Webseite mit interessanten Informationen gefunden hast, achte darauf, wer die Webseite erstellt hat. Sind die Informationen zuverlässig (Online-Lexikon, seriöse Zeitung, usw.) oder handelt es sich eher um persönliche Meinungen (Forum, Blog, usw.)?
3.   Kopiere nicht einfach ganze Artikel aus dem Internet. Mache dir Notizen zu den wichtigsten Informationen und gebe sie anschließend in deinen eigenen Worten wieder.
4.   Ordne dein Material und suche gezielt weiter, falls du zusätzliche Informationen brauchst.

Grammar

Liebe Schülerin, lieber Schüler,

in diesem Grammatik-Anhang findest du ausführliche Erklärungen zu allen grammatischen Themen, die in Green Line 4 behandelt werden. Die Grammatikkapitel (G) helfen dir, die Grammatik zu verstehen, einzelne Punkte nachzuholen oder bestimmte Regeln für Hausaufgaben und die Vorbereitung von Tests und Klassenarbeiten nachzuschlagen.

Regeln sind mit einem blauen Punkt (O) gekennzeichnet. Ein Ausrufezeichen (!) bedeutet, dass du hier besonders aufpassen musst. Die englische Zusammenfassung der wichtigsten Regeln findest du in der **English summary**. Mit **Test yourself** überprüfst du, ob du alles verstanden hast. Die Lösungen hierzu findest du ab Seite 259.

Grammatical terms

English term		Example	Deutsche Bezeichnung
defining and non-defining relative clauses	G8	Diego is the boy **who took us around New York**. Diego, who knows NY like the back of his hand, showed the girls great places.	notwendige und nicht-notwendige Relativsätze
gerund	G5	**Living** in New York is great. I just **love being** here.	Gerundium
gerund or infinitive	G7	Stop **shouting**! Let's stop **to have** something to eat.	gerund oder Infinitiv mit to
indirect speech	G1–G4		Indirekte Rede
statements	G1	They **said** (that) there **was** free wifi!	Aussagen
expressions of time and place	G2	He told me (that) they had been to Paris **the day before**.	Zeit- und Ortsangaben
questions	G3	Grandma **asked** me when my flight **was**.	Fragen
commands and requests	G4	She **told** him **to call** her back.	Befehle, Aufforderungen und Bitten
infinitive with and without *to*	G6	Would you like **to go** to the movie theater after school? – Sorry, I can't. My parents always make me come straight home.	Infinitiv mit und ohne to
past perfect progressive	G9	José was tired because he **had been driving** around New York all day.	Verlaufsform des Plusquamperfekts

Unit 1

G1 You told us there was free wifi!

→ Seiten 10–12

Aussagen in der indirekten Rede

Statements in indirect speech

Direct speech:	**Indirect speech:**
Steve's parents: We**'re** worried about Steve, Ms Woodruff. He **can't** live without **his** phone. He**'s** addicted to it.	Your parents told me (that) they **were** worried about you. They said (that) you **couldn't** live without **your** phone and they thought (that) you **were** addicted to it.

Wenn du wiedergeben möchtest, was ein anderer dir mitgeteilt hat, verwendest du gewöhnlich nicht die direkte, sondern die indirekte Rede.

- *Die indirekte Rede besteht aus einem **Einführungssatz** (Hauptsatz) (They told me … / They said …), und einem **Nebensatz**, der mit oder ohne* that *eingeleitet werden kann (… that they were worried about you).*

- Anders *als im Deutschen steht zwischen dem Einführungssatz und dem Nebensatz **kein** Komma.*

- *Wenn du eine Aussage in der indirekten Rede wiedergibst, musst du Personalpronomen und Possessivbegleiter anpassen (**we → they**; **his → your**).*

○ *Steht das Einleitungsverb im* **simple past**, *ändert sich die Zeitform im Nebensatz folgendermaßen:*

Direkte Rede Direct speech	*Indirekte Rede* Indirect speech
simple present → Steve's parents: We **are** worried about Steve.	**simple past** Steve's parents told Ms Woodruff that they **were** worried about Steve.
present progressive → We think he **is spending** too much time on his phone.	**past progressive** They thought he **was spending** too much time on his phone.
present perfect → I **have tried** to take his phone away, …	**past perfect** His mum explained that she **had tried** to take his phone away, …
simple past → … but that **didn't work**.	**past perfect** … but that **hadn't worked**.
can → We **can't** help him.	**could** They said they **couldn't** help him.
will → Ms Woodruff: OK, I**'ll** talk to him.	**would** Ms Woodruff promised that she **would** talk to him.

English summary

You use indirect speech when you want to report what somebody has said.

When the reporting verb is in the simple past (He said that … / They told her that … / She thought …), the verbs used in the original speech usually move one tense further back (**present → past; past → past perfect simple; will → would; can → could**).

Steve: *I'm on the ferry to Calais. I'll call you back later.*

Steve told Eddie that he was on the ferry to Calais and that he'd call him back later.

Test yourself **A message from Jack**
When Jack (the narrator of the story) arrived in France, he sent this message to his mother. What did she tell Jack's father when he came home?

Start like this: Jack sent me a message this afternoon. He said that …

I had a good trip and arrived safely. I haven't had time to look around yet, so I can't tell you much, but the hostel is clean and the people are very friendly. I'll call again later, but I don't know when because we're going into town for dinner and I'm not sure when we'll be back.

G2 Steve's blog

→ Seiten 10–12

Zeit- und Ortsangaben in der indirekten Rede
Expressions of time and place in indirect speech

Friday morning:	**Friday afternoon:**	**A few days later:**
Steve: We **had** horsemeat for dinner **yesterday**.	Steve told me that they **had had** horsemeat for dinner **yesterday**.	Last Friday Steve told me that they **had had** horsemeat for dinner **the day before**.

Wenn die indirekte Rede sich auf eine Aussage aus der Vergangenheit bezieht, musst du auch die Zeit- und Ortsangaben im Satz verändern.

○ *Die Zeitangaben ändern sich folgendermaßen:*

today → that day	this evening → that evening
tomorrow → the next day	three days ago → three days before
yesterday → the day before	last week / year → the week / year before
next year → the following year	now → then

○ *Auch Ortsangaben ändern sich, wenn die Aussage später an einem anderen Ort wiedergegeben wird:* here → there.

○ *Weitere Wörter, die meist in der indirekten Rede verändert werden, um sie dem Standpunkt des Berichtenden anzupassen, sind:* this → that; these → those; come → go *und* bring → take.

It's quite cold over **here**.
This is unusual for the time of year. So when you **come**, you shouldn't forget to **bring** some warm clothes,
Michel Lebrun

Listen boys and girls,
I've had an e-mail from Monsieur Lebrun. He said that it was quite cold over **there**. **That** was unusual for the time of year. So when we **go**, we shouldn't forget to **take** some warm clothes.

○── **English summary** ──○

In indirect speech, adverbs of time often change too, e.g. **today → that day**, **yesterday → the day before** etc.
But if you report something **on the same day** as it was said, the adverbs of time **don't** change.
Other words that you may need to change are:
this → that; here → there; come → go; bring → take.

Steve: *I'm going to France tomorrow.*

(the same day)
Steve said he was going to France tomorrow.

(a week later):
Steve said he was going to France the next day.

Test yourself *While Steve was in France last week, he sent this text message to his friend Eddie. A week later Eddie met Amarjit. What did he tell him?*

Start like this: Steve sent me a message from France last week. He said that …

The athletics event started yesterday and our team is doing well. But it's very cold here. If I ever come back to this place, I'll bring warmer clothes. I wish I had listened to Ms W.

G3   He asked me what the purpose of my visit was

→ Seiten 13–15

Fragen in der indirekten Rede
Questions in indirect speech

Direct question:	Indirect speech:
Steve's grandma: When **is** your flight, Rafiq?	Grandma **asked** me when my flight **was**.
How **are** you **getting** to the airport?	She **asked** me how I **was getting** to the airport.
Have you **weighed** your suitcase?	She **asked** me **if** I **had weighed** my suitcase.
Are you nervous about the trip?	She **asked** me **if** I **was** nervous about the trip.
Did you **find** a nice present for Aunt Sadia?	She **wanted to know if** I **had found** a nice present for Aunt Sadia.
When **will** you be back?	She **wanted to know** when I **would** be back.

Fragen werden in der indirekten Rede als Aussagesätze wiedergegeben.

○ *Das Verb im **Einführungssatz** (Hauptsatz) muss deutlich machen, dass es sich um eine indirekte Frage handelt* (Grandma **asked** me … / She **wanted to know** …).

○ *Das Fragewort* (what, when, where, why …) *wird in der indirekten Frage als Bindewort zwischen Haupt- und Nebensatz übernommen. Steht **kein** Fragewort, leitest du den Nebensatz mit **if** ein.*

○ *Die Wortstellung im Nebensatz ist die gleiche wie in einem Aussagesatz: Das **Subjekt** steht immer **vor** dem **Verb**. Umschreibungen mit* do / does / did *fallen weg.*

○ *Wie bei indirekten Aussagesätzen (→ G1) werden bei indirekten Fragen die Zeitformen meist um eine Zeitstufe zurückverschoben, wenn das Einleitungsverb im* simple past *steht.*

○ **English summary** ○

1. If you report questions that begin with a question word (what, when, how …), you use **asked / wanted to know + question word**.
2. If there is no question word, you use **if**.
3. The word order in indirect questions is the same as in statements: Subject – Verb.
4. The verb in the direct question moves one tense further back.

Steve's grandma: *How long is the flight to Dhaka?*
Grandma **wanted to know how long** the flight to Dhaka **was**.

Steve's grandma: *Will you be able to sleep on the plane?*
She asked Rafiq if he **would** be able to sleep on the plane.

Test yourself   *When Rafiq arrives at Dhaka airport, the man at passport control asks him a lot of questions. What does Rafiq tell his uncle and aunt later?*

Start like this: The man at passport control asked me …

1. Why are you travelling alone?
2. Where are you from?
3. How long do you plan to stay?
4. Do you have family in Bangladesh?
5. Can you speak Bengali?
6. Is anybody meeting you at the airport?

G4   He told me to go into a side room

→ Seiten 13–15

Befehle, Aufforderungen und Bitten in der indirekten Rede
Commands and requests in indirect speech

Direct command / request:	Indirect command / request:
Steve's grandma: Don't spend all your money in the first week. Please send me some photos from Bangladesh.	She **told** him (Rafiq) **not to spend** all his money in the first week. Grandma **asked** him (Rafiq) **to send** her some photos from Bangladesh.

Befehle, Aufforderungen und Bitten werden in der indirekten Rede als Infinitivkonstruktion mit **to** *oder* **not to** *wiedergegeben.*

○ *In der indirekten Rede verwendest du meist* **tell somebody to do something** *für Befehle und Aufforderungen und* **ask somebody to do something** *für Bitten.*

○ *Enthält der Befehlssatz ein Verbot (also eine Verneinung), wird* **don't** *zu* **not to** *(Don't shout →* ... not to shout).

○ *Dem Einleitungsverb* (told, asked) **folgt** *kein Nebensatz, sondern ein* **Personenobjekt + to-Infinitiv** (She asked **Rafiq to send** ...).

○ *Wird* **kein** *Eigenname genannt, verwendest du ein* **Pronomen** *in der* **Objektform** (me, you, him, her, us, them) (She asked **him** ...).

❗ *Beachte, dass es hier keine Zeitverschiebung gibt, da der Befehl selbst durch einen Infinitiv wiedergegeben wird.*
Für weitere Verben im Satz gelten jedoch die Regeln für indirekte Aussagesätze (→ G1).
Grandma: **Don't spend** all your money on things you **don't** need.
Grandma told Rafiq **not to spend** all his money on things he **didn't** need.

○ **English summary** ○ ─────────────────────────

In indirect speech, you use **to tell somebody (not) to do something** for indirect commands and **to ask somebody (not) to do something** for indirect requests.

Flight attendant: *Fasten your seatbelt, please, and don't use your phone during take-off and landing.*
The flight attendant **asked** *Rafiq* **to fasten** *his seatbelt and* **told** *him* **not to use** *his phone during take-off and landing.*

Test yourself   *What did Rafiq's mum say to him at the airport?*
Put her words into indirect speech.

Start like this: Rafiq's mum asked ...

1. Please say hello to everyone from us.
2. Be careful with your passport. Don't lose it.
3. Please call me as soon as you get to Dhaka.
4. Have fun while you're there and take lots of photos.

Unit 2

G5 Living here isn't bad

→ Seiten 44–46

Das Gerundium
The gerund (verb + -ing)

Living in rural Pennsylvania isn't bad. But I really **miss seeing** my friends at home and I'm **scared of changing** too much. What's Pittsburgh like? I'm **thinking of coming** to visit soon. How about **meeting up** there?

Pittsburgh is amazing. I just **love being** here. It's really cool. But I still can't **get used to living** on the 22nd floor! I'm afraid I'm very busy here, so **meeting up** isn't easy right now.

Das **gerund** *(verb + -ing) ist eine Verbform, die es im Deutschen nicht gibt.*
Im Satz kann es verschiedene Funktionen haben. Es wird folgendermaßen verwendet:
1. *als Subjekt (***Living*** here isn't …),*
2. *als Objekt nach bestimmten Verben (I miss* **seeing** *…),*
3. *nach Präpositionen (I'm scared of* **changing** *… / I'm thinking of* **coming** *… /*
   How about **meeting** *…).*

- *Das* **gerund** *sieht aus wie das* present participle (playing, taking, running) *und wird genauso gebildet. Es gelten auch die gleichen Schreibregeln:*
  try + -ing → trying   liv**e** + -ing → living   ge**t** + -ing → ge**tt**ing

- *Im Deutschen wird das* **gerund** *mit dem **Infinitiv** wiedergegeben:*
  I miss **seeing** my friends.   *Ich vermisse es, meine Freunde **zu sehen**.*
  Living here isn't bad.   *Es ist nicht schlecht hier **zu leben**.*

a) *Das* gerund *als Subjekt des Satzes*

Meeting up isn't easy right now.	*Sich zu treffen ist im Moment nicht einfach.*
Finding new friends can be difficult.	*Neue Freunde zu finden kann schwierig sein.*
Living in America is awesome.	*In Amerika zu leben ist toll.*

- *Als Subjekt des Satzes steht das* **gerund** *am Satzanfang und wird wie ein Nomen gebraucht.*

- *Es kann allein stehen (***Meeting up***), zusammen mit einem Nomen verwendet werden (***Finding new friends***) und auch eine adverbiale Bestimmung bei sich haben (***Living** in America**).*

b) *Das gerund als Objekt des Satzes nach bestimmten Verben*

Matt **enjoys**	**being** in Pittsburgh.	*Matt ist gerne in Pittsburgh.*
Sophie **didn't mind**	**moving** to America.	*Sophie hatte nichts dagegen, nach Amerika umzuziehen.*
Lena **keeps**	**thinking about** her friends in Germany.	*Lena denkt immer wieder an ihre Freunde in Deutschland.*
She **misses**	**hanging out** with them.	*Sie vermisst es, Zeit mit ihnen zu verbringen.*

- *Als Objekt des Satzes steht **nach bestimmten Verben** das* gerund *anstelle eines Infinitivs mit to, z.B.* Matt **enjoys** being *in Pittsburgh (nicht: Matt enjoys to be …).*
- *Häufig sind es Verben, die allgemeine Vorlieben oder Abneigungen ausdrücken, wie* enjoy, like, dislike, love, hate.
- *Weitere Verben, nach denen ein **Verb** als* gerund *stehen **muss**, sind:* keep, miss, imagine *und* suggest.

c) *Das gerund als Objekt nach Präpositionen*

1. *Adjektiv + Präposition + gerund*

Lena is **scared of**	**changing** too much.	*Lena hat Angst davor, sich zu sehr zu verändern.*
Sophie is **tired of**	**living** in the middle of nowhere.	*Sophie hat es satt, am Ende der Welt zu wohnen.*
Matt isn't **worried about**	**being** bored in Pittsburgh.	*Matt macht sich keine Sorgen, dass er sich in Pittsburgh langweilen könnte.*

- *Weitere Verbindungen von Adjektiv + Präposition, nach denen ein* gerund *stehen **muss**, sind:* good at, interested in, crazy about.

2. *Verb + Präposition + gerund*

Lena is **looking forward to**	**seeing** Matt again.	*Lena freut sich darauf, Matt wiederzusehen.*
But Matt doesn't **feel like**	**meeting** up with her.	*Aber Matt hat keine Lust, sich mit ihr zu treffen.*
He is **thinking of**	**inviting** Sophie to a baseball game.	*Er denkt darüber nach, Sophie zu einem Baseballspiel einzuladen.*

- *Weitere Verbindungen von Verb + Präposition, nach denen ein* gerund *steht, sind:* talk about, get used to, dream of, forgive somebody for, worry about.

❗ *Bei* look forward **to** *(sich freuen **auf**) und* get used **to** *(sich gewöhnen **an**) ist das* **to** *eine Präposition, die zum vorangestellten Verb gehört und auf die das* gerund *folgt:*
Sophie can't get used **to** **sharing** a room with her messy cousin.
She's looking forward **to** **moving** to Pittsburgh soon.

English summary

The gerund has the same form as the present participle: going, living etc. It can be used …

1. as the subject of the sentence.   **Living** in rural Pennsylvania is OK.
2. as the object of the sentence after certain verbs, e.g. *enjoy, like, hate, imagine, mind*.   Lena doesn't mind **being** there.
3. after prepositions
   a) adjective + preposition + gerund   She isn't worried about **having to** travel for two hours to get there.
   b) verb + preposition + gerund   She's looking forward to **going** to the mall.

Test yourself   *Use a gerund to rewrite the sentences.*

Example: What would you like to do today? (be interested in)
→ What would you be interested in doing today?

1. Why don't we visit a museum? (How about)
2. I don't really want to go to a museum today. (feel like)
3. OK, then, what would you like to do? (suggest)
4. Mom tells me every day about the spectacular views from Mt. Washington. (keep)
5. My mom goes there a lot too. (love)
6. She talks about the place all the time. (never stop)

G6   That's the worst thing to do!

→ Seiten 48–50

Der Infinitiv mit und ohne to
The infinitive with and without *to*

Scott and Eva don't **want me to talk** to Henry and Tyler. They say that's the **worst thing to do**. I don't **want to listen** to them. But to be honest I'm **not sure what to do**.

I'm glad I don't have your problems, Matt, but mine aren't much better, you know. I **can** never **meet** friends after school because my parents always **make me come** straight home. They won't **let me do** anything.

*Der **Infinitiv** ist die Grundform des Verbs. Im Englischen findet sich der Infinitiv in zwei Formen:*
mit to *(to be, to go, to play) und* **ohne** to *(be, go, play).*
*Der **Infinitiv mit** to steht nach zahlreichen Verben, Adjektiven und Nomen.*
*Der **Infinitiv ohne** to wird vor allem nach Hilfsverben (can, must, should), aber auch nach anderen Verben wie* let *oder* make *+ Objekt gebraucht.*

a) *Der Infinitiv mit* **to** *nach bestimmten Verben*

Would you **like**	**to watch** the movie on TV this evening?
No, I**'d prefer**	**to go** to the movie theater.
OK. I'll **try**	**to get** some tickets.

- *Verben auf die der* **Infinitiv mit** **to** *folgt, können in folgende Gruppen unterteilt werden:*
  1. **Wünsche und Absichten**, *z. B.* want, would like, hope, decide, expect, offer, plan, promise
  2. **Vorlieben**, *die sich auf konkrete Situationen beziehen, z. B.* choose, prefer
  3. **Versuche** *oder* **Bemühungen**, *z. B.* try, learn, manage.

b) *Der Infinitiv mit* **to** *nach Verb + Fragewort oder nach* **whether**

Direkte Frage	Indirekte Frage	mit can, should, must, have to mit Infinitiv + to
Where do I have to go?	Matt doesn't **know**	**where** he has to go. **where to go**.
Who can I ask?	He **isn't sure**	who he can ask. **who to ask**.
Should I sit with Henry and Tyler?	He **wonders**	**if** he should sit with Henry and Tyler. **whether to sit** with Henry and Tyler.

- *Nach* **know, be sure, decide, wonder** *+ Fragewort* (what, when, where, which, whether) *steht der* **Infinitiv mit** **to** *oft anstelle einer indirekten Frage (mit can, should, must, have to).*

❗ *Bei Entscheidungsfragen wird bei der Infinitivkonstruktion* if *(ob) durch* **whether** *ersetzt.*

c) *Der Infinitiv mit* **to** *nach Superlativen*

Hauptsatz + Relativsatz	Hauptsatz + Infinitiv mit to
You are the first person who has said that.	You are **the first** (person) **to say** that.
I was the only one who ordered meat.	I was **the only one to order** meat.
That's the worst thing that you can do.	That's **the worst thing to do**.

- *Nach* **the first, the last, the only one** *und nach* **Superlativen** (the worst thing, the most important thing) *ersetzt der* **Infinitiv mit** **to** *einen Relativsatz.*

d) *Der Infinitiv mit* **to** *nach Verb + Objekt*

Verb	Objekt	Infinitiv mit to
Henry and Tyler **want**	**people**	**to think** about sweatshops and child labor.
They **would like**	**them**	**to join** their protest at the mall.
Scott and Eva **expect**	**Matt**	**to ignore** them.

○ *Auf die folgenden Verben kann die Verbindung von **Objekt** + **Infinitiv mit** to folgen:*
  ask *(bitten)*, expect, prefer, tell, warn, want *und* would like.

🛑 *Nach* want *(wollen, dass) und* would like *(möchten, dass) darfst du keinen Nebensatz mit* that
anschließen. Vergleiche:

Matt: Scott and Eva want **me to drop** Henry and Tyler.
       Scott und Eva wollen, **dass ich** Henry und Tyler fallen lasse.

e) ***Der Infinitiv ohne* to *nach* let *und* make *+ Objekt***

Verb	Objekt	Infinitiv ohne to
Sophie's parents won't **let**	her	**meet** her friends after school.
They **make**	her	**come** straight home.
Do your parents **let**	you	**do** what you want?
Or do they **make**	you	**come** home early too?

○ *Nach* make *+ Objekt (veranlassen, zwingen) und* let *+ Objekt (zulassen, erlauben) wird der*
  Infinitiv ohne* to *gebraucht.

English summary

The infinitive with *to* is used …

1. after certain verbs, e.g. *want, expect, decide, would like / would prefer*
2. after certain verbs + questions words
3. after superlatives *(the first / last / only one / the best thing)*
4. after *want, would like, expect, ask, tell* + object

Sophie's parents always **want to know** where she is. They**'d like to take** control of her life.
Sophie **isn't sure what to do**.
She's **the only one to have** parents who are so strict.
She **would like them to relax** more.

The infinitive without *to* is used …

1. after modal verbs *(can, should, must, have to)*
2. after *let / make* + object

They **should trust** her.

They should **let her go out** with her friends.

Test yourself *Complete the second sentence so that the meaning is similar to the first.*
Use infinitive constructions.

1. I'll be home before 6 p.m., I promise.   I promise …
2. I didn't know what I could say.   I didn't know what …
3. My parents say that I shouldn't watch too much TV.   My parents don't want …
4. I was surprised when he invited me to his party.   I didn't expect …
5. They always say that she can do what she wants.   They always let …
6. Our football coach says we have to train every day.   Our football coach makes …
7. The best thing that we can do is say nothing at all.   The best thing …

G7   Gerund or infinitive: It depends on the meaning

→ Seite 51

Das gerund *oder der Infinitiv mit* to: *Bedeutungsunterschiede*

Dad, I've got a problem with my computer. I've **tried turning** it off and **starting** it up again, but that hasn't worked.

I'm sorry, Sophie. I'm really busy at the moment. But I'll **try to find** some time this afternoon. Maybe I can help you then.

Nach einigen wenigen Verben (forget, go on, mean, remember, stop, try) *wird je nach Bedeutung entweder ein* **gerund** *oder ein* **Infinitiv mit to** *verwendet.*

a) *Nach* go on, mean, stop *und* try *hängt die* **Bedeutung des Verbs** *davon ab, ob ihm ein* **gerund** *oder ein* **Infinitiv mit to** *folgt.*

to go on doing sth *etwas fortsetzen / weitermachen*	to go on to do sth *etwas anschließend machen*
They **went on** **talking**. Sie redeten weiter.	Then they **went on** **to talk about** child labor. Anschließend sprachen sie über Kinderarbeit.

to mean doing sth *bedeuten*	to mean to do sth *wollen, beabsichtigen*
That **means** **walking**. Das bedeutet, dass wir laufen müssen.	I **meant** **to send** you a text, but I forgot. Ich wollte dir eine SMS schicken, aber …

to stop doing sth *aufhören, etwas zu tun*	to stop to do something *anhalten, um etwas Neues zu tun*
Stop **shouting**! Hör auf, zu schreien!	Let's **stop** **to have** a drink. Lasst uns anhalten, um etwas zu trinken.

to try doing sth *eine Methode ausprobieren*	to try to do sth *eine konkrete Handlung ausprobieren*
If you can't sleep, **try** **counting** sheep. … probier's mal mit Schäfchen zählen.	I **tried** **to sleep** in the car, but it wasn't possible. Ich habe versucht, im Auto zu schlafen, aber …

b) *Nach* remember *und* forget *steht das* **gerund** *für eine Handlung, die* **bereits stattgefunden** *hat und an die man sich erinnert. Der* **Infinitiv mit** to *weist hingegen auf eine Handlung hin, die* **beabsichtigt ist** *und* **noch bevorsteht**.

to remember doing sth *sich erinnern an*	to remember to do sth *daran denken, etwas zu tun*
Sophie can't **remember visiting** London. She was too young. *Sophie kann sich nicht daran erinnern, dass sie London besucht hat. …*	Please **remember to learn** the irregular verbs for the test. *Denkt bitte daran, die unregelmäßigen Verben für den Test zu lernen.*

to forget doing sth *vergessen, wie man etwas getan hat*	to forget to do sth *vergessen, etwas zu tun*
Lena will never **forget having to say goodbye** to her friends in Hamburg. *Lena wird nie vergessen, wie sie sich von ihren Freunden … verabschieden musste.*	Please don't **forget to tidy** your room before your friends arrive. *Vergiss nicht, dein Zimmer aufzuräumen, bevor deine Freunde kommen.*

❗ *Nach* to begin, to start *und* to like *(im Sinne von „genießen") kann sowohl das* **gerund** *als auch der* **Infinitiv mit** to *stehen. Die Bedeutung ist in beiden Fällen gleich!*

It started to rain. It started raining.
I like to go to the movie theater. I like going to the movie theater.

○ **English summary** ○

Some English verbs such as *forget, go on, mean, remember, stop* and *try* can be followed by a gerund or by an infinitive with *to*, but with a change in meaning.

We **stopped to buy** some eggs from the farm.
We've **stopped buying** them from the supermarket.

Test yourself *After Lena received Matt's e-mail, this is what she wrote in her diary.*
Put the verb into the right form: gerund or infinitive with to.

Dear Diary,
Bad news! I got a mail from Matt today and it seems he can't stop (think) about Sophie. I'm sure Matt didn't mean (hurt) me, but … When I told Madison, she said I should try (forget) him. But how? M. thinks I should try (do) yoga! She says she can remember (feel) upset about something once, and it really helped her. But I'm not sure. I'm not really sure about anything at the moment: Should I go on (write) him? Should I tell him how I feel? I don't know. The only thing I know right now is that it's really late and I mustn't forget (set) my alarm clock! Madison's mom is driving us to the mall outside Pittsburgh tomorrow. We want (get) there early and it's two hours in the car, so that means (leave) at 8 a.m.! Oh well, at least we can stop (have) breakfast somewhere on the way.

Unit 3

G8   **The boy who … / Diego, who …**   → Seiten 72–74

Notwendige und nicht-notwendige Relativsätze
Defining and non-defining relative clauses

Diego is the boy **who took us around New York**. He showed us sights in New York (**which**) **you would never find in a guidebook**.

Diego, **who knows New York like the back of his hand**, showed the two girls some great places. All the sights were amazing, but Rockefeller Center, **which they visited last**, was just awesome.

> *Relativsätze sind Nebensätze, die ihr **Bezugswort** im Hauptsatz a) näher bestimmen*
> (**the boy** who took us around New York) *oder b) zusätzlich beschreiben* (**Diego**, who knows New York like the back of his hand, …).
> *Im Englischen nennt man diese zwei Arten von Relativsätzen* **defining** *und* **non-defining**
> **relative clauses**.

a)   **Defining relative clauses**

> **Two girls** who / that are spending the day in New York visit a diner.
>
> **A boy** (who / that) they meet there takes them on a tour of the city.
>
> Some of the **sights** (which / that) he shows them are amazing.

○   **Defining relative clauses** *bestimmen ihr vorangestelltes **Bezugswort** im Hauptsatz näher.
   Sie legen fest, wer oder was gemeint ist. Ohne den Relativsatz wäre in den obigen
   Beispielen nicht klar, von welchen beiden Mädchen, von welchem Jungen oder von welchen
   Sehenswürdigkeiten genau die Rede ist.*

○   *Relativsätze, die ihr Bezugswort näher bestimmen, stehen **ohne Komma**. Beim Sprechen
   macht man keine Pause.*

○ **Defining relative clauses** *werden durch Relativpronomen wie* **who** *oder* **that** *(bei Personen) und* **which** *oder* **that** *(bei Sachen) eingeleitet, wenn sie das Subjekt im Relativsatz sind. Sind die Relativpronomen* who, which, that *das Objekt im Relativsatz, können sie weggelassen werden (*a boy (**who / that**) they meet …; some of the sights (**that**) he shows …*). Diese Relativsätze nennt man* **contact clauses**.

b) **Non-defining relative clauses**

Rylee and Lea, who are spending the day in New York, visit a diner.
Diego, who they meet there, takes them on a tour of the city.
At **Rockefeller Center**, which they visit last, they have a scary experience.

○ *Bei* non-defining relative clauses *ist das vorangestellte* **Bezugswort bereits definiert**. *Auch ohne den Relativsatz bleibt klar, wer oder was gemeint ist:* Rylee and Lea, Diego *und das* Rockefeller Center. *Die Relativsätze bestimmen daher ihr Bezugswort* **nicht** *näher. Sie enthalten lediglich eine zusätzliche oder ergänzende Information, die ebenso gut in Klammern stehen oder entfallen könnte, ohne dass die Aussage im Hauptsatz verändert wird.*

○ *Relativsätze, die Zusatzinformationen enthalten, werden vom Hauptsatz immer* **durch Kommas abgetrennt**. *Beim Sprechen wird eine Pause gemacht.*

○ *Im Gegensatz zu* defining relative clauses *beginnen* non-defining relative clauses **immer mit einem Relativpronomen**: *Für Personen verwendet man* **who**. *Für Dinge verwendet man* **which**. *Das Relativpronomen* **that** *ist in einem* non-defining relative clause *nicht möglich*.

○ **English summary** ○

There are two types of relative clauses: **defining** and **non-defining**.

1. Defining relative clauses tell you which person or thing the speaker is talking about. **No comma** is used between the noun and the relative clause.	Lea is a German girl **who / that** comes from Berlin.
2. Non-defining relative clauses are used after nouns that are definite already. They give extra information about a person or thing. You always need a **comma** to separate the main clause from the relative clause.	Lea, **who** is German, is Rylee's cousin from Berlin.
3. Non-defining relative clauses always begin with a relative pronoun. You use *who* for people and *which* for things. You **never** use *that*.	They walked to the Alvin Ailey Dance Studio, **which** is close to Central Park.

Test yourself *Copy these sentences into your exercise book. Underline the noun(s) to which the relative clauses refer (das Bezugswort) and add commas where needed.*

1. Last year we visited New York which is the largest city in the USA.
2. We stayed with some friends who live there.
3. They showed us some amazing sights which we would never have found on our own.
4. But they also took us to famous sights like Rockefeller Center which was awesome too.
5. In Times Square we saw the Naked Cowboy who is really only *almost* naked.
6. He is a street performer who has become one of New York's biggest tourist attractions.

G9 How long had they been doing that?

→ Seiten 76–78

Die Verlaufsform des Plusquamperfekts
The past perfect progressive

> When Emilio arrived home, he felt tired. He **had been working** hard all day.

Das **past perfect** *wird verwendet, um Vorzeitigkeit vor einem bestimmten Zeitpunkt in der Vergangenheit auszudrücken.*
Mit dem **past perfect simple** *(I had done) betonst du* **das Ergebnis** *einer abgeschlossenen Handlung, z. B. Emilio felt tired. He* **had had** *a hard day.*
Mit dem **past perfect progressive** *(I had been doing) betonst du den* **Verlauf** *oder die* **Dauer** *dieser Handlung, z. B. Emilio felt tired. He* **had been working** *hard all day.*

○ *Das* past perfect progressive *bildest du aus* **had been** + **present participle** (verb + -ing)

Aussage:	He **had been listening**.
Verneinung:	He **hadn't been listening**.
Ergänzungsfrage:	How long **had** he **been listening**?
Entscheidungsfrage mit Kurzantwort:	**Had** he **been listening**? Yes, he **had**. / No, he **hadn't**.

○ Das **past perfect progressive** benutzt du für Handlungen, die vor einem Zeitpunkt in der Vergangenheit angefangen haben und bis zu diesem Zeitpunkt andauerten. Hierbei wird die Dauer der Handlung häufig durch eine Zeitangabe betont, z.B. for ten years, since 2015, all day / week / year, all the time usw.

Past perfect progressive + *Zeitangabe*	*Vergangenheit*
Emilio **had been waiting** for 20 minutes … *wartete schon seit …*	before his first passenger arrived.
His second passenger **hadn't been sitting** in his taxi **for long** … *hatte noch nicht lange im Taxi gesessen …*	when he started to ask lots of questions.

○ Der Gebrauch des **past perfect progressive** ist mit der Verwendung des **present perfect progressive** vergleichbar. Die beschriebenen Handlungen dauern jedoch nicht bis in die Gegenwart an, sondern nur bis zu einem Zeitpunkt in der Vergangenheit.

Present (now) ←←←	Present perfect progressive
Emilio **is** tired	because he **has been driving** around New York all day.
Past (yesterday) ←←←	Past perfect progressive
Emilio **was** tired	because he **had been driving** around New York all day.

❗ Beachte, dass du das **past perfect progressive** wie alle Verlaufsformen **nur bei Tätigkeitsverben** verwenden kannst (z.B. wait, work, live). Bei Verben, die keine Tätigkeit, sondern einen Zustand bezeichnen (z.B. be, know, belong) benutzt du das **past perfect simple**, z.B. Emilio had only been at the taxi stand for a few minutes when his next passenger got in.

English summary

You use the past perfect progressive to stress how long an activity continued before another event in the past happened. It is often used with an expression of time, e.g. *since, for, all day* etc.

Last week Diego found a new assistant for his diner. He **had been looking for** help since the summer.

Test yourself Use the past perfect simple or the past perfect progressive to complete the text.

After Julia and Andrea from Germany (walk) around Manhattan all morning, they were very hungry. So they decided to go to Diego's Diner, which they (read) about in the guidebook they (buy) the day before. When they got there at 12:30, the diner was already very busy. Some of the people (wait) to get their lunch for quite some time. The girls (learn) English since the age of ten, so they had no language problems. But when they tried to order, nobody seemed to notice them. Finally, after they (try) to get a waiter's attention for about 15 minutes, a friendly Hispanic American came to their table and took their order.

Vocabulary

Im *Vocabulary* findest du alle wichtigen englischen Wörter und Redewendungen aus *Green Line* 4. Sie stehen in der Reihenfolge, in der sie im Buch vorkommen. Diese Wörter solltest du lernen und anwenden können. Andere nützliche Wörter und Begriffe (z. B. Arbeitsanweisungen), die du **nicht** auswendig lernen musst, findest du ab S. 256.

Auf das *Vocabulary* folgt das **Dictionary (English – German, German – English)**. Falls du ein Wort vergessen hast, kannst du in diesen alphabetischen Wortlisten nachsehen.

Englische Begriffe wie *e-mail*, *cool* oder *cornflakes*, die du auch im Deutschen verwendest, stehen nicht im *Vocabulary*. Du kannst ihre Aussprache und Übersetzung aber im *Dictionary* nachschlagen. Das gleiche gilt für Wörter, die auf Englisch und Deutsch fast gleich geschrieben und ausgesprochen werden, wie z. B. *park* oder *partner*.

In den drei Teilen von **Text smart** musst du nicht alle neuen Vokabeln auswendig lernen. Die Wörter und Ausdrücke, die im *Vocabulary* aufgelistet sind, sind die wichtigsten und sie solltest du lernen und anwenden können. Alle anderen neuen Wörter aus *Text smart* kannst du ebenfalls hinten im *Dictionary* ab S. 191 nachschlagen.

Abkürzungen und Zeichen

pl	Mehrzahl (Plural)	↔	ist das Gegenteil von
sg	Einzahl (Singular)	→	ist verwandt mit
AE	amerikanisch-englisches Wort	=	entspricht
coll/ugs	umgangssprachlich	≠	entspricht nicht
5	In dieser Übung kommen die Wörter vor.	*Fr./Lat.*	verwandte Wörter in anderen Fremdsprachen
!	Achtung!		

Englische Laute

Konsonanten

[b]	**b**ed	[p]	**p**icture
[d]	**d**ay	[r]	**r**ed
[ð]	**th**e	[s]	**s**ix
[f]	**f**amily	[ʃ]	**sh**e
[g]	**g**o	[t]	**t**en
[ŋ]	morni**ng**	[tʃ]	**ch**air
[h]	**h**ouse	[v]	**v**ideo
[j]	**y**ou	[w]	**w**e, **o**ne
[k]	**c**an, mil**k**	[z]	ea**s**y
[l]	**l**etter	[ʒ]	revi**s**ion
[m]	**m**an	[dʒ]	**p**age
[n]	**n**o	[θ]	**th**ank you

Vokale

[ɑː]	c**ar**	[i]	happ**y**
[æ]	**a**pple	[iː]	t**ea**cher
[e]	p**e**n	[ɒ]	d**o**g
[ə]	**a**gain	[ɔː]	b**a**ll
[ɜː]	g**ir**l	[ʊ]	b**oo**k
[ʌ]	b**u**t	[u]	Jan**u**ary
[ɪ]	**i**t	[uː]	t**oo**, tw**o**

Doppellaute

[aɪ]	**I**, m**y**
[aʊ]	n**ow**, m**ou**se
[eɪ]	n**a**me, th**ey**
[eə]	th**ere**, p**air**
[ɪə]	h**ere**, id**ea**
[əʊ]	hell**o**
[ɔɪ]	b**oy**
[ʊə]	s**ure**

[ː]	der vorangehende Laut ist lang, z. B. *you* [juː]
[‿]	der Bindebogen zeigt, dass zwei Wörter in der Aussprache verbunden werden
[']	die folgende Silbe trägt den Hauptakzent
[ˌ]	die folgende Silbe trägt den Nebenakzent

Der Aussprachestandard in *Green Line* ist *British English*. Auch Wörter, die den Zusatz *AE* haben, werden entsprechend lautschriftlich dargestellt.

Unit 1 On the move

Introduction

on the move [ˌɒnˌðə ˈmuːv]	unterwegs	He has to travel a lot in his job. He is always *on the move*.
travelling *(no pl)* [ˈtrævlɪŋ]	(das) Reisen	*travelling* → to travel
foreign [ˈfɒrɪn]	ausländisch; fremd	A lot of British schools teach French as the first *foreign* language.
seasick [ˈsiːsɪk]	seekrank	People sometimes feel *seasick* when they're travelling on boats or ships in bad weather.
luggage *(no pl)* [ˈlʌgɪdʒ]	Gepäck	
to be afraid (of) [biˌəˈfreɪdˌəv]	(sich) fürchten; Angst haben (vor)	He's *afraid of* dogs.
plane [pleɪn]	Flugzeug	We're on our way to the airport. Our *plane* leaves in two hours.
departure lounge [dɪˈpɑːtʃəˌlaʊndʒ]	Abflughalle	
passport [ˈpɑːspɔːt]	Pass; Reisepass	If you want to travel from Germany to New York, you'll need a *passport*.
boarding card [ˈbɔːdɪŋˌkɑːd]	Bordkarte	A *boarding card* is the ticket you need before you get onto the plane.
desk [desk]	Schalter	
visa [ˈviːzə], **visas** [ˈviːzəz] *(pl)*	Visum, Visa *(Pl.)*; Einreisebewilligung	You can't enter the USA without a *visa*.
passenger [ˈpæsndʒə]	Passagier/-in; Fahrgast	a person who is travelling by plane, train, bus, etc.
flight attendant [ˈflaɪtˌəˌtendnt]	Flugbegleiter/-in	The *flight attendant* looks after the passengers on a plane.
customs *(sg)* [ˈkʌstəmz]	Zoll	**!** *Customs* steht immer ohne Artikel und hat keine Pluralform: *Customs* **is** on your right.
suitcase [ˈsuːtkeɪs]	Koffer	Have you packed your *suitcase* yet?
ferry [ˈferi]	Fähre	= a boat that takes passengers and cars across a river or a narrow part of sea
control [kənˈtrəʊl]	Kontrolle	If you want to travel by plane, you have to go through passport *control*.
arrivals hall [əˈraɪvlzˌhɔːl]	Ankunftshalle	*arrivals hall* → arrival → to arrive
currency [ˈkʌrnsi]	Währung	The *currency* in the UK is the British Pound.
duty-free [ˌdjuːtiˈfriː]	zollfrei	Every airport has *duty-free* shops.

Station 1: You told us there was free wifi!

athletics *(no pl)* [æθˈletɪks]	Leichtathletik	**!** *Athletics* **is** an important part of PE in British schools.
vending machine [ˈvendɪŋ məˌʃiːn]	Automat	Let's get some drinks from the *vending machine*.
to **spill** [spɪl], **spilt** [spɪlt], **spilt** [spɪlt]	verschütten; auslaufen	Don't put too much water in the glass or you'll *spill* it.
to **hang on** [ˌhæŋ ˈɒn]	(einen Augenblick) warten	*Hang on*. I'll ask them.
coast [kəʊst]	Küste	= where the land meets the sea *coast* → coastal path
shutter [ˈʃʌtə]	Fensterladen	If it's hot outside, you should keep the *shutters* closed.
abroad [əˈbrɔːd]	im Ausland; ins Ausland	**!** They live *abroad*. (= im Ausland) They went *abroad*. (= ins Ausland)
groan [grəʊn]	Stöhnen	= a 'slow' sound that shows you are hurt, unhappy or disappointed
hostel [ˈhɒstl]	Herberge	A *hostel* is cheaper than a hotel.
addict [ˈædɪkt]	Süchtige/-r; Abhängige/-r	Steve is a phone *addict*.
to **mutter** [ˈmʌtə]	murmeln	to speak – to talk – to shout – *to mutter*
latest [ˈleɪtɪst]	neueste/-r/-s	What's the *latest* news from your brother in Australia?
closed [kləʊzd]	geschlossen; zu	*closed* ↔ open *closed* → to close
big deal [bɪg ˈdiːl]	große Sache	That's no *big deal*. = It's not a problem.
apart from [əˈpɑːt frəm]	abgesehen von; außer	I'm going to the supermarket later. What else do we need *apart from* bread, milk and sugar?
soup [suːp]	Suppe	A bowl of hot *soup* does you good on a cold day.
herb [hɜːb]	Kraut	*Herbs* are plants that people add to food to make it taste good.
garlic [ˈgɑːlɪk]	Knoblauch	The soup had too much *garlic* in it.
style [staɪl]	Stil	She always wears her own *style* of clothes.
to **be called** [bi ˈkɔːld]	heißen; genannt werden	What's your sister *called*?
sleep [sliːp]	Schlaf	*sleep* → to sleep

Station 2: Idiot nephew?

nephew [ˈnefjuː]	Neffe	= the son of your sister or your brother
although [ɔːlˈðəʊ]	obwohl	Jenny's father speaks very good English *although* he's German.
purpose [ˈpɜːpəs]	Ziel; Absicht; Zweck	If you have a *purpose*, you have a reason to do something.
date of birth [ˌdeɪt əv ˈbɜːθ]	Geburtsdatum	*date of birth* → birthday

suspicious [səˈspɪʃəs]	misstrauisch; argwöhnisch	When Rafiq told the man he was only 13, he started to get *suspicious*.
side room [ˈsaɪd ˌrʊm]	Nebenraum	We celebrated my birthday in a *side room* of the restaurant.
security [sɪˈkjʊərəti]	Sicherheit; Schutz; Wachdienst; Wach-; Sicherheits-	The *security* people at the airport are very strict.
immigration office [ˌɪmɪˈgreɪʃn ˌɒfɪs]	Einwanderungsbehörde	The officials asked Rafiq's aunt to come to the *immigration office*.
immigration [ˌɪmɪˈgreɪʃn]	Immigration; Einwanderung; Einreise	The USA is a popular country for *immigration*.
truth [truːθ]	Wahrheit	*truth* ↔ lie *truth* → true
10 **quite** [kwaɪt]	ziemlich; ganz; völlig	The old centre of Dhaka is *quite* small.
traffic [ˈtræfɪk]	Verkehr	= all the cars, buses, etc. that are moving on a road
to **search for** [ˈsɜːtʃ fə]	suchen (nach)	*to search for* = to look for

Nouns and verbs with the same form

answer	to answer	hope	to hope	reply	to reply
change	to change	interest	to interest	rescue	to rescue
chat	to chat	interview	to interview	run	to run
compromise	to compromise	joke	to joke	search	to search
dance	to dance	land	to land	show	to show
design	to design	lie	to lie	smile	to smile
dream	to dream	link	to link	surprise	to surprise
drink	to drink	look	to look	talk	to talk
e-mail	to e-mail	love	to love	test	to test
end	to end	name	to name	travel	to travel
exchange	to exchange	order	to order	use	to use
film	to film	plan	to plan	visit	to visit
fight	to fight	plant	to plant	walk	to walk
guide	to guide	post	to post	work	to work
help	to help	rain	to rain		

11 **traveller** [ˈtrævlə]	Reisende/-r	*traveller* → to travel
to **bother** [ˈbɒðə]	stören; belästigen	Sorry to *bother* you, but I need your help.
to **suggest** [səˈdʒest]	vorschlagen	*to suggest* → suggestion
chewing gum [ˈtʃuːɪŋ ˌgʌm]	Kaugummi	*Chewing gum* isn't allowed at our school.
take-off [ˈteɪk ˌɒf]	Start; Abheben	
landing [ˈlændɪŋ]	Landung	*landing* ↔ take-off

out of [ˈaʊt‿əv]	aus … heraus	Take a pencil *out of* your pencil case, please.
12 to **contain** [kənˈteɪn]	enthalten	What does this box *contain*? = What's in the box?
gate [geɪt]	Gate; Flugsteig; Ausgang	Our plane leaves from *Gate* 9.
delay [dɪˈleɪ]	Verzögerung; Verspätung	The train will be half an hour late. We apologise for the *delay*.

At the airport

arrival(s hall)	Ankunft(shalle)
boarding (card)	Boarding/Bordkarte
customs	Zoll
delay	Verspätung
departure (lounge)	Abflug(halle)
desk	Schalter
duty free	Duty Free
flight	Flug
flight attendant	Flugbegleiter/-in
gate	Gate
immigration office	Einwanderungsbehörde
landing	Landung
passenger	Passagier/-in
passport	Pass/Ausweis
plane	Flugzeug
security control	Sicherheitskontrolle
suitcase	Koffer
take-off	Start
visa	Visum

Have you ever travelled by plane? Write 4–5 sentences.

Story: Where I belong

where I belong [ˌweər‿aɪ bɪˈlɒŋ]	wo ich hingehöre	
responsible [rɪsˈpɒnsəbl]	verantwortlich; verantwortungsvoll	Who is *responsible* for the pets?
to **accept** [əkˈsept]	akzeptieren; hinnehmen; annehmen	I had to *accept* my father's decision.
mask [mɑːsk]	Maske	He showed no feelings. His face looked like a *mask*.
smuggler [ˈsmʌglə]	Schmuggler/-in	I'm reading an exciting adventure story about *smugglers*.
overloaded [ˌəʊvəˈləʊdɪd]	überladen	The bus was completely *overloaded*.
shark [ʃɑːk]	Hai	

crushed [krʌʃt]	eingequetscht; eingeklemmt	The girl was *crushed* between two men and couldn't move.
to **rock** [rɒk]	schaukeln	The wind was very strong and the boat *rocked* badly.
to **smash** [smæʃ]	zerschlagen; zerschmettern	The waves *smashed* against the boat.
to **be sick** [bi ˈsɪk]	sich übergeben	I *was sick* in the car.
to **close oneself away from** [ˌkləʊz əˈweɪ frəm]	sich abschotten von	I *closed myself away from* what was happening around me.
to **give sb a piggyback** [gɪv ˌə ˈpɪgibæk]	jmdn. Huckepack nehmen	
checkpoint [ˈtʃekpɔɪnt]	Kontrollpunkt	*checkpoint* → to check
seat [si:t]	Sitz; Sitzplatz	the place where you sit (in a train, plane, theatre, etc.)
except [ɪkˈsept]	außer; bis auf	Everybody's here, *except* Jenny.
air-conditioning [ˌeəkənˈdɪʃnɪŋ]	Klimaanlage	I'm cold. Please turn off the *air-conditioning*.
to **concentrate** [ˈkɒnsntreɪt]	(sich) konzentrieren	Khadija *concentrated* on what Uncle had told her.
rain [reɪn]	Regen	*rain* → to rain
steady [ˈstedi]	kontinuierlich; unaufhörlich	
depressing [dɪˈpresɪŋ]	deprimierend; bedrückend	It rained for more than a week, which was very *depressing* for everyone.
drizzle [ˈdrɪzl]	Nieselregen	
ground [graʊnd]	Boden; Erdboden	My phone fell onto the *ground* and broke.
to **cover** [ˈkʌvə]	abdecken; bedecken; zudecken	
concrete [ˈkɒŋkri:t]	Beton	The streets in a city are *covered* with concrete.
official [əˈfɪʃl]	Beamter/Beamtin	The *officials* just looked at her passport and then let her into the country.
to **pretend** [prɪˈtend]	vortäuschen; tun als ob	Let's *pretend* to be on holiday.
useless [ˈju:sləs]	nutzlos	*useless* ↔ useful
invisible [ɪnˈvɪzəbl]	unsichtbar	If something becomes *invisible*, you can't see it any more.
phone box [ˈfəʊn ˌbɒks]	Telefonzelle	
to **fetch** [fetʃ]	holen; abholen	Wait at the station. I'm going to *fetch* you.
button [ˈbʌtn]	Knopf	
Somali [səˈmɑ:li]	Somali	In Somalia people speak *Somali*.
straight [streɪt]	gerade; direkt; geradewegs	Go *straight* to school, you're late.
2 **refugee** [ˌrefjʊˈdʒi:]	Flüchtling	A lot of *refugees* have come to live in our town.
5 **climate** [ˈklaɪmət]	Klima	= the kind of weather that is typical of a country or area
to **be homesick** [bi ˈhəʊmsɪk]	Heimweh haben	*Are* you *homesick* when you're away from home?

Action UK! The guitar lesson

	guitar [gɪˈtɑː]	Gitarre	
1	**I go wherever the wind takes me.** [aɪ ˌɡəʊ weəˌrevə ðə wɪnd ˈteɪks miː]	Ich lasse mich treiben.	Let's *go wherever the wind takes us.*
2	**future** [ˈfjuːtʃə]	zukünftig	Talk about your *future* plans.
	origin [ˈɒrɪdʒɪn]	Ursprung; Herkunft; Abstammung	The girl is of African *origin.*
	destination [ˌdestɪˈneɪʃn]	Ziel; Reiseziel	Where are you travelling to? What's your *destination?*
	outgoing [aʊtˈɡəʊɪŋ]	kontaktfreudig	*outgoing* ↔ shy
	easy-going [ˌiːziˈɡəʊɪŋ]	locker; unkompliziert	Who is more *easy-going* – your dad or your mum?
	odd [ɒd]	seltsam; komisch	*odd* = strange
3	to **be set (in)** [bi ˈset ɪn]	spielen (in); seinen Schauplatz haben (in)	"Star Trek" *is set in* the future.
	unreal [ˌʌnˈrɪəl]	irreal	*unreal* ↔ real
	specific [spəˈsɪfɪk]	spezifisch; speziell	
	era [ˈɪərə]	Ära; Zeitalter	The Industrial Revolution was an exciting *era* in British history.
	lavish [ˈlævɪʃ]	üppig; verschwenderisch	Only rich people can afford *lavish* lifestyles.
	magic [ˈmædʒɪk]	Magie; Zauberei	*magic* → magical
	supernatural [ˈsuːpəˌnætʃrl]	übernatürlich	Fantasy stories are usually about people with magical or *supernatural* powers.
	force [fɔːs]	Kraft; Macht	The hero couldn't defeat the supernatural *forces.*
	mythical [ˈmɪθɪkl]	sagenhaft; sagenumwoben	

Skills: How to tell a travel story

1	**the other day** [ðiˌʌðə ˈdeɪ]	neulich	! False friend: *the other day* ≠ am anderen Tag
	It turned out that ... [ɪt ˌtɜːndˌˈaʊt ðæt]	Es stellte sich heraus, dass ...	
2	**war** [wɔː]	Krieg	World *War* II
3	**Egyptian** [ɪˈdʒɪpʃn]	Ägypter/-in; ägyptisch	= from Egypt
	dominoes [ˈdɒmɪnəʊz]	Domino	
	to **order** [ˈɔːdə]	bestellen	At the restaurant, I *ordered* a burger and a glass of water.
	Arab [ˈærəb]	arabisch	Egypt is an *Arab* country.

Unit task: True or not true?

	convincing [kənˈvɪnsɪŋ]	überzeugend	The story doesn't sound *convincing.* *Lat.* convincere

Across cultures 1 Dos and don'ts

dos and don'ts [ˌduːz_ənd ˈdəʊnts]	Ge- und Verbote; was man tun und was man nicht tun sollte	The *dos and don'ts* are the things you should and shouldn't do.
1 **behaviour** *(no pl)* [bɪˈheɪvjə]	Verhalten; Benehmen; Betragen	*behaviour* → to behave
to **point at sb/sth** [ˈpɔɪnt æt]	mit dem Finger auf jmdn./etw. zeigen	Don't *point at* people. It's rude.
to **stand in the way of sb/sth** [ˌstænd ɪn ðə ˈweɪ_əv]	jmdm./etw. im Weg stehen	Excuse me, you're *standing in my way*.
to **hold open** [ˌhəʊld_ˈəʊpn]	aufhalten	You should always *hold* the door *open* for others.
to **talk with your mouth full** [ˌtɔːk wɪð jɔː ˈmaʊθ fʊl]	mit vollem Mund sprechen	Never *talk with your mouth full*.
to **litter** [ˈlɪtə]	verschmutzen; verunreinigen; Müll herumliegen lassen	Don't *litter* the playground. Take your rubbish home with you.
ear [ɪə]	Ohr	
2 to **guess** [ges]	annehmen	You look tired. I *guess* you want to go home.
custom [ˈkʌstəm]	Gewohnheit; Brauch; Sitte	People often wear funny costumes at Halloween. It's a *custom*.
4 **icebreaker** [ˈaɪsˌbreɪkə]	Eisbrecher *(Sätze, um mit jmdm. ins Gespräch zu kommen)*	*Icebreakers* are phrases which people use to start a conversation.
glad [glæd]	froh	I'm *glad* you aren't angry with me.
crowded [ˈkraʊdɪd]	überfüllt	= full of people
5 **leaflet** [ˈliːflət]	Broschüre; Informationsblatt; Prospekt	
manners *(pl)* [ˈmænəz]	Manieren; Benehmen	It's good *manners* to say hello.

Text smart 1 Drama

Introduction

2 to **entertain** [ˌentəˈteɪn]	unterhalten	Theatre plays *entertain* the audience. *to entertain* → entertainment
to **stage** [steɪdʒ]	aufführen	This year our tutor group is going to *stage* a play by Shakespeare.
to **mess sth up** [ˌmes_ˈʌp]	etw. durcheinanderbringen; etw. vergeigen	= to do sth badly or wrong
performance [pəˈfɔːməns]	Aufführung; Vorstellung	All the actors gave great *performances* in the school play.

director [dɪˈrektə]	Regisseur/-in	When a film is made, the *director* tells everyone what to do.
lines *(pl)* [laɪnz]	Text	They've learnt their *lines* by heart.
protagonist [prəʊˈtægnɪst]	Protagonist/-in; Hauptfigur	The *protagonist* is the main character in a play or story.

Station 1

| **devil** [ˈdevl] | Teufel |  |

teenage [ˈtiːneɪdʒ]	jugendlich; Jugend-	Your *teenage* years are the time from age 13 to age 19.
dilemma [daɪˈlemə]	Dilemma; Zwickmühle	Claire is in a *dilemma*: should she go to the party or not?
to **face** [feɪs]	gegenüber stehen; konfrontiert werden mit	This is a problem we have to *face*.
angel [ˈeɪndʒl]	Engel	

4	to **phone** [fəʊn]	anrufen; telefonieren	*to phone* = to call *to phone* → (tele)phone
	tonight [təˈnaɪt]	heute Abend; heute Nacht	*tonight* = this evening
	conscience [ˈkɒnʃns]	Gewissen	Does Claire have a bad *conscience* when she lies to her parents?
5	**motivation** [ˌməʊtɪˈveɪʃn]	Motivation; Beweggründe	
	unsure [ʌnˈʃʊə]	unsicher	I'm *unsure* about what to do. = I'm not sure about what I should do.
	convinced [kənˈvɪnst]	überzeugt	*convinced* → to convince
	tempted [ˈtemptɪd]	in Versuchung gebracht	She feels *tempted* to lie to her parents.
	to **tempt** [tempt]	in Versuchung führen; reizen	Rob *tempts* Claire to break the rules.

Station 2

6	**motive** [ˈməʊtɪv]	Motiv; Beweggrund	
	to **take a risk** [ˌteɪk ə ˈrɪsk]	ein Risiko eingehen	If you *take a risk*, you do something that could be dangerous.
	to **exaggerate** [ɪgˈzædʒreɪt]	übertreiben	If you *exaggerate* something, you make it sound better or worse than it really is. *Fr.* exagérer
	sensible [ˈsensɪbl]	vernünftig	**!** engl. *sensible* ≠ dt. *sensibel* *sensible* ↔ stupid
	Let's face it. [lets ˈfeɪs ɪt]	Machen wir uns doch nichts vor.	*Let's face it*: nobody likes this situation.

white lie [ˌwaɪt ˈlaɪ]	Notlüge	= a small lie that you use when you don't want to hurt somebody's feelings
7 mean [miːn]	gemein	*mean* = nasty
pushy [ˈpʊʃi]	aufdringlich; penetrant; aggressiv	Try to get what you want – but don't be too *pushy*!
argument [ˈɑːgjəmənt]	Argument	You use *arguments* to explain the reasons for your opinion.
9 tempting [ˈtemptɪŋ]	verführerisch	*tempting* → tempted → to tempt

Station 3

10 to warn [wɔːn]	warnen	They *warned* me of the dangers. 
hardly [ˈhɑːdli]	kaum	I can *hardly* believe it.
dishonest [dɪˈsɒnɪst]	unehrlich	*dishonest* ↔ honest
to do well [ˌduː ˈwel]	gute Leistungen erbringen	They would like to *do* really *well* on the project.
schoolwork [ˈskuːlwɜːk]	Schularbeiten	
12 bit by bit [ˌbɪt baɪ ˈbɪt]	Stück für Stück	They've learnt their lines *bit by bit*.
fake [feɪk]	falsch; gefälscht	A *fake* person pretends to be somebody that he or she isn't. *fake* → to fake

Station 4

13 youth [juːθ]	Jugend	= the period in your life before you become an adult
to support [səˈpɔːt]	unterstützen	Do your parents *support* you in what you do?
tolerant [ˈtɒlrnt]	tolerant	**!** Achtung Betonung.
There's no need to ... [ˌðeəz nəʊ ˈniːd tə]	Es gibt keinen Grund zu ...	*There's no need to* shout. I'm listening to you.
to expect [ɪkˈspekt]	erwarten	What you *expect* is what you think will happen.
to ring [rɪŋ], rang [ræŋ], rung [rʌŋ]	anrufen	= to call sb on the phone
out of order [ˌaʊt əv ˈɔːdə]	kaputt; außer Betrieb	The vending machine is *out of order*. It isn't working.
14 shocked [ʃɒkt]	schockiert; geschockt	
guilty [ˈgɪlti]	schuldig	I didn't feel *guilty* because I hadn't done anything wrong.

Options

16 casting [ˈkɑːstɪŋ]	Casting; Rollenbesetzung	= the job of choosing actors to play particular roles

Across cultures 2 The USA: Country of contrasts

contrast ['kɒntrɑːst]	Kontrast; Unterschied; Gegensatz	**!** Notice the stress on the first syllable. *Fr.* contraste *(m)*
the US (= the United States) [ðə juːˈes]	die USA (= die Vereinigten Staaten)	*The US* is a country of contrasts.
urban ['ɜːbn]	städtisch; Stadt-	Towns and cities are *urban* areas. *Lat.* urbs *(f)*
endless ['endləs]	endlos	School lessons sometimes seem *endless*. *endless* → end
sparse [spɑːs]	dünn; spärlich	I only have *sparse* information on this topic.
populated ['pɒpjəleɪtɪd]	bevölkert; besiedelt	
rural ['rʊərl]	ländlich	*rural* ↔ urban *Fr.* rural/-e
single ['sɪŋgl]	einzeln; einzig; alleinstehend	a *single* room = ein Einzelzimmer not a *single* person = kein einziger Mensch I'm *single*. = Ich bin alleinstehend.
tractor ['træktə]	Traktor	
desert ['dezət]	Wüste	
(the) Southwest [ˌsaʊθˈwest]	(der) Südwesten; im Südwesten; südwestlich	*southwest* → northwest
temperature ['temprətʃə]	Temperatur	What's the *temperature* today? *Fr.* température *(f)*
degree Fahrenheit (°F) ['færnhaɪt]	Grad Fahrenheit	110 *°F* is about 43°C.
cactus ['kæktəs]	Kaktus	
cool [kuːl]	kühl	The weather can be cold, *cool*, warm or hot.
zone [zəʊn]	Zone	There are different climate *zones* in the US.
immigrant ['ɪmɪgrənt]	Immigrant/-in; Einwanderer/-in	**!** He's an *immigrant* **from** Asia. He's an *immigrant* **to** the US. *Fr.* immigrant *(m)*; *Lat.* immigrare
European [jʊərəˈpiːən]	Europäer/-in; europäisch; aus Europa	*European* → Europe
cultural ['kʌltʃrl]	kulturell	There are *cultural* differences between people who come from different countries.
redwood (tree) ['redwʊd ˌtriː]	Mammutbaum	= a huge tree that grows in California
foot [fʊt], **feet** [fiːt] *(pl)*	Fuß *(Längenmaß: 30,48 cm)*	I'm 1.82 m tall, that's about 6 *feet*.

	skyscraper [ˈskaɪskreɪpə]	Wolkenkratzer	The Empire State Building is the most famous *skyscraper* in New York.
	state [steɪt]	Staat; Bundesstaat; Land	The US has 50 *states*.
	to **fly** [flaɪ], **flew** [fluː], **flown** [fləʊn]	hissen	Flags *are flown* on a lot of public buildings and on homes in the US.
	a (day/week/year) [ə ˈdeɪ/ wiːk/jɪə]	pro (Tag/Woche/Jahr)	An apple *a day* keeps the doctor away. = Einen Apfel pro Tag und man bleibt gesund.
	population [ˌpɒpjəˈleɪʃn]	Bevölkerung; Population	*population* → populated *Fr.* population *(f)*
	billionaire [ˈbɪliəneə]	Milliardär/-in	
1	**scenery** [ˈsiːnri]	Landschaft	= what you see around you when you're somewhere with a view, e.g. out in the country
	simply [ˈsɪmpli]	einfach nur	Americans usually call their country *simply* 'America'.
	dense [dens]	dicht	*dense* ↔ sparse
	in the country [ˌɪn ðə ˈkʌntri]	auf dem Land	
	mountainous [ˈmaʊntɪnəs]	bergig	
	flat [flæt]	flach; platt	Countryside with no hills is *flat*.
	gigantic [dʒaɪˈgæntɪk]	gigantisch; riesig	Those mountains are *gigantic*!
	wealthy [ˈwelθi]	wohlhabend; reich	*wealthy* ↔ poor
	wasteful [ˈweɪstfl]	verschwenderisch	Don't be *wasteful* with water!
	luxury [ˈlʌkʃri]	Luxus	Wealthy people often spend their money on all kinds of *luxury*.
	to **represent** [ˌreprɪˈzent]	repräsentieren; darstellen; stehen für	*to represent* = to stand for *Fr.* représenter
	to **symbolize** *(AE)* [ˈsɪmbəlaɪz]	symbolisieren	*to symbolise* → symbol *Fr.* symboliser
2	**harsh** [hɑːʃ]	rau; hart	Don't be so *harsh* with him. He already feels bad enough.
	extreme [ɪkˈstriːm]	extrem; radikal	
	standard of living [ˌstændəd əv ˈlɪvɪŋ]	Lebensstandard	In Germany, we enjoy a high *standard of living*.
4	to **become friends** [bɪˌkʌm ˈfrendz]	sich anfreunden; Freundschaft schließen	Tristan and Callum *became friends* some years ago.
	vacation *(AE)* [vəˈkeɪʃn]	Ferien; Urlaub	Summer *vacation* at American schools is at least two, sometimes three months.
	dude *(coll)* [duːd]	Mann; Alter *(ugs.)*	Hey, *dude*! What's up?
	awesome [ˈɔːsəm]	super; spitze	*awesome* = great
	US [juːˈes]	US-amerikanisch	Most *US* teens don't know what it's like to have school uniforms.
	to **have no clue** [ˌhæv nəʊ ˈkluː]	keine Ahnung haben	What's the time? – I *have no clue*.

route planner [ˈruːt ˌplænə]	Routenplaner	
Brit [brɪt]	Brite/Britin *(ugs.)*	
colonist [ˈkɒlənɪst]	Siedler/-in; Kolonist/-in	*colonist* → colony (n)
corn [kɔːn]	Korn; Mais; Getreide	
wheat [wiːt]	Weizen	In the Midwest you can see endless corn and *wheat* fields.
to **ride** [raɪd], **rode** [rəʊd], **ridden** [ˈrɪdn]	fahren; reiten	You can *ride* a bike or a horse.
epic [ˈepɪk]	episch; *hier:* geil	The party was *epic*!
massive [ˈmæsɪv]	riesig; massiv; *hier:* super	*massive* = awesome
complete [kəmˈpliːt]	vollständig; komplett; völlig	Is your picture of America *complete*?

Unit 2 Kids in America

kid [kɪd]	Jugendliche/-r; Kind	Hey *kids*, let's go swimming! *kid* = child

Introduction

1	**impression** [ɪmˈpreʃn]	Impression; Eindruck	What is your *impression* of the US?
3	**orientation** [ˌɔːriənˈteɪʃn]	Orientierung; Orientierungs-	At the *orientation* weekend teenagers get information about teen life in the US.
	to **give a talk** [ˌɡɪv ə ˈtɔːk]	einen Vortrag halten	I'm nervous. I have to *give a talk* at school.
	suburb [ˈsʌbɜːb]	Vorort	Wimbledon is a *suburb* of London.
	suburban [səˈbɜːbn]	Vorstadt-	*Suburban* houses often have lots of space. *suburban* → suburb
	front yard *(AE)* [ˌfrʌnt ˈjɑːd]	Vorgarten	*front yard* ↔ backyard
	shopping mall [ˈʃɒpɪŋ ˌmɔːl]	Einkaufszentrum	
	middle school *(AE)* [ˈmɪdl ˌskuːl]	Mittelschule *(weiterführende Schule in den USA, Mittelstufe)*	Children at *middle school* in the US are usually 13 to 14 years old.
	high school *(AE)* [ˈhaɪ ˌskuːl]	High School *(weiterführende Schule in den USA, Oberstufe)*	= a school in the US for students between the ages of 15 and 18
	hallway [ˈhɔːlweɪ]	Flur; Diele; Korridor	
	hall pass [ˈhɔːl pɑːs]	Erlaubnis, sich während des Unterrichts auf dem Flur aufzu-halten	During lessons students are not allowed to be in the hallway without a *hall pass*.
	dress code [ˈdres ˌkəʊd]	Kleiderordnung; Bekleidungs-vorschriften	The school has a *dress code*, so she can't wear such a short skirt.
	restroom *(AE)* [ˈrestrʊm]	Toilette	

Urban vs. rural

urban centers
city life
crowded, densely populated,
  not enough space
short distances
skyscrapers, tall buildings, downtown
suburb, suburban

rural areas
country life, in the country
farms, corn/wheat fields, mountains
long distances, endless roads
sparsely populated,
  open spaces/lots of space

Write five sentences with these words or phrases.

Station 1: Living here isn't bad

movie *(AE)* ['muːvi]	Film	In *movies*, teen life is often shown as all fun and games.
walk-in closet [ˌwɔːkɪn ˈklɒzɪt]	begehbarer Kleiderschrank	American houses often have *walk-in closets*.
to **be around** [ˌbiː əˈraʊnd]	da sein; zusammen sein mit	There *aren't* many restaurants *around*, just a few.
not until [ˌnɒt ˌənˈtɪl]	nicht vor; erst um/im	My birthday *isn't until* six weeks!
store *(AE)* [stɔː]	Laden; Geschäft	There's a cool new *store* at the mall. Let's check it out!
drive [draɪv]	Fahrt; Anfahrt; Autofahrt	*drive* → to drive
along for the ride [əˌlɒŋ fə ðə ˈraɪd]	mit dabei	My brother doesn't always want me *along for the ride*.
ride [raɪd]	Fahrt; Ritt	*ride* → to ride
curfew [ˈkɜːfjuː]	Sperrstunde; Ausgangssperre	In Germany, the *curfew* for teenagers between sixteen and eighteen is 10 p.m. They have to be home by 10 o'clock.
to **meet up** [ˌmiːtˈʌp]	sich treffen	
downtown *(AE)* [ˌdaʊnˈtaʊn]	im Stadtzentrum	Don't you think malls are boring? Shopping *downtown* is cooler!
to **get used to sth** [ˌget ˈjuːzd tə]	sich an etw. gewöhnen	I don't like to get up early in the morning, but I *got used to* it.
floor [flɔː]	Stockwerk	**!** What you call the first *floor* in Germany is the second *floor* in the US.
elevator *(AE)* [ˈelɪveɪtə]	Aufzug; Lift	
luckily [ˈlʌkɪli]	glücklicherweise	*Luckily*, he found his money and could pay for his lunch.
movie theater *(AE)* [ˈmuːvi ˌθɪətə]	Kino	Let's go to the movies. – OK, which *movie theater*?
soccer *(AE)* [ˈsɒkə]	Fußball	*Soccer* is becoming very popular in the US.
I'm afraid … [ˌaɪm əˈfreɪd]	Leider …	*I'm afraid* I'm very busy right now.
to **keep in touch** [ˌkiːp ɪn ˈtʌtʃ]	in Kontakt bleiben	Let's *keep in touch*.

to **keep** [ki:p], **kept** [kept], **kept** [kept]	*hier:* weiter tun; immer wieder tun	*Keep* smiling, and everything will be fine! = Everything feels better when you smile.
no wonder [ˌnəʊ ˈwʌndə]	kein Wunder	Your dad is American; *no wonder* your English is so good.
Pilgrim [ˈpɪlgrɪm]	Pilger/-in	In 1620 the *Pilgrims* left England for America.
to **practice a religion** [ˌpræktɪs ə rɪˈlɪdʒn]	eine Religion ausüben	
survivor [səˈvaɪvə]	Überlebende/-r	*survivor → to survive*
Native American [ˌneɪtɪv əˈmerɪkən]	Ureinwohner/-in Amerikas; Indianer/-in; indianisch	
harvest [ˈhɑːvɪst]	Ernte	
to **give thanks** [ˌgɪv ˈθæŋks]	danken	At Thanksgiving people *give thanks* for the good things in their lives.
Indian [ˈɪndiən]	Indianer/-in; indianisch	! The terms ‚*Indian*' and ‚Native American' are both fine for describing the original population of what is now the US.
menu [ˈmenjuː]	Speisekarte	
dish [dɪʃ]	Gericht; Speise	What's your favorite *dish*?
instead of [ɪnˈsted əv]	statt; anstatt; an Stelle von	This year we're going to go on vacation in the winter *instead of* the summer.
social media [ˌsəʊʃl ˈmiːdiə]	soziale Netzwerke	Why aren't you on *social media* like everybody else? – Why do I have to do what everybody else does?
to **mind** [maɪnd]	etwas dagegen haben; einem etwas ausmachen	Do you *mind* if I open the window? – No, I don't *mind*.
in the middle of nowhere [ɪn ðə ˌmɪdl əv ˈnəʊweə]	mitten im Nirgendwo	
to **find one's way around** [ˌfaɪnd wʌnz ˌweɪ əˈraʊnd]	sich zurechtfinden	I know New York very well. I know how to *find my way around* in New York.
to **be tired of** [bi ˈtaɪəd əv]	es müde sein (zu); es leid sein (zu); es satt haben (zu)	I'm really *tired of* cleaning up your room all the time. = I really don't want to clean up your room anymore.
likes *(pl)* [laɪks]	Vorlieben	
dislikes *(pl)* [dɪˈslaɪks]	Abneigungen	What are your likes and *dislikes*? = What do you like and what don't you like?
to **unpack** [ʌnˈpæk]	auspacken	
to **dislike** [dɪˈslaɪk]	nicht mögen	*to dislike ↔ to like*
to **dream** [driːm], **dreamt** [dremt], **dreamt** [dremt]	träumen	I *dream* of having my own restaurant one day. = I really want my own restaurant one day. ! *to dream, dreamt/dreamed, dreamt/dreamed*
to **be crazy about** [bi ˈkreɪzi əbaʊt]	verrückt sein nach; abfahren auf	He's *crazy about* posting new selfies. = He loves it when he can post new selfies.
insecure [ˌɪnsɪˈkjʊə]	unsicher	Meeting new people makes me feel *insecure*.
foreground [ˈfɔːgraʊnd]	Vordergrund	*foreground ↔ background*

Likes and dislikes

There are different ways to express likes and dislikes. Sometimes you can use the same verb, sometimes there are totally different ways to express things.

I'm **interested in** meeting new friends.

Living here isn't bad / is cool.
I **like/love** having a big bedroom.
I **hate/dislike** sharing my room.
I **miss** seeing my old friends.
I'm **scared of** changing too much.
I **enjoyed** meeting you.
How about meeting up?
I haven't **got used to** living on the 22nd floor.

I **look forward to** starting school.
I'm **good at** swimming.
Don't **worry about** losing your old friends.

I **keep** forgetting your dad is American.

I **didn't mind** moving to America.
I **don't feel like** going anywhere.
He's **tired of** answering her questions.

I **dream of** going to Australia.
She's **crazy about** going shopping.

I'm **interested in** new friends. / It's great to meet new friends.

Life here isn't bad/is cool.
I **like/love** my big bedroom.
A bedroom on my own **would be great**.
I **miss** my old friends.
I'm **scared of** too many changes.
It was **great** to meet you.
Let's meet up.
I haven't **got used to** our apartment on the 22nd floor.

I **look forward to** my first day at school.
I'm a **good** swimmer.
Don't **worry about** your old friends; you won't lose them.

I **always forget about** the fact that your dad is American.

A new life in America **was no problem** for me.
I don't **want to** go anywhere.
He **doesn't like** it when he has to answer her questions.

I **dream of** a trip to Australia.
She **loves** shopping. / She **loves** it when she can go to cool stores.

Can you think of other ways to say these two sentences?
1. She talked about organizing a party.
2. Stop worrying.

Station 2: That's the worst thing to do!

committee [kəˈmɪti]	Komitee; Ausschuss	*Fr.* comité *(m)*
8th-grader *(AE)* [ˈeɪtθˌɡreɪdə]	Achtklässler/-in	An *8th-grader* is a student in the 8th year of school.
period *(AE)* [ˈpɪəriəd]	Stunde; Unterrichtsstunde	At our school, first *period* starts at 8:00 a.m.
geek [ɡiːk]	Außenseiter/-in	Just because a person isn't super popular doesn't mean he/she is a *geek*.
What a … [ˈwɒt̬ə]	Was für ein/-e …	*What a* dilemma!
shopper [ˈʃɒpə]	Käufer/-in	*shopper → shopping → shop*
child labor *(AE)* [ˌtʃaɪld ˈleɪbə]	Kinderarbeit	
sweatshop [ˈswetʃɒp]	Ausbeuterbetrieb	
to **demonstrate** [ˈdemənstreɪt]	demonstrieren	
right [raɪt]	Recht	Child labor goes against the *rights* of children.
(11) **whether** [ˈweðə]	ob	*whether* = if *(in indirect speech)*

Phrases with superlatives

Why don't you come with us? You're **the only one** to stay at home.	Warum kommst du nicht mit? Du bist die Einzige, die zu Hause bleibt.
If you don't want to walk, it's **the cheapest thing** to take the bus.	Wenn du nicht zu Fuß gehen willst, ist es am günstigsten, den Bus zu nehmen.
On the weekends my dad is always **the first** to get up. My sister is **the last** to have breakfast.	Am Wochenende steht mein Vater immer als Erster auf. Meine Schwester frühstückt als Letzte.
My friends are great. They're **the funniest people** to go out with.	Meine Freunde sind toll! Mit ihnen ist es am lustigsten auszugehen.
Don't stay home alone. It's **the worst thing** to do when you're sad.	Bleib nicht allein zu Hause. Das ist das Schlimmste, was du tun kannst, wenn du traurig bist.
Should I stay or should I go? What's **the best thing** to do?	Soll ich bleiben oder gehen? Was ist am besten?

Write three more sentences with superlative phrases.

Phrases with question words

Matt didn't know **what** to think.	Er wusste nicht, **was** er davon halten sollte.
He was wondering **who** to sit with in the cafeteria.	Er fragte sich, zu **wem** er sich in der Cafeteria setzen sollte/konnte.
He wanted to know **where** to go.	Er wollte wissen, **wohin** er gehen sollte.
He wasn't sure **how much** money to bring.	Er war sich nicht sicher, **wie viel** Geld er mitbringen sollte/musste.
He didn't know **when** to use his locker.	Er wusste nicht, **wann** er seinen Spind benutzen sollte/durfte.
He didn't know **whether** to use his own laptop.	Er wusste nicht, **ob** er seinen eigenen Laptop benutzen sollte/konnte.

Write three more sentences with question words.

13 to **prefer** [prɪˈfɜː]	vorziehen	= to like more/better *Fr.* préférer
14 to **control** [kənˈtrəʊl]	kontrollieren; steuern	My parents *control* everything I do.
might [maɪt]	könnte/-n (vielleicht)	Maybe he'll play well in the match. He *might* even win it!
15 to **argue** [ˈɑːgjuː]	argumentieren; streiten	In a discussion, you use arguments to *argue* for or against something.
16 to **clean out** [ˌkliːnˈaʊt]	ausräumen; entrümpeln	
clothing drive [ˈkləʊðɪŋ ˌdraɪv]	Kleidersammlung	Let's clean out our attic for the *clothing drive*.
homeless shelter [ˈhəʊmləs ˌʃeltə]	Obdachlosenunterkunft	= a place where homeless people can sleep
homeless [ˈhəʊmləs]	obdachlos	

to **wish** [wɪʃ]	(sich) wünschen	*to wish* → wish
to **donate** [dəˈneɪt]	spenden; stiften	= to give money, food, etc. to sb
benefit [ˈbenɪfɪt]	Vorteil; Nutzen; Unterstützung	What's the *benefit* of a clothing drive?
pound [paʊnd]	Pfund *(Maßeinheit)*	In the US, people weigh things in *pounds*, not in kilos.
item [ˈaɪtəm]	Gegenstand; Objekt	We'll get a few cents for every *item* we donate.
drop-off [ˈdrɒpɒf]	Abgabe	The *drop-off* point for clothes is in the cafeteria.

Story: Nightmare at the mall!

nightmare [ˈnaɪtmeə]	Alptraum	= a scary dream
1 **believable** [brˈliːvəbl]	glaubwürdig	The novel has *believable* characters. *believable* → to believe
exaggerated [ɪgˈzædʒreɪtɪd]	übertrieben	*Fr.* exagéré/-e
unrealistic [ˌʌnrɪəˈlɪstɪk]	unrealistisch	Your plan won't work because it's *unrealistic*.
coincidence [kəʊˈɪnsɪdns]	Zufall	There are too many unrealistic *coincidences* in this movie!
to **open** [ˈəʊpn]	eröffnen	He's going to *open* a new sports store.
to **sign** [saɪn]	unterschreiben; unterzeichnen	Please *sign* the letter. *Fr.* signer; *Lat.* signare
amazed [əˈmeɪzd]	erstaunt; verblüfft	
scared [skeəd]	verängstigt; ängstlich	This film is scary. I feel *scared*.
right [raɪt]	direkt	I'm looking for my pen. – It's *right* next to your exercise book.
cheer [tʃɪə]	Jubel; Hurraruf	
dizzy [ˈdɪzi]	schwindelig	Some people feel *dizzy* if they look down from a skyscraper.
down [daʊn]	nieder	*Down* with child labor!
to **escape (from)** [ɪˈskeɪp frəm]	fliehen; entfliehen; flüchten; entkommen	= to run away from sth or sb
protester [ˈprəʊtestə]	Protestierende/-r; Demonstrant/-in	**!** Be careful with the pronunciaton.
to **touch** [tʌtʃ]	berühren; antippen	Don't *touch* the dog, it bites.
troublemaker [ˈtrʌblmeɪkə]	Unruhestifter/-in	*troublemaker* → trouble
to **leave sb alone** [ˌliːv ə'ləʊn]	jmdn. in Ruhe lassen	*Leave me alone*!
obvious [ˈɒbviəs]	offensichtlich	= easy to see or understand *obvious* = clear
twice [twaɪs]	zweimal	= two times
2 **mess** [mes]	Unordnung; Durcheinander; Schweinerei	There's a *mess* in my room. I'll have to tidy it up.
to **mix** [mɪks]	zusammenpassen	These colors don't *mix*.

Action USA! Go on, text her!

	Go on! [ˌgəʊˈɒn]	Los!	*Go on*, don't wait too long!
1	**attractive** [əˈtræktɪv]	attraktiv	**!** Be careful with the word stress.
	boyfriend [ˈbɔɪfrend]	Freund *(in einer Paarbeziehung)*	Is he just a friend, or your *boyfriend*?
	attitude [ˈætɪtjuːd]	Haltung; Einstellung	Your *attitude* to/towards life is the way you feel about it. *Fr.* attitude *(f)*
2	to **overdo** [əʊvəˈduː], **overdid** [əʊvəˈdɪd], **overdone** [əʊvəˈdʌn]	übertreiben; zu weit gehen	Don't you think that's *overdoing* it? I mean, it's a great party outfit, but for school?
3	**date** [deɪt]	Verabredung; Date	Have you got a *date* for the dance yet?

Skills: How to write in the appropriate style

1	**content** [ˈkɒntent]	Inhalt	= the information or ideas e.g. in a book, film, photo, etc.
	toothpaste [ˈtuːθpeɪst]	Zahnpasta	
3	**ironic** [ˌaɪˈrɒnɪk]	ironisch	I love writers with an *ironic* sense of humor.
	informative [ɪnˈfɔːmətɪv]	informativ	Brochures are usually *informative*.
	natural [ˈnætʃrl]	natürlich; Natur-	**!** Be careful with the pronunciation. *natural* → nature
	individual [ˌɪndɪˈvɪdʒuəl]	Einzelperson; Einzelne/-r; Individuum	Each person is an *individual* with his/her own personality.
	pose [pəʊz]	Pose; Haltung	
	season [ˈsiːzn]	Saison; Jahreszeit	Summer is the warmest *season*.
	championship [ˈtʃæmpiənʃɪp]	Meisterschaft	She was the youngest player ever to win the national *championship*.

Unit task: An American-style yearbook

	double [ˈdʌbl]	Doppel-; zweimal	The pictures don't fit on one page, I'll need a *double* page for them.
	concert [ˈkɒnsət]	Konzert	

Important differences

	AE 🇺🇸		BE 🇬🇧	
Different spelling	center		centre	
	Dr.		Dr	
	Mr./Mrs./Ms.		Mr/Mrs/Ms	
	neighbor(hood)		neighbour(hood)	
	to symbolize		to symbolise	
Different words	apartment	mom	flat	mum
	downtown	movie	city centre	film
	elevator	movie theater	lift	cinema
	front yard	period	garden	lesson
	high school	restroom	grammar school	bathroom, toilets
	middle school	soccer	comprehensive school	football
	8th-grader, 8th-grade student	store	Year 8 student	shop
		vacation		holiday

Text smart 2 Advertisements

ad(vertisement) [əd'vɜːtɪsmənt]	Anzeige; Werbespot	
product ['prɒdʌkt]	Produkt; Erzeugnis	! Be careful with the pronunciation. *product* → to produce
just about anywhere [ˌdʒʌstˌəˌbaʊt 'eniweə]	praktisch überall	You can see advertisements for products *just about anywhere* you look.
advertiser ['ædvətaɪzə]	Werbefachmann/-frau	
to win sb over [ˌwɪnˌ'əʊvə]	jmdn. für sich gewinnen; jmdn. überzeugen	Advertisers try to *win* customers *over*.

Introduction

1	brand [brænd]	Marke	= a particular product or line of products made by one company and sold under a special name
	immediately [ɪ'miːdiətli]	sofort; gleich	I don't want to wait any longer. Let's go *immediately*.
	to give away [ˌgɪvˌə'weɪ]	verteilen; verschenken	
	sample ['sɑːmpl]	Probe; Muster	My favorite chocolate company is giving away free *samples* today.
	chocolate bar ['tʃɒklət ˌbɑː]	Schokoriegel	

to **fall for** [ˈfɔːl fə]	hereinfallen auf	You didn't *fall for* that trick, did you?
hair [heə]	Haar; Haare	! Ihre Haare **sind** lang. = Her *hair* **is** long.
to **advertise** [ˈædvətaɪz]	Werbung machen; werben; anpreisen; inserieren	Have you heard about that new phone? They *advertise* it a lot on TV.
receptive [rɪˈseptɪv]	empfänglich	*receptive* → to receive
temptation [tempˈteɪʃn]	Versuchung	*temptation* → to tempt
sceptical [ˈskeptɪkl]	skeptisch	= when you have your doubts about sth
advertising (no pl) [ˈædvətaɪzɪŋ]	Werbung; Reklame	*advertising* → to advertise → advertisement → advertiser

You, one, they

In English there are different words for the German word 'man'. Sometimes you can also translate it with a passive sentence.

You can see advertisements for products just about anywhere **you** look.	**Man** sieht Werbung praktisch überall, wohin **man** schaut.
On the radio, **they** mentioned a big sale at a clothes store.	Im Radio erwähnte **man** einen großen Ausverkauf in einem Kleiderladen./Im Radio **wurde** ein großer Ausverkauf in einem Kleiderladen erwähnt.
One can never know what will happen.	**Man** kann nie wissen, was passieren wird.

'You' and 'they' are very common, but 'one' is for a more formal kind of English, e.g. for business, in formal writing and sometimes in literature too.

Station: Did you see that new ad?

to **spice up** [ˌspaɪsˈʌp]	aufpeppen	*Spice up* your style with some color!
highly [ˈhaɪli]	höchst-	*highly* = very, extremely
brand-new [ˌbrændˈnjuː]	brandneu	
available [əˈveɪləbl]	erhältlich; verfügbar	If sth is *available*, you can get it or buy it.
glamorous [ˈɡlæmrəs]	glamourös	She looks so *glamorous*, like a movie star!
lovely [ˈlʌvli]	schön; hübsch	Thank you, that's a *lovely* present.
nerd [nɜːd]	Nerd *(Person, die intelligent, aber sozial unbeholfen ist)*	
2 **target** [ˈtɑːɡɪt]	Ziel; Ziel-	Who is the *target* group of this advertisement?
eye-catcher [ˈaɪkætʃə]	Blickfang; Hingucker	Her dress is an *eye-catcher*.
visual [ˈvɪʒuəl]	Bild	Ads depend a lot on *visuals*.
ad copy [ˈæd ˌkɒpi]	Werbetext	We've got the visuals for the new ad, but we still need the *ad copy* for it.
image [ˈɪmɪdʒ]	Bild; Abbildung	*Fr.* image *(f)*
billboard [ˈbɪlbɔːd]	Plakatwand	= large outdoor sign for advertisements
4 **approach** [əˈprəʊtʃ]	Herangehensweise; Vorgehensweise; Ansatz; Annäherung	We get the same results but we have different *approaches*. *Fr.* approche *(f)*

truckload ['trʌkləʊd]	Lastwagenladung	The shop gets *truckloads* of new clothes every day so the customers always find something new.
arrival [ə'raɪvl]	Ankommende/-r; Neuzugang	*arrival* → to arrive
to **settle for less** [ˌsetl fə 'les]	sich mit weniger zufrieden geben	I want the best, so why should I *settle for less*?
effective [ɪ'fektɪv]	effektiv; wirkungsvoll	Featuring famous people in ads can be very *effective*.
to **attract** [ə'trækt]	anziehen	What target group are they trying to *attract*?
fabulous ['fæbjələs]	sagenhaft; fantastisch	*Fr.* fabuleux/fabuleuse
5 effectiveness [ɪ'fektɪvnəs]	Effektivität; Wirksamkeit	*effectiveness* → effective

Options

| trash *(AE)* [træʃ] | Abfall; Müll | There's so much *trash* on TV! |
| ugly ['ʌgli] | hässlich | *ugly* ↔ beautiful |

Across cultures 3 School life – dos and don'ts

1 corridor ['kɒrɪdɔ:]	Gang; Flur; Korridor	
gym(nasium) [dʒɪm; dʒɪm'neɪziəm]	Turnhalle	= the room in a school where PE lessons often take place
lab(oratory) [læb; lə'bɒrətri]	Labor	
cell phone *(AE)* ['selfəʊn]	Mobiltelefon; Handy	If you can't reach him at home, try him on his *cell phone*.
to **skip** [skɪp]	auslassen; schwänzen	The girls decided to *skip* class after lunch. Bad idea! That always means trouble.
to **cheat** [tʃi:t]	mogeln; betrügen	She *cheated* on the test, so she had to repeat it. She's *cheating* on her boyfriend. = She's going out with sb else, but her boyfriend doesn't know.
to **get caught** [ˌget 'kɔ:t]	erwischt werden; ertappt werden	She *got caught* by the teacher while she was cheating on a test.
principal *(AE)* ['prɪnsɪpl]	Schulleiter/-in	= the boss of a school in the US
to **be suspended** [bi sə'spendɪd]	suspendiert werden; zeitweilig vom Unterricht ausgeschlossen werden	One of my classmates *was suspended* for two weeks for skipping class so often.
detention [dɪ'tenʃn]	Nachsitzen; Haft; Verhaftung	The whole class got *detention* today.
2 lunchtime ['lʌnʃtaɪm]	Mittagszeit; Mittagspause	At *lunchtime* the students eat in the cafeteria.
to **complete** [kəm'pli:t]	fertigstellen; vervollständigen; vollenden	After ten years the director finally *completed* his epic, 3-hour film.

consequence [ˈkɒnsɪkwəns]	Konsequenz; Folge	
otherwise [ˈʌðəwaɪz]	sonst	I have to do my homework now. *Otherwise* I won't be able to go to the mall later.
3 to **stand in line** *(AE)* [ˌstænd ˌɪn ˈlaɪn]	anstehen; Schlange stehen; (sich) anstellen	In the US, you'll be unpopular very quicklyif you don't *stand in line*.
to **switch off** [ˌswɪtʃ ˈɒf]	ausschalten	*to switch off* = to turn off
5 to **be about to do sth** [bi ˌəˈbaʊt tə]	im Begriff sein, etw. zu tun	Can you help me with my presentation? – I'm *about to go* shopping; I'll help you later.
to **get into trouble** [ˌget ˌɪntə ˈtrʌbl]	in Schwierigkeiten geraten	
so (that) [ˌsəʊ ˈðæt]	damit; so dass	Some students fake hall passes *so that* they can skip classes.
cheat sheet [ˈtʃiːt ʃiːt]	Spickzettel	I've never used a *cheat sheet* in my life!
You'd better … *(= You had better)* [ˈjuːd ˌbetə]	Du solltest lieber …	It's late. *I'd better* go home.
If I were you … [ˌɪf aɪ wɜː ˈjuː]	Wenn ich du wäre …	*If I were you*, I wouldn't say a word to my parents.
No risk, no fun! [nəʊ ˌrɪsk nəʊ ˈfʌn]	Wer nicht wagt, der nicht gewinnt.	You never take any risks. *No risk, no fun!*
mad [mæd]	wütend	He's *mad* at me. = He's angry with me.
I can't see the point of … [aɪ ˌkɑːnt siː ðə ˈpɔɪnt əv]	Ich sehe keinen Sinn darin …	*I can't see the point of* talking to the teacher. He won't change his mind.
waste [weɪst]	Verschwendung	It's a *waste* of time telling him what to do. He'll never change!

Unit 3   City of dreams: New York

Introduction

intersection [ˌɪntəˈsekʃn]	Kreuzung	= where two or more roads meet
district [ˈdɪstrɪkt]	Distrikt; Bezirk	**!** Be careful with the word stress.
lung [lʌŋ]	Lunge	*Lungs* need fresh air.
1 **a pocketful of** [ə ˈpɒkɪtfl̩ əv]	Unmengen von/an	*a pocketful of* = a lot of
gonna (= going to) *(coll)* [ˈgɒnə]	wird/werden	**!** *Gonna* is often used in conversations and in songs.
to **make it** [ˈmeɪk ɪt]	es schaffen	If I can *make it* here, I can *make it* anywhere.
by any means [baɪ ˌenɪ ˈmiːnz]	mit allen Mitteln	I'm going to make it in show business *by any means*, I don't care how!
to **inspire** [ɪnˈspaɪə]	inspirieren; anregen	= to give the idea for sth (e.g. a poem or a song)

melting pot ['meltɪŋ ˌpɒt]	Schmelztiegel	= a place where people from different origins come together to live and form a new culture
jungle ['dʒʌŋgl]	Dschungel	A lot of people call New York a 'concrete *jungle*'.

Station 1: Saving the best for last

to **save the best for last** [ˌseɪv ðə ˌbest fə 'lɑːst]	sich das Beste bis zum Schluss aufheben	
to **take the day off** [ˌteɪk ðə ˌdeɪ 'ɒf]	sich den Tag freinehmen	Diego isn't working. He's *taken the day off*.
diner *(AE)* ['daɪnə]	einfaches Restaurant mit Theke und Tischen	I have breakfast in the *diner* around the corner every morning before I go to work.
conference ['kɒnfrns]	Konferenz; Tagung	*Fr.* conférence *(f)*
guidebook ['gaɪdbʊk]	Reiseführer	In a *guidebook* you can find all the important sights of a city.
to **gasp** [gɑːsp]	tief Luft holen; keuchen	"Oh no! That's terrible!" she *gasped*.
classical ['klæsɪkl]	klassisch	
bank [bæŋk]	Bank	! *bank* (Geldinstitut) ≠ *bench* (Bank zum Sitzen).
sculpture ['skʌlptʃə]	Skulptur	! Be careful with the pronunciation.
since [sɪns]	da	! '*Since*' has two meanings: – *since* I was little = seit … – *since* it's too late = da …
naked ['neɪkɪd]	nackt	! Be careful with the pronunciation: two syllables!
for free [fə 'friː]	umsonst; kostenlos	
on a shoestring [ˌɒn ə 'ʃuːstrɪŋ]	für/mit wenig Geld	Living *on a shoestring* isn't easy in an expensive city like New York.
to **time** [taɪm]	den richtigen Zeitpunkt wählen	If we *time* it right, we'll be at the Empire State Building before it closes.
block [blɒk]	Block; Häuserblock	= an area of land (in a town) with streets on all sides
enthusiasm [ɪn'θjuːziæzm]	Enthusiasmus; Begeisterung	He talks about his city with so much *enthusiasm*!
just in time [ˌdʒʌst ˌɪn 'taɪm]	gerade rechtzeitig	I got to the airport *just in time*. People were already getting on the plane.
sunset ['sʌnset]	Sonnenuntergang	
to **sneak** [sniːk], **snuck** [snʌk], **snuck** [snʌk]	schleichen; schmuggeln	He *snuck* into his bedroom quietly; his parents never knew he'd been gone.
service ['sɜːvɪs]	Service; Dienstleistung; Dienst	*Fr.* service *(m)*; *Lat.* servitium *(nt)*
Leave that to me. [ˌliːv ðæt tə 'miː]	Überlass das mir.	Oh no, what are we going to do? – *Leave that to me*. I always know what to do.
bright [braɪt]	hell; leuchtend; strahlend	In the summer, the sun is very *bright*.
2 **tour company** ['tʊə ˌkʌmpəni]	Reiseanbieter	I like *tour companies* that offer unusual tours.
3 to **be located** [bi ləʊ'keɪtɪd]	gelegen sein; liegen	Where *is* the museum *located*? = Where exactly is the museum? *to be located in* → location *(n)*

4	**subway** (AE) ['sʌbweɪ]	U-Bahn	
✕	to **groan** [grəʊn]	stöhnen	= a sound that shows you're hurt, unhappy or disappointed
6	**statue** ['stætʃuː]	Statue; Standbild	Oh look, that's not a *statue*; it's a man!
	liberty ['lɪbəti]	Freiheit	*Fr.* liberté *(f)*
	artist ['ɑːtɪst]	Künstler/-in	*artist* → art
	tablet ['tæblət]	Tafel	The Statue of Liberty is holding a torch and a *tablet*.
	spike [spaɪk]	Spitze; Stachel	The Statue of Liberty's crown has seven *spikes*.
	to **base on** ['beɪsˌɒn]	stützen auf	The character in the story is *based on* a real person.
	goddess ['gɒdes]	Göttin	What's the name of the Roman *goddess* of liberty?
✕	to **be known as** [bi 'nəʊnˌæz]	bekannt sein als	
	enlightenment [ɪn'laɪtnmənt]	Aufklärung; Erleuchtung	The Statue of Liberty's torch stands for *enlightenment*.
8	**ethnic** ['eθnɪk]	ethnisch; Volks-; *hier:* exotisch	What's your *ethnic* background? – I'm half German and half Spanish.
	from the outside [ˌfrəm ðiˌ aʊt'saɪd]	von außen	*From the outside*, the restaurant doesn't look very nice.
✕	**delicious** [dɪ'lɪʃəs]	köstlich	Mmm, this cake is *delicious*.
✕	**fried** [fraɪd]	gebraten *(in der Pfanne)*	*Fried* food is delicious – but you mustn't eat too much of it.
	pastry ['peɪstri]	Teig; Teigtasche	
	filling ['fɪlɪŋ]	Füllung	This pastry has a vegetarian *filling*.
✕	**Jewish** ['dʒuːɪʃ]	jüdisch	A bagel with lox is typical *Jewish* food.
	truck (AE) [trʌk]	*hier:* Wagen	Are there any food *trucks* in the area?
	cart [kɑːt]	Karrenw	an ice-cream *cart*
	New Yorker [ˌnjuːˈjɔːkə]	New Yorker/-in	= a person who is from New York City
	to **combine** [kəm'baɪn]	kombinieren; verbinden	Can you *combine* red and pink?
	flavor (AE) ['fleɪvə]	Geschmack; Aroma	Two ice creams, please. – What *flavor*? – One chocolate and one banana.
	specialty (AE) ['speʃlti]	Spezialität; Besonderheit	
	combination [ˌkɒmbɪ'neɪʃn]	Kombination; Verbindung	*combination* → to combine
10	**hometown** ['həʊmtaʊn]	Heimatstadt	*hometown* → home
✕	**spot** [spɒt]	Fleck; Ort	We found a quiet *spot* in the park and sat down on the grass.

Station 2: Life is a trip

	to **lift** [lɪft]	heben; hochheben; anheben	You can really hurt yourself if you try to *lift* something that's too heavy.
	trunk (AE) [trʌŋk]	Kofferraum	

to **be done with** [bi ˈdʌn wɪð]	fertig sein mit	I'*m done with* you, I don't want to see you again!
break [breɪk]	Durchbruch	He'd been hoping for his big *break* for five years.
rejection [rɪˈdʒektʃn]	Ablehnung; Absage	He got one *rejection* after the other.
to **come true** [ˌkʌm ˈtruː]	wahr werden; in Erfüllung gehen	Wouldn't it be wonderful if our dreams always *came true*?
good luck [ˌɡʊd ˈlʌk]	(viel) Glück	Emilio wished the man *good luck*.
sidewalk *(AE)* [ˈsaɪdwɔːk]	Gehweg; Gehsteig	
businessman [ˈbɪznɪsmæn]	Geschäftsmann	The passenger looked like a successful *businessman*.
not necessarily [ˌnɒt nesəˈserəli]	nicht notwendigerweise; nicht unbedingt	Seeing New York on a shoestring is impossible! – That's *not necessarily* true. Central Park, for example, is free.
however [haʊˈevə]	jedoch	The man had lots of money. *However*, he wasn't happy with his life.
bill *(AE)* [bɪl]	Geldschein; Rechnung	The suitcase was full of 100$ *bills*. We'd like to pay. Can you bring us the *bill*, please?
change [tʃeɪndʒ]	Münzgeld; Wechselgeld	That'll be $8.50, please. – Here's $10.00. Keep the *change*.
to **get in** [ˌɡetˈɪn]	einsteigen	Agree on the price before you *get in* a taxi.
yet [jet]	doch; und trotzdem; und dennoch	*Yet* is used to add sth that seems surprising after what has been said.
to **complain** [kəmˈpleɪn]	sich beschweren; sich beklagen	My soup was cold, so I *complained*.
to **shop** [ʃɒp]	einkaufen; shoppen	New York City is a great place to *shop*.
needless to say [ˌniːdləs tə ˈseɪ]	natürlich; selbstverständlich	When we got home, our teenage kids were having a huge, loud party. *Needless to say*, we weren't happy!
tip [tɪp]	Trinkgeld	In the US, before you leave a café or restaurant, it's normal to leave a *tip* of at least 15%, often 20%.
16 **grade** *(AE)* [ɡreɪd]	Note	! The best *grade* in American schools is A+; the worst is F (there's no E). Some schools use a number system: 4.00 is the best; 0.00 the worst.
18 **busker** [ˈbʌskə]	Straßenmusikant/-in	= sb who plays music or sings for money in city streets or stations
to **perform** [pəˈfɔːm]	aufführen; auftreten	If you *perform* a play, you act it in front of people who come to watch it.
freeway *(AE)* [ˈfriːweɪ]	Autobahn	
to **transport** [trænˈspɔːt]	transportieren; befördern	= to take from one place to another *Fr.* transporter
lorry [ˈlɒri]	Lastwagen	
19 to **fail to do sth** [ˈfeɪl tə]	versäumen, etw. zu tun; es nicht schaffen, etw. zu tun	A lot of actors *fail to* find success.
rags to riches [ˌræɡz təˈrɪtʃɪz]	vom Tellerwäscher zum Millionär	There are lots of Hollywood movies with a *rags to riches* storyline.

to **make a living (from)** [ˌmeɪk ə ˈlɪvɪŋ frəm]	seinen Lebensunterhalt bestreiten (mit)	She *makes a living* from piano lessons.
either ... or ... [ˈaɪðə/ˈiːðə ... ɔː]	entweder ... oder ...	You have to decide now: You can have *either* this one *or* that one, but not both.

Story: Asphalt Tribe

3	**panel** [ˈpænl]	Bild *(eines Comics)*	
	lead-in [ˈliːdɪn]	Einführung; Einleitung	
	shape [ʃeɪp]	Form	
	sequence [ˈsiːkwəns]	Abfolge; Reihenfolge	The *sequence* of comic panels is very important.
	consecutive [kənˈsekjʊtɪv]	aufeinanderfolgend; fortlaufend	The panels here are arranged *consecutively*.
	to **overlap** [ˌəʊvəˈlæp]	(sich) überlappen	The pictures in the book *overlap*, which I think looks cool.
	to **lay** [leɪ], **laid** [leɪd], **laid** [leɪd]	legen	
	to **make use of** [meɪk ˈjuːz əv]	benutzen; verwenden	What tricks do they *make use of*?
	long shot [ˈlɒŋ ʃɒt]	Totale *(Kameraeinstellung)*	Let's use a *long shot* for this scene so we can see everything that's going on.
	medium shot [ˈmiːdiəm ʃɒt]	Halbtotale *(Kameraeinstellung)*	
	medium [ˈmiːdiəm]	mittel; mittelgroß	What size do you wear: small, *medium* or large?
	effect [ɪˈfekt]	Effekt; Wirkung	You should always think of the *effects* of your actions before you do something. *Fr.* effet *(m)*
	stylistic [staɪˈlɪstɪk]	Stil-; stilistisch	*stylistic* → style
	speed [spiːd]	Geschwindigkeit	This movie has a lot of *speed*.

Action USA! New Yorkers don't do things like that!

1	to **cringe** [krɪndʒ]	schaudern; sich ducken	If you *cringe* about sth, you feel very embarrassed by it. Usually, it's what sb else has done.
2	**unexpected** [ˌʌnɪkˈspektɪd]	unerwartet	*unexpected* → to expect

Skills: How to conduct a podcast interview

	to **conduct** [kənˈdʌkt]	durchführen; ausführen	*to conduct* an interview
1	**path** [pɑːθ]	Pfad; Weg	Rita's *path* to success was long and hard.
2	**follow-up** [ˈfɒləʊʌp]	Fortsetzung; Folge-	*follow-up* → to follow → the following
	talk [tɔːk]	Gespräch; Unterhaltung	*talk* → to talk

Important differences

	AE 🇺🇸		BE 🇬🇧	
Different spelling	flavor, labor		flavour, labour	
	specialty		speciality	
	to realize		to realise	
	to practice		to practise	
	traveling		travelling	
Different words	bill	sidewalk	note	pavement
	cell phone	subway	mobile phone	underground
	freeway	trash	motorway	rubbish
	grade	truck	class	lorry
	intersection	trunk	crossroad	boot
	period	yard	lesson	garden
	principal		head teacher	

Text smart 3 Internet texts

Introduction

	reliable [rɪˈlaɪəbl]	verlässlich; zuverlässig; vertrau-enswürdig	He's very *reliable*. He always does what he says he'll do.
1	**inconvenient** [ˌɪnkənˈviːniənt]	unbequem; lästig	Hi, can I ask you something? – Er, it's a bit *inconvenient* right now. Later?
	up-to-date [ˌʌptəˈdeɪt]	modern; zeitgemäß; aktuell	
	tutorial [tjuːˈtɔːriəl]	Tutorium; Tutorial	I often watch *tutorials* about cooking on the Internet.
3	**moon landing** [ˈmuːn ˌlændɪŋ]	Mondlandung	
	science [saɪəns]	Wissenschaft; Naturwissenschaft	*science* → scientist *Fr.* science *(f); Lat.* scientia *(f)*
	astronaut [ˈæstrənɔːt]	Astronaut/-in	
	human [ˈhjuːmən]	Mensch	Neil Armstrong was the first *human* on the moon.
	to be considered (to be) sth [bi kənˈsɪdəd tə]	als etw. gelten	Germany *is considered to* be one of the richest countries in the world.

Station 1: An online wiki text

	wiki (text) ['wɪkɪ ˌtekst]	Wikitext	
	mission ['mɪʃn]	Mission; Auftrag	Our *mission* as a team is to win the championship.
	to **touch down** [tʌtʃ 'daʊn]	landen	In 1969 Apollo 11 *touched down* on the moon.
	surface ['sɜːfɪs]	Oberfläche	*Fr.* surface (f)
	to **announce** [ə'naʊns]	ankündigen; durchsagen	*to announce* → announcement *Fr.* annoncer; *Lat.* ad + nuntiare
	to **step** [step]	treten; steigen	*to step* → step
	president ['prezɪdnt]	Präsident/-in	! Watch the word stress.
	priority [praɪ'ɒrəti]	Priorität; Vorrang	The moon landing was one of President John F. Kennedy's top *priorities*.
	to **challenge** ['tʃælɪndʒ]	herausfordern	*to challenge* → challenge
	engineer [ˌendʒɪ'nɪə]	Ingenieur/-in; Techniker/-in	
	political [pə'lɪtɪkl]	politisch	Do you like watching TV programs about *political* problems?
5	**hoax** [həʊks]	Täuschung; Trick	Some people say that the moon landing was a *hoax*.
	conspiracy [kən'spɪrəsi]	Verschwörung	Is there a *conspiracy* against the Queen? *Fr.* conspiration (f); *Lat.* conspiratio (f)
	theory ['θɪəri]	Theorie	
	to **stage** [steɪdʒ]	inszenieren; aufführen	How difficult would it be to *stage* something like the moon landing?
	the public [ðə 'pʌblɪk]	die Öffentlichkeit	Stars sometimes want to hide from *the public*. *Fr.* public (m); *Lat.* publicum (nt)
	to **involve** [ɪn'vɒlv]	involvieren; einbeziehen; beteiligen	If you *involve* sb in sth, you include them, e.g. in a situation or activity.
	cover-up ['kʌvərʌp]	Vertuschung	*cover-up* → to cover
	government ['ɡʌvnmənt]	Regierung	= a group of people whose job it is to run a country and deal with its problems
6	**complicated** ['kɒmplɪkeɪtɪd]	kompliziert	The rules of this game are too *complicated*!
	impossible [ɪm'pɒsəbl]	unmöglich	*impossible* ↔ possible *Fr.* impossible
	to **make sense** [ˌmeɪk 'sens]	Sinn ergeben; einleuchten	If sth *makes sense*, you can understand it.
	at the time [ˌət ðə 'taɪm]	damals	
	to **run** [rʌn]	betreiben; leiten; führen	My parents *run* a restaurant.
	tech [tek]	Technologie; Technik	The US is famous for its *tech* companies, e.g. in Silicon Valley or Seattle.
7	**respect** [rɪ'spekt]	Respekt	Honest bloggers will enjoy their readers' *respect*.
	entertaining [ˌentə'teɪnɪŋ]	unterhaltsam	*entertaining* ↔ boring
8	**function** ['fʌŋkʃn]	Funktion	Every text has a *function*.
	to **trick** [trɪk]	austricksen; täuschen	*to trick* → trick
	to **estimate** ['estɪmeɪt]	schätzen	I *estimate* her stay in hospital to take a week.

| to **question** [ˈkwestʃən] | fragen; hinterfragen | Our trainer always *questions* our motivation. |
| **critical** [ˈkrɪtɪkl] | kritisch | *critical* → self-critical |

Station 2: Online ratings

10	to **rate** [reɪt]	bewerten; einstufen	*to rate* → rating
11	**space** [speɪs]	Weltraum; Weltall	There's endless space in *space*.
	space program [ˈspeɪs prəʊɡræm]	Raumfahrtprogramm	There's a Mars *space program*, but will there ever really be a human on Mars?
12	**breathtaking** [ˈbreθˌteɪkɪŋ]	atemberaubend	The visuals in the movie were *breathtaking*.
	well-written [ˌwelˈrɪtn]	gut geschrieben	I think the story is *well-written*.
	disappointing [ˌdɪsəˈpɔɪntɪŋ]	enttäuschend	How was the movie? – It was very *disappointing*. A waste of time!
14	**special effect** [ˌspeʃlˌɪˈfekt]	Spezialeffekt	In action movies the *special effects* are often as important as the story.
	well-developed [ˌweldɪˈveləpt]	gut entwickelt; ausgereift	You know a character is *well-developed* when he/she seems believable, like sb you know.
	undeveloped [ˌʌndɪˈveləpt]	unentwickelt; unausgereift	*undeveloped* ↔ well-developed
	badly-written [ˌbædliˈrɪtn]	schlecht geschrieben	*badly-written* ↔ well-written
	weak [wiːk]	schwach	*weak* ↔ strong

How words can start or end

You can use prefixes and suffixes to make new words from the same word family.

adjectives

in-	direct, convenient, secure	help, hope, thank, use	**-ful**
im-	possible	help, end, use	**-less**
ir-	regular	health, luck, cloud	**-y**
un-	expected, developed, realistic		
dis-	honest		

verbs

dis-	appear, agree, obey	! Be careful with the pronunciation:
re-	build, read, tell, write	In English, you don't put the stress on the prefix.
un-	wrap, pack	<u>hon</u>est – dis<u>hon</u>est
mis-	behave, understand	

nouns

re-	action, discovery	interview, report, sing	**-er**
ex-	change	champion, friend, relation	**-ship**
in-	dependence	surf, swim(m)	**-ing**
		invent, narrat(e), surviv(e)	**-or**
		demonstrat(e), organiz(e)	**-ion/-ation**
		settle, improve	**-ment**

Write sentences with one word from each group.

Across cultures 4 What you say and how you say it

	register [ˈredʒɪstə]	Sprachebene; Register	It's important to change your *register* to match the situation you're in. That means you should always use the right language for the right situation.
2	**Canadian** [kəˈneɪdiən]	kanadisch; Kanadier/-in	= sb or sth from Canada
	to **pronounce** [prəˈnaʊns]	aussprechen	**!** Be careful with the spelling: to pron**ou**nce [aʊ] – pron**u**nciation [ʌ]
	schedule *(AE)* [ˈʃedjuːl; ˈskedʒuːl]	Stundenplan; Fahrplan; Termin- kalender	
	though [ðəʊ]	doch; jedoch; obwohl	I tried my best, but I just couldn't win the race. I don't mind *though*. Winning isn't everything.
	water fountain [ˈwɔːtə ˌfaʊntɪn]	Wasserspender	
4	**informal** [ɪnˈfɔːml]	informell; zwanglos	*informal* ↔ formal
	nope *(infml)* [nəʊp]	nee; nö	= a very informal word for 'no'
	It sucks. *(slang)* [ɪt ˈsʌks]	Das ist zum Kotzen.	**!** Only use this phrase when you talk to your friends.
	ain't (= isn't/aren't) [eɪnt]	ist nicht; sind nicht	**!** It isn't good English to use *ain't*, but one hears it quite often. It's typical to use it in ‚double negative' sentences which are incorrect grammar: „I'm not doing anything for her!" → „I *ain't* doing nothing for her!"
	totally [ˈtəʊtli]	völlig; total	*totally* = completely
	whatever [wɒtˈevə]	was/wie auch immer; egal (was/welche)	
	no more [ˌnəʊ ˈmɔː]	nicht mehr	*no more* = not anymore
	(I) didn't mean to … [aɪ ˌdɪdnt ˈmiːn tə]	Ich wollte nicht …	Sorry! *I didn't mean to* be rude.
	auntie [ˈɑːnti]	Tantchen	
	not … either [nɒt … ˈaɪðə; nɒt … ˈiːðə]	auch nicht	He doesn't like her. She doesn*'t* like him *either*.
	to **mind sth** [maɪnd]	auf etw. aufpassen	*Mind* your language: Don't be rude.

Dictionary

In dieser alphabetischen Wortliste findest du das gesamte Vokabular von *Green Line* 1, 2, 3 und 4.
Namen stehen in einer extra Liste am Ende des *Dictionary*.
Einträge, die aus mehreren Wörtern bestehen, kannst du meist unter verschiedenen
Stichwörtern nachschlagen. So ist z.B. *after all* unter *after* und unter *all* eingetragen.
Die Fundstellen stehen immer hinter dem jeweiligen Wort und zeigen dir an, wo es zum ersten Mal vorkommt, z.B.:
air-conditioning [ˌeəkən'dɪʃnɪŋ] Klimaanlage **IV U1**, 17 kommt zum ersten Mal vor in Band 4, Unit 1, Seite 17
advertising *(no pl)* ['ædvətaɪzɪŋ] Werbung; Reklame **IVTS2**, 64 kommt zum ersten Mal vor in Band 4, Text smart 2, Seite 64
U = Unit, AC = Across cultures, TS = Text smart
Die mit * gekennzeichneten Verben sind unregelmäßig.
Die mit ° gekennzeichneten Vokabeln sind rezeptiv.
Die mit ⟨ ⟩ gekennzeichneten Vokabeln sind fakultativ.

A

a [ə] ein/-e I
　a bit [ə 'bɪt] ein bisschen; ein wenig II
　a couple of [ə 'kʌpl əv] ein paar I
　a few [ə 'fjuː] ein paar; wenige; einige I
　a girl from Germany [ə ˌgɜːl frəm 'dʒɜːməni] ein Mädchen aus Deutschland I
　a group of three [ə ˌgruːp əv 'θriː] eine Dreiergruppe I
　a little [ə 'lɪtl] ein wenig; etwas I
　a lot [ə 'lɒt] viel I
　a lot of [ə 'lɒt əv] viel/-e; eine Menge I
　a (day/week/year) [ə 'deɪ/wiːk/jɪə] pro (Tag/Woche/Jahr) **IV AC2**, 39
　a lot to learn [ə ˌlɒt tə 'lɜːn] viel zu lernen I
a.m. [ˌeɪ'em] vormittags *(Uhrzeit)* I
*to be able to (do sth) [bi ˌeɪbl tə] fähig sein zu; können; dürfen I
aboard [ə'bɔːd] an Bord I
about [ə'baʊt] ungefähr; circa; etwa I
　out and about [ˌaʊt ən ə'baʊt] unterwegs II
about [ə'baʊt] über; von I
　*to be about to do sth [bi ə'baʊt tə] im Begriff sein, etw. zu tun **IV AC3**, 69
　What about …? ['wɒt ˌəbaʊt] Wie wär's mit …?; Was ist mit …? I
　What is … about? [ˌwɒt ɪz …ə'baʊt] Worum geht es in/im …? I
above [ə'bʌv] oben II
abroad [ə'brɔːd] im Ausland; ins Ausland **IV U1**, 10
absolutely [ˌæbsə'luːtli] absolut; völlig II
accent ['æksnt] Akzent III
to accept [ək'sept] akzeptieren; hinnehmen; annehmen **IV U1**, 16
accident ['æksɪdnt] Unfall II
account settings [ə'kaʊnt ˌsetɪŋz] Profileinstellungen III
across [ə'krɒs] auf der anderen Seite von; über; hinüber; herüber; quer durch I
　Across cultures [əˌkrɒs 'kʌltʃəz] Interkulturelles I

to act [ækt] spielen *(Theater)* I; sich verhalten; handeln °**IV AC3**, 68
　to act like ['ækt laɪk] tun als ob II
　to act out [ˌækt 'aʊt] nachspielen II
　acting a scene [ˌæktɪŋ ə 'siːn] eine Theaterszene spielen I
acting ['æktɪŋ] Schauspielen III
action ['ækʃn] Handlung; Action; Aktion I
active ['æktɪv] aktiv III
activity [æk'tɪvəti] Aktivität I
actor ['æktə] Schauspieler II
actual ['æktʃuəl] tatsächlich; wirklich; eigentlich °**IV U3**, 92
ad [ˌæd'vɜːtɪsmənt] Anzeige; Werbespot **IVTS2**, 64
　ad copy ['æd ˌkɒpi] Werbetext **IVTS2**, 65
AD (= Anno Domini) [ˌeɪ'diː] nach Christus III
to add [æd] hinzufügen; ergänzen I
addict ['ædɪkt] Süchtige/-r; Abhängige/-r **IV U1**, 10
additional [ə'dɪʃnl] zusätzlich II
address [ə'dres] Adresse I
adjective ['ædʒɪktɪv] Adjektiv; Eigenschaftswort II
adult ['ædʌlt] Erwachsene/-r II
adventure [əd'ventʃə] Abenteuer II
adverb ['ædvɜːb] Adverb II
advert ['ædvɜːt] Anzeige; Werbespot III
to advertise ['ædvətaɪz] Werbung machen; werben; anpreisen; inserieren **IVTS2**, 64
advertisement [əd'vɜːtɪsmənt] Anzeige; Werbespot **IVTS2**, 64
advertiser ['ædvətaɪzə] Werbefachmann/-frau **IVTS2**, 64
advertising *(no pl)* ['ædvətaɪzɪŋ] Werbung; Reklame **IVTS2**, 64
advice [əd'vaɪs] Rat; Ratschlag II
to afford [ə'fɔːd] sich leisten III
*to be afraid (of) [bi ə'freɪd əv] (sich) fürchten; Angst haben (vor) **IV U1**, 8
I'm afraid … [aɪm ə'freɪd] Leider … **IV U2**, 44
after ['ɑːftə] nach *(zeitlich)* I
　after all [ˌɑːftər 'ɔːl] doch; schließlich; immerhin I
　after that [ˌɑːftə 'ðæt] danach I

afternoon [ˌɑːftə'nuːn] Nachmittag I
　this afternoon [ðɪs 'ɑːftənuːn] heute Nachmittag I
afterwards ['ɑːftəwədz] danach; hinterher °**IVTS2**, 67
again [ə'gen] wieder; noch einmal; noch mal I
　over and over again [ˌəʊvər ən ˌəʊvər ə'gen] immer wieder III
against [ə'genst] gegen II
　against all odds [əˌgenst ɔːl 'ɒdz] entgegen allen Erwartungen III
age [eɪdʒ] Alter; Zeitalter III
　Bronze Age ['brɒnz eɪdʒ] Bronzezeit *(ca. 2200–800 v. Chr.)* III
　golden age [ˌgəʊldn 'eɪdʒ] goldenes Zeitalter III
travel agency ['trævl ˌeɪdʒnsi] Reisebüro III
travel agent's ['trævl ˌeɪdʒnts] Reisebüro III
aggressive [ə'gresɪv] aggressiv II
ago [ə'gəʊ] vor *(zeitlich)* II
agony aunt ['ægəni ˌɑːnt] Kummerkastentante II
to agree (on) [ə'griː] sich einigen (auf) III
to agree (with) [ə'griː] einer Meinung sein (mit); zustimmen III
ain't (= isn't/aren't) [eɪnt] ist nicht; sind nicht **IV AC4**, 107
air [eə] Luft III
air-conditioning [ˌeəkən'dɪʃnɪŋ] Klimaanlage **IV U1**, 17
air-force base ['eəfɔːs ˌbeɪs] Luftwaffenstützpunkt ⟨**IVTS3**, 102⟩
airport ['eəpɔːt] Flughafen II
aka [ˌeɪkeɪ'eɪ] alias °**IV U3**, 79
alarm clock [ə'lɑːm ˌklɒk] Wecker II
alien ['eɪliən] Außerirdische/-r; außerirdisches Wesen I
all [ɔːl] alle/-s; ganz I
　after all [ˌɑːftər 'ɔːl] doch; schließlich; immerhin I
　all alone [ˌɔːl ə'ləʊn] ganz allein ⟨**IVTS3**, 104⟩
　all day [ˌɔːl 'deɪ] den ganzen Tag II
　all night [ˌɔːl 'naɪt] die ganze Nacht I
　all over [ˌɔːl'əʊvə] überall (in) I

all the time [ˌɔ:l ðə ˈtaɪm] die ganze Zeit **II**
at **all** [ət ˈɔ:l] überhaupt **I**
all of them [ˈɔ:l əv ˌðem] alle **I**
all of us [ˈɔ:l əv ˌʌs] wir alle **III**
to pledge **allegiance** [ˌpledʒ əˈli:dʒns] Treueschwur leisten ⟨**IV U2**, 49⟩
bowling **alley** [ˈbəʊlɪŋ ˌæli] Bowlingbahn **I**
*to be **allowed** to (do sth) [bi əˈlaʊd tə]
dürfen **II**
almost [ˈɔ:lməʊst] fast; beinahe **II**
alone [əˈləʊn] allein; ohne fremde Hilfe **I**
all **alone** [ˌɔ:l əˈləʊn] ganz allein
⟨**IVTS3**, 104⟩
*to leave sb **alone** [ˌli:v əˈləʊn] jmdn. in
Ruhe lassen **IV U2**, 53
along [əˈlɒŋ] entlang **I**
*to sing **along** [ˌsɪŋ əˈlɒŋ] mitsingen **III**
along for the ride [əˌlɒŋ fə ðə ˈraɪd] mit
dabei **IV U2**, 44
alphabet [ˈælfəbet] Alphabet **I**
alphabetical [ˌælfəˈbetɪkl] alphabetisch **II**
already [ɔ:lˈredi] schon; bereits **I**
also [ˈɔ:lsəʊ] auch **II**
although [ɔ:lˈðəʊ] obwohl **IV U1**, 13
always [ˈɔ:lweɪz] immer; ständig **I**
amazed [əˈmeɪzd] erstaunt; verblüfft
IV U2, 52
amazing [əˈmeɪzɪŋ] unglaublich; toll;
erstaunlich **II**
ambulance [ˈæmbjələns] Krankenwagen **III**
American [əˈmerɪkən] Amerikanisch; amerikanisch; aus Amerika; Amerikaner/-in **II**
Native **American** [ˌneɪtɪv əˈmerɪkən]
Ureinwohner/-in Amerikas; Indianer/-in;
indianisch **IV U2**, 45
among [əˈmʌŋ] unter; inmitten **III**
amount (of) [əˈmaʊnt] Menge °**IVTS3**, 105
an [ən] ein/-e **I**
to **analyze** (AE) [ˈænlaɪz] analysieren
°**IV U2**, 43
ancient [ˈeɪnʃnt] alt; altertümlich; antik
⟨**IVTS3**, 102⟩
and [ænd; ənd] und **I**
angel [ˈeɪndʒl] Engel **IVTS1**, 31
anger (no pl) [ˈæŋgə] Zorn; Wut **III**
angry [ˈæŋgri] wütend; zornig; verärgert;
böse **I**
*to make sb **angry** [meɪk ˈæŋgri] jmdn.
wütend machen; jmdn. verärgern **III**
animal [ˈænɪməl] Tier **I**
animal shelter [ˈænɪml ˌʃeltə] Tierheim **III**
ankle [ˈæŋkl] Fußgelenk; Fußknöchel **II**
to twist your **ankle** [ˌtwɪst jɔ:r ˈæŋkl] sich
den Knöchel verrenken **II**
to **announce** [əˈnaʊns] ankündigen; durchsagen **IVTS3**, 101
announcement [əˈnaʊnsmənt] Ankündigung; Durchsage **III**
anonymous [ənˈɒnɪməs] anonym **II**
another [əˈnʌðə] ein/-e andere/-r/-s; noch
ein/-e; ein/-e andere/-r/-s **I**
answer [ˈɑ:nsə] Antwort **I**

short **answer** [ˌʃɔ:t ˈɑ:nsə] Kurzantwort **I**
to **answer** [ˈɑ:nsə] antworten; beantworten **I**
to **answer** the phone [ˌɑ:nsə ðə ˈfəʊn]
einen Anruf entgegennehmen **I**
answering machine [ˈɑ:nsrɪŋ məˌʃi:n]
Anrufbeantworter **I**
anthem [ˈænθəm] Hymne **III**
any [ˈeni] irgendein/-e/-er; irgendwelche **I**
not **any** more [ˌnɒt eni ˈmɔ:] nicht mehr **I**
not … **any** [nɒt … eni] kein/-e/-en **I**
not **anymore** (AE) [ˌnɒt eniˈmɔ:] nicht mehr
IV AC2, 39
anyone else [ˌeniwʌn ˈels] jemand anderes **II**
Anything else? [ˌeniθɪŋ ˈels] Sonst noch
etwas? **I**
not … **anything** [ˌnɒt ˈeniθɪŋ] nichts **I**
anyway [ˈeniweɪ] trotzdem; jedenfalls;
sowieso **II**
anywhere [ˈeniweə] irgendwo; überall (egal,
wo) **II**
just about **anywhere** [ˌdʒʌst əˌbaʊt
ˈeniweə] praktisch überall **IVTS2**, 64
apart from [əˈpɑ:t frəm] abgesehen von;
außer **IV U1**, 11
apartment (AE) [əˈpɑ:tmənt] Apartment;
Wohnung **IV U2**, 43
to **apologise** [əˈpɒlədʒaɪz] sich entschuldigen **II**
app [æp] App **II**
apple [ˈæpl] Apfel **I**
approach [əˈprəʊtʃ] Herangehensweise;
Vorgehensweise; Ansatz; Annäherung
IVTS2, 66
appropriate [əˈprəʊpriət] angemessen **III**
April [ˈeɪprəl] April **I**
Arab [ˈærəb] arabisch **IV U1**, 20
architect [ˈɑ:kɪtekt] Architekt/-in **II**
How **are** you? [ˌhaʊ ˈɑ: jə] Wie geht es dir?;
Wie geht es euch?; Wie geht es Ihnen? **I**
area [ˈeəriə] Areal; Gebiet; Fläche **II**
run **area** [ˈrʌn ˌeəriə] Gehege; Auslauf **III**
to **argue** [ˈɑ:gju:] argumentieren; streiten
IV U2, 51
argument [ˈɑ:gjəmənt] Auseinandersetzung; Streit; Argument **III**
arm [ɑ:m] Arm **II**
around [əˈraʊnd] um … herum; umher **I**
*to be **around** [bi əˈraʊnd] da sein; zusammen sein mit **IV U2**, 44
*to find one's way **around** [ˌfaɪnd wʌnz ˌweɪ
əˈraʊnd] sich zurechtfinden **IV U2**, 46
to turn **around** [ˌtɜ:n (ə)ˈraʊnd] (sich) umdrehen; wenden **II**
to **arrange** [əˈreɪndʒ] arrangieren; anordnen
III
to **arrest** [əˈrest] festnehmen; verhaften **II**
arrival [əˈraɪvl] Ankunft **IV U1**, 9; Ankom-
mende/-r; Neuzugang **IVTS2**, 66
arrivals hall [əˈraɪvlz ˌhɔ:l] Ankunftshalle
IV U1, 9
to **arrive** [əˈraɪv] ankommen **III**

arrow [ˈærəʊ] Pfeil **III**
Art [ɑ:t] Kunstunterricht **I**
art [ɑ:t] Kunst **II**
article [ˈɑ:tɪkl] Artikel; Bericht (in einer
Zeitschrift, Zeitung) **II**
reference **article** [ˈrefrns ˌɑ:tɪkl] Referenzartikel **III**
artist [ˈɑ:tɪst] Künstler/-in **IV U3**, 74
as [æz; əz] als **II**
as if [əzˈɪf] als ob **III**
as … **as** [əz … əz] so … wie **I**
as [æz] während; indem **I**; wie **II**
as long **as** [əz ˈlɒŋ əz] solange ⟨**IVTS1**, 34⟩
as soon **as** [əz ˈsu:n əz] sobald **II**
to **ask** [ɑ:sk] fragen; bitten **I**
Ask about … [ˈɑ:sk əˌbaʊt] Frage/Fragt
nach … **I**
to **ask** for [ˈɑ:sk fə] fragen nach; bitten
um **I**
*to be **asleep** [ˌbi əˈsli:p] schlafen **II**
*to fall **asleep** [ˌfɔ:l əˈsli:p] einschlafen **I**
aspect [ˈæspekt] Aspekt; Gesichtspunkt
°**IV U2**, 42
asphalt [ˈæsfælt] Asphalt ⟨**IV U3**, 80⟩
assembly [əˈsembli] Versammlung; Morgen-
appell **II**
assistant [əˈsɪstnt] Assistent/-in; Ver -
käufer/-in **II**
astronaut [ˈæstrənɔ:t] Astronaut/-in
IVTS3, 100
at [æt; ət] in; auf; bei; an; um (bei Uhrzeitangaben) **I**
at 7:30 [ət ˌsevn ˈθɜ:ti] um halb acht **I**
at all [ətˈɔ:l] überhaupt **I**
at first [ət ˈfɜ:st] zuerst; zunächst **II**
at home [ət ˈhəʊm] zu Hause **I**
at last [ət ˈlɑ:st] endlich; schließlich **I**
at least [ət ˈli:st] mindestens; wenigstens
II
at the back of [ət ðə ˈbæk əv] hinten; am
Ende; im hinteren Teil **II**
at the moment [ət ðə ˈməʊmənt] im
Moment; gerade **I**
at the same time [ət ðə ˌseɪm ˈtaɪm] zur
selben Zeit; gleichzeitig **I**
at the time [ˌət ðə ˈtaɪm] damals
IVTS3, 102
at the weekend [ət ðə ˌwi:kˈend] am
Wochenende **I**
athletics (no pl) [æθˈletɪks] Leichtathletik
IV U1, 10
atlas [ˈætləs] Atlas **II**
atmosphere [ˈætməsfɪə] Atmosphäre;
Stimmung **II**
to **attack** [əˈtæk] angreifen **III**
flight **attendant** [ˈflaɪt əˌtendnt] Flugbe-
gleiter/-in **IV U1**, 9
attention [əˈtenʃn] Aufmerksamkeit; Beachtung **II**
*to pay **attention** to sb/sth [ˌpeɪ əˈtenʃn
tʊ] jmdn./etw. beachten **III**
attic [ˈætɪk] Dachboden **II**

attitude ['ætɪtjuːd] Haltung; Einstellung **IV U2**, 55

to attract [ə'trækt] anziehen **IVTS2**, 66

attraction [ə'trækʃn] Attraktion; Sehenswürdigkeit **II**

attractive [ə'træktɪv] attraktiv **IV U2**, 55

audience ['ɔːdiəns] Publikum **II**

audio ['ɔːdiəʊ] Audio-; Hör- **I**

  audio tour ['ɔːdiəʊ ˌtʊə] Audioführung **II**

audio-visual effect [ˌɔːdiəʊvɪʒuəl ɪ'fekt] audiovisueller Effekt **II**

audition [ɔː'dɪʃn] Vorsprechen; Vorsingen; Vortanzen **III**

August ['ɔːgəst] August **I**

aunt [ɑːnt] Tante **I**

  agony aunt ['ægəniˌɑːnt] Kummerkastentante **II**

auntie ['ɑːnti] Tantchen **IV AC4**, 107

Australian [ɒs'treɪliən] australisch; Australier/-in **III**

author ['ɔːθə] Autor/-in **III**

available [ə'veɪləbl] erhältlich; verfügbar **IVTS2**, 65

to avoid [ə'vɔɪd] vermeiden; meiden; aus dem Weg gehen **III**

to stay awake [ˌsteɪ ə'weɪk] wach bleiben ⟨**IV U3**, 90⟩

award [ə'wɔːd] Auszeichnung; Preis **II**

to be aware of sth [bi ə'weərˌəv] sich etw. bewusst sein °**IVTS2**, 65

away [ə'weɪ] weg **I**

  *to give away [ˌgɪv ə'weɪ] verteilen; verschenken **IVTS2**, 64; verraten; preisgeben °**IV U3**, 93

  right away [ˌraɪt ə'weɪ] sofort; gleich **I**

  *to run away [ˌrʌn ə'weɪ] wegrennen **I**

  straight away [ˌstreɪt ə'weɪ] sofort; gleich **III**

  *to throw away [θrəʊ ə'weɪ] wegwerfen **I**

awesome ['ɔːsəm] super; spitze **IV AC2**, 41

awful ['ɔːfl] schrecklich; furchtbar **I**

axe [æks] Axt **III**

B

baby ['beɪbi] Baby; Säugling **I**

back [bæk] Rückseite; Rücken **III**

  at the back of [ət ðə 'bækˌəv] hinten; am Ende; im hinteren Teil **II**

  back to back [ˌbæk tʊ 'bæk] Rücken an Rücken **I**

to back down [ˌbæk 'daʊn] einen Rückzieher machen ⟨**IVTS1**, 32⟩

back [bæk] zurück **I**

back then [bæk 'ðen] damals **III**

*to go right back to [ˌgəʊ raɪt 'bæk tə] zurückgehen auf **III**

to turn back [tɜːn 'bæk] umkehren; zurückgehen **II**

backache ['bækeɪk] Rückenschmerzen; Rückenweh **II**

background ['bækgraʊnd] Hintergrund **I**

backing ['bækɪŋ] Hintergrund-; Background- **III**

  backing dancer ['bækɪŋˌdɑːnsə] Backgroundtänzer/-in **III**

backpack ['bækpæk] Rucksack **III**

backyard [bæk'jɑːd] Garten; Hinterhof **III**

bacon ['beɪkn] Schinkenspeck; Speck **I**

bad [bæd] schlecht; böse; schlimm *(ugs.)* **I**

  Too bad! [ˌtuː 'bæd] Zu dumm!; Schade! **I**

badly-written ['bædliˌrɪtn] schlecht geschrieben **IVTS3**, 105

badminton ['bædmɪntən] Badminton **III**

bag [bæg] Tasche; Tüte **I**

  tea bag ['tiːˌbæg] Teebeutel **III**

bagel ['beɪgl] Bagel *(weiches, ringförmiges Brötchen)* ⟨**IV U3**, 75⟩

bagpipes *(pl)* ['bægpaɪps] Dudelsack **III**

baked beans *(pl)* [ˌbeɪkt 'biːnz] weiße Bohnen in Tomatensoße **I**

ball [bɔːl] Ball **I**

  *to keep the ball bouncing [ˌkiːp ðə bɔːl 'baʊntsɪŋ] *hier:* das Gespräch am Laufen halten **II**

to ban [bæn] bannen; verbieten; sperren **III**

banana [bə'nɑːnə] Banane **I**

band [bænd] Band; Musikgruppe **III**

Bang! [bæŋ] Peng! **II**

bank [bæŋk] Ufer **II**; Bank **IV U3**, 72

  word bank ['wɜːdˌbæŋk] Wortsammlung **III**

chocolate bar ['tʃɒklətˌbɑː] Schokoriegel **IVTS2**, 64

snack bar ['snækˌbɑː] Café; Imbissstube **I**

barbed wire [ˌbɑːbd 'waɪə] Stacheldraht ⟨**IV U3**, 90⟩

bare [beə] nackt; bloß **III**

bargain ['bɑːgɪn] Schnäppchen **I**

to bark [bɑːk] bellen **I**

air-force base ['eəfɔːsˌbeɪs] Luftwaffenstützpunkt ⟨**IVTS3**, 102⟩

to base on ['beɪsˌɒn] stützen auf **IV U3**, 74

baseball ['beɪsbɔːl] Baseball **IV U2**, 46

based on ['beɪstˌɒn] basierend auf; beruhend auf °**IV AC2**, 40

basic ['beɪsɪk] grundlegend; Grund- **II**

basics *(pl)* ['beɪsɪks] Grundlagen **III**

basketball ['bɑːskɪtbɔːl] Basketball **I**

bath [bɑːθ] Bad; Badewanne **I**

baths *(pl)* [bɑːθs] Badehaus; Therme **III**

bathroom ['bɑːθrʊm] Bad; Badezimmer **I**

battery ['bætri] Batterie; Akku **II**

battle ['bætl] Schlacht; Kampf **III**

BC (= before Christ) [ˌbiː'siː] vor Christus **III**

*to be [biː] sein **I**

  *to be able to (do sth) [biˌeɪbl tə] fähig sein zu; können; dürfen **II**

  *to be about [biːˌə'baʊt] sich handeln um **I**

  *to be about to do sth [biˌə'baʊt tə] im Begriff sein, etw. zu tun **IV AC3**, 69

  *to be afraid (of) [biˌə'freɪdˌəv] (sich) fürchten; Angst haben (vor) **IV U1**, 8

*to be allowed to (do sth) [biˌə'laʊd tə] dürfen **II**

*to be around [ˌbiː ə'raʊnd] da sein; zusammen sein mit **IV U2**, 44

*to be asleep [ˌbi ə'sliːp] schlafen **II**

to be aware of sth [biˌə'weərˌəv] sich etw. bewusst sein °**IVTS2**, 65

*to be born [bi 'bɔːn] geboren werden **III**

*to be called [bi 'kɔːld] heißen; genannt werden **III**

*to be called to do sth [bi 'kɔːld tə duː] auserwählt sein, etw. zu tun **III**

*to be connected [bi kə'nektɪd] zusammenhängen; in Zusammenhang stehen **II**

*to be considered (to be) sth [bi kən'sɪdəd tə] als etw. gelten **IVTS3**, 100

*to be crazy about [bi 'kreɪziˌəbaʊt] verrückt sein nach; abfahren auf **IV U2**, 47

*to be done with [bi 'dʌn wɪð] fertig sein mit **IV U3**, 76

*to be fed up (with) [bi fed ˌʌp wɪð] sauer sein (auf); die Nase voll haben (von) **III**

*to be gone [biː 'gɒn] verschwunden sein; weg sein **II**

*to be good at [bi 'gʊdˌət] gut sein in **I**

*to be grounded [bi 'graʊndɪd] Hausarrest haben **III**

*to be hard on sb [bi 'hɑːdˌɒn] streng mit jmdm. sein **III**

*to be homesick [bi 'həʊmsɪk] Heimweh haben **IV U1**, 18

*to be in [biˌ'ɪn] dabei sein; mitmachen **II**

*to be in charge (of) [biˌɪn 'tʃɑːdʒ əv] die Verantwortung tragen (für); zuständig sein (für) **III**

*to be in sb's shoes [ˌbiː ɪn sʌmbɒdɪz 'ʃuːz] an jmds. Stelle sein; in jmds. Haut stecken **III**

*to be in the way [biːˌɪn ðə 'weɪ] im Weg sein/stehen **I**

*to be interested in [bi 'ɪntrəstɪdˌɪn] interessiert sein an; sich interessieren für **II**

*to be into [biːˌ'ɪntə] mögen; stehen auf **I**

*to be jealous (of) [biː 'dʒeləs] eifersüchtig sein (auf); neidisch sein (auf) **I**

*to be known as [bi 'nəʊnˌəz] bekannt sein als **IV U3**, 74

*to be late [biː 'leɪt] zu spät dran sein; zu spät kommen **I**

*to be like [bi 'laɪk] sein **III**

*to be located [bi ləʊ'keɪtɪd] gelegen sein; liegen **IV U3**, 73

*to be lucky [biˌ'lʌki] Glück haben **II**

*to be made of [bi 'meɪdˌəv] bestehen aus **III**

*to be on [biˌ'ɒn] an sein; laufen **II**

*to be on fire [biːˌɒn 'faɪə] brennen **III**

*to be right [biː 'raɪt] recht haben **I**

*to be scared (of) [biː 'skeədˌəv] Angst haben (vor) **I**

*to be set (in) [bi 'set ɪn] spielen (in); seinen Schauplatz haben (in) **IV U1**, 19 *to **be** sick [bi 'sɪk] sich übergeben **IV U1**, 16

*to **be** sorry [bi: 'sɒri] leid tun **I**

*to **be** stressed out [bi ,strest 'aʊt] völlig gestresst sein **III**

*to **be** surprised [bi sə'praɪzd] überrascht sein **II**

*to **be** suspended [bi sə'spendɪd] suspendiert werden; zeitweilig vom Unterricht ausgeschlossen werden **IV AC3**, 68

*to **be** tired of [bi 'taɪəd ˌəv] es müde sein (zu); es leid sein (zu); es satt haben (zu) **IV U2**, 46

*to **be** trapped [bi 'træpt] eingeschlossen sein; in der Falle sitzen **III**

*to **be** unlucky [bi: ʌn'lʌki] Pech haben **I**

*to **be** up to [bi ,ʌp tə] vorhaben **II**

*to **be** used to (+ -ing) [bi 'ju:s ˌtə] gewöhnt sein an; gewohnt sein **III**

*to **be** walled in [ˌbi wɔːld 'ɪn] von Wänden eingeschlossen sein 〈**IV U3**, 90〉

*to **be** worried [bi 'wʌrid] beunruhigt sein; besorgt sein **I**

*to **be** worth [bi: 'wɜːθ] wert sein **I**

*to **be** wrong [bi: 'rɒŋ] unrecht haben; sich irren **I**

Be careful! [bi: 'keəfl] Vorsicht!; Pass/Passt auf! **I**

Be polite. [bi: pə'laɪt] Sei/Seid höflich. **I**

Here you **are**. [ˌhɪə juˌ'ɑː] Bitte schön. **I**

How **are** you? [ˌhaʊ ˌ'ɑː jə] Wie geht es dir?; Wie geht es euch?; Wie geht es Ihnen? **I**

How much **is/are** …? [ˌhaʊ 'mʌtʃ ɪz/ɑː] Wie viel (kostet/kosten) …? **I**

I'm from … [ˌaɪm frɒm] Ich bin aus … **I**

Is this how you (do) …? [ɪz 'ðɪs haʊ jʊ ˌduː] Machst du so …? **I**

beach [biːtʃ] Strand **II**

baked **beans** (pl) [ˌbeɪkt 'biːnz] weiße Bohnen in Tomatensoße **I**

bear [beə] Bär **II**

*to **beat** [biːt] schlagen; besiegen **II**

beautiful ['bjuːtɪfl] schön; hübsch; wunderbar **II**

because [bɪ'kɒz] weil; da **I**

because of [bɪ'kɒz ˌəv] wegen **II**

*to **become** [bɪ'kʌm] werden **II**

*to **become** extinct [bɪˌkʌm ɪk'stɪŋkt] aussterben **III**

*to **become** friends [bɪˌkʌm 'frendz] sich anfreunden; Freundschaft schließen **IV AC2**, 41

bed [bed] Bett **I**

*to go to **bed** [ˌgəʊ tə 'bed] ins Bett gehen **I**

bedroom ['bedrʊm] Schlafzimmer **I**

bee [biː] Biene **II**

Beefeater ['biːˌfiːtə] königlicher Leibgardist **II**

before [bɪ'fɔː] schon einmal; vorher; zuvor **II**

before [bɪ'fɔː] vor (zeitlich); bevor **I**

*to **begin** [bɪ'gɪn] beginnen; anfangen **II**

beginning [bɪ'gɪnɪŋ] Anfang; Beginn **II**

to **behave** [bɪ'heɪv] sich benehmen; sich verhalten **III**

behavior (no pl) (AE) [bɪ'heɪvjə] Verhalten; Benehmen; Betragen **IV AC3**, 69

behaviour (no pl) [bɪ'heɪvjə] Verhalten; Benehmen; Betragen **IV AC1**, 22

behind [bɪ'haɪnd] hinter **I**

*to leave **behind** [ˌliːv bɪ'haɪnd] zurücklassen **II**

believable [bɪ'liːvəbl] glaubwürdig **IV U2**, 52

to **believe** [bɪ'liːv] glauben **II**

He couldn't **believe** his eyes. [hi ˌkʊdnt bɪˌliːv hɪz 'aɪz] Er traute seinen Augen nicht. **II**

bell [bel] Glocke **II**

saved by the **bell** [ˌseɪvd baɪ ðə 'bel] noch mal Glück gehabt **III**

to **belong** (to) [bɪ'lɒŋ (tə)] gehören (zu) **II**

where I **belong** [ˌweər aɪ bɪ'lɒŋ] wo ich hingehöre **IV U1**, 16

below [bɪ'ləʊ] unterhalb; unten **I**

belt [belt] Gürtel **II**

bench [bentʃ] Bank; Sitzbank **III**

benefit ['benɪfɪt] Vorteil; Nutzen; Unterstützung **IV U2**, 51

besides [bɪ'saɪdz] neben **III**

(the) **best** [best] (der/die/das) Beste **II**

to save the **best** for last [ˌseɪv ðə ˌbest fə 'lɑːst] sich das Beste bis zum Schluss aufheben **IV U3**, 72

best [best] beste/-r/-s; am besten **I**

Best wishes [ˌbest 'wɪʃɪz] Viele Grüße; Herzliche Grüße **III**

the **best** … ever ['best … ˌevə] der/die/das beste … überhaupt **II**

I **bet** [aɪ 'bet] ich wette **II**

better ['betə] besser; lieber **I**

You'd **better** … (= You had better) ['juːd ˌbetə] Du solltest lieber … **IV AC3**, 69

between [bɪ'twiːn] zwischen **I**

in **between** [ˌɪn bɪ'twiːn] dazwischen **III**

bicycle motocross [ˌbaɪsɪkl 'məʊtəʊkrɒs] Fahrradmotocross **II**

big [bɪg] groß **I**

big deal [ˌbɪg 'diːl] große Sache **IV U1**, 11

bike [baɪk] Fahrrad **I**

mountain **biking** ['maʊntɪn ˌbaɪkɪŋ] Mountainbikefahren **III**

bilingual [baɪ'lɪŋgwl] zweisprachig **II**

bill (AE) [bɪl] Geldschein; Rechnung **IV U3**, 76

billboard ['bɪlbɔːd] Plakatwand **IV TS2**, 65

billion ['bɪliən] Milliarde **III**

billionaire [ˌbɪliəneə] Milliardär/-in **IV AC2**, 39

biographical [ˌbaɪəʊ'græfɪkl] biografisch **III**

bird [bɜːd] Vogel **II**

birdwatching ['bɜːdˌwɒtʃɪŋ] Vogelbeobachtung **II**

date of **birth** [ˌdeɪt əv 'bɜːθ] Geburtsdatum **IV U1**, 13

birthday ['bɜːθdeɪ] Geburtstag **I**

Happy **Birthday**! [ˌhæpi 'bɜːθdeɪ] Alles Gute zum Geburtstag!; Herzlichen Glückwunsch zum Geburtstag! **I**

biscuit ['bɪskɪt] Keks **I**

a **bit** [ə 'bɪt] ein bisschen; ein wenig **II**

bit by bit [ˌbɪt baɪ 'bɪt] Stück für Stück **IV TS1**, 35

to **bitch** (coll) [bɪtʃ] meckern; sich aufregen über 〈**IV U3**, 87〉

*to **bite** [baɪt] beißen **II**

black [blæk] schwarz **I**

*to go **black** [ˌgəʊ 'blæk] schwarz werden **II**

block [blɒk] Block; Häuserblock **IV U3**, 72

building **block** ['bɪldɪŋ blɒk] Baustein **II**

to **block** [blɒk] blockieren; abblocken **II**

blog [blɒg] Blog; Internettagebuch **III**

blogger ['blɒgə] Blogger/-in °**IV TS3**, 102

bloke (fam) [bləʊk] Typ (ugs.) **III**

blond [blɒnd] blond **III**

blood [blʌd] Blut **III**

*to **blow** out [ˌbləʊ 'aʊt] ausblasen; auspusten **I**

blue [bluː] blau **I**

blurred [blɜːd] verschwommen; verwischt **III**

BMX [ˌbiːem'eks] BMX **II**

board [bɔːd] Brett; Tafel **III**

tourist **board** ['tʊərɪst bɔːd] Touristeninformation **III**

boarding ['bɔːdɪŋ] Boarding **IV U1**, 9

boarding card ['bɔːdɪŋ ˌkɑːd] Bordkarte **IV U1**, 9

boat [bəʊt] Boot **I**

boating lake ['bəʊtɪŋ ˌleɪk] See zum Rudern **I**

body ['bɒdi] Körper **III**

human **body** [ˌhjuːmən 'bɒdi] menschlicher Körper **II**

bodyguard ['bɒdigɑːd] Bodyguard **IV U2**, 52

bold [bəʊld] fett gedruckt **III**

bonfire ['bɒnfaɪə] Lagerfeuer; Freudenfeuer **I**

book [bʊk] Buch **I**

exercise **book** ['eksəsaɪz ˌbʊk] Übungsheft **I**

to **book** [bʊk] buchen; reservieren **III**

to **boom** [buːm] dröhnen **III**

boot [buːt] Stiefel; Kofferraum **III**

bored [bɔːd] gelangweilt **I**

boring ['bɔːrɪŋ] langweilig **I**

*to be **born** [bi 'bɔːn] geboren werden **III**

to **borrow** ['bɒrəʊ] (sich) ausleihen **II**

boss [bɒs] Boss; Chef **III**

bossy ['bɒsi] herrisch; rechthaberisch **III**

both [bəʊθ] beide **II**

to **bother** ['bɒðə] stören; belästigen **IV U1**, 15

bottle ['bɒtl] Flasche **I**

to **bounce** [baʊns] springen; hüpfen **III**

*to keep the ball **bouncing** [ˌkiːp ðə bɔːl ˈbaʊntsɪŋ] *hier:* das Gespräch am Laufen halten **III**

bowl [bəʊl] Schale; Schälchen; Schüssel **I**
  to play **bowls** [ˌpleɪ ˈbəʊlz] Bowling spielen **III**

bowling alley [ˈbəʊlɪŋ ˌæli] Bowlingbahn **I**

box [bɒks] Box; Kasten; Schachtel; Kiste **I**
  phone **box** [ˈfəʊn ˌbɒks] Telefonzelle **IV U1**, 17

boxing [ˈbɒksɪŋ] Boxen **II**
  round of **boxing** [ˌraʊnd ˌəv ˈbɒksɪŋ] Boxrunde **II**

boy [bɔɪ] Junge **I**
  cabin **boy** [ˈkæbɪn ˌbɔɪ] Schiffsjunge **I**

boyfriend [ˈbɔɪfrend] Freund *(in einer Paarbeziehung)* **IV U2**, 55

bracelet [ˈbreɪslət] Armband **I**

bracket [ˈbrækɪt] Klammer **III**

brain(s) [breɪn] Gehirn; Verstand ⟨**IV U1**, 12⟩

to **brainstorm** [ˈbreɪnstɔːm] Ideen sammeln °**IV U2**, 57

brand [brænd] Marke **IV TS2**, 64

brand-new [ˌbrændˈnjuː] brandneu **IV TS2**, 65

brave [breɪv] mutig; tapfer **I**

bread [bred] Brot **I**
  bread roll [ˈbred rəʊl] Brötchen **III**

break [breɪk] Pause **II**; Durchbruch **IV U3**, 76
  half-term **break** [ˌhɑːftɜːm ˈbreɪk] Halbjahresferien **I**
  lunch **break** [ˈlʌnʃbreɪk] Mittagspause **I**

*to **break** [breɪk] brechen; zerbrechen **I**

broken [ˈbrəʊkn] gebrochen; kaputt **I**

breakfast [ˈbrekfəst] Frühstück **I**
  *to have **breakfast** [ˌhæv ˈbrekfəst] frühstücken **I**

breath [breθ] Atem; Atemzug **III**
  *to take a **breath** [ˌteɪk ə ˈbreθ] Luft holen; Atem holen **III**
  Take a deep **breath**. [ˌteɪk ə ˌdiːp ˈbreθ] Atme(t) tief ein. **II**

to **breathe** [briːð] atmen **II**

breathtaking [ˈbreθˌteɪkɪŋ] atemberaubend **IV TS3**, 104

bridge [brɪdʒ] Brücke **II**

bright [braɪt] hell; leuchtend; strahlend **IV U3**, 72

*to **bring** [brɪŋ] bringen; mitbringen **I**
  *to **bring** round [ˌbrɪŋ ˈraʊnd] mitbringen ⟨**IV TS1**, 36⟩

on the **brink** of [ˌɒn ðə ˈbrɪŋk ˌəv] am Rande von; kurz vor **III**

Brit [brɪt] Brite/Britin *(ugs.)* **IV AC2**, 41

British [ˈbrɪtɪʃ] britisch; Brite/Britin **I**

brochure [ˈbrəʊʃə] Broschüre; Prospekt **I**

broken [ˈbrəʊkn] gebrochen; kaputt **I**

Bronze Age [ˈbrɒnz eɪdʒ] Bronzezeit *(ca. 2200–800 v. Chr.)* **III**

brother [ˈbrʌðə] Bruder **I**

brown [braʊn] braun **I**

bucket [ˈbʌkɪt] Eimer **II**

*to **build** [bɪld] bauen **II**; aufbauen **III**

building [ˈbɪldɪŋ] Gebäude **I**

building block [ˈbɪldɪŋ blɒk] Baustein **II**

cyber **bully** [ˌsaɪbə ˈbʊli] *jemand, der andere in sozialen Netzwerken belästigt oder mobbed* **II**

*to give the **bumps** [ˌɡɪv ðə ˈbʌmps] hochleben lassen **I**

a **bunch** of junk [əˌbʌnʃ ˌəv ˈdʒʌŋk] ein Haufen Müll ⟨**IV U3**, 84⟩

burger [ˈbɜːɡə] Hamburger **I**

*to **burn** [bɜːn] brennen; verbrennen **III**
  *to **burn** down [ˌbɜːn ˈdaʊn] abbrennen; niederbrennen **III**

bus [bʌs] Bus **I**
  bus station [ˈbʌs ˌsteɪʃn] Busbahnhof **I**

bush [bʊʃ] Busch *(Buschlandschaft)*; Wildnis **III**

business [ˈbɪznɪs] Geschäft; Business **III**

businessman [ˈbɪznɪsmæn] Geschäftsmann **IV U3**, 76

busker [ˈbʌskə] Straßenmusikant/-in **IV U3**, 79

busy [ˈbɪzi] belebt; beschäftigt **I**

but [bʌt] aber **I**

butter [ˈbʌtə] Butter **III**

button [ˈbʌtn] Knopf **IV U1**, 17

*to **buy** [baɪ] kaufen **I**

buyer [ˈbaɪə] Käufer/-in **I**

by [baɪ] bei; neben; an; von **III**

by (bike) [baɪ] mit *(dem Fahrrad)* **I**
  by the river [baɪ ðə ˈrɪvə] am Fluss **II**
  by any means [baɪ ˌeni ˈmiːnz] mit allen Mitteln **IV U3**, 70

Bye! [baɪ] Tschüss! **II**

C

cabin boy [ˈkæbɪn ˌbɔɪ] Schiffsjunge **I**

cache [kæʃ] Cache **III**

cactus [ˈkæktəs] Kaktus **IV AC2**, 38

café [ˈkæfeɪ] Café **I**

cafeteria [ˌkæfəˈtɪəriə] Cafeteria **I**

cake [keɪk] Kuchen; Torte **I**

calendar [ˈkæləndə] Kalender **III**

(phone) **call** [ˈfəʊn ˌkɔːl] Anruf; Telefonanruf **I**

to **call** [kɔːl] nennen; anrufen; rufen **I**
  *to be **called** [bi ˈkɔːld] heißen; genannt werden **III**
  *to be **called** to do sth [bi ˈkɔːld tə duː] auserwählt sein, etw. zu tun **III**

caller [ˈkɔːlə] Anrufer/-in **I**

call-in [ˈkɔːlɪn] *Sendung, bei der sich das Publikum telefonisch beteiligen kann* **III**

to **calm** down [ˌkɑːm ˈdaʊn] sich beruhigen **II**

camel racing [ˈkæml ˌreɪsɪŋ] Kamelrennen **II**

camera [ˈkæmrə] Fotoapparat; Kamera **II**
  caught on **camera** [ˌkɔːt ɒn ˈkæmrə] ertappt; mit der Kamera festgehalten **II**

summer **camp** [ˈsʌmə kæmp] Sommerferienlager **II**

to **camp** [kæmp] campen; zelten **III**

to **campaign** (for) [kæmˈpeɪn fɔː] demonstrieren (für); aufmerksam machen (auf); sich engagieren (für) **III**

camping [ˈkæmpɪŋ] Camping; Zelten **II**

can [kæn] Dose; Büchse **I**
  tin **can** [ˈtɪn kæn] Blechdose **III**

can [kæn; kən] können; dürfen **I**
  can't [kɑːnt] kann nicht; können nicht **I**
  Can you name …? [ˈkæn jʊ ˌneɪm] Kannst du … nennen? **I**

Canadian [kəˈneɪdiən] kanadisch; Kanadier/-in **IV AC4**, 106

candle [ˈkændl] Kerze **I**

candlelight *(no pl)* [ˈkændlaɪt] Kerzenlicht **II**

cannot [ˈkænɒt] kann nicht; können nicht **II**

capital [ˈkæpɪtl] Hauptstadt **II**

capital letter [ˌkæpɪtl ˈletə] Großbuchstabe **I**

capitalistic [ˌkæpɪtlˈɪstɪk] kapitalistisch ⟨**IV U3**, 87⟩

captain [ˈkæptɪn] Kapitän/-in; Mannschaftsführer/-in **I**

caption [ˈkæpʃn] Bildunterschrift; Untertitel **III**

to **capture** [ˈkæptʃə] ergreifen; einfangen **III**

car [kɑː] Auto **I**

card [kɑːd] Karte; Spielkarte **I**
  boarding **card** [ˈbɔːdɪŋ ˌkɑːd] Bordkarte **IV U1**, 9
  prompt **card** [ˈprɒmpt kɑːd] Stichwortkarte; Rollenkarte **II**

*to take **care** of sb [ˌteɪk ˈkeər ˌəv] sich um jmdn. kümmern; für jmdn. sorgen **III**

to **care** (about) [ˈkeər əˌbaʊt] wichtig nehmen; sich kümmern (um); sich interessieren (für) **III**

career [kəˈrɪə] Beruf; Laufbahn; Karriere **III**

careful [ˈkeəfl] vorsichtig; sorgfältig **II**
  Be **careful!** [bi ˈkeəfl] Vorsicht!; Pass/Passt auf! **I**

carnival [ˈkɑːnɪvl] Karneval **II**

carpet [ˈkɑːpɪt] Teppich **II**

carrot [ˈkærət] Karotte; Möhre **I**

to **carry** [ˈkæri] tragen **III**

cart [kɑːt] Karren **IV U3**, 75

cartoon [kɑːˈtuːn] Cartoon; Zeichentrickfilm **III**

cash *(no pl)* [kæʃ] Bargeld ⟨**IV U3**, 84⟩

plaster **cast** [ˈplɑːstə kɑːst] Gipsverband **III**

casting [ˈkɑːstɪŋ] Casting; Rollenbesetzung **IV TS1**, 37

castle [ˈkɑːsl] Schloss; Burg **II**

cat [kæt] Katze **I**

*to **catch** [kætʃ] fangen **II**; mitbekommen *(ugs.)*; mitkriegen *(ugs.)* **III**; erwischen ⟨**IV U3**, 83⟩

catchy [ˈkætʃi] eingängig; einprägsam **III**

category [ˈkætəɡri] Kategorie; Klasse **II**

caught on camera [ˌkɔːt ɒn ˈkæmrə] ertappt; mit der Kamera festgehalten **II**

*to get **caught** [ˌɡet ˈkɔːt] erwischt werden; ertappt werden **IV AC3**, 68

to **cause** [kɔːz] verursachen II
cave [keɪv] Höhle III
to **celebrate** ['seləbreɪt] feiern I
celebration [ˌseləˈbreɪʃn] Feier ⟨IV U3, 90⟩
celebrity [səˈlebrəti] Prominente/-r; berühmte Person III
cell [sel] Zelle ⟨IV U3, 90⟩
   cell phone (AE) ['selfəʊn] Mobiltelefon; Handy IV AC3, 68
Celt [kelt] Kelte/Keltin III
Celtic ['keltɪk; 'seltɪk] keltisch II
cent [sent] Cent (Währung) I
center (AE) ['sentə] Zentrum; Center IV AC2, 38
central ['sentrl] zentral; Zentral- II
centre ['sentə] Zentrum; Center I
   community **centre** [kəˈmjuːnəti ˌsentə] Gemeindezentrum I
   leisure **centre** ['leʒə ˌsentə] Freizeitzentrum I
   tourist information **centre** [ˌtʊərɪst ɪnfəˈmeɪʃn ˌsentə] Touristeninformation I
century ['senʃri] Jahrhundert II
cereal (no pl) ['sɪəriəl] Frühstückszerealie; Getreideprodukt (z. B. Cornflakes oder Müsli) I
chair [tʃeə] Stuhl; Sessel I
challenge ['tʃælɪndʒ] Herausforderung II
to **challenge** ['tʃælɪndʒ] herausfordern IV TS3, 101
champion ['tʃæmpiən] Gewinner/-in; Sieger/-in; Champion III
championship ['tʃæmpiənʃip] Meisterschaft IV U2, 56
chance [tʃɑːns] Chance; Gelegenheit; Möglichkeit II
change [tʃeɪndʒ] Änderung; Veränderung; Wechsel III; Münzgeld; Wechselgeld IV U3, 76
to **change** [tʃeɪndʒ] wechseln; (sich) ändern II
   to **change** one's mind [tʃeɪndʒ wʌnz ˈmaɪnd] seine Meinung ändern III
to **change** (onto) [tʃeɪndʒ (ˈɒntʊ)] umsteigen (in) II
chant [tʃɑːnt] Sprechgesang II
chaos ['keɪɒs] Chaos; Durcheinander III
chapter ['tʃæptə] Kapitel III
character ['kærəktə] Charakter; Figur I
characteristic [ˌkærəktəˈrɪstɪk] typisches Merkmal °IV TS3, 103
*to be in **charge** (of) [bɪ ˌɪn ˈtʃɑːdʒ əv] die Verantwortung tragen (für); zuständig sein (für) III
charity ['tʃærɪti] Wohltätigkeitsverein; wohltätige Zwecke; Wohlfahrt I
   charity shop ['tʃærɪti ʃɒp] Second-Hand-Laden I
lucky **charm** [ˌlʌki ˈtʃɑːm] Glücksbringer; Talisman I
to **chase** [tʃeɪs] jagen; nachjagen I
chat [tʃæt] Chat III

chat room ['tʃæt rʊm] Chatroom II
video **chat** ['vɪdiəʊ ˌtʃæt] Videochat II
to **chat** [tʃæt] plaudern; chatten (sich online unterhalten) I
cheap [tʃiːp] billig; preiswert I
to **cheat** [tʃiːt] mogeln; betrügen IV AC3, 68
   cheat sheet ['tʃiːt ʃiːt] Spickzettel IV AC3, 69
to **check** [tʃek] überprüfen; prüfen; kontrollieren I
   to **check** out (coll) [tʃek ˈaʊt] prüfen; abchecken; auschecken III
   to **check** with ['tʃek wɪð] nachfragen bei ⟨IV TS1, 34⟩
Check-in ['tʃekɪn] Einchecken I
checklist ['tʃeklɪst] Checkliste II
Check-out ['tʃekaʊt] Auschecken I
checkpoint ['tʃekpɔɪnt] Kontrollpunkt IV U1, 16
cheer [tʃɪə] Jubel; Hurraruf IV U2, 52
to **cheer** [tʃɪə] anfeuern; jubeln; zujubeln II
   to **cheer** sb up [tʃɪər ˈʌp] jmdn. aufheitern III
Cheers! [tʃɪəz] Danke! III
cheese [tʃiːz] Käse I
chess [tʃes] Schach II
chewing gum ['tʃuːɪŋ ˌgʌm] Kaugummi IV U1, 15
chick (slang) [tʃɪk] Puppe (Jargon); Mieze (Jargon) ⟨IV U3, 84⟩
chicken ['tʃɪkɪn] Huhn; Hähnchen I
   chicken tikka masala [ˌtʃɪkɪn ˌtɪkə məˈsɑːlə] indisches Hühnchengericht I
child, **children** (pl) ['tʃaɪld; 'tʃɪldrən] Kind I
   child labor (AE) [tʃaɪld ˈleɪbə] Kinderarbeit IV U2, 48
   only **child** ['əʊnli ˌtʃaɪld] Einzelkind I
to **chill** out [tʃɪl ˈaʊt] chillen III
chimney ['tʃɪmni] Kamin; Schornstein III
chips (pl) (BE) [tʃɪps] Pommes frites I
chocolate ['tʃɒklət] Schokolade I
   chocolate bar ['tʃɒklət ˌbɑː] Schokoriegel IV TS2, 64
choice [tʃɔɪs] Wahl; Auswahl II
*to **choose** [tʃuːz] auswählen; wählen II
chorus ['kɔːrəs] Refrain III
   in **chorus** [ɪn ˈkɔːrəs] im Chor IV TS1, 33
Christmas ['krɪsməs] Weihnachten I
church [tʃɜːtʃ] Kirche I
cinema ['sɪnəmə] Kino I
circle ['sɜːkl] Kreis; Ring I
   *to go round in **circles** [gəʊ ˌraʊnd ɪn ˈsɜːklz] sich im Kreis drehen III
city ['sɪti] Stadt; Großstadt I
to **claim** [kleɪm] behaupten °IV TS3, 102
to **clap** [klæp] klatschen I
   Clap your hands. [ˌklæp jɔː ˈhændz] Klatsch/Klatscht in die Hände. I
clarification [ˌklærɪfɪˈkeɪʃn] Klärung; Klarstellung IV U1, 15
class [klɑːs] Klasse; Schulklasse I; hier: Unterricht II

class display ['klɑːs dɪˌspleɪ] Ausstellung in der Klasse I
class poster ['klɑːs ˌpəʊstə] Klassenposter I
classical ['klæsɪkl] klassisch IV U3, 72
classmate ['klɑːsmeɪt] Klassenkamerad/-in; Mitschüler/-in I
classroom ['klɑːsrʊm] Klassenzimmer I
contact **clause** ['kɒntækt ˌklɔːz] Relativsatz ohne Relativpronomen II
defining relative **clause** [dɪˈfaɪnɪŋ ˈrelətɪv ˌklɔːz] notwendiger Relativsatz II
if-**clause** ['ɪfˌklɔːz] if-Satz II
main **clause** [ˌmeɪn ˈklɔːz] Hauptsatz III
non-defining relative **clause** [ˌnɒndɪˈfaɪnɪŋ ˈrelətɪv ˌklɔːz] nicht notwendiger Relativsatz °IV U3, 73
clay pipe ['kleɪ paɪp] Tonpfeife II
to **clean** [kliːn] säubern; reinigen I
   to **clean** out [ˌkliːn ˈaʊt] ausräumen; entrümpeln IV U2, 51
clean [kliːn] sauber III
to **clear** out [ˌklɪər ˈaʊt] ausräumen; entrümpeln I
clear [klɪə] klar; deutlich I
clever ['klevə] schlau; klug II
click [klɪk] Klicken; Klick II
to **click** on ['klɪk ˌɒn] anklicken III
cliff [klɪf] Klippe; Kliff III
climate ['klaɪmət] Klima IV U1, 18
climax ['klaɪmæks] Höhepunkt III
to **climb** [klaɪm] klettern; besteigen; steigen II
climbing ['klaɪmɪŋ] Klettern II
clique [kliːk] Clique IV U2, 48
clock [klɒk] Uhr I
   alarm **clock** [əˈlɑːm klɒk] Wecker II
   o'**clock** [əˈklɒk] Uhr (Zeitangabe bei vollen Stunden) I
to **clone** [kləʊn] klonen III
close [kləʊs] schmaler Durchgang III
to **close** [kləʊz] schließen; zumachen I
   to **close** oneself away from [ˌkləʊz əˈweɪ frəm] sich abschotten von IV U1, 16
close [kləʊs] eng; knapp I; nahe II
   Look **closely** … [ˌlʊk ˈkləʊsli] Schau(t) genau … I
   That was **close**! [ˌðæt wəz ˈkləʊs] Das war knapp! I
closed [kləʊzd] geschlossen; zu IV U1, 11
closet ['klɒzɪt] Schrank; Wandschrank IV U2, 44
   walk-in **closet** [ˌwɔːkɪn ˈklɒzɪt] begehbarer Kleiderschrank IV U2, 44
close-up ['kləʊsʌp] Nahaufnahme II
clothes (pl) [kləʊðz] Kleider; Kleidung I
clothing ['kləʊðɪŋ] Kleidung IV U2, 51
   clothing drive ['kləʊðɪŋ ˌdraɪv] Kleidersammlung IV U2, 51
cloud [klaʊd] Wolke III
   word **cloud** ['wɜːd ˌklaʊd] Wörterwolke II
cloudy ['klaʊdi] bedeckt; bewölkt II

clown [klaʊn] Clown **II**

club [klʌb] Klub; Verein; AG **I**
Cooking **Club** [ˈkʊkɪŋ ˌklʌb] Koch-AG **I**

clue [klu:] Hinweis; Spur **II**
*to have no **clue** [ˌhæv nəʊ ˈklu:] keine
Ahnung haben **IV AC2**, 41

coach [kəʊtʃ] Trainer/-in **I**; Reisebus **II**

coast [kəʊst] Küste **IV U1**, 10

coastal path [ˌkəʊstl ˈpɑː:θ] Küstenweg **III**

coastline [ˈkəʊstlaɪn] Küste; Küstenverlauf
III

coconut [ˈkəʊkənʌt] Kokosnuss **II**

dress code [ˈdres ˌkəʊd] Kleiderordnung;
Bekleidungsvorschriften **IV U2**, 43

coffee [ˈkɒfi] Kaffee **I**

coin [kɔɪn] Münze **I**

coincidence [kəʊˈɪnsɪdns] Zufall **IV U2**, 52

coke [ˈkəʊk] Cola **I**

cold [kəʊld] Erkältung **II**; Kälte ⟨**IV U3**, 90⟩

cold [kəʊld] kalt **II**

to collect [kəˈlekt] sammeln **I**

collection [kəˈlekʃn] Kollektion; Sammlung **II**

collocation [ˌkɒləˈkeɪʃn] Wortverbindung **II**

colonist [ˈkɒlənɪst] Siedler/-in; Kolonist/-in
IV AC2, 41

colony [ˈkɒləni] Kolonie **II**

colour [ˈkʌlə] Farbe **I**
What **colour** is …? [ˌwɒt ˈkʌlər ɪz] Welche
Farbe hat …? **I**

colourful [ˈkʌləfl] farbenfroh; bunt **I**

column [ˈkɒləm] Spalte **III**

combination [ˌkɒmbɪˈneɪʃn] Kombination;
Verbindung **IV U3**, 75

to combine [kəmˈbaɪn] kombinieren; verbinden **IV U3**, 75

*to come [kʌm] kommen **I**
*to **come** down [kʌm ˈdaʊn] herunterkommen **I**
*to **come** in [kʌm ˈɪn] hereinkommen **III**
*to **come** true [kʌm ˈtru:] wahr werden; in
Erfüllung gehen **IV U3**, 76
*to **come** up [kʌm ˈʌp] vorkommen **III**
Come off it! [kʌm ˈɒf ɪt] Komm wieder
runter! ⟨**IV U3**, 86⟩
Come on! [kʌm ˈɒn] Komm schon!; Komm
jetzt! **I**

comedian [kəˈmi:diən] Komiker/-in; Comedian **II**

comedy [ˈkɒmədi] Komödie **III**
comedy show [ˈkɒmədi ˌʃəʊ] Comedy
Show **II**

comfortable [ˈkʌmftəbl] komfortabel;
bequem **II**

comic [ˈkɒmɪk] Comicheft **II**

comma [ˈkɒmə] Komma °**IV U3**, 73

command [kəˈmɑː:nd] Befehl **IV U1**, 9
command module [kəˈmɑː:nd ˌmɒdju:l]
Kommandokapsel ⟨**IVTS3**, 101⟩

commander [kəˈmɑː:ndə] Kommandant/-in
⟨**IVTS3**, 101⟩

comment [ˈkɒment] Kommentar **II**

to comment (on) [ˈkɒment ˌ(ɒn)] kommentieren **II**

committee [kəˈmɪti] Komitee; Ausschuss
IV U2, 48

*to have in common [ˌhæv ɪn ˈkɒmən]
gemeinsam haben **III**

to communicate [kəˈmju:nɪkeɪt] kommunizieren; sich verständigen **II**

communication [kəˌmju:nɪˈkeɪʃn] Kommunikation **II**

community centre [kəˈmju:nəti ˌsentə]
Gemeindezentrum **I**

company [ˈkʌmpəni] Gesellschaft; Firma;
Unternehmen **III**
tour **company** [ˈtʊə ˌkʌmpəni] Reiseanbieter **IV U3**, 73

comparative [kəmˈpærətɪv] Komparativ **II**

to compare (with/to) [kəmˈpeə] vergleichen
(mit) **I**

comparison [kəmˈpærɪsn] Vergleich **II**

to compete (with) [kəmˈpi:t] konkurrieren
(mit); sich messen (mit); in Wettbewerb
treten (mit) **II**

competition [ˌkɒmpəˈtɪʃn] Wettbewerb;
Turnier **II**

competitive [kəmˈpetɪtɪv] leistungsorientiert; konkurrierend **III**

to complain [kəmˈpleɪn] sich beschweren;
sich beklagen **IV U3**, 76

to complete [kəmˈpli:t] fertigstellen; vervollständigen; vollenden **IV AC3**, 68

complete [kəmˈpli:t] vollständig; komplett;
völlig **IV AC2**, 41

completely [kəmˈpli:tli] völlig **III**

complicated [ˈkɒmplɪkeɪtɪd] kompliziert
IVTS3, 102

compound word [ˈkɒmpaʊnd wɜ:d] Kompositum (zusammengesetztes Wort) **II**

compromise [ˈkɒmprəmaɪz] Kompromiss **II**

to compromise [ˈkɒmprəmaɪz] Kompromisse eingehen **III**

computer [kəmˈpju:tə] Computer **I**

computing power [kəmˈpju:tɪŋ ˌpaʊə]
Rechenleistung ⟨**IVTS3**, 102⟩

con [kɒn] Argument dagegen **II**

to concentrate [ˈkɒnsntreɪt] (sich) konzentrieren **IV U1**, 17

concert [ˈkɒnsət] Konzert **IV U2**, 57

concrete [ˈkɒnkri:t] Beton **IV U1**, 17

conditional sentence [kənˌdɪʃnl ˈsentəns]
Bedingungssatz **III**

to conduct [kənˈdʌkt] durchführen; ausführen **IV U3**, 92

conference [ˈkɒnfrns] Konferenz; Tagung
IV U3, 72

confident [ˈkɒnfɪdnt] selbstsicher; selbstbewusst **II**

confused [kənˈfju:zd] verwirrt; wirr; konfus
III

*to be connected [bi kəˈnektɪd] zusammen-
hängen; in Zusammenhang stehen **II**

connection [kəˈnekʃn] Verbindung **III**

conscience [ˈkɒnʃns] Gewissen **IVTS1**, 31

consecutive [kənˈsekjʊtɪv] aufeinanderfolgend; fortlaufend **IV U3**, 89

consequence [ˈkɒnsɪkwəns] Konsequenz;
Folge **IV AC3**, 68

*to be considered (to be) sth [bi kənˈsɪdəd
tə] als etw. gelten **IVTS3**, 100

conspiracy [kənˈspɪrəsi] Verschwörung
IVTS3, 102

construction [kənˈstrʌkʃn] Konstruktion
°**IV U2**, 43

contact [ˈkɒntækt] Kontakt **II**
contact clause [ˈkɒntækt ˌklɔ:z] Relativsatz ohne Relativpronomen **II**

to contain [kənˈteɪn] enthalten **IV U1**, 15

content [ˈkɒntent] Inhalt **IV U2**, 56

contest [ˈkɒntest] Wettkampf; Wettbewerb **I**

continent [ˈkɒntɪnənt] Kontinent; Erdteil
IV U3, 74

to continue [kənˈtɪnju:] fortfahren; andauern; weitermachen **III**; weitergehen
IV U1, 18

contrast [ˈkɒntrɑː:st] Kontrast; Unterschied;
Gegensatz **IV AC2**, 38

control [kənˈtrəʊl] Kontrolle **IV U1**, 9
mission **control** [ˌmɪʃn kənˈtrəʊl] Bodenkontrollzentrum ⟨**IVTS3**, 101⟩

to control [kənˈtrəʊl] kontrollieren; beherr-
schen ⟨**IV U1**, 12⟩; steuern **IV U2**, 50

conversation [ˌkɒnvəˈseɪʃn] Konversation;
Gespräch; Unterhaltung **I**
to hog a **conversation** [ˌhɒg ə kɒnvəˈseɪʃn]
ein Gespräch für sich in Beschlag nehmen; ein Gespräch dominieren **I**

to convert [kənˈvɜ:t] umwandeln; verwan-
deln; umsetzen in ⟨**IV U3**, 90⟩

to convince [kənˈvɪns] überzeugen **II**

convinced [kənˈvɪnst] überzeugt **IVTS1**, 31

convincing [kənˈvɪnsɪŋ] überzeugend
IV U1, 21

to cook [kʊk] kochen **II**

cooker [ˈkʊkə] Herd **I**

cooking [ˈkʊkɪŋ] Kochen **I**
Cooking Club [ˈkʊkɪŋ ˌklʌb] Koch-AG **I**

*to leave it to cool [ˌli:v ɪt tə ˈku:l] kalt
stellen **I**

cool [ku:l] cool; super **I**; kühl **IV AC2**, 38

cop (coll) [kɒp] Polizist/-in (ugs.) ⟨**IV U3**, 88⟩

ad copy [ˈæd ˌkɒpi] Werbetext **IVTS2**, 65

to copy [ˈkɒpi] abschreiben; kopieren **I**

corn [kɔ:n] Korn; Mais; Getreide **IV AC2**, 41

corner [ˈkɔ:nə] Ecke **II**

Cornish [ˈkɔ:nɪʃ] in Cornwall **III**

Correct … [kəˈrekt] Korrigiere/Korrigiert … **I**

correct [kəˈrekt] richtig; korrekt **I**

corridor [ˈkɒrɪdɔ:] Gang; Flur; Korridor
IV AC3, 68

*to cost [kɒst] kosten **I**

costume [ˈkɒstju:m] Kostüm **I**

cough [kɒf] Husten **II**

could [kʊd] könnte/-n **II**; konnte/-n **III**

to count (on) [ˈkaʊnt ˌɒn] zählen (auf) **I**

country, countries (pl) ['kʌntri; 'kʌntriz]
Land I
in the country [ɪn ðə 'kʌntri] auf dem
Land IV AC2, 40
countryside ['kʌntrisaɪd] Land III
couple ['kʌpl] Paar III
a couple of [ə 'kʌpl_əv] ein paar I
course [kɔ:s] Kurs II
of course [əv 'kɔ:s] natürlich; selbstverständlich I
court [kɔ:t] Spielfeld II
cousin ['kʌzn] Cousin/Cousine I
cover ['kʌvə] Cover; Titelblatt III
cover version ['kʌvə ˌvɜ:ʃn] Coverversion
III
to cover ['kʌvə] abdecken; bedecken;
zudecken III
to cover up for sb [ˌkʌvər_'ʌp_fə] jmdn.
decken ⟨IV TS1, 31⟩
cover-up ['kʌvərʌp] Vertuschung IV TS3, 102
cow [kaʊ] Kuh III
cowboy ['kaʊbɔɪ] Cowboy; Rinderhirte
IV U3, 72
crack [kræk] Knacken; Krachen III
cracking ['krækɪŋ] knackend; brechend III
cramp [kræmp] Krampf II
cranberry ['krænbri] Cranberry ⟨IV U2, 45⟩
crane [kreɪn] Kran III
to crash [kræʃ] abstürzen II; zusammenstoßen III
crazy ['kreɪzi] verrückt I
*to be crazy about [bi 'kreɪzi_əbaʊt] ver-
rückt sein nach; abfahren auf IV U2, 47
*to go crazy [ˌgəʊ 'kreɪzi] ausflippen;
durchdrehen; verrückt werden II
cream [kri:m] Creme; Sahne I
ice cream [aɪs 'kri:m] Eis; Eiscreme I
to create [kri'eɪt] schaffen; erschaffen;
erfinden I
creative [kri'eɪtɪv] kreativ I
credit ['kredɪt] Guthaben II
cricket ['krɪkɪt] Cricket II
crime [kraɪm] Verbrechen; Kriminalität III
criminal ['krɪmɪnəl] Kriminelle/-r; Verbre-
cher/-in III
to cringe [krɪndʒ] schaudern; sich ducken
IV U3, 91
crisp (BE) [krɪsp] Kartoffelchip I
criterion [kraɪ'tɪəriən], criteria [kraɪ'tɪəriə]
(pl) Kriterium; Argument III
critical ['krɪtɪkl] kritisch IV TS3, 103
croissant ['krwæsɑ̃] Croissant ⟨IV U3, 75⟩
cronut ['krəʊnʌt] Cronut ⟨IV U3, 75⟩
to crop (a photo) [krɒp] (ein Foto) zurechtschneiden I
cross [krɒs] Kreuz III
to cross [krɒs] überqueren; kreuzen II
*to keep your fingers crossed [ki:p jɔ:
ˌfɪŋgəz 'krɒst] die Daumen drücken I
crowd [kraʊd] Menschenmenge II
crowded ['kraʊdɪd] überfüllt IV AC1, 23
crown [kraʊn] Krone III

crown jewels [ˌkraʊn 'dʒu:əlz] Kronjuwelen II
cruel ['kru:əl] grausam III
crushed [krʌʃt] eingequetscht; eingeklemmt
IV U1, 16
to cry [kraɪ] schreien; rufen II; weinen III
CU (= See you) ['si: ju:] Bis dann!; Bis … I
cultural ['kʌltʃrl] kulturell IV AC2, 38
culture ['kʌltʃə] Kultur I
Across cultures [əˌkrɒs 'kʌltʃəz] Interkulturelles I
cup [kʌp] Tasse III
cupboard ['kʌbəd] Küchenschrank; Schrank I
curfew ['kɜ:fju:] Sperrstunde; Ausgangssperre IV U2, 44
currency ['kʌrnsi] Währung IV U1, 9
curry ['kʌri] Curry (Gewürz oder Gericht) I
custard ['kʌstəd] Vanillesoße; Vanillepudding I
custom ['kʌstəm] Gewohnheit; Brauch; Sitte
IV AC1, 22
customer ['kʌstəmə] Kunde/Kundin III
customs (sg) ['kʌstəmz] Zoll IV U1, 9
*to cut (off) [kʌt (ɒf)] schneiden; abschnei-
den II
*to cut up [kʌt_'ʌp] zerschneiden °IV U3, 91
cute [kju:t] niedlich; süß I
cyber bully [ˌsaɪbə 'bʊli] jemand, der andere
in sozialen Netzwerken belästigt oder
mobbed II
to cycle ['saɪkl] Fahrrad fahren IV U2, 46
cycling ['saɪklɪŋ] Radfahren I

D

dad [dæd] Papa I
dance [dɑ:ns] Tanz; Tanzveranstaltung III
to dance [dɑ:ns] tanzen I
to dance to ['dɑ:ns tə] tanzen zu III
I like singing and dancing. [aɪ laɪk ˌsɪŋɪŋ
ənd 'dɑ:nsɪŋ] Ich singe und tanze gern. I
dancer ['dɑ:nsə] Tänzer/-in II
backing dancer ['bækɪŋ ˌdɑ:nsə] Back-
groundtänzer/-in III
danger ['deɪndʒə] Gefahr III
dangerous ['deɪndʒrəs] gefährlich I
the dark [ðə 'dɑ:k] Dunkelheit II
dark [dɑ:k] dunkel II
darkness ['dɑ:knəs] Dunkelheit III
date [deɪt] Datum I; Verabredung; Date
IV U2, 55
date of birth [ˌdeɪt_əv 'bɜ:θ] Geburtsdatum IV U1, 13
daughter ['dɔ:tə] Tochter III
day [deɪ] Tag I
all day [ˌɔ:l 'deɪ] den ganzen Tag II
one day [wʌn 'deɪ] eines Tages II
*to take the day off [ˌteɪk ðə ˌdeɪ 'ɒf] sich
den Tag freinehmen IV U3, 72
the other day [ˌðiˌʌðə 'deɪ] neulich
IV U1, 20
these days [ˌði:z 'deɪz] zurzeit III

a (day/week/year) [ə 'deɪ/wi:k/jɪə] pro
(Tag/Woche/Jahr) IV AC2, 39
a day out in … [ə ˌdeɪ_'aʊt ɪn] ein Tag
in … II
the next day [ðə ˌnekst 'deɪ] am nächsten
Tag II
dead [ded] tot II
big deal [bɪg 'di:l] große Sache IV U1, 11
*to deal (with) [di:l] sich befassen mit;
umgehen mit II
Oh dear! [əʊ 'dɪə] Oje! III
Dear … [dɪə] Lieber …; Liebe … (Anrede in
Briefen) I
Dear Sir or Madam [dɪə ˌsɜ:r_ɔ: 'mædəm]
Sehr geehrte Dame, sehr geehrter Herr III
death [deθ] Tod III
December [dɪ'sembə] Dezember I
to decide [dɪ'saɪd] (sich) entscheiden I
decision [dɪ'sɪʒn] Entscheidung III
*to make a decision [ˌmeɪk_ə dɪ'sɪʒn] eine
Entscheidung treffen II
deck [dek] Deck II
to decorate ['dekəreɪt] dekorieren; verzieren; schmücken I
decorations (pl) [ˌdekə'reɪʃnz] Dekoration;
Schmuck I
deep [di:p] tief III
to defeat [dɪ'fi:t] besiegen III
defining relative clause [dɪˌfaɪnɪŋ 'relətɪv
ˌklɔ:z] notwendiger Relativsatz II
definitely ['defɪnətli] bestimmt; definitiv;
eindeutig III
definition [ˌdefɪ'nɪʃn] Definition III
degree Fahrenheit (°F) ['færnhaɪt] Grad
Fahrenheit IV AC2, 38
delay [dɪ'leɪ] Verzögerung; Verspätung
IV U1, 15
to delete [dɪ'li:t] löschen III
deli ['deli] Feinkostgeschäft ⟨IV U3, 85⟩
delicate ['delɪkət] empfindlich ⟨IV U3, 86⟩
delicious [dɪ'lɪʃəs] köstlich IV U3, 75
to demonstrate ['demənstreɪt] demonstrieren IV U2, 48
dense [dens] dicht IV AC2, 40
to depart [dɪ'pɑ:t] abfahren III
departure [dɪ'pɑ:tʃə] Abflug; Abreise IV U1, 9
departure lounge [dɪ'pɑ:tʃə ˌlaʊndʒ]
Abflughalle IV U1, 9
to depend (on) [dɪ'pend_(ɒn)] abhängen
von III
depressing [dɪ'presɪŋ] deprimierend; bedrückend IV U1, 17
to describe [dɪ'skraɪb] beschreiben I
description [dɪ'skrɪpʃn] Beschreibung II
desert ['dezət] Wüste IV AC2, 38
to deserve [dɪ'zɜ:v] verdienen III
design [dɪ'zaɪn] Design; Gestaltung; Entwurf II
to design [dɪ'zaɪn] entwerfen; gestalten II
designer [dɪ'zaɪnə] Designer/-in III
web designer ['web dɪˌzaɪnə] Webdesigner III

desk [desk] Schalter **IV U1**, 9

destination [ˌdestɪˈneɪʃn] Ziel; Reiseziel **IV U1**, 19

detail [ˈdiːteɪl] Detail; Einzelheit **II**

detective [dɪˈtektɪv] Detektiv/-in; Detektivgeschichte; Kriminalroman; Kriminalfilm; Krimi **III**

   private **detective** [ˌpraɪvət dɪˈtektɪv] Privatdetektiv/-in **III**

detention [dɪˈtenʃn] Nachsitzen; Haft; Verhaftung **IV AC3**, 68

devil [ˈdevl] Teufel **IV TS1**, 31

diagram [ˈdaɪəɡræm] Diagramm **I**

dialect [ˈdaɪəlekt] Dialekt **III**

dialogue [ˈdaɪəlɒɡ] Dialog; Gespräch **I**

diary [ˈdaɪəri] Tagebuch **III**

   diary entry [ˈdaɪəri entri] Tagebucheintrag **III**

dice [daɪs] Würfel **II**

   Roll two **dice**. [ˌrəʊl ˌtuː ˈdaɪs] Würfle/ Würfelt mit zwei Würfeln. **I**

   throw the **dice** twice [ˌθrəʊ ðə daɪs ˈtwaɪs] würfle zweimal **II**

dictionary [ˈdɪkʃnri] Wörterbuch **I**

to die [daɪ] sterben **III**

difference [ˈdɪfrəns] Unterschied **I**

different [ˈdɪfrnt] anders; unterschiedlich; verschieden **I**

difficult [ˈdɪfɪklt] schwierig **II**

*to **dig** [dɪɡ] graben **II**

dilemma [daɪˈlemə] Dilemma; Zwickmühle **IV TS1**, 31

diner (AE) [ˈdaɪnə] einfaches Restaurant mit Theke und Tischen **IV U3**, 72

dinner [ˈdɪnə] Abendessen **I**

dinosaur [ˈdaɪnəsɔː] Dinosaurier **II**

direct [dɪˈrekt] direkt **III**

   direct speech [dɪˌrekt ˈspiːtʃ] direkte Rede **IV U1**, 11

direction [dɪˈrekʃn] Richtung **I**

   stage **direction** [ˈsteɪdʒ dɪˌrekʃn] Regieanweisung **III**

director [dɪˈrektə] Regisseur/-in **IV TS1**, 30

dirt [dɜːt] Schmutz; Dreck **III**

dirty [ˈdɜːti] dreckig; schmutzig **II**

to disagree [ˌdɪsəˈɡriː] anderer Meinung sein; nicht einverstanden sein **III**

disappointed [ˌdɪsəˈpɔɪntɪd] enttäuscht **I**

disappointing [ˌdɪsəˈpɔɪntɪŋ] enttäuschend **IV TS3**, 104

disaster [dɪˈzɑːstə] Desaster; Katastrophe; Unglück **II**

to discover [dɪˈskʌvə] entdecken **II**

discovery [dɪˈskʌvri] Entdeckung **III**

to discuss [dɪˈskʌs] diskutieren **I**

discussion [dɪˈskʌʃn] Diskussion **II**

dish [dɪʃ] Gericht; Speise **IV U2**, 45

dishonest [dɪˈsɒnɪst] unehrlich **IV TS1**, 34

to dislike [dɪˈslaɪk] nicht mögen **IV U2**, 47

dislikes (pl) [dɪˈslaɪks] Abneigungen **IV U2**, 46

to disobey [ˌdɪsəˈbeɪ] nicht gehorchen; ungehorsam sein **III**

display [dɪˈspleɪ] Ausstellung **II**

   class **display** [ˈklɑːs dɪˌspleɪ] Ausstellung in der Klasse **I**

distance [ˈdɪstns] Distanz; Entfernung **II**

district [ˈdɪstrɪkt] Distrikt; Bezirk **IV U3**, 70

to divide (up) [dɪˈvaɪd] aufteilen **III**

dizzy [ˈdɪzi] schwindelig **IV U2**, 52

DJ [diːˈdʒeɪ] DJ; Discjockey **III**

*to **do** [duː] machen; tun **I**

   *to be **done** with [bi ˈdʌn wɪð] fertig sein mit **IV U3**, 76

   *to **do** about [ˈduː əˌbaʊt] unternehmen wegen **II**

   *to **do** our hair [ˌduː ˌaʊə ˈheə] uns frisieren; unsere Haare machen **I**

   *to **do** the shopping [ˌduː ðə ˈʃɒpɪŋ] Einkäufe machen; Besorgungen machen **III**

   *to **do** well [duː ˈwel] gute Leistungen erbringen **IV TS1**, 34

   Don't worry! [ˈdəʊnt ˈwʌri] Keine Sorge! **I**

   dos and **don'ts** [ˌduːz ənd ˈdəʊnts] Geund Verbote; was man tun und was man nicht tun sollte **IV AC1**, 22

   We **did** it! [ˌwiː ˈdɪd ɪt] Wir haben es geschafft! **II**

   You can **do** it! [juː kən ˈduː ɪt] Du schaffst es! **III**

doctor [ˈdɒktə] Arzt/Ärztin **II**

to document [ˈdɒkjəment] dokumentieren; festhalten ⟨**IV TS3**, 101⟩

dog [dɒɡ] Hund **I**

   hot **dog** [ˈhɒt ˌdɒɡ] Hot Dog (Würstchen im Brötchen) ⟨**IV U3**, 75⟩

   to walk the **dog** [wɔːk ðə ˈdɒɡ] den Hund ausführen; mit dem Hund spazieren gehen **I**

I'm dog-tired. [ˌaɪm ˌdɒɡˈtaɪəd] Ich bin hundemüde. **I**

dollar [ˈdɒlə] Dollar (Währung) **III**

dolphin [ˈdɒlfɪn] Delfin **III**

dominoes [ˈdɒmɪnəʊz] Domino **IV U1**, 20

to donate [dəˈneɪt] spenden; stiften **IV U2**, 51

door [dɔː] Tür **I**

   front **door** [ˌfrʌnt ˈdɔː] Haustür **II**

   next **door** [ˌnekst ˈdɔː] (von) nebenan **III**

doorbell [ˈdɔːbel] Türklingel **III**

double [ˈdʌbl] Doppel-; zweimal **IV U2**, 57

doubt [daʊt] Zweifel **III**

doughnut [ˈdəʊnʌt] Donut (frittierter Teigkringel) ⟨**IV U3**, 75⟩

down [daʊn] nach unten; herunter; hinunter **II**; nieder **IV U2**, 52

   *to come **down** [ˌkʌm ˈdaʊn] herunterkommen **I**

   *to go **down** [ˌɡəʊ ˈdaʊn] hinuntergehen; nach unten gehen; entlanggehen **I**

   to note **down** [ˌnəʊt ˈdaʊn] notieren; aufschreiben **II**

   to pull **down** [ˌpʊl ˈdaʊn] abreißen **III**

   *to sit **down** [ˌsɪt ˈdaʊn] sich hinsetzen; sich setzen **I**

   to slow **down** [ˌsləʊ ˈdaʊn] langsamer werden; bremsen ⟨**IV U3**, 90⟩

   to touch **down** [tʌtʃ ˈdaʊn] landen **IV TS3**, 101

   *to write **down** [ˌraɪt ˈdaʊn] aufschreiben **I**

to download [ˌdaʊnˈləʊd] herunterladen (aus dem Internet) **II**

downstairs [ˌdaʊnˈsteəz] nach unten; im Untergeschoss; unten **II**

downtown (AE) [ˌdaʊnˈtaʊn] im Stadtzentrum **IV U2**, 44

draft [drɑːft] Entwurf; Konzept **I**

drama [ˈdrɑːmə] Theater; Drama **II**

dramatic [drəˈmætɪk] dramatisch **II**

*to **draw** [drɔː] zeichnen **I**; ziehen **III**

   *to **draw** the reader into the story/action [drɔː ðə ˌriːdə ɪntə ðə ˈstɔːri/ˈækʃn] den Leser/die Leserin in die Geschichte/ Handlung hineinziehen **III**

drawing [ˈdrɔːɪŋ] Zeichnung **I**

dreadlocks (pl) [ˈdredlɒks] Rastalocken ⟨**IV U3**, 90⟩

dream [driːm] Traum **II**

*to **dream** [driːm] träumen **IV U2**, 47

dress [dres] Kleid **III**

   dress code [ˈdres ˌkəʊd] Kleiderordnung; Bekleidungsvorschriften **IV U2**, 43

   fancy **dress** [ˈfænsi dres] Verkleidung; Kostüm **II**

to drift [drɪft] schweben; treiben ⟨**IV U1**, 12⟩

drink [drɪŋk] Getränk **I**

*to **drink** [drɪŋk] trinken **I**

drive [draɪv] Fahrt; Anfahrt; Autofahrt **IV U2**, 44

   clothing **drive** [ˈkləʊðɪŋ ˌdraɪv] Kleidersammlung **IV U2**, 51

*to **drive** [draɪv] fahren **III**

   *to **drive** off [draɪv ˈɒf] wegfahren **III**

driver [ˈdraɪvə] Fahrer/-in **II**

drizzle [ˈdrɪzl] Nieselregen **IV U1**, 17

to drop [drɒp] fallen (lassen) **II**

   to **drop** out (of) [drɒp ˈaʊt əv] abbrechen **III**

drop-off [ˈdrɒpɒf] Abgabe **IV U2**, 51

to drown [draʊn] ertrinken; ertränken **III**

drums (pl) [drʌmz] Schlagzeug **III**

dry [draɪ] trocken **III**

dude (coll) [duːd] Mann; Alter (ugs.) **IV AC2**, 41

dumpster [ˈdʌmpstə] Müllcontainer ⟨**IV U3**, 85⟩

during (+ noun) [ˈdjʊərɪŋ] während (+ Nomen) **II**

duty-free [ˌdjuːtiˈfriː] zollfrei **IV U1**, 9

DVD [ˌdiːviːˈdiː] DVD **I**

E

e.g. (= for example) [ˌiːˈdʒiː] z.B. (= zum Beispiel) I

each [iːtʃ] jede/-r/-s I
  each other [iːtʃˈʌðə] einander; sich; sich gegenseitig I

each [iːtʃ] pro Person; pro Stück I

ear [ɪə] Ohr IV AC1, 22

early [ˈɜːli] früh I
  this early [ˈðɪs ˌɜːli] so früh III

to earn [ɜːn] verdienen I

earth [ɜːθ] Erdboden; Erde; die Erde II
  What on earth …? [wɒt ˌɒn ˈɜːθ] Was um alles in der Welt …? II

east [iːst] Osten; Ost- I

Easter [ˈiːstə] Ostern I

easy [ˈiːzi] einfach; leicht I

easy-going [ˌiːziˈɡəʊɪŋ] locker; unkompliziert IV U1, 19

*to eat [iːt] essen; fressen I

Eco [ˈiːkəʊ] Öko- II

to edit out [ˌedɪt ˈaʊt] herausschneiden III

education (no pl) [ˌedʒʊˈkeɪʃn] Erziehung; Bildung III

effect [ɪˈfekt] Effekt; Wirkung IV U3, 89
  audio-visual effect [ˌɔːdiəʊvɪʒuəl ɪˈfekt] audiovisueller Effekt II
  special effect [ˌspeʃl ɪˈfekt] Spezialeffekt IV TS3, 105

effective [ɪˈfektɪv] effektiv; wirkungsvoll IV TS2, 66

effectiveness [ɪˈfektɪvnəs] Effektivität; Wirksamkeit IV TS2, 67

egg [eɡ] Ei I

Egyptian [ɪˈdʒɪpʃn] Ägypter/-in; ägyptisch IV U1, 20

eight [eɪt] acht I

not … either [nɒt … ˈaɪðə; nɒt … ˈiːðə] auch nicht IV AC4, 107

either … or … [ˈaɪðə/ˈiːðə … ɔː] entweder … oder … IV U3, 79

elderly [ˈeldəli] älter III

electric [ɪˈlektrɪk] elektrisch III

electrician [ɪˌlekˈtrɪʃn] Elektriker/-in III

electricity [ɪˌlekˈtrɪsəti] Elektrizität; Strom III

electrics [ɪˈlektrɪks] Elektrik III

electronic [ɪˌlekˈtrɒnɪk] elektronisch II

element [ˈelɪmənt] Element III

elephant [ˈelɪfənt] Elefant III

elevator (AE) [ˈelɪveɪtə] Aufzug; Lift IV U2, 44

eleven [ɪˈlevn] elf I

else [els] andere/-r/-s; sonst noch III
  nobody else [ˈnəʊbədi els] niemand anderes III
  what else [wɒt ˈels] was sonst; was noch I

e-mail [ˈiːmeɪl] E-Mail I

to e-mail [ˈiːmeɪl] mailen; per E-Mail schicken II

embarrassed [ɪmˈbærəst] verlegen II

embarrassing [ɪmˈbærəsɪŋ] peinlich II

emotion [ɪˈməʊʃn] Gefühl; Emotion ⟨IV TS3, 104⟩

emotional [ɪˈməʊʃnl] emotional; Gefühls- III

emperor [ˈemprə] Kaiser III

empire [ˈempaɪə] Reich; Kaiserreich III

empty [ˈemti] leer III

encyclopaedia [ɪnˌsaɪkləˈpiːdiə] Enzyklopädie; Lexikon °IV TS3, 101

end [end] Ende; Schluss I
  in the end [ˌɪn ðiˈend] schließlich; zum Schluss I

to end [end] enden; beenden II
  to end up [ˌend ˈʌp] enden; landen II

ending [ˈendɪŋ] Ende; Schluss (einer Geschichte) I
  happy ending [ˌhæpi ˈendɪŋ] Happy End III

endless [ˈendləs] endlos IV AC2, 38

enemy [ˈenəmi] Feind/-in III

energy [ˈenədʒi] Energie; Kraft III

search engine [ˈsɜːtʃ ˌendʒɪn] Suchmaschine °IV U2, 42

steam engine [ˈstiːm ˌendʒɪn] Dampfmaschine III

engineer [ˌendʒɪˈnɪə] Ingenieur/-in; Techniker/-in IV TS3, 101

engineering [ˌendʒɪˈnɪərɪŋ] Technik; Maschinenbau ⟨IV TS3, 102⟩

English [ˈɪŋglɪʃ] englisch; Englisch; aus England; Engländer/-in I
  English-speaking [ˈɪŋglɪʃˌspiːkɪŋ] englischsprachig I
  I'm English. [aɪm ˈɪŋglɪʃ] Ich bin Engländer/-in. I

to enjoy [ɪnˈdʒɔɪ] genießen; sich freuen an II
  to enjoy oneself [ɪnˈdʒɔɪ] Spaß haben; sich amüsieren III

enlightenment [ɪnˈlaɪtnmənt] Aufklärung; Erleuchtung IV U3, 74

enough [ɪˈnʌf] genug; genügend I

to enter [ˈentə] hineingehen; betreten; eintreten; hier: mitmachen II

to entertain [ˌentəˈteɪn] unterhalten IV TS1, 30

entertainer [ˌentəˈteɪnə] Entertainer/-in; Unterhaltungskünstler/-in IV U3, 72

entertaining [ˌentəˈteɪnɪŋ] unterhaltsam IV TS3, 103

entertainment (no pl) [ˌentəˈteɪnmənt] Unterhaltung III

enthusiasm [ɪnˈθjuːziæzm] Enthusiasmus; Begeisterung IV U3, 72

entrance [ˈentrəns] Eingang; Eintritt III

entry [ˈentri] Eintrag III
  diary entry [ˈdaɪəri entri] Tagebucheintrag III

environment [ɪnˈvaɪrnmənt] Umwelt; Umgebung III

epic [ˈepɪk] episch; hier: geil IV AC2, 41

equipment [ɪˈkwɪpmənt] Ausstattung; Ausrüstung II

er [ɜː] äh I

era [ˈɪərə] Ära; Zeitalter IV U1, 19

escalator [ˈeskəleɪtə] Rolltreppe I

escape [ɪˈskeɪp] Flucht III

to escape (from) [ɪˈskeɪp frəm] fliehen; entfliehen; flüchten; entkommen IV U2, 52

to estimate [ˈestɪmeɪt] schätzen IV TS3, 103

etc. (= et cetera) [ɪtˈsetrə] usw. (= und so weiter) II

ethnic [ˈeθnɪk] ethnisch; Volks-; hier: exotisch IV U3, 75

euro [ˈjʊərəʊ] Euro (Währung) I

European [ˌjʊərəˈpiːən] Europäer/-in; europäisch; aus Europa IV AC2, 38

even [ˈiːvn] sogar; selbst I

evening [ˈiːvnɪŋ] Abend I
  in the evenings [ɪn ðiˈiːvnɪŋz] abends I

event [ɪˈvent] Ereignis; Veranstaltung I

ever [ˈevə] jemals I
  the best … ever [ˈbest … ˌevə] der/die/das beste … überhaupt III

every [ˈevri] jede/-r/-s I

everybody [ˈevrɪbɒdi] jeder; alle II

everyday [ˈevrɪdeɪ] alltäglich III

everyone [ˈevrɪwʌn] jeder; alle I

everything [ˈevrɪθɪŋ] alles I

everywhere [ˈevrɪweə] überall I

exactly [ɪɡˈzæktli] genau II

to exaggerate [ɪɡˈzædʒəreɪt] übertreiben IV TS1, 32

exaggerated [ɪɡˈzædʒəreɪtɪd] übertrieben IV U2, 52

exam [ɪɡˈzæm] Examen; Prüfung II

example [ɪɡˈzɑːmpl] Beispiel I
  for example [fər ɪɡˈzɑːmpl] zum Beispiel II

excellent [ˈekslnt] exzellent; hervorragend ⟨IV TS3, 104⟩

excellent piece of quick thinking [ˈekslnt piːs əv kwɪk ˈθɪŋkɪŋ] ausgezeichnete Reaktionsschnelligkeit ⟨IV TS1, 36⟩

except [ɪkˈsept] außer; bis auf IV U1, 17

excerpt [ˈeksɜːpt] Auszug °IV U3, 89

exchange [ɪksˈtʃeɪndʒ] Austausch; Austausch- III
  exchange student [ɪksˈtʃeɪndʒ ˌstjuːdnt] Austauschschüler/-in III
  student exchange [ˈstjuːdnt ɪksˈtʃeɪndʒ] Schüleraustausch III

to exchange [ɪksˈtʃeɪndʒ] austauschen II

excited [ɪkˈsaɪtɪd] aufgeregt; begeistert I

excitement (no pl) [ɪkˈsaɪtmənt] Aufregung III

exciting [ɪkˈsaɪtɪŋ] spannend; aufregend I

Excuse me … [ɪkˈskjuːz mi] Entschuldigung!; Entschuldigen Sie! I

exercise [ˈeksəsaɪz] Übung; Aufgabe I
  exercise book [ˈeksəsaɪz ˌbʊk] Übungsheft I

to expect [ɪkˈspekt] erwarten III

expectation [ˌekspekˈteɪʃn] Erwartung °IV U2, 50

expensive [ɪkˈspensɪv] teuer I

experience [ɪkˈspɪərɪəns] Erfahrung II

to experience [ɪkˈspɪərɪəns] erfahren; erleben III

expert [ˈekspɜːt] Experte/Expertin II

to explain [ɪkˈspleɪn] erklären I

exploration [ˌekspləˈreɪʃn] Erforschung; Erkundung 〈IV TS3, 104〉

to explore [ɪkˈsplɔː] auf Entdeckungsreise gehen; sich umschauen; erkunden; erforschen I

to express [ɪkˈspres] ausdrücken II

expression [ɪkˈspreʃn] Ausdruck; Wendung; Äußerung II

facial expression [ˌfeɪʃl ɪkˈspreʃn] Gesichtsausdruck III

*to become extinct [bɪˌkʌm ɪkˈstɪŋkt] aussterben III

extinction (no pl) [ɪksˈtɪŋkʃn] Aussterben III

extra [ˈekstrə] extra; zusätzlich I

extreme [ɪkˈstriːm] extrem; radikal IV AC2, 40

eye [aɪ] Auge II

to roll one's eyes [ˌrəʊl wʌnzˈaɪz] die Augen verdrehen II

He couldn't believe his eyes. [hi ˌkʊdnt bɪˌliːv hɪzˈaɪz] Er traute seinen Augen nicht. II

eyebrow [ˈaɪbraʊ] Augenbraue 〈IV U3, 90〉

eye-catcher [ˈaɪkætʃə] Blickfang; Hingucker IV TS2, 65

eyewitness [ˈaɪwɪtnəs] Augenzeuge/Augenzeugin II

F

fabulous [ˈfæbjələs] sagenhaft; fantastisch IV TS2, 66

face [feɪs] Gesicht I

Put … face down. [pʊt ˌfeɪs ˈdaʊn] Lege/Legt … umgedreht hin. I

to face [feɪs] gegenüber stehen; konfrontiert werden mit IV TS1, 31

Let's face it. [lets ˈfeɪs ɪt] Machen wir uns doch nichts vor. IV TS1, 32

face-to-face [ˌfeɪstəˈfeɪs] hier: persönlich; von Angesicht zu Angesicht II

facial expression [ˌfeɪʃl ɪkˈspreʃn] Gesichtsausdruck III

fact [fækt] Fakt; Tatsache II

factory [ˈfæktri] Fabrik; Werk III

factual [ˈfæktʃʊəl] sachlich III

factual text [ˌfæktʃʊəl ˈtekst] Sachtext III

degree Fahrenheit (°F) [ˈfærnhaɪt] Grad Fahrenheit IV AC2, 38

to fail to do sth [ˈfeɪl tə] versäumen, etw. zu tun; es nicht schaffen, etw. zu tun IV U3, 79

fair [feə] gerecht; fair I

fair play [feə ˈpleɪ] Fairplay III

to fake [feɪk] vortäuschen; fälschen II

fake [feɪk] falsch; gefälscht IV TS1, 35

*to fall [fɔːl] fallen; hinfallen I

*to fall asleep [ˌfɔːl əˈsliːp] einschlafen I

*to fall down [ˌfɔːl ˈdaʊn] stürzen; hinunterfallen III

*to fall for [ˈfɔːl fə] hereinfallen auf IV TS2, 64

*to fall off [ˌfɔːl ˈɒf] herunterfallen; hinunterfallen II

*to fall over [ˌfɔːl ˈəʊvə] hinfallen; umkippen I

family [ˈfæmli] Familie I

family tree [ˈfæmli ˌtriː] Stammbaum I

host family [ˈhəʊst ˌfæmli] Gastfamilie III

famous [ˈfeɪməs] berühmt I

fan [fæn] Fan; Anhänger/-in II

to fancy (+ ing) (infml) (BE) [ˈfænsi] Lust haben zu 〈IV TS1, 31〉

fancy dress [ˈfænsi dres] Verkleidung; Kostüm II

fantastic [fænˈtæstɪk] fantastisch; großartig II

fantasy [ˈfæntəsi] Fantasie; Traum- I; Fantasy III

fanzine [fænˈziːn] Fanzeitschrift II

FAQ [ˌefəˈkjuː] Liste mit häufig gestellten Fragen III

in the far west [ɪn ðə fɑː ˈwest] im äußersten Westen III

far [fɑː] weit II

so far [ˌsəʊ ˈfɑː] bis jetzt II

fare [feə] Fahrpreis III

farewell [ˌfeəˈwel] Lebewohl; Abschied 〈IV TS1, 36〉

farm [fɑːm] Farm; Bauernhof I

farmer [ˈfɑːmə] Farmer/-in; Landwirt/-in II

fascinating [ˈfæsɪneɪtɪŋ] faszinierend III

fashion [ˈfæʃn] Mode II

fast [fɑːst] schnell I

father [ˈfɑːðə] Vater I

their fault [ˌðeə ˈfɔːlt] ihre Schuld 〈IV TS1, 36〉

favourite [ˈfeɪvrɪt] Favorit/-in; Günstling III

favourite [ˈfeɪvrɪt] Lieblings- I

My favourite … [maɪ ˈfeɪvrɪt] Mein/e Lieblings … I

What's your favourite …? [ˈwɒts jə ˌfeɪvrɪt] Was ist dein/e Lieblings…? I

fear [fɪə] Angst; Furcht; Befürchtung II

fearful [ˈfɪəfl] ängstlich III

feast [fiːst] Festmahl 〈IV U3, 85〉

feather [ˈfeðə] Feder III

feature [ˈfiːtʃə] Eigenschaft; Merkmal III

to feature [ˈfiːtʃə] zeigen; aufweisen III

February [ˈfebruri] Februar I

*to be fed up (with) [bi fed ˈʌp wɪð] sauer sein (auf); die Nase voll haben (von) III

fee [fiː] Gebühr III

school fees (pl) [ˈskuːl fiːz] Schulgeld; Schulgebühren III

*to feed [fiːd] füttern; ernähren III

feedback [ˈfiːdbæk] Feedback; Rückmeldung II

*to feel [fiːl] fühlen; sich fühlen I

*to feel left out [ˌfiːl left ˈaʊt] sich ausgeschlossen fühlen II

*to feel sick [ˌfiːl ˈsɪk] Übelkeit verspüren; sich schlecht fühlen II

*to feel sorry for [ˌfiːl ˈsɒri fɔː] Mitleid haben mit; bedauern III

feeling [ˈfiːlɪŋ] Gefühl II

ferry [ˈferi] Fähre IV U1, 9

festival [ˈfestɪvl] Festival; Fest I

to fetch [fetʃ] holen; abholen IV U1, 17

fever [ˈfiːvə] Fieber II

few [fjuː] wenige II

a few [ə ˈfjuː] ein paar; wenige; einige I

fiction (no pl) [ˈfɪkʃn] Erzählliteratur; Erfindung; Prosa; Fiktion III

science fiction [ˌsaɪəns ˈfɪkʃn] Science-Fiction (Zukunftsdichtung) II

fictional [ˈfɪkʃnl] fiktional; fiktiv; erdichtet III

field [fiːld] Feld; Spielfeld; Wiese; Weide; Acker II

fifteen [ˌfɪfˈtiːn] fünfzehn I

fight [faɪt] Kampf; Streit II

*to fight [faɪt] kämpfen; (sich) streiten II

figure [ˈfɪgə] Figur; Gestalt II; Ziffer; Zahl III

wax figure [ˈwæks ˌfɪgə] Wachsfigur II

to fill [fɪl] (sich) füllen III

to fill in [ˌfɪl ˈɪn] ausfüllen II

filling [ˈfɪlɪŋ] Füllung IV U3, 75

film [fɪlm] Film I

to film [fɪlm] filmen; drehen III

filmmaker [ˈfɪlmˌmeɪkə] Filmemacher/-in II

final [ˈfaɪnl] endgültig II; letzte/-r/-s III

finally [ˈfaɪnli] schließlich; endlich; zum Schluss; letztlich II

*to find [faɪnd] finden; herausfinden I

*to find one's way around [ˌfaɪnd wʌnz ˌweɪ əˈraʊnd] sich zurechtfinden IV U2, 46

*to find out [ˌfaɪnd ˈaʊt] herausfinden I

fine [faɪn] gut; in Ordnung; schön I

I'm fine. [ˌaɪm ˈfaɪn] Mir geht's gut. I

finger [ˈfɪŋgə] Finger I

*to keep your fingers crossed [kiːp jɔː ˌfɪŋgəz ˈkrɒst] die Daumen drücken I

finish line [ˈfɪnɪʃ ˌlaɪn] Ziellinie II

to finish [ˈfɪnɪʃ] beenden; enden; fertigstellen; aufhören I

finished [ˈfɪnɪʃt] fertig II

fire [faɪə] Feuer III

*to be on fire [ˌbiː ɒn ˈfaɪə] brennen III

fireworks (pl) [ˈfaɪəwɜːks] Feuerwerk I

first [fɜːst] zuerst; als Erstes; erste/-r/-s I

at first [ət ˈfɜːst] zuerst; zunächst II

first language [ˌfɜːst ˈlæŋgwɪdʒ] Muttersprache II

first person narrator [ˌfɜːst ˌpɜːsn nəˈreɪtə] Ich-Erzähler/-in III

fish, fish (pl) [fɪʃ] Fisch I

fishing [ˈfɪʃɪŋ] Angeln; Fischen; Fischerei III

to fit [fɪt] passen II

*to get fit [ˌget ˈfɪt] in Form kommen; fit werden I

five [faɪv] fünf I

to **fix** [fɪks] reparieren; befestigen II

flag [flæg] Flagge; Fahne III

flair [fleə] Flair; Atmosphäre II

flame [fleɪm] Flamme III

flash [flæʃ] Blitz; Lichtblitz III

flashback ['flæʃbæk] Rückblende; Flashback III

flat [flæt] Wohnung I

flat [flæt] flach; platt **IV AC2**, 40

flavor (AE) ['fleɪvə] Geschmack; Aroma **IV U3**, 75

flea market ['fli: ˌmɑːkɪt] Flohmarkt I

flight [flaɪt] Flug III

 flight attendant ['flaɪt əˌtendnt] Flugbegleiter/-in **IV U1**, 9

floor [flɔː] Fußboden I; Stockwerk **IV U2**, 44

to **flow** out [fləʊ ˈaʊt] hinausfließen II

flower ['flaʊə] Blume II

*to **fly** [flaɪ] fliegen III

*to **fly** [flaɪ] hissen **IV AC2**, 39

flyer ['flaɪə] Flyer I

focus ['fəʊkəs] Blickpunkt; Schwerpunkt; Fokus III

 out of **focus** [ˌaʊt əv ˈfəʊkəs] unscharf III

to **focus** (on) ['fəʊkəs ɒn] sich konzentrieren (auf) II

folder ['fəʊldə] Ordner; Mappe I

to **follow** ['fɒləʊ] folgen; hinterhergehen; befolgen II

the **following** [ðə ˈfɒləʊɪŋ] folgende/-r/-s III

follow-up ['fɒləʊʌp] Fortsetzung; Folge- **IV U3**, 92

food [fuːd] Essen; Lebensmittel I; Futter III

foot [fʊt], **feet** [fiːt] (pl) Fuß (Längenmaß: 30,48 cm) **IV AC2**, 39

 *to keep one's **feet** or hands still [ˌkiːp wʌnz ˈfiːtːɔː ˈhændz stɪl] die Beine und Hände ruhig halten III

 on **foot** [ɒn ˈfʊt] zu Fuß II

foot, feet (pl) [fʊt; fiːt] Fuß I

football ['fʊtbɔːl] Fußball I

for [fɔː; fə] für I; wegen II

for (+ Zeitraum) [fɔː; fə] seit III

 for example [fər ɪgˈzɑːmpl] zum Beispiel II

 for free [fə ˈfriː] umsonst; kostenlos **IV U3**, 72

for … [fɔː; fə] … lang II

force [fɔːs] Kraft; Macht **IV U1**, 19

weather **forecast** ['weðə ˌfɔːkɑːst] Wettervorhersage III

foreground ['fɔːgraʊnd] Vordergrund **IV U2**, 47

foreign ['fɒrɪn] ausländisch; fremd **IV U1**, 8

 foreign language [ˌfɒrɪn ˈlæŋgwɪdʒ] Fremdsprache II

forest ['fɒrɪst] Wald II

forever [fəˈrevə] für immer; ewig II

*to **forget** [fəˈget] vergessen I

*to **forgive** [fəˈgɪv] vergeben; verzeihen II

fork [fɔːk] Gabel III

form [fɔːm] Form I; Formular III

negative **form** ['negətɪv ˌfɔːm] verneinte Form I

past **form** ['pɑːst fɔːm] Vergangenheitsform II

possessive **form** [pəˌsesɪv ˈfɔːm] Possessivform I

short **form** ['ʃɔːt fɔːm] Kurzform I

to **form** [fɔːm] formen; bilden II

formal ['fɔːml] formal; formell; förmlich II

forum ['fɔːrəm] Forum II

forward ['fɔːwəd] vorwärts III

 to look **forward** to [ˌlʊk ˈfɔːwəd tə] sich freuen auf III

to **found** [faʊnd] gründen III

water **fountain** ['wɔːtə ˌfaʊntɪn] Wasserspender **IV AC4**, 106

four [fɔː] vier I

 Four and six is ten. [ˌfɔːr ənd ˌsɪks ɪz ˈten] Vier plus sechs ist zehn. I

four-walled ['fɔːwɔːld] mit vier Wänden ⟨**IV U3**, 90⟩

fox [fɒks] Fuchs II

freeze frame ['friːz ˌfreɪm] Standbild III

free [friː] frei; kostenlos II

 free time [ˌfriː 'taɪm] Freizeit I

 for **free** [fə 'friː] umsonst; kostenlos **IV U3**, 72

freedom (no pl) ['friːdəm] Freiheit; Unabhängigkeit III

freeway (AE) ['friːweɪ] Autobahn **IV U3**, 79

freeze frame ['friːz ˌfreɪm] Standbild III

French [frenʃ] französisch; Französisch II

frequently asked [ˌfriːkwəntliˈɑːskt] häufig gefragt II

fresh [freʃ] frisch I

Friday ['fraɪdeɪ] Freitag I

fridge [frɪdʒ] Kühlschrank I

fried [fraɪd] gebraten (in der Pfanne) **IV U3**, 75

friend [frend] Freund/-in I

 *to become **friends** [bɪˌkʌm ˈfrendz] sich anfreunden; Freundschaft schließen **IV AC2**, 41

 *to make **friends** [ˌmeɪk ˈfrendz] Freundschaft schließen II

 That's what **friends** are for. [ˌðæts wɒt ˈfrendz ˌɑː fɔː] Dafür sind Freunde da. I

friendly ['frendli] freundlich; nett II

friendship ['frendʃɪp] Freundschaft II

fringe [frɪndʒ] Rand-; Alternativ- III

from [frɒm; frəm] aus; von I

 from the outside [ˌfrəm ðiˌaʊtˈsaɪd] von außen **IV U3**, 75

 from … to [frəm … tə] von … bis I

 Where … **from**? [ˌweə … ˈfrɒm] Woher …? I

 from around the world [frɒm əˌraʊnd ðə ˈwɜːld] aus aller Welt III

front [frʌnt] Vorderseite; Front-; Vorder- III

 front door [ˌfrʌnt ˈdɔː] Haustür II

 front yard (AE) [ˌfrʌnt ˈjɑːd] Vorgarten **IV U2**, 43

in **front** of [ɪn ˈfrʌnt əv] vor I

fruit [fruːt] Frucht; Obst I

full (of) [fʊl əv] voll (von) I

 to talk with your mouth **full** [ˌtɔːk wɪð jɔː ˈmaʊθ fʊl] mit vollem Mund sprechen **IV AC1**, 22

fun [fʌn] Freude; Spaß I

 *to have **fun** [ˌhæv ˈfʌn] Spaß haben; sich amüsieren I

 It's **fun**. [ɪts ˈfʌn] Es macht Spaß. I

 No risk, no **fun**! [ˌnəʊ ˌrɪsk nəʊ ˈfʌn] Wer nicht wagt, der nicht gewinnt. **IV AC3**, 69

fun [fʌn] lustig; witzig; fröhlich I

function ['fʌŋkʃn] Funktion **IV TS3**, 103

funny ['fʌni] lustig; witzig I; merkwürdig; komisch III

further ['fɜːðə] weiter (weg) III

future ['fjuːtʃə] Zukunft III

future ['fjuːtʃə] zukünftig **IV U1**, 19

G

gadget ['gædʒɪt] Gerät; technische Spielerei III

Gaelic ['geɪlɪk] gälisch; Gälisch III

gallery walk ['gælri ˌwɔːk] Museumsrundgang; Vernissage I

game [geɪm] Spiel I

 guessing **game** ['gesɪŋ ˌgeɪm] Ratespiel II

gap [gæp] Lücke; Spalt; Abstand I

garage ['gærɑːʒ] Garage I

garden ['gɑːdn] Garten I

garlic ['gɑːlɪk] Knoblauch **IV U1**, 11

to **gasp** [gɑːsp] tief Luft holen; keuchen **IV U3**, 72

gate [geɪt] Gate; Flugsteig; Ausgang **IV U1**, 15

geek [giːk] Außenseiter/-in **IV U2**, 48

general ['dʒenrl] allgemein °**IV U3**, 92

generation [ˌdʒenəˈreɪʃn] Generation III

generous ['dʒenrəs] großzügig III

genius ['dʒiːniəs] Genie II

genre ['ʒɑ̃ːnrə] Gattung III

gentleman ['dʒentlmən], **gentlemen** ['dʒentlmen] (pl) Gentleman; feiner Herr III

geocaching ['dʒiːˌəʊkæʃɪŋ] Geocaching III

geography [dʒiˈɒgrəfi] Geografie; Erdkunde III

German ['dʒɜːmən] deutsch; Deutsch; aus Deutschland; Deutsche/-r I

gerund ['dʒerənd] Gerundium °**IV U2**, 43

gesture ['dʒestʃə] Geste; Gebärde **IV TS1**, 33

*to **get** [get] holen; bringen; bekommen; besorgen; kaufen I; werden III

 *to **get** around [ˌget əˈraʊnd] hier: sich fortbewegen II

 *to **get** away with [ˌget əˈweɪ wɪð] davonkommen mit II

 *to **get** caught [ˌget ˈkɔːt] erwischt werden; ertappt werden **IV AC3**, 68

*to **get** fit [ˌget ˈfɪt] in Form kommen; fit werden **I**
*to **get** in [ˌget ˈɪn] einsteigen **IV U3**, 76
*to **get** in the way [ˌget ɪn ðə ˈweɪ] stören; im Weg stehen **II**
*to **get** into [ˌget ˈɪntə] einsteigen; hineingelangen **I**
*to **get** into trouble [ˌget ɪntə ˈtrʌbl] in Schwierigkeiten geraten **IV AC3**, 69
*to **get** involved with sb [ˌget ɪnˈvɒlvd wɪð] sich einlassen mit jmdm. ⟨**IVTS1**, 34⟩
*to **get** lost [ˌget ˈlɒst] verloren gehen; sich verirren **III**
*to **get** off (a bus/train) [ˌget ˈɒf] aussteigen (aus einem Bus/Zug) **II**
*to **get** on (the bus) [ˌget ˈɒn] einsteigen (in den Bus) **III**
*to **get** on people's nerves [ˌget ɒn ˌsʌmbɒdiz ˈnɜːvz] jemandem auf die Nerven gehen **I**
*to **get** organised [get ˈɔːɡənaɪzd] sich organisieren **III**
*to **get** out of [get ˌaʊt əv] aussteigen **II**
*to **get** right [get ˈraɪt] richtig beantworten **III**
*to **get** started [get ˈstɑːtɪd] anfangen **II**
*to **get** sth out of one's head [get ˌaʊt əv wʌnz ˈhed] etw. aus dem Kopf bekommen **III**
*to **get** there [ˈget ðeə] hinkommen **I**
*to **get** to [ˈget tə] kommen zu; kommen nach; erreichen **I**
*to **get** to know [get tə ˈnəʊ] kennenlernen **III**
*to **get** up [getˌˈʌp] aufstehen (aus dem Bett) **I**
*to **get** used to sth [get ˈjuːzd tə] sich an etw. gewöhnen **IV U2**, 44
Time to **get** up! [ˌtaɪm tə getˌˈʌp] Es ist Zeit aufzustehen! **I**
ghost [ɡəʊst] Geist **II**
giant [dʒaɪənt] Riesen-; riesig ⟨**IVTS3**, 101⟩
gig [ɡɪɡ] Auftritt; Gig **III**
gigantic [dʒaɪˈɡæntɪk] gigantisch; riesig **IV AC2**, 40
girl [ɡɜːl] Mädchen **I**
a **girl** from Germany [ə ˌɡɜːl frəm ˈdʒɜːməni] ein Mädchen aus Deutschland **I**
girlfriend [ˈɡɜːlfrend] Freundin (in einer Paarbeziehung) **II**
gist [dʒɪst] das Wesentliche **II**
*to **give** [ɡɪv] geben; schenken **I**
*to **give** a talk [ˌɡɪv ə ˈtɔːk] einen Vortrag halten **IV U2**, 43
*to **give** away [ˌɡɪv əˈweɪ] verteilen; verschenken **IVTS2**, 64; verraten; preisgeben °**IV U3**, 93
*to **give** reasons [ˌɡɪv ˈriːznz] Gründe nennen/angeben ⟨**IV U3**, 90⟩
*to **give** sb a piggyback [ˌɡɪv ə ˈpɪɡibæk] jmdn. Huckepack nehmen **IV U1**, 16

*to **give** sb funny looks [ˌɡɪv fʌni ˈlʊks] jmdn. schief anschauen **III**
*to **give** thanks [ˌɡɪv ˈθæŋks] danken **IV U2**, 45
*to **give** the bumps [ˌɡɪv ðə ˈbʌmps] hochleben lassen **I**
*to **give** up [ˌɡɪv ˈʌp] aufgeben **III**
glad [ɡlæd] froh **IV AC1**, 23
glamorous [ˈɡlæmrəs] glamourös **IVTS2**, 65
to **glance** at [ˈɡlɑːns ət] einen Blick werfen auf; blicken auf ⟨**IV U3**, 90⟩
glass [ɡlɑːs] Glas **I**
glasses (pl) [ˈɡlɑːsɪz] Brille **II**
to **glint** [ɡlɪnt] glitzern ⟨**IV U3**, 90⟩
glossary [ˈɡlɒsri] Glossar; Stichwortverzeichnis **IVTS1**, 30
glove [ɡlʌv] Handschuh **I**
*to **go** [ɡəʊ] gehen; fahren **I**
*to **go** black [ˌɡəʊ ˈblæk] schwarz werden **II**
*to **go** crazy [ˌɡəʊ ˈkreɪzi] ausflippen; durchdrehen; verrückt werden **II**
*to **go** down [ˌɡəʊ ˈdaʊn] hinuntergehen; nach unten gehen; entlanggehen **I**
*to **go** for a walk [ˌɡəʊ fərˌə ˈwɔːk] spazieren gehen **II**
*to **go** on [ˌɡəʊ ˈɒn] weitergehen; weitermachen; weiterführen; fortfahren **I**
*to **go** out [ˌɡəʊˌˈaʊt] ausgehen; hinausgehen **III**
*to **go** over to [ˌɡəʊ ˈəʊvə tə] hinübergehen zu; zu jmdm. nach Hause gehen **II**
*to **go** right back to [ˌɡəʊ raɪt ˈbæk tə] zurückgehen auf **III**
*to **go** round in circles [ˌɡəʊ ˌraʊnd ɪn ˈsɜːklz] sich im Kreis drehen **III**
*to **go** shopping [ˌɡəʊ ˈʃɒpɪŋ] einkaufen gehen **I**
*to **go** swimming [ˌɡəʊ ˈswɪmɪŋ] Schwimmen gehen **I**
*to **go** to bed [ˌɡəʊ tə ˈbed] ins Bett gehen **I**
*to **go** together [ˌɡəʊ təˈɡeðə] zueinander passen; zueinander gehören **I**
*to **go** with [ˈɡəʊ wɪð] passen zu; gehören zu **I**
*to **go** wrong [ˌɡəʊ ˈrɒŋ] schiefgehen **II**
*to let **go** (of) [ˌlet ˈɡəʊ (əv)] loslassen **II**
Go on! [ˌɡəʊ ˈɒn] Los! **IV U2**, 55
It's **gone**. [ɪts ˈɡɒn] Es ist weg. **II**
What's **going** on? [wɒts ˌɡəʊɪŋˈɒn] Was ist los?; Was geht ab? **III**
goal [ɡəʊl] Tor; Ziel **I**
God [ɡɒd] Gott ⟨**IV U2**, 49⟩
goddess [ˈɡɒdes] Göttin **IV U3**, 74
gold [ɡəʊld] Gold **III**
golden [ˈɡəʊldn] golden; Gold- ⟨**IV U1**, 12⟩
golden age [ˌɡəʊldn ˈeɪdʒ] goldenes Zeitalter **III**
golf [ɡɒlf] Golf **III**
*to be **gone** [biː ˈɡɒn] verschwunden sein; weg sein **II**

gonna (= going to) (coll) [ˈɡɒnə] wird/ werden **IV U3**, 70
good [ɡʊd] gut **I**
*to be **good** at [biː ˈɡʊdˌət] gut sein in **I**
good luck [ˌɡʊd ˈlʌk] viel Glück **IV U3**, 76
Good morning. [ɡʊd ˈmɔːnɪŋ] Guten Morgen. **I**
goodbye [ɡʊdˈbaɪ] auf Wiedersehen **I**
gorge scrambling [ˈɡɔːdʒ ˌskræmblɪŋ] Schluchtenklettern **II**
government [ˈɡʌvnmənt] Regierung **IVTS3**, 102
to **grab** [ɡræb] greifen; ergreifen; schnappen **II**
grade (AE) [ɡreɪd] Note **IV U3**, 78
8th-**grader** (AE) [ˈeɪtθˌɡreɪdə] Achtklässler/-in **IV U2**, 48
grammar [ˈɡræmə] Grammatik **II**
grammar school [ˈɡræmə ˌskuːl] Gymnasium **III**
grandad [ˈɡrændæd] Opa **I**
grandma [ˈɡrænmɑː] Oma **I**
grandparents (pl) [ˈɡrænˌpeərənts] Großeltern **I**
granny [ˈɡræni] Oma **I**
graphic novel [ˌɡræfɪk ˈnɒvl] Bildergeschichte; Comic **III**
gratitude [ˈɡrætɪtjuːd] Dankbarkeit **III**
great [ɡreɪt] großartig; toll; super **I**
It's **great** for … [ɪts ˈɡreɪt fə] Es ist super zum/für … **I**
green [ɡriːn] grün **I**
Greenwich Mean Time (= GMT) [ˌɡrenɪdʒ ˈmiːn ˌtaɪm] westeuropäische Zeit **I**
greeting [ˈɡriːtɪŋ] Gruß **I**
grey [ɡreɪ] grau **I**
grid [ɡrɪd] Gitter; Tabelle; Raster **I**
groan [ɡrəʊn] Stöhnen **IV U1**, 10
to **groan** [ɡrəʊn] stöhnen **IV U3**, 74
ground [ɡraʊnd] Boden; Erdboden **IV U1**, 17
*to be **grounded** [biː ˈɡraʊndɪd] Hausarrest haben **III**
group [ɡruːp] Gruppe; Klasse **I**
a **group** of three [ə ˌɡruːp əv ˈθriː] eine Dreiergruppe **I**
tutor **group** [ˈtjuːtə ˌɡruːp] Klasse (in einer englischen Schule) **I**
to **group** (around) [ɡruːp (əˈraʊnd)] gruppieren (um) **III**
*to **grow** [ɡrəʊ] wachsen; anbauen; züchten **III**
*to **grow** up [ˌɡrəʊˌˈʌp] aufwachsen; erwachsen werden **III**
guard [ɡɑːd] Wache; Wächter/-in **II**
to **guess** [ɡes] raten; erraten; vermuten **I**; annehmen **IV AC1**, 22
guessing game [ˈɡesɪŋ ˌɡeɪm] Ratespiel **II**
guest [ɡest] Gast **III**
guide [ɡaɪd] Führer/-in; Reiseführer **II**
to **guide** [ɡaɪd] führen; leiten **III**
guidebook [ˈɡaɪdbʊk] Reiseführer **IV U3**, 72
guilty [ˈɡɪlti] schuldig **IVTS1**, 37

guinea pig [ˈgɪni ˌpɪg] Meerschweinchen **I**
guitar [gɪˈtɑː] Gitarre **IV U1**, 19
chewing **gum** [ˈtʃuːɪŋ ˌgʌm] Kaugummi
IV U1, 15
guy [gaɪ] Typ; Kerl; (Pl.) Leute **II**
gym(nasium) [dʒɪm; dʒɪmˈneɪziəm] Turnhalle **IV AC3**, 68

H

haggis [ˈhægɪs] Haggis (schottisches Gericht aus in einem Schafsmagen gekochten Schafsinnereien und Haferschrot) **III**
hair [ˌduː ˌaʊə ˈheə] Haar(e) **I**
*to do our **hair** [ˌduː ˌaʊə ˈheə] uns frisieren; unsere Haare machen **I**
hair [heə] Haar; Haare **IV TS2**, 64
hairbrush [ˈheəbrʌʃ] Haarbürste **III**
half, **halves** (pl) (of) [hɑːf; hɑːvz] die Hälfte **I**
half an hour [ˌhɑːf ən ˈaʊə] eine halbe Stunde **III**
half [hɑːf] halb **I**
half past [ˌhɑːf ˈpɑːst] halb (bei Uhrzeitangaben) **I**
half-sister [ˈhɑːfˌsɪstə] Halbschwester **I**
half-term break [ˌhɑːftɜːm ˈbreɪk] Halbjahresferien **I**
*to meet **halfway** [ˌmiːt hɑːfˈweɪ] sich auf halbem Weg treffen **III**
hall [hɔːl] Halle; Saal **II**; Flur; Diele; Korridor **III**
arrivals **hall** [əˈraɪvlz ˌhɔːl] Ankunftshalle **IV U1**, 9
hall pass [ˈhɔːl pɑːs] Erlaubnis, sich während des Unterrichts auf dem Flur aufzuhalten **IV U2**, 43
hallway [ˈhɔːlweɪ] Flur; Diele; Korridor **IV U2**, 43
ham [hæm] Schinken **III**
hammer [ˈhæmə] Hammer **II**
hand [hænd] Hand **I**
Clap your **hands**. [ˌklæp jɔː ˈhændz] Klatsch/Klatscht in die Hände. **I**
On the one **hand** …, (but) on the other **hand** … [ɒn ðə ˌwʌn ˌhænd … (bʌt) ɒn ðiˌʌðə ˌhænd …] Einerseits …, (aber) andererseits … **II**
*to **hang** on [ˌhæŋ ˈɒn] (einen Augenblick) warten **IV U1**, 10
*to **hang** out (with) (infml) [ˌhæŋ ˈaʊt wɪð] sich herumtreiben (mit); rumhängen (mit); sich treffen (mit) **III**
*to **hang** up [ˌhæŋ ˈʌp] aufhängen **II**
to **happen** [ˈhæpn] geschehen; passieren **I**
happy [ˈhæpi] glücklich; froh; fröhlich **I**
happy ending [ˌhæpi ˈendɪŋ] Happy End **III**
Happy Birthday! [ˌhæpi ˈbɜːθdeɪ] Alles Gute zum Geburtstag!; Herzlichen Glückwunsch zum Geburtstag! **I**
harbour [ˈhɑːbə] Hafen **III**

hard [hɑːd] hart; schwer; schwierig; hier: stark **II**
*to be **hard** on sb [bi ˈhɑːd ɒn] streng mit jmdm. sein **III**
hardly [ˈhɑːdli] kaum **IV TS1**, 34
harsh [hɑːʃ] rau; hart **IV AC2**, 40
harvest [ˈhɑːvɪst] Ernte **IV U2**, 45
hat [hæt] Hut **I**
to **hate** [heɪt] hassen; nicht mögen **II**
*to **have** [hæv] haben **I**
*to **have** a look (at) [ˌhæv ə ˈlʊk] anschauen **II**
*to **have** a point [ˌhæv ə ˈpɔɪnt] nicht ganz unrecht haben **III**
*to **have** breakfast [ˌhæv ˈbrekfəst] frühstücken **I**
*to **have** fun [ˌhæv ˈfʌn] Spaß haben; sich amüsieren **I**
*to **have** got [hæv ˈgɒt] besitzen; haben **I**
*to **have** in common [ˌhæv ɪn ˈkɒmən] gemeinsam haben **III**
*to **have** no clue [ˌhæv nəʊ ˈkluː] keine Ahnung haben **IV AC2**, 41
*to **have** to [ˈhæv tə] müssen **II**
Have a good time. [ˌhæv ə gʊd ˈtaɪm] Viel Spaß. ⟨**IV TS1**, 36⟩
*to **have** (a sweet) [hæv] (ein Bonbon) nehmen; (ein Bonbon) essen **I**
he [hiː] er **I**
head [hed] Kopf **I**
*to get sth out of one's **head** [get ˌaʊt əv wʌnz ˈhed] etw. aus dem Kopf bekommen **III**
head of state [ˌhed əv ˈsteɪt] Staatsoberhaupt **II**
With a very big **head**! [ˌwɪð ə ˌveri bɪg ˈhed] Und ein Angeber! **II**
to **head** for [ˈhed fə] zusteuern auf ⟨**IV TS1**, 34⟩
headache (no pl) [ˈhedeɪk] Kopfschmerzen; Kopfweh **II**
heading [ˈhedɪŋ] Überschrift; Titel **II**
headline [ˈhedlaɪn] Schlagzeile **III**
headphones (pl) [ˈhedfəʊnz] Kopfhörer **II**
health [helθ] Gesundheit **II**
healthy [ˈhelθi] gesund **I**
*to **hear** [hɪə] hören **I**
I **hear** … [aɪ ˈhɪə] Ich habe gehört, dass … **I**
heart [hɑːt] Herz; hier: Zentrum **II**
*to learn … by **heart** [ˌlɜːn baɪ ˈhɑːt] auswendig lernen **I**
heating [ˈhiːtɪŋ] Heizung **III**
underfloor **heating** (no pl) [ˌʌndəflɔː ˈhiːtɪŋ] Fußbodenheizung **III**
heavy [ˈhevi] schwer; stark **III**
hectic [ˈhektɪk] hektisch ⟨**IV U3**, 81⟩
hedgehog [ˈhedʒhɒg] Igel **III**
height [haɪt] Höhe ⟨**IV TS3**, 102⟩
Hello. [helˈəʊ] Hallo. **I**
*to say **hello** (to) [ˌseɪ helˈəʊ tə] grüßen; Grüße ausrichten (an) **I**

help [help] Hilfe **I**
to **help** [help] helfen **I**
to **help** out [ˌhelp ˈaʊt] aushelfen **III**
helpful [ˈhelpfl] hilfsbereit; hilfreich **I**
helpless [ˈhelpləs] hilflos **I**
her [hɜː] ihr/-e; sie **I**
herb [hɜːb] Kraut **IV U1**, 11
here [hɪə] hier **I**
right **here** [ˌraɪt ˈhɪə] genau hier **II**
Here you are. [ˌhɪə juˈɑː] Bitte schön. **I**
Here's … [ˈhɪəz] Hier ist … **I**
hero, **heroes** (pl) [ˈhɪərəʊ, ˈhɪərəʊz] Held **III**
heroine [ˈherəʊɪn] Heldin **III**
to **hesitate** [ˈhezɪteɪt] zögern **III**
Hey! [heɪ] Hi.; He!; Hallo. **I**
Hi. [haɪ] Hi.; Hallo. **I**
hibernation [ˌhaɪbəˈneɪʃn] Winterschlaf **III**
*to **hide** [haɪd] (sich) verstecken **III**
high [haɪ] hoch; groß **II**
high school (AE) [ˈhaɪ ˌskuːl] High School (weiterführende Schule in den USA, Oberstufe) **IV U2**, 43
high tide [ˈhaɪ ˌtaɪd] Flut **II**
the **high** street [ðə ˈhaɪ ˌstriːt] die Haupteinkaufsstraße **III**
highlight [ˈhaɪlaɪt] Highlight; Höhepunkt **II**
highly [ˈhaɪli] höchst- **IV TS2**, 65
hiking [ˈhaɪkɪŋ] Wandern **III**
hill [hɪl] Berg; Hügel **III**
him [hɪm] ihn; ihm **I**
himself [hɪmˈself] er/sich (selbst); selber **II**
hint [hɪnt] Hinweis; Andeutung; Tipp **III**
his [hɪz] sein/-e **I**
historic [hɪˈstɒrɪk] historisch **III**
historical [hɪˈstɒrɪkl] historisch; geschichtlich **I**
history [ˈhɪstri] Geschichte **II**
living **history** show [ˌlɪvɪŋ ˈhɪstəri ˌʃəʊ] Show, in der historischer Alltag nachgespielt wird **III**
*to **hit** [hɪt] schlagen; treffen **I**
hoax [həʊks] Täuschung; Trick **IV TS3**, 102
hobby, **hobbies** (pl) [ˈhɒbi; ˈhɒbiz] Hobby **I**
hockey [ˈhɒki] Hockey **II**
to **hog** a conversation [ˌhɒg ə kɒnvəˈseɪʃn] ein Gespräch für sich in Beschlag nehmen; ein Gespräch dominieren **III**
*to **hold** [həʊld] halten; festhalten **I**
*to **hold** onto [ˌhəʊld ˈɒntə] (sich) festhalten an **III**
*to **hold** open [ˌhəʊld ˈəʊpn] aufhalten **IV AC1**, 22
hole [həʊl] Loch **II**
holiday [ˈhɒlədeɪ] Urlaub; Feiertag **I**
holidays (pl) [ˈhɒlədeɪz] Ferien **I**
home [həʊm] Zuhause; Heim **I**
at **home** [ət ˈhəʊm] zu Hause **I**
home [həʊm] nach Hause **I**
homeless [ˈhəʊmləs] obdachlos **IV U2**, 51
homeless shelter [ˈhəʊmləs ˌʃeltə] Obdachlosenunterkunft **IV U2**, 51
homepage [ˈhəʊmpeɪdʒ] Homepage **I**

*to be **homesick** [bi ˈhəʊmsɪk] Heimweh haben **IV U1**, 18
hometown [ˈhəʊmtaʊn] Heimatstadt **IV U3**, 75
homework [ˈhəʊmwɜːk] Hausaufgabe(n) **I**
honest [ˈɒnɪst] ehrlich **III**
honey [ˈhʌni] Honig **III**
to **hook** [hʊk] *hier:* fesseln **III**
hope [həʊp] Hoffnung **II**
to **hope** [həʊp] hoffen **I**
hopeful [ˈhəʊpfl] hoffnungsvoll **I**
horn [hɔːn] Horn **III**
horrified [ˈhɒrɪfaɪd] entsetzt **I**
horror [ˈhɒrə] Horrorgeschichte; Horrorfilm; Horror **III**
horse [hɔːs] Pferd **I**
hospital [ˈhɒspɪtl] Hospital; Krankenhaus **II**
host family [ˈhəʊst ˌfæmli] Gastfamilie **III**
hostel [ˈhɒstl] Herberge **IV U1**, 10
hostile [ˈhɒstaɪl] feindlich; ablehnend ⟨**IV TS3**, 104⟩
hot [hɒt] heiß **III**
  hot dog [ˈhɒt ˌdɒg] Hot Dog *(Würstchen im Brötchen)* ⟨**IV U3**, 75⟩
hotel [həʊˈtel] Hotel **II**
hour [aʊə] Stunde **II**
  half an **hour** [ˌhɑːf ən ˈaʊər] eine halbe Stunde **III**
house [haʊs] Haus **I**
to move (**house**) [muːv (haʊs)] umziehen **III**
how [haʊ] wie **I**
  How many …? [ˌhaʊ ˈmeni] Wie viele …? **I**
  How are you? [ˌhaʊ ˈɑː jə] Wie geht es dir?; Wie geht es euch?; Wie geht es Ihnen? **I**
  How much (is/are) …? [ˌhaʊ ˈmʌtʃ ɪz/ɑː] Wie viel (kostet/kosten) …? **I**
  How old are you? [haʊ ˈəʊld ə ˌjuː] Wie alt bist du?; Wie alt sind Sie? **I**
  How to … [ˈhaʊ tə] Wie man … **I**
  Is this **how** you (do) …? [ɪz ˈðɪs haʊ jʊ ˌduː] Machst du so …? **I**
  that's **how** [ðæts ˈhaʊ] so **II**
however [haʊˈevə] jedoch **IV U3**, 76
to **hug** [hʌg] umarmen **I**
huge [hjuːdʒ] riesig; riesengroß; gewaltig **II**
to **hum** [hʌm] summen **I**
human [ˈhjuːmən] Mensch **IV TS3**, 100
human body [ˌhjuːmən ˈbɒdi] menschlicher Körper **II**
Humanities *(pl)* [hjuːˈmænətiz] Sozialwissenschaften **II**
humour *(no pl)* [ˈhjuːmə] Humor; Stimmung **III**
  sense of **humour** *(no pl)* [ˌsens əv ˈhjuːmə] Sinn für Humor **III**
hundreds of [ˈhʌndrədz əv] Hunderte (von) **III**
hungry [ˈhʌŋgri] hungrig **I**
to **hurry** [ˈhʌri] eilen; sich beeilen **I**
*to **hurt** [hɜːt] verletzen; weh tun **II**

hurt [hɜːt] verletzt **II**
husband [ˈhʌzbənd] Ehemann **II**

I

I [aɪ] ich **I**
  I don't know! [aɪ ˌdəʊnt ˈnəʊ] Ich weiß (es) nicht! **I**
  I don't like … [aɪ ˈdəʊnt laɪk] Ich mag … nicht.; Ich mache … nicht gern. **I**
  I hear … [aɪ ˈhɪə] Ich habe gehört, dass … **I**
  I like … [aɪ ˈlaɪk] Mir gefällt …; Ich mag … **I**
  I love you. [aɪ ˈlʌv ju] Ich liebe dich.; Ich mag dich. **I**
  I love … [aɪ ˈlʌv] Ich liebe …; Ich mag … total gern. **I**
  I'd like to … (= I would like to) [aɪd ˈlaɪk tə] Ich möchte …; Ich würde gern … **I**
  I'd rather [aɪd ˈrɑːðə] ich würde lieber **III**
  I'm (not) scared of … [ˌaɪm (nɒt) ˈskeəd əv] Ich habe (keine) Angst vor … **I**
  I'm afraid … [ˌaɪm əˈfreɪd] Leider … **IV U2**, 44
  I'm dog-tired. [ˌaɪm ˌdɒgˈtaɪəd] Ich bin hundemüde. **I**
  I'm English. [aɪm ˈɪŋglɪʃ] Ich bin Engländer/-in. **I**
  I'm fine. [aɪm ˈfaɪn] Mir geht's gut. **I**
  I'm from … [ˌaɪm frɒm] Ich bin aus … **I**
  I'm sorry! [aɪm ˈsɒri] Tut mir leid! **I**
  I'm … [aɪm] Ich bin … **I**
ice [aɪs] Eis **I**
  ice cream [ˌaɪs ˈkriːm] Eis; Eiscreme **I**
  ice rink [ˈaɪs ˌrɪŋk] Eisbahn; Schlittschuhbahn **I**
icebreaker [ˈaɪsˌbreɪkə] Eisbrecher *(Sätze, um mit jmdm. ins Gespräch zu kommen)* **IV AC1**, 23
idea [aɪˈdɪə] Idee; Einfall **I**
  no **idea** [ˌnəʊ aɪˈdɪə] keine Ahnung **II**
to **identify** with [aɪˈdentɪfaɪ wɪð] sich identifizieren mit **III**
identity [aɪˈdentəti] Identität **II**
idiot [ˈɪdiət] Idiot/-in **II**
if [ɪf] wenn; falls; ob **I**
  as **if** [əzˈɪf] als ob **III**
  if-clause [ˈɪfklɔːz] if-Satz **III**
  If I were you … [ˌɪf aɪ wɜː ˈjuː] Wenn ich du wäre … **IV AC3**, 69
to **ignore** [ɪgˈnɔː] ignorieren; außer Acht lassen **III**
ill [ɪl] krank **III**
illegal [ɪˈliːgl] illegal; unrechtmäßig; rechtswidrig **III**
image [ˈɪmɪdʒ] Bild; Abbildung **IV TS2**, 65
imagination [ɪˌmædʒɪˈneɪʃn] Fantasie; Vorstellungskraft **III**
imaginative [ɪˈmædʒɪnətɪv] einfallsreich; fantasievoll **III**

to **imagine** [ɪˈmædʒɪn] sich (etwas) vorstellen **I**
immediately [ɪˈmiːdiətli] sofort; gleich **IV TS2**, 64
immigrant [ˈɪmɪgrənt] Immigrant/-in; Einwanderer/-in **IV AC2**, 38
immigration [ˌɪmɪˈgreɪʃn] Immigration; Einwanderung; Einreise **IV U1**, 13
  immigration office [ˌɪmɪˈgreɪʃn ˌɒfɪs] Einwanderungsbehörde **IV U1**, 13
imperative [ɪmˈperətɪv] Imperativ; Befehlsform **I**
impolite [ˌɪmpˈlaɪt] unhöflich **III**
important [ɪmˈpɔːtnt] wichtig **I**
impossible [ɪmˈpɒsəbl] unmöglich **IV TS3**, 102
impressed [ɪmˈprest] beeindruckt **II**
impression [ɪmˈpreʃn] Impression; Eindruck **IV U2**, 42
to **improve** [ɪmˈpruːv] sich verbessern; verbessern **I**
improvement [ɪmˈpruːvmənt] Verbesserung °**IV TS2**, 67
in [ɪn] in; im; rein; herein **I**
  in between [ˌɪn bɪˈtwiːn] dazwischen **III**
  in chorus [ɪn ˈkɔːrəs] im Chor **IV TS1**, 33
  in front of [ɪn ˈfrʌnt əv] vor **I**
  in need [ɪn ˈniːd] bedürftig; in Not **II**
  in secret [ɪn ˈsiːkrət] heimlich **II**
  in the country [ˌɪn ðə ˈkʌntri] auf dem Land **IV AC2**, 40
  in the end [ˌɪn ðiˈend] schließlich; zum Schluss **II**
  in the evenings [ɪn ðiˈiːvnɪŋz] abends **I**
  in the mornings [ɪn ðə ˈmɔːnɪŋz] morgens; vormittags **I**
  in the photo(s) [ˌɪn ðə ˈfəʊtəʊ(z)] auf dem Foto/den Fotos **I**
  in the street [ɪn ðə ˈstriːt] in der Straße; auf der Straße **I**
to **include** [ɪnˈkluːd] einschließen; beinhalten; aufnehmen; einbeziehen **III**
inconvenient [ˌɪnkənˈviːniənt] unbequem; lästig **IV TS3**, 100
in-crowd [ˈɪnkraʊd] Szene; die Angesagten; die Beliebten **III**
independence *(no pl)* [ˌɪndɪˈpendəns] Unabhängigkeit **III**
independent [ˌɪndɪˈpendənt] unabhängig **III**
Indian [ˈɪndiən] Inder/-in; indisch **I**; Indianer/-in; indianisch **IV U2**, 45
indirect [ˈɪndɪrekt] indirekt **IV U1**, 11
  indirect speech [ˌɪndɪrekt ˈspiːtʃ] indirekte Rede **IV U1**, 11
individual [ˌɪndɪˈvɪdʒuəl] Einzelperson; Einzelne/-r; Individuum **IV U2**, 56
individual [ˌɪndɪˈvɪdʒuəl] individuell; einzeln **II**
indivisible [ˌɪndɪˈvɪzəbl] unteilbar ⟨**IV U2**, 49⟩
industry [ˈɪndəstri] Industrie; Branche; Gewerbe **III**
infinitive [ɪnˈfɪnətɪv] Infinitiv **I**

to **influence** ['ɪnfluəns] beeinflussen **II**

informal [ɪn'fɔ:ml] informell; zwanglos **IV AC4**, 107

information (no pl) [ˌɪnfə'meɪʃn] Information; Informationen **I**

informative [ɪn'fɔ:mətɪv] informativ **IV U2**, 56

ingredient [ɪn'gri:dɪənt] Zutat **III**

injury ['ɪndʒəri] Verletzung **II**

inline skating ['ɪnlaɪn ˌskeɪtɪŋ] Inlineskate-fahren **I**

insecure [ˌɪnsɪ'kjʊə] unsicher **IV U2**, 47

inside [ɪn'saɪd] innen; im Innern; hinein; nach drinnen; in; drin **I**

to **inspire** [ɪn'spaɪə] inspirieren; anregen **IV U3**, 70

instead [ɪn'sted] stattdessen **III**
  instead of [ɪn'sted ˌəv] statt; anstatt; an Stelle von **IV U2**, 45

instruction [ɪn'strʌkʃn] Instruktion; Anweisung **I**

instructor [ɪn'strʌktə] Lehrer/-in; Betreuer/-in **II**

interest ['ɪntrəst] Interesse **II**

to **interest** ['ɪntrəst] (sich) interessieren **II**

*to be **interested** in [bɪ'ɪntrəstɪd ɪn] interessiert sein an; sich interessieren für **II**

interesting ['ɪntrəstɪŋ] interessant **I**

international [ˌɪntə'næʃnl] international **I**

internet ['ɪntənet] Internet **I**

intersection [ˌɪntə'sekʃn] Kreuzung **IV U3**, 70

interview ['ɪntəvju:] Interview; Befragung **I**

to **interview** ['ɪntəvju:] interviewen; befragen **I**

interviewee [ˌɪntəvju'i:] Befragte/-r; Interviewte/-r °**IV U3**, 93

interviewer ['ɪntəvju:ə] Interviewer/-in; Befrager/-in °**IV U3**, 92

into ['ɪntə] in; in … hinein **I**
  *to be **into** [bɪ:ˌ'ɪntə] mögen; stehen auf **I**
  You're **into** … ['jɔ:rˌ'ɪntə] Du magst …; Du stehst auf … **I**

to **introduce** [ˌɪntrə'dju:s] einführen; einleiten **IV U1**, 11
  Introduce … [ˌɪntrə'dju:s] Stelle/Stellt … vor. **I**

introduction [ˌɪntrə'dʌkʃn] Einführung; Einleitung; Vorstellung **II**

to **invade** [ɪn'veɪd] einmarschieren (in); eindringen (in); überfallen **III**

to **invent** [ɪn'vent] erfinden **III**

invention [ɪn'venʃn] Erfindung **III**

inventor [ɪn'ventə] Erfinder/-in **III**

invisible [ɪn'vɪzəbl] unsichtbar **IV U1**, 17

invitation [ˌɪnvɪ'teɪʃn] Einladung **I**

to **invite** [ɪn'vaɪt] einladen **I**

to **involve** [ɪn'vɒlv] involvieren; einbeziehen; beteiligen **IV TS3**, 102

*to get **involved** with sb [get ɪn'vɒlvd wɪð] sich einlassen mit jmdm. ⟨**IV TS1**, 34⟩

inward ['ɪnwəd] ankommend **III**

Irish ['aɪrɪʃ] irisch; Irisch **III**

ironic [ˌaɪ'rɒnɪk] ironisch **IV U2**, 56

irregular [ɪ'regjələ] unregelmäßig **I**

Is this how you (do) …? [ɪz 'ðɪs haʊ jʊ ˌdu:] Machst du so …? **I**

island ['aɪlənd] Insel **III**

it [ɪt] es **I**
  *to make **it** ['meɪk ˌɪt] es schaffen **IV U3**, 70
  It's fun. [ɪts 'fʌn] Es macht Spaß. **I**
  It's great for … [ɪts 'greɪt fə] Es ist super zum/für … **I**
  It's your turn. [ɪts 'jɔ: tɜ:n] Du bist dran. **I**
  It's, like, so wild to … [ɪts laɪk səʊ 'waɪld tə] Es ist echt klasse … ⟨**IV AC4**, 107⟩
  It's …/They're … [ɪts/ðeə] Es kostet …/ Sie kosten … **I**

IT (= Information Technology) [ˌaɪ'ti:] Informatik; Informationstechnik **III**

item ['aɪtəm] Gegenstand; Objekt **IV U2**, 51

its [ɪts] sein/-e; ihr/-e **I**

ivory (no pl) ['aɪvri] Elfenbein **III**

J

jacket ['dʒækɪt] Jacke **III**

jam [dʒæm] Marmelade; Konfitüre **III**

January ['dʒænjuri] Januar **I**

*to be **jealous** (of) [bɪ: 'dʒeləs] eifersüchtig sein (auf); neidisch sein (auf) **I**

jelly ['dʒeli] Tortenguss; Götterspeise; Wackelpudding; Gelee **I**

jewel ['dʒu:əl] Juwel; Edelstein **III**
  crown **jewels** [ˌkraʊn 'dʒu:əlz] Kronjuwelen **II**

jewellery ['dʒu:əlri] Schmuck **I**

Jewish ['dʒu:ɪʃ] jüdisch **IV U3**, 75

job [dʒɒb] Arbeit; Aufgabe; Job **I**

mouth **jogging** ['maʊθ ˌdʒɒgɪŋ] Training für den Mund **I**

to **join** [dʒɔɪn] beitreten; sich anschließen; verbinden **II**

joke [dʒəʊk] Witz **I**

to **joke** [dʒəʊk] scherzen **II**

journey ['dʒɜ:ni] Reise; Fahrt **III**

to **judge** [dʒʌdʒ] beurteilen; bewerten **III**

juggling ['dʒʌglɪŋ] Jonglieren **II**

juice [dʒu:s] Saft **I**

July [dʒʊ'laɪ] Juli **I**

to **jump** [dʒʌmp] springen **I**
  to **jump** back [ˌdʒʌmp'bæk] zurückspringen; hier: zurückschrecken **II**
  to **jump** the queue [ˌdʒʌmp ðə 'kju:] sich vordrängeln **I**

June [dʒu:n] Juni **I**

jungle ['dʒʌŋgl] Dschungel **IV U3**, 70

a bunch of **junk** [əˌbʌnʃˌəv 'dʒʌŋk] ein Haufen Müll ⟨**IV U3**, 84⟩

piece of **junk** [ˌpi:s əv 'dʒʌŋk] Stück Schrott **III**

just [dʒʌst] gerade; nur; einfach **I**
  just about anywhere [ˌdʒʌstˌəˌbaʊt 'eniweə] praktisch überall **IV TS2**, 64

just in time [ˌdʒʌstˌɪn 'taɪm] gerade rechtzeitig **IV U3**, 72

justice ['dʒʌstɪs] Gerechtigkeit ⟨**IV U2**, 49⟩

juvenile ['dʒu:vnaɪl] Jugend- ⟨**IV U3**, 88⟩

K

keen [ki:n] begeistert; leidenschaftlich ⟨**IV TS1**, 36⟩

*to **keep** [ki:p] behalten; aufbewahren; halten **I**
  *to **keep** away from [ˌki:pˌə'weɪ frəm] (sich) fernhalten von **III**
  *to **keep** going [ˌki:p 'gəʊɪŋ] aufrechterhalten **II**
  *to **keep** in mind [ˌki:pˌɪn 'maɪnd] beachten; im Gedächtnis behalten °**IV U3**, 79
  *to **keep** in touch [ˌki:pˌɪn 'tʌtʃ] in Kontakt bleiben **IV U2**, 44
  *to **keep** one's feet or hands still [ˌki:p wʌnz 'fi:tˌɔ: 'hændz stɪl] die Beine und Hände ruhig halten **III**
  *to **keep** out (of) [ˌki:p'aʊt əv] draußen bleiben; draußen halten **III**
  *to **keep** the ball bouncing [ˌki:p ðə bɔ:l 'baʊnsɪŋ] hier: das Gespräch am Laufen halten **III**
  *to **keep** up (with) [ˌki:pˌ'ʌp (wɪð)] mithalten (mit); Schritt halten (mit) **II**
  *to **keep** your fingers crossed [ˌki:p jɔ: ˌfɪŋgəz 'krɒst] die Daumen drücken **I**

*to **keep** [ki:p] hier: weiter tun; immer wieder tun **IV U2**, 44

key [ki:] Schlüssel **II**
  key ring ['ki: ˌrɪŋ] Schlüsselbund; Schlüsselanhänger **III**
  key word ['ki: wɜ:d] Stichwort; Schlüsselbegriff **I**

to **kick** [kɪk] schießen; treten **II**

kid [kɪd] Jugendliche/-r; Kind **IV U2**, 42

to **kill** [kɪl] töten; umbringen **III**

kilometre (km) ['kɪləˌmi:tə; kɪ'lɒmɪtə] Kilometer **III**

kilt [kɪlt] Kilt; Schottenrock **III**

kind [kaɪnd] Art; Sorte **I**
  kind of ['kaɪndˌəv] ziemlich ⟨**IV U3**, 90⟩

king [kɪŋ] König **I**

kitchen ['kɪtʃɪn] Küche **I**

knife [naɪf], **knives** [naɪvz] (pl) Messer **III**

knight [naɪt] Ritter **III**

knob [nɒb] Griff **II**

*to **know** [nəʊ] kennen; wissen **I**
  *to be **known** as [bɪ 'nəʊnˌəz] bekannt sein als **IV U3**, 74
  *to get to **know** [get tə 'nəʊ] kennenlernen **III**
  I don't **know**! [aɪˌdəʊnt 'nəʊ] Ich weiß (es) nicht! **I**
  You **know** how to … [ju: 'nəʊ ˌhaʊ tə] Du weißt, wie man …; Ihr wisst, wie man … **I**

koala [kəʊ'ɑ:lə] Koala **III**

Korean [kəˈriːən] koreanisch; Koreanisch; Koreaner/-in **II**
South **Korean** [saʊθ kəˈriːən] Südkoreaner/-in; südkoreanisch; Südkoreanisch **II**

L

lab(oratory) [læb; ləˈbɒrətri] Labor **IV AC3**, 68
child **labor** (AE) [tʃaɪld ˈleɪbə] Kinderarbeit **IV U2**, 48
laboratory [læb; ləˈbɒrətri] Labor **IV AC3**, 68
ladder [ˈlædə] Leiter **II**
lady [ˈleɪdi] Lady; Dame **III**
lady-in-waiting [ˌleɪdiɪnˈweɪtɪŋ] Hofdame **III**
laid-back [ˌleɪdˈbæk] entspannt; locker **III**
lake [leɪk] See **I**
boating **lake** [ˈbəʊtɪŋ ˌleɪk] See zum Rudern **I**
lamb [læm] Lamm; Lämmchen **I**
land [lænd] Land **I**
to **land** [lænd] landen **II**
landing [ˈlændɪŋ] Landung **IV U1**, 15
moon **landing** [ˈmuːn ˌlændɪŋ] Mondlandung **IV TS3**, 100
landscape [ˈlændskeɪp] Landschaft **III**
language [ˈlæŋgwɪdʒ] Sprache **I**
first **language** [ˌfɜːst ˈlæŋgwɪdʒ] Muttersprache **II**
foreign **language** [ˌfɒrɪn ˈlæŋgwɪdʒ] Fremdsprache **II**
official **language** [əˌfɪʃl ˈlæŋgwɪdʒ] Amtssprache **II**
laptop [ˈlæptɒp] Laptop **II**
large [lɑːdʒ] groß; riesig **II**
lassi [ˈlʌsi] Lassi **I**
last [lɑːst] letzte/-r/-s **I**
at **last** [ət ˈlɑːst] endlich; schließlich **I**
to save the best for **last** [ˌseɪv ðə ˌbest fə ˈlɑːst] sich das Beste bis zum Schluss aufheben **IV U3**, 72
late [leɪt] spät; zu spät **I**
*to be **late** [bi: ˈleɪt] zu spät dran sein; zu spät kommen **I**
later [ˈleɪtə] später **I**
latest [ˈleɪtɪst] neueste/-r/-s **IV U1**, 11
to **laugh** [lɑːf] lachen **I**
lavish [ˈlævɪʃ] üppig; verschwenderisch **IV U1**, 19
*to **lay** [leɪ] legen **IV U3**, 89
layer (of) [ˈleɪər ˌəv] Schicht (aus); Lage (aus) **III**
layout [ˈleɪaʊt] Layout; Anordnung **III**
lazy [ˈleɪzi] faul **III**
lead part [ˌliːd ˈpɑːt] Hauptrolle **III**
*to **lead** [liːd] führen; anführen **III**
*to **lead** off [liːd ˈɒf] wegführen **III**
lead [liːd] Haupt- **III**
lead-in [ˈliːdɪn] Einführung; Einleitung **IV U3**, 89
leaflet [ˈliːflət] Broschüre; Informationsblatt; Prospekt **IV AC1**, 23

leap [liːp] Sprung; Satz ⟨**IV TS3**, 101⟩
*to **learn** [lɜːn] lernen **I**
*to **learn** a lesson from [ˌlɜːn ə ˈlesn frəm] lernen aus ⟨**IV U3**, 86⟩
*to **learn** about [ˈlɜːn əˌbaʊt] erfahren über **III**
*to **learn** … by heart [ˈlɜːn baɪ ˈhɑːt] auswendig lernen **I**
a lot to **learn** [ə ˌlɒt tə ˈlɜːn] viel zu lernen **I**
at **least** [ət ˈliːst] mindestens; wenigstens **II**
*to **leave** [liːv] verlassen; lassen; abfahren; losgehen **II**
*to **leave** a message [ˌliːv ə ˈmesɪdʒ] eine Nachricht hinterlassen **I**
*to **leave** behind [ˌliːv bɪˈhaɪnd] zurücklassen **III**
*to **leave** it to cool [ˌliːv ˌɪt tə ˈkuːl] kalt stellen **I**
*to **leave** out [ˌliːv ˈaʊt] auslassen; weglassen °**IV U2**, 54
*to **leave** sb alone [ˌliːv ə ˈləʊn] jmdn. in Ruhe lassen **IV U2**, 53
*to **leave** space [liːv ˈspeɪs] Platz lassen **I**
Leave that to me. [ˌliːv ðæt tə ˈmiː] Überlass das mir. **IV U3**, 72
left [left] linke/-r/-s; links **I**
on the **left** [ɒn ðə ˈleft] auf der linken Seite; links **I**
left [left] übrig **I**
left-hand [ˈlefthænd] linke/-r/-s °**IV U2**, 45
leg [leg] Bein **II**
legend [ˈledʒənd] Legende; Sage **III**
leisure [ˈleʒə] Freizeit; Freizeit- **I**
leisure centre [ˈleʒə ˌsentə] Freizeitzentrum **I**
lemon [ˈlemən] Zitrone **II**
lemonade [ˌleməˈneɪd] Limonade **I**
*to **lend** [ˈlend tə] leihen; verleihen **III**
less [les] weniger **III**
to settle for **less** [ˌsetl fə ˈles] sich mit weniger zufrieden geben **IV TS2**, 66
lesson [ˈlesn] Unterrichtsstunde; Schulstunde; Unterricht **I**
*to learn a **lesson** from [ˌlɜːn ə ˈlesn frəm] lernen aus ⟨**IV U3**, 86⟩
*to **let** [let] lassen **I**
*to **let** go (of) [ˌlet ˈgəʊ (əv)] loslassen **II**
Let's face it. [lets ˈfeɪs ɪt] Machen wir uns doch nichts vor. **IV TS1**, 32
Let's … [lets] Lass/Lasst uns … **I**
letter [ˈletə] Buchstabe **I**; Brief **II**
capital **letter** [ˌkæpɪtl ˈletə] Großbuchstabe **I**
liberty [ˈlɪbəti] Freiheit **IV U3**, 74
library [ˈlaɪbri] Bibliothek; Bücherei **III**
lie [laɪ] Lüge **III**
white **lie** [ˌwaɪt ˈlaɪ] Notlüge **IV TS1**, 32
to **lie** [laɪ] lügen **II**
*to **lie** [laɪ] liegen **II**
life, **lives** (pl) [laɪf, laɪvz] Leben **II**
lifeboat [ˈlaɪfbəʊt] Rettungsboot **I**

lifebuoy [ˈlaɪfbɔɪ] Rettungsring **I**
lifestyle [ˈlaɪfstaɪl] Lebensstil; Lifestyle **III**
to **lift** [lɪft] heben; hochheben; anheben **IV U3**, 76
light [laɪt] Licht; Lampe **II**
light [laɪt] leicht **III**
to **lighten** [ˈlaɪtn] aufhellen **III**
lightning (no pl) [ˈlaɪtnɪŋ] Blitz **II**
to **like** [laɪk] mögen; gern haben **I**
would **like** [wʊd ˈlaɪk] würde-/st/-n/-t gern; hätte-/st/-n/-t gern **I**
I don't **like** … [aɪ ˈdəʊnt laɪk] Ich mag … nicht.; Ich mache … nicht gern. **I**
I **like** singing and dancing. [aɪ laɪk ˌsɪŋɪŋ ənd ˈdɑːnsɪŋ] Ich singe und tanze gern. **I**
I **like** … [aɪ ˈlaɪk] Mir gefällt …; Ich mag … **I**
I'd **like** to … (= I would like to) [aɪd ˈlaɪk tə] Ich möchte …; Ich würde gern … **I**
Would you **like** …? [ˌwʊd jʊ ˈlaɪk] Möchtest du …?; Möchten Sie …?; Möchtet ihr …? **II**
like [laɪk] wie **I**
*to be **like** [bi ˈlaɪk] sein **III**
like that [laɪk ˈðæt] so **I**
like this [laɪk ˈðɪs] so **I**
What was it **like**? [ˌwɒt wɒz ɪt ˈlaɪk] Wie war es? **III**
likes (pl) [laɪks] Vorlieben **IV U2**, 46
limit [ˈlɪmɪt] Limit; Grenze **III**
line [laɪn] Zeile; Linie **I**
finish **line** [ˈfɪnɪʃ laɪn] Ziellinie **II**
opening **line** [ˈəʊpnɪŋ ˌlaɪn] der erste Satz **III**
*to stand in **line** (AE) [ˌstænd ɪn ˈlaɪn] anstehen; Schlange stehen; (sich) anstellen **IV AC3**, 69
time **line** [ˈtaɪm ˌlaɪn] Zeitstrahl **I**
lines (pl) [laɪnz] Text **IV TS1**, 30
to **line** up [laɪnˈʌp] (sich) aufstellen **III**
link [lɪŋk] Link; Verbindung **II**
to **link** [lɪŋk] verbinden **II**
linking word [ˈlɪŋkɪŋ ˌwɜːd] Bindewort **I**
lion [ˈlaɪən] Löwe **II**
list [lɪst] Liste **I**
to **listen** (to) [ˈlɪsn] zuhören; anhören **I**
Listen again. [ˌlɪsn əˈgen] Hör/Hört noch einmal zu. **I**
to **listen** for [ˈlɪsn fə] horchen auf **I**
listener [ˈlɪsənə] Zuhörer/-in **II**
listening [ˈlɪsnɪŋ] Hören **I**
litre (l) [ˈliːtə] Liter **III**
to **litter** [ˈlɪtə] verschmutzen; verunreinigen; Müll herumliegen lassen **IV AC1**, 22
little [ˈlɪtl] klein **I**
a **little** [ə ˈlɪtl] ein wenig; etwas **I**
little [ˈlɪtl] wenig °**IV U3**, 91
to **live** [lɪv] wohnen; leben **I**
standard of **living** [ˌstændəd əv ˈlɪvɪŋ] Lebensstandard **IV AC2**, 40
live [laɪv] live **III**
lively [ˈlaɪvli] lebendig **II**

living room ['lɪvɪŋ rʊm] Wohnzimmer I
*to make a living (from) [ˌmeɪk ə 'lɪvɪŋ frəm] seinen Lebensunterhalt bestreiten (mit) IV U3, 79
living history show [ˌlɪvɪŋ 'hɪstəri ˌʃəʊ] Show, in der historischer Alltag nachgespielt wird III
local ['ləʊkl] örtlich; lokal III
*to be located [bi ləʊ'keɪtɪd] gelegen sein; liegen IV U3, 73
location [ləʊ'keɪʃn] Handlungsort; Lage; Standort II
loch [lɒx; lɒk] See (in Schottland) III
locked [lɒkt] abgeschlossen II
locker ['lɒkə] Schließfach; Spind I
loft [lɒft] Dachboden I
logbook ['lɒgbʊk] Logbuch °IV TS3, 102
logic ['lɒdʒɪk] Logik III
LOL (= laughing out loud) [lɒl] LOL II
Londoner ['lʌndənə] Londoner/-in I
lonely ['ləʊnli] einsam I
long [lɒŋ] lang I
  as long as [əz 'lɒŋ ˌəz] solange (IV TS1, 34)
  long shot ['lɒŋ ˌʃɒt] Totale (Kameraeinstellung) IV U3, 89
  (not) any longer [nɒt ˌeni 'lɒŋɡə] (nicht) mehr; (nicht) länger III
look [lʊk] Blick I
  *to give sb funny looks [ˌgɪv fʌni 'lʊks] jmdn. schief anschauen III
  *to have a look (at) [ˌhæv ə 'lʊk] anschauen II
  *to take a look at [ˌteɪk ə 'lʊk ˌæt] einen Blick werfen auf II
to look [lʊk] schauen; sehen; aussehen I
  Look! [lʊk] Schau/Schaut mal! I
  to look after [ˌlʊk 'ɑːftə] aufpassen auf; hüten; sich kümmern um I
  to look at ['lʊk ˌət] anschauen; ansehen I
  to look for ['lʊk fɔː] suchen nach I
  to look forward to [ˌlʊk 'fɔːwəd tə] sich freuen auf II
  to look out [ˌlʊk 'aʊt] aufpassen II
  to look up [ˌlʊk 'ʌp] nachschlagen; nachschauen I
  Look closely … [ˌlʊk 'kləʊsli] Schau(t) genau … II
  what the man looked like [ˌwɒt ðə mæn 'lʊkt laɪk] wie der Mann aussah II
looks (pl) [lʊks] Aussehen III
lord [lɔːd] Lord; Herr III
lorry ['lɒri] Lastwagen IV U3, 79
*to lose [luːz] verlieren II
lost [lɒst] verloren (IV TS3, 104)
  *to get lost [ˌget 'lɒst] verloren gehen; sich verirren III
a lot [ə 'lɒt] viel I
a lot of [ə 'lɒt ˌəv] viel/-e; eine Menge I
lots (of) ['lɒts ˌəv] viel/-e; jede Menge I
loud [laʊd] laut I
  *to read/sing out loud [ˌriːd/sɪŋ ˌaʊt 'laʊd] laut vorsingen III

departure lounge [dɪ'pɑːtʃə ˌlaʊndʒ] Abflughalle IV U1, 9
love [lʌv] Liebe III
Love … [lʌv] Liebe Grüße (am Briefende); Herzliche Grüße (am Briefende) I
to love [lʌv] lieben; gern mögen I
  would love [wʊd 'lʌv] würde-/-st/-n/-t sehr gern; hätte-/-st-/-n/-t sehr gern I
  I love you. [aɪ 'lʌv ju] Ich liebe dich.; Ich mag dich. I
  I love … [aɪ 'lʌv] Ich liebe …; Ich mag … total gern. I
lovebirds (pl) ['lʌvˌbɜːdz] Turteltauben II
lovely ['lʌvli] schön; hübsch IV TS2, 65
low [ləʊ] niedrig II
  low tide ['ləʊ ˌtaɪd] Ebbe II
lox [lɑːks] Räucherlachs (IV U3, 75)
good luck [ˌgʊd 'lʌk] viel Glück IV U3, 76
What luck! [wɒt 'lʌk] Was für ein Glück! III
luckily ['lʌkɪli] glücklicherweise IV U2, 44
lucky … ['lʌki] … der/die Glückliche I
  *to be lucky [bi 'lʌki] Glück haben II
  lucky charm [ˌlʌki 'tʃɑːm] Glücksbringer; Talisman I
  … is/are lucky. [ɪz/ɑː 'lʌki] … hat/haben Glück. I
luggage (no pl) ['lʌgɪdʒ] Gepäck IV U1, 8
lunch [lʌnʃ] Mittagessen I
  lunch break ['lʌnʃbreɪk] Mittagspause I
lunchtime ['lʌnʃtaɪm] Mittagszeit; Mittagspause IV AC3, 68
lung [lʌŋ] Lunge IV U3, 71
the lungs (pl) [ðə 'lʌŋz] die Lunge III
luxury ['lʌkʃri] Luxus IV AC2, 40
(song) lyrics (pl) [sɒŋ 'lɪrɪks] Liedtext III

M

machine [mə'ʃiːn] Automat; Maschine; Apparat; Gerät I
  answering machine ['ɑːnsrɪŋ məˌʃiːn] Anrufbeantworter I
  vending machine ['vendɪŋ məˌʃiːn] Automat IV U1, 10
  washing machine ['wɒʃɪŋ məˌʃiːn] Waschmaschine II
mad [mæd] verrückt II; wütend IV AC3, 69
Dear Sir or Madam [dɪə ˌsɜːrˌɔː 'mædəm] Sehr geehrte Dame, sehr geehrter Herr III
made up from [ˌmeɪdˌʌp frəm] zusammengesetzt aus °IV TS3, 102
magazine [mægə'ziːn] Zeitschrift I
maggot ['mægət] Made (IV U3, 86)
magic ['mædʒɪk] Magie; Zauberei IV U1, 19
magical ['mædʒɪkəl] magisch; Zauber- III
to mail ['iːmeɪl] mailen; per E-Mail schicken II
main [meɪn] Haupt- I
  main clause ['meɪn ˌklɔːz] Hauptsatz III
*to make [meɪk] machen; tun; bilden; hier: ergeben I

*to be made of [bi 'meɪd ˌəv] bestehen aus III
*to make a decision [ˌmeɪk ə dɪ'sɪʒn] eine Entscheidung treffen II
*to make a living (from) [ˌmeɪk ə 'lɪvɪŋ frəm] seinen Lebensunterhalt bestreiten (mit) IV U3, 79
*to make a wish [ˌmeɪk ə 'wɪʃ] sich etwas wünschen I
*to make friends [ˌmeɪk 'frendz] Freundschaft schließen I
*to make it ['meɪk ˌɪt] es schaffen IV U3, 70
*to make money [ˌmeɪk 'mʌni] Geld verdienen I
*to make notes [ˌmeɪk 'nəʊts] Notizen machen I
*to make sb angry [meɪk 'æŋgri] jmdn. wütend machen; jmdn. verärgern III
*to make sense [ˌmeɪk 'sens] Sinn ergeben; einleuchten IV TS3, 102
*to make somebody do something [meɪk] jmdn. dazu bringen, etw. zu tun II
*to make sure [ˌmeɪk 'ʃɔː] sich versichern I
*to make trouble [ˌmeɪk 'trʌbl] Ärger machen; in Schwierigkeiten bringen I
*to make use of [meɪk 'juːz ˌəv] benutzen; verwenden IV U3, 89
shopping mall ['ʃɒpɪŋ ˌmɔːl] Einkaufszentrum IV U2, 43
man, men (pl) [mæn; men] Mann I
  what the man looked like [ˌwɒt ðə mæn 'lʊkt laɪk] wie der Mann aussah II
manga ['mæŋgə] Manga (japanischer Comic) II
mango ['mæŋgəʊ] Mango I
manicure ['mænɪkjʊə] Maniküre (IV U3, 86)
mankind [mæn'kaɪnd] Menschheit (IV TS3, 101)
manners (pl) ['mænəz] Manieren; Benehmen IV AC1, 23
software manual ['sɒftweə ˌmænjuəl] Softwarehandbuch III
many ['meni] viele I
  How many …? [ˌhaʊ 'meni] Wie viele …? I
map [mæp] Stadtplan; Landkarte I
  mind map ['maɪnd mæp] Wörternetz (eine Art Schaubild) I
marathon ['mærəθn] Marathon II
March [mɑːtʃ] März I
to march [mɑːtʃ] marschieren III
mark [mɑːk] Note III
marked [mɑːkt] markiert °IV AC4, 106
market ['mɑːkɪt] Markt I
  flea market ['fliː ˌmɑːkɪt] Flohmarkt I
marmalade ['mɑːməleɪd] Marmelade aus Zitrusfrüchten III
to marry ['mæri] heiraten III
mashed potatoes (pl) [ˌmæʃt pə'teɪtəʊz] Kartoffelpüree III
mask [mɑːsk] Maske IV U1, 16
massive ['mæsɪv] riesig; massiv; hier: super IV AC2, 41

raven **master** [ˈreɪvn ˌmɑːstə] Herr der Raben II

match [mætʃ] Spiel; Match II

to **match** [mætʃ] zuordnen; passen zu; entsprechen I

mate [meɪt] Schiffsoffizier; Maat I

material [məˈtɪəriəl] Material II

Maths [mæθs] Mathematik; Mathe II

What's the **matter?** [wɒts ðə ˈmætə] Was ist los?; Was hast du? III

It doesn't **matter.** [ɪt ˌdʌznt ˈmætə] Es ist egal. III

May [meɪ] Mai I

may [meɪ] (vielleicht) können; dürfen II

maybe [ˈmeɪbi] vielleicht I

mayo [ˈmeɪəʊ] Mayonnaise ⟨IV U3, 87⟩

me [miː] ich; mich; mir I

meal [miːl] Mahlzeit; Essen II

ready **meal** [ˌredi ˈmiːl] Fertiggericht I

*to **mean** [miːn] bedeuten; meinen II

(I) didn't **mean** to … [aɪ ˌdɪdnt ˈmiːn tə] Ich wollte nicht … IV AC4, 107

mean [miːn] gemein IV TS5, 33

meaning [ˈmiːnɪŋ] Bedeutung; Sinn II

by any **means** [baɪ ˌeni ˈmiːnz] mit allen Mitteln IV U3, 70

meat (no pl) [miːt] Fleisch III

mechanic [məˈkænɪk] Mechaniker/-in; Kfz-Mechaniker/-in II

media [ˈmiːdiə] Medien II

social **media** [ˌsəʊʃl ˈmiːdiə] soziale Netzwerke IV U2, 46

mediation [ˌmiːdiˈeɪʃn] Sprachmittlung I

medicine (no pl) [ˈmedsn] Medizin; Medikamente III

medieval [ˌmediˈiːvl] mittelalterlich III

medium [ˈmiːdiəm] mittel; mittelgroß IV U3, 89

medium shot [ˈmiːdiəm ʃɒt] Halbtotale (Kameraeinstellung) IV U3, 89

*to **meet** [miːt] treffen; sich treffen I

*to **meet** halfway [ˌmiːt hɑːfˈweɪ] sich auf halbem Weg treffen III

*to **meet** up [ˌmiːt ˈʌp] sich treffen IV U2, 44

melody [ˈmelədi] Melodie III

melting pot [ˈmeltɪŋ ˌpɒt] Schmelztiegel IV U3, 70

member [ˈmembə] Mitglied II

memory [ˈmemri] Erinnerung; Gedächtnis II

menacing [ˈmenɪsɪŋ] drohend ⟨IV U3, 90⟩

to **mention** [ˈmenʃn] erwähnen II

menu [ˈmenjuː] Speisekarte IV U2, 45

merchant [ˈmɜːtʃənt] Kaufmann; Händler II

mess [mes] Unordnung; Durcheinander; Schweinerei IV U2, 54

to **mess** sth up [ˌmes ˈʌp] etw. durcheinanderbringen; etw. vergeigen IV TS1, 30

message [ˈmesɪdʒ] Botschaft; Nachricht I

*to leave a **message** [ˌliːv ə ˈmesɪdʒ] eine Nachricht hinterlassen I

*to take a **message** [ˌteɪk ə ˈmesɪdʒ] eine Nachricht entgegennehmen; jmdm. etw. ausrichten I

text (**message**) [ˈtekst ˌmesɪdʒ] SMS; Kurznachricht I

messy [ˈmesi] unordentlich III

metre [ˈmiːtə] Meter II

middle [ˈmɪdl] Mitte I

middle school (AE) [ˈmɪdl ˌskuːl] Mittelschule (weiterführende Schule in den USA, Mittelstufe) IV U2, 43

in the **middle** of nowhere [ɪn ðə ˌmɪdl əv ˈnəʊweə] mitten im Nirgendwo IV U2, 46

midnight [ˈmɪdnaɪt] Mitternacht III

might [maɪt] könnte/-n (vielleicht) IV U2, 50

It **might** as well be … [ɪt maɪt əs ˈwel biː …] Es könnte/-n auch … sein. III

mile [maɪl] Meile (brit. Längenmaß) II

milk [mɪlk] Milch I

to **milk** [mɪlk] melken III

million [ˈmɪljən] Million II

I've done this a **million** times before. [ˌaɪv dʌn ðɪs ə ˌmɪljən taɪmz bɪˈfɔː] Ich habe das schon eine Million Mal gemacht. II

millionaire [ˌmɪljəˈneə] Millionär/-in III

mind [maɪnd] Geist; Verstand III

to change one's **mind** [tʃeɪndʒ wʌnz ˈmaɪnd] seine Meinung ändern III

*to keep in **mind** [ˌkiːp ɪn ˈmaɪnd] beachten; im Gedächtnis behalten °IV U3, 79

mind map [ˈmaɪnd mæp] Wörternetz (eine Art Schaubild) I

*to rise up in one's **mind** [raɪz ˌʌp ɪn wʌnz ˈmaɪnd] jmdm. in den Sinn kommen III

to **mind** [maɪnd] etwas dagegen haben; einem etwas ausmachen IV U2, 46

to **mind** sth [maɪnd] auf etw. aufpassen IV AC4, 107

I don't **mind** … (+ -ing) [aɪ dəʊnt ˈmaɪnd] Ich habe nichts dagegen (zu) …; Mir macht es nichts aus (zu) … III

mine [maɪn] Mine III

mine [maɪn] mein/-er/-e/-es II

mini [ˈmɪni] Mini- II

mining [ˈmaɪnɪŋ] Bergbau III

minute [ˈmɪnɪt] Minute I

mirror [ˈmɪrə] Spiegel III

miserable [ˈmɪzrəbl] elend; armselig; jämmerlich ⟨IV TS1, 32⟩

Miss [mɪs] Fräulein (Anrede) III

to **miss** [mɪs] verpassen; versäumen II; vermissen III

missing [ˈmɪsɪŋ] fehlend; verschwunden II

What is **missing?** [wɒt ɪz ˈmɪsɪŋ] Was fehlt? I

mission [ˈmɪʃn] Mission; Auftrag IV TS3, 101

mission control [ˌmɪʃn kənˈtrəʊl] Bodenkontrollzentrum ⟨IV TS3, 101⟩

mist [mɪst] Nebel; Dunst ⟨IV U3, 90⟩

mistake [mɪˈsteɪk] Fehler I

misunderstood [ˌmɪsʌndəˈstʊd] missverstanden III

mix [mɪks] Mix III

to **mix** [mɪks] Umgang haben ⟨IV TS1, 34⟩; zusammenpassen IV U2, 54

to **mix** (up) [mɪksˈʌp] mischen; vermischen III

mobile [ˈməʊbaɪl] Handy; Mobiltelefon II

modal [ˈməʊdl] Modalverb II

model [ˈmɒdl] Modell; Tonmodell; Model I

modelling [ˈmɒdəlɪŋ] Modeln III

modern [ˈmɒdn] modern II

module [ˈmɒdjuːl] Modul; Element ⟨IV TS3, 101⟩

command **module** [kəˈmɑːnd ˌmɒdjuːl] Kommandokapsel ⟨IV TS3, 101⟩

mom (AE) [mɒm] Mama IV AC2, 41

moment [ˈməʊmənt] Moment; Augenblick II

at the **moment** [ət ðə ˈməʊmənt] im Moment; gerade I

monarch [ˈmɒnək] Monarch/-in III

Monday [ˈmʌndeɪ] Montag I

on **Mondays** [ɒn ˈmʌndeɪz] montags I

money [ˈmʌni] Geld I

*to make **money** [ˌmeɪk ˈmʌni] Geld verdienen I

pocket **money** [ˈpɒkɪt ˌmʌni] Taschengeld I

to raise **money** [ˌreɪz ˈmʌni] Geld sammeln II

monster [ˈmɒnstə] Monster; Ungeheuer I

montage [mɒnˈtɑːʒ] Montage °IV U3, 91

month [mʌnθ] Monat II

monument [ˈmɒnjəmənt] Monument; Denkmal III

mood [muːd] Stimmung; Laune II

moon [muːn] Mond IV TS3, 100

moon landing [ˈmuːn ˌlændɪŋ] Mondlandung IV TS3, 100

moonlight [ˈmuːnlaɪt] Mondlicht III

more [mɔː] mehr; weitere I

no **more** [nəʊ ˈmɔː] nicht mehr IV AC4, 107

not any **more** [ˌnɒt eni ˈmɔː] nicht mehr I

more … than [ˈmɔː ðən] mehr … als I

morning [ˈmɔːnɪŋ] Morgen; Vormittag I

in the **mornings** [ɪn ðə ˈmɔːnɪŋz] morgens; vormittags I

Good **morning.** [ɡʊd ˈmɔːnɪŋ] Guten Morgen. I

(the) **most** [ðə ˈməʊst] der/die/das meiste; die meisten I

mother [ˈmʌðə] Mutter I

to **motivate** [ˈməʊtɪveɪt] motivieren I

motivation [ˌməʊtɪˈveɪʃn] Motivation; Beweggründe IV TS1, 31

motive [ˈməʊtɪv] Motiv; Beweggrund IV TS1, 32

bicycle **motocross** [ˌbaɪsɪkl ˈməʊtəʊkrɒs] Fahrradmotocross II

mountain [ˈmaʊntɪn] Berg II

mountain biking [ˈmaʊntɪn ˌbaɪkɪŋ] Mountainbikefahren III

mountainous [ˈmaʊntɪnəs] bergig IV AC2, 40

mouse *(sg)*, mice *(pl)* [maʊs; maɪs] Maus/
Mäuse I

mouth [maʊθ] Mund I
  mouth jogging [ˈmaʊθ ˌdʒɒɡɪŋ] Training
  für den Mund I
  to talk with your mouth full [ˌtɔːk wɪð jɔː
  ˈmaʊθ fʊl] mit vollem Mund sprechen
  IV AC1, 22

move [muːv] Bewegung I
  on the move [ɒn ˌðə ˈmuːv] unterwegs
  IV U1, 8

to move [muːv] (sich) bewegen I
  to move in/into [muːvˈɪn/ˈɪntə] einziehen
  in III

to move (house) [muːv (haʊs)] umziehen III

movie *(AE)* [ˈmuːvi] Film IV U2, 44
  movie theater *(AE)* [ˈmuːvi ˌθɪətə] Kino
  IV U2, 44

Mr [ˈmɪstə] Herr *(Anrede)* I

Mrs [ˈmɪsɪz] Frau *(Anrede)* I

much [mʌtʃ] viel I
  that much [ðæt ˈmʌtʃ] so viel III

mud [mʌd] Schlamm II

muddy [ˈmʌdi] schlammig II

mudlark [ˈmʌdlɑːk] *jemand, der im
Schlamm nach Sachen sucht, die er dann
verkaufen kann* II

muesli [ˈmjuːzli] Müsli III

mug [mʌɡ] Becher III

multi-ethnic [ˌmʌltiˈeθnɪk] Vielvölker-;
international II

mum [mʌm] Mama I

mummy [ˈmʌmi] Mama; Mami; Mutti III

murder [ˈmɜːdə] Mord II

museum [mjuːˈziːəm] Museum I

music [ˈmjuːzɪk] Musik I

musical [ˈmjuːzɪkl] musikalisch; Musik- III

musician [mjuːˈzɪʃn] Musiker/-in II

must [mʌst] müssen I

mustn't [ˈmʌsnt] nicht dürfen I

to mutter [ˈmʌtə] murmeln IV U1, 10

my [maɪ] mein/-e I
  My favourite … [maɪ ˈfeɪvrɪt] Mein/e
  Lieblings … I
  My name is … [maɪ ˈneɪmˌɪz] Ich hei-
  ße … I

myself [maɪˈself] ich/mir/mich (selbst);
selber II

mysterious [mɪˈstɪəriəs] mysteriös; geheimnisvoll III

mystery [ˈmɪstri] Mysterium; Rätsel; Geheimnis III

mythical [ˈmɪθɪkl] sagenhaft; sagenumwoben IV U1, 19

N

naked [ˈneɪkɪd] nackt IV U3, 72

name [neɪm] Name I
  name day [ˈneɪm ˌdeɪ] Namenstag I
  My name is … [maɪ ˈneɪmˌɪz] Ich heiße … I

What's your name? [wɒts jə ˈneɪm] Wie
heißt du?; Wie heißen Sie? I

to name [neɪm] nennen; benennen I

narrative perspective [ˌnærətɪv pəˈspektɪv]
Erzählperspektive III

narrator [nəˈreɪtə] Erzähler/-in III
  first person narrator [ˌfɜːst ˌpɜːsn nəˈreɪtə]
  Ich-Erzähler/-in III
  third person narrator [ˌθɜːd ˌpɜːsn
  nəˈreɪtə] Er/Sie-Erzähler/-in III

narrow [ˈnærəʊ] eng; schmal III

NASA *(= National Aeronautics and Space
Administration)* [ˈnæsə] NASA IV TS3, 100

nasty [ˈnɑːsti] garstig; gemein II

nation [ˈneɪʃn] Nation ‹IV U2, 49›

national [ˈnæʃnl] national; landesweit I

Native American [ˌneɪtɪvˌəˈmerɪkən]
Ureinwohner/-in Amerikas; Indianer/-in;
indianisch IV U2, 45

natural [ˈnætʃrl] natürlich; Natur- IV U2, 56

nature [ˈneɪtʃə] Natur II

near [nɪə] nahe; in der Nähe von I

nearly [ˈnɪəli] fast; annähernd II

not necessarily [ˌnɒt nesəˈserəli] nicht notwendigerweise; nicht unbedingt IV U3, 76

necessary [ˈnesəsri] nötig; notwendig; erfor-
derlich °IV TS3, 105

neck [nek] Hals; Nacken; Genick ‹IV U3, 90›

necklace [ˈnekləs] Halskette III

in need [ɪn ˈniːd] bedürftig; in Not II

There's no need to … [ˌðeəz nəʊ ˈniːd tə] Es
gibt keinen Grund zu … IV TS1, 36

with special needs [wɪð ˌspeʃl ˈniːdz]
behindert II

to need (to do) [niːd] (tʊn) müssen I
  needn't [ˈniːdnt] nicht brauchen; nicht
  müssen II

to need (to) [niːd] brauchen; benötigen I

needless to say [ˌniːdləs tə ˈseɪ] natürlich;
selbstverständlich IV U3, 76

negative [ˈneɡətɪv] negativ; verneint III
  negative form [ˈneɡətɪv ˌfɔːm] verneinte
  Form I

neighborhood *(AE)* [ˈneɪbəhʊd] Nachbarschaft IV U2, 43

neighbour *(BE)* [ˈneɪbə] Nachbar/-in I

neighbourhood [ˈneɪbəhʊd] Nachbarschaft
III

nephew [ˈnefjuː] Neffe IV U1, 13

nerd [nɜːd] Nerd *(Person, die intelligent,
aber sozial unbeholfen ist)* IV TS2, 65

*to get on people's nerves [ˌget ɒn
ˈsʌmbɒdiz ˈnɜːvz] jemandem auf die
Nerven gehen I

nervous [ˈnɜːvəs] nervös; aufgeregt II

net [net] Netz II

netball [ˈnetbɔːl] Korbball I

social network [ˌsəʊʃl ˈnetwɜːk] soziales
Netzwerk II

never [ˈnevə] nie; niemals I

new [njuː] neu I

New Year's Eve [ˌnjuːˌjɪəzˌˈiːv] Silvester
‹IV U3, 90›

New Yorker [ˌnjuːˈjɔːkə] New Yorker/-in
IV U3, 75

news *(sg)* [njuːz] Nachrichten; Neuigkeiten
II
  news report [ˈnjuːz rɪˌpɔːt] Tatsachenbericht; Nachrichtenbeitrag; Meldung III

newspaper [ˈnjuːsˌpeɪpə] Zeitung III

next [nekst] nächste/-r/-s; der/die
Nächste(n) I
  next door [ˌnekst ˈdɔː] (von) nebenan III
  next to [ˈnekst tə] neben I
  the next day [ðə ˌnekst ˈdeɪ] am nächsten
  Tag II

next [nekst] als Nächstes I

nice [naɪs] nett; schön; lieb I

night [naɪt] Nacht I
  all night [ˌɔːl ˈnaɪt] die ganze Nacht I
  night walk [ˈnaɪt wɔːk] Nachtwanderung
  II

nightmare [ˈnaɪtmeə] Alptraum IV U2, 52

nine [naɪn] neun I

2nite *(= tonight)* [təˈnaɪt] heute Abend I

no [nəʊ] kein/-e I
  no more [nəʊ ˈmɔː] nicht mehr IV AC4, 107
  no way [nəʊ ˈweɪ] auf keinen Fall; keineswegs ‹IV U2, 54›; keine Möglichkeit; kein
  Weg ‹IV TS3, 102›
  no idea [ˌnəʊ aɪˈdɪə] keine Ahnung II
  no wonder [ˌnəʊ ˈwʌndə] kein Wunder
  IV U2, 44

no [nəʊ] nein I

nobody [ˈnəʊbədi] niemand II
  nobody else [ˈnəʊbədi els] niemand
  anderes III

noise [nɔɪz] Lärm; Geräusch II

noisy [ˈnɔɪzi] laut III

non- [nɒn] nicht- II

non-defining relative clause [ˌnɒndɪfaɪnɪŋ
ˈrelətɪv ˌklɔːz] nicht notwendiger Relativsatz °IV U3, 73

nope *(infml)* [nəʊp] nee; nö IV AC4, 107

normal [ˈnɔːml] normal II

normally [ˈnɔːmli] normalerweise IV AC1, 22

Norman [ˈnɔːmən] Normanne/Normannin;
normannisch III

north [nɔːθ] Norden; Nord- II

north [nɔːθ] nördlich; im Norden III

nose [nəʊz] Nase II
  to wrinkle one's nose [ˌrɪŋkl wʌnz ˈnəʊz]
  die Nase rümpfen ‹IV U3, 90›

not [nɒt] nicht I
  not any more [ˌnɒtˌeni ˈmɔː] nicht mehr I
  not anymore *(AE)* [ˌnɒtˌeniˈmɔː] nicht
  mehr IV AC2, 39
  not necessarily [ˌnɒt nesəˈserəli] nicht
  notwendigerweise; nicht unbedingt
  IV U3, 76
  not until [ˌnɒtˌənˈtɪl] nicht vor; erst um/
  im IV U2, 44
  not … any [nɒt … eni] kein/-e/-en I

not … anything [nɒt 'eniθɪŋ] nichts **I**
not … either [nɒt … 'aɪðə; nɒt … 'i:ðə] auch nicht **IV AC4**, 107
not … yet [nɒt 'jet] noch nicht **II**
note [nəʊt] Notiz; Anmerkung **I**
 *to make **notes** [ˌmeɪk 'nəʊts] Notizen machen **I**
 *to take **notes** [ˌteɪk 'nəʊts] sich Notizen machen **I**
to **note** down [nəʊt 'daʊn] notieren; aufschreiben **II**
nothing ['nʌθɪŋ] nichts **I**
to **notice** ['nəʊtɪs] bemerken; wahrnehmen **II**
noticeboard ['nəʊtɪsbɔːd] schwarzes Brett **II**
noun [naʊn] Nomen; Hauptwort **I**
novel ['nɒvl] Roman **III**
 graphic **novel** [ˌgræfɪk 'nɒvl] Bildergeschichte; Comic **III**
November [nə'vembə] November **I**
now [naʊ] jetzt; nun **I**
 right **now** [raɪt 'naʊ] jetzt gleich; sofort; gerade **II**
nowhere ['nəʊweə] nirgendwo; nirgendwohin **III**
 in the middle of **nowhere** [ɪn ðə ˌmɪdl̩ əv 'nəʊweə] mitten im Nirgendwo **IV U2**, 46
number ['nʌmbə] Zahl; Nummer **I**
nurse [nɜːs] Krankenschwester; Krankenpfleger **III**
nut [nʌt] Nuss **I**

O

o'clock [ə'klɒk] Uhr *(Zeitangabe bei vollen Stunden)* **I**
oak [əʊk] Eiche **III**
object ['ɒbdʒɪkt] Objekt **II**; Gegenstand **III**
 object pronoun [ˌɒbdʒɪkt 'prəʊnaʊn] Objektpronomen **III**
obvious ['ɒbviəs] offensichtlich **IV U2**, 53
October [ɒk'təʊbə] Oktober **I**
against all **odds** [əˌgenst ɔːl 'ɒdz] entgegen allen Erwartungen **III**
odd [ɒd] seltsam; komisch **IV U1**, 19
of [ɒv; əv] von **I**
 of course [əv 'kɔːs] natürlich; selbstverständlich **I**
 of one's own [əv wʌnz 'əʊn] eigen **III**
*to take **off** [teɪk 'ɒf] abnehmen; herunternehmen; ausziehen **I**
*to take the day **off** [teɪk ðə ˌdeɪ 'ɒf] sich den Tag freinehmen **IV U3**, 72
to turn **off** [tɜːn 'ɒf] abschalten; ausschalten **II**
special **offer** [ˌspeʃl̩ 'ɒfə] Sonderangebot **I**
to **offer** ['ɒfə] anbieten **II**
office ['ɒfɪs] Büro **I**
 immigration **office** [ˌɪmɪˈgreɪʃn ˌɒfɪs] Einwanderungsbehörde **IV U1**, 13
 ticket **office** ['tɪkɪt ˌɒfɪs] Kartenschalter **III**

police **officer** [pə'liːs ˌɒfɪsə] Polizeibeamter; Polizist/-in **II**
official [ə'fɪʃl] Schiedsrichter/-in **II**; Beamter/Beamtin **IV U1**, 17
official [ə'fɪʃl] offiziell **III**
 official language [əˌfɪʃl 'læŋgwɪdʒ] Amtssprache **II**
offline ['ɒflaɪn] offline **II**
often ['ɒfn] oft; häufig **II**
oh [əʊ] null *(bei Telefonnummern und Uhrzeitangaben)* **I**
Oh! [əʊ] O! **I**
 Oh dear! [əʊ 'dɪə] Oje! **III**
ointment ['ɔɪntmənt] Salbe **II**
OK [əʊ'keɪ] o.k.; in Ordnung **I**
okay [ə'keɪ] okay **IV TS1**, 31
old [əʊld] alt **I**
 How **old** are you? [haʊ ˌəʊld ə 'juː] Wie alt bist du?; Wie alt sind Sie? **I**
11-year-**old** [ɪˌlevn'jɪərəʊld] 11-Jährige/-r **II**
OMG! (Oh my god!) [əʊ maɪ 'gɒd] OMG! (Oh mein Gott!) **IV U2**, 56
*to put **on** [pʊt 'ɒn] anziehen **III**
on [ɒn] auf; an; am; in; im **I**
 *to be **on** [bi 'ɒn] an sein; laufen **II**
 on Mondays [ɒn 'mʌndeɪz] montags **I**
 on my own [ɒn maɪ 'əʊn] allein; für mich **II**
 on the brink of [ɒn ðə 'brɪŋk əv] am Rande von; kurz vor **III**
 on the left [ɒn ðə 'left] auf der linken Seite; links **I**
 on the right [ɒn ðə 'raɪt] auf der rechten Seite; rechts **I**
 on time [ɒn 'taɪm] pünktlich **II**
 on top [ɒn 'tɒp] oben; obendrauf **I**
 Come **on**! [kʌm 'ɒn] Komm schon!; Komm jetzt! **I**
 on a shoestring [ɒn ə 'ʃuːstrɪŋ] für/mit wenig Geld **IV U3**, 72
 on the move [ɒn ðə 'muːv] unterwegs **IV U1**, 8
once [wʌns] einmal; einst **I**
one [wʌn] eins **I**
one *(sg)*/**ones** *(pl)* [wʌn/wʌnz] eine/-r/-s **II**
one-way ticket ['wʌnweɪ ˌtɪkɪt] einfache Fahrkarte **I**
online [ɒn'laɪn] online **II**
only ['əʊnli] einzige/-r/-s **II**
only ['əʊnli] erst; bloß; nur **I**
 only child ['əʊnli ˌtʃaɪld] Einzelkind **I**
onto ['ɒntə] auf … hinauf ⟨**IV TS3**, 101⟩
Oops! [uːps] Hoppla!; Huch! **I**
to **open** ['əʊpn] öffnen; aufmachen **I**; *hier:* beginnen **III**; eröffnen **IV U2**, 52
open ['əʊpn] offen; geöffnet; aufgeschlagen **I**
 *to hold **open** [ˌhəʊld 'əʊpn] aufhalten **IV AC1**, 22
opening ['əʊpnɪŋ] Öffnung; Beginn **III**
 opening line ['əʊpnɪŋ ˌlaɪn] der erste Satz **III**

opinion [ə'pɪnjən] Meinung **II**
opposite ['ɒpəzɪt] gegenüber; auf der anderen Seite von **I**
optimistic [ˌɒptɪ'mɪstɪk] optimistisch **III**
option ['ɒpʃn] Möglichkeit; Wahl; Option **III**
or [ɔː] oder **I**
 either … **or** … ['aɪðə/'iːðə … ɔː] entweder … oder … **IV U3**, 79
orange ['ɒrɪndʒ] Orange **I**
orange ['ɒrɪndʒ] orange **I**
orbit ['ɔːbɪt] Umlaufbahn; Orbit ⟨**IV TS3**, 101⟩
order ['ɔːdə] Reihenfolge; Ordnung **I**; Befehl **III**
 out of **order** [ˌaʊt əv 'ɔːdə] kaputt; außer Betrieb **IV TS1**, 36
 word **order** ['wɜːdˌɔːdə] Wortstellung; Satzstellung **I**
to **order** ['ɔːdə] bestellen **IV U1**, 20
organisation [ˌɔːgnaɪ'zeɪʃn] Organisation **III**
to **organise** ['ɔːgənaɪz] organisieren **I**
*to get **organised** [get 'ɔːgənaɪzd] sich organisieren **III**
orientation [ˌɔːriən'teɪʃn] Orientierung; Orientierungs- **IV U2**, 43
origin ['ɒrɪdʒɪn] Ursprung; Herkunft; Abstammung **IV U1**, 19
original [ə'rɪdʒnl] Original **III**
original [ə'rɪdʒnl] original; ursprünglich **III**
originally [ə'rɪdʒnli] ursprünglich **II**
other ['ʌðə] anders; andere/-r/-s; weitere **I**
 each **other** [iːtʃ'ʌðə] einander; sich; sich gegenseitig **I**
 the **others** [ðiˌ'ʌðəz] die anderen **I**
otherwise ['ʌðəwaɪz] sonst **IV AC3**, 68
Ouch! [aʊtʃ] Aua! **I**
our [aʊə; ɑː] unser/-e **I**
out [aʊt] außerhalb; heraus; hinaus; nach draußen **I**
 to clean **out** [ˌkliːn 'aʊt] ausräumen; entrümpeln **IV U2**, 51
 to clear **out** [klɪər 'aʊt] ausräumen; entrümpeln **I**
 to drop **out** (of) [drɒp 'aʊt əv] abbrechen **III**
 *to hang **out** (with) *(infml)* [ˌhæŋ 'aʊt wɪð] sich herumtreiben (mit); rumhängen (mit); sich treffen (mit) **III**
 *to leave **out** [ˌliːv 'aʊt] auslassen; weglassen °**IV U2**, 54
 out and about [ˌaʊt ən ə'baʊt] unterwegs **II**
 out of ['aʊt əv] aus … heraus **IV U1**, 15
 out of focus [ˌaʊt əv 'fəʊkəs] unscharf **III**
 out of order [ˌaʊt əv 'ɔːdə] kaputt; außer Betrieb **IV TS1**, 36
 a day **out** in … [ə ˌdeɪ 'aʊt ɪn] ein Tag in … **II**
outdoor [ˌaʊt'dɔː] Freiluft-; Outdoor- **II**
outfit ['aʊtfɪt] Outfit; Kleidung **II**
outgoing [aʊt'gəʊɪŋ] kontaktfreudig **IV U1**, 19

outlaw ['aʊtlɔː] Geächtete/-r; Gesetz-lose/-r III

out-of-character [ˌaʊtəˈkærəktə] unge-wöhnlich °IV U2, 54

from the outside [ˌfrəm ðiˌaʊtˈsaɪd] von außen IV U3, 75

outside [aʊtˈsaɪd] nach draußen; draußen; außerhalb I

outward ['aʊtwəd] abfahrend III

over ['əʊvə] hinüber; über I; vorüber; vorbei II

*to go over to [ˌgəʊ ˈəʊvə tə] hinüberge-hen zu; zu jmdm. nach Hause gehen II

over and over again [ˌəʊvərˌənˌəʊvərˌəˈgen] immer wieder III

*to win sb over [ˌwɪnˈəʊvə] jmdn. für sich gewinnen; jmdn. überzeugen IVTS2, 64

overall [ˌəʊvrˈɔːl] insgesamt ⟨IVTS3, 104⟩

*to overdo [əʊvəˈduː] übertreiben; zu weit gehen IV U2, 55

to overlap [əʊvəˈlæp] (sich) überlappen IV U3, 89

overloaded [ˌəʊvəˈləʊdɪd] überladen IV U1, 16

overnight [əʊvəˈnaɪt] über Nacht III

to overreact [əʊvəriˈækt] überreagieren II

own [əʊn] eigene/-r/-s I

of one's own [əv wʌnzˈəʊn] eigen III

on my own [ɒn maɪˈəʊn] allein; für mich II

P

p.m. [ˌpiːˈem] nachmittags (Uhrzeit); abends (Uhrzeit) I

packet ['pækɪt] Päckchen; Paket; Packung I

page [peɪdʒ] Seite I

pain [peɪn] Schmerz II

to paint [peɪnt] anmalen; malen I

painting ['peɪntɪŋ] Malerei; Gemälde II

pair [peə] Paar I

pair work ['peə wɜːk] Partnerarbeit II

to pair [peə] Paare bilden III

palm tree ['pɑːm ˌtriː] Palme III

panel ['pænl] Bild (eines Comics) IV U3, 89

to panic ['pænɪk] panisch werden II

piece of paper [ˌpiːsˌəv ˈpeɪpə] Stück Papier I

paper ['peɪpə] Papier I

paradise ['pærədaɪs] Paradies II

paragraph ['pærəgrɑːf] Paragraf; Absatz °IVTS3, 103

parcel ['pɑːsl] Paket; Päckchen I

parents (pl) ['peərənts] Eltern I

park [pɑːk] Park I

part [pɑːt] Teil; Stadtteil I; Rolle III

lead part [ˌliːd ˈpɑːt] Hauptrolle III

*to take part (in) [teɪk ˈpɑːt (ɪn)] teil-nehmen (an) I

partially sighted [ˌpɑːʃəli ˈsaɪtɪd] sehbehin-dert II

to participate [pɑːˈtɪsɪpeɪt] teilnehmen II

past participle [ˌpɑːst pɑːˈtɪsɪpl] Partizip II

particular [pəˈtɪkjələ] bestimmte/-r/-s III

partly ['pɑːtli] teilweise ⟨IVTS1, 32⟩

partner ['pɑːtnə] Partner/-in I

party ['pɑːti] Party; Feier I; Partei III

hall pass ['hɔːl pɑːs] Erlaubnis, sich während des Unterrichts auf dem Flur aufzuhalten IV U2, 43

to pass [pɑːs] zupassen; zuspielen II

to pass (on) [pɑːsˌɒn] weitergeben I

passenger ['pæsndʒə] Passagier/-in; Fahr-gast IV U1, 9

passive ['pæsɪv] Passiv III

passive ['pæsɪv] passiv III

passport ['pɑːspɔːt] Pass; Reisepass IV U1, 9

past [pɑːst] Vergangenheit II

past form ['pɑːst fɔːm] Vergangenheits-form II

past participle [ˌpɑːst pɑːˈtɪsɪpl] Partizip II

past perfect [ˌpɑːst ˈpɜːfɪkt] Plusquam-perfekt III

past perfect progressive [ˌpɑːst ˌpɜːfɪkt prəˈgresɪv] Verlaufsform des Plusquam-perfekts °IV U3, 77

past progressive [ˌpɑːst prəˈgresɪv] Ver-laufsform der Vergangenheit II

simple past [ˌsɪmpl ˈpɑːst] Vergangen-heitsform II

past [pɑːst] nach (bei Uhrzeitangaben); vorbei (an); vorüber (an) I

half past [ˌhɑːf ˈpɑːst] halb (bei Uhrzeit-angaben) I

quarter past/to ['kwɔːtə pɑːst/tə] Viertel nach/vor I

pasta ['pæstə] Pasta; Nudeln I

pastry ['peɪstri] Teig; Teigtasche IV U3, 75

patchwork ['pætʃwɜːk] Flicken-; Patchwork- ⟨IV U3, 90⟩

path [pɑːθ] Pfad; Weg IV U3, 92

coastal path [ˌkəʊstl ˈpɑːθ] Küstenweg III

pattern ['pætn] Muster III

pause [pɔːz] Pause III

pawn shop ['pɔːn ʃɒp] Pfandhaus; Pfand-leihe III

*to pay (for) [peɪ] bezahlen I

*to pay attention to sb/sth [peɪˌəˈtenʃn tʊ] jmdn./etw. beachten III

*to pay out [peɪˈaʊt] ausgeben ⟨IVTS1, 34⟩

PC (= Personal Computer) [piːˈsiː] PC II

PE (= Physical Education) [ˌpiːˈiː; ˌfɪzɪklˌedʒʊˈkeɪʃn] Sportunterricht II

peach [piːtʃ] Pfirsich III

peer pressure ['pɪə ˌpreʃə] Gruppenzwang III

to peer-edit ['pɪərˌedɪt] gegenseitig kontrol-lieren II

pen [pen] Füller I

penny, pence (pl) ['peni; pens] Penny (brit. Währungseinheit); Pence (brit. Währungs-einheit) I

pencil ['pensl] Bleistift; Buntstift I

pencil-case ['pensl ˌkeɪs] Federmäppchen; Mäppchen I

penicillin [ˌpenɪˈsɪlɪn] Penicillin III

penny, pence (pl) ['peni; pens] Penny (brit. Währungseinheit); Pence (brit. Währungs-einheit) I

penthouse ['penthaʊs] Penthouse; Woh-nung mit Dachterrasse IV U3, 79

people (pl) ['piːpl] Leute; Menschen I

per [pɜː; pə] pro III

past perfect [ˌpɑːst ˈpɜːfɪkt] Plusquamper-fekt III

past perfect progressive [ˌpɑːst ˌpɜːfɪkt prəˈgresɪv] Verlaufsform des Plusquam-perfekts °IV U3, 77

present perfect [ˌpreznt ˈpɜːfɪkt] das Perfekt II

present perfect progressive [ˌpreznt ˌpɜːfɪkt prəˈgresɪv] Verlaufsform des Perfekts III

perfect ['pɜːfɪkt] perfekt; vollkommen I

to perform [pəˈfɔːm] aufführen; auftreten IV U3, 79

performance [pəˈfɔːməns] Aufführung; Vorstellung IVTS1, 30

perhaps [pəˈhæps] vielleicht III

period ['pɪəriəd] Periode; Zeitspanne III

period (AE) ['pɪəriəd] Stunde; Unterrichts-stunde IV U2, 48

person, people (pl) ['pɜːsn; 'piːpl] Person; Mensch I

first person narrator [ˌfɜːst ˌpɜːsn nəˈreɪtə] Ich-Erzähler/-in III

third person narrator [ˌθɜːd ˌpɜːsn nəˈreɪtə] Er/Sie-Erzähler/-in III

personal ['pɜːsnl] persönlich I

personality [ˌpɜːsnˈæləti] Persönlichkeit III

perspective [pəˈspektɪv] Perspektive; Blick-winkel I

narrative perspective [ˌnærətɪv pəˈspektɪv] Erzählperspektive III

to persuade [pəˈsweɪd] überreden II

persuasive [pəˈsweɪsɪv] überzeugend III

pet [pet] Haustier I

phone [fəʊn] Telefon; Handy I

to answer the phone [ˌɑːnsə ðə ˈfəʊn] einen Anruf entgegennehmen I

cell phone (AE) ['selfəʊn] Mobiltelefon; Handy IV AC3, 68

phone box ['fəʊn ˌbɒks] Telefonzelle IV U1, 17

phone call ['fəʊn ˌkɔːl] Anruf; Telefonan-ruf I

rotary phone ['rəʊtri fəʊn] Telefon mit Wählscheibe III

to phone [fəʊn] anrufen; telefonieren IVTS1, 31

photo ['fəʊtəʊ] Foto; Fotografie I

in the photo(s) [ˌɪn ðə ˈfəʊtəʊ(z)] auf dem Foto/den Fotos I

photo shoot ['fəʊtəʊ ˌʃuːt] Fotoshooting; Fotoaufnahmen III

photo story ['fəʊtəʊ ˌstɔːri] Fotostory; Bildgeschichte I

*to take **photos** [ˌteɪk ˈfəʊtəʊz] fotografieren; Fotos machen **I**

to **photobomb** [ˈfəʊtəʊbɒm] ins Foto laufen **III**

photographer [fəˈtɒgrəfə] Fotograf/-in **III**

phrase [freɪz] Redewendung; Ausdruck; Satz **I**
Useful **phrases** [ˌjuːsfl ˈfreɪsɪz] nützliche Ausdrücke **I**

piano [piˈænəʊ] Klavier; Piano **IV U3**, 77

to **pick** [pɪk] auswählen; aussuchen **II**
to **pick** up [ˌpɪk ˈʌp] aufheben; mitnehmen; abholen **III**
pick-up [ˈpɪkʌp] Pick-up; Wiederaufnehmen **I**

picnic [ˈpɪknɪk] Picknick **I**

picture [ˈpɪktʃə] Bild; Foto **I**

pie [paɪ] Kuchen; Pastete **I**
pumpkin **pie** [ˌpʌmpkɪn ˈpaɪ] Kürbiskuchen ⟨**IV U2**, 45⟩

piece [piːs] Stück **I**
excellent **piece** of quick thinking [ˌekslnt piːs əv kwɪk ˈθɪŋkɪŋ] ausgezeichnete Reaktionsschnelligkeit ⟨**IVTS1**, 36⟩
piece of junk [ˌpiːs əv ˈdʒʌŋk] Stück Schrott **III**
piece of paper [ˌpiːs əv ˈpeɪpə] Stück Papier **I**

pier [pɪə] Pier; Hafendamm **I**

piercing [ˈpɪəsɪŋ] Piercing ⟨**IV U3**, 90⟩

pig [pɪg] Schwein **I**
guinea **pig** [ˈgɪni ˌpɪg] Meerschweinchen **I**

*to give sb a **piggyback** [gɪv ə ˈpɪgibæk] jmdn. Huckepack nehmen **IV U1**, 16

Pilgrim [ˈpɪlgrɪm] Pilger/-in ⟨**IV U2**, 45⟩

pill [pɪl] Pille; Tablette **II**

pilot [ˈpaɪlət] Pilot/-in **II**

pineapple [ˈpaɪnæpl] Ananas **III**

pink [pɪŋk] pink; rosa **I**

pipe [paɪp] Rohr; Rohrleitung; Pfeife **II**
clay **pipe** [ˈkleɪ paɪp] Tonpfeife **II**

pitch [pɪtʃ] Spielfeld; Platz **II**

pizza [ˈpiːtsə] Pizza **I**

place [pleɪs] Ort; Stelle; Platz **I**
starting **place** [ˈstɑːtɪŋ pleɪs] Startpunkt **III**
*to take **place** [ˌteɪk ˈpleɪs] stattfinden **I**

to **place** [pleɪs] legen **III**

placemat [ˈpleɪsmæt] Placemat; Platzdeckchen **I**

plan [plæn] Plan; Entwurf **I**

to **plan** [plæn] planen **I**

plane [pleɪn] Flugzeug **IV U1**, 8

planet [ˈplænɪt] Planet **II**

planner [ˈplænə] Handbuch; Kalender **I**
route **planner** [ˈruːt ˌplænə] Routenplaner **IV AC2**, 41

plant [plɑːnt] Pflanze **III**

to **plant** [plɑːnt] pflanzen; anpflanzen **II**

plaster cast [ˈplɑːstə kɑːst] Gipsverband **III**

plate [pleɪt] Teller **III**

platform [ˈplætfɔːm] Plattform; Bahnsteig **III**

play [pleɪ] Theaterstück **III**
fair **play** [feə ˈpleɪ] Fairplay **III**
play on words [ˌpleɪ ɒn ˈwɜːdz] Wortspiel **III**
role **play** [ˈrəʊl ˌpleɪ] Rollenspiel **I**

to **play** [pleɪ] spielen **I**
to **play** a trick (on) [ˌpleɪ ə ˈtrɪk ɒn] einen Streich spielen **I**
to **play** bowls [ˌpleɪ ˈbəʊlz] Bowling spielen **II**

player [ˈpleɪə] Spieler/-in; Mitspieler/-in **II**

Please. [pliːz] Bitte. **I**

to **pledge** allegiance [ˌpledʒ əˈliːdʒns] Treueschwur leisten ⟨**IV U2**, 49⟩

plot [plɒt] Handlung **III**

plumber [ˈplʌmə] Installateur/-in; Klempner/-in **III**

plumbing [ˈplʌmɪŋ] Sanitärarbeit **III**

plural [ˈplʊərəl] Plural; Mehrzahl **I**

poaching (no pl) [ˈpəʊtʃɪŋ] Wilderei **III**

pocket [ˈpɒkɪt] Tasche; Hosentasche **III**
pocket money [ˈpɒkɪt ˌmʌni] Taschengeld **I**

a **pocketful** of [ə ˈpɒkɪtfl əv] Unmengen von/an **IV U3**, 70

podcast [ˈpɒdkɑːst] Podcast **IV U3**, 92

poem [ˈpəʊɪm] Gedicht **I**

point [pɔɪnt] Punkt; Zeitpunkt **II**
*to have a **point** [ˌhæv ə ˈpɔɪnt] nicht ganz unrecht haben **III**
point of view [ˌpɔɪnt əv ˈvjuː] Standpunkt; Ansicht; Perspektive **II**
to the **point** [tə ðə ˈpɔɪnt] prägnant; treffend **II**
turning **point** [ˈtɜːnɪŋ ˌpɔɪnt] Wendepunkt **III**
I can't see the **point** of … [aɪ ˌkɑːnt siː ðə ˈpɔɪnt əv] Ich sehe keinen Sinn darin … **IV AC3**, 69

to **point** at sb/sth [ˈpɔɪnt æt] mit dem Finger auf jmdn./etw. zeigen **IV AC1**, 22

to **point** out sth [ˌpɔɪnt ˈaʊt] hinweisen auf etw. °**IV AC2**, 41

Point to … [ˈpɔɪnt tə] Zeige/Zeigt auf … **I**

Point. [pɔɪnt] Zeige/Zeigt darauf. **I**

police [pəˈliːs] Polizei **I**
police officer [pəˈliːs ˌɒfɪsə] Polizeibeamter; Polizist/-in **II**

polite [pəˈlaɪt] höflich **I**
Be **polite**. [biː pəˈlaɪt] Sei/Seid höflich. **I**

political [pəˈlɪtɪkl] politisch **IVTS3**, 101

pollution [pəˈluːʃn] Verschmutzung **II**

pond [pɒnd] Teich **II**

pony [ˈpəʊni] Pony **I**
pony trekking [ˈpəʊni ˌtrekɪŋ] Ponyreiten im Gelände **III**

swimming **pool** [ˈswɪmɪŋ ˌpuːl] Swimmingpool; Schwimmbecken **III**

the **poor** [ðə pʊə] die Armen **III**

poor [pɔː; pʊə] arm **III**

popular [ˈpɒpjələ] beliebt; populär **I**

populated [ˈpɒpjəleɪtɪd] bevölkert; besiedelt **IV AC2**, 38

population [ˌpɒpjəˈleɪʃn] Bevölkerung; Population **IV AC2**, 39

pose [pəʊz] Pose; Haltung **IV U2**, 56

positive [ˈpɒzətɪv] positiv **II**

possessive form [pəˌsesɪv ˈfɔːm] Possessivform **I**

possibility [ˌpɒsəˈbɪləti] Möglichkeit **III**

possible [ˈpɒsəbl] möglich **I**

post [pəʊst] Post (Eintrag im Internet) **I**

to **post** [pəʊst] online stellen; posten **II**

postcard [ˈpəʊstkɑːd] Postkarte **III**

poster [ˈpəʊstə] Poster **I**
class **poster** [ˈklɑːs ˌpəʊstə] Klassenposter **I**

postman [ˈpəʊstmən] Briefträger **II**

melting **pot** [ˈmeltɪŋ ˌpɒt] Schmelztiegel **IV U3**, 70

potato [pəˈteɪtəʊ], **potatoes** [pəˈteɪtəʊz] (pl) Kartoffel **III**
mashed **potatoes** (pl) [ˌmæʃt pəˈteɪtəʊz] Kartoffelpüree **III**
sweet **potatoes** (pl) [ˈswiːt pəˌteɪtəʊz] Süßkartoffeln ⟨**IV U2**, 45⟩

pound [paʊnd] Pfund (Maßeinheit) **IV U2**, 51

pound (£) [paʊnd] Pfund (brit. Währungseinheit) **I**

to **pour** [pɔː] einschenken; eingießen; schütten **I**

power [paʊə] Kraft; Macht; Stärke **III**
computing **power** [kəmˈpjuːtɪŋ ˌpaʊə] Rechenleistung ⟨**IVTS3**, 102⟩
power cut [ˈpaʊə ˌkʌt] Stromausfall **II**
Word **power** [ˈwɜːd ˌpaʊə] die Kraft der Wörter (Wortschatzübung) **I**
those in **power** [ˌðəʊz ɪn ˈpaʊə] die Regierenden; die Herrschenden **III**

powerful [ˈpaʊəfl] stark; mächtig **III**

practical [ˈpræktɪkl] praktisch **II**

practice [ˈpræktɪs] Training; Übung **III**

to **practice** (AE) [ˈpræktɪs] üben; ausüben; praktizieren; trainieren **IV U2**, 45
to **practice** a religion [ˌpræktɪs ə rɪˈlɪdʒn] eine Religion ausüben **IV U2**, 45

to **practise** [ˈpræktɪs] üben; trainieren **I**

practising [ˈpræktɪsɪŋ] Üben **I**

to **pray** [preɪ] beten **III**

to **preach** [priːtʃ] predigen ⟨**IVTS1**, 36⟩

prediction [prɪˈdɪkʃn] Vorhersage; Voraussage **III**

to **prefer** [prɪˈfɜː] vorziehen **IV U2**, 50

prehistoric [ˌpriːhɪˈstɒrɪk] vorgeschichtlich **III**

to **prepare** [prɪˈpeə] vorbereiten; zubereiten **I**

preposition [ˌprepəˈzɪʃn] Präposition **I**

pre-reading [ˌpriːˈriːdɪŋ] vor dem Lesen **I**

prescription [prɪˈskrɪpʃn] Rezept (für Arzneimittel) **II**

present ['preznt] Geschenk I; Gegenwart; Präsens II
present perfect [,preznt 'pɜːfɪkt] das Perfekt II
present progressive [,preznt prə'gresɪv] Verlaufsform des Präsens/der Gegenwart I
present perfect progressive [,preznt ,pɜːfɪkt prə'gresɪv] Verlaufsform des Perfekts III
simple **present** [,sɪmpl 'preznt] Gegenwart; Präsens I
to **present** [prɪ'zent] präsentieren; vorstellen I
present ['preznt] heutig; Gegenwarts- III
presentation [,prezn'teɪʃn] Präsentation; Vortrag I
presenter [prɪ'zentə] Moderator/-in I
president ['prezɪdnt] Präsident/-in IVTS3, 101
to **press** [pres] drücken; pressen II
peer **pressure** ['pɪə ,preʃə] Gruppenzwang III
to **pretend** [prɪ'tend] vortäuschen; tun als ob IVU1, 17
pretty ['prɪti] hübsch III
pretty ['prɪti] ziemlich; ganz schön ⟨IVTS3, 104⟩
price [praɪs] Preis I
primary school ['praɪmri ,skuːl] Grundschule I
principal (AE) ['prɪnsɪpl] Schulleiter/-in IVAC3, 68
print [prɪnt] gedruckt; Druck- II
priority [praɪ'ɒrəti] Priorität; Vorrang IVTS3, 101
prison ['prɪzn] Gefängnis II
prisoner ['prɪznə] Gefangene/-r ⟨IVU3, 90⟩
private detective [,praɪvət dɪ'tektɪv] Privatdetektiv/-in III
prize [praɪz] Preis; Gewinn I
pro [prəʊ] Argument dafür II
probably ['prɒbəbli] möglicherweise; wahrscheinlich II
problem ['prɒbləm] Problem; Schwierigkeit II
to **produce** [prə'djuːs] herstellen; produzieren II
product ['prɒdʌkt] Produkt; Erzeugnis IVTS2, 64
production [prə'dʌkʃn] Produktion; Inszenierung IVTS1, 30
profile ['prəʊfaɪl] Profil; Porträt I
program (AE) ['prəʊgræm] Programm; Sendung IVTS3, 104
space **program** ['speɪs prəʊgræm] Raumfahrtprogramm IVTS3, 104
programme ['prəʊgræm] Programm; Sendung II
progress ['prəʊgres] Fortschritt II
past perfect **progressive** [,pɑːst ,pɜːfɪkt prə'gresɪv] Verlaufsform des Plusquamperfekts °IVU3, 77

past **progressive** [,pɑːst prə'gresɪv] Verlaufsform der Vergangenheit II
present perfect **progressive** [,preznt ,pɜːfɪkt prə'gresɪv] Verlaufsform des Perfekts III
present **progressive** [,preznt prə'gresɪv] Verlaufsform des Präsens/der Gegenwart I
project ['prɒdʒekt] Projekt I
to **promise** ['prɒmɪs] versprechen III
prompt [prɒmpt] Stichwort III
prompt card ['prɒmpt kɑːd] Stichwortkarte; Rollenkarte III
pronoun ['prəʊnaʊn] Pronomen; Fürwort °IVU2, 50
object **pronoun** [ɒbdʒɪkt 'prəʊnaʊn] Objektpronomen III
reflexive **pronoun** [rɪ,fleksɪv 'prəʊnaʊn] Reflexivpronomen III
relative **pronoun** [,relətɪv 'prəʊnaʊn] Relativpronomen II
to **pronounce** [prə'naʊns] aussprechen IVAC4, 106
pronunciation [prə,nʌnsi'eɪʃn] Aussprache I
prop [prɒp] Requisite III
protagonist [prəʊ'tægnɪst] Protagonist/-in; Hauptfigur IVTS1, 30
protest ['prəʊtest] Protest III
protester ['prəʊtestə] Protestierende/-r; Demonstrant/-in IVU2, 52
proud (of) ['praʊd əv] stolz (auf) II
the **public** [ðə 'pʌblɪk] die Öffentlichkeit IVTS3, 102
public ['pʌblɪk] öffentlich II
public transport (no pl) [,pʌblɪk 'trænspɔːt] öffentliche Verkehrsmittel II
pudding ['pʊdɪŋ] Pudding; Nachtisch I
to **pull** [pʊl] ziehen I
to **pull** down [,pʊl 'daʊn] abreißen III
pumpkin pie [,pʌmpkɪn 'paɪ] Kürbiskuchen ⟨IVU2, 45⟩
purple ['pɜːpl] violett; lila I
purpose ['pɜːpəs] Ziel; Absicht; Zweck IVU1, 13
to **push** [pʊʃ] stoßen; schieben; schubsen II
to **push** oneself ['pʊʃ wʌn,self] sich alles abverlangen; sich Mühe geben III
pushy ['pʊʃi] aufdringlich; penetrant; aggressiv IVTS1, 33
*to **put** [pʊt] setzen; stellen; legen I
Put in … [pʊt 'ɪn] Setze/Setzt ein … I
Put it in … [pʊt ɪt 'ɪn] Lege/Legt es in …; Stelle/Stellt es in … I
*to **put** on [pʊt 'ɒn] anziehen III
*to **put** through [pʊt 'θruː] verbinden I
*to **put** up [pʊt 'ʌp] aufstellen; errichten; aufhängen II
Put … face down. [pʊt ,feɪs 'daʊn] Lege/Legt … umgedreht hin. I
puzzle ['pʌzl] Rätsel; Puzzle I
pyjamas (pl) [pɪ'dʒɑːməz] Schlafanzug; Pyjama II

Q

quality ['kwɒləti] Qualität I
quarter past/to ['kwɔːtə pɑːst/tə] Viertel nach/vor I
queen [kwiːn] Königin II
question ['kwestʃən] Frage I
question tag ['kwestʃən ,tæg] Frageanhängsel; Bestätigungsfrage II
to **question** ['kwestʃən] fragen; hinterfragen IVTS3, 103
questionnaire [,kwestʃə'neə] Fragebogen III
queue [kjuː] Schlange; Warteschlange I
to jump the **queue** [dʒʌmp ðə 'kjuː] sich vordrängeln I
quick [kwɪk] schnell I
quickly ['kwɪkli] schnell II
quiet [kwaɪət] still; ruhig; leise I
quill [kwɪl] Federkiel III
quite [kwaɪt] ziemlich; ganz; völlig IVU1, 14
quiz [kwɪz] Quiz; Rätsel I
quotation [kwə'teɪʃn] Zitat; Belegstelle °IVU3, 79
quote [kwəʊt] Zitat II

R

rabbit ['ræbɪt] Kaninchen I
race [reɪs] Wettlauf; Rennen II
camel **racing** ['kæml ,reɪsɪŋ] Kamelrennen II
racquet ['rækɪt] Schläger II
radio ['reɪdiəʊ] Radio II
raffle ['ræfl] Tombola I
rags to riches [,rægz tə 'rɪtʃɪz] vom Tellerwäscher zum Millionär IVU3, 79
rain [reɪn] Regen IVU1, 17
to **rain** [reɪn] regnen II
rainbow ['reɪnbəʊ] Regenbogen III
raincoat ['reɪnkəʊt] Regenmantel III
to **raise** money [reɪz 'mʌni] Geld sammeln II
rap [ræp] Rap I
to **rap** [ræp] rappen I
rat [ræt] Ratte I
to **rate** [reɪt] bewerten; einstufen IVTS3, 104
I'd **rather** [aɪd 'rɑːðə] ich würde lieber III
rating ['reɪtɪŋ] Kritik III
raven ['reɪvn] Rabe II
raven master ['reɪvn ,mɑːstə] Herr der Raben II
RE (= Religious Education) [ɑːr'iː; rɪ,lɪdʒəs edʒʊ'keɪʃn] Religion (Schulfach) II
to **reach** [riːtʃ] erreichen; dran kommen II
to **react** [ri'ækt] reagieren III
reaction [ri'ækʃn] Reaktion II
*to **read** [riːd] lesen I
*to **read** out loud [,riːd/sɪŋ aʊt 'laʊd] laut vorsingen III
reader ['riːdə] Leser/-in I
*to draw the **reader** into the story/action [drɔː ðə ,riːdə ɪntə ðə 'stɔːri/'ækʃn] den

Leser/die Leserin in die Geschichte/ Handlung hineinziehen III
reading ['riːdɪŋ] Lesen I
ready ['redi] fertig; bereit II
  ready meal [ˌredi 'miːl] Fertiggericht I
real [rɪəl] echt; richtig; wirklich II
to **realise** ['rɪəlaɪz] erkennen; realisieren III
realistic [ˌrɪə'lɪstɪk] realistisch II
to **realize** (AE) ['rɪəlaɪz] erkennen; realisieren **IV U2**, 52
really ['rɪəli] wirklich I
reason ['riːzn] Grund II
  *to give **reasons** [gɪv 'riːznz] Gründe nennen/angeben ⟨**IV U3**, 90⟩
*to **rebuild** [ˌriː'bɪld] wieder aufbauen III
to **receive** [rɪ'siːv] empfangen; erhalten; bekommen II
recently ['riːsntli] kürzlich; neulich °**IV TS3**, 105
receptive [rɪ'septɪv] empfänglich **IV TS2**, 64
recipe ['resɪpi] Rezept III
to **recite** [rɪ'saɪt] vortragen; rezitieren III
to **record** [rɪ'kɔːd] aufnehmen; aufzeichnen II
recorder [rɪ'kɔːdə] Flöte III
recording [rɪ'kɔːdɪŋ] Aufnahme; Aufzeichnung I
  recording studio [rɪ'kɔːdɪŋ ˌstjuːdiəʊ] Aufnahmestudio; Tonstudio I
recycling [ˌriː'saɪklɪŋ] Recycling; Wiederaufbereitung II
red [red] rot I
redwood (tree) ['redwʊd ˌtriː] Mammutbaum **IV AC2**, 39
to **reef** the sails [ˌriːf ðə 'seɪlz] die Segel einholen I
to **refer** to [rɪ'fɜː tə] sich beziehen auf °**IV TS3**, 103
reference article ['refrns ˌɑːtɪkl] Referenzartikel III
referendum [ˌrefr'endəm] Referendum; Volksentscheid III
reflexive [rɪ'fleksɪv] reflexiv; Reflexiv- III
  reflexive pronoun [rɪˌfleksɪv 'prəʊnaʊn] Reflexivpronomen I
refugee [ˌrefjʊ'dʒiː] Flüchtling **IV U1**, 18
region ['riːdʒn] Region; Gegend II
register ['redʒɪstə] Sprachebene; Register **IV AC4**, 106
registration [ˌredʒɪs'treɪʃn] Anwesenheitskontrolle II
regular ['regjələ] regelmäßig; gleichmäßig I
regulator ['regjəleɪtə] Regulator/-in; Aufsicht führende Person °**IV TS3**, 101
to **rehearse** [rɪ'hɜːs] proben III
reign [reɪn] Herrschaft; Regierungszeit III
to **reign** [reɪn] herrschen; regieren III
rejection [rɪ'dʒektʃn] Ablehnung; Absage **IV U3**, 76
to **relate** to [rɪ'leɪt tə] Zugang finden zu III
relationship [rɪ'leɪʃnʃɪp] Beziehung II

defining **relative** clause [dɪ'faɪnɪŋ 'relətɪv ˌklɔːz] notwendiger Relativsatz II
non-defining **relative** clause [ˌnɒndɪfaɪnɪŋ 'relətɪv ˌklɔːz] nicht notwendiger Relativsatz °**IV U3**, 73
relative pronoun [ˌrelətɪv 'prəʊnaʊn] Relativpronomen II
to **relax** [rɪ'læks] sich entspannen; sich ausruhen; sich beruhigen II
reliable [rɪ'laɪəbl] verlässlich; zuverlässig; vertrauenswürdig **IV TS3**, 100
religion [rɪ'lɪdʒn] Religion **IV U2**, 45
  to practice a **religion** [ˌpræktɪs ə rɪ'lɪdʒn] eine Religion ausüben **IV U2**, 45
religious [rɪ'lɪdʒəs] religiös; gläubig I
to **rely** (on) [rɪ'laɪ ˌɒn] sich verlassen (auf); vertrauen (auf) III
to **remember** [rɪ'membə] sich erinnern (an); sich merken; denken an I
  Remember? [rɪ'membə] Erinnerst du dich?; Erinnert ihr euch? I
to **remind** (sb of sth/sb) [rɪ'maɪnd əv] (jmdn. an etw./jmdn.) erinnern III
to **rent** (out) [ˌrent 'aʊt] mieten III
to **repeat** [rɪ'piːt] wiederholen II
repetition [ˌrepɪ'tɪʃn] Wiederholung **IV U1**, 15
to **replace** (by/with) [rɪ'pleɪs] ersetzen (durch) ⟨**IV U3**, 90⟩
reply [rɪ'plaɪ] Antwort; Erwiderung; Entgegnung I
to **reply** [rɪ'plaɪ] antworten; erwidern; entgegnen I
report [rɪ'pɔːt] Bericht; Meldung II
  news **report** ['njuːz rɪˌpɔːt] Tatsachenbericht; Nachrichtenbeitrag; Meldung III
  travel **report** [ˌtrævl rɪ'pɔːt] Reisebericht II
to **report** [rɪ'pɔːt] berichten; wiedergeben **IV U1**, 9
reporter [rɪ'pɔːtə] Reporter/-in II
to **represent** [ˌreprɪ'zent] repräsentieren; darstellen; stehen für **IV AC2**, 40
republic [rɪ'pʌblɪk] Republik ⟨**IV U2**, 49⟩
request [rɪ'kwest] Bitte **IV U1**, 9
*to **reread** [ˌriː'riːd] noch einmal lesen III
rescue ['reskjuː] Rettung II
to **rescue** ['reskjuː] retten III
research (no pl) [rɪ'sɜːtʃ] Recherche; Forschung; Untersuchung III
respect [rɪ'spekt] Respekt **IV TS3**, 103
response [rɪ'spɒns] Antwort; Erwiderung; Rückmeldung °**IV TS3**, 103
responsible [rɪs'pɒnsəbl] verantwortlich; verantwortungsvoll **IV U1**, 16
the **rest** [rest] der Rest I
restaurant ['restrɒnt] Restaurant; Gaststätte I
restroom (AE) ['restrʊm] Toilette **IV U2**, 43
result [rɪ'zʌlt] Ergebnis; Resultat II
*to **retell** [ˌriː'tel] nacherzählen; nochmals erzählen I
return ticket [rɪ'tɜːn ˌtɪkɪt] Hin- und Rückfahrkarte III

to **return** [rɪ'tɜːn] zurückkehren; zurückfahren III
revision [rɪ'vɪʒn] Wiederholung II
*to **rewrite** [ˌriː'raɪt] umschreiben; neu schreiben III
rhino ['raɪnəʊ] Rhinozeros; Nashorn III
rhyme [raɪm] Reim I
  rhyme scheme ['raɪm skiːm] Reimschema III
to **rhyme** [raɪm] (sich) reimen III
rhyming ['raɪmɪŋ] sich reimend 100
rhythm ['rɪðm] Rhythmus I
the **rich** [ðə rɪtʃ] die Reichen III
rich [rɪtʃ] reich III
  rags to **riches** [ˌrægz tə 'rɪtʃɪz] vom Tellerwäscher zum Millionär **IV U3**, 79
ride [raɪd] Fahrt; Ritt **IV U2**, 44
  along for the **ride** [əˌlɒŋ fə ðə 'raɪd] mit dabei **IV U2**, 44
*to **ride** [raɪd] fahren; reiten **IV AC2**, 41
rigging ['rɪgɪŋ] Takelage I
right [raɪt] Recht **IV U2**, 48
right [raɪt] richtig; korrekt; rechts; rechte/-r/-s I
  *to be **right** [bi 'raɪt] recht haben I
  *to get **right** [get 'raɪt] richtig beantworten III
  on the **right** [ɒn ðə 'raɪt] auf der rechten Seite; rechts I
  right away [raɪt ə'weɪ] sofort; gleich I
  right here [ˌraɪt 'hɪə] genau hier II
  right now [raɪt 'naʊ] jetzt gleich; sofort; gerade II
right [raɪt] direkt **IV U2**, 52
ring [rɪŋ] Ring III
  key **ring** ['kiː ˌrɪŋ] Schlüsselbund; Schlüsselanhänger III
*to **ring** [rɪŋ] klingeln; läuten I; anrufen **IV TS1**, 36
ice **rink** ['aɪs ˌrɪŋk] Eisbahn; Schlittschuhbahn I
*to **rise** [raɪz] steigen; sich erheben III
  *to **rise** up in one's mind [raɪz ˌʌp ɪn wʌnz 'maɪnd] jmdm. in den Sinn kommen III
No **risk**, no fun! [nəʊ ˌrɪsk nəʊ 'fʌn] Wer nicht wagt, der nicht gewinnt. **IV AC3**, 69
*to take a **risk** [ˌteɪk ə 'rɪsk] ein Risiko eingehen **IV TS1**, 32
river ['rɪvə] Fluss I
  by the **river** [baɪ ðə 'rɪvə] am Fluss II
road [rəʊd] Straße II
to **roar** [rɔː] dröhnen; brüllen; rauschen III
roaring ['rɔːrɪŋ] dröhnend; tosend; donnernd III
roast turkey [ˌrəʊst 'tɜːki] Putenbraten ⟨**IV U2**, 45⟩
robber ['rɒbə] Räuber/-in III
robot ['rəʊbɒt] Roboter; Automat ⟨**IV U3**, 90⟩
rock [rɒk] Fels; Stein ⟨**IV TS3**, 101⟩
rock [rɒk] Rock (Musik) III
  rock 'n' roll [ˌrɒk ən 'rəʊl] Rock 'n' Roll II
to **rock** [rɒk] schaukeln **IV U1**, 16

rocky ['rɒki] felsig; steinig **III**
role [rəʊl] Rolle **I**
  role play ['rəʊl ˌpleɪ] Rollenspiel **I**
  to swap **roles** [ˌswɒp 'rəʊlz] Rollen tauschen **I**
bread **roll** ['bred rəʊl] Brötchen **III**
rock 'n' **roll** [ˌrɒk ən 'rəʊl] Rock 'n' Roll **II**
to **roll** off [rəʊl] hinunterrollen; herunterrollen **II**
to **roll** one's eyes [ˌrəʊl wʌnz ˌaɪz] die Augen verdrehen **II**
Roll two dice. [ˌrəʊl ˌtuː 'daɪs] Würfle/Würfelt mit zwei Würfeln. **I**
Roman ['rəʊmən] Römer/-in; römisch **II**
romance [rə'mæns] Liebesgeschichte; Liebesfilm **III**
Romanian [rʊ'meɪnɪən] Rumäne/Rumänin; rumänisch; Rumänisch **II**
roof [ruːf] Dach **III**
room [ruːm; rʊm] Zimmer; Raum **I**
  chat **room** ['tʃæt rʊm] Chatroom **II**
  living **room** ['lɪvɪŋ rʊm] Wohnzimmer **I**
  side **room** ['saɪd ˌrʊm] Nebenraum **IV U1**, 13
roommate ['ruːmmeɪt] Zimmergenosse/Zimmergenossin **I**
rope [rəʊp] Seil **III**
rotary phone ['rəʊtri fəʊn] Telefon mit Wählscheibe **III**
rough [rʌf] rau; derb; grob 〈**IV TS1**, 31〉
round [raʊnd] Runde **II**
  round of boxing [ˌraʊnd əv 'bɒksɪŋ] Boxrunde **II**
the **Round** Table [ðə ˌraʊnd 'teɪbl] die Tafelrunde **III**
*to bring **round** [ˌbrɪŋ 'raʊnd] mitbringen 〈**IV TS1**, 36〉
*to go **round** in circles [gəʊ ˌraʊnd ɪn 'sɜːklz] sich im Kreis drehen **III**
to turn **round** [tɜːn ˌ(ə)'raʊnd] (sich) umdrehen; wenden **II**
round [raʊnd] um … herum **II**
route [ruːt] Strecke; Route **II**
  route planner ['ruːt ˌplænə] Routenplaner **IV AC2**, 41
routine [ruː'tiːn] Routine **IV U1**, 16
royal ['rɔɪəl] königlich **I**
rubber ['rʌbə] Radiergummi **I**
rubbish ['rʌbɪʃ] Müll; Gerümpel **I**
rude [ruːd] unhöflich; unverschämt **I**
rugby ['rʌgbi] Rugby **II**
to **ruin** ['ruːɪn] ruinieren; zerstören **II**
rule [ruːl] Regel **I**
  What's the **rule** for …? [wɒts ðə 'ruːl fə] Was ist die Regel für …? **I**
to **rule** [ruːl] herrschen; regieren **III**
ruler ['ruːlə] Lineal **I**
run [rʌn] Rennen; Lauf **II**
  run area ['rʌn ˌeəriə] Gehege; Auslauf **III**
*to **run** [rʌn] rennen; laufen **I**; betreiben; leiten; führen **IV TS3**, 102
  *to **run** away [ˌrʌn ə'weɪ] wegrennen **I**

runner ['rʌnə] Läufer/-in **II**
running ['rʌnɪŋ] Laufen; Rennen **II**
rural ['rʊərl] ländlich **IV AC2**, 38

S

sad [sæd] traurig **I**
safe [seɪf] sicher; ungefährlich **II**
to reef the **sails** [ˌriːf ðə 'seɪlz] die Segel einholen **I**
to **sail** [seɪl] segeln; umsegeln **III**
sailboat ['seɪlbəʊt] Segelboot **III**
sailor ['seɪlə] Seemann; Matrose **I**
salad ['sæləd] Salat **I**
sale [seɪl] Verkauf **II**
the **same** [ðə 'seɪm] der-/die-/dasselbe; der/die/das gleiche **I**
the **same** way as [ˌðə seɪm 'weɪ æz] genauso wie **II**
samosa [sə'məʊsə] mit Kartoffeln oder Hackfleisch gefüllte indische Teigtasche 〈**IV U3**, 75〉
sample ['sɑːmpl] Probe; Muster **IV TS2**, 64
sandal ['sændl] Sandale **III**
sandwich ['sænwɪdʒ] Sandwich; belegtes Brot **I**
sandy ['sændi] sandig; Sand- **III**
Saturday ['sætədeɪ] Samstag **I**
sauce [sɔːs] Soße **III**
sausage ['sɒsɪdʒ] Wurst; Bratwurst **III**
to **save** [seɪv] retten; bergen **I**; sparen **III**
  to **save** the best for last [ˌseɪv ðə ˌbest fə 'lɑːst] sich das Beste bis zum Schluss aufheben **IV U3**, 72
  saved by the bell [ˌseɪvd baɪ ðə 'bel] noch mal Glück gehabt **III**
sax ['sæks] Saxofon **I**
saxophone ['sæksəfəʊn] Saxofon **I**
*to **say** [seɪ] sagen; aufsagen; sprechen **I**
  needless to **say** [ˌniːdləs tə 'seɪ] natürlich; selbstverständlich **IV U3**, 76
  *to **say** hello (to) [ˌseɪ hel'əʊ tə] grüßen; Grüße ausrichten (an) **I**
saying ['seɪɪŋ] Redensart; Sprichwort **III**
to **scan** [skæn] scannen; nach Details durchsuchen **II**
scared [skeəd] verängstigt; ängstlich **IV U2**, 52
  *to be **scared** (of) [bi: 'skeəd əv] Angst haben (vor) **I**
  I'm (not) **scared** of … [ˌaɪm (nɒt) 'skeəd əv] Ich habe (keine) Angst vor … **I**
scary ['skeəri] unheimlich; gruselig; beängstigend **II**
scene [siːn] Szene; Schauplatz **II**
  acting a **scene** [ˌæktɪŋ ə 'siːn] eine Theaterszene spielen **I**
scenery ['siːnri] Landschaft **IV AC2**, 40
sceptical ['skeptɪkl] skeptisch **IV TS2**, 64
schedule (AE) ['ʃedjuːl; 'skedʒuːl] Stundenplan; Fahrplan; Terminkalender **IV AC4**, 106

rhyme **scheme** ['raɪm skiːm] Reimschema **III**
schnitzel ['ʃnɪtsl] Schnitzel 〈**IV U3**, 75〉
school [skuːl] Schule **I**
  grammar **school** ['græmə ˌskuːl] Gymnasium **III**
  high **school** (AE) ['haɪ ˌskuːl] High School (weiterführende Schule in den USA, Oberstufe) **IV U2**, 43
  middle **school** (AE) ['mɪdl ˌskuːl] Mittelschule (weiterführende Schule in den USA, Mittelstufe) **IV U2**, 43
  primary **school** ['praɪmri ˌskuːl] Grundschule **I**
  school fees (pl) ['skuːl fiːz] Schulgeld; Schulgebühren **III**
schoolbag ['skuːlbæg] Schultasche **I**
schoolwork ['skuːlwɜːk] Schularbeiten **IV TS1**, 34
Science [saɪəns] Naturwissenschaften **II**
science [saɪəns] Wissenschaft; Naturwissenschaft **IV TS3**, 100
  science fiction [ˌsaɪəns 'fɪkʃn] Science-Fiction (Zukunftsdichtung) **II**
scientist ['saɪəntɪst] Wissenschaftler/-in **III**
score [skɔː] Punktestand; Spielstand **II**
Scot [skɒt] Schotte/Schottin **III**
Scottish ['skɒtɪʃ] schottisch **III**
gorge **scrambling** ['gɔːdʒ ˌskræmblɪŋ] Schluchtenklettern **II**
to **scream** [skriːm] schreien; kreischen **II**
script [skrɪpt] Drehbuch; Skript **III**
sculpture ['skʌlptʃə] Skulptur **IV U3**, 72
sea [siː] Meer **I**
search [sɜːtʃ] Suche; Such- **II**
  search engine ['sɜːtʃ ˌendʒɪn] Suchmaschine °**IV U2**, 42
to **search** for ['sɜːtʃ fə] suchen (nach) **IV U1**, 14
seasick ['siːsɪk] seekrank **IV U1**, 8
season ['siːzn] Saison; Jahreszeit **IV U2**, 56
seat [siːt] Sitz; Sitzplatz **IV U1**, 16
second ['seknd] zweite/-r/-s **I**
secret ['siːkrət] Geheimnis **II**
  in **secret** [ɪn 'siːkrət] heimlich **II**
secret ['siːkrət] geheim **III**
section ['sekʃn] Abschnitt; Paragraf **II**
security [sɪ'kjʊərəti] Sicherheit; Schutz; Wachdienst; Wach-; Sicherheits- **IV U1**, 13
*to **see** [siː] sehen **I**
  See you! ['siː jə] Bis dann!; Bis … **I**
  I can't **see** the point of … [aɪ ˌkɑːnt siː ðə 'pɔɪnt əv] Ich sehe keinen Sinn darin … **IV AC3**, 69
  Wait and **see**! [ˌweɪt ənd 'siː] Warte ab! **I**
to **seem** [siːm] scheinen **III**
self [self], **selves** [selvz] (pl) das Selbst **III**
self-critical ['self,krɪtɪkl] selbstkritisch **II**
self-evaluation [ˌselfɪˌvæljuˈeɪʃn] Selbsteinschätzung **I**
selfie ['selfi] Selfie **II**
*to **sell** [sel] verkaufen **I**

seller ['selə] Verkäufer/-in *(auf einem Flohmarkt)* I
*to **send** [send] schicken; senden I
  *to **send** off [send ˌɒf] abschicken III
sense [sens] Sinn III
  *to make **sense** [ˌmeɪk 'sens] Sinn ergeben; einleuchten IV TS3, 102
  sense of humour *(no pl)* [ˌsens əv 'hjuːmə] Sinn für Humor III
sensible ['sensɪbl] vernünftig IV TS1, 32
sentence ['sentəns] Satz I
  conditional **sentence** [kənˌdɪʃnl 'sentəns] Bedingungssatz III
to **separate** ['sepreɪt] (sich) trennen °IV U3, 73
separate ['seprət] separat; getrennt; verschieden II
September [sep'tembə] September I
sequence ['siːkwəns] Sequenz; Szene III; Abfolge; Reihenfolge IV U3, 89
series ['sɪəriːz], **series** ['sɪəriːz] *(pl)* Serie III
serious ['sɪəriəs] ernsthaft; ernst I
service ['sɜːvɪs] Service; Dienstleistung; Dienst IV U3, 72
set [set] Umgebung; Rahmen; Aufnahmeort; Drehort III
  a **set** of [ə 'set əv] eine Liste von III
*to be **set** (in) [bi 'set ɪn] spielen (in); seinen Schauplatz haben (in) IV U1, 19
*to **set** off [set ˌɒf] *hier:* ein Feuerwerk zünden III
*to **set** up [set ˌʌp] einrichten; aufbauen I
setting ['setɪŋ] Schauplatz; Rahmen II
  account **settings** [əˈkaʊnt ˌsetɪŋz] Profileinstellungen III
to **settle** for less [ˌsetl fə 'les] sich mit weniger zufrieden geben IV TS2, 66
seven ['sevn] sieben I
several ['sevrl] einige; mehrere; verschiedene II
shadow ['ʃædəʊ] Schatten III
*to **shake** [ʃeɪk] schütteln ⟨IV U3, 90⟩
shampoo [ʃæm'puː] Shampoo IV TS2, 64
shape [ʃeɪp] Form IV U3, 89
to **share** [ʃeə] teilen II
shark [ʃɑːk] Hai IV U1, 16
sharp [ʃɑːp] scharf; schneidend III
she [ʃiː] sie I
sheep, **sheep** *(pl)* [ʃiːp] Schaf II
cheat **sheet** *(AE)* ['tʃiːt ʃiːt] Spickzettel IV AC3, 69
animal **shelter** ['ænɪml ˌʃeltə] Tierheim III
homeless **shelter** ['həʊmləs ˌʃeltə] Obdachlosenunterkunft IV U2, 51
*to **shine** [ʃaɪn] scheinen; glänzen II
shinty ['ʃɪnti] Shinty *(eine Art Hockey)* III
ship [ʃɪp] Schiff I
shipbuilding ['ʃɪpbɪldɪŋ] Schiffsbau III
shit *(vulg)* [ʃɪt] Scheiße; Scheißdreck ⟨IV U3, 84⟩
shock [ʃɒk] Schock II
shocked [ʃɒkt] schockiert; geschockt IV TS1, 37

shoe [ʃuː] Schuh I
  *to be in sb's **shoes** [ˌbiː ɪn sʌmbɒdiz 'ʃuːz] an jmds. Stelle sein; in jmds. Haut stecken III
  in Jay's **shoes** [ɪn dʒeɪz 'ʃuːz] an Jays Stelle III
on a **shoestring** [ɒn ə 'ʃuːstrɪŋ] für/mit wenig Geld IV U3, 72
photo **shoot** ['fəʊtəʊ ˌʃuːt] Fotoshooting; Fotoaufnahmen III
*to **shoot** [ʃuːt (ət)] schießen (auf) III
shop [ʃɒp] Geschäft; Laden I
  charity **shop** ['tʃærɪti ʃɒp] Second-Hand-Laden I
  pawn **shop** ['pɔːn ʃɒp] Pfandhaus; Pfandleihe III
to **shop** [ʃɒp] einkaufen; shoppen IV U3, 76
shopper ['ʃɒpə] Käufer/-in IV U2, 48
shopping ['ʃɒpɪŋ] Einkaufen; Einkäufe I
  *to do the **shopping** [ˌduː ðə 'ʃɒpɪŋ] Einkäufe machen; Besorgungen machen III
  *to go **shopping** [ˌgəʊ 'ʃɒpɪŋ] einkaufen gehen I
  shopping mall ['ʃɒpɪŋ ˌmɔːl] Einkaufszentrum IV U2, 43
shore [ʃɔː] Ufer; Küste II
short [ʃɔːt] kurz I
  short answer [ˌʃɔːt 'ɑːnsə] Kurzantwort I
  short form ['ʃɔːt fɔːm] Kurzform I
shorts *(pl)* [ʃɔːts] Shorts; kurze Hose II
shot [ʃɒt] Einstellung; Kameraeinstellung II; Aufnahme III
  long **shot** ['lɒŋ ʃɒt] Totale *(Kameraeinstellung)* IV U3, 89
  medium **shot** ['miːdiəm ʃɒt] Halbtotale *(Kameraeinstellung)* IV U3, 89
should [ʃʊd] sollte; solltest; sollten; solltet II
  shouldn't ['ʃʊdnt] sollte(n) nicht II
shoulder ['ʃəʊldə] Schulter II
to **shout** [ʃaʊt] schreien; rufen I
show [ʃəʊ] Show; Schau; Aufführung II
  comedy **show** ['kɒmədi ˌʃəʊ] Comedy Show II
  living history **show** [ˌlɪvɪŋ 'hɪstəri ˌʃəʊ] Show, in der historischer Alltag nachgespielt wird III
  talent **show** ['tælənt ˌʃəʊ] Talentwettbewerb I
to **show** [ʃəʊ] zeigen I
  to **show** off [ʃəʊ ˌɒf] angeben II
shower ['ʃaʊə] Dusche I
show-off ['ʃəʊ ˌɒf] Angeber/-in III
to **shuffle** ['ʃʌfl] mischen III
shutter ['ʃʌtə] Fensterladen IV U1, 10
shy [ʃaɪ] schüchtern II
sick [sɪk] krank; unwohl II
  *to be **sick** [bi 'sɪk] sich übergeben IV U1, 16
  *to feel **sick** [ˌfiːl 'sɪk] Übelkeit verspüren; sich schlecht fühlen II
side [saɪd] Seite II

side room ['saɪd ˌruːm] Nebenraum IV U1, 13
sidewalk *(AE)* ['saɪdwɔːk] Gehweg; Gehsteig IV U3, 76
sight [saɪt] Sehenswürdigkeit; Anblick II; *hier:* Blick III
sighting ['saɪtɪŋ] Sichten °IV TS3, 105
sightseeing ['saɪtsiːɪŋ] Sightseeing-; Besichtigungs- II
sign [saɪn] Zeichen; Schild II
to **sign** [saɪn] unterschreiben; unterzeichnen IV U2, 52
signal ['sɪgnl] Signal; Empfang III
  signal word ['sɪgnəl ˌwɜːd] Signalwort I
silence *(no pl)* ['saɪləns] Stille; Schweigen; Ruhe III
silent ['saɪlənt] still; ruhig; schweigsam; stumm III
silk [sɪlk] Seide ⟨IV TS1, 34⟩
silly ['sɪli] Dummkopf II
silly ['sɪli] dumm; doof; albern I
silver ['sɪlvə] Silber II
similar ['sɪmɪlə] ähnlich II
similarity [ˌsɪmɪ'lærəti] Ähnlichkeit; Gemeinsamkeit °IV TS2, 67
simple ['sɪmpl] einfach; simpel III
  simple past [ˌsɪmpl 'pɑːst] Vergangenheitsform II
  simple present [ˌsɪmpl 'preznt] Gegenwart; Präsens I
simply ['sɪmpli] einfach nur IV AC2, 40
since [sɪns] da IV U3, 72
since (+ *Zeitpunkt*) [sɪns] seit; seitdem III
*to **sing** [sɪŋ] singen I
  *to **sing** along [sɪŋ ə'lɒŋ] mitsingen III
  *to **sing** out loud [ˌriːd/sɪŋ aʊt 'laʊd] laut vorsingen III
  I like **singing** and dancing. [aɪ laɪk ˌsɪŋɪŋ ənd 'dɑːnsɪŋ] Ich singe und tanze gern. I
singer ['sɪŋə] Sänger/-in II
single ['sɪŋgl] einzeln; einzig; alleinstehend IV AC2, 38
  single ticket ['sɪŋgl ˌtɪkɪt] einfache Fahrkarte II
*to **sink** [sɪŋk] untergehen; sinken III
Dear **Sir** or Madam [dɪə ˌsɜːr ɔː 'mædəm] Sehr geehrte Dame, sehr geehrter Herr III
sister ['sɪstə] Schwester I
  half-**sister** ['hɑːf ˌsɪstə] Halbschwester I
*to **sit** [sɪt] sitzen I
  Sit! [sɪt] Sitz! *(Befehl für Hunde)*; Platz! *(Befehl für Hunde)* I
  *to **sit** down [sɪt 'daʊn] sich hinsetzen; sich setzen I
  *to **sit** face to face [sɪt feɪs tə ˌfeɪs] sich gegenüber sitzen I
site [saɪt] Webseite II
situation [ˌsɪtjuˈeɪʃn] Situation I
six [sɪks] sechs I
  Four and **six** is ten. [ˌfɔːr ənd ˌsɪks ɪz 'ten] Vier plus sechs ist zehn. I
size [saɪz] Größe; Kleidergröße I

to **skate** [skeɪt] Inlineskates fahren; Schlittschuh laufen **I**

skateboard [ˈskeɪtbɔːd] Skateboard **II**

skateboarding [ˈskeɪtbɔːdɪŋ] Skateboardfahren **I**

skates (pl) [skeɪts] Inlineskates; Rollschuhe; Schlittschuhe **I**

(inline) **skating** [ˈɪnlaɪn ˌskeɪtɪŋ] Inlineskatefahren **I**

skill [skɪl] Fertigkeit; Geschick **I**

to **skim** [skɪm] überfliegen **II**

to **skip** [skɪp] auslassen; schwänzen **IV AC3**, 68

skirt [skɜːt] Rock **III**

sky [skaɪ] Himmel **III**

skyscraper [ˈskaɪskreɪpə] Wolkenkratzer **IV AC2**, 39

slave [sleɪv] Sklave/Sklavin **III**

sleep [sliːp] Schlaf **IV U1**, 11

*to **sleep** [sliːp] schlafen **I**

sleepover [ˈsliːpˌəʊvə] Übernachtung **I**

to **slice** [slaɪs] in Scheiben schneiden **I**

slide [slaɪd] Rutschbahn **I**
water **slide** [ˈwɔːtə ˌslaɪd] Wasserrutsche **I**

*to **slide** [slaɪd] gleiten lassen ⟨**IV U3**, 90⟩

to **slip** into [slɪpˈɪntə] schlüpfen in °**IV TS2**, 67

slogan [ˈsləʊgən] Slogan; Werbespruch **II**

time **slot** [ˈtaɪm slɒt] Zeitfenster **II**

to **slow** down [sləʊ ˈdaʊn] langsamer werden; bremsen ⟨**IV U3**, 90⟩

slow [sləʊ] langsam **I**
to step into a story **slowly** [stepˌɪntʊ ə ˌstɔːri ˈsləʊli] eine Geschichte langsam entwickeln **III**

small [smɔːl] klein **I**
small talk [ˈsmɔːl ˌtɔːk] Smalltalk **III**

smart [smɑːt] schlau; klug; intelligent **III**

smartcard [ˈsmɑːtkɑːd] Chipkarte **II**

smartphone [ˈsmɑːtfəʊn] Smartphone **II**

to **smash** [smæʃ] zerschlagen; zerschmettern **IV U1**, 16

*to **smell** [smel] riechen; duften **III**

smile [smaɪl] Lächeln **I**

to **smile** [smaɪl] lächeln **I**

smoke [sməʊk] Rauch **III**

smoky [ˈsməʊki] verraucht **III**

smuggler [ˈsmʌglə] Schmuggler/-in **IV U1**, 16

snack [snæk] Snack; Imbiss **I**
snack bar [ˈsnæk ˌbɑː] Café; Imbissstube **I**

word **snake** [ˈwɜːd ˌsneɪk] Wortschlange **I**

to **sneak** around [sniːk əˈraʊnd] herumschleichen **II**

*to **sneak** [sniːk] schleichen; schmuggeln **IV U3**, 72

to **snore** [snɔː] schnarchen **I**

snow [snəʊ] Schnee **III**

so [səʊ] so; also **I**
so far [səʊ ˈfɑː] bis jetzt **II**
so is [ˈsəʊ ɪz] ebenso wie **III**

so (that) [ˌsəʊ ˈðæt] damit; so dass **IV AC3**, 69

to **soak** up [səʊkˈʌp] aufsaugen **III**

soccer (AE) [ˈsɒkə] Fußball **IV U2**, 44

social [ˈsəʊʃl] sozial; gesellschaftlich **IV U2**, 46
social media [ˌsəʊʃl ˈmiːdiə] soziale Netzwerke **IV U2**, 46
social network [ˌsəʊʃl ˈnetwɜːk] soziales Netzwerk **II**

society [səˈsaɪəti] Verein; Gesellschaft **III**

sofa [ˈsəʊfə] Sofa; Couch **I**

software [ˈsɒftweə] Software (Computerprogramme) ⟨**IV TS3**, 102⟩
software manual [ˈsɒftweə ˌmænjuəl] Softwarehandbuch **III**

soldier [ˈsəʊldʒə] Soldat/-in **III**

solution [səˈluːʃn] Lösung **II**

to **solve** [sɒlv] lösen **III**

Somali [səˈmɑːli] Somali **IV U1**, 17

some [sʌm; səm] einige; ein paar; etwas **I**

somebody [ˈsʌmbədi] jemand **I**

someone [ˈsʌmwʌn] jemand **II**

something [ˈsʌmθɪŋ] etwas **I**

sometimes [ˈsʌmtaɪmz] manchmal **I**

somewhere [ˈsʌmweə] irgendwo **II**

son [sʌn] Sohn **III**

song [sɒŋ] Song; Lied **I**
theme **song** [ˈθiːm sɒŋ] Titelmelodie °**IV U3**, 91

soon [suːn] bald **II**
as **soon** as [əz ˈsuːnˌəz] sobald **II**

Sorry! [ˈsɒri] Entschuldigung!; Tut mir leid! **I**
*to be **sorry** [biː ˈsɒri] leid tun **I**
*to feel **sorry** for [ˌfiːl ˈsɒri fɔː] Mitleid haben mit; bedauern **II**
I'm **sorry**! [ˌaɪm ˈsɒri] Tut mir leid! **I**

sort [sɔːt] Sorte; Art ⟨**IV TS1**, 34⟩

to **sort** into [sɔːt ˈɪntʊ] einsortieren; sortieren nach **III**

sound [saʊnd] Ton; Geräusch; Klang **I**

to **sound** [saʊnd] klingen **I**

soup [suːp] Suppe **IV U1**, 11

source [sɔːs] Quelle **III**

south [saʊθ] Süden; Süd- **II**
South Korean [ˌsaʊθ kəˈriːən] Südkoreaner/-in; südkoreanisch; Südkoreanisch **II**

(the) **Southwest** [ˌsaʊθˈwest] (der) Südwesten; im Südwesten; südwestlich **IV AC2**, 38

souvenir [ˌsuːvnˈɪə] Souvenir; Andenken **II**

space [speɪs] Raum; Fläche; Platz; Ort **II**
*to leave **space** [liːv ˈspeɪs] Platz lassen **I**

space [speɪs] Weltraum; Weltall **IV TS3**, 104
space program [ˈspeɪs prəʊgræm] Raumfahrtprogramm **IV TS3**, 104

spaceship [ˈspeɪsʃɪp] Raumschiff **II**

Spanish [ˈspænɪʃ] spanisch; Spanisch; die Spanier **III**

sparse [spɑːs] dünn; spärlich **IV AC2**, 38

*to **speak** [spiːk] sprechen **I**

speaker [ˈspiːkə] Redner/-in; Sprecher/-in **I**

speaking [ˈspiːkɪŋ] Sprechen **I**

spear [spɪə] Speer **III**

special [ˈspeʃl] besonders; speziell **I**

special effect [ˈspeʃl ɪˈfekt] Spezialeffekt **IV TS3**, 105

special offer [ˌspeʃl ˈɒfə] Sonderangebot **I**
with **special** needs [wɪð ˌspeʃl ˈniːdz] behindert **II**

specialty (AE) [ˈspeʃlti] Spezialität; Besonderheit **IV U3**, 75

specific [spəˈsɪfɪk] spezifisch; speziell **IV U1**, 19

spectacular [spekˈtækjələ] spektakulär **III**

speech [spiːtʃ] Rede **III**
direct **speech** [dɪˌrekt ˈspiːtʃ] direkte Rede **IV U1**, 11
indirect **speech** [ˌɪndɪrekt ˈspiːtʃ] indirekte Rede **IV U1**, 11
speech bubble [ˈspiːtʃ ˌbʌbl] Sprechblase **I**

speed [spiːd] Geschwindigkeit **IV U3**, 89

*to **spell** [spel] buchstabieren **I**

spelling [ˈspelɪŋ] Rechtschreibung **I**

*to **spend** [spend] ausgeben (Geld) **I**; verbringen (Zeit) **I**

to **spice** up [spaɪsˈʌp] aufpeppen **IV TS2**, 65

spider [ˈspaɪdə] Spinne **III**

spike [spaɪk] Spitze; Stachel **IV U3**, 74

*to **spill** [spɪl] verschütten; auslaufen **IV U1**, 10

spoken [ˈspəʊkn] gesprochen **II**

sponge [spʌndʒ] Rühr-; Biskuit- **I**

spontaneous [spɒnˈteɪniəs] spontan **III**

spoon [spuːn] Löffel **III**

sport [spɔːt] Sport; Sportart **I**

spot [spɒt] Fleck; Ort **IV U3**, 75

spray [spreɪ] Spray ⟨**IV U3**, 86⟩

spring [sprɪŋ] Frühling **III**

squirrel [ˈskwɪrəl] Eichhörnchen **I**

stadium [ˈsteɪdiəm] Stadion **II**

stage [steɪdʒ] Bühne **III**
stage direction [ˈsteɪdʒ dɪˌrekʃn] Regieanweisung **III**

to **stage** [steɪdʒ] aufführen **IV TS1**, 30; inszenieren **IV TS3**, 102

stairs (pl) [steəz] Treppe **III**

*to **stand** [stænd] stehen **I**
*to **stand** in line (AE) [ˌstændˌɪn ˈlaɪn] anstehen; Schlange stehen; (sich) anstellen **IV AC3**, 69
*to **stand** in the way of sb/sth [ˌstænd ɪn ðə ˈweɪˌəv] jmdm./etw. im Weg stehen **IV AC1**, 22
*to **stand** up [ˌstændˈʌp] aufstehen (von einer Sitzgelegenheit) **I**

standard of living [ˌstændədˌəv ˈlɪvɪŋ] Lebensstandard **IV AC2**, 40

star [stɑː] Star; Stern **I**

to **stare** [steə] starren; anstarren **I**

start [stɑːt] Anfang; Start **III**

to **start** [stɑːt] anfangen; beginnen; starten **I**; hier: gründen **III**
*to get **started** [ˌget ˈstɑːtɪd] anfangen **II**
starting place [ˈstɑːtɪŋ pleɪs] Startpunkt **III**

state [steɪt] Staat; Bundesstaat; Land **IV AC2**, 39

head of **state** [ˌhed əv 'steɪt] Staatsoberhaupt **II**

statement ['steɪtmənt] Aussage; Behauptung; Erklärung **II**

station ['steɪʃn] Haltestelle; Bahnhof; Station **I**; Sender **II**

bus **station** ['bʌs ˌsteɪʃn] Busbahnhof **I**

statue ['stætʃuː] Statue; Standbild **IV U3**, 74

to **stay** [steɪ] bleiben **I**; übernachten **III**

to **stay** awake [ˌsteɪ ə'weɪk] wach bleiben ⟨**IV U3**, 90⟩

to **stay** away from [ˌsteɪ ə'weɪ frəm] fernbleiben von; meiden **II**

to **stay** in touch (with) [ˌsteɪ ɪn 'tʌtʃ (wɪð)] in Kontakt bleiben (mit) **II**

to **stay** with [ˈsteɪ wɪð] wohnen bei **II**

Stay the way you are. [ˌsteɪ ðə weɪ ju 'ɑː] Bleib wie du bist. **III**

steady ['stedi] kontinuierlich; unaufhörlich **IV U1**, 17

steak [steɪk] Steak **I**

*to **steal** [stiːl] stehlen **II**

steam [stiːm] Dampf **III**

steam engine ['stiːmˌendʒɪn] Dampfmaschine **III**

step [step] Stufe; Schritt **I**

step-by-**step** [ˌstepbaɪ'step] Schritt-für-Schritt- **II**

to **step** [step] treten; steigen **IVTS3**, 101

to **step** into a story slowly [stepˌɪntʊ ə ˌstɔːri 'sləʊli] eine Geschichte langsam entwickeln **III**

stepmum ['stepmʌm] Stiefmutter **I**

*to **stick** [stɪk] stecken ⟨**IV U3**, 88⟩

still [stɪl] Standbild **II**

still [stɪl] still **I**

still [stɪl] noch; immer noch **I**; dennoch **II**

*to keep one's feet or hands **still** [ˌkiːp wʌnz ˈfiːt ɔː ˈhændz stɪl] die Beine und Hände ruhig halten **III**

*to **sting** [stɪŋ] stechen **III**

stomach ['stʌmək] Magen; Bauch **II**

stomachache ['stʌməkeɪk] Bauchschmerzen; Bauchweh **II**

stone [stəʊn] Stein; Stein- **III**

stop [stɒp] Haltestelle; Halt **II**

to **stop** [stɒp] aufhören (mit); anhalten; stoppen **I**

Stop and think [ˌstɒp ənd 'θɪŋk] Warte/ Wartet und denk/denkt nach. **I**

Stop it! ['stɒp ɪt] Mach/Macht das aus!; Hör/Hört auf! **I**

store (AE) [stɔː] Laden; Geschäft **IV U2**, 44

storm [stɔːm] Sturm **I**

story, **stories** (pl) ['stɔːri; 'stɔːriz] Story; Geschichte; Erzählung **I**

photo **story** ['fəʊtəʊ ˌstɔːri] Fotostory; Bildgeschichte **I**

to step into a **story** slowly [stepˌɪntʊ ə ˌstɔːri 'sləʊli] eine Geschichte langsam entwickeln **III**

storyline ['stɔːrilaɪn] Handlung °**IV U2**, 54

straight [streɪt] gerade; direkt; geradewegs **IV U1**, 17

straight away [ˌstreɪt ə'weɪ] sofort; gleich **III**

straight on [streɪt 'ɒn] geradeaus **I**

strange [streɪndʒ] fremd; seltsam; merkwürdig **I**

street [striːt] Straße (in der Stadt) **I**

in the **street** [ˌɪn ðə 'striːt] in der Straße; auf der Straße **I**

the high **street** [ðə ˌhaɪ 'striːt] die Haupteinkaufsstraße **III**

streetlight ['striːtlaɪt] Straßenlampe ⟨**IV U3**, 90⟩

stress [stres] Betonung **III**

to **stress** [stres] betonen; hervorheben **III**

*to be **stressed** out [bi ˌstrestˈaʊt] völlig gestresst sein **III**

strict [strɪkt] streng; strikt **III**

stringy ['strɪŋi] strähnig ⟨**IV U3**, 90⟩

strong [strɒŋ] stark **II**

structure ['strʌktʃə] Struktur; Aufbau; Gliederung **III**

to **structure** ['strʌktʃə] strukturieren; gliedern °**IVTS3**, 105

stuck in the middle of … [ˌstʌk ɪn ðə 'mɪdl̩ əv] mitten in … stecken; feststecken in … **III**

student ['stjuːdnt] Schüler/-in; Student/-in **I**

exchange **student** [ɪks'tʃeɪndʒ ˌstjuːdnt] Austauschschüler/-in **III**

student exchange ['stjuːdnt ɪksˌtʃeɪndʒ] Schüleraustausch **III**

studies (pl) ['stʌdiz] Studium; Lernen; Arbeit für die Schule **II**

studio ['stjuːdiəʊ] Studio; Atelier **IV U3**, 72

recording **studio** [rɪˈkɔːdɪŋ ˌstjuːdiəʊ] Aufnahmestudio; Tonstudio **I**

to **study** ['stʌdi] studieren; lernen **III**

stuff [stʌf] Zeug **I**

stupid ['stjuːpɪd] dumm; blöd **II**

style [staɪl] Stil **IV U1**, 11

stylistic [staɪ'lɪstɪk] Stil-; stilistisch **IV U3**, 89

subject ['sʌbdʒɪkt] Schulfach; Subjekt; Satzgegenstand **II**; Thema **III**

substitute ['sʌbstɪtjuːt] Ersatz; Ersatz- **II**

suburb ['sʌbɜːb] Vorort **IV U2**, 43

suburban [sə'bɜːbn] Vorstadt- **IV U2**, 43

subway (AE) ['sʌbweɪ] U-Bahn **IV U3**, 74

to **succeed** (in) [sək'siːd ɪn] Erfolg haben (in/bei/mit) **III**

success [sək'ses] Erfolg **III**

successful [sək'sesfl] erfolgreich **III**

such [sʌtʃ] solch; solche/-r/-s **II**

It **sucks**. (slang) [ɪt 'sʌks] Das ist zum Kotzen. **IV AC4**, 107

suddenly ['sʌdnli] plötzlich; auf einmal **I**

sugar ['ʃʊgə] Zucker **III**

to **suggest** [sə'dʒest] vorschlagen **IV U1**, 15

suggestion [sə'dʒestʃn] Vorschlag; Anregung **I**

suitcase ['suːtkeɪs] Koffer **IV U1**, 9

to **sum up** [ˌsʌmˈʌp] zusammenfassen **II**

summary ['sʌmri] Zusammenfassung **IVTS1**, 37

summer ['sʌmə] Sommer **II**

summer camp ['sʌmə kæmp] Sommerferienlager **II**

sun [sʌn] Sonne **II**

Sunday ['sʌndeɪ] Sonntag **I**

sunflower ['sʌnflaʊə] Sonnenblume **III**

sunset ['sʌnset] Sonnenuntergang **IV U3**, 72

super ['suːpə] super **IV U2**, 44

superlative [suː'pɜːlətɪv] Superlativ **II**

supermarket ['suːpəˌmɑːkɪt] Supermarkt **I**

supernatural ['suːpəˌnætʃrl] übernatürlich **IV U1**, 19

superpower ['suːpəˌpaʊə] Supermacht **II**

supper ['sʌpə] spätes Abendessen ⟨**IV U3**, 86⟩

to **supply** [sə'plaɪ] versorgen **III**

to **support** [sə'pɔːt] unterstützen **IVTS1**, 36

sure [ʃʊə; ʃɔː] sicher **I**

*to make **sure** [meɪk 'ʃɔː] sich versichern **I**

I'm (not) **sure** … [ˌaɪm nɒt 'ʃʊə] Ich bin mir (nicht) sicher … **III**

surface ['sɜːfɪs] Oberfläche **IVTS3**, 101

surfing ['sɜːfɪŋ] Surfen **III**

surgery ['sɜːdʒəri] Arztpraxis; Praxis; Praxisräume **I**

surprise [sə'praɪz] Überraschung **I**

to **surprise** [sə'praɪz] überraschen **II**

*to be **surprised** [bi sə'praɪzd] überrascht sein **II**

surprising [sə'praɪzɪŋ] überraschend **II**

survey ['sɜːveɪ] Umfrage; Studie **I**

to **survive** [sə'vaɪv] überleben **III**

survivor [sə'vaɪvə] Überlebende/-r **IV U2**, 45

*to be **suspended** [bi sə'spendɪd] suspendiert werden; zeitweilig vom Unterricht ausgeschlossen werden **IV AC3**, 68

suspense [sə'spens] Spannung **III**

suspicious [sə'spɪʃəs] misstrauisch; argwöhnisch **IV U1**, 13

to **swap** [swɒp] tauschen °**IVTS2**, 67

to **swap** roles [ˌswɒp 'rəʊlz] Rollen tauschen **I**

sweatshop ['swetʃɒp] Ausbeuterbetrieb **IV U2**, 48

sweet [swiːt] süß **I**

sweet potatoes (pl) ['swiːt pəˌteɪtəʊz] Süßkartoffeln ⟨**IV U2**, 45⟩

sweets (pl) [swiːts] Süßigkeiten; Bonbons **I**

*to **swim** [swɪm] schwimmen **I**

swimming ['swɪmɪŋ] Schwimmen **I**

*to go **swimming** [ˌgəʊ 'swɪmɪŋ] Schwimmen gehen **I**

swimming pool ['swɪmɪŋ ˌpuːl] Swimmingpool; Schwimmbecken **III**

switch [swɪtʃ] Schalter **III**

to **switch** off [ˈswɪtʃ ˈɒf] ausschalten
IV AC3, 69
syllable [ˈsɪləbl] Silbe **III**
symbol [ˈsɪmbl] Symbol **II**
to **symbolize** (AE) [ˈsɪmbəlaɪz] symbolisieren
IV AC2, 40
system [ˈsɪstəm] System ⟨**IV U3**, 90⟩

T

table [ˈteɪbl] Tisch **I**
the Round **Table** [ðə ˌraʊnd ˈteɪbl] die
Tafelrunde **III**
tablet [ˈtæblət] Tablet **II**; Tafel **IV U3**, 74
taco [ˈtækəʊ] Taco (mexikanische gefüllte
Teigtasche) ⟨**IV U3**, 75⟩
taekwondo [ˌtækwʌnˈduː] Taekwondo **II**
question **tag** [ˈkwestʃən ˌtæg] Frageanhängsel; Bestätigungsfrage **II**
tail [teɪl] Schwanz; Schweif **I**
*to **take** [teɪk] nehmen; mitnehmen; wegnehmen; bringen; mitbringen **I**; dauern;
(Zeit) brauchen **II**
*to **take** a breath [ˌteɪk ə ˈbreθ] Luft holen;
Atem holen **III**
*to **take** a look at [ˌteɪk ə ˈlʊk ˌæt] einen
Blick werfen auf **II**
*to **take** a message [ˌteɪk ə ˈmesɪdʒ] eine
Nachricht entgegennehmen; jmdm. etw.
ausrichten **I**
*to **take** a risk [ˌteɪk ə ˈrɪsk] ein Risiko
eingehen **IVTS1**, 32
*to **take** a test [ˌteɪk ə ˈtest] einen Test
machen **II**
*to **take** a vote [ˌteɪk ə ˈvəʊt] abstimmen **I**
*to **take** care of sb [ˌteɪk ˈkeər əv] sich um
jmdn. kümmern; für jmdn. sorgen **III**
*to **take** notes [ˌteɪk ˈnəʊts] sich Notizen
machen **I**
*to **take** off [ˌteɪk ˈɒf] abnehmen; herunternehmen; ausziehen **I**
*to **take** part (in) [ˌteɪk ˈpɑːt (ɪn)] teilnehmen (an) **II**
*to **take** photos [ˌteɪk ˈfəʊtəʊz] fotografieren; Fotos machen **I**
*to **take** place [ˌteɪk ˈpleɪs] stattfinden **I**
*to **take** the day off [ˌteɪk ðə ˌdeɪ ˈɒf] sich
den Tag freinehmen **IV U3**, 72
Take turns. [ˌteɪk ˈtɜːnz] Wechselt euch
ab. **I**
Take a deep breath. [ˌteɪk ə ˌdiːp ˈbreθ]
Atme(t) tief ein. **II**
take-off [ˈteɪk ˌɒf] Start; Abheben **IV U1**, 15
talent [ˈtælənt] Talent **I**
talent show [ˈtælənt ˌʃəʊ] Talentwettbewerb **I**
talk [tɔːk] Vortrag; Rede **IV U2**, 43; Gespräch;
Unterhaltung **IV U3**, 92
*to give a **talk** [ˌgɪv ə ˈtɔːk] einen Vortrag
halten **IV U2**, 43
small **talk** [ˈsmɔːl ˌtɔːk] Smalltalk **III**
to **talk** [tɔːk] sprechen; reden **I**

to **talk** about … [ˈtɔːk əbaʊt] sprechen
über; erzählen von **I**
to **talk** to [ˈtɔːk tə] reden mit **I**
to **talk** with your mouth full [ˌtɔːk wɪð jɔː
ˈmaʊθ ˈfʊl] mit vollem Mund sprechen
IV AC1, 22
talker [ˈtɔːkə] Sprecher/-in **III**
talking [ˈtɔːkɪŋ] Sprechen **I**
tall [tɔːl] groß; hoch **II**
to **tap** [tæp] antippen **II**
target [ˈtɑːgɪt] Ziel; Ziel- **IVTS2**, 65
tartan [ˈtɑːtn] Schottenkaro (bestimmtes
Muster eines Clans); karierter Schottenstoff **III**
task [tɑːsk] Aufgabe; Auftrag **I**
to **taste** [teɪst] schmecken; probieren **III**
tattoo [tætˈuː] Tattoe; Tätowierung **III**
to **tattoo** [tætˈuː] tätowieren ⟨**IV U3**, 90⟩
taxi [ˈtæksi] Taxi **II**
tea [tiː] Tee **I**
tea bag [ˈtiː ˌbæg] Teebeutel **III**
*to **teach** [tiːtʃ] unterrichten; lehren; beibringen **II**
*to **teach** somebody a lesson [ˌtiːtʃ ə ˈlesn]
jmdm. eine Lehre/Lektion erteilen **II**
teacher [ˈtiːtʃə] Lehrer/-in **I**
team [tiːm] Team; Gruppe **II**
tear [tɪə] Träne ⟨**IV U3**, 84⟩
to **tease** sb [tiːz] jmdn. aufziehen; jmdn.
hänseln; jmdn. ärgern **III**
tech [tek] Technologie; Technik **IVTS3**, 102
technique [tekˈniːk] Methode; Technik
°**IV U3**, 91
Technology [tekˈnɒlədʒi] Technik; Computerunterricht **I**
technology [tekˈnɒlədʒi] Technologie **II**
teen [tiːn] Jugend- **II**; Teenager; Jugendli-
che/-r **III**
teenage [ˈtiːneɪdʒ] jugendlich; Jugend-
IVTS1, 31
teenager [ˈtiːnˌeɪdʒə] Teenager; Jugend-
liche/-r **I**
telephone [ˈtelɪfəʊn] Telefon **I**
*to **tell** [tel] erzählen; sagen; mitteilen **I**
Tell me about … [ˈtel miː əˌbaʊt] Erzähle
mir von … **I**
temperature [ˈtemprətʃə] Temperatur
IV AC2, 38
to **tempt** [tempt] in Versuchung führen;
reizen **IVTS1**, 31
temptation [tempˈteɪʃn] Versuchung
IVTS2, 64
tempted [ˈtemptɪd] in Versuchung gebracht
IVTS1, 31
tempting [ˈtemptɪŋ] verführerisch **IVTS1**, 33
ten [ten] zehn **I**
ten times [ten ˈtaɪmz] zehnmal **I**
Four and six is **ten**. [ˌfɔːr ənd ˌsɪks ɪz ˈten]
Vier plus sechs ist zehn. **I**
tennis [ˈtenɪs] Tennis **I**
tense [tens] Zeit; Zeitform (grammatisch) **II**
term [tɜːm] Begriff **IVTS1**, 30

terrible [ˈterəbl] schrecklich; schlimm;
furchtbar ⟨**IVTS1**, 34⟩; ⟨**IVTS3**, 104⟩
test [test] Test; Klassenarbeit; Prüfung **I**
*to take a **test** [ˌteɪk ə ˈtest] einen Test
machen **II**
to **test** [test] testen; prüfen **III**
text [tekst] Text **I**
factual **text** [ˌfæktʃəl ˈtekst] Sachtext **III**
text (message) [ˈtekst ˌmesɪdʒ] SMS;
Kurznachricht **I**
wiki (**text**) [ˈwɪki ˌtekst] Wikitext **IVTS3**, 101
to **text** [tekst] eine SMS schicken **II**
than [ðæn] als (bei Vergleichen) **II**
more … **than** [ˈmɔː ðən] mehr … als **I**
*to give **thanks** [ˌgɪv ˈθæŋks] danken
IV U2, 45
to **thank** [θæŋk] danken **II**
Thank you. [ˈθæŋk juː] Danke. **I**
thankful [ˈθæŋkfl] dankbar **I**
Thanks. [θæŋks] Danke. **I**
that [ðæt] so (Betonung) **III**
that much [ðæt ˈmʌtʃ] so viel **III**
that [ðæt; ðət] dass **II**
so (**that**) [ˌsəʊ ˈðæt] damit; so dass
IV AC3, 69
that [ðæt] das; jenes **I**
after **that** [ˌɑːftə ˈðæt] danach **I**
like **that** [laɪk ˈðæt] so **I**
That was close! [ˌðæt wəz ˈkləʊs] Das war
knapp! **I**
that's how [ˌðæts ˈhaʊ] so **II**
That's what friends are for. [ˌðæts wɒt
ˈfrendz ˌɑː ˌfɔː] Dafür sind Freunde da. **I**
that's why [ˌðæts ˈwaɪ] deshalb **II**
That's … [ˌðæts] Das macht … **I**
that [ðæt] der; dem; den; die; das (Relativpronomen) **II**
the [ðə; ði] der; die (auch Pl.); das **I**
the others [ðiˈʌðəz] die anderen **I**
the same [ðə ˈseɪm] der-/die-/dasselbe;
der/die/das gleiche **I**
the … **the** [ðə … ðə] je … desto **II**
theater (AE) [ˈθɪətə] Theater **IV U3**, 70
movie **theater** (AE) [ˈmuːvi ˌθɪətə] Kino
IV U2, 44
theatre [ˈθɪətə] Theater **I**
their [ðeə] ihr/-e (Pl.) **I**
their fault [ˌðeə ˈfɔːlt] ihre Schuld
⟨**IVTS1**, 36⟩
them [ðem] sie (Pl.); ihnen **I**
theme [θiːm] Thema; Motto **I**
theme song [ˈθiːm sɒŋ] Titelmelodie
°**IV U3**, 91
then [ðen] dann; danach **I**
back **then** [ˌbæk ˈðen] damals **III**
theorist [ˈθɪərɪst] Theoretiker/-in ⟨**IVTS3**, 102⟩
theory [ˈθɪəri] Theorie **IVTS3**, 102
there [ðeə] da; dort; dahin; dorthin **I**
there is/are [ðərˈɪz/ˈɑː] da ist/sind; es
gibt **I**
There's no need to … [ˌðeəz nəʊ ˈniːd tə]
Es gibt keinen Grund zu … **IVTS1**, 36

these [ðiːz] diese (hier) I
  these days [ˌðiːz ˈdeɪz] zurzeit III
they [ðeɪ] sie (Pl.) I
  It's …/They're … [ɪts/ðeə] Es kostet …/
  Sie kosten … I
thick [θɪk] dick (nicht für Personen) III
thief [θiːf], thieves [θiːvz] (pl) Dieb/-in
  ⟨IV U3, 82⟩
thing [θɪŋ] Ding; Sache I
*to think [θɪŋk] denken; nachdenken;
  glauben I
  Stop and think [ˌstɒp ənd ˈθɪŋk] Warte/
  Wartet und denk/denkt nach. I
  *to think of [ˈθɪŋk əv] halten von; denken
  über I
  *to think of [ˈθɪŋk əv] (sich) ausdenken;
  sich etwas einfallen lassen II
  Think of … [ˈθɪŋk əv] Denke/Denkt
  an … I
  *to think up [θɪŋk ˈʌp] (sich) ausdenken;
  sich einfallen lassen °IVTS2, 66
excellent piece of quick thinking [ˌekslnt
  piːs əv kwɪk ˈθɪŋkɪŋ] ausgezeichnete
  Reaktionsschnelligkeit ⟨IVTS1, 36⟩
third [θɜːd] dritte/-r/-s I
  third person narrator [θɜːd ˌpɜːsn
  nəˈreɪtə] Er/Sie-Erzähler/-in III
thirsty [ˈθɜːsti] durstig III
thirteen [ˌθɜːˈtiːn] dreizehn I
this [ðɪs] dies; diese/-r/-s I
  this afternoon [ðɪs ˈɑːftənuːn] heute
  Nachmittag II
  this early [ˈðɪs ˌɜːli] so früh III
  This is … [ˈðɪs ɪz] Das (hier) ist … I
thistle [ˈθɪsl] Distel III
those [ðəʊz] diese dort; jene I
  those in power [ˈðəʊz ɪn ˈpaʊə] die Regierenden; die Herrschenden III
though [ðəʊ] doch; jedoch; obwohl
  IV AC4, 106
thought [θɔːt] Gedanke II
thousands of [ˈθaʊzndz əv] tausende
  (von) I
three [θriː] drei I
through [θruː] durch I
*to throw (at) [θrəʊ] werfen (nach) I
  *to throw away [θrəʊ əˈweɪ] wegwerfen I
  throw the dice twice [θrəʊ ðə daɪs ˈtwaɪs]
  würfle zweimal II
thumb [θʌm] Daumen II
thunder (no pl) [ˈθʌndə] Donner II
Thursday [ˈθɜːzdeɪ] Donnerstag I
to tick [tɪk] abhaken II
ticket [ˈtɪkɪt] Los; Ticket; Eintrittskarte
  I; Fahrschein III
  one-way ticket [ˈwʌnweɪ ˌtɪkɪt] einfache
  Fahrkarte III
  return ticket [rɪˈtɜːn ˌtɪkɪt] Hin- und Rückfahrkarte III
  single ticket [ˈsɪŋgl ˌtɪkɪt] einfache Fahrkarte III
  ticket office [ˈtɪkɪt ˌɒfɪs] Kartenschalter III

high tide [ˈhaɪ ˌtaɪd] Flut II
low tide [ˈləʊ ˌtaɪd] Ebbe II
to tidy (a room) [ˈtaɪdi] aufräumen; in Ordnung bringen I
to tie (to) [ˈtaɪ tə] binden (an); fesseln (an)
  III
tight [taɪt] eng ⟨IV U3, 90⟩
till [tɪl] bis I
time [taɪm] Zeit I; Mal II
  all the time [ˌɔːl ðə ˈtaɪm] die ganze Zeit II
  at the same time [ət ðə ˌseɪm ˈtaɪm] zur
  selben Zeit; gleichzeitig I
  at the time [ət ðə ˈtaɪm] damals
  IVTS3, 102
  free time [ˌfriː ˈtaɪm] Freizeit I
  on time [ɒn ˈtaɪm] pünktlich II
  ten times [ten ˈtaɪmz] zehnmal I
  time line [ˈtaɪm ˌlaɪn] Zeitstrahl I
  time slot [ˈtaɪm slɒt] Zeitfenster II
  Have a good time. [ˌhæv ə gʊd ˈtaɪm] Viel
  Spaß. ⟨IVTS1, 36⟩
  I can't wait till next time. [aɪ kɑːnt ˌweɪt
  tɪl nekst ˈtaɪm] Ich kann es bis zum
  nächsten Mal kaum erwarten. II
  just in time [dʒʌst ɪn ˈtaɪm] gerade rechtzeitig IV U3, 72
  Time to get up! [ˌtaɪm tə ˌgetˈʌp] Es ist
  Zeit aufzustehen! I
  What time? [ˌwɒt ˈtaɪm] Um wie viel Uhr? I
  What's the time? [ˌwɒts ðə ˈtaɪm] Wie spät
  ist es?; Wie viel Uhr ist es? I
to time [taɪm] den richtigen Zeitpunkt
  wählen IV U3, 72
timetable [ˈtaɪmˌteɪbl] Stundenplan; Fahrplan I
tin [tɪn] Zinn III
  tin can [ˈtɪn kæn] Blechdose III
tinned [tɪnd] Dosen-; aus der Dose I
tiny [ˈtaɪni] klein; winzig III
tip [tɪp] Tipp; Ratschlag I; Trinkgeld IV U3, 76
to tiptoe [ˈtɪptəʊ] auf Zehenspitzen gehen II
tired [taɪəd] müde I
  *to be tired of [bi ˈtaɪəd əv] es müde sein
  (zu); es leid sein (zu); es satt haben (zu)
  IV U2, 46
title [ˈtaɪtl] Titel; Überschrift II
to [tʊ; tə] zu; nach; auf; in; vor (bei Uhrzeitangaben) I
  from … to [frəm … tə] von … bis I
  quarter past/to [ˈkwɔːtə pɑːst/tə] Viertel
  nach/vor I
  to the point [tə ðə ˈpɔɪnt] prägnant;
  treffend III
toast [təʊst] Toast I
tobacco (no pl) [təˈbækəʊ] Tabak III
today [təˈdeɪ] heute I
together [təˈgeðə] zusammen; miteinander;
  gemeinsam I
toilet [ˈtɔɪlət] Toilette I
tolerant [ˈtɒlrnt] tolerant IVTS1, 36
tomato, tomatoes (pl) [təˈmɑːtəʊ;
  təˈmɑːtəʊz] Tomate I

tomorrow [təˈmɒrəʊ] morgen I
tone [təʊn] Ton; Signalton °IV U2, 56
tonight [təˈnaɪt] heute Abend; heute Nacht
  IVTS1, 31
too [tuː] auch; zu I
  Too bad! [ˌtuː ˈbæd] Zu dumm!; Schade! I
  You too? [ju ˈtuː] Du auch? I
tool [tuːl] Werkzeug; Gerät III
toothpaste [ˈtuːθpeɪst] Zahnpasta IV U2, 56
top [tɒp] Spitze; oberer Teil; oberes Ende I
  on top [ɒn ˈtɒp] oben; obendrauf I
to top up [tɒpˈʌp] aufladen I
topic [ˈtɒpɪk] Thema II
torch [tɔːtʃ] Fackel; Taschenlampe II
totally [ˈtəʊtli] völlig; total IV AC4, 107
*to keep in touch [ˌkiːpˌɪn ˈtʌtʃ] in Kontakt
  bleiben IV U2, 44
to stay in touch (with) [ˌsteɪ ɪn ˈtʌtʃ (wɪð)] in
  Kontakt bleiben (mit) II
to touch [tʌtʃ] berühren; antippen IV U2, 52
  to touch down [tʌtʃ ˈdaʊn] landen
  IVTS3, 101
tour [tʊə] Tour; Fahrt; Rundgang II
  audio tour [ˈɔːdiəʊ ˌtʊə] Audioführung II
  tour company [ˈtʊə ˌkʌmpəni] Reiseanbieter IV U3, 73
tourism [ˈtʊərɪzm] Tourismus III
tourist [ˈtʊərɪst] Tourist/-in I
  tourist board [ˈtʊərɪst bɔːd] Touristeninformation III
  tourist information centre [ˌtʊərɪst
  ɪnfəˈmeɪʃn ˌsentə] Touristeninformation I
towards [təˈwɔːdz] in Richtung; auf … zu;
  darauf zu II
tower [ˈtaʊə] Turm III
town [taʊn] Stadt I
toy [tɔɪ] Spielzeug I
to trace [treɪs] verfolgen; nachspüren I
tractor [ˈtræktə] Traktor IV AC2, 38
to trade [treɪd] austauschen II
tradition [trəˈdɪʃn] Tradition I
traditional [trəˈdɪʃnl] traditionell III
traffic [ˈtræfɪk] Verkehr IV U1, 14
walking trail [ˈwɔːkɪŋ treɪl] Wanderweg III
train [treɪn] Zug I
to train [treɪn] trainieren II
trainer [ˈtreɪnə] Turnschuh III
training [ˈtreɪnɪŋ] Training II
to translate [trænzˈleɪt] übersetzen I
translation [trænzˈleɪʃn] Übersetzung I
transport [ˈtrænspɔːt] Verkehrsmittel;
  Transport III
  public transport (no pl) [ˌpʌblɪk
  ˈtrænspɔːt] öffentliche Verkehrsmittel II
to transport [trænˈspɔːt] transportieren;
  befördern IV U3, 79
*to be trapped [bi ˈtræpt] eingeschlossen
  sein; in der Falle sitzen III
trash (AE) [træʃ] Abfall; Müll IVTS2, 67
travel [ˈtrævl] (das) Reisen; Reise II
  travel agency [ˈtrævlˌeɪdʒnsi] Reisebüro
  III

travel agent's ['trævl ̩eɪdʒnts] Reisebüro **III**

travel report [ˌtrævl rɪ'pɔːt] Reisebericht **II**

to **travel** ['trævl] fahren; reisen **II**

traveller ['trævlə] Reisende/-r **IV U1**, 15

travelling (no pl) ['trævlɪŋ] (das) Reisen **IV U1**, 9

treasure ['treʒə] Schatz **II**

treat [triːt] hier: Leckerli; Belohnung **III**

tree [triː] Baum **I**

family **tree** ['fæmli ˌtriː] Stammbaum **I**

palm **tree** ['pɑːm ˌtriː] Palme **III**

redwood **tree** ['redwʊd ˌtriː] Mammutbaum **IV AC2**, 39

pony **trekking** ['pəʊni ˌtrekɪŋ] Ponyreiten im Gelände **III**

trial [traɪəl] Qualifikation **II**

tribe [traɪb] Stamm; Volksstamm **III**

trick [trɪk] Trick; Streich **I**

to play a **trick** (on) [ˌpleɪ ə 'trɪk ˌɒn] einen Streich spielen **I**

to **trick** [trɪk] austricksen; täuschen **IV TS3**, 103

trifle ['traɪfl] Trifle (englischer Nachtisch) **I**

trip [trɪp] Trip; Reise; Ausflug; Fahrt **II**

triumph ['traɪəmf] Triumph 〈**IV TS3**, 101〉

trouble ['trʌbl] Ärger; Probleme; Schwierigkeiten **II**

*to get into **trouble** [ˌget ɪntə 'trʌbl] in Schwierigkeiten geraten **IV AC3**, 69

*to make **trouble** [ˌmeɪk 'trʌbl] Ärger machen; in Schwierigkeiten bringen **I**

troublemaker ['trʌblmeɪkə] Unruhestifter/-in **IV U2**, 53

trousers (pl) ['traʊzəz] Hose **III**

trowel ['traʊəl] kleiner Spaten **II**

truck (AE) [trʌk] hier: Wagen **IV U3**, 75

truckload ['trʌkləʊd] Lastwagenladung **IV TS2**, 66

true [truː] wahr **II**

*to come **true** [ˌkʌm 'truː] wahr werden; in Erfüllung gehen **IV U3**, 76

trunk (AE) [trʌŋk] Kofferraum **IV U3**, 76

to **trust** [trʌst] vertrauen **III**

truth [truːθ] Wahrheit **IV U1**, 13

to **try** [traɪ] versuchen; probieren **I**

to **try** on [ˌtraɪ 'ɒn] anprobieren **II**

to **try** out [ˌtraɪ 'aʊt] ausprobieren **III**

Try … [traɪ] Versuch es mal mit …; Probier mal … **I**

T-shirt ['tiːʃɜːt] T-Shirt **I**

the **Tube** [ðə 'tjuːb] die Londoner U-Bahn **II**

Tudor ['tjuːdə] Tudor- **III**

Tuesday ['tjuːzdeɪ] Dienstag **I**

tune [tjuːn] Melodie **III**

tunnel ['tʌnl] Tunnel **I**

roast **turkey** [ˌrəʊst 'tɜːki] Putenbraten 〈**IV U2**, 45〉

It's your **turn**. [ˌɪts 'jɔː tɜːn] Du bist dran. **I**

Take **turns**. [ˌteɪk 'tɜːnz] Wechselt euch ab. **I**

Your **turn**. ['jɔː tɜːn] Du bist dran. **I**

to **turn** [tɜːn] einbiegen; abbiegen **I**

to **turn** (a)round [tɜːn ̩(ə)'raʊnd] (sich) umdrehen; wenden **II**

to **turn** back [tɜːn 'bæk] umkehren; zurückgehen **II**

to **turn** into [ˌtɜːn 'ɪntə] ändern in; umwandeln in **IV U1**, 14

to **turn** off [ˌtɜːn 'ɒf] abschalten; ausschalten **II**

to **turn** to ['tɜːn tə] sich wenden an; sich zuwenden **III**

turning point ['tɜːnɪŋ ˌpɔɪnt] Wendepunkt **III**

It **turned** out that … [ɪt ˌtɜːnd ̩'aʊt ðæt] Es stellte sich heraus, dass … **IV U1**, 20

to **turn** [tɜːn] drehen; (sich) umdrehen **III**

tusk [tʌsk] Stoßzahn **III**

tutor ['tjuːtə] Klassenlehrer/-in **I**

tutor group ['tjuːtə ˌgruːp] Klasse (in einer englischen Schule) **I**

tutorial [tjuː'tɔːriəl] Tutorium; Tutorial **IV TS3**, 100

TV [tiː'viː] Fernsehen; Fernseher **I**

to watch **TV** [ˌwɒtʃ tiː'viː] fernsehen **I**

twelve [twelv] zwölf **I**

twice [twaɪs] zweimal **IV U2**, 53

twin [twɪn] Zwilling; Zwillings- **III**

to **twist** your ankle [ˌtwɪst jɔːr 'æŋkl] sich den Knöchel verrenken **II**

two [tuː] zwei **I**

the **two** of them [ðə 'tuː ̩əv ðəm] beide **II**

two of which ['tuː ̩əv wɪtʃ] zwei von ihnen **III**

type [taɪp] Typ; Art; Sorte **III**

typical ['tɪpɪkl] typisch **I**

typically ['tɪpɪkli] typisch **III**

U

u (= you) [juː; jə] du; Sie; ihr **I**

UFO [ˌjuːef'əʊ] UFO **II**

ugly ['ʌgli] hässlich **IV TS2**, 67

umbrella [ʌm'brelə] Regenschirm 〈**IV U3**, 90〉

unable [ʌn'eɪbl] unfähig; nicht in der Lage 〈**IV TS3**, 104〉

unbelievable [ˌʌnbɪ'liːvəbl] unglaublich; unglaubwürdig 〈**IV TS3**, 102〉

uncle ['ʌŋkl] Onkel **I**

under ['ʌndə] unter **I**

underfloor heating (no pl) [ˌʌndəflɔː 'hiːtɪŋ] Fußbodenheizung **III**

underground ['ʌndəgraʊnd] U-Bahn **II**

to **underline** [ˌʌndə'laɪn] unterstreichen **III**

*to **understand** [ˌʌndə'stænd] verstehen **I**

understanding [ˌʌndə'stændɪŋ] Verständnis **II**

undeveloped [ˌʌndɪ'veləpt] unentwickelt; unausgereift **IV TS3**, 105

unexpected [ˌʌnɪk'spektɪd] unerwartet **IV U3**, 91

unfair [ʌn'feə] unfair **II**

unfamiliar [ˌʌnfə'mɪliə] nicht vertraut; unbekannt **III**

unfriendly [ʌn'frendli] unfreundlich **II**

uniform ['juːnɪfɔːm] Uniform **I**

unit ['juːnɪt] Lektion; Kapitel; Einheit **I**

*to be **unlucky** [biː ʌn'lʌki] Pech haben **I**

unofficial [ˌʌnə'fɪʃl] inoffiziell **III**

to **unpack** [ʌn'pæk] auspacken **IV U2**, 46

unreal [ˌʌn'rɪəl] irreal **IV U1**, 19

unrealistic [ˌʌnrɪə'lɪstɪk] unrealistisch **IV U2**, 52

unsure [ʌn'ʃʊə] unsicher **IV TS1**, 31

until [ʌn'tɪl] bis; erst wenn **II**

not **until** [ˌnɒt ən'tɪl] nicht vor; erst um/im **IV U2**, 44

to **unwrap** [ʌn'ræp] auswickeln; auspacken **I**

up [ʌp] hinauf; nach oben **II**

*to cut **up** [ˌkʌt 'ʌp] zerschneiden °**IV U3**, 91

to end **up** [ˌend 'ʌp] enden; landen **II**

*to get **up** [ˌget 'ʌp] aufstehen (aus dem Bett) **I**

*to give **up** [ˌgɪv 'ʌp] aufgeben **III**

to look **up** [ˌlʊk 'ʌp] nachschlagen; nachschauen **I**

What's **up**? [ˌwɒts 'ʌp] Was ist los? **III**

*to **upset** [ʌp'set] aus der Fassung bringen **III**

upset [ʌp'set] aufgebracht; bestürzt **II**

upstairs [ʌp'steəz] nach oben; im Obergeschoss; oben **II**

up-to-date [ˌʌptə'deɪt] modern; zeitgemäß; aktuell **IV TS3**, 100

urban ['ɜːbn] städtisch; Stadt- **IV AC2**, 38

us [ʌs] uns **I**

US [juː'es] US-amerikanisch **IV AC2**, 41

use [juːs] Verwendung; Gebrauch; Nutzen °**IV U3**, 77

*to make **use** of [meɪk 'juːz ̩əv] benutzen; verwenden **IV U3**, 89

to **use** [juːz] benutzen; verwenden; gebrauchen **I**

*to be **used** to (+ -ing) [biː 'juːs tə] gewöhnt sein an; gewohnt sein **III**

*to get **used** to sth [ˌget 'juːzd tə] sich an etw. gewöhnen **IV U2**, 44

useful ['juːsfl] nützlich; hilfreich **I**

Useful phrases [ˌjuːsfl 'freɪsɪz] nützliche Ausdrücke **I**

useless ['juːsləs] nutzlos **IV U1**, 17

usual ['juːʒl] üblich **III**

usually ['juːʒli] normalerweise; gewöhnlich; meistens **I**

V

vacation (AE) [və'keɪʃn] Ferien; Urlaub **IV AC2**, 41

van [væn] Lieferwagen; Transporter; Kleinbus 〈**IV U3**, 88〉

vegetable ['vedʒtəbl] Gemüse **III**

vegetarian [ˌvedʒɪ'teəriən] Vegetarier/-in **III**

vegetarian [ˌvedʒɪ'teəriən] vegetarisch **III**

vending machine ['vendɪŋ məˌʃiːn] Automat **IV U1**, 10

verb [vɜːb] Verb I
verse [vɜːs] Vers; Strophe III
version ['vɜːʃn] Version III
cover version ['kʌvə ˌvɜːʃn] Coverversion III
versus (vs.) ['vɜːsəs] gegen III
very ['veri] sehr I
very much [ˌveri 'mʌtʃ] sehr I
vet [vet] Tierarzt/Tierärztin I
Victorian [vɪk'tɔːriən] viktorianisch; Viktorianer/-in III
video ['vɪdiəʊ] Video II
video chat ['vɪdiəʊ ˌtʃæt] Videochat II
view [vjuː] Aussicht; Sicht; Ausblick; Blick II
point of view [ˌpɔɪnt əv 'vjuː] Standpunkt; Ansicht; Perspektive II
viewer ['vjuːə] Zuschauer/-in II
viewing ['vjuːɪŋ] Hör-/Sehverstehen I
village ['vɪlɪdʒ] Dorf I
villain ['vɪlən] Bösewicht III
violence (no pl) ['vaɪələns] Gewalt III
violent ['vaɪələnt] gewaltsam; gewalttätig; brutal III
visa ['viːzə], visas ['viːzəz] (pl) Visum, Visa (Pl.); Einreisebewilligung IV U1, 9
visit ['vɪzɪt] Besuch I
to visit ['vɪzɪt] besichtigen; besuchen I
visitor ['vɪzɪtə] Besucher/-in I
visual ['vɪʒuəl] Bild IV TS2, 65
vitamin ['vɪtəmɪn] Vitamin III
vocabulary [və'kæbjələri] Vokabular; Wortschatz I
voice [vɔɪs] Stimme I
volleyball ['vɒlibɔːl] Volleyball I
*to take a vote [ˌteɪk ə 'vəʊt] abstimmen I
to vote [vəʊt] abstimmen; wählen I
voyage ['vɔɪɪdʒ] Reise; Fahrt ⟨IV TS3, 104⟩

W

to wait (for) [weɪt] warten (auf) I
I can't wait till next time. [aɪ kɑːnt ˌweɪt tɪl nekst 'taɪm] Ich kann es bis zum nächsten Mal kaum erwarten. II
Wait and see! [ˌweɪt ənd 'siː] Warte ab! I
*to wake up [weɪk 'ʌp] aufwachen; aufwecken III
gallery walk ['gæləri ˌwɔːk] Museumsrundgang; Vernissage I
*to go for a walk [ˌgəʊ fər ə 'wɔːk] spazieren gehen II
night walk ['naɪt wɔːk] Nachtwanderung II
to walk [wɔːk] gehen; laufen I
to walk the dog [wɔːk ðə 'dɒg] den Hund ausführen; mit dem Hund spazieren gehen I
walk-in closet [ˌwɔːkɪn 'klɒzɪt] begehbarer Kleiderschrank IV U2, 44
walking ['wɔːkɪŋ] Wandern II
walking trail ['wɔːkɪŋ treɪl] Wanderweg III
wall [wɔːl] Wand; Mauer I; Online-Pinnwand III

*to be walled in [ˌbi wɔːld 'ɪn] von Wänden eingeschlossen sein ⟨IV U3, 90⟩
wanna (= want to) (infml) ['wɒnə] will/wollen ⟨IV U1, 12⟩
to want (to) ['wɒnt tə] wollen; mögen I
war [wɔː] Krieg IV U1, 20
wardrobe ['wɔːdrəʊb] Kleiderschrank I
to warm up [ˌwɔːm 'ʌp] aufwärmen; sich aufwärmen I
warm [wɔːm] warm III
warm-up ['wɔːmˌʌp] Aufwärmübung I
to warn [wɔːn] warnen IV TS1, 34
warrior ['wɒriə] Krieger III
to wash [wɒʃ] waschen; sich waschen I
to wash up [ˌwɒʃ'ʌp] angespült werden II
washing machine [ˌwɒʃɪŋ məˌʃiːn] Waschmaschine II
waste [weɪst] Verschwendung IV AC3, 69
to waste [weɪst] verschwenden II
wasteful ['weɪstfl] verschwenderisch IV AC2, 40
to watch [wɒtʃ] beobachten; (sich) ansehen; zuschauen I
to watch TV [ˌwɒtʃ tiːˈviː] fernsehen I
water ['wɔːtə] Wasser I
water fountain ['wɔːtə ˌfaʊntɪn] Wasserspender IV AC4, 106
water slide ['wɔːtə ˌslaɪd] Wasserrutsche I
wave [weɪv] Welle I
wax [wæks] Wachs II
wax figure ['wæks ˌfɪgə] Wachsfigur II
way [weɪ] Weg; Art und Weise I
*to be in the way [bi ˌɪn ðə 'weɪ] im Weg sein/stehen I
*to find one's way around [ˌfaɪnd wʌnz ˌweɪ əˈraʊnd] sich zurechtfinden IV U2, 46
*to get in the way [get ˌɪn ðə 'weɪ] stören; im Weg stehen II
no way [ˌnəʊ 'weɪ] auf keinen Fall; keineswegs ⟨IV U2, 54⟩; keine Möglichkeit; kein Weg ⟨IV TS3, 102⟩
in other ways [ɪn ˌʌðə weɪz] auf andere Weise II
the same way as [ðə seɪm 'weɪ æz] genauso wie II
we [wiː; wi] wir I
We're from … ['wɪə frəm] Wir sind aus … I
weak [wiːk] schwach IV TS3, 105
wealthy ['welθi] wohlhabend; reich IV AC2, 40
weapon ['wepən] Waffe III
*to wear [weə] anhaben; tragen (Kleidung) I
weather ['weðə] Wetter I
weather forecast ['weðə ˌfɔːkɑːst] Wettervorhersage III
web [web] Netz; Spinnennetz III
web designer ['web dɪˌzaɪnə] Webdesigner III
website ['websaɪt] Website; Internetauftritt I
wedding ['wedɪŋ] Hochzeit I

Wednesday ['wenzdeɪ] Mittwoch I
week [wiːk] Woche I
weekday ['wiːkdeɪ] Wochentag II
weekend [ˌwiːk'end] Wochenende I
at the weekend [ət ðə ˌwiːk'end] am Wochenende I
to weigh [weɪ] wiegen III
weight [weɪt] Gewicht III
weird [wɪəd] merkwürdig; seltsam; sonderbar II
Welcome! ['welkəm] Willkommen! II
to welcome ['welkəm] willkommen heißen II
You're welcome. [jɔː 'welkəm] Bitte schön.; Nichts zu danken.; Gern geschehen. I
*to do well [ˌdu: 'wel] gute Leistungen erbringen IV TS1, 34
well-developed [ˌweldɪ'veləpt] gut entwickelt; ausgereift IV TS3, 105
well-written [ˌwel'rɪtn] gut geschrieben IV TS3, 104
well [wel] tja; nun I
Welsh [welʃ] walisisch; Walisisch; Waliser/-in II
west [west] Westen; West- I
in the far west [ɪn ðə fɑː 'west] im äußersten Westen III
wet [wet] nass II
what [wɒt] was; welche/-r/-s; was für ein I
What a … ['wɒt ə] Was für ein/-e … IV U2, 48
What about … ? ['wɒt əbaʊt] Wie wär's mit … ?; Was ist mit … ? I
What are …? ['wɒt ɑː] Welche … sind es? I
What colour is …? [ˌwɒt 'kʌlər ɪz] Welche Farbe hat …? I
what else [wɒt 'els] was sonst; was noch I
What is missing? [ˌwɒt ɪz 'mɪsɪŋ] Was fehlt? I
What is … about? [wɒt ɪz … əˈbaʊt] Worum geht es in/im …? I
what it's like [ˌwɒt ɪts 'laɪk] wie das ist II
What luck! [wɒt 'lʌk] Was für ein Glück! III
What on earth …? [ˌwɒt: ɒn ˌ'ɜːθ] Was um alles in der Welt …? II
What time? [wɒt 'taɪm] Um wie viel Uhr? I
what to … ['wɒt tə] was man … I
What was it like? [ˌwɒt wɒz ɪt 'laɪk] Wie war es? III
What's that? [wɒts 'ðæt] Was ist das? I
What's the rule for …? [ˌwɒts ðə 'ruːl fə] Was ist die Regel für …? I
What's up? [ˌwɒts'ʌp] Was ist los? III
What's your favourite …? [ˌwɒts jə ˌfeɪvrɪt] Was ist dein/-e Lieblings…? I
What's your name? [ˌwɒts jə 'neɪm] Wie heißt du?; Wie heißen Sie? I
What's going on? [wɒts ˌgəʊɪŋ 'ɒn] Was ist los?; Was geht ab? III
What's the matter? [ˌwɒts ðə 'mætə] Was ist los?; Was hast du? III

What's the time? [ˌwɒts ðə 'taɪm] Wie spät ist es?; Wie viel Uhr ist es? **I**

… **what** to do. ['wɒt tə du:] … was ich tun soll. **II**

what the man looked like [ˌwɒt ðə mæn 'lʊkt laɪk] wie der Mann aussah **II**

whatever [wɒt'evə] wie auch immer; egal (was/welche) **IV AC4**, 107

wheat [wi:t] Weizen **IV AC2**, 41

wheel [wi:l] Rad; Steuerrad; Steuer **I**

wheelchair ['wi:ltʃeə] Rollstuhl **II**

when [wen] wenn; wann; als **I**

whenever [wen'evə] wann immer; jedes Mal, wenn; so oft **II**

where [weə] wo; wohin **I**

Where … from? [ˌweə … 'frɒm] Woher …? **I**

where I belong [ˌweər aɪ bɪ'lɒŋ] wo ich hingehöre **IV U1**, 16

… **where** to go. [ˌweə tə 'gəʊ] … wohin ich gehen kann. **II**

I go **wherever** the wind takes me. [aɪ ˌgəʊ weəˌrevə ðə wɪnd 'teɪks mi:] Ich lasse mich treiben. **IV U1**, 19

whether ['weðə] ob **IV U2**, 49

which [wɪtʃ] welche/-r/-s **I**

which [wɪtʃ] der; die; das; dem; den (Relativpronomen) **II**

a while [ə 'waɪl] eine Weile **II**

while [waɪl] während **I**

to whip [wɪp] schlagen **I**

whisky ['wɪski] Whisky **III**

to whisper ['wɪspə] flüstern **I**

white [waɪt] weiß **I**

white lie [ˌwaɪt 'laɪ] Notlüge **IV TS1**, 32

who [hu:] wer; wem; wen **I**

Who … for? [ˌhu: 'fɔ:] Für wen …? **I**

Who is it? [ˌhu: ˌɪz ɪt] Wer ist es? **I**

Who's in? [hu:z ˌɪn] Wer macht mit?; Wer ist dabei? **II**

who [hu:] der; dem; den; die (Relativpronomen) **II**

whole [həʊl] ganz **I**

whom [hu:m] wem; wen **IV TS1**, 37

whoosh [wʊʃ] wusch **I**

whose [hu:z] wessen °**IV U2**, 44

whose [hu:z] dessen; deren (Relativpronomen) **II**

why [waɪ] warum **I**

that's **why** [ðæts 'waɪ] deshalb **II**

wide [waɪd] breit; weit; ausgedehnt **III**

wife, wives (pl) [waɪf, waɪvz] Ehefrau **II**

wifi ['waɪfaɪ] WLAN **IV U1**, 10

wiki (text) ['wɪki ˌtekst] Wikitext **IV TS3**, 101

wild [waɪld] wild **III**

It's, like, so **wild** to … [ˌɪts laɪk səʊ 'waɪld tə] Es ist echt klasse … ⟨**IV AC4**, 107⟩

wildlife ['waɪldlaɪf] Tierwelt (in freier Wildbahn) **II**

will [wɪl] werden (futurisch) **III**

*to win [wɪn] gewinnen; siegen **I**

*to **win** sb over [wɪn ˌəʊvə] jmdn. für sich gewinnen; jmdn. überzeugen **IV TS2**, 64

wind [wɪnd] Wind **III**

I go wherever the **wind** takes me. [aɪ ˌgəʊ weəˌrevə ðə wɪnd 'teɪks mi:] Ich lasse mich treiben. **IV U1**, 19

window ['wɪndəʊ] Fenster **I**

windsurfing ['wɪndsɜ:fɪŋ] Windsurfen **III**

wine [waɪn] Wein **I**

winner ['wɪnə] Gewinner/-in; Sieger/-in **I**

winter ['wɪntə] Winter **III**

barbed wire [ˌbɑːbd 'waɪə] Stacheldraht ⟨**IV U3**, 90⟩

wish [wɪʃ] Wunsch **I**

*to make a **wish** [ˌmeɪk ə 'wɪʃ] sich etwas wünschen **I**

Best **wishes** [ˌbest 'wɪʃɪz] Viele Grüße; Herzliche Grüße **III**

to wish [wɪʃ] (sich) wünschen **IV U2**, 51

with [wɪð] mit; bei **I**

within [wɪ'ðɪn] innerhalb °**IV AC4**, 106

without [wɪ'ðaʊt] ohne **I**

witness ['wɪtnəs] Zeuge/Zeugin **II**

wizard ['wɪzəd] Zauberer **III**

wobbly ['wɒbli] wackelig **II**

woman, women (pl) ['wʊmən; 'wɪmɪn] Frau **I**

no wonder [ˌnəʊ 'wʌndə] kein Wunder **IV U2**, 44

wonderful ['wʌndəfl] wunderbar **II**

wood [wʊd] Wald; Wäldchen **III**

wood [wʊd] Holz **III**

wooden ['wʊdn] hölzern; aus Holz **III**

Woof! [wʊf] Wau! **I**

word [wɜ:d] Wort **I**

compound **word** ['kɒmpaʊnd wɜ:d] Kompositum (zusammengesetztes Wort) **II**

key **word** ['ki: wɜ:d] Stichwort; Schlüsselbegriff **I**

linking **word** ['lɪŋkɪŋ ˌwɜ:d] Bindewort **I**

play on **words** [ˌpleɪ ɒn 'wɜ:dz] Wortspiel **III**

signal **word** ['sɪgnəl ˌwɜ:d] Signalwort **I**

word bank ['wɜ:d ˌbæŋk] Wortsammlung **III**

word cloud ['wɜ:d ˌklaʊd] Wörterwolke **II**

word order ['wɜ:dˌɔ:də] Wortstellung; Satzstellung **I**

Word power ['wɜ:d ˌpaʊə] die Kraft der Wörter (Wortschatzübung) **I**

word snake ['wɜ:d ˌsneɪk] Wortschlange **I**

word-building ['wɜ:dˌbɪldɪŋ] Wortbildung **II**

work [wɜ:k] Arbeit **I**

pair **work** ['peə wɜ:k] Partnerarbeit **I**

to work [wɜ:k] arbeiten **I**; funktionieren **II**

to **work** out [wɜ:kˌaʊt] herausfinden; ausarbeiten **II**; funktionieren; klappen **III**

workbook ['wɜ:kbʊk] Arbeitsheft; Übungsheft **IV TS1**, 37

workshop ['wɜ:kʃɒp] Workshop **I**

world [wɜ:ld] Erde; Welt **I**

from around the **world** [frɒm əˌraʊnd ðə 'wɜ:ld] aus aller Welt **III**

worm [wɜ:m] Wurm **I**

worried ['wʌrid] beunruhigt; besorgt **III**

*to be **worried** [bi 'wʌrid] beunruhigt sein; besorgt sein **II**

to worry ['wʌri] sich Sorgen machen **II**

Don't **worry**! [dəʊnt 'wʌri] Keine Sorge! **I**

the worst [ðə 'wɜ:st] der/die/das schlimmste; der/die/das schlechteste **II**

*to be worth [bi: 'wɜ:θ] wert sein **I**

would [wʊd] würde/-st/-n/-t **III**

would like [wʊd 'laɪk] würde/-st/-n/-t gern; hätte/-st/-n/-t gern **I**

would love [wʊd 'lʌv] würde/-st/-n/-t sehr gern; hätte/-st-/-n/-t sehr gern **I**

Would you like …? [wʊd jʊ 'laɪk] Möchtest du …?; Möchten Sie …?; Möchtet ihr …? **II**

wounded ['wu:ndɪd] verwundet; verletzt **III**

Wow! [waʊ] Wow! **I**

to wrap [ræp] einwickeln; einpacken **I**

wrapping ['ræpɪŋ] Verpackung; Hülle **I**

to wrinkle one's nose [ˌrɪŋkl wʌnz 'nəʊz] die Nase rümpfen ⟨**IV U3**, 90⟩

wrist [rɪst] Handgelenk **II**

*to write [raɪt] schreiben **I**

*to **write** down [ˌraɪt 'daʊn] aufschreiben **I**

writer ['raɪtə] Autor/-in; Verfasser/-in **III**

writing ['raɪtɪŋ] Schreiben **I**

wrong [rɒŋ] falsch **I**

*to be **wrong** [bi: 'rɒŋ] unrecht haben; sich irren **I**

*to go **wrong** [ˌgəʊ 'rɒŋ] schiefgehen **I**

X

XOXO [ˌhʌgzˌən 'kɪsɪz] Umarmungen und Küsse (am Ende von E-Mails und SMS) **I**

Y

yard [jɑ:d] Garten; Hof **IV U2**, 43

front **yard** (AE) [ˌfrʌnt 'jɑ:d] Vorgarten **IV U2**, 43

yeah (infml) [jeə] ja **I**

year [jɪə] Jahr; Schuljahr **I**

New **Year's** Eve [ˌnju: ˌjɪəz'i:v] Silvester ⟨**IV U3**, 90⟩

11-year-old [ɪˌlevn'jɪərəʊld] 11-Jährige/-r **II**

18-year-old [ˌeɪti:n 'jɪərˌəʊld] 18-jährig **II**

yearbook ['jɪəbʊk] Jahrbuch **II**

yellow ['jeləʊ] gelb **I**

yes [jes] ja **I**

yesterday ['jestədeɪ] gestern **II**

yet [jet] schon; noch **II**

not … **yet** [nɒt 'jet] noch nicht **II**

yet [jet] doch; und trotzdem; und dennoch **IV U3**, 76

yoghurt ['jɒgət] Joghurt **I**

you [ju:; jə] du; ihr; Sie **I**

You know how to … [ju: ˈnəʊ ˌhaʊ tə] Du weißt, wie man …; Ihr wisst, wie man … I

You too? [ju: ˈtu:] Du auch? I

You'd better … (= You had better) [ˈjuːd ˌbetə] Du solltest lieber … IV AC3, 69

You're into … [ˈjɔːrˌɪntə] Du magst …; Du stehst auf … I

You're welcome. [jɔ: ˈwelkəm] Bitte schön.; Nichts zu danken.; Gern geschehen. I

You're … [jɔːr] Sie sind …; Du bist … I

young [jʌŋ] jung I

your [jɔ:; jə] dein/-e; euer/eure; Ihr/-e I

What's **your** name? [ˌwɒts jə ˈneɪm] Wie heißt du?; Wie heißen Sie? I

Your turn. [ˈjɔ: tɜːn] Du bist dran. I

yours [jɔːz] dein/-er/-e/-es; eure/-r/-s; Ihr/-e II

Yours … [jɔːz] Viele Grüße … (am Ende von Briefen und Mails) II

yourself [jɔːˈself] du/dir/dich/Sie/sich (selbst); selber I

yourselves [jɔːˈselvz] ihr/euch/Sie/sich (selbst); selber III

youth [ju:θ] Jugend IV TS1, 36

Z

zero [ˈzɪərəʊ] null I

zone [zəʊn] Zone IV AC2, 38

zoo [zu:] Zoo; Tierpark II

to **zoom** in (on) [zu:mˌɪn ɒn] heranzoomen (auf) III

Boys' names

Abdi [ˈæbdi] IV U1, 16

Abdirahman [ˌæbdirəˈmɑːn] IV U1, 17

Ahmed [ˈæmed] IV U1, 16

Amarjit [əˈmɑːdʒɪt] IV U1, 10

Amir [ˌɑːˈmiːr] II

Austin [ˈɒstɪn] IV U2, 56

Ben [ben] I

Bob [bɒb] I

Brad [bræd] III

Brodie [ˈbrəʊdi] IV AC4, 107

Callum [ˈkæləm] IV AC2, 41

Damian [ˈdeɪmiən] I

Daniel [ˈdænjəl] IV U3, 92

Dave [deɪv] I

David [ˈdeɪvɪd] I

Desmond [ˈdezmənd] I

Diego [diˈeɪgəʊ] IV U3, 72

Ed [ed] II

Eddie [ˈedi] IV U1, 10

Emilio [ɪˈmɪliəʊ] IV U3, 76

Ethan [ˈiːθn] III

Finn [fɪn] III

Frank [fræŋk] II

Harrison [ˈhærɪsn] IV U3, 79

Henry [ˈhenri] I

Jack [dʒæk] I

Jago [ˈdʒeɪgəʊ] III

James [dʒeɪmz] III

Jamie [ˈdʒeɪmi] I

Jay [dʒeɪ] I

Jim [dʒɪm] III

John [dʒɒn] II

Josh [dʒɒʃ] IV U2, 43

Lawrence [ˈlɔːrəns] IV U3, 91

Luke [luːk] I

Mario [ˈmæriəʊ] III

Mark [mɑːk] IV TS3, 104

Marley [ˈmɑːli] II

Marlon [ˈmɑːlən] IV TS3, 100

Masud [məˈsuːd] IV U1, 14

Matt [mæt] III

Max [mæks] III

Mick [mɪk] II

Mike [maɪk] II

Nathan [ˈneɪθn] II

Nick [nɪk] II

Peter [ˈpiːtə] II

Rick [rɪk] III

Rob [rɒb] IV TS1, 31

Scott [skɒt] IV U2, 48

Sean [ʃɔːn] III

Shahid [ʃɑːˈhiːd] I

Simon [ˈsaɪmən] IV TS1, 30

Steve [stiːv] I

Stuart [ˈstuːət] III

Thomas [ˈtɒməs] III

Tim [tɪm] IV TS3, 100

Todd [tɒd] ⟨IV U3, 90⟩

Tony [ˈtəʊni] I

Tristan [ˈtrɪstən] IV AC2, 41

Tyler [ˈtaɪlə] I

Wesley [ˈwezli] IV U2, 55

Will [wɪl] II

Girls' names

Alice [ˈælɪs] II

Alicia [əˈlɪsiə; əˈlɪʃə] I

Alva [ˈælvə] III

Amber [ˈæmbə] I

Anna [ˈænə] I

Anne [æn] I

Annie [ˈæni] III

Anya [ˈænjə] IV U1, 13

Ashley [ˈæʃli] IV U3, 73

Carol [ˈkærəl] I

Ceri [ˈkeri] II

Christine [krɪˈstiːn] IV U3, 91

Ciara [sˈjærə] IV U1, 19

Claire [ˈkleə] I

Emily [ˈemɪli] I

Eva [ˈiːvə] IV U2, 48

Fowsia [faʊˈziɑ] IV U1, 16

Frances [ˈfrɑːnsɪs] I

Gwen [gwen] I

Hayley [ˈheɪli] IV U1, 19

Helen [ˈhelɪn] III

Holly [ˈhɒli] I

Irina [ɪˈriːnə] I

Ivy [ˈaɪvi] III

Janie [ˈdʒeɪni] IV U2, 56

Jean [dʒiːn] III

Jenny [ˈdʒeni] IV U1, 15

Jessica [ˈdʒesɪkə] IV U2, 55

Judith [ˈdʒuːdɪθ] III

Julie [ˈdʒuːli] I

June [dʒuːn] IV AC4, 107

Kate [keɪt] II

Kelly [ˈkeli] IV U3, 78

Khadija [kəˈdiːdʒə] IV U1, 16

Kirsty [ˈkɜːsti] III

Laura [ˈlɔːrə] I

Lauren [ˈlɔːrən] II

Leanne [liˈæn] IV U2, 55

Lou [luː] I

Lucy [ˈluːsi] I

Madison [ˈmædɪsn] IV U2, 44

Maisie [ˈmeɪzi] II

Margaret [ˈmɑːgrət] III

Mary [ˈmeəri] II

Maryan [ˈmærjən] IV U1, 16

Megan [ˈmegən] II

Meredith [ˈmerədɪθ] IV U3, 77

Mila [ˈmiːlə] I

Mina [ˈmiːnə] II

Nancy [ˈnænsi] IV U3, 74

Olivia [ɒlˈɪviə] I

Pia [ˈpiːə] I

Polly [ˈpɒli] II

Rita [ˈriːtə] IV U3, 92

Rose [rəʊz] I

Ruby [ˈruːbi] II

Rylee [ˈraɪli] IV U3, 72

Sabra [ˈsæbrə] IV U1, 16

Sadia [ˈseɪdjə] IV U1, 14

Sally [ˈsæli] I

Sarah [ˈseərə] IV U3, 91

Sophie [ˈsəʊfi] IV U2, 44

Tamara [təˈmɑːrə] III

Tina [ˈtiːnə] III

Violet [ˈvaɪələt] III

Vivien [ˈvɪvjən] III

Surnames

Ashton [ˈæʃtən] II

Azad [əˈzɑːd] I

Blanchard [ˈblænʃəd] IV U3, 79

Elliot [ˈeliət] I

Ford [fɔːd] IV U2, 56

Francis [ˈfrɑːnsɪs] III

Fraser [ˈfreɪzə] I

Green [griːn] I

Jones [dʒəʊnz] IV U1, 12

Karp [kɑːp] III

King [kɪŋ] III

Mahmoud [məˈmuːd] IV U1, 17

Miller [ˈmɪlə] III

Moreno [məˈriːnəʊ] IV U3, 92

Mussa ['muːsə] **IV U1**, 16
Nicholls ['nɪkəlz] **III**
Parker ['pɑːkə] **II**
Preston ['prestən] **I**
Pulsford ['pʌlsfɔːd] **III**
Richardson ['rɪtʃədsn] **I**
Strasser ['stræsə] ⟨**IV U3**, 90⟩
Swindon ['swɪndən] **I**
Thompson ['tɒmsən] **II**
Walker ['wɔːkə] **II**
Watney ['wɒtni] **IV TS3**, 104
Woodruff ['wʊdrʌf] **IV U1**, 10
Wright [raɪt] **II**

Place names

Aberdeen [ˌæbə'diːn] *Stadt in Schottland* **III**
Bedloe Island [ˌbedləʊˌˈaɪlənd] **IV U3**, 74
Birchview ['bɜːtʃvjuː] *Stadt in den USA*
    IV U2, 44
Birmingham ['bɜːmɪŋəm] **III**
Boston ['bɒstn] *Stadt in den USA* **IV AC2**, 41
Bradford ['brædfəd] **II**
Bristol ['brɪstl] **III**
Broadway ['brɔːdweɪ] *Straße in NYC*
    IV AC2, 41
Brooklyn ['brʊklɪn] *Stadtteil von New York*
    IV TS2, 65
Calais ['kæleɪ] *frz. Küstenstadt am Ärmelka-
    nal* **IV U1**, 10
Cambridge ['keɪmbrɪdʒ] *Stadt in den USA*
    IV U2, 44
Camden Market ['kæmdən ˌmɑːkɪt] **II**
Chicago [ʃɪ'kɑːgəʊ] *Stadt in den USA*
    IV AC2, 39
Cologne [kə'ləʊn] Köln **I**
Covent Garden [ˌkɒvnt 'gɑːdn] **II**
Cracow ['krækɒv; 'krɑːkaʊ] Krakau **I**
Dhaka ['dɑːkə] **IV U1**, 14
Dover ['dəʊvə] *englische Küstenstadt am
    Ärmelkanal* **IV U1**, 10
Dubai [duːˈbaɪ] **IV U1**, 16
Edinburgh ['edɪnbrə] **III**
Ellis Island [ˌelɪsˌˈaɪlənd] *Insel vor New York
    City* **IV AC2**, 38
Glasgow ['glɑːzgəʊ] *Stadt in Schottland* **III**
Heathrow [ˌhiːˈθrəʊ] *Flughafen in London*
    IV U1, 15
Hollywood ['hɒliwʊd] **II**
Houston ['hjuːstn] *Stadt in den USA*
    IV TS3, 101
Hyde Park [ˌhaɪd 'pɑːk] **II**
Isle of Man [ˌaɪlˌəv 'mæn] **III**
Lakeview ['leɪkvjuː] *Stadt in den USA*
    IV U2, 51
Liberty Island [ˌlɪbətiˌˈaɪlənd] **IV U3**, 74
Liverpool ['lɪvəpuːl] **III**
London ['lʌndən] **I**
Lower Manhattan [ˌləʊə mæn'hætn]
    IV U3, 74
Manhattan [mæn'hætn] *Stadtteil von New
    York* **IV TS2**, 65

Midtown Manhattan [ˌmɪdtaʊn mæn'hætn]
    IV U3, 71
New York [ˌnju: 'jɔːk] **III**
Nottingham ['nɒtɪŋəm] **III**
Philadelphia [ˌfɪlə'delfiə] *Stadt in den USA*
    IV TS2, 65
Pittsburgh ['pɪtsbɜːg] *Stadt in den USA*
    IV U2, 44
Roswell ['rɒzwel] *Stadt in den USA*
    IV TS3, 105
San Diego [ˌsæn di'eɪgəʊ] *Stadt in den USA*
    IV AC2, 41
Seattle [si'ætl] **IV U1**, 15
Stratford-upon-Avon [ˌstrætfədəpɒn'eɪvn]
    Geburtsort Shakespeares **III**
Washington, D.C. [ˌwɒʃɪŋtən ˌdiːˈsiː] *Haupt-
    stadt der USA* **IV TS2**, 65
Wimbledon ['wɪmbldən] **I**

Geographical names

Africa ['æfrɪkə] Afrika **III**
Alabama [ˌælə'bæmə] *US-amerik. Bundes-
    staat* **IV U3**, 72
America [ə'merɪkə] **II**
Arizona [ˌærɪ'zəʊnə] *US-Bundesstaat*
    IV AC2, 38
Asia ['eɪʒə] Asien **IV AC2**, 38
Atlantic Ocean [ətˌlæntɪk 'əʊʃn] Atlantischer
    Ozean **III**
Australia [ɒs'treɪliə] Australien **II**
Austria ['ɔːstriə] Österreich **II**
Bangladesh [bæŋglə'deʃ] Bangladesch
    IV U1, 13
Britain ['brɪtn] Großbritannien **I**
British Empire [ˌbrɪtɪʃ'empaɪə] britisches
    Königreich **II**
British Isles [ˌbrɪtɪʃ'aɪlz] Britische Inseln **III**
California [ˌkælɪ'fɔːniə] Kalifornien *(US-
    amerik. Bundesstaat)* **IV AC2**, 39
Canada ['kænədə] Kanada **I**
China ['tʃaɪnə] China **I**
Cornwall ['kɔːnwɔːl] **III**
Cuba ['kjuːbə] Kuba **IV U3**, 92
Egypt ['iːdʒɪpt] Ägypten **IV U1**, 20
England ['ɪŋglənd] England **I**
European Union (EU) [ˌjʊərəpiən 'juːnjən
    (iːjuː)] Europäische Union **II**
France [frɑːns] Frankreich **II**
Germany ['dʒɜːməni] Deutschland **I**
Great Britain (GB) [ˌgreɪt 'brɪtn] Großbritan-
    nien **III**
India ['ɪndiə] Indien **II**
Italy ['ɪtəli] Italien **II**
Kenya ['kenjə] Kenia **IV U1**, 16
Latin America [ˌlætɪn ə'merɪkə] Lateiname-
    rika **IV AC2**, 38
Loch Ness [ˌlɒx 'nes; ˌlɒk 'nes] *See in Schott-
    land* **III**
(the) Midwest [ˌmɪd'west] (der) Mittlere
    Westen **IV AC2**, 41

Mount Rainier [ˌmaʊnt reɪ'niə] *Berg in den
    USA* **IV AC2**, 38
New Mexico [ˌnju: 'meksɪkəʊ] *US-amerik.
    Bundesstaat* **IV TS3**, 105
North Sea [ˌnɔːθ 'siː] Nordsee **III**
Northern Ireland [ˌnɔːðn 'aɪələnd] Nordir-
    land **III**
the Pacific Northwest [ðə pəˌsɪfɪk nɔːθ'west]
    Pazifischer Nordwesten **IV AC2**, 38
Pennsylvania [ˌpensɪl'veɪniə] *US-amerik.
    Bundesstaat* **IV U2**, 44
Poland ['pəʊlənd] Polen **I**
Republic of Ireland [rɪˌpʌblɪkˌəv 'aɪələnd]
    Republik Irland **III**
the Rockies (= the Rocky Mountains) [ðə
    'rɒkiz] *Gebirge in the USA* **IV AC2**, 41
Russia ['rʌʃə] Russland **IV AC2**, 39
Scandinavia [ˌskændɪ'neɪviə] Skandinavien
    III
Scotland ['skɒtlənd] Schottland **III**
Somalia [sə'mɑːliə] Somalia **IV U1**, 16
South Africa [ˌsaʊθ 'æfrɪkə] Südafrika **II**
Soviet Union [ˌsəʊviət 'juːnjən] Sowjetunion
    IV TS3, 101
Spain [speɪn] Spanien **II**
Sweden ['swiːdn] Schweden **IV AC2**, 39
Thames [temz] **I**
United Kingdom (UK) [juː'keɪ] Vereinigtes
    Königreich von Großbritannien und
    Nordirland **I**
the US (= the United States) [ðə juː'es] die
    USA (= die Vereinigten Staaten) **IV AC2**, 38
USA (United States of America) [ˌjuːes'eɪ
    (juːˌnaɪtɪd steɪtsˌəv ə'merɪkə)] USA (Verei-
    nigte Staaten von Amerika) **II**
Wales [weɪlz] **I**
Washington State [ˌwɒʃɪŋtən 'steɪt] *US-
    Bundesstaat* **IV AC2**, 38
Wisconsin [wɪ'skɒnsɪn] *US-amerik. Bundes-
    staat* **IV U3**, 76

Other names

Apollo 11 [əˌpɒləʊ ɪ'levn] *Raumfähre*
    IV TS3, 101
Area 51 [ˌeəriə ˌfɪfti'wʌn] **IV TS3**, 102
Astor Place Cube [ˌæstə pleɪs 'kjuːb] *Kunst-
    werk* **IV U3**, 72
Auguste Bartholdi [ɔːˌgʊst bɑː'təʊldi] *frz.
    Bildhauer* **IV U3**, 74
Big Ben [ˌbɪg 'ben] **II**
British Airways [ˌbrɪtɪʃ'eəweɪz] *Fluggesell-
    schaft* **IV U1**, 15
Buckingham Palace [ˌbʌkɪŋəm 'pælɪs] **II**
Capricorn One [ˌkæprɪkɔːn 'wʌn] *Filmtitel*
    IV TS3, 104
Central Park [ˌsentrl 'pɑːk] *Park in New York*
    IV U3, 71
Chinatown ['tʃaɪnataʊn] **IV U3**, 71
Chrysler Building ['kraɪslə ˌbɪldɪŋ] *Wolken-
    kratzer in New York* **IV U3**, 71

Cold War [ˌkəʊld ˈwɔː] Kalter Krieg **IVTS3**, 101

Columbia [kəˈlʌmbiə] *Raumkapsel* **IVTS3**, 101

Docklands Light Railway *(DLR)* [ˌdɒklændz ˌlaɪt ˈreɪlweɪ] *Regionalbahn im Osten Londons* **I**

Eagle [ˈiːgl] *Raumkapsel* **IVTS3**, 101

Empire State Building [ˌempaɪə ˈsteɪt ˌbɪldɪŋ] *Wolkenkratzer in NYC* **IV AC2**, 39

Empire State of Mind [ˌempaɪə ˌsteɪt ˌəv ˈmaɪnd] *Liedtitel* **IV U3**, 70

Fashion Fabulous [ˌfæʃn ˈfæbjələs] **IVTS2**, 66

the Globe Theatre [ðə ˌgləʊb ˈθɪətə] **III**

God Save the Queen [ˈgɒd seɪv ðə ˌkwiːn] Gott schütze die Königin *(britische Nationalhymne)* **III**

the Houses of Parliament [ðə ˌhaʊzɪz ˌəv ˈpɑːləmənt] *britisches Parlamentsgebäude* **II**

Independence Day [ˌɪndɪˈpendəns ˌdeɪ] amerikanischer Unabhängigkeitstag **IV AC2**, 41

Industrial Revolution [ɪnˌdʌstriəl revlˈuːʃn] *die industrielle Revolution* **III**

Juillard School [ˈdʒuːljəd ˌskuːl] *Hochschule für Tanz* **IV U3**, 72

London Eye [ˌlʌndən ˈaɪ] **II**

Mars [mɑːz] **IVTS3**, 104

Meridian Line [məˌrɪdiən ˈlaɪn] *Nullmeridian* **I**

Metropolitan Museum of Art [metrəˌpɒlɪtn mjuːˌziːˌəmˌəvˌˈɑːt] *Museum in New York* **IV U3**, 72

OG [əʊˈdʒiː] **IV U3**, 79

Park Avenue [pɑːkˌˈævənjuː] *Straße in New York* **IV U3**, 76

Pledge of Allegiance [ˌpledʒˌəvˌəˈliːdʒns] *Treueeid auf die amerikanische Flagge* **IV U2**, 48

Retro 4ever [ˌretrəʊ fəˈrevə] **IVTS2**, 65

Rockefeller Center [ˌrɒkəfelə ˈsentə] *Gebäude in New York* **IV U3**, 72

Statue of Liberty [ˌstætʃuːˌəv ˈlɪbəti] *Freiheitsstatue* **IV U3**, 74

Thanksgiving [ˌθæŋksˈgɪvɪŋ] *amerik. Erntedankfest* **IV U2**, 44

The Martian [ðə ˈmɑːʃn] *Filmtitel* **IVTS3**, 104

The Naked Cowboy [ðə ˌneɪkɪd ˈkaʊbɔɪ] **IV U3**, 72

The Wind in the Willows [ðə ˌwɪnd ɪn ðə ˈwɪləʊz] *engl. Kinderbuchklassiker* **IVTS1**, 30

Times Square [ˌtaɪmz ˈskweə] *Platz in New York* **IV U3**, 70

the Tower of London [ðə ˌtaʊərˌəv ˈlʌndən] **II**

Wall Street [ˈwɔːl ˌstriːt] *Straße in New York* **IV U3**, 74

Wayne Larson [ˌweɪn ˈlɑːsn] **IV U2**, 52

Weezer [ˈwiːzə] **IV U1**, 12

World War II [ˌwɜːld ˌwɔː ˈtuː] *Zweiter Weltkrieg* **II**

Famous names

Alicia Keys [əˌlɪʃə ˈkiːz] *US-amerik. Sängerin* **IV U3**, 70

Alvin Ailey [ˌælvɪn ˈeɪli] *Tänzer* **IV U3**, 72

Anne Boleyn [ˌæn ˈbɒlɪn] *Mutter von Elizabeth I.* **III**

Anne Hathaway [ˌæn ˈhæðəweɪ] *Shakespeares Frau* **III**

Buzz Aldrin [ˌbʌz ˈɔːldrɪn] *amerik. Astronaut* **IVTS3**, 101

Dave Draper [ˌdeɪv ˈdreɪpə] **IVTS1**, 31

Elizabeth I [ɪˌlɪzəbəθ ðə ˈfɜːst] **II**

Francis Drake [ˌfrɑːnsɪs ˈdreɪk] **III**

Henry VIII [ˌhenri ði ˈeɪtθ] *Heinrich VIII.* **III**

John F. Kennedy (JFK) [ˌdʒɒnˌef ˈkenədi; ˌdʒeɪˌef keɪ] **IV U3**, 74

King Arthur [ˌkɪŋ ˈɑːθə] *König Artus* **III**

King Edward [kɪŋ ˈedwəd] **III**

Matt Damon [ˌmæt ˈdeɪmən] *US-amerik. Schauspieler* **IVTS3**, 104

Michael Collins [ˌmaɪkl ˈkɒlɪnz] *amerik. Astronaut* **IVTS3**, 101

Neil Armstrong [niːlˌˈɑːmstrɒŋ] *amerik. Astronaut* **IVTS3**, 100

Prince Albert [ˌprɪns ˈælbət] **II**

Queen Victoria [ˌkwiːn vɪkˈtɔːriə] **II**

Sherlock Holmes [ˌʃɜːlɒk ˈhəʊmz] **III**

William Shakespeare [ˌwɪljəm ˈʃeɪkspɪə] *englischer Dramatiker (1564–1616)* **III**

William the Conqueror [ˌwɪljəm ðə ˈkɒŋkrə] **II**

A

abbiegen to turn **I**
Abbildung image **IV TS2**, 65
abblocken to block **II**
abbrechen to drop out (of) **III**
abbrennen *to burn down **III**
abchecken to check out (of) (coll) **III**
abdecken to cover **III**
Abend evening **I**
    heute **Abend** 2nite (= tonight) **I**; tonight
    IV TS1, 31
Abendessen dinner **I**
abends in the evenings **I**
abends (Uhrzeit) p.m. **I**
Abenteuer adventure **II**
aber but **I**
abfahren *to leave **II**; to depart **III**
    abfahren auf *to be crazy about **IV U2**, 47
abfahrend outward **III**
Abfall trash (AE) **IV TS2**, 67
Abflug departure **IV U1**, 9
Abflughalle departure lounge **IV U1**, 9
Abfolge sequence **IV U3**, 89
Abgabe drop-off **IV U2**, 51
abgeschlossen locked **II**
abgesehen von apart from **IV U1**, 11
abhaken to tick **II**
abhängen von to depend (on) **III**
Abhängige/-r addict **IV U1**, 10
Abheben take-off **IV U1**, 15
abholen to pick up **III**; to fetch **IV U1**, 17
Ablehnung rejection **IV U3**, 76
abnehmen *to take off **I**
Abneigungen dislikes (pl) **IV U2**, 46
Abreise departure **IV U1**, 9
abreißen to pull down **III**
Absage rejection **IV U3**, 76
abschalten to turn off **II**
abschicken *to send off **III**
abschneiden *to cut (off) **II**
Abschnitt section **II**
sich **abschotten** von to close oneself away
    from **IV U1**, 16
abschreiben to copy **I**
Absicht purpose **IV U1**, 13
absolut absolutely **II**
Abstammung origin **IV U1**, 19
Abstand gap **I**
abstimmen *to take a vote; to vote **I**
abstürzen to crash **II**
sich alles **abverlangen** to push oneself **III**
außer **Acht** lassen to ignore **III**
acht eight **I**
Achtklässler/-in 8th-grader (AE) **IV U2**, 48
Acker field **II**
Action action **I**
Adjektiv adjective **II**
Adresse address **I**
Adverb adverb **II**
AG club **I**
aggressiv aggressive **II**; pushy **IV TS1**, 33

Ägypter/-in Egyptian **IV U1**, 20
ägyptisch Egyptian **IV U1**, 20
äh er **I**
ähnlich similar **II**
keine **Ahnung** no idea **II**
keine **Ahnung** haben *to have no clue
    IV AC2, 41
Akku battery **II**
Aktion action **I**
aktiv active **III**
Aktivität activity **I**
aktuell up-to-date **IV TS3**, 100
Akzent accent **III**
akzeptieren to accept **IV U1**, 16
albern silly **I**
alle all of them; everyone **I**; everybody **II**
alle/-s all **I**
    wir **alle** all of us **III**
allein alone **I**; on my own **II**
alleinstehend single **IV AC2**, 38
alles everything **I**
alltäglich everyday **III**
Alphabet alphabet **I**
alphabetisch alphabetical **II**
Alptraum nightmare **IV U2**, 52
als as **II**
als (bei Vergleichen) than **II**
als when **I**
    als ob as if **III**
also so **I**
alt old **I**
    Wie **alt** bist du? How old are you? **I**
    Wie **alt** sind Sie? How old are you? **I**
Alter age **III**
Alter (ugs.) dude (coll) **IV AC2**, 41
älter elderly **III**
Alternativ- fringe **III**
am on **I**
    am besten best **I**
    am Fluss by the river **II**
    am Wochenende at the weekend **I**
aus **Amerika** American **II**
    Ureinwohner/-in **Amerikas** Native Ameri-
    can **IV U2**, 45
Amerikaner/-in American **II**
amerikanisch American **II**
Amtssprache official language **II**
sich **amüsieren** *to have fun **I**; to enjoy
    oneself **III**
an on; at **I**; by **III**
    an Bord aboard **I**
    an Stelle von instead of **IV U2**, 45
    an sein *to be on **II**
Ananas pineapple **III**
anbauen *to grow **III**
anbieten to offer **II**
Anblick sight **II**
andauern to continue **III**
Andenken souvenir **II**
die **anderen** the others **I**
andere/-r/-s other **I**; else **III**
    ein/-e **andere**/-r/-s another **I**

Einerseits …, (aber) **andererseits** … On the
    one hand …, (but) on the other hand …
    II
ändern in to turn into **IV U1**, 14
    seine Meinung **ändern** to change one's
    mind **III**
    (sich) **ändern** to change **II**
anders different; other **I**
Änderung change **III**
Andeutung hint **III**
Anfahrt drive **IV U2**, 44
Anfang beginning **II**; start **III**
anfangen to start **I**; *to get started; *to
    begin **II**
anfeuern to cheer **II**
sich **anfreunden** *to become friends
    IV AC2, 41
anführen *to lead **III**
angeben to show off **II**
Angeber/-in show-off **III**
    Und ein **Angeber**! With a very big head! **II**
Angeln fishing **III**
angemessen appropriate **III**
die **Angesagten** in-crowd **III**
von **Angesicht** zu **Angesicht** face-to-face **II**
angespült werden to wash up **II**
angreifen to attack **III**
Angst fear **II**
    Angst haben (vor) *to be scared (of) **I**; *to
    be afraid (of) **IV U1**, 8
    Ich habe (keine) **Angst** vor … I'm (not)
    scared of … **I**
ängstlich fearful **III**; scared **IV U2**, 52
anhaben *to wear **I**
anhalten to stop **I**
Anhänger/-in fan **II**
anheben to lift **IV U3**, 76
anhören to listen (to) **I**
anklicken to click on **III**
ankommen to arrive **III**
ankommend inward **III**
Ankommende/-r arrival **IV TS2**, 66
ankündigen to announce **IV TS3**, 101
Ankündigung announcement **III**
Ankunft arrival **IV U1**, 9
Ankunftshalle arrivals hall **IV U1**, 9
anmalen to paint **I**
Anmerkung note **I**
annähernd nearly **II**
Annäherung approach **IV TS2**, 66
annehmen to accept **IV U1**, 16; to guess
    IV AC1, 22
anonym anonymous **II**
anordnen to arrange **III**
Anordnung layout **III**
anpflanzen to plant **II**
anpreisen to advertise **IV TS2**, 64
anprobieren to try on **II**
anregen to inspire **IV U3**, 70
Anregung suggestion **I**
Anruf phone call **I**

einen **Anruf** entgegennehmen to answer the phone I
Anrufbeantworter answering machine I
anrufen to call I; to phone **IV TS1**, 31; *to ring **IV TS1**, 36
Anrufer/-in caller I
Ansatz approach **IV TS2**, 66
anschauen to look at I; *to have a look (at) II
jmdn. schief/komisch **anschauen** *to give sb funny looks III
sich **anschließen** to join II
ansehen to look at I
(sich) **ansehen** to watch I
Ansicht point of view II
anstarren to stare I
anstatt instead of **IV U2**, 45
anstehen *to stand in line (AE) **IV AC3**, 69
(sich) **anstellen** *to stand in line (AE) **IV AC3**, 69
antippen to tap II; to touch **IV U2**, 52
Antwort answer; reply I
antworten to answer; to reply I
Anweisung instruction I
Anwesenheitskontrolle registration II
Anzeige advert III; ad **IV TS2**, 64
anziehen *to put on III; to attract **IV TS2**, 66
Apartment apartment (AE) **IV U2**, 43
Apfel apple I
App app II
Apparat machine I
April April I
Ära era **IV U1**, 19
arabisch Arab **IV U1**, 20
Arbeit job; work I
Arbeit für die Schule studies (pl) II
arbeiten to work I
Arbeitsheft workbook **IV TS1**, 37
Architekt/-in architect II
Areal area II
Ärger trouble II
Ärger machen *to make trouble I
jmdn. **ärgern** to tease sb III
Argument criterion, criteria (pl); argument III
Argument dafür pro II
Argument dagegen con II
argumentieren to argue **IV U2**, 51
argwöhnisch suspicious **IV U1**, 13
Arm arm II
arm poor III
die **Armen** the poor III
armselig miserable ⟨**IV TS1**, 32⟩
Aroma flavor (AE) **IV U3**, 75
arrangieren to arrange III
Art kind I; type III
Art und Weise way I
Artikel article II
Arzt/Ärztin doctor II
Arztpraxis surgery I
Assistent/-in assistant II
Astronaut/-in astronaut **IV TS3**, 100
Atelier studio **IV U3**, 72

Atem breath III
Atem holen *to take a breath III
atemberaubend breathtaking **IV TS3**, 104
Atemzug breath III
Atlantischer Ozean Atlantic Ocean III
Atlas atlas II
atmen to breathe II
Atmosphäre flair; atmosphere II
Attraktion attraction II
attraktiv attractive **IV U2**, 55
Aua! Ouch! II
auch too I; also II
auch nicht not … either **IV AC4**, 107
Du **auch**? You too? I
Audio- audio I
Audioführung audio tour II
audiovisueller Effekt audio-visual effect II
auf on; at; to I
auf dem Foto/den Fotos in the photo(s) I
auf der anderen Seite von across; opposite I
auf der Straße in the street I
auf einmal suddenly I
auf Wiedersehen goodbye I
auf … zu towards II
Aufbau structure III
aufbauen *to set up I; *to build III
wieder **aufbauen** *to rebuild III
aufbewahren *to keep I
aufdringlich pushy **IV TS1**, 33
aufeinanderfolgend consecutive **IV U3**, 89
aufführen to stage **IV TS1**, 30; **IV TS3**, 102; to perform **IV U3**, 79
Aufführung show II; performance **IV TS1**, 30
Aufgabe task; exercise; job I
aufgeben *to give up III
aufgebracht upset II
aufgeregt excited I; nervous II
aufgeschlagen open I
aufhalten *to hold open **IV AC1**, 22
aufhängen *to put up; *to hang up II
jmdn. **aufheitern** to cheer sb up III
aufheben to pick up III
aufhellen to lighten III
aufhören to finish I
Hör/Hört auf! Stop it! I
aufhören (mit) to stop I
Aufklärung enlightenment **IV U3**, 74
aufladen to top up II
aufmachen to open I
aufmerksam machen (auf) to campaign (for) III
Aufmerksamkeit attention II
Aufnahme recording I; shot III
Aufnahmeort set III
Aufnahmestudio recording studio I
aufnehmen to record II; to include III
auf etw. **aufpassen** to mind sth **IV AC4**, 107
aufpassen auf to look after I
Pass/Passt auf! Be careful! I
aufpassen to look out II
aufpeppen to spice up **IV TS2**, 65

aufräumen to tidy (a room) I
aufrechterhalten *to keep going II
aufregend exciting I
Aufregung excitement (no pl) III
aufsagen *to say I
aufsaugen to soak up III
aufschreiben *to write down I; to note down II
aufstehen (aus dem Bett) *to get up I
Es ist Zeit **aufzustehen**! Time to get up! I
aufstehen (von einer Sitzgelegenheit) *to stand up I
aufstellen *to put up II
(sich) **aufstellen** to line up III
aufteilen to divide (up) III
Auftrag task I; mission **IV TS3**, 101
auftreten to perform **IV U3**, 79
Auftritt gig III
aufwachen *to wake up III
aufwachsen *to grow up III
aufwärmen to warm up I
sich **aufwärmen** to warm up I
Aufwärmübung warm-up I
aufwecken *to wake up III
aufweisen to feature III
aufzeichnen to record II
Aufzeichnung recording I
jmdn. **aufziehen** to tease sb III
Aufzug elevator (AE) **IV U2**, 44
Auge eye II
die **Augen** verdrehen to roll one's eyes III
Er traute seinen **Augen** nicht. He couldn't believe his eyes. II
Augenblick moment II
Augenzeuge/Augenzeugin eyewitness II
August August I
aus from I
aus Cornwall Cornish III
aus … heraus out of **IV U1**, 15
aus aller Welt from around the world III
ausarbeiten to work out II
Ausbeuterbetrieb sweatshop **IV U2**, 48
ausblasen *to blow out I
Ausblick view II
Auschecken Check-out I
auschecken to check out (coll) III
(sich) **ausdenken** *to think of II
Ausdruck phrase I; expression II
nützliche **Ausdrücke** Useful phrases I
ausdrücken to express II
Auseinandersetzung argument III
auserwählt sein, etw. zu tun *to be called to do sth III
ausflippen *to go crazy II
Ausflug trip II
ausführen to conduct **IV U3**, 92
den Hund **ausführen** to walk the dog I
ausfüllen to fill in II
Ausgang gate **IV U1**, 15
Ausgangssperre curfew **IV U2**, 44
ausgeben (Geld) *to spend I
ausgedehnt wide III

ausgehen *to go out **III**
ausgereift well-developed **IV TS3**, 105
sich ausgeschlossen fühlen *to feel left out **II**
zeitweilig vom Unterricht ausgeschlossen werden *to be suspended **IV AC3**, 68
aushelfen to help out **III**
im Ausland abroad **IV U1**, 10
ins Ausland abroad **IV U1**, 10
ausländisch foreign **IV U1**, 8
auslassen to skip **IV AC3**, 68
Auslauf run area **III**
auslaufen *to spill **IV U1**, 10
(sich) ausleihen to borrow **II**
einem etwas ausmachen to mind **IV U2**, 46
Mach/Macht das aus! Stop it! **I**
auspacken to unwrap **I**; to unpack **IV U2**, 46
ausprobieren to try out **III**
auspusten *to blow out **I**
ausräumen to clear out **I**; to clean out **IV U2**, 51
jmdm. etw. ausrichten *to take a message **I**
sich ausruhen to relax **II**
Ausrüstung equipment **II**
Aussage statement **II**
ausschalten to turn off **II**; to switch off **IV AC3**, 69
Ausschuss committee **IV U2**, 48
aussehen to look **I**
Aussehen looks (pl) **III**
von außen from the outside **IV U3**, 75
Außenseiter/-in geek **IV U2**, 48
außer Acht lassen to ignore **III**
außer apart from **IV U1**, 11; except **IV U1**, 17
außer Betrieb out of order **IV TS1**, 36
im äußersten Westen in the far west **III**
außerhalb outside; out **I**
Außerirdische/-r alien **I**
Äußerung expression **II**
Aussicht view **II**
Aussprache pronunciation **I**
aussprechen to pronounce **IV AC4**, 106
Ausstattung equipment **II**
aussteigen *to get out of **II**
aussteigen (aus einem Bus/Zug) *to get off (a bus/train) **II**
Ausstellung display **II**
Ausstellung in der Klasse class display **I**
Aussterben extinction (no pl) **III**
aussterben *to become extinct **III**
aussuchen to pick **II**
Austausch exchange **III**
Austausch- exchange **III**
austauschen to exchange; to trade **II**
Austauschschüler/-in exchange student **III**
Australier/-in Australian **III**
australisch Australian **III**
austricksen to trick **IV TS3**, 103
ausüben to practice (AE) **IV U2**, 45
eine Religion ausüben to practice a religion **IV U2**, 45
Auswahl choice **II**

auswählen *to choose; to pick **II**
auswendig lernen *to learn … by heart **I**
auswickeln to unwrap **I**
Auszeichnung award **II**
ausziehen *to take off **I**
Auto car **I**
Autobahn freeway (AE) **IV U3**, 79
Autofahrt drive **IV U2**, 44
Automat machine **I**; vending machine **IV U1**, 10
Autor/-in author; writer **III**
Axt axe **III**

B

Baby baby **I**
Background- backing **III**
Backgroundtänzer/-in backing dancer **III**
Bad bath **I**
Badehaus baths (pl) **III**
Badewanne bath **I**
Badezimmer bathroom **I**
Badminton badminton **I**
Bahnhof station **I**
Bahnsteig platform **III**
bald soon **II**
Ball ball **I**
Banane banana **I**
Band band **III**
Bank bench **III**; bank **IV U3**, 72
bannen to ban **III**
Bär bear **II**
Baseball baseball **IV U2**, 46
Basketball basketball **I**
Batterie battery **II**
Bauch stomach **II**
Bauchschmerzen stomachache **II**
Bauchweh stomachache **II**
bauen *to build **II**
Bauernhof farm **I**
Baum tree **I**
Baustein building block **II**
jmdn./etw. beachten *to pay attention to sb/sth **III**
Beachtung attention **II**
Beamter/Beamtin official **IV U1**, 17
beängstigend scary **II**
beantworten to answer **I**
richtig beantworten *to get right **III**
Becher mug **III**
bedauern *to feel sorry for **III**
bedecken to cover **III**
bedeckt cloudy **II**
bedeuten *to mean **II**
Bedeutung meaning **II**
Bedingungssatz conditional sentence **III**
bedrückend depressing **IV U1**, 17
bedürftig in need **II**
sich beeilen to hurry **I**
beeindruckt impressed **II**
beeinflussen to influence **II**
beenden to finish **I**; to end **II**

sich befassen mit *to deal (with) **II**
Befehl order **III**; command **IV U1**, 9
Befehlsform imperative **III**
befestigen to fix **II**
befolgen to follow **II**
befördern to transport **IV U3**, 79
befragen to interview **I**
Befragung interview **I**
Befürchtung fear **II**
begehbarer Kleiderschrank walk-in closet **IV U2**, 44
begeistert excited **I**
Begeisterung enthusiasm **IV U3**, 72
Beginn beginning **II**; opening **III**
beginnen to start **I**; *to begin **II**
Begriff term **IV TS1**, 30
im Begriff sein, etw. zu tun *to be about to do sth **IV AC3**, 69
behalten *to keep **I**
Behauptung statement **II**
behindert with special needs **II**
bei with; at **I**; by **III**
beibringen *to teach **II**
beide both **II**
beide the two of them **II**
Bein leg **II**
die Beine und Hände ruhig halten *to keep one's feet or hands still **III**
beinahe almost **II**
beinhalten to include **III**
Beispiel example **I**
zum Beispiel for example **II**
beißen *to bite **II**
beitreten to join **II**
bekannt sein als *to be known as **IV U3**, 74
sich beklagen to complain **IV U3**, 76
Bekleidungsvorschriften dress code **IV U2**, 43
bekommen *to get **I**; to receive **II**
etw. aus dem Kopf bekommen *to get sth out of one's head **III**
belästigen to bother **IV U1**, 15
belebt busy **I**
beliebt popular **I**
die Beliebten in-crowd **III**
bellen to bark **I**
Belohnung treat **III**
bemerken to notice **II**
Benehmen behaviour (no pl) **IV AC1**, 22; manners (pl) **IV AC1**, 23; behavior (no pl) (AE) **IV AC3**, 69
sich benehmen to behave **III**
benötigen to need (to) **I**
benutzen to use **I**; *to make use of **IV U3**, 89
beobachten to watch **I**
bequem comfortable **II**
bereit ready **II**
bereits already **I**
Berg mountain **II**; hill **III**
Bergbau mining **III**
bergen to save **I**
bergig mountainous **IV AC2**, 40

Bericht report **II**
Bericht *(in einer Zeitschrift, Zeitung)* article **II**
berichten to report **IV U1**, 9
Beruf career **III**
sich beruhigen to relax; to calm down **II**
berühmt famous **I**
  berühmte Person celebrity **III**
berühren to touch **IV U2**, 52
beschäftigt busy **I**
beschreiben to describe **I**
Beschreibung description **II**
sich beschweren to complain **IV U3**, 76
besichtigen to visit **I**
Besichtigungs- sightseeing **II**
besiedelt populated **IV AC2**, 38
besiegen *to beat **II**; to defeat **III**
besitzen *to have got **I**
Besonderheit specialty *(AE)* **IV U3**, 75
besonders special **I**
besorgen *to get **I**
besorgt worried **III**
  besorgt sein *to be worried **II**
Besorgungen machen *to do the shopping **III**
besser better **I**
Bestätigungsfrage question tag **II**
(der/die/das) Beste (the) best **II**
  sich das Beste bis zum Schluss aufheben to save the best for last **IV U3**, 72
bestehen aus *to be made of **III**
besteigen to climb **I**
bestellen to order **IV U1**, 20
beste/-r/-s best **I**
  am besten best **I**
  der/die/das beste … überhaupt the best … ever **III**
bestimmt definitely **III**
bestimmte/-r/-s particular **III**
bestürzt upset **II**
Besuch visit **I**
besuchen to visit **I**
Besucher/-in visitor **I**
beteiligen to involve **IV TS3**, 102
beten to pray **III**
Beton concrete **IV U1**, 17
betonen to stress **III**
Betonung stress **III**
Betragen behaviour *(no pl)* **IV AC1**, 22; behavior *(no pl) (AE)* **IV AC3**, 69
betreiben *to run **IV TS3**, 102
betreten to enter **II**
Betreuer/-in instructor **II**
außer Betrieb out of order **IV TS1**, 36
betrügen to cheat **IV AC3**, 68
Bett bed **I**
  ins Bett gehen *to go to bed **I**
beunruhigt worried **III**
  beunruhigt sein *to be worried **II**
beurteilen to judge **III**
bevölkert populated **IV AC2**, 38
Bevölkerung population **IV AC2**, 39

bevor before **I**
(sich) bewegen to move **I**
Beweggrund motive **IV TS1**, 32
Beweggründe motivation **IV TS1**, 31
Bewegung move **I**
bewerten to judge **III**; to rate **IV TS3**, 104
bewölkt cloudy **II**
bezahlen *to pay (for) **I**
Beziehung relationship **II**
  eine Beziehung finden zu to relate to **III**
Bezirk district **IV U3**, 70
Bibliothek library **III**
Biene bee **II**
Bild picture **I**; visual; image **IV TS2**, 65
Bild *(eines Comics)* panel **IV U3**, 89
bilden *to make **I**; to form **II**
Bildergeschichte graphic novel **III**
Bildgeschichte photo story **I**
Bildung education *(no pl)* **III**
Bildunterschrift caption **III**
billig cheap **I**
binden (an) to tie (to) **III**
Bindewort linking word **I**
biografisch biographical **III**
Bis … CU *(= See you)*; See you! **I**
  Bis dann! CU *(= See you)*; See you! **I**
bis till **I**; until **II**
  bis jetzt so far **II**
  von … bis from … to **I**
  bis auf except **IV U1**, 17
Biskuit- sponge **I**
ein bisschen a bit **II**
Bitte request **IV U1**, 9
Bitte. Please. **I**
  Bitte schön. Here you are.; You're welcome. **I**
bitten to ask **I**
  bitten um to ask for **I**
blau blue **I**
Blechdose tin can **III**
bleiben to stay **I**
  draußen bleiben *to keep out (of) **III**
  Bleib wie du bist. Stay the way you are. **III**
Bleistift pencil **I**
Blick look **I**; view **II**
  einen Blick werfen auf *to take a look at **II**
hier: Blick sight **II**
Blickfang eye-catcher **IV TS2**, 65
Blickpunkt focus **III**
Blickwinkel perspective **II**
Blitz lightning *(no pl)* **II**; flash **III**
Block block **IV U3**, 72
blockieren to block **II**
blöd stupid **II**
Blog blog **III**
blond blond **III**
bloß bare **III**
bloß only **I**
Blume flower **II**
Blut blood **III**
BMX BMX **II**
Boarding boarding **IV U1**, 9

Boden ground **IV U1**, 17
Bodyguard bodyguard **IV U2**, 52
weiße Bohnen in Tomatensoße baked beans *(pl)* **I**
Bonbons sweets *(pl)* **I**
Boot boat **I**
an Bord aboard **I**
Bordkarte boarding card **IV U1**, 9
böse angry; bad **I**
Bösewicht villain **III**
Boss boss **III**
Botschaft message **I**
Bowling spielen to play bowls **III**
Bowlingbahn bowling alley **I**
Box box **I**
Boxen boxing **II**
Boxrunde round of boxing **II**
Branche industry **III**
brandneu brand-new **IV TS2**, 65
Bratwurst sausage **III**
Brauch custom **IV AC1**, 22
brauchen to need (to) **I**
  nicht brauchen needn't **I**
  (Zeit) brauchen *to take **II**
braun brown **I**
brechen *to break **I**
brechend cracking **III**
breit wide **III**
brennen *to burn; *to be on fire **III**
Brett board **III**
  schwarzes Brett noticeboard **II**
Brief letter **II**
Briefträger postman **II**
Brille glasses *(pl)* **II**
bringen *to bring; *to get; *to take **I**
  in Schwierigkeiten bringen *to make trouble **II**
  jmdn. dazu bringen, etw. zu tun *to make somebody do something **II**
Brite/Britin British **I**
britisch British **I**
Bronzezeit *(ca. 2200–800 v. Chr.)* Bronze Age **III**
Broschüre brochure **I**; leaflet **IV AC1**, 23
Brot bread **I**
  belegtes Brot sandwich **I**
Brötchen bread roll **III**
Brücke bridge **II**
Bruder brother **I**
brüllen to roar **III**
brutal violent **III**
Buch book **I**
buchen to book **III**
Bücherei library **III**
Büchse can **I**
Buchstabe letter **I**
buchstabieren *to spell **I**
Bühne stage **III**
Bundesstaat state **IV AC2**, 39
bunt colourful **I**
Buntstift pencil **I**
Burg castle **II**

Büro office **I**
Bus bus **I**
Busbahnhof bus station **I**
Busch (*Buschlandschaft*) bush **III**
Business business **III**
Butter butter **III**

C

Cache cache **III**
Café café; snack bar **I**
Cafeteria cafeteria **I**
campen to camp **III**
Camping camping **II**
Cartoon cartoon **III**
Casting casting **IV TS1**, 37
Cent (*Währung*) cent **I**
Center centre **I**; center (*AE*) **IV AC2**, 38
Champion champion **III**
Chance chance **II**
Chaos chaos **III**
Charakter character **I**
Chat chat **III**
Chatroom chat room **II**
chatten (*sich online unterhalten*) to chat **I**
Checkliste checklist **II**
Chef boss **III**
chillen to chill out **III**
Chipkarte smartcard **II**
im **Chor** in chorus **IV TS1**, 33
nach **Christus** AD (= Anno Domini) **III**
vor **Christus** BC (= before Christ) **III**
circa about **I**
Clique clique **IV U2**, 48
Clown clown **II**
Cola coke **I**
Comedian comedian **II**
Comedy Show comedy show **II**
Comic comic **II**; graphic novel **III**
Comicheft comic **II**
Computer computer **I**
Computerunterricht Technology **II**
cool cool **I**
aus **Cornwall** Cornish **III**
Couch sofa **I**
Cousin/Cousine cousin **I**
Cover cover **III**
Coverversion cover version **III**
Cowboy cowboy **IV U3**, 72
Creme cream **I**
Cricket cricket **II**
Curry (*Gewürz oder Gericht*) curry **I**

D

da sein *to be around **IV U2**, 44
da because **I**; since **IV U3**, 72
da there **I**
  da ist/sind there is/are **I**
dabei sein *to be in **II**
  mit **dabei** along for the ride **IV U2**, 44
Dach roof **III**

Dachboden loft **I**; attic **II**
Wohnung mit **Dachterrasse** penthouse
  IV U3, 79
etwas **dagegen** haben to mind **IV U2**, 46
  Ich habe nichts **dagegen** (zu) … I don't
  mind … (*+ -ing*) **III**
dahin there **I**
damals back then **III**; at the time **IV TS3**, 102
Dame lady **III**
  Sehr geehrte **Dame**, sehr geehrter Herr
  Dear Sir or Madam **III**
damit so (that) **IV AC3**, 69
Dampf steam **III**
Dampfmaschine steam engine **III**
danach then; after that **I**
dankbar thankful **I**
Dankbarkeit gratitude **III**
Danke! Cheers! **III**
Danke. Thank you.; Thanks. **I**
danken to thank **II**; *to give thanks **IV U2**, 45
  Nichts zu **danken**. You're welcome. **I**
dann then **I**
darauf zu towards **II**
das the **I**
das that **II**
  Das (hier) ist … This is … **I**
  Das macht … That's … **I**
  Das war knapp! That was close! **I**
das (*Relativpronomen*) which **II**
dass that **I**
Date date **IV U2**, 55
Datum date **I**
dauern *to take **II**
Daumen thumb **II**
  die **Daumen** drücken *to keep your
  fingers crossed **I**
davonkommen mit *to get away with **II**
dazwischen in between **III**
Deck deck **I**
Definition definition **III**
definitiv definitely **III**
dein/-e your **I**
dein/-er/-e/-es yours **II**
Dekoration decorations (*pl*) **I**
dekorieren to decorate **I**
Delfin dolphin **III**
dem (*Relativpronomen*) who; which **II**
Demonstrant/-in protester **IV U2**, 52
demonstrieren to demonstrate **IV U2**, 48
  demonstrieren (für) to campaign (for) **III**
den (*Relativpronomen*) who; which **II**
denken *to think **I**
  Denke/Denkt an … Think of … **I**
  denken an to remember **I**
  denken über *to think of **I**
Denkmal monument **III**
dennoch still **II**
  und **dennoch** yet **IV U3**, 76
deprimierend depressing **IV U1**, 17
der the **I**

der; **dem**; **den**; **die**; **das** (*Relativpronomen*)
  that **II**
der (*Relativpronomen*) who; which **II**
deren (*Relativpronomen*) whose **II**
der-/die-/dasselbe the same **I**
Desaster disaster **II**
deshalb that's why **II**
Design design **II**
Designer/-in designer **III**
dessen (*Relativpronomen*) whose **II**
Detail detail **II**
  nach **Details** durchsuchen to scan **II**
Detektiv/-in detective **II**
Detektivgeschichte detective **III**
deutlich clear **I**
Deutsch German **I**
deutsch German **I**
Deutsche/-r German **I**
aus **Deutschland** German **I**
Dezember December **I**
Diagramm diagram **I**
Dialekt dialect **III**
Dialog dialogue **I**
dicht dense **IV AC2**, 40
dick (*nicht für Personen*) thick **III**
die (*auch Pl.*) the **I**
die (*Relativpronomen*) who; which **II**
Diele hall **III**; hallway **IV U2**, 43
Dienst service **IV U3**, 72
Dienstag Tuesday **I**
Dienstleistung service **IV U3**, 72
dies this **I**
diese (*hier*) these **I**
  diese dort those **I**
dlese/-r/-s this **I**
Dilemma dilemma **IV TS1**, 31
Ding thing **I**
Dinosaurier dinosaur **II**
direkt direct **III**
direkte Rede direct speech **IV U1**, 11
direkt straight **IV U1**, 17; right **IV U2**, 52
Discjockey DJ **III**
Diskussion discussion **II**
diskutieren to discuss **I**
Distanz distance **II**
Distel thistle **III**
Distrikt district **IV U3**, 70
DJ DJ **III**
doch after all **I**
doch yet **IV U3**, 76; though **IV AC4**, 106
dokumentieren to document (**IV TS3**, 101)
Dollar (*Währung*) dollar **III**
ein Gespräch **dominieren** to hog a conver-
  sation **III**
Domino dominoes **IV U1**, 20
Donner thunder (*no pl*) **II**
donnernd roaring **III**
Donnerstag Thursday **I**
doof silly **I**
Doppel- double **IV U2**, 57
Dorf village **I**
dort there **I**

dorthin there **I**
Dose can **I**
 aus der **Dose** tinned **I**
Dosen- tinned **I**
Drama drama **II**
dramatisch dramatic **II**
dran kommen to reach **II**
Du bist **dran**. Your turn.; It's your turn. **I**
draußen outside **I**
 draußen bleiben *to keep out (of) **III**
 draußen halten *to keep out (of) **III**
 nach **draußen** out **I**
Dreck dirt **III**
dreckig dirty **II**
Drehbuch script **III**
drehen to film; to turn **III**
 sich im Kreis **drehen** *to go round in circles **III**
Drehort set **III**
drei three **I**
eine **Dreiergruppe** a group of three **I**
dreizehn thirteen **I**
drin inside **I**
dritte/-r/-s third **I**
dröhnen to boom; to roar **III**
dröhnend roaring **III**
Druck- print **II**
drücken to press **II**
 die Daumen **drücken** *to keep your fingers crossed **I**
Dschungel jungle **IV U3**, 70
du you; u (= you) **I**
 Du auch? You too? **I**
 Du bist dran. Your turn.; It's your turn. **I**
 Du bist … You're … **I**
 Du solltest lieber … You'd better … (= You had better) **IV AC3**, 69
 Du weißt, wie man … You know how to … **I**
du/dir/dich/Sie/sich (selbst) yourself **I**
sich **ducken** to cringe **IV U3**, 91
Dudelsack bagpipes (pl) **III**
duften *to smell **III**
dumm silly **I**; stupid **II**
 Zu **dumm**! Too bad! **I**
Dummkopf silly **II**
dunkel dark **II**
Dunkelheit the dark **II**; darkness **III**
dünn sparse **IV AC2**, 38
Dunst mist (**IV U3**, 90)
durch through **I**
Durchbruch break **IV U3**, 76
durchdrehen *to go crazy **II**
Durcheinander chaos **III**; mess **IV U2**, 54
etw. **durcheinanderbringen** to mess sth up **IV TS1**, 30
durchführen to conduct **IV U3**, 92
schmaler **Durchgang** close **III**
Durchsage announcement **III**
durchsagen to announce **IV TS3**, 101
nach Details **durchsuchen** to scan **II**

dürfen can **I**; *to be allowed to (do sth); *to be able to (do sth); may **II**
 nicht **dürfen** mustn't **I**
durstig thirsty **III**
Dusche shower **I**
DVD DVD **I**

E

Ebbe low tide **II**
ebenso wie so is **III**
echt real **II**
Ecke corner **II**
Edelstein jewel **III**
(der Garten) **Eden** Eden **III**
Effekt effect **IV U3**, 89
 audiovisueller **Effekt** audio-visual effect **II**
effektiv effective **IV TS2**, 66
Effektivität effectiveness **IV TS2**, 67
egal (was/welche) whatever **IV AC4**, 107
 Es ist **egal**. It doesn't matter. **III**
Ehefrau wife, wives (pl) **II**
Ehemann husband **II**
ehrlich honest **III**
Ei egg **I**
Eiche oak **III**
Eichhörnchen squirrel **I**
eifersüchtig sein (auf) *to be jealous (of) **I**
eigen of one's own **III**
eigene/-r/-s own **I**
Eigenschaft feature **III**
Eigenschaftswort adjective **II**
eilen to hurry **I**
Eimer bucket **II**
ein/-e a; an **I**
 ein paar a couple of **I**
 ein wenig a little **I**
 ein/-e andere/-r/-s another **I**
 noch **ein**/-e another **I**
einander each other **I**
einbeziehen to include **III**; to involve **IV TS3**, 102
einbiegen to turn **I**
Einchecken Check-in **I**
eindeutig definitely **III**
eindringen (in) to invade **III**
Eindruck impression **IV U2**, 42
eine/-r/-s one (sg)/ones (pl) **II**
Einerseits …, (aber) andererseits … On the one hand …, (but) on the other hand … **II**
einfach easy **I**; simple **III**
 einfache Fahrkarte one-way ticket; single ticket **III**
 einfach nur simply **IV AC2**, 40
einfach just **I**
Einfall idea **I**
sich etwas **einfallen** lassen *to think of **II**
einfallsreich imaginative **III**
einfangen to capture **III**
einführen to introduce **IV U1**, 11

Einführung introduction **II**; lead-in **IV U3**, 89
Eingang entrance **III**
eingängig catchy **III**
eingeklemmt crushed **IV U1**, 16
eingequetscht crushed **IV U1**, 16
eingeschlossen sein *to be trapped **III**
eingießen to pour **I**
Einheit unit **I**
die Segel **einholen** to reef the sails **I**
einige some; a few **I**; several **III**
sich **einigen** (auf) to agree (on) **III**
Einkäufe machen *to do the shopping **III**
Einkäufe shopping **I**
Einkaufen shopping **I**
einkaufen to shop **IV U3**, 76
 einkaufen gehen *to go shopping **I**
Einkaufszentrum shopping mall **IV U2**, 43
einladen to invite **I**
Einladung invitation **I**
einleiten to introduce **IV U1**, 11
Einleitung introduction **II**; lead-in **IV U3**, 89
einleuchten *to make sense **IV TS3**, 102
einmal once **I**
einmarschieren (in) to invade **III**
einpacken to wrap **I**
einprägsam catchy **III**
Einreise immigration **IV U1**, 13
Einreisebewilligung visa, visas (pl) **IV U1**, 9
einrichten *to set up **I**
eins one **I**
einschenken to pour **I**
einschlafen *to fall asleep **I**
einschließen to include **III**
einsortieren to sort into **III**
einst once **I**
einsteigen *to get into **I**; *to get in **IV U3**, 76
einsteigen (in den Bus) *to get on (the bus) **III**
Einstellung shot **II**; attitude **IV U2**, 55
einstufen to rate **IV TS3**, 104
Eintrag entry **III**
eintreten to enter **II**
Eintritt entrance **II**
Eintrittskarte ticket **I**
nicht **einverstanden** sein to disagree **III**
Einwanderer/-in immigrant **IV AC2**, 38
Einwanderung immigration **IV U1**, 13
Einwanderungsbehörde immigration office **IV U1**, 13
einwickeln to wrap **I**
Einzelheit detail **II**
Einzelkind only child **I**
einzeln individual **II**; single **IV AC2**, 38
Einzelne/-r individual **IV U2**, 56
Einzelperson individual **IV U2**, 56
einziehen in to move in/into **III**
einzig single **IV AC2**, 38
einzige/-r/-s only **II**
Eis ice; ice cream **I**
Eisbahn ice rink **I**

Eisbrecher *(Sätze, um mit jmdm. ins Gespräch zu kommen)* icebreaker **IV AC1**, 23
Eiscreme ice cream **I**
Elefant elephant **III**
Elektrik electrics **III**
Elektriker/-in electrician **III**
elektrisch electric **III**
Elektrizität electricity **III**
elektronisch electronic **II**
Element element **III**
elf eleven **I**
Elfenbein ivory *(no pl)* **III**
Eltern parents *(pl)* **I**
E-Mail e-mail **I**
   per **E-Mail** schicken to mail **II**
emotional emotional **III**
Empfang signal **III**
empfangen to receive **II**
empfänglich receptive **IV TS2**, 64
Ende ending; end **I**
   am **Ende** at the back of **II**
enden to finish **I**; to end up; to end **II**
endgültig final **II**
endlich at last **I**; finally **II**
endlos endless **IV AC2**, 38
Energie energy **III**
eng close **I**; narrow **III**
sich engagieren *(für)* to campaign (for) **III**
Engel angel **IV TS1**, 31
aus England English **I**
Brite/Britin *(ugs.)* Brit **IV AC2**, 41
Engländer/-in English **I**
   Ich bin **Engländer/-in**. I'm English. **I**
Englisch English **I**
englisch English **I**
englischsprachig English-speaking **I**
entdecken to discover **II**
Entdeckung discovery **III**
auf **Entdeckungsreise** gehen to explore **I**
Entertainer/-in entertainer **IV U3**, 72
Entfernung distance **II**
entfliehen to escape (from) **IV U2**, 52
entgegen allen Erwartungen against all odds **III**
eine Nachricht **entgegennehmen** *to take a message* **I**
   einen Anruf **entgegennehmen** to answer the phone **I**
entgegnen to reply **I**
Entgegnung reply **I**
enthalten to contain **IV U1**, 15
Enthusiasmus enthusiasm **IV U3**, 72
entkommen to escape (from) **IV U2**, 52
entlang along **I**
entlanggehen *to go down **I***
entrümpeln to clear out **I**; to clean out **IV U2**, 51
(sich) entscheiden to decide **I**
Entscheidung decision **III**
   eine **Entscheidung** treffen *to make a decision* **II**

Entschuldigen Sie! Excuse me … **I**
sich entschuldigen to apologise **III**
Entschuldigung! Sorry!; Excuse me … **I**
entsetzt horrified **I**
sich entspannen to relax **II**
entspannt laid-back **III**
entsprechen to match **I**
enttäuschend disappointing **IV TS3**, 104
enttäuscht disappointed **I**
entweder … oder … either … or … **IV U3**, 79
entwerfen to design **II**
eine Geschichte langsam **entwickeln** to step into a story slowly **III**
gut **entwickelt** well-developed **IV TS3**, 105
Entwurf plan; draft **I**; design **II**
episch epic **IV AC2**, 41
er he **I**
Erdboden earth **II**; ground **IV U1**, 17
Erde world **I**; earth **II**
   die **Erde** earth **II**
erdichtet fictional **III**
Erdkunde geography **III**
Erdteil continent **IV U3**, 74
Ereignis event **I**
erfahren to experience **III**
   erfahren über *to learn about* **III**
Erfahrung experience **II**
erfinden to create **I**; to invent **III**
Erfinder/-in inventor **III**
Erfindung invention; fiction *(no pl)* **III**
Erfolg success **III**
   Erfolg haben (in/bei/mit) to succeed (in) **III**
erfolgreich successful **III**
erforschen to explore **I**
in **Erfüllung** gehen *to come true* **IV U3**, 76
ergänzen to add **I**
Ergebnis result **II**
ergreifen to grab **II**; to capture **III**
erhalten to receive **II**
erhältlich available **IV TS2**, 65
sich erheben *to rise* **III**
(jmdn. an etw./jmdn.) erinnern to remind (sb of sth/sb) **III**
   sich erinnern (an) to remember **I**
   Erinnerst du dich? Remember? **I**
   Erinnert ihr euch? Remember? **I**
Erinnerung memory **II**
Erkältung cold **II**
erkennen to realise **III**; to realize *(AE)* **IV U2**, 52
erklären to explain **I**
Erklärung statement **II**
erkunden to explore **I**
Erlaubnis, *sich während des Unterrichts auf dem Flur aufzuhalten* hall pass **IV U2**, 43
erleben to experience **III**
Erleuchtung enlightenment **IV U3**, 74
ernähren *to feed* **III**
ernst serious **I**
ernsthaft serious **I**

Ernte harvest **IV U2**, 45
eröffnen to open **IV U2**, 52
erraten to guess **I**
erreichen *to get to* **I**; to reach **II**
errichten *to put up* **II**
Ersatz substitute **II**
Ersatz- substitute **II**
erschaffen to create **I**
erst only **I**
   erst um/im not until **IV U2**, 44
   erst wenn until **II**
erstaunlich amazing **II**
erstaunt amazed **IV U2**, 52
erste/-r/-s first **I**
   als **Erstes** first **I**
ertappt caught on camera **II**
   ertappt werden *to get caught* **IV AC3**, 68
ertränken to drown **III**
ertrinken to drown **III**
erwachsen werden *to grow up* **III**
Erwachsene/-r adult **II**
erwähnen to mention **II**
erwarten to expect **III**
entgegen allen **Erwartungen** against all odds **III**
erwidern to reply **I**
Erwiderung reply **I**
erwischt werden *to get caught* **IV AC3**, 68
erzählen *to tell* **I**
   erzählen von to talk about … **I**
   nochmals **erzählen** *to retell* **I**
   Erzähle mir von … Tell me about … **I**
Erzähler/-in narrator **I**
   Er/Sie-**Erzähler/-in** third person narrator **III**
Erzählliteratur fiction *(no pl)* **III**
Erzählperspektive narrative perspective **III**
Erzählung story, stories *(pl)* **I**
Erzeugnis product **IV TS2**, 64
Erziehung education *(no pl)* **III**
es it **I**
Essen food **I**; meal **II**
(ein Bonbon) essen *to have (a sweet)* **I**
essen *to eat* **I**
ethnisch ethnic **IV U3**, 75
etwa about **I**
etwas some; something; a little **I**
euer/eure your **I**
eure/-r/-s yours **II**
Euro *(Währung)* euro **I**
aus Europa European **IV AC2**, 38
Europäer/-in European **IV AC2**, 38
europäisch European **IV AC2**, 38
ewig forever **II**
Examen exam **II**
hier: exotisch ethnic **IV U3**, 75
Experte/Expertin expert **II**
extra extra **I**
extrem extreme **IV AC2**, 40

F

Fabrik factory **III**
Fackel torch **II**
fähig sein zu *to be able to (do sth) **II**
Fahne flag **III**
Fähre ferry **IV U1**, 9
fahren *to go **I**; to travel **II**; *to drive **III**; *to ride raid **IV AC2**, 41
   Fahrrad **fahren** to cycle **IV U2**, 46
   Grad **Fahrenheit** degree Fahrenheit (°F) **IV AC2**, 38
Fahrer/-in driver **II**
Fahrgast passenger **IV U1**, 9
einfache **Fahrkarte** one-way ticket; single ticket **III**
Fahrplan timetable **I**; schedule (AE) **IV AC4**, 106
Fahrpreis fare **III**
Fahrrad bike **I**
   Fahrrad **fahren** to cycle **IV U2**, 46
Fahrradmotocross bicycle motocross **II**
Fahrschein ticket **III**
Fahrt trip; tour **II**; journey **III**; drive; ride **IV U2**, 44
fair fair **I**
Fairplay fair play **III**
Fakt fact **II**
in der **Falle** sitzen *to be trapped **III**
fallen *to fall **I**
   fallen (lassen) to drop **II**
falls if **I**
falsch wrong **I**; fake **IV TS1**, 35
fälschen to fake **II**
Familie family **I**
Fan fan **II**
fangen *to catch **II**
Fantasie fantasy **I**; imagination **III**
fantasievoll imaginative **III**
fantastisch fantastic **II**; fabulous **IV TS2**, 66
Fantasy fantasy **III**
Fanzeitschrift fanzine **II**
Farbe colour **I**
   Welche **Farbe** hat …? What colour is …? **I**
farbenfroh colourful **I**
Farm farm **I**
Farmer/-in farmer **II**
aus der **Fassung** bringen *to upset **III**
fast nearly; almost **II**
Fastnachtsdienstag Shrove Tuesday **I**
faszinierend fascinating **III**
faul lazy **III**
Favorit/-in favourite **III**
Februar February **I**
Feder feather **III**
Federkiel quill **III**
Federmäppchen pencil-case **I**
Feedback feedback **II**
Was **fehlt?** What is missing? **I**
fehlend missing **II**
Fehler mistake **I**
Feier party **I**

feiern to celebrate **I**
Feiertag holiday **I**
Feind/-in enemy **III**
Feld field **II**
felsig rocky **III**
Fenster window **I**
Fensterladen shutter **IV U1**, 10
Ferien holidays (pl) **I**; vacation (AE) **IV AC2**, 41
fernbleiben von to stay away from **II**
(sich) **fernhalten** von *to keep away from **III**
Fernsehen TV **I**
fernsehen to watch TV **I**
Fernseher TV **I**
fertig ready; finished **II**
   fertig sein mit *to be done with **IV U3**, 76
Fertiggericht ready meal **I**
Fertigkeit skill **I**
fertigstellen to finish **I**; to complete **IV AC3**, 68
fesseln (an) to tie (to) **III**
Fest festival **I**
festhalten *to hold **I**
   (sich) **festhalten** an *to hold onto **III**
Festival festival **I**
festnehmen to arrest **II**
feststecken in … stuck in the middle of … **III**
fett gedruckt bold **III**
Feuer fire **III**
Feuerwerk fireworks (pl) **I**
   hier: ein **Feuerwerk** zünden *to set off **III**
Fieber fever **II**
Figur character **I**; figure **II**
Fiktion fiction (no pl) **III**
fiktional fictional **III**
fiktiv fictional **III**
Film film **I**; movie (AE) **IV U2**, 44
Filmemacher/-in filmmaker **II**
filmen to film **III**
finden *to find **I**
Finger finger **I**
Firma company **III**
Fisch fish, fish (pl) **I**
Fischen fishing **III**
Fischerei fishing **III**
fit werden *to get fit **I**
flach flat **IV AC2**, 40
Fläche space; area **II**
Flagge flag **III**
Flair flair **II**
Flamme flame **III**
Flasche bottle **I**
Flashback flashback **III**
Fleck spot **IV U3**, 75
Fleisch meat (no pl) **III**
fliegen *to fly **III**
fliehen to escape (from) **IV U2**, 52
Flohmarkt flea market **I**
Flöte recorder **III**
Flucht escape **III**
flüchten to escape (from) **IV U2**, 52

Flüchtling refugee **IV U1**, 18
Flug flight **III**
Flugbegleiter/-in flight attendant **IV U1**, 9
Flughafen airport **II**
Flugsteig gate **IV U1**, 15
Flugzeug plane **IV U1**, 8
Flur hall **III**; hallway **IV U2**, 43; corridor **IV AC3**, 68
Fluss river **I**
   am **Fluss** by the river **II**
flüstern to whisper **I**
Flut high tide **II**
Flyer flyer **I**
Fokus focus **III**
Folge consequence **IV AC3**, 68
Folge- follow-up **IV U3**, 92
folgen to follow **II**
folgende/-r/-s the following **III**
Form form **I**; shape **IV U3**, 89
   in **Form** kommen *to get fit **I**
   verneinte **Form** negative form **I**
formal formal **II**
formell formal **II**
formen to form **II**
förmlich formal **II**
Formular form **III**
Forschung research (no pl) **III**
hier: sich **fortbewegen** *to get around **II**
fortfahren *to go on **I**; to continue **III**
fortlaufend consecutive **IV U3**, 89
Fortschritt progress **II**
Fortsetzung follow-up **IV U3**, 92
Forum forum **I**
Foto photo; picture **I**
   auf dem **Foto**/den **Fotos** in the photo(s) **I**
   Fotos machen *to take photos **I**
   ins **Foto** laufen to photobomb **III**
Fotoapparat camera **II**
Fotoaufnahmen photo shoot **III**
Fotograf/-in photographer **III**
Fotografie photo **I**
fotografieren *to take photos **I**
Fotoshooting photo shoot **III**
Fotostory photo story **I**
Frage question **I**
Frageanhängsel question tag **II**
Fragebogen questionnaire **III**
fragen to ask **I**; to question **IV TS3**, 103
   Frage/Fragt nach … Ask about … **I**
   fragen nach to ask for **I**
Französisch French **II**
französisch French **II**
Frau woman, women (pl) **I**
Frau (Anrede) Mrs **I**
Fräulein (Anrede) Miss **III**
frei free **I**
Freiheit freedom (no pl) **III**; liberty **IV U3**, 74
Freiluft- outdoor **II**
sich den Tag **freinehmen** *to take the day off **IV U3**, 72
Freitag Friday **I**
Freizeit free time; leisure **I**

Freizeitzentrum leisure centre **I**
fremd strange **I**; foreign **IV U1**, 8
Fremdsprache foreign language **II**
fressen *to eat **I**
Freude fun **I**
Freudenfeuer bonfire **I**
sich **freuen auf** to look forward to **II**
    sich **freuen an** to enjoy **II**
Freund (in einer Paarbeziehung) boyfriend
    IV U2, 55
Freund/-in friend **I**
    Dafür sind **Freunde** da. That's what
    friends are for. **I**
Freundin (in einer Paarbeziehung) girlfriend
    II
freundlich friendly **II**
Freundschaft friendship **II**
    Freundschaft schließen *to make friends
    II; *to become friends **IV AC2**, 41
frisch fresh **I**
uns **frisieren** *to do our hair **I**
froh happy **I**; glad **IV AC1**, 23
fröhlich happy; fun **I**
Front- front **III**
Frucht fruit **I**
früh early **I**
    so **früh** this early **III**
Frühling spring **III**
Frühstück breakfast **I**
frühstücken *to have breakfast **I**
Frühstückszerealie cereal (no pl) **I**
Fuchs fox **II**
fühlen *to feel **I**
    sich **fühlen** *to feel **I**
    sich ausgeschlossen **fühlen** *to feel left
    out **II**
    sich schlecht **fühlen** *to feel sick **II**
führen to guide; *to lead **III**; *to run
    IV TS3, 102
Führer/-in guide **II**
(sich) **füllen** to fill **III**
Füller pen **I**
Füllung filling **IV U3**, 75
fünf five **I**
fünfzehn fifteen **I**
Funktion function **IV TS3**, 103
funktionieren to work **II**; to work out **III**
für for **I**
    für mich on my own **II**
    Für wen …? Who … for? **I**
Furcht fear **II**
furchtbar awful **I**
(sich) **fürchten** *to be afraid (of) **IV U1**, 8
Fuß foot, feet (pl) **I**
    zu **Fuß** on foot **II**
Fuß (Längenmaß: 30,48 cm) foot, feet (pl)
    IV AC2, 39
Fußball football **I**; soccer (AE) **IV U2**, 44
Fußboden floor **I**
Fußbodenheizung underfloor heating (no
    pl) **III**
Fußgelenk ankle **II**

Fußknöchel ankle **II**
Futter food **III**
füttern *to feed **III**

G

Gabel fork **III**
Gälisch Gaelic **III**
gälisch Gaelic **III**
Gang corridor **IV AC3**, 68
ganz all **I**
    den **ganzen** Tag all day **II**
ganz quite **IV U1**, 14
ganz whole **I**
Garage garage **I**
garstig nasty **II**
Garten garden **I**; backyard **III**; yard **IV U2**, 43
Gast guest **III**
Gastfamilie host family **III**
Gaststätte restaurant **I**
Gate gate **IV U1**, 15
Gattung genre **III**
Geächtete/-r outlaw **III**
Gebärde gesture **IV TS1**, 33
Gebäude building **I**
geben *to give **I**
    es **gibt** there is/are **I**
Gebiet area **II**
geboren werden *to be born **III**
Ge- und Verbote dos and don'ts **IV AC1**, 22
gebraten (in der Pfanne) fried **IV U3**, 75
gebrauchen to use **I**
gebrochen broken **I**
Gebühr fee **III**
Geburtsdatum date of birth **IV U1**, 13
Geburtstag birthday **I**
    Alles Gute zum **Geburtstag**! Happy
    Birthday! **I**
    Herzlichen Glückwunsch zum **Geburtstag**!
    Happy Birthday! **I**
Gedächtnis memory **II**
Gedanke thought **II**
Gedicht poem **I**
gedruckt print **II**
Sehr **geehrte** Dame, sehr **geehrter** Herr
    Dear Sir or Madam **III**
Gefahr danger **III**
gefährlich dangerous **I**
Mir **gefällt** … I like … **I**
gefälscht fake **IV TS1**, 35
Gefängnis prison **II**
Gefühl feeling **II**
Gefühls- emotional **III**
gegen against **II**; versus (vs.) **III**
Gegend region **II**
Gegensatz contrast **IV AC2**, 38
sich **gegenseitig** each other **I**
Gegenstand object **III**; item **IV U2**, 51
gegenüber stehen to face **IV TS1**, 31
gegenüber opposite **I**
Gegenwart present **II**
Gegenwarts- present **III**

Gehege run area **III**
geheim secret **III**
Geheimnis secret **II**; mystery **III**
geheimnisvoll mysterious **III**
gehen *to go; to walk **I**
    aus dem Weg **gehen** to avoid **III**
    ins Bett **gehen** *to go to bed **I**
    nach unten **gehen** *to go down **I**
    zu jmdm. nach Hause **gehen** *to go over
    to **II**
    Wie **geht** es dir? How are you? **I**
    Wie **geht** es euch? How are you? **I**
    Wie **geht** es Ihnen? How are you? **I**
nicht **gehorchen** to disobey **III**
gehören (zu) to belong (to) **II**
    gehören zu *to go with **I**
    zueinander **gehören** *to go together **I**
Gehsteig sidewalk (AE) **IV U3**, 76
Gehweg sidewalk (AE) **IV U3**, 76
hier: **geil** epic **IV AC2**, 41
Geist ghost **II**; mind **III**
gelangweilt bored **I**
gelb yellow **I**
Geld money **I**
    Geld sammeln to raise money **II**
    Geld verdienen *to make money **I**
    für/mit wenig **Geld** on a shoestring
    IV U3, 72
Geldschein bill (AE) **IV U3**, 76
Gelee jelly **I**
Gelegenheit chance **II**
als etw. **gelten** *to be considered (to be) sth
    IV TS3, 100
Gemälde painting **II**
gemein nasty **II**; mean **IV TS1**, 33
Gemeindezentrum community centre **I**
gemeinsam together **I**
    gemeinsam haben *to have in common
    III
Gemüse vegetable **III**
genannt werden *to be called **III**
genau exactly **II**
    genau hier right here **II**
genauso wie the same way as **II**
Generation generation **III**
Genie genius **II**
genießen to enjoy **II**
Gentleman gentleman, gentlemen (pl) **III**
genug enough **I**
genügend enough **I**
Geocaching geocaching **III**
geöffnet open **I**
Geografie geography **III**
Gepäck luggage (no pl) **IV U1**, 8
gerade straight **IV U1**, 17
gerade just; at the moment **I**; right now **II**
    gerade rechtzeitig just in time **IV U3**, 72
geradeaus straight on **I**
geradewegs straight **IV U1**, 17
Gerät machine **I**; tool; gadget **III**
Geräusch sound **I**; noise **II**
gerecht fair **I**

Gericht dish **IV U2**, 45
Gern geschehen. You're welcome. **I**
gern haben to like **I**
    gern mögen to love **I**
    hätte/-st/-n/-t **gern** would like **I**
    hätte/-st-/-n/-t sehr **gern** would love **I**
    würde/-st/-n/-t **gern** would like **I**
    würde/-st/-n/-t sehr **gern** would love **I**
Gerümpel rubbish **I**
Geschäft shop **I**; business **III**; store (AE) **IV U2**, 44
Geschäftsmann businessman **IV U3**, 76
geschehen to happen **I**
Geschenk present **I**
Geschichte story, stories (pl) **I**; history **II**
    eine **Geschichte** langsam entwickeln to step into a story slowly **III**
geschichtlich historical **I**
Geschick skill **I**
geschlossen closed **IV U1**, 11
Geschmack flavor (AE) **IV U3**, 75
geschockt shocked **IV TS1**, 37
gut **geschrieben** well-written **IV TS3**, 104
    schlecht **geschrieben** badly-written **IV TS3**, 105
Geschwindigkeit speed **IV U3**, 89
Gesellschaft society; company **III**
gesellschaftlich social **IV U2**, 46
Gesetzlose/-r outlaw **III**
Gesicht face **I**
Gesichtsausdruck facial expression **III**
Gespräch dialogue; conversation **I**; talk **IV U3**, 92
    ein **Gespräch** dominieren to hog a conversation **III**
    ein **Gespräch** für sich in Beschlag nehmen to hog a conversation **III**
    hier: das **Gespräch** am Laufen halten *to keep the ball bouncing **III**
gesprochen spoken **II**
Gestalt figure **II**
gestalten to design **II**
Gestaltung design **II**
Geste gesture **IV TS1**, 33
gestern yesterday **II**
völlig **gestresst** sein *to be stressed out **III**
gesund healthy **I**
Gesundheit health **II**
Getränk drink **I**
Getreide corn **IV AC2**, 41
getrennt separate **II**
Gewalt violence (no pl) **III**
gewaltig huge **II**
gewaltsam violent **III**
gewalttätig violent **III**
Gewerbe industry **III**
Gewicht weight **III**
Gewinn prize **I**
gewinnen *to win **I**
    jmdn. für sich **gewinnen** *to win sb over **IV TS2**, 64
Gewinner/-in winner **I**; champion **III**

Gewissen conscience **IV TS1**, 31
sich an etw. **gewöhnen** *to get used to sth **IV U2**, 44
Gewohnheit custom **IV AC1**, 22
gewöhnlich usually **I**
gewohnt sein *to be used to (+ -ing) **III**
gewöhnt sein an *to be used to (+ -ing) **III**
Gig gig **III**
gigantisch gigantic **IV AC2**, 40
Gipsverband plaster cast **III**
Gitarre guitar **IV U1**, 19
Gitter grid **I**
glamourös glamorous **IV TS2**, 65
glänzen *to shine **II**
Glas glass **I**
glauben *to think; to believe **I**
gläubig religious **I**
glaubwürdig believable **IV U2**, 52
der/die/das **gleiche** the same **I**
gleich right away **I**; straight away **III**; immediately **IV TS2**, 64
    jetzt **gleich** right now **II**
gleichmäßig regular **II**
gleichzeitig at the same time **I**
Gliederung structure **III**
Glocke bell **II**
Glossar glossary **IV TS1**, 30
Glück haben *to be lucky **II**
    noch mal **Glück** gehabt saved by the bell **III**
    (viel) **Glück** good luck **IV U3**, 76
    Was für ein **Glück**! What luck! **III**
    … hat/haben **Glück**. … is/are lucky. **I**
glücklich happy **I**
glücklicherweise luckily **IV U2**, 44
Glücksbringer lucky charm **I**
Gold gold **III**
goldenes Zeitalter golden age **III**
Golf golf **III**
Götterspeise jelly **I**
Göttin goddess **IV U3**, 74
graben *to dig **II**
Grad Fahrenheit degree Fahrenheit (°F) **IV AC2**, 38
Grammatik grammar **II**
grau grey **I**
grausam cruel **III**
greifen to grab **II**
Grenze limit **III**
Griff knob **II**
groß big **I**; tall; high; large **II**
    große Sache big deal **IV U1**, 11
großartig great **I**; fantastic **II**
Großbuchstabe capital letter **I**
Größe size **I**
Großeltern grandparents (pl) **I**
Großstadt city **I**
großzügig generous **III**
grün green **I**
Grund reason **II**
    Es gibt keinen **Grund** zu … There's no need to … **IV TS1**, 36

Grund- basic **II**
gründen to found **III**; to start **III**
Grundlagen basics (pl) **III**
grundlegend basic **II**
Grundschule primary school **I**
Gruppe group **I**; team **II**
Gruppenzwang peer pressure **III**
gruppieren (um) to group (around) **III**
gruselig scary **II**
Gruß greeting **I**
    Grüße ausrichten (an) *to say hello (to) **I**
    Herzliche **Grüße** Best wishes **III**
    Herzliche **Grüße** (am Briefende) Love … **I**
    Liebe **Grüße** (am Briefende) Love … **I**
    Viele **Grüße** Best wishes **III**
    Viele **Grüße** … (am Ende von Briefen und Mails) Yours … **II**
grüßen *to say hello (to) **I**
Günstling favourite **III**
Gürtel belt **III**
gut good; fine **I**
    gut entwickelt well-developed **IV TS3**, 105
    gut geschrieben well-written **IV TS3**, 104
    gut sein in *to be good at **I**
    gute Leistungen erbringen *to do well **IV TS1**, 34
    Guten Morgen. Good morning. **I**
    Mir geht's **gut**. I'm fine. **I**
Guthaben credit **II**
Gymnasium grammar school **III**

H

Haar hair **IV TS2**, 64
Haar(e) hair **I**
Haarbürste hairbrush **III**
Haare hair **IV TS2**, 64
    unsere **Haare** machen *to do our hair **I**
haben *to have got; *to have **I**
    hätte/-st/-n/-t gern would like **I**
    hätte/-st-/-n/-t sehr gern would love **I**
    nicht ganz Unrecht **haben** *to have a point **III**
Hafen harbour **III**
Hafendamm pier **I**
Haft detention **IV AC3**, 68
Haggis (schottisches Gericht aus in einem Schafsmagen gekochten Schafsinnereien und Haferschrot) haggis **III**
Hähnchen chicken **I**
Hai shark **IV U1**, 16
halb half **I**
    halb (bei Uhrzeitangaben) half past **I**
    eine **halbe** Stunde half an hour **III**
Halbjahresferien half-term break **I**
Halbschwester half-sister **I**
Halbtotale (Kameraeinstellung) medium shot **IV U3**, 89
die **Hälfte** half, halves (pl) (of) **I**
Halle hall **II**
Hallo. Hello.; Hi.; Hey! **I**
Halskette necklace **III**

Halt stop II
halten *to hold; *to keep I
   halten von *to think of I
Haltestelle station I; stop II
Haltung attitude IV U2, 55; pose IV U2, 56
Hamburger burger I
Hammer hammer II
Hand hand I
   Klatsch/Klatscht in die **Hände**. Clap your
   hands. I
Handbuch planner I
sich **handeln** um *to be about I
Handgelenk wrist II
Händler merchant II
Handlung action I; plot III
Handlungsort location II
Handschuh glove I
Handy phone I; mobile II; cell phone (AE)
   IV AC3, 68
jmdn. **hänseln** to tease sb III
Happy End happy ending III
hart hard II; harsh IV AC2, 40
hassen to hate II
hässlich ugly IV TS2, 67
häufig often I
   häufig gefragt frequently asked I
Haupt- main I; lead III
die **Haupteinkaufsstraße** the high street III
Hauptfigur protagonist IV TS1, 30
Hauptrolle lead part III
Hauptsatz main clause III
Hauptstadt capital II
Hauptwort noun I
Haus house I
   nach **Hause** home I
   zu **Hause** at home I
   zu jmdm. nach **Hause** gehen *to go over
   to II
Hausarrest haben *to be grounded III
Hausaufgabe(n) homework I
Häuserblock block IV U3, 72
Haustier pet I
Haustür front door II
in jmds. **Haut** stecken *to be in sb's shoes III
He! Hey! I
heben to lift IV U3, 76
Heim home I
Heimatstadt hometown IV U3, 75
heimlich in secret II
Heimweh haben *to be homesick IV U1, 18
heiraten to marry III
heiß hot III
heißen *to be called III
   Ich **heiße** … My name is … I
   Wie **heißen** Sie? What's your name? I
   Wie **heißt** du? What's your name? I
Heizung heating III
Held hero, heroes (pl) III
Heldin heroine III
helfen to help I
hell bright IV U3, 72
Herangehensweise approach IV TS2, 66

heranzoomen (auf) to zoom in (on) III
heraus out I
herausfinden *to find; *to find out I; to work
   out II
herausfordern to challenge IV TS3, 101
Herausforderung challenge II
herausschneiden to edit out III
Es **stellte** sich **heraus**, dass … It turned out
   that … IV U1, 20
Herberge hostel IV U1, 10
Herd cooker I
herein in I
hereinfallen auf *to fall for IV TS2, 64
hereinkommen *to come in III
Herkunft origin IV U1, 19
Herr lord III
   feiner **Herr** gentleman, gentlemen (pl) III
   Herr der Raben raven master II
   Sehr geehrte Dame, sehr geehrter **Herr**
   Dear Sir or Madam III
Herr (Anrede) Mr I
herrisch bossy III
Herrschaft reign II
herrschen to rule; to reign III
die **Herrschenden** those in power III
herstellen to produce III
um … **herum** around I
herumschleichen to sneak around II
sich **herumtreiben** (mit) *to hang out (with)
   (infml) III
herunter down II
herunterfallen *to fall off II
herunterkommen *to come down I
herunterladen (aus dem Internet) to
   download II
herunternehmen *to take off I
herunterrollen to roll off II
hervorheben to stress III
Herz heart II
Herzliche Grüße Best wishes III
   Herzliche Grüße (am Briefende) Love … I
heute today I
   heute Abend 2nite (= tonight) I; tonight
   IV TS1, 31
   heute Nachmittag this afternoon II
   heute Nacht tonight IV TS1, 31
heutig present III
Hi. Hi.; Hey! I
hier here I
   genau **hier** right here II
   Hier ist … Here's … I
High School (weiterführende Schule in den
   USA, Oberstufe) high school (AE) IV U2, 43
Highlight highlight II
Hilfe help I
   ohne fremde **Hilfe** alone I
hilflos helpless I
hilfreich useful; helpful I
hilfsbereit helpful I
Himmel sky III
hinauf up II
hinaus out I

hinausfließen to flow out II
hinausgehen *to go out III
hinein inside I
hineingehen to enter II
hineingelangen *to get into I
den Leser/die Leserin in die Geschichte/
   Handlung **hineinziehen** *to draw the
   reader into the story/action III
Hin- und Rückfahrkarte return ticket III
hinfallen *to fall over; *to fall I
wo ich **hingehöre** where I belong IV U1, 16
Hingucker eye-catcher IV TS2, 65
hinkommen *to get there I
hinnehmen to accept IV U1, 16
sich **hinsetzen** *to sit down I
hinten at the back of II
hinter behind I
hinterfragen to question IV TS3, 103
Hintergrund background I
Hintergrund- backing III
hinterhergehen to follow II
Hinterhof backyard III
hinüber over; across I
hinübergehen zu *to go over to II
hinunter down II
hinunterfallen *to fall off II; *to fall down III
hinuntergehen *to go down I
hinunterrollen to roll off II
Hinweis clue II; hint III
hinzufügen to add I
hissen *to fly flai IV AC2, 39
historisch historical I; historic III
Hobby hobby, hobbies (pl) I
hoch tall; high II
hochheben to lift IV U3, 76
hochleben lassen *to give the bumps I
höchst- highly IV TS2, 65
Hochzeit wedding I
Hockey hockey II
Hof yard IV U2, 43
Hofdame lady-in-waiting III
hoffen to hope I
Hoffnung hope II
hoffnungsvoll hopeful I
höflich polite I
   Sei/Seid **höflich**. Be polite. I
Höhepunkt highlight II; climax III
Höhle cave III
holen *to get I; to fetch IV U1, 17
Holz wood III
   aus **Holz** wooden III
hölzern wooden III
Homepage homepage I
Honig honey III
Hoppla! Oops! I
Hör- audio I
horchen auf to listen for I
Hören listening I
hören *to hear I
   Ich habe **gehört**, dass … I hear … I
Horn horn III
Horror horror III

Horrorfilm horror **III**
Horrorgeschichte horror **III**
Hör-/Sehverstehen viewing **I**
Hose trousers (pl) **III**
   kurze **Hose** shorts (pl) **II**
Hosentasche pocket **III**
Hospital hospital **II**
Hotel hotel **II**
hübsch beautiful **II**; pretty **III**; lovely
   IV TS2, 65
Huch! Oops! **I**
jmdn. **Huckepack** nehmen *to give sb a
   piggyback **IV U1**, 16
Hügel hill **III**
Huhn chicken **I**
Hülle wrapping **I**
Humor humour (no pl) **III**
   Sinn für **Humor** sense of humour (no pl)
   III
Hund dog **I**
   den **Hund** ausführen to walk the dog **I**
   mit dem **Hund** spazieren gehen to walk
   the dog **I**
Ich bin **hundemüde**. I'm dog-tired. **I**
Hunderte (von) hundreds of **III**
hungrig hungry **I**
hüpfen to bounce **III**
Hurraruf cheer **IV U2**, 52
Husten cough **II**
Hut hat **I**
hüten to look after **I**
Hymne anthem **III**

I

ich I; me **I**
   Ich bin aus … I'm from … **I**
   Ich bin Engländer/-in. I'm English. **I**
   Ich heiße … My name is … **I**
   Ich mache … nicht gern. I don't like … **I**
   Ich mag … nicht. I don't like … **I**
   Ich möchte … I'd like to … (= I would
   like to) **I**
   Ich weiß (es) nicht! I don't know! **I**
   Ich würde gern … I'd like to … (= I would
   like to) **I**
   ich würde lieber I'd rather **III**
Ich-Erzähler/-in first person narrator **III**
Idee idea **I**
sich **identifizieren mit** to identify with **III**
Identität identity **II**
Idiot/-in idiot **II**
if-Satz if-clause **III**
Igel hedgehog **III**
ignorieren to ignore **III**
ihm him **I**
ihn him **I**
ihnen them **I**
ihr you; u (= you) **I**
Ihr/-e your **I**; yours **II**
ihr/-e her; its **I**
ihr/-e (Pl.) their **I**

illegal illegal **III**
im in; on **I**
   im Begriff sein, etw. zu tun *to be about
   to do sth **IV AC3**, 69
   im Chor in chorus **IV TS1**, 33
   im Innern inside **I**
   im Moment at the moment **I**
   im Weg sein/stehen *to be in the way **I**
Imbiss snack **I**
Imbissstube snack bar **I**
immer always **I**
   für **immer** forever **II**
   immer noch still **I**
   immer wieder over and over again **III**
   immer wieder tun *to keep ki:p **IV U2**, 44
immerhin after all **I**
Immigrant/-in immigrant **IV AC2**, 38
Immigration immigration **IV U1**, 13
Imperativ imperative **III**
Impression impression **IV U2**, 42
in in; on; at; to; into; inside **I**
   in Cornwall Cornish **I**
   in der Nähe von near **I**
   in der Straße in the street **I**
   in Kontakt bleiben *to keep in touch
   IV U2, 44
   in Not in need **II**
   in … hinein into **I**
   in Ordnung OK; fine **I**
indem as **I**
Inder/-in Indian **I**
Indianer/-in Native American; Indian
   IV U2, 45
indianisch Native American; Indian **IV U2**, 45
indirekt indirect **IV U1**, 11
   indirekte Rede indirect speech **IV U1**, 11
indisch Indian **I**
individuell individual **II**
Individuum individual **IV U2**, 56
Industrie industry **III**
Infinitiv infinitive **I**
Informatik IT (= Information Technology) **III**
Information information (no pl) **I**
Informationen information (no pl) **I**
Informationsblatt leaflet **IV AC1**, 23
Informationstechnik IT (= Information
   Technology) **III**
informativ informative **IV U2**, 56
informell informal **IV AC4**, 107
Ingenieur/-in engineer **IV TS3**, 101
Inhalt content **IV U2**, 56
Inlineskates fahren to skate **I**
Inlineskatefahren inline skating **I**
Inlineskates skates (pl) **I**
inmitten among **III**
innen inside **I**
inoffiziell unofficial **III**
Insel island **III**
inserieren to advertise **IV TS2**, 64
inspirieren to inspire **IV U3**, 70
Installateur/-in plumber **III**
Instruktion instruction **I**

inszenieren to stage **IV TS3**, 102
Inszenierung production **IV TS1**, 30
intelligent smart **III**
interessant interesting **I**
Interesse interest **II**
(sich) **interessieren** to interest **II**
   sich **interessieren** (für) to care (about) **II**
   sich **interessieren** für *to be interested
   in **II**
interessiert sein an *to be interested in **II**
Interkulturelles Across cultures **I**
international international **I**; multi-ethnic **II**
Internet internet **I**
Internetauftritt website **I**
Internettagebuch blog **III**
Interview interview **I**
interviewen to interview **I**
involvieren to involve **IV TS3**, 102
irgendein/-e/-er any **I**
irgendwelche any **I**
irgendwo anywhere; somewhere **II**
Irisch Irish **III**
irisch Irish **III**
ironisch ironic **IV U2**, 56
irreal unreal **IV U1**, 19
sich **irren** *to be wrong **I**

J

ja yes; yeah (infml) **I**
Jacke jacket **III**
jagen to chase **I**
Jahr year **I**
Jahrbuch yearbook **II**
Jahreszeit season **IV U2**, 56
Jahrhundert century **II**
18-jährig 18-year-old **II**
11-Jährige/-r 11-year-old **II**
Januar January **I**
je … desto the … the **II**
jedenfalls anyway **II**
jede/-r/-s every; each **I**
jeder everyone **I**; everybody **II**
   jede Menge lots (of) **I**
   jedes Mal, wenn whenever **II**
jedoch however **IV U3**, 76; though **IV AC4**, 106
jemals ever **II**
jemand somebody **I**; someone **II**
   jemand anderes anyone else **II**
jene those **I**
jenes that **I**
jetzt now **I**
   jetzt gleich right now **II**
Job job **I**
Joghurt yoghurt **I**
Jonglieren juggling **II**
Jubel cheer **IV U2**, 52
jubeln to cheer **II**
jüdisch Jewish **IV U3**, 75
Jugend youth **IV TS1**, 36
Jugend- teen **II**; teenage **IV TS1**, 31
jugendlich teenage **IV TS1**, 31

Jugendliche/-r teenager I; teen III; kid **IV U2**, 42
Juli July I
jung young I
Junge boy I
Juni June I
Juwel jewel III

K

Kaffee coffee I
Kaiser emperor III
Kaiserreich empire III
Kaktus cactus **IV AC2**, 38
Kalender planner I; calendar III
kalt cold II
    kalt stellen *to leave it to cool I
Kamelrennen camel racing II
Kamera camera II
    mit der **Kamera** festgehalten caught on camera II
Kameraeinstellung shot II
Kamin chimney III
Kampf fight II; battle III
kämpfen *to fight II
Kanadier/-in Canadian **IV AC4**, 106
kanadisch Canadian **IV AC4**, 106
Kaninchen rabbit I
Kapitän/-in captain I
Kapitel unit I; chapter III
kaputt broken I; out of order **IV TS1**, 36
Karneval carnival II
Karotte carrot I
Karren cart **IV U3**, 75
Karriere career III
Karte card I
Kartenschalter ticket office III
Kartoffel potato, potatoes (pl) III
Kartoffelchip crisp (BE) I
Kartoffelpüree mashed potatoes (pl) III
Käse cheese I
Kasten box I
Katastrophe disaster II
Kategorie category II
Katze cat I
kaufen *to buy; *to get I
Käufer/-in buyer I; shopper **IV U2**, 48
Kaufmann merchant II
Kaugummi chewing gum **IV U1**, 15
kaum hardly **IV TS1**, 34
kein/-e no I
    kein Wunder no wonder **IV U2**, 44
    keine Ahnung no idea II
    keine Ahnung haben *to have no clue **IV AC2**, 41
    Keine Sorge! Don't worry! I
kein/-e/-en not ... any I
Keks biscuit I
Kelte/Keltin Celt III
keltisch Celtic II
kennen *to know I
kennenlernen *to get to know III

Kerl guy II
Kerze candle I
Kerzenlicht candlelight (no pl) II
keuchen to gasp **IV U3**, 72
Kfz-Mechaniker/-in mechanic II
Kilometer kilometre (km) III
Kilt kilt III
Kind child, children (pl) I; kid **IV U2**, 42
Kinderarbeit child labor (AE) **IV U2**, 48
Kino cinema I; movie theater (AE) **IV U2**, 44
Kirche church I
Kiste box I
Klammer bracket III
Klang sound I
klappen to work out III
klar clear I
Klarstellung clarification **IV U1**, 15
Klärung clarification **IV U1**, 15
Klasse group; class I
Klasse (in einer englischen Schule) tutor group I
    Ausstellung in der **Klasse** class display I
Klassenarbeit test I
Klassenkamerad/-in classmate I
Klassenlehrer/-in tutor I
Klassenposter class poster I
Klassenzimmer classroom I
klassisch classical **IV U3**, 72
klatschen to clap I
    Klatsch/Klatscht in die Hände. Clap your hands. I
Klavier piano **IV U3**, 77
Kleid dress I
Kleider clothes (pl) I
Kleidergröße size I
Kleiderordnung dress code **IV U2**, 43
Kleidersammlung clothing drive **IV U2**, 51
Kleiderschrank wardrobe I
    begehbarer **Kleiderschrank** walk-in closet **IV U2**, 44
Kleidung clothes (pl) I; outfit II; clothing **IV U2**, 51
klein small; little I; tiny III
Klempner/-in plumber III
Klettern climbing II
klettern to climb I
Klick click II
Klicken click II
Kliff cliff III
Klima climate **IV U1**, 18
Klimaanlage air-conditioning **IV U1**, 17
klingeln *to ring I
klingen to sound I
Klippe cliff III
klonen to clone III
Klub club I
klug clever II; smart III
Knacken crack III
knackend cracking III
knapp close I
    Das war **knapp**! That was close! I
Knoblauch garlic **IV U1**, 11

sich den **Knöchel** verrenken to twist your ankle II
Knopf button **IV U1**, 17
Koala koala III
Koch-AG Cooking Club I
Kochen cooking I
kochen to cook II
Koffer suitcase **IV U1**, 9
Kofferraum boot III; trunk (AE) **IV U3**, 76
Kokosnuss coconut II
Kollektion collection II
Kolonie colony II
Kolonist/-in colonist **IV AC2**, 41
Kombination combination **IV U3**, 75
kombinieren to combine **IV U3**, 75
komfortabel comfortable II
Komiker/-in comedian II
komisch funny III; odd **IV U1**, 19
    jmdn. **komisch** anschauen *to give sb funny looks III
Komitee committee **IV U2**, 48
kommen *to come I
    kommen nach *to get to I
    kommen zu *to get to I
    Komm jetzt! Come on! I
    Komm schon! Come on! I
Kommentar comment II
kommentieren to comment (on) II
Kommunikation communication II
kommunizieren to communicate II
Komödie comedy III
Komparativ comparative II
komplett complete **IV AC2**, 41
kompliziert complicated **IV TS3**, 102
Kompositum (zusammengesetztes Wort) compound word II
Kompromiss compromise II
    Kompromisse eingehen to compromise III
Konferenz conference **IV U3**, 72
Konfitüre jam III
konfrontiert werden mit to face **IV TS1**, 31
konfus confused III
König king I
Königin queen II
königlich royal I
    königlicher Leibgardist Beefeater II
konkurrieren (mit) to compete (with) III
konkurrierend competitive III
können can I; *to be able to (do sth) II
    kann nicht can't I; cannot II
    können nicht can't I; cannot II
könnte/-n could II
    könnte/-n (vielleicht) might **IV U2**, 50
    (vielleicht) **können** may II
    Es **könnte/-n** auch ... sein. It might as well be ... III
konnte/-n could III
Konsequenz consequence **IV AC3**, 68
Kontakt contact II
    in **Kontakt** bleiben *to keep in touch **IV U2**, 44

in **Kontakt** bleiben (mit) to stay in touch (with) **II**
kontaktfreudig outgoing **IV U1**, 19
Kontinent continent **IV U3**, 74
kontinuierlich steady **IV U1**, 17
Kontrast contrast **IV AC2**, 38
Kontrolle control **IV U1**, 9
kontrollieren to check **I**; to control **IV U2**, 50
gegenseitig **kontrollieren** to peer-edit **II**
Kontrollpunkt checkpoint **IV U1**, 16
Konversation conversation **I**
(sich) **konzentrieren** to concentrate **IV U1**, 17
sich **konzentrieren** (auf) to focus (on) **II**
Konzept draft **I**
Konzert concert **IV U2**, 57
Kopf head **I**
etw. aus dem **Kopf** bekommen *to get sth out of one's head **III**
Kopfhörer headphones (pl) **II**
Kopfschmerzen headache (no pl) **II**
Kopfweh headache (no pl) **II**
kopieren to copy **I**
Korbball netball **I**
Koreaner/-in Korean **II**
Koreanisch Korean **II**
koreanisch Korean **II**
Korn corn **IV AC2**, 41
Körper body **III**
menschlicher **Körper** human body **II**
korrekt correct; right **I**
Korridor hall **III**; hallway **IV U2**, 43; corridor **IV AC3**, 68
Korrigiere/Korrigiert … Correct … **I**
kosten *to cost **I**
Es **kostet** …/Sie **kosten** … It's …/They're … **I**
Wie viel **kostet/kosten** …? How much is/are …? **I**
kostenlos free **I**; for free **IV U3**, 72
köstlich delicious **IV U3**, 75
Kostüm costume **I**; fancy dress **II**
Das ist zum **Kotzen**. It sucks. (slang) **IV AC4**, 107
Krachen crack **III**
Kraft power; energy **III**; force **IV U1**, 19
Krampf cramp **I**
Kran crane **III**
krank sick **II**; ill **III**
Krankenhaus hospital **II**
Krankenpfleger nurse **III**
Krankenschwester nurse **III**
Krankenwagen ambulance **III**
Kraut herb **IV U1**, 11
kreativ creative **I**
Kreis circle **I**
sich im **Kreis** drehen *to go round in circles **III**
kreischen to scream **II**
Kreuz cross **III**
kreuzen to cross **II**
Kreuzung intersection **IV U3**, 70
Krieg war **IV U1**, 20

Krieger warrior **III**
Krimi detective **III**
Kriminalfilm detective **III**
Kriminalität crime **III**
Kriminalroman detective **III**
Kriminelle/-r criminal **III**
Kriterium criterion, criteria (pl) **III**
Kritik rating **III**
kritisch critical **IV TS3**, 103
Krone crown **III**
Kronjuwelen crown jewels **II**
Küche kitchen **I**
Kuchen cake; pie **I**
Küchenschrank cupboard **I**
Kuh cow **III**
kühl cool **IV AC2**, 38
Kühlschrank fridge **I**
Kultur culture **I**
kulturell cultural **IV AC2**, 38
Kummerkastentante agony aunt **II**
sich **kümmern** (um) to care (about) **II**
sich **kümmern** um to look after **I**
sich um jmdn. **kümmern** *to take care of sb **II**
Kunde/Kundin customer **III**
Kunst art **II**
Künstler/-in artist **IV U3**, 74
Kunstunterricht Art **I**
Kurs course **II**
kurz short **I**
kurz vor on the brink of **III**
Kurzantwort short answer **I**
Kurzform short form **I**
Kurznachricht text (message) **I**
Küste shore **II**; coastline **III**; coast **IV U1**, 10
Küstenverlauf coastline **III**
Küstenweg coastal path **III**

L

Labor laboratory **IV AC3**, 68
Lächeln smile **I**
lächeln to smile **I**
lachen to laugh **I**
Laden shop **I**; store (AE) **IV U2**, 44
Lady lady **III**
Lage location **II**
Lage (aus) layer (of) **III**
Lagerfeuer bonfire **I**
Lamm lamb **I**
Lämmchen lamb **I**
Lampe light **II**
Land country, countries (pl); land **I**; countryside **III**; state **IV AC2**, 39
auf dem **Land** in the country **IV AC2**, 40
landen to end up; to land **II**; to touch down **IV TS3**, 101
landesweit national **I**
Landkarte map **I**
ländlich rural **IV AC2**, 38
Landschaft landscape **III**; scenery **IV AC2**, 40
Landung landing **IV U1**, 15

Landwirt/-in farmer **II**
lang long **I**
(nicht) **länger** (not) any longer **III**
… **lang** for … **II**
langsam slow **I**
eine Geschichte **langsam** entwickeln to step into a story slowly **III**
langweilig boring **I**
Laptop laptop **II**
Lärm noise **II**
lassen *to let **I**; *to leave **II**
Lass/Lasst uns … Let's … **I**
Lassi lassi **I**
lästig inconvenient **IV TS3**, 100
Lastwagen lorry **IV U3**, 79
Lastwagenladung truckload **IV TS2**, 66
Lauf run **II**
Laufbahn career **III**
Laufen running **II**
laufen *to run; to walk **I**; *to be on **II**
ins Foto **laufen** to photobomb **III**
Läufer/-in runner **II**
Laune mood **II**
laut loud **I**; noisy **III**
laut vorsingen *to sing out loud **III**
läuten *to ring **I**
Layout layout **III**
Leben life, lives (pl) **II**
leben to live **I**
lebendig lively **II**
Lebensmittel food **I**
Lebensstandard standard of living **IV AC2**, 40
Lebensstil lifestyle **III**
seinen **Lebensunterhalt** bestreiten (mit) *to make a living (from) **IV U3**, 79
hier: **Leckerli** treat **III**
leer empty **III**
legen *to put **I**; to place **III**; *to lay **IeI IV U3**, 89
Lege/Legt es in … Put it in … **I**
Legende legend **III**
jmdm. eine **Lehre**/Lektion erteilen *to teach somebody a lesson **II**
lehren *to teach **II**
Lehrer/-in teacher **I**; instructor **II**
königlicher **Leibgardist** Beefeater **II**
leicht easy **I**; light **III**
Leichtathletik athletics (no pl) **IV U1**, 10
es **leid** sein (zu) *to be tired of **IV U2**, 46
leid tun *to be sorry **I**
Tut mir **leid**! Sorry!; I'm sorry! **I**
Leider … I'm afraid … **IV U2**, 44
leihen *to lend **III**
leise quiet **I**
sich **leisten** to afford **III**
gute **Leistungen** erbringen *to do well **IV TS1**, 34
leistungsorientiert competitive **III**
leiten to guide **III**; *to run **IV TS3**, 102
Leiter ladder **II**
Lektion unit **I**

jmdm. eine Lehre/**Lektion** erteilen *to teach somebody a lesson **II**

Lernen studies *(pl)* **II**

lernen *to learn **I**; to study **III**

  viel zu **lernen** a lot to learn **I**

  auswendig **lernen** *to learn … by heart **I**

Lesen reading **I**

  vor dem **Lesen** pre-reading **I**

lesen *to read **I**

  noch einmal **lesen** *to reread **III**

Leser/-in reader **I**

  den **Leser**/die **Leserin** in die Geschichte/ Handlung hineinziehen *to draw the reader into the story/action **III**

letzte/-r/-s last **I**; final **III**

letztlich finally **II**

leuchtend bright **IV U3**, 72

Leute people *(pl)* **I**

Licht light **II**

Lichtblitz flash **III**

lieb nice **I**

  Lieber … Dear … **I**

  Liebe … *(Anrede in Briefen)* Dear … **I**

  Liebe Grüße *(am Briefende)* Love … **I**

Liebe love **III**

lieben to love **I**

  Ich **liebe** dich. I love you. **I**

  Ich **liebe** … I love … **I**

lieber better **I**

  ich würde **lieber** I'd rather **III**

Liebesfilm romance **III**

Liebesgeschichte romance **III**

Lieblings- favourite **I**

  Mein/e **Lieblings** … My favourite … **I**

  Was ist dein/-e **Lieblings**…? What's your favourite …? **I**

Lied song **I**

Liedtext (song) lyrics *(pl)* **III**

liegen *to lie **II**; *to be located **IV U3**, 73

  gelegen sein *to be located **IV U3**, 73

Lifestyle lifestyle **III**

Lift elevator *(AE)* **IV U2**, 44

lila purple **I**

Limit limit **III**

Limonade lemonade **I**

Lineal ruler **I**

Linie line **I**

Link link **II**

linke/-r/-s left **I**

  auf der **linken** Seite on the left **I**

links on the left; left **I**

Liste list **I**

  eine **Liste** von a set of **III**

  Liste mit häufig gestellten Fragen FAQ **III**

Liter litre (l) **III**

live live **III**

Loch hole **II**

locker laid-back **III**; easy-going **IV U1**, 19

Löffel spoon **III**

Logik logic **III**

lokal local **III**

LOL LOL (= laughing out loud) **II**

Londoner/-in Londoner **I**

Lord lord **III**

Los ticket **I**

Los! Go on! **IV U2**, 55

löschen to delete **III**

lösen to solve **III**

losgehen *to leave **II**

loslassen *to let go (of) **II**

Lösung solution **II**

Löwe lion **II**

Lücke gap **I**

Luft air **III**

  Luft holen *to take a breath **III**

  tief **Luft** holen to gasp **IV U3**, 72

Lüge lie **III**

lügen to lie **II**

die **Lunge** the lungs *(pl)* **III**; lung **IV U3**, 71

lustig funny; fun **I**

Luxus luxury **IV AC2**, 40

M

Maat mate **I**

machen *to do; *to make **I**

  Fotos **machen** *to take photos **I**

  sich Notizen **machen** *to take notes **I**

  Machen wir uns doch nichts vor. Let's face it. **IV TS1**, 32

  Machst du so …? Is this how you (do) …? **I**

  Mir **macht** es nichts aus (zu) … I don't mind … (+ -ing) **III**

Macht power **III**; force **IV U1**, 19

mächtig powerful **III**

Mädchen girl **I**

Magen stomach **II**

Magie magic **IV U1**, 19

magisch magical **III**

Mahlzeit meal **II**

Mai May **I**

mailen to mail **II**

Mais corn **IV AC2**, 41

Mal time **II**

malen to paint **I**

Malerei painting **II**

Mama mum **I**; mummy **III**; mom *(AE)* **IV AC2**, 41

Mami mummy **III**

Mammutbaum redwood tree **IV AC2**, 39

manchmal sometimes **I**

Manga *(japanischer Comic)* manga **II**

Mango mango **I**

Manieren manners *(pl)* **IV AC1**, 23

Mann man, men *(pl)* **I**; dude *(coll)* **IV AC2**, 41

Mannschaftsführer/-in captain **I**

Mäppchen pencil-case **I**

Mappe folder **I**

Marathon marathon **II**

Marke brand **IV TS2**, 64

Markt market **I**

Marmelade jam **III**

Marmelade aus Zitrusfrüchten marmalade **III**

marschieren to march **III**

März March **I**

Maschine machine **I**

Maske mask **IV U1**, 16

massiv massive **IV AC2**, 41

Match match **II**

Material material **II**

Mathe Maths **II**

Mathematik Maths **II**

Matrose sailor **I**

Mauer wall **I**

Maus/Mäuse mouse *(sg)*, mice *(pl)* **I**

Mechaniker/-in mechanic **II**

Medien media **II**

Medikamente medicine *(no pl)* **III**

Medizin medicine *(no pl)* **III**

Meer sea **I**

Meerschweinchen guinea pig **I**

mehr more **I**

  nicht **mehr** no more **IV AC4**, 107

  (nicht) **mehr** (not) any longer **III**

  mehr … als more … than **I**

mehrere several **II**

Mehrzahl plural **I**

meiden to stay away from **II**; to avoid **III**

Meile *(brit. Längenmaß)* mile **II**

mein/-e my **I**

  Mein/e Lieblings… My favourite … **I**

mein/-er/-e/-es mine **II**

meinen *to mean **II**

Meinung opinion **II**

  anderer **Meinung** sein to disagree **III**

  einer **Meinung** sein (mit) to agree (with) **II**

  seine **Meinung** ändern to change one's mind **III**

die **meisten** (the) most **I**

der/die/das **meiste** (the) most **I**

meistens usually **I**

Meisterschaft championship **IV U2**, 56

Meldung report **II**; news report **III**

melken to milk **III**

Melodie tune; melody **III**

eine **Menge** a lot of **I**

  jede **Menge** lots (of) **I**

Mensch person, people *(pl)* **I**; human **IV TS3**, 100

Menschen people *(pl)* **I**

Menschenmenge crowd **II**

menschlicher Körper human body **II**

sich **merken** to remember **I**

Merkmal feature **III**

merkwürdig strange **I**; weird **II**; funny **III**

sich **messen** (mit) to compete (with) **III**

Messer knife, knives *(pl)* **III**

Meter metre **II**

mich me **I**

mieten to rent (out) **III**

Milch milk **I**

Milliardär/-in billionaire **IV AC2**, 39

Milliarde billion III
Million million II
Ich habe das schon eine **Million** Mal gemacht. I've done this a million times before. II
Millionär/-in millionaire III
vom Tellerwäscher zum **Millionär** rags to riches IV U3, 79
mindestens at least II
Mine mine III
Mini- mini II
Minute minute I
mir me I
Mir geht's gut. I'm fine. I
mischen to shuffle; to mix (up) III
Mission mission IV TS3, 101
misstrauisch suspicious IV U1, 13
missverstanden misunderstood III
mit with I
mit allen Mitteln by any means IV U3, 70
mit dabei along for the ride IV U2, 44
mit (dem Fahrrad) by (bike) I
mitbekommen (ugs.) *to catch III
mitbringen *to bring; *to take I
miteinander together I
Mitglied member II
mithalten (mit) *to keep up (with) II
mitkriegen (ugs.) *to catch III
Mitleid haben mit *to feel sorry for III
mitmachen *to be in II; to enter II
mitnehmen *to take I; to pick up III
Mitschüler/-in classmate I
mitsingen *to sing along III
Mitspieler/-in player II
Mittagessen lunch I
Mittagspause lunch break I; lunchtime IV AC3, 68
Mittagszeit lunchtime IV AC3, 68
Mitte middle I
mitteilen *to tell I
mit allen **Mitteln** by any means IV U3, 70
mittel medium IV U3, 89
mittelalterlich medieval III
mittelgroß medium IV U3, 89
Mittelschule (weiterführende Schule in den USA, Mittelstufe) middle school (AE) IV U2, 43
mitten im Nirgendwo in the middle of nowhere IV U2, 46
mitten in … stecken stuck in the middle of … III
Mitternacht midnight III
Mittwoch Wednesday I
Mix mix III
Mobiltelefon mobile II; cell phone (AE) IV AC3, 68
Modalverb modal II
Mode fashion II
Model model I
Modell model I
Modeln modelling III
Moderator/-in presenter I

modern modern II; up-to-date IV TS3, 100
mogeln to cheat IV AC3, 68
mögen to like; *to be into; to want (to) I
gern **mögen** to love I
nicht **mögen** to hate II; to dislike IV U2, 47
Du **magst** … You're into … I
Ich **mag** dich. I love you. I
Ich **mag** … I like … I
Ich **mag** … nicht. I don't like … I
Ich **mag** … total gern. I love … I
Ich **möchte** … I'd like to … (= I would like to) I
Möchten Sie …? Would you like …? II
Möchtest du …? Would you like …? II
Möchtet ihr …? Would you like …? II
möglich possible I
möglicherweise probably II
Möglichkeit chance II; possibility; option III
Möhre carrot I
Moment moment II
im **Moment** at the moment I
Monarch/-in monarch III
Monat month II
Mond moon IV TS3, 100
Mondlandung moon landing IV TS3, 100
Mondlicht moonlight III
Monster monster I
Montag Monday I
montags on Mondays I
Monument monument III
Mord murder III
Morgen morning I
Guten **Morgen**. Good morning. I
morgen tomorrow I
morgens in the mornings I
Motiv motive IV TS1, 32
Motivation motivation IV TS1, 31
motivieren to motivate I
Motto theme I
Mountainbikefahren mountain biking III
müde tired I
es **müde** sein (zu) *to be tired of IV U2, 46
sich **Mühe** geben to push oneself III
Müll rubbish I; trash (AE) IV TS2, 67
Müll herumliegen lassen to litter IV AC1, 22
Mund mouth I
mit vollem **Mund** sprechen to talk with your mouth full IV AC1, 22
Münze coin I
Münzgeld change IV U3, 76
murmeln to mutter IV U1, 10
Museum museum I
Museumsrundgang gallery walk I
Musik music I
Musik- musical III
musikalisch musical III
Musiker/-in musician II
Musikgruppe band III
Müsli muesli III
müssen must I; *to have to II

(tun) **müssen** to need (to do) I
nicht **müssen** needn't I
Muster pattern III; sample IV TS2, 64
mutig brave I
Mutter mother I
Muttersprache first language II
Mutti mummy III
mysteriös mysterious III
Mysterium mystery III

N

nach to I
nach draußen outside; out I
nach drinnen inside I
nach Hause home I
nach oben up; upstairs II
nach unten down II; downstairs II
nach (bei Uhrzeitangaben) past I
nach (zeitlich) after I
Nachbar/-in neighbour (BE) I
Nachbarschaft neighbourhood III; neighborhood (AE) IV U2, 43
nachdenken *to think I
Warte/Wartet und **denk/denkt nach**. Stop and think I
nacherzählen *to retell I
nachjagen to chase I
Nachmittag afternoon I
heute **Nachmittag** this afternoon II
nachmittags (Uhrzeit) p.m. I
Nachricht message I
eine **Nachricht** entgegennehmen *to take a message I
eine **Nachricht** hinterlassen *to leave a message I
Nachrichten news (sg) II
Nachrichtenbeitrag news report III
nachschauen to look up I
nachschlagen to look up I
Nachsitzen detention IV AC3, 68
nachspielen to act out II
nachspüren to trace I
nächste/-r/-s next I
der/die **Nächste(n)** next I
als **Nächstes** next I
am **nächsten** Tag the next day II
Nacht night I
die ganze **Nacht** all night I
heute **Nacht** tonight IV TS1, 31
über **Nacht** overnight III
Nachtisch pudding I
Nachtwanderung night walk II
nackt bare III; naked IV U3, 72
Nahaufnahme close-up II
in der **Nähe** von near I
nahe near I; close II
Name name I
Namenstag name day I
Nase nose II
die **Nase** voll haben (von) *to be fed up (with) III

Nashorn rhino III
nass wet II
national national I
Natur nature II
Natur- natural IV U2, 56
natürlich natural IV U2, 56
natürlich of course I; needless to say
    IV U3, 76
Naturwissenschaft science IV TS3, 100
Naturwissenschaften Science II
neben next to I; besides; by III
(von) nebenan next door III
Nebenraum side room IV U1, 13
nee nope (infml) IV AC4, 107
Neffe nephew IV U1, 13
negativ negative III
nehmen *to take I
    (ein Bonbon) **nehmen** *to have (a sweet) I
neidisch sein (auf) *to be jealous (of) I
nein no I
benennen to name I
nennen to name; to call I
Nerd (Person, die intelligent, aber sozial
    unbeholfen ist) nerd IV TS2, 65
jemandem auf die **Nerven** gehen *to get on
    people's nerves I
nervös nervous II
nett nice I; friendly II
Netz net II; web III
soziale **Netzwerke** social media IV U2, 46
soziales **Netzwerk** social network II
neu new I
    neu schreiben *to rewrite III
neueste/-r/-s latest IV U1, 11
Neuigkeiten news (sg) II
neulich the other day IV U1, 20
neun nine I
Neuzugang arrival IV TS2, 66
New Yorker/-in New Yorker IV U3, 75
nicht not I
    auch **nicht** not … either IV AC4, 107
    nicht gehorchen to disobey III
    nicht mehr not any more I; not anymore
    (AE) IV AC2, 39; no more IV AC4, 107
    nicht mögen to hate II; to dislike IV U2, 47
    nicht notwendigerweise not necessarily
    IV U3, 76
    nicht unbedingt not necessarily IV U3, 76
    nicht vor not until IV U2, 44
    noch **nicht** not … yet II
nicht- non- II
nichts nothing; not … anything I
    Nichts zu danken. You're welcome. I
nie never I
nieder down IV U2, 52
niederbrennen *to burn down III
niedlich cute I
niedrig low II
niemals never I
niemand nobody II
    niemand anderes nobody else III
Nieselregen drizzle IV U1, 17

mitten im **Nirgendwo** in the middle of
    nowhere IV U2, 46
nirgendwo nowhere III
nirgendwohin nowhere III
nö nope (infml) IV AC4, 107
noch still I; yet II
    noch ein/-e another I
    noch einmal again I
    noch mal again I
    noch nicht not … yet II
    noch mal Glück gehabt saved by the bell
    III
Nomen noun I
Nord- north II
Norden north II
    im **Norden** north III
nördlich north III
Nordsee North Sea III
normal normal II
normalerweise usually I; normally IV AC1, 22
Normanne/Normannin Norman III
normannisch Norman III
in **Not** in need II
Note mark III; grade (AE) IV U3, 78
notieren to note down II
Notiz note I
    Notizen machen *to make notes I
    sich **Notizen** machen *to take notes I
Notlüge white lie IV TS1, 32
notwendiger Relativsatz defining relative
    clause II
nicht **notwendigerweise** not necessarily
    IV U3, 76
November November I
Nudeln pasta I
null zero I
null (bei Telefonnummern und Uhrzeitanga-
    ben) oh I
Nullmeridian Meridian Line I
Nummer number I
nun now I
nun well I
nur only; just I
Nuss nut I
Nutzen benefit IV U2, 51
nützlich useful I
    nützliche Ausdrücke Useful phrases I
nutzlos useless IV U1, 17

O

O! Oh! I
o.k. OK I
ob if I; whether IV U2, 49
obdachlos homeless IV U2, 51
Obdachlosenunterkunft homeless shelter
    IV U2, 51
oben on top I; above; upstairs II
    nach **oben** up II
obendrauf on top I
oberer Teil top I
oberes Ende top I

Oberfläche surface IV TS3, 101
im **Obergeschoss** upstairs II
Objekt object II; item IV U2, 51
Objektpronomen object pronoun III
Obst fruit I
obwohl although IV U1, 13; though
    IV AC4, 106
oder or I
    entweder … **oder** … either … or …
    IV U3, 79
offen open I
offensichtlich obvious IV U2, 53
öffentlich public II
die **Öffentlichkeit** the public IV TS3, 102
offiziell official III
offline offline II
öffnen to open I
Öffnung opening III
oft often I
    so **oft** whenever II
ohne without I
    ohne fremde Hilfe alone I
Ohr ear IV AC1, 22
Oje! Oh dear! I
okay okay IV TS1, 31
Öko- Eco II
Oktober October I
Oma grandma; granny I
OMG! (Oh mein Gott!) OMG! (Oh my god!)
    IV U2, 56
Onkel uncle I
Online-Pinnwand wall III
    online stellen to post II
online online II
Opa grandad I
optimistisch optimistic III
Option option III
Orange orange I
orange orange I
Ordner folder I
Ordnung order I
    in **Ordnung** fine I
    in **Ordnung** bringen to tidy (a room) I
Organisation organisation III
organisieren to organise I
    sich **organisieren** *to get organised III
Orientierung orientation IV U2, 43
Orientierungs- orientation IV U2, 43
Original original III
original original III
Ort place I; space II; spot IV U3, 75
örtlich local III
Ost- east I
Osten east I
Ostern Easter I
Outdoor- outdoor II
Outfit outfit II

P

Paar pair I; couple III
    Paare bilden to pair III

ein **paar** some; a few; a couple of **I**
Päckchen packet; parcel **I**
Packung packet **I**
Paket packet; parcel **I**
Palme palm tree **III**
panisch werden to panic **II**
Papa dad **I**
Papier paper **I**
  Stück **Papier** piece of paper **I**
Paradies paradise **II**
Paragraf section **II**
Park park **I**
Partei party **III**
Partizip past participle **II**
Partner/-in partner **I**
Partnerarbeit pair work **II**
Party party **I**
Pass passport **IV U1**, 9
Passagier/-in passenger **IV U1**, 9
passen to fit **II**
  passen zu *to go with; to match **I**
  zueinander **passen** *to go together **I**
passieren to happen **I**
Passiv passive **III**
Pasta pasta **I**
Pastete pie **I**
Pause break **II**; pause **III**
PC PC *(= Personal Computer)* **II**
Pech haben *to be unlucky **I**
peinlich embarrassing **II**
Pence *(brit. Währungseinheit)* penny, pence *(pl)* **I**
penetrant pushy **IV TS1**, 33
Penicillin penicillin **III**
Penny *(brit. Währungseinheit)* penny, pence *(pl)* **I**
Penthouse penthouse **IV U3**, 79
perfekt perfect **I**
Periode period **III**
Person person, people *(pl)* **I**
  berühmte **Person** celebrity **III**
  pro **Person** each **I**
persönlich personal **I**; face-to-face **II**
Persönlichkeit personality **III**
Perspektive perspective; point of view **II**
Pfad path **IV U3**, 92
Pfandhaus pawn shop **III**
Pfandleihe pawn shop **III**
Pfeife pipe **II**
Pfeil arrow **III**
Pferd horse **I**
Pfirsich peach **III**
Pflanze plant **III**
pflanzen to plant **II**
Pfund *(brit. Währungseinheit)* pound (£) **I**
Pfund *(Maßeinheit)* pound **IV U2**, 51
Piano piano **IV U3**, 77
Picknick picnic **I**
Pick-up pick-up **I**
Pier pier **I**
Pilger/-in Pilgrim **IV U2**, 45
Pille pill **II**

Pilot/-in pilot **II**
pink pink **I**
Online-**Pinnwand** wall **III**
Pizza pizza **I**
Placemat placemat **I**
Platzdeckchen placemat **I**
Plakatwand billboard **IV TS2**, 65
Plan plan **I**
planen to plan **I**
Planet planet **II**
platt flat **IV AC2**, 40
Plattform platform **III**
Platz place **I**; space; pitch **II**
Platz! *(Befehl für Hunde)* Sit! **I**
plaudern to chat **I**
plötzlich suddenly **I**
Plural plural **I**
Plusquamperfekt past perfect **III**
Podcast podcast **IV U3**, 92
Polen Poland **I**
politisch political **IV TS3**, 101
Polizei police **II**
Polizeibeamter police officer **II**
Polizist/-in police officer **II**
Pommes frites chips *(pl) (BE)* **I**
Pony pony **I**
Ponyreiten im Gelände pony trekking **III**
populär popular **I**
Population population **IV AC2**, 39
Porträt profile **I**
Pose pose **IV U2**, 56
positiv positive **II**
Possessivform possessive form **I**
Post *(Eintrag im Internet)* post **I**
Poster poster **I**
Postkarte postcard **III**
prägnant to the point **III**
praktisch practical **II**
  praktisch überall just about anywhere **IV TS2**, 64
praktizieren to practice *(AE)* **IV U2**, 45
Präposition preposition **I**
Präsens present **II**
Präsentation presentation **I**
präsentieren to present **I**
Präsident/-in president **IV TS3**, 101
Praxis surgery **I**
Praxisräume surgery **I**
Preis price; prize **I**; award **II**
preiswert cheap **I**
pressen to press **II**
Priorität priority **IV TS3**, 101
Privatdetektiv/-in private detective **III**
pro per **III**
  pro Person each **I**
  pro Stück each **I**
  pro (Tag/Woche/Jahr) a (day/week/year) **IV AC2**, 39
Probe sample **IV TS2**, 64
proben to rehearse **III**
probieren to try **I**; to taste **III**
Problem problem **I**

Probleme trouble **II**
Produkt product **IV TS2**, 64
Produktion production **IV TS1**, 30
produzieren to produce **III**
Profil profile **I**
Profileinstellungen account settings **III**
Programm programme **II**; program *(AE)* **IV TS3**, 104
Projekt project **I**
Prominente/-r celebrity **III**
Prosa fiction *(no pl)* **III**
Prospekt brochure **I**; leaflet **IV AC1**, 23
Protagonist/-in protagonist **IV TS1**, 30
Protest protest **III**
Protestierende/-r protester **IV U2**, 52
prüfen to check **I**; to test; to check out *(coll)* **III**
Prüfung test **I**; exam **II**
Publikum audience **II**
Pudding pudding **I**
Punkt point **II**
Punktestand score **II**
pünktlich on time **II**
Puzzle puzzle **I**
Pyjama pyjamas *(pl)* **II**

Q

Qualifikation trial **II**
Qualität quality **I**
Quelle source **III**
quer durch across **I**
Quiz quiz **I**

R

Rabe raven **II**
  Herr der **Raben** raven master **II**
Rad wheel **I**
Radfahren cycling **I**
Radiergummi rubber **I**
radikal extreme **IV AC2**, 40
Radio radio **II**
Rahmen setting **II**; set **III**
am **Rande von** on the brink of **III**
Rand- fringe **III**
Rap rap **I**
rappen to rap **I**
Raster grid **I**
Rat advice **II**
raten to guess **I**
Ratespiel guessing game **II**
Ratschlag tip **I**; advice **II**
Rätsel puzzle; quiz **I**; mystery **III**
Ratte rat **I**
rau harsh **IV AC2**, 40
Räuber/-in robber **III**
Rauch smoke **III**
Raum room **I**; space **II**
Raumfahrtprogramm space program **IV TS3**, 104
Raumschiff spaceship **II**

rauschen to roar **III**
reagieren to react **III**
Reaktion reaction **II**
realisieren to realise **III**; to realize *(AE)*
   IV U2, 52
realistisch realistic **II**
Recherche research *(no pl)* **III**
Rechnung bill *(AE)* **IV U3**, 76
Recht right **IV U2**, 48
recht haben *to be right **I**
rechte/-r/-s right **I**
rechthaberisch bossy **III**
rechts on the right; right **I**
   auf der **rechten** Seite on the right **I**
Rechtschreibung spelling **I**
rechtswidrig illegal **III**
gerade rechtzeitig just in time **IV U3**, 72
Recycling recycling **II**
Rede speech **III**; talk **IV U2**, 43
   direkte **Rede** direct speech **IV U1**, 11
   indirekte **Rede** indirect speech **IV U1**, 11
reden to talk **I**
   reden mit to talk to **I**
Redensart saying **III**
Redewendung phrase **I**
Redner/-in speaker **I**
Referendum referendum **III**
Referenzartikel reference article **III**
reflexiv reflexive **III**
Reflexiv- reflexive **III**
Reflexivpronomen reflexive pronoun **III**
Refrain chorus **III**
Regel rule **I**
regelmäßig regular **I**
Regen rain **IV U1**, 17
Regenbogen rainbow **III**
Regenmantel raincoat **III**
Regieanweisung stage direction **III**
regieren to rule; to reign **III**
die Regierenden those in power **III**
Regierung government **IV TS3**, 102
Regierungszeit reign **III**
Region region **II**
Regisseur/-in director **IV TS1**, 30
Register register **IV AC4**, 106
regnen to rain **II**
Reich empire **III**
reich rich **III**; wealthy **IV AC2**, 40
die Reichen the rich **III**
Reihenfolge order **I**; sequence **IV U3**, 89
Reim rhyme **I**
(sich) reimen to rhyme **III**
sich reimend rhyming **III**
Reimschema rhyme scheme **III**
rein in **I**
reinigen to clean **I**
Reise trip; travel **II**; journey **III**
Reiseanbieter tour company **IV U3**, 73
Reisebericht travel report **II**
Reisebüro travel agent's; travel agency **III**
Reisebus coach **II**
Reiseführer guide **II**; guidebook **IV U3**, 72

(das) Reisen travel **II**; travelling *(no pl)*
   IV U1, 9
reisen to travel **II**
Reisende/-r traveller **IV U1**, 15
Reisepass passport **IV U1**, 9
Reiseziel destination **IV U1**, 19
reiten *to ride **IV AC2**, 41
reizen to tempt **IV TS1**, 31
Reklame advertising *(no pl)* **IV TS2**, 64
Relativpronomen relative pronoun **II**
notwendiger Relativsatz defining relative
   clause **II**
Religion religion **IV U2**, 45
   eine **Religion** ausüben to practice a
   religion **IV U2**, 45
Religion *(Schulfach)* RE *(= Religious Educa-*
   tion) **II**
religiös religious **I**
Rennen race; running; run **II**
rennen *to run **I**
reparieren to fix **II**
Reporter/-in reporter **II**
repräsentieren to represent **IV AC2**, 40
Requisite prop **III**
reservieren to book **III**
Respekt respect **IV TS3**, 103
der Rest the rest **I**
Restaurant restaurant **I**
   einfaches **Restaurant** mit Theke und
   Tischen diner *(AE)* **IV U3**, 72
Resultat result **II**
retten to save **I**; to rescue **III**
Rettung rescue **II**
Rettungsboot lifeboat **I**
Rettungsring lifebuoy **I**
Rezept recipe **III**
Rezept *(für Arzneimittel)* prescription **II**
rezitieren to recite **III**
Rhinozeros rhino **III**
Rhythmus rhythm **I**
richtig correct; right **I**; real **II**
   richtig beantworten *to get right **III**
Richtung direction **I**
   in Richtung towards **II**
riechen *to smell **III**
riesengroß huge **II**
riesig huge; large **II**; gigantic **IV AC2**, 40;
   massive **IV AC2**, 41
Rinderhirte cowboy **IV U3**, 72
Ring circle **I**; ring **III**
ein Risiko eingehen *to take a risk **IV TS1**, 32
Ritt ride **IV U2**, 44
Ritter knight **III**
Rock skirt **III**
Rock *(Musik)* rock **III**
Rock 'n' Roll rock 'n' roll **II**
Rohr pipe **II**
Rohrleitung pipe **II**
Rolle role **I**; part **III**
   Rollen tauschen to swap roles **I**
Rollenbesetzung casting **IV TS1**, 37
Rollenkarte prompt card **II**

Rollenspiel role play **I**
Rollschuhe skates *(pl)* **I**
Rollstuhl wheelchair **II**
Rolltreppe escalator **I**
Roman novel **III**
Römer/-in Roman **II**
römisch Roman **II**
rosa pink **I**
rot red **I**
Route route **II**
Routenplaner route planner **IV AC2**, 41
Routine routine **IV U1**, 16
Rückblende flashback **III**
Rücken back **III**
   Rücken an Rücken back to back **I**
Rückenschmerzen backache **II**
Rückenweh backache **II**
Hin- und Rückfahrkarte return ticket **III**
Rückmeldung feedback **II**
Rucksack backpack **III**
Rückseite back **II**
rufen to shout; to call **I**; to cry **II**
Rugby rugby **II**
Ruhe silence *(no pl)* **III**
   jmdn. in Ruhe lassen *to leave sb alone
   IV U2, 53
ruhig quiet **I**; silent **III**
   die Beine und Hände ruhig halten *to
   keep one's feet or hands still **III**
Rühr- sponge **I**
ruinieren to ruin **II**
Rumäne/Rumänin Romanian **II**
Rumänisch Romanian **II**
rumänisch Romanian **II**
rumhängen (mit) *to hang out (with) *(infml)*
   III
Runde round **II**
Rundgang tour **II**
Rutschbahn slide **I**

S

Saal hall **II**
Sache thing **I**
   große Sache big deal **IV U1**, 11
sachlich factual **III**
Sachtext factual text **III**
Saft juice **I**
Sage legend **III**
sagen *to say; *to tell **I**
sagenhaft mythical **IV U1**, 19; fabulous
   IV TS2, 66
sagenumwoben mythical **IV U1**, 19
Sahne cream **I**
Saison season **IV U2**, 56
Salat salad **I**
Salbe ointment **II**
sammeln to collect **I**
   Geld sammeln to raise money **II**
Sammlung collection **II**
Samstag Saturday **I**
Sand- sandy **III**

Sandale sandal **III**
sandig sandy **III**
Sandwich sandwich **I**
Sänger/-in singer **II**
Sanitärarbeit plumbing **III**
es **satt** haben (zu) *to be tired of **IV U2**, 46
Satz phrase; sentence **I**
    if-**Satz** if-clause **III**
    der erste **Satz** opening line **III**
Satzgegenstand subject **II**
Satzstellung word order **I**
sauber clean **III**
säubern to clean **I**
sauer sein (auf) *to be fed up (with) **III**
Säugling baby **I**
Saxofon saxophone; sax **I**
scannen to scan **II**
Schach chess **II**
Schachtel box **I**
Schade! Too bad! **I**
Schaf sheep, sheep (pl) **II**
schaffen to create **I**
    es nicht **schaffen**, etw. zu tun to fail to do
    sth **IV U3**, 79
    es **schaffen** *to make it **IV U3**, 70
    Du **schaffst** es! You can do it! **III**
    Wir haben es **geschafft**! We did it! **II**
Schälchen bowl **I**
Schale bowl **I**
Schalter switch **III**; desk **IV U1**, 9
scharf sharp **III**
Schatten shadow **III**
Schatz treasure **II**
schätzen to estimate **IV TS3**, 103
Schau show **II**
schaudern to cringe **IV U3**, 91
schauen to look **I**
    Schau/**Schaut** mal! Look! **I**
    Schau(t) genau … Look closely … **II**
schaukeln to rock **IV U1**, 16
Schauplatz setting; scene **II**
    seinen **Schauplatz** haben (in) *to be set
    (in) **IV U1**, 19
Schauspielen acting **III**
Schauspieler actor **II**
in **Scheiben** schneiden to slice **I**
scheinen *to shine **II**; to seem **III**
schenken *to give **I**
scherzen to joke **II**
Schicht (aus) layer (of) **III**
schicken *to send **I**
schieben to push **II**
Schiedsrichter/-in official **II**
jmdn. **schief** anschauen *to give sb funny
    looks **III**
schiefgehen *to go wrong **I**
schießen *to kick **I**
schießen (auf) *to shoot **III**
Schiff ship **I**
Schiffsbau shipbuilding **III**
Schiffsjunge cabin boy **I**
Schiffsoffizier mate **I**

Schild sign **II**
Schinken ham **III**
Schinkenspeck bacon **I**
Schlacht battle **III**
Schlaf sleep **IV U1**, 11
Schlafanzug pyjamas (pl) **II**
schlafen *to sleep **I**; *to be asleep **II**
Schlafzimmer bedroom **I**
schlagen *to hit; to whip **I**; *to beat **II**
Schläger racquet **II**
Schlagzeile headline **III**
Schlagzeug drums (pl) **III**
Schlamm mud **II**
schlammig muddy **II**
Schlange queue **I**
    Schlange stehen *to stand in line (AE)
    IV AC3, 69
schlau clever **II**; smart **III**
schlecht bad **I**
    der/die/das **schlechteste** the worst **II**
    schlecht geschrieben badly-written
    IV TS3, 105
    sich **schlecht** fühlen *to feel sick **II**
schleichen *to sneak **IV U3**, 72
schließen to close **I**
Schließfach locker **I**
schließlich at last; after all **I**; in the end;
    finally **II**
schlimm (ugs.) bad **I**
    der/die/das **schlimmste** the worst **II**
Schlittschuh laufen to skate **I**
Schlittschuhbahn ice rink **I**
Schlittschuhe skates (pl) **I**
Schloss castle **II**
Schluchtenklettern gorge scrambling **II**
Schluss end **I**
    zum **Schluss** in the end; finally **II**
    sich das Beste bis zum **Schluss** aufheben
    to save the best for last **IV U3**, 72
Schluss (einer Geschichte) ending **I**
Schlüssel key **II**
Schlüsselanhänger key ring **III**
Schlüsselbegriff key word **I**
Schlüsselbund key ring **III**
schmal narrow **III**
    schmaler Durchgang close **III**
schmecken to taste **III**
Schmelztiegel melting pot **IV U3**, 70
Schmerz pain **II**
Schmuck jewellery; decorations (pl) **I**
schmücken to decorate **I**
schmuggeln *to sneak **IV U3**, 72
Schmuggler/-in smuggler **IV U1**, 16
Schmutz dirt **III**
schmutzig dirty **II**
Schnäppchen bargain **I**
schnappen to grab **II**
schnarchen to snore **I**
Schnee snow **III**
schneiden *to cut (off) **II**
    in Scheiben **schneiden** to slice **I**
schneidend sharp **III**

schnell fast; quick **I**
schnell quickly **II**
Schock shock **II**
schockiert shocked **IV TS1**, 37
Schokolade chocolate **I**
Schokoriegel chocolate bar **IV TS2**, 64
schön nice; fine **I**; beautiful **II**; lovely
    IV TS2, 65
schon already **I**; yet **II**
    schon einmal before **II**
High **School** (weiterführende Schule in den
    USA, Oberstufe) high school (AE) **IV U2**, 43
Schornstein chimney **III**
Schotte/**Schottin** Scot **III**
Schottenkaro (bestimmtes Muster eines
    Clans) tartan **III**
Schottenrock kilt **III**
karierter **Schottenstoff** tartan **III**
schottisch Scottish **III**
Schrank cupboard **I**; closet **IV U2**, 44
schrecklich awful **I**
Schreiben writing **I**
schreiben *to write **I**
schreien to shout **I**; to scream; to cry **II**
Schritt step **I**
    Schritt halten (mit) *to keep up (with) **II**
    Schritt-für-**Schritt**- step-by-step **II**
Stück **Schrott** piece of junk **III**
schubsen to push **II**
schüchtern shy **II**
Schuh shoe **I**
Schularbeiten schoolwork **IV TS1**, 34
schuldig guilty **IV TS1**, 37
Schule school **I**
Schüler/-in student **I**
Schüleraustausch student exchange **III**
Schulfach subject **II**
Schulgebühren school fees (pl) **III**
Schulgeld school fees (pl) **III**
Schuljahr year **I**
Schulklasse class **I**
Schulleiter/-in principal (AE) **IV AC3**, 68
Schulstunde lesson **I**
Schultasche schoolbag **I**
Schulter shoulder **II**
Schüssel bowl **I**
schütten to pour **I**
Schutz security **IV U1**, 13
schwach weak **IV TS3**, 105
Schwanz tail **I**
schwänzen to skip **IV AC3**, 68
schwarz black **I**
    schwarz werden *to go black **II**
    schwarzes Brett noticeboard **II**
Schweif tail **I**
Schweigen silence (no pl) **III**
schweigsam silent **III**
Schwein pig **I**
Schweinerei mess **IV U2**, 54
schwer hard **II**; heavy **III**
Schwerpunkt focus **III**
Schwester sister **I**

schwierig hard; difficult II
Schwierigkeit problem I
Schwierigkeiten trouble II
   in **Schwierigkeiten** bringen *to make trouble I
   in **Schwierigkeiten** geraten *to get into trouble **IV AC3**, 69
Schwimmbecken swimming pool III
Schwimmen swimming I
   Schwimmen gehen *to go swimming I
schwimmen *to swim I
schwindelig dizzy **IV U2**, 52
Science-Fiction *(Zukunftsdichtung)* science fiction II
sechs six I
Second-Hand-Laden charity shop I
See lake I
   See zum Rudern boating lake I
seekrank seasick **IV U1**, 8
Seemann sailor I
die **Segel** einholen to reef the sails I
Segelboot sailboat III
segeln to sail III
sehbehindert partially sighted II
sehen *to see; to look I
   Ich **sehe** keinen Sinn darin … I can't see the point of … **IV AC3**, 69
Sehenswürdigkeit sight; attraction II
sehr very; very much I
   Sehr geehrte Dame, **sehr** geehrter Herr Dear Sir or Madam III
Hör-/**Sehverstehen** viewing I
Seil rope III
sein *to be I; *to be like III
   ist nicht ain't (= isn't/aren't) **IV AC4**, 107
   Sei/Seid höflich. Be polite. I
   sind nicht ain't (= isn't/aren't) **IV AC4**, 107
sein/-e his; its I
seit for (+ Zeitraum) III; since (+ Zeitpunkt) III
seitdem since (+ Zeitpunkt) III
Seite page I; side II
   auf der anderen **Seite** von across; opposite I
selber yourself I; himself; myself II; yourselves III
das **Selbst** self self, selves selvz (pl) III
selbst even I
   du/dir/dich/Sie/sich (**selbst**) yourself I
   ihr/euch/Sie/sich (**selbst**) yourselves III
   er/sich (**selbst**) himself II
   ich/mir/mich (**selbst**) myself II
selbstbewusst confident II
Selbsteinschätzung self-evaluation I
selbstkritisch self-critical II
selbstsicher confident II
selbstverständlich of course I; needless to say **IV U3**, 76
Selfie selfie II
seltsam strange I; weird II; odd **IV U1**, 19
senden *to send I
Sender station II

Sendung programme II; program (AE) **IV TS3**, 104
separat separate II
September September I
Sequenz sequence III
Serie series, series (pl) III
Service service **IV U3**, 72
Sessel chair I
setzen *to put I
   sich **setzen** *to sit down I
Shampoo shampoo **IV TS2**, 64
Shinty (eine Art Hockey) shinty III
shoppen to shop **IV U3**, 76
Shorts shorts (pl) II
Show show II
   Comedy **Show** comedy show II
sich each other I
sicher sure I; safe II
   Ich bin mir (nicht) **sicher** … I'm (not) sure … III
Sicherheit security **IV U1**, 13
Sicherheits- security **IV U1**, 13
Sicht view II
Sie you; u (= you) I
sie her; she I
sie (Pl.) they I; them I
sieben seven I
Siedler/-in colonist **IV AC2**, 41
siegen *to win I
Sieger/-in winner I; champion III
Sightseeing- sightseeing II
Signal signal III
Signalwort signal word I
Silbe syllable III
Silber silver II
simpel simple III
singen *to sing I
sinken *to sink III
Sinn meaning II; sense III
   jmdm. in den **Sinn** kommen *to rise up in one's mind III
   Sinn ergeben *to make sense **IV TS3**, 102
   Sinn für Humor sense of humour (no pl) III
   Ich sehe keinen **Sinn** darin … I can't see the point of … **IV AC3**, 69
Sitte custom **IV AC1**, 22
Situation situation I
Sitz seat **IV U1**, 16
Sitzbank bench III
Sitz! (Befehl für Hunde) Sit! I
sitzen *to sit I
   sich gegenüber **sitzen** *to sit face to face I
Sitzplatz seat **IV U1**, 16
Skateboard skateboard II
Skateboardfahren skateboarding I
skeptisch sceptical **IV TS2**, 64
Sklave/Sklavin slave III
Skript script III
Skulptur sculpture **IV U3**, 72
Slogan slogan II
Smalltalk small talk III

Smartphone smartphone II
SMS text (message) I
   eine **SMS** schicken to text II
Snack snack I
so like this; so; like that I; that's how II
   so dass so (that) **IV AC3**, 69
   so früh this early III
   so oft whenever II
   so … wie as … as I
   so viel that much III
sobald as soon as II
Sofa sofa I
sofort right away I; right now II; straight away III; immediately **IV TS2**, 64
Softwarehandbuch software manual III
sogar even I
Sohn son III
solch such II
solche/-r/-s such II
Soldat/-in soldier III
sollte/solltest/solltet should II
   Du **solltest** lieber … You'd better … (= You had better) **IV AC3**, 69
   sollte(n) nicht shouldn't II
Somali Somali **IV U1**, 17
Sommer summer II
Sommerferienlager summer camp II
Sonderangebot special offer I
sonderbar weird II
Song song I
Sonne sun II
Sonnenblume sunflower III
Sonnenuntergang sunset **IV U3**, 72
Sonntag Sunday I
sonst otherwise **IV AC3**, 68
   sonst noch else III
   Sonst noch etwas? Anything else? I
Keine **Sorge**! Don't worry! I
sich **Sorgen** machen to worry II
für jmdn. **sorgen** *to take care of sb III
sorgfältig careful II
Sorte kind I; type III
sortieren nach to sort into III
Soße sauce III
Souvenir souvenir II
sowieso anyway II
sozial social **IV U2**, 46
   soziale Netzwerke social media **IV U2**, 46
   soziales Netzwerk social network II
Sozialwissenschaften Humanities (pl) II
Spalt gap I
Spalte column III
die **Spanier** Spanish III
Spanisch Spanish III
spanisch Spanish III
spannend exciting I
Spannung suspense III
sparen to save III
spärlich sparse **IV AC2**, 38
Spaß fun I
   Spaß haben *to have fun I; to enjoy oneself III

Es macht **Spaß**. It's fun. **I**
spät late **I**
  zu **spät** late **I**
  zu **spät** kommen *to be late **I**
  Wie **spät** ist es? What's the time? **I**
  zu **spät** dran sein *to be late **I**
kleiner **Spaten** trowel **II**
später later **I**
spazieren gehen *to go for a walk **II**
  mit dem Hund **spazieren** gehen to walk the dog **I**
Speck bacon **I**
Speer spear **III**
Speise dish **IV U2**, 45
Speisekarte menu **IV U2**, 45
spektakulär spectacular **III**
spenden to donate **IV U2**, 51
sperren to ban **III**
Sperrstunde curfew **IV U2**, 44
Spezialeffekt special effect **IV TS3**, 105
Spezialität specialty (AE) **IV U3**, 75
speziell special **I**; specific **IV U1**, 19
spezifisch specific **IV U1**, 19
Spickzettel cheat sheet **IV AC3**, 69
Spiegel mirror **III**
Spiel game **I**; match **II**
spielen to play **I**
  einen Streich **spielen** to play a trick (on) **I**
spielen (in) *to be set (in) **IV U1**, 19
spielen (Theater) to act **I**
  eine Theaterszene **spielen** acting a scene **I**
Spieler/-in player **II**
technische **Spielerei** gadget **III**
Spielfeld field; court; pitch **II**
Spielkarte card **I**
Spielstand score **II**
Spielzeug toy **I**
Spind locker **I**
Spinne spider **III**
Spinnennetz web **III**
Spitze top **I**; spike **IV U3**, 74
spitze awesome **IV AC2**, 41
spontan spontaneous **III**
Sport sport **I**
Sportart sport **I**
Sportunterricht PE (= Physical Education) **II**
Sprache language **I**
Sprachebene register **IV AC4**, 106
Sprachmittlung mediation **I**
Sprechblase speech bubble **I**
Sprechen speaking; talking **I**
sprechen *to say; to talk; *to speak **I**
  mit vollem Mund **sprechen** to talk with your mouth full **IV AC1**, 22
  sprechen über to talk about … **I**
Sprecher/-in speaker **I**; talker **III**
Sprechgesang chant **II**
Sprichwort saying **III**
springen to jump **I**; to bounce **III**
Spur clue **II**
Staat state **IV AC2**, 39

Staatsoberhaupt head of state **II**
Stachel spike **IV U3**, 74
Stadion stadium **II**
Stadt city; town **I**
Stadt- urban **IV AC2**, 38
städtisch urban **IV AC2**, 38
Stadtplan map **I**
Stadtteil part **I**
im **Stadtzentrum** downtown (AE) **IV U2**, 44
Stamm tribe **III**
Stammbaum family tree **I**
Standbild still **II**; freeze frame **III**; statue **IV U3**, 74
ständig always **I**
Standort location **II**
Standpunkt point of view **II**
Star star **I**
stark strong **II**; powerful; heavy **III**
Stärke power **III**
starren to stare **I**
Start start **III**; take-off **IV U1**, 15
starten to start **I**
Startpunkt starting place **III**
Station station **I**
statt instead of **IV U2**, 45
stattdessen instead **III**
stattfinden *to take place **I**
Statue statue **IV U3**, 74
Steak steak **I**
stechen *to sting **III**
  mitten in **stecken** stuck in the middle of … **III**
stehen *to stand **I**
  gegenüber **stehen** to face **IV TS1**, 31
  jmdm./etw. im Weg **stehen** *to stand in the way of sb/sth **IV AC1**, 22
  stehen auf *to be into **I**
  stehen für to represent **IV AC2**, 40
  Du **stehst** auf … You're into … **I**
stehlen *to steal **II**
steigen to climb **I**; *to rise **III**; to step **IV TS3**, 101
Stein stone **III**
Stein- stone **III**
steinig rocky **III**
Stelle place **I**
  an **Stelle** von instead of **IV U2**, 45
  an Jays **Stelle** in Jay's shoes **III**
  an jmds. **Stelle** sein *to be in sb's shoes **III**
stellen *to put **I**
  online **stellen** to post **II**
  Stelle/Stellt es in … Put it in … **I**
sterben to die **III**
Stern star **I**
Steuer wheel **I**
steuern to control **IV U2**, 50
Steuerrad wheel **I**
Stichwort key word **I**; prompt **III**
Stichwortkarte prompt card **II**
Stichwortverzeichnis glossary **IV TS1**, 30
Stiefel boot **III**
Stiefmutter stepmum **I**

stiften to donate **IV U2**, 51
Stil style **IV U1**, 11
Stil- stylistic **IV U3**, 89
stilistisch stylistic **IV U3**, 89
still quiet; still **I**; silent **III**
Stille silence (no pl) **III**
Stimme voice **I**
Stimmung mood; atmosphere **II**; humour (no pl) **III**
Stockwerk floor **IV U2**, 44
Stöhnen groan **IV U1**, 10
stöhnen to groan **IV U3**, 74
stolz (auf) proud (of) **II**
stoppen to stop **I**
stören *to get in the way **II**; to bother **IV U1**, 15
Story story, stories (pl) **I**
stoßen to push **II**
Stoßzahn tusk **III**
strahlend bright **IV U3**, 72
Strand beach **II**
Straße road **II**
Straße (in der Stadt) street **I**
  auf der **Straße** in the street **I**
  in der **Straße** in the street **I**
Straßenmusikant/-in busker **IV U3**, 79
Strecke route **II**
Streich trick **I**
  einen **Streich** spielen to play a trick (on) **I**
Streit fight **II**; argument **III**
streiten to argue **IV U2**, 51
  (sich) **streiten** *to fight **II**
streng strict **III**
  streng mit jmdm. sein *to be hard on sb **III**
strikt strict **III**
Strom electricity **III**
Stromausfall power cut **II**
Strophe verse **III**
Struktur structure **III**
Stück piece **I**
  pro **Stück** each **I**
  Stück für **Stück** bit by bit **IV TS1**, 35
  Stück Papier piece of paper **I**
  Stück Schrott piece of junk **III**
Student/-in student **I**
Studie survey **I**
studieren to study **III**
Studio studio **IV U3**, 72
Studium studies (pl) **II**
Stufe step **I**
Stuhl chair **I**
stumm silent **III**
Stunde hour **II**; period (AE) **IV U2**, 48
  eine halbe **Stunde** half an hour **III**
Stundenplan timetable **I**; schedule (AE) **IV AC4**, 106
Sturm storm **I**
stürzen *to fall down **III**
stützen auf to base on **IV U3**, 74
Such- search **II**
Suche search **II**

suchen (nach) to search for **IV U1**, 14
  suchen nach to look for **I**
Süchtige/-r addict **IV U1**, 10
Süd- south **II**
Süden south **II**
Südkoreaner/-in South Korean **II**
Südkoreanisch South Korean **II**
südkoreanisch South Korean **II**
(der) Südwesten (the) Southwest **IV AC2**, 38
im Südwesten (the) Southwest **IV AC2**, 38
südwestlich (the) Southwest **IV AC2**, 38
summen to hum **II**
super great; cool **I**; awesome **IV AC2**, 41;
  massive **IV AC2**, 41; super **IV U2**, 44
Superlativ superlative **II**
Supermacht superpower **II**
Supermarkt supermarket **I**
Suppe soup **IV U1**, 11
Surfen surfing **III**
suspendiert werden *to be suspended
  IV AC3, 68
süß cute; sweet **I**
Süßigkeiten sweets *(pl)* **I**
Swimmingpool swimming pool **III**
Symbol symbol **II**
symbolisieren to symbolize *(AE)* **IV AC2**, 40
Szene scene **I**; in-crowd; sequence **III**

T

Tabak tobacco *(no pl)* **III**
Tabelle grid **I**
Tablet tablet **II**
Tablette pill **II**
Taekwondo taekwondo **II**
Tafel board **III**; tablet **IV U3**, 74
die Tafelrunde the Round Table **III**
Tag day **I**
  sich den Tag freinehmen *to take the day
  off **IV U3**, 72
  am nächsten Tag the next day **II**
  den ganzen Tag all day **II**
  ein Tag in … a day out in … **II**
  eines Tages one day **II**
  pro (Tag/Woche/Jahr) a (day/week/year)
  IV AC2, 39
Tagebuch diary **III**
Tagebucheintrag diary entry **III**
Tagung conference **IV U3**, 72
Takelage rigging **I**
Talent talent **I**
Talentwettbewerb talent show **I**
Talisman lucky charm **I**
Tantchen auntie **IV AC4**, 107
Tante aunt **I**
Tanz dance **III**
tanzen to dance **I**
  tanzen zu to dance to **III**
Tänzer/-in dancer **II**
Tanzveranstaltung dance **III**
tapfer brave **I**
Tasche bag **I**; pocket **III**

Taschengeld pocket money **I**
Taschenlampe torch **II**
Tasse cup **III**
Tätowierung tattoo **III**
Tatsache fact **II**
Tatsachenbericht news report **III**
Tattoe tattoo **III**
Rollen tauschen to swap roles **I**
täuschen to trick **IV TS3**, 103
Täuschung hoax **IV TS3**, 102
tausende (von) thousands of **I**
Taxi taxi **II**
Team team **II**
Technik Technology **II**; engineering; tech
  IV TS3, 102
Techniker/-in engineer **IV TS3**, 101
technische Spielerei gadget **III**
Technologie technology **II**; tech **IV TS3**, 102
Tee tea **I**
Teebeutel tea bag **III**
Teenager teenager **I**; teen **III**
Teich pond **I**
Teig pastry **IV U3**, 75
Teigtasche pastry **IV U3**, 75
Teil part **I**
  im hinteren Teil at the back of **II**
teilen to share **II**
teilnehmen to participate **II**
teilnehmen (an) *to take part (in) **II**
Telefon phone; telephone **I**
  Telefon mit Wählscheibe rotary phone **III**
Telefonanruf phone call **I**
telefonieren to phone **IV TS1**, 31
Telefonzelle phone box **IV U1**, 17
Teller plate **III**
vom Tellerwäscher zum Millionär rags to
  riches **IV U3**, 79
Temperatur temperature **IV AC2**, 38
Tennis tennis **I**
Teppich carpet **II**
Terminkalender schedule *(AE)* **IV AC4**, 106
Test test **I**
  einen Test machen *to take a test **II**
testen to test **III**
teuer expensive **I**
Teufel devil **IV TS1**, 31
Text text **I**; lines *(pl)* **IV TS1**, 30
Theater theatre **I**; drama **II**; theater *(AE)*
  IV U3, 70
Theaterstück play **III**
eine Theaterszene spielen acting a scene **I**
Thema theme **I**; topic **II**; subject **III**
Theorie theory **IV TS3**, 102
Therme baths *(pl)* **III**
Ticket ticket **I**
tief deep **III**
  tief Luft holen to gasp **IV U3**, 72
Tier animal **I**
Tierarzt/Tierärztin vet **I**
Tierheim animal shelter **III**
Tierpark zoo **II**
Tierwelt *(in freier Wildbahn)* wildlife **II**

Tipp tip **I**; hint **III**
Tisch table **I**
Titel heading **I**; title **II**
Titelblatt cover **III**
tja well **I**
Toast toast **I**
Tochter daughter **III**
Tod death **III**
Toilette toilet **I**; restroom *(AE)* **IV U2**, 43
tolerant tolerant **IV TS1**, 36
toll great **I**; amazing **II**
Tomate tomato, tomatoes *(pl)* **I**
Tombola raffle **I**
Ton sound **I**
Tonmodell model **I**
Tonpfeife clay pipe **II**
Tonstudio recording studio **I**
Tor goal **I**
Torte cake **I**
Tortenguss jelly **I**
tosend roaring **III**
tot dead **II**
total totally **IV AC4**, 107
Totale *(Kameraeinstellung)* long shot
  IV U3, 89
töten to kill **III**
Tour tour **II**
Tourismus tourism **III**
Tourist/-in tourist **I**
Touristeninformation tourist information
  centre **I**; tourist board **III**
Tradition tradition **I**
traditionell traditional **III**
tragen to carry **II**
tragen *(Kleidung)* *to wear **I**
Trainer/-in coach **I**
trainieren to practise **I**; to train **II**; to practice *(AE)* **IV U2**, 45
Training training **II**; practice **III**
Traktor tractor **IV AC2**, 38
Transport transport **III**
transportieren to transport **IV U3**, 79
Er traute seinen Augen nicht. He couldn't
  believe his eyes. **II**
Traum dream **II**
Traum- fantasy **I**
träumen *to dream dri:m **IV U2**, 47
traurig sad **I**
treffen *to meet; *to hit **I**
  sich auf halbem Weg treffen *to meet
  halfway **III**
  sich treffen *to meet **I**; *to meet up
  IV U2, 44
  sich treffen (mit) *to hang out (with)
  (infml) **III**
treffend to the point **III**
Ich lasse mich treiben. I go wherever the
  wind takes me. **IV U1**, 19
Treppe stairs *(pl)* **III**
treten to kick **II**; to step **IV TS3**, 101
Trick trick **I**; hoax **IV TS3**, 102
Trifle *(englischer Nachtisch)* trifle **I**

trinken *to drink **I**
Trinkgeld tip **IV U3**, 76
Trip trip **II**
trocken dry **III**
trotzdem anyway **II**
   und **trotzdem** yet **IV U3**, 76
Tschüss! Bye! **II**
T-Shirt T-shirt **I**
Tudor- Tudor **III**
tun *to do; *to make **I**
   tun als ob to act like **II**; to pretend
   IV U1, 17
   was man **tun** und was man nicht **tun** sol-
   lte dos and don'ts **IV AC1**, 22
Tunnel tunnel **I**
Tür door **I**
Türklingel doorbell **III**
Turm tower **III**
Turnhalle gym(nasium) **IV AC3**, 68
Turnier competition **II**
Turnschuh trainer **III**
Turteltauben lovebirds *(pl)* **II**
Tüte bag **I**
Tutorial tutorial **IV TS3**, 100
Tutorium tutorial **IV TS3**, 100
Typ guy **II**; type **III**
Typ *(ugs.)* bloke *(fam)* **III**
typisch typical **I**
typisch typically **III**

U

U-Bahn underground **II**; subway *(AE)*
   IV U3, 74
   die Londoner **U-Bahn** the Tube **II**
Übelkeit verspüren *to feel sick **II**
Üben practising **I**
üben to practise **I**; to practice *(AE)* **IV U2**, 45
über about; over; across **I**
   über Nacht overnight **III**
überall everywhere **I**
überall (in) all over **I**
überall (egal, wo) anywhere **II**
   praktisch **überall** just about anywhere
   IV TS2, 64
überfallen to invade **III**
überfliegen to skim **II**
überfüllt crowded **IV AC1**, 23
sich übergeben *to be sick **IV U1**, 16
überhaupt at all **I**
überladen overloaded **IV U1**, 16
(sich) überlappen to overlap **IV U3**, 89
Überlass das mir. Leave that to me. **IV U3**, 72
überleben to survive **III**
Überlebende/-r survivor **IV U2**, 45
übernachten to stay **III**
Übernachtung sleepover **I**
übernatürlich supernatural **IV U1**, 19
überprüfen to check **I**
überqueren to cross **II**
überraschen to surprise **II**
überraschend surprising **II**

überrascht sein *to be surprised **II**
Überraschung surprise **I**
überreagieren to overreact **II**
überreden to persuade **II**
Überschrift heading **I**; title **II**
übersetzen to translate **I**
Übersetzung translation **I**
übertreiben to exaggerate **IV TS1**, 32; *to
   overdo **IV U2**, 55
übertrieben exaggerated **IV U2**, 52
jmdn. überzeugen *to win sb over **IV TS2**, 64
überzeugen to convince **II**
überzeugend persuasive **III**; convincing
   IV U1, 21
überzeugt convinced **IV TS1**, 31
üblich usual **III**
übrig left **I**
Übung exercise **I**; practice **III**
Übungsheft exercise book **I**; workbook
   IV TS1, 37
Ufer bank; shore **II**
UFO UFO **II**
Uhr clock **I**
   Um wie viel **Uhr**? What time? **I**
   Wie viel **Uhr** ist es? What's the time? **I**
Uhr *(Zeitangabe bei vollen Stunden)*
   o'clock **I**
um *(bei Uhrzeitangaben)* at **I**
   um halb acht at 7:30 **I**
   um … herum around **I**; round **II**
   Um wie viel Uhr? What time? **I**
umarmen to hug **I**
umbringen to kill **III**
(sich) umdrehen to turn round **II**; to turn **III**
Umfrage survey **I**
Umgebung environment; set **III**
umgehen mit *to deal (with) **II**
umher around **I**
umkehren to turn back **II**
umkippen *to fall over **I**
sich umschauen to explore **I**
umschreiben *to rewrite **III**
umsegeln to sail **III**
umsonst for free **IV U3**, 72
umsteigen (in) to change (onto) **II**
umwandeln in to turn into **IV U1**, 14
Umwelt environment **III**
umziehen to move (house) **III**
unabhängig independent **III**
Unabhängigkeit freedom *(no pl)*; independence *(no pl)* **III**
unaufhörlich steady **IV U1**, 17
unausgereift undeveloped **IV TS3**, 105
nicht unbedingt not necessarily **IV U3**, 76
unbekannt unfamiliar **III**
unbequem inconvenient **IV TS3**, 100
und and **I**
unehrlich dishonest **IV TS1**, 34
unentwickelt undeveloped **IV TS3**, 105
unerwartet unexpected **IV U3**, 91
unfair unfair **II**
Unfall accident **II**

unfreundlich unfriendly **II**
ungefähr about **I**
ungefährlich safe **II**
Ungeheuer monster **I**
ungehorsam sein to disobey **III**
unglaublich amazing **II**
Unglück disaster **II**
unheimlich scary **II**
unhöflich rude **I**; impolite **III**
Uniform uniform **I**
unkompliziert easy-going **IV U1**, 19
Unmengen von/an a pocketful of **IV U3**, 70
unmöglich impossible **IV TS3**, 102
unordentlich messy **III**
Unordnung mess **IV U2**, 54
unrealistisch unrealistic **IV U2**, 52
nicht ganz **unrecht** haben *to have a point
   III
unrecht haben *to be wrong **I**
unrechtmäßig illegal **III**
unregelmäßig irregular **I**
Unruhestifter/-in troublemaker **IV U2**, 53
uns us **I**
unscharf out of focus **III**
unser/-e our **I**
unsicher unsure **IV TS1**, 31; insecure **IV U2**, 47
unsichtbar invisible **IV U1**, 17
unten downstairs **II**
   nach **unten** down **II**
   nach **unten** gehen *to go down **I**
unten below **I**
unter under **I**; among **III**
untergehen *to sink **III**
im Untergeschoss downstairs **II**
unterhalb below **I**
unterhalten to entertain **IV TS1**, 30
unterhaltsam entertaining **IV TS3**, 103
Unterhaltung conversation **I**; entertainment
   (no pl) **III**; talk **IV U3**, 92
Unterhaltungskünstler/-in entertainer
   IV U3, 72
Unternehmen company **III**
unternehmen wegen *to do about **II**
Unterricht lesson **I**; class **II**
   zeitweilig vom **Unterricht** ausgeschlossen
   werden *to be suspended **IV AC3**, 68
unterrichten *to teach **II**
Unterrichtsstunde lesson **I**; period *(AE)*
   IV U2, 48
Unterschied difference **I**; contrast **IV AC2**, 38
unterschiedlich different **I**
unterschreiben to sign **IV U2**, 52
unterstreichen to underline **III**
unterstützen to support **IV TS1**, 36
Unterstützung benefit **IV U2**, 51
Untersuchung research *(no pl)* **III**
Untertitel caption **III**
unterwegs out and about **II**; on the move
   IV U1, 8
unterzeichnen to sign **IV U2**, 52
unverschämt rude **I**
unwohl sick **II**

üppig lavish **IV U1**, 19
Ureinwohner/-in Amerikas Native American **IV U2**, 45
Urlaub holiday **I**; vacation *(AE)* **IV AC2**, 41
   Seid ihr im **Urlaub**? Are you on holiday? **I**
   Sind Sie im **Urlaub**? Are you on holiday? **I**
Ursprung origin **IV U1**, 19
ursprünglich original **III**
ursprünglich originally **II**
US-amerikanisch US **IV AC2**, 41
usw. *(= und so weiter)* etc. *(= et cetera)* **II**

V

Vanillepudding custard **I**
Vanillesoße custard **I**
Vater father **I**
Vegetarier/-in vegetarian **III**
vegetarisch vegetarian **III**
Verabredung date **IV U2**, 55
Veränderung change **III**
verängstigt scared **IV U2**, 52
Veranstaltung event **I**
verantwortlich responsible **IV U1**, 16
die **Verantwortung** tragen (für) *to be in charge (of) **III**
verantwortungsvoll responsible **IV U1**, 16
jmdn. verärgern *to make sb angry **III**
verärgert angry **I**
Verb verb **I**
verbessern to improve **I**
   sich **verbessern** to improve **I**
verbieten to ban **III**
verbinden *to put through **I**; to join; to link **II**; to combine **IV U3**, 75
Verbindung link **II**; connection **III**; combination **IV U3**, 75
verblüfft amazed **IV U2**, 52
Ge- und **Verbote** dos and don'ts **IV AC1**, 22
Verbrechen crime **III**
Verbrecher/-in criminal **III**
verbrennen *to burn **III**
verbringen *(Zeit)* *to spend **II**
verdienen to earn **I**; to deserve **II**
   Geld **verdienen** *to make money **I**
die Augen **verdrehen** to roll one's eyes **III**
Verein club **I**; society **III**
Verfasser/-in writer **III**
verfolgen to trace **I**
verfügbar available **IV TS2**, 65
verführerisch tempting **IV TS1**, 33
Vergangenheit past **II**
Vergangenheitsform simple past; past form **II**
vergeben *to forgive **II**
etw. vergeigen to mess sth up **IV TS1**, 30
vergessen *to forget **I**
Vergleich comparison **II**
vergleichen (mit) to compare (with/to) **I**
verhaften to arrest **II**
Verhaftung detention **IV AC3**, 68

Verhalten behaviour *(no pl)* **IV AC1**, 22; behavior *(no pl)* *(AE)* **IV AC3**, 69
sich verhalten to behave **III**
sich verirren *to get lost **III**
Verkauf sale **II**
verkaufen *to sell **I**
Verkäufer/-in assistant **II**
Verkäufer/-in *(auf einem Flohmarkt)* seller **I**
Verkehr traffic **IV U1**, 14
Verkehrsmittel transport **III**
   öffentliche **Verkehrsmittel** public transport *(no pl)* **II**
Verkleidung fancy dress **II**
verlassen *to leave **II**
   sich **verlassen** (auf) to rely (on) **III**
verlässlich reliable **IV TS3**, 100
verlegen embarrassed **II**
verleihen *to lend **III**
verletzen *to hurt **II**
verletzt hurt **II**; wounded **III**
Verletzung injury **II**
verlieren *to lose **II**
verloren gehen *to get lost **III**
vermeiden to avoid **III**
vermieten to rent (out) **III**
vermischen to mix (up) **III**
vermissen to miss **III**
vermuten to guess **I**
verneint negative **III**
   verneinte Form negative form **I**
Vernissage gallery walk **I**
vernünftig sensible **IV TS1**, 32
Verpackung wrapping **I**
verpassen to miss **II**
verraucht smoky **III**
sich den Knöchel verrenken to twist your ankle **II**
verrückt crazy **I**; mad **II**
   verrückt sein nach *to be crazy about **IV U2**, 47
   verrückt werden *to go crazy **II**
Vers verse **III**
Versammlung assembly **II**
versäumen to miss **II**
   versäumen, etw. zu tun to fail to do sth **IV U3**, 79
verschenken *to give away **IV TS2**, 64
verschieden different **I**; separate **II**
verschiedene several **II**
verschmutzen to litter **IV AC1**, 22
Verschmutzung pollution **II**
verschütten *to spill **IV U1**, 10
verschwenden to waste **II**
verschwenderisch lavish **IV U1**, 19; wasteful **IV AC2**, 40
Verschwendung waste **IV AC3**, 69
verschwommen blurred **III**
Verschwörung conspiracy **IV TS3**, 102
verschwunden missing **II**
   verschwunden sein *to be gone **II**
sich versichern *to make sure **I**
Version version **III**

versorgen to supply **III**
Verspätung delay **IV U1**, 15
versprechen to promise **III**
Verstand mind **III**
sich verständigen to communicate **II**
Verständnis understanding **II**
(sich) verstecken *to hide **III**
verstehen *to understand **I**
versuchen to try **II**
Versuchung temptation **IV TS2**, 64
   in **Versuchung** führen to tempt **IV TS1**, 31
   in **Versuchung** gebracht tempted **IV TS1**, 31
verteilen *to give away **IV TS2**, 64
vertrauen to trust **III**
vertrauen (auf) to rely (on) **III**
vertrauenswürdig reliable **IV TS3**, 100
nicht vertraut unfamiliar **III**
Vertuschung cover-up **IV TS3**, 102
verunreinigen to litter **IV AC1**, 22
verursachen to cause **II**
vervollständigen to complete **IV AC3**, 68
verwenden to use **I**; *to make use of **IV U3**, 89
verwirrt confused **III**
verwischt blurred **III**
verwundet wounded **III**
verzeihen *to forgive **II**
verzieren to decorate **I**
Verzögerung delay **IV U1**, 15
Video video **II**
Videochat video chat **II**
viel/-e lots (of); a lot of **I**
viel a lot **I**; much **I**
   so viel that much **III**
   viel zu lernen a lot to learn **I**
   viel Glück good luck **IV U3**, 76
viele many **I**
   Viele Grüße Best wishes **III**
vielleicht maybe **I**; perhaps **III**
Vielvölker- multi-ethnic **II**
vier four **I**
Viertel nach/vor quarter past/to **I**
Viktorianer/-in Victorian **III**
viktorianisch Victorian **III**
violett purple **III**
Visum, Visa *(Pl.)* visa, visas *(pl)* **IV U1**, 9
Vitamin vitamin **III**
Vogel bird **II**
Vogelbeobachtung birdwatching **II**
Vokabular vocabulary **I**
Volks- ethnic **IV U3**, 75
Volksentscheid referendum **III**
Volksstamm tribe **III**
voll (von) full (of) **I**
vollenden to complete **IV AC3**, 68
Volleyball volleyball **I**
völlig complete **IV AC2**, 41
völlig absolutely **II**; completely **III**; quite **IV U1**, 14; totally **IV AC4**, 107
vollkommen perfect **I**
vollständig complete **IV AC2**, 41

von from; about; of **I**; by **III**
  von … bis from … to **I**
vor in front of **I**
vor *(bei Uhrzeitangaben)* to **I**
vor *(zeitlich)* before **I**; ago **II**
  nicht **vor** not until **IV U2**, 44
  vor dem Lesen pre-reading **I**
Voraussage prediction **III**
vorbei over **II**
vorbei (an) past **I**
vorbereiten to prepare **I**
Vorder- front **III**
Vordergrund foreground **IV U2**, 47
Vorderseite front **III**
sich **vordrängeln** to jump the queue **I**
Vorgarten front yard *(AE)* **IV U2**, 43
Vorgehensweise approach **IV TS2**, 66
vorgeschichtlich prehistoric **III**
vorhaben *to be up to **II**
vorher before **II**
Vorhersage prediction **III**
vorkommen *to come up **III**
laut **vorlesen** *to read out loud **III**
Vorlieben likes *(pl)* **IV U2**, 46
Vormittag morning **I**
vormittags in the mornings **I**
vormittags *(Uhrzeit)* a.m. **I**
Vorort suburb **IV U2**, 43
Vorrang priority **IV TS3**, 101
Vorschlag suggestion **I**
vorschlagen to suggest **IV U1**, 15
Vorsicht! Be careful! **I**
vorsichtig careful **II**
Vorsingen audition **I**
laut **vorsingen** *to sing out loud **III**
Vorsprechen audition **III**
Vorstadt- suburban **IV U2**, 43
vorstellen to present **I**
  sich (etwas) **vorstellen** to imagine **I**
  Stelle/Stellt … vor. Introduce … **I**
Vorstellung introduction **II**; performance **IV TS1**, 30
Vorstellungskraft imagination **III**
Vortanzen audition **III**
vortäuschen to fake **II**; to pretend **IV U1**, 17
Vorteil benefit **IV U2**, 51
Vortrag presentation **I**; talk **IV U2**, 43
  einen **Vortrag** halten *to give a talk **IV U2**, 43
vortragen to recite **III**
vorüber over **II**
vorüber (an) past **I**
vorwärts forward **III**
vorziehen to prefer **IV U2**, 50

W

Wach- security **IV U1**, 13
Wachdienst security **IV U1**, 13
Wache guard **II**
Wachs wax **II**
wachsen *to grow **III**

Wachsfigur wax figure **II**
Wächter/-in guard **II**
wackelig wobbly **II**
Wackelpudding jelly **I**
Waffe weapon **III**
hier: **Wagen** truck *(AE)* **IV U3**, 75
Wer nicht **wagt**, der nicht gewinnt. No risk, no fun! **IV AC3**, 69
Wahl choice **II**; option **III**
wählen to vote **I**; *to choose **II**
  den richtigen Zeitpunkt **wählen** to time **IV U3**, 72
Telefon mit **Wählscheibe** rotary phone **III**
wahr true **II**
  wahr werden *to come true **IV U3**, 76
während *(+ Nomen)* during *(+ noun)* **II**
während while; as **I**
Wahrheit truth **IV U1**, 13
wahrnehmen to notice **II**
wahrscheinlich probably **II**
Währung currency **IV U1**, 9
Wald forest **II**; wood **III**
Wäldchen wood **III**
Waliser/-in Welsh **II**
Walisisch Welsh **II**
walisisch Welsh **II**
Wand wall **I**
Wandern walking **II**; hiking **III**
Wanderweg walking trail **III**
Wandschrank closet **IV U2**, 44
wann when **I**
  wann immer whenever **II**
warm warm **III**
warnen to warn **IV TS1**, 34
warten (auf) to wait (for) **I**
  (einen Augenblick) **warten** *to hang on **IV U1**, 10
  Warte/Wartet und denk/denkt nach. Stop and think **I**
  Warte ab! Wait and see! **I**
Warteschlange queue **I**
warum why **I**
was what **I**
  was auch immer whatever **IV AC4**, 107
  was für ein what **I**
  Was fehlt? What is missing? **I**
  Was für ein Glück! What luck! **III**
  Was für ein/-e … What a … **IV U2**, 48
  Was geht ab? What's going on? **III**
  Was hast du? What's the matter? **III**
  Was ist das? What's that? **I**
  Was ist dein/-e Lieblings…? What's your favourite …? **I**
  Was ist die Regel für …? What's the rule for …? **I**
  Was ist los? What's the matter?; What's up?; What's going on? **III**
  Was ist mit …? What about …? **I**
  was noch what else **I**
  was sonst what else **I**
  Was um alles in der Welt …? What on earth …? **II**

waschen to wash **I**
  sich **waschen** to wash **I**
Waschmaschine washing machine **II**
Wasser water **I**
Wasserrutsche water slide **I**
Wasserspender water fountain **IV AC4**, 106
Wau! Woof! **I**
Webdesigner web designer **III**
Webseite site **II**
Website website **I**
Wechsel change **III**
Wechselgeld change **IV U3**, 76
wechseln to change **II**
  Wechselt euch ab. Take turns. **I**
Wecker alarm clock **II**
Weg way **I**; path **IV U3**, 92
  im **Weg** sein/stehen *to be in the way **I**
  im **Weg** stehen *to get in the way **II**
weg away **I**
  weg sein *to be gone **II**
  Es ist **weg**. It's gone. **II**
wegen because of; for **II**
wegfahren *to drive off **III**
wegführen *to lead off **III**
wegnehmen *to take **III**
wegrennen *to run away **I**
wegwerfen *to throw away **I**
weh tun *to hurt **II**
Weide field **II**
Weihnachten Christmas **I**
weil because **I**
eine **Weile** a while **II**
Wein wine **I**
weinen to cry **III**
auf andere **Weise** in other ways **II**
weiß white **I**
weit far **II**; wide **III**
  weiter (weg) further **III**
  zu **weit** gehen *to overdo **IV U2**, 55
hier: **weiter** tun *to keep **IV U2**, 44
weitere more; other **I**
weiterführen *to go on **I**
weitergeben to pass (on) **I**
weitergehen *to go on **I**; to continue **IV U1**, 18
weitermachen *to go on **I**; to continue **III**
Weizen wheat **IV AC2**, 41
welche/-r/-s what; which **I**
  Welche Farbe hat …? What colour is …? **I**
  Welche … sind es? What are …? **I**
Welle wave **I**
Welt world **I**
  aus aller **Welt** from around the world **III**
  Was um alles in der **Welt** …? What on earth …? **II**
Weltall space **IV TS3**, 104
Weltraum space **IV TS3**, 104
wem who **I**; whom **IV TS1**, 37
wen who **I**; whom **IV TS1**, 37
  Für **wen** …? Who … for? **I**
wenden to turn round **II**
  sich **wenden** an to turn to **III**

Wendepunkt turning point **III**
Wendung expression **II**
ein **wenig** a little **I**; a bit **II**
  für/mit **wenig** Geld on a shoestring
  IV U3, 72
wenige a few **I**; few **II**
weniger less **III**
wenigstens at least **II**
wenn when; if **I**
  Wenn ich du wäre … If I were you …
  IV AC3, 69
wer who **I**
  Wer ist dabei? Who's in? **II**
  Wer ist es? Who is it? **I**
  Wer macht mit? Who's in? **II**
Werbefachmann/-frau advertiser **IV TS2**, 64
werben to advertise **IV TS2**, 64
Werbespot advert **III**; ad **IV TS2**, 64
Werbespruch slogan **II**
Werbetext ad copy **IV TS2**, 65
Werbung advertising (no pl) **IV TS2**, 64
  Werbung machen to advertise **IV TS2**, 64
werden *to become **II**; *to get **III**
werden (futurisch) will **III**
wird/werden gonna (= going to) (coll)
  IV U3, 70
würde/-st/-n/-t would **III**
werfen (nach) *to throw (at) **I**
Werk factory **III**
Werkzeug tool **III**
wert sein *to be worth **I**
das **Wesentliche** gist **II**
West- west **I**
Westen west **I**
  im äußersten **Westen** in the far west **III**
westeuropäische Zeit Greenwich Mean
  Time (= GMT) **I**
Wettbewerb contest **I**; competition **II**
  in **Wettbewerb** treten (mit) to compete
  (with) **III**
ich **wette** I bet **II**
Wetter weather **I**
Wettervorhersage weather forecast **III**
Wettkampf contest **I**
Wettlauf race **II**
Whisky whisky **III**
wichtig important **I**
  wichtig nehmen to care (about) **II**
wie like **I**; as **II**
wie how **I**
  wie auch immer whatever **IV AC4**, 107
  Wie viele …? How many …? **I**
  Wie alt bist du? How old are you? **I**
  Wie alt sind Sie? How old are you? **I**
  wie das ist what it's like **II**
  Wie geht es dir? How are you? **I**
  Wie geht es euch? How are you? **I**
  Wie geht es Ihnen? How are you? **I**
  Wie heißen Sie? What's your name? **I**
  Wie heißt du? What's your name? **I**
  Wie man … How to … **I**
  Wie spät ist es? What's the time? **I**

Wie viel (kostet/kosten) …? How much
  is/are …? **I**
Wie viel Uhr ist es? What's the time? **I**
Wie war es? What was it like? **III**
Wie wär's mit …? What about …? **I**
wieder again **I**
Wiederaufbereitung recycling **II**
Wiederaufnehmen pick-up **I**
wiedergeben to report **IV U1**, 9
wiederholen to repeat **II**
Wiederholung revision **II**; repetition
  IV U1, 15
auf **Wiedersehen** goodbye **I**
wiegen to weigh **III**
Wiese field **II**
Wikitext wiki (text) **IV TS3**, 101
wild wild **III**
Wilderei poaching (no pl) **III**
Wildnis bush **III**
Willkommen! Welcome! **II**
willkommen heißen to welcome **II**
Wind wind **III**
Windsurfen windsurfing **III**
Winter winter **III**
Winterschlaf hibernation **III**
winzig tiny **III**
wir we **I**
  Wir sind aus … We're from … **I**
wirklich real **II**
wirklich really **I**
Wirksamkeit effectiveness **IV TS2**, 67
Wirkung effect **IV U3**, 89
wirkungsvoll effective **IV TS2**, 66
wirr confused **III**
wissen *to know **I**
  Du **weißt**, wie man … You know how
  to … **I**
  Ich **weiß** (es) nicht! I don't know! **I**
  Ihr **wisst**, wie man … You know how
  to … **I**
Wissenschaft science **IV TS3**, 100
Wissenschaftler/-in scientist **III**
Witz joke **I**
witzig funny; fun **I**
WLAN wifi **IV U1**, 10
wo where **I**
  wo ich hingehöre where I belong **IV U1**, 16
Woche week **I**
Wochenende weekend **I**
  am **Wochenende** at the weekend **I**
Wochentag weekday **II**
Woher …? Where … from? **I**
wohin where **I**
Wohlfahrt charity **I**
wohlhabend wealthy **IV AC2**, 40
wohltätige Zwecke charity **I**
Wohltätigkeitsverein charity **I**
wohnen to live **I**
  wohnen bei to stay with **II**
Wohnung flat **I**; apartment (AE) **IV U2**, 43
  Wohnung mit Dachterrasse penthouse
  IV U3, 79

Wohnzimmer living room **I**
Wolke cloud **III**
Wolkenkratzer skyscraper **IV AC2**, 39
wollen to want (to) **I**
  Ich **wollte** nicht … (I) didn't mean to …
  IV AC4, 107
Workshop workshop **I**
Wort word **I**
Wortbildung word-building **II**
Wörterbuch dictionary **I**
Wörternetz (eine Art Schaubild) mind map **I**
Wörterwolke word cloud **II**
Wortsammlung word bank **III**
Wortschatz vocabulary **I**
Wortschlange word snake **I**
Wortspiel play on words **III**
Wortstellung word order **I**
Wortverbindung collocation **II**
Worum geht es in/im …? What is …
  about? **I**
Wow! Wow! **I**
kein **Wunder** no wonder **IV U2**, 44
wunderbar beautiful; wonderful **II**
Wunsch wish **I**
(sich) **wünschen** to wish **IV U2**, 51
  sich etwas **wünschen** *to make a wish **I**
würde/-st/-n/-t gern would like **I**
  Ich **würde** gern … I'd like to … (= I would
  like to) **I**
  würde/-st/-n/-t sehr gern would love **I**
Würfel dice **II**
würfle zweimal throw the dice twice **II**
  Würfle/Würfelt mit zwei Würfeln. Roll
  two dice. **I**
Wurm worm **I**
Wurst sausage **III**
wusch whoosh **I**
Wüste desert **IV AC2**, 38
Wut anger (no pl) **III**
wütend angry **I**; mad **IV AC3**, 69
  jmdn. **wütend** machen *to make sb angry
  III

Z

z.B. (= zum Beispiel) e.g. (= for example) **I**
Zahl number **I**; figure **III**
zählen (auf) to count (on) **I**
Zahnpasta toothpaste **IV U2**, 56
Zauber- magical **III**
Zauberei magic **IV U1**, 19
Zauberer wizard **III**
auf **Zehenspitzen** gehen to tiptoe **II**
zehn ten **I**
zehnmal ten times **I**
Zeichen sign **II**
Zeichentrickfilm cartoon **III**
zeichnen *to draw **III**
Zeichnung drawing **I**
zeigen to show **I**; to feature **III**
  mit dem Finger auf jmdn./etw. **zeigen** to
  point at sb/sth **IV AC1**, 22

Zeige/Zeigt auf … Point to … **I**
Zeige/Zeigt darauf. Point. **I**
Zeile line **I**
Zeit time **I**; tense **II**
 (**Zeit**) brauchen *to take **II**
 zur selben **Zeit** at the same time **I**
 die ganze **Zeit** all the time **II**
 Es ist **Zeit** aufzustehen! Time to get up! **I**
Zeitalter age **III**; era **IV U1**, 19
 goldenes **Zeitalter** golden age **III**
Zeitfenster time slot **II**
Zeitform (*grammatisch*) tense **II**
zeitgemäß up-to-date **IV TS3**, 100
Zeitpunkt point **II**
 den richtigen **Zeitpunkt** wählen to time
 IV U3, 72
Zeitschrift magazine **I**
Zeitspanne period **III**
Zeitstrahl time line **I**
Zeitung newspaper **III**
zeitweilig vom Unterricht ausgeschlossen
 werden *to be suspended **IV AC3**, 68
Zelten camping **II**
zelten to camp **III**
zentral central **II**
Zentral- central **II**
Zentrum centre **I**; center (*AE*) **IV AC2**, 38
zerbrechen *to break **I**
Zeuge/Zeugin witness **II**
ziehen to pull **I**; *to draw **III**
Ziel goal **I**; purpose **IV U1**, 13; destination
 IV U1, 19; target **IV TS2**, 65
Ziel- target **IV TS2**, 65
Ziellinie finish line **II**
ziemlich quite **IV U1**, 14
Ziffer figure **III**
Zimmer room **I**

Zimmergenosse/Zimmergenossin roommate **I**
Zinn tin **III**
Zitrone lemon **II**
zögern to hesitate **III**
Zoll customs (*sg*) **IV U1**, 9
zollfrei duty-free **IV U1**, 9
Zone zone **IV AC2**, 38
Zoo zoo **II**
Zorn anger (*no pl*) **III**
zornig angry **I**
zu closed **IV U1**, 11
zu too **I**
 Zu dumm! Too bad! **I**
zu to **I**
 zu Hause at home **I**
zubereiten to prepare **I**
züchten *to grow **III**
Zucker sugar **III**
zudecken to cover **III**
zuerst first **I**; at first **II**
Zufall coincidence **IV U2**, 52
sich mit weniger **zufrieden** geben to settle
 for less **IV TS2**, 66
Zug train **I**
Zugang finden zu to relate to **III**
Zuhause home **I**
zuhören to listen (to) **I**
Zuhörer/-in listener **II**
zujubeln to cheer **II**
Zukunft future **III**
zukünftig future **IV U1**, 19
zum Beispiel for example **II**
zumachen to close **I**
zunächst at first **II**
hier: ein Feuerwerk **zünden** *to set off **III**
zuordnen to match **I**
zupassen to pass **II**
sich **zurechtfinden** *to find one's way
 around **IV U2**, 46
(ein Foto) **zurechtschneiden** to crop (a
 photo) **III**

zurück back **I**
zurückfahren to return **III**
zurückgehen to turn back **II**
 zurückgehen auf *to go right back to **III**
zurückkehren to return **III**
zurücklassen *to leave behind **III**
hier: **zurückschrecken** to jump back **II**
zurückspringen to jump back **II**
zurzeit these days **III**
zusammen sein mit *to be around **IV U2**, 44
zusammen together **I**
zusammenfassen to sum up **II**
Zusammenfassung summary **IV TS1**, 37
in **Zusammenhang** stehen *to be connected
 II
zusammenhängen *to be connected **II**
zusammenpassen to mix **IV U2**, 54
zusammenstoßen to crash **III**
zusätzlich extra **I**; additional **II**
zuschauen to watch **I**
Zuschauer/-in viewer **II**
zuspielen to pass **II**
zuständig sein (für) *to be in charge (of) **III**
zustimmen to agree (with) **II**
Zutat ingredient **III**
zuverlässig reliable **IV TS3**, 100
zuvor before **II**
sich **zuwenden** to turn to **III**
zwanglos informal **IV AC4**, 107
Zweck purpose **IV U1**, 13
zwei two **I**
 zwei von ihnen two of which **III**
Zweifel doubt **III**
zweimal twice **IV U2**, 53; double **IV U2**, 57
zweisprachig bilingual **II**
zweite/-r/-s second **I**
Zwickmühle dilemma **IV TS1**, 31
Zwilling twin **III**
Zwillings- twin **III**
zwischen between **I**
zwölf twelve **I**

In the classroom

Asking for help and information

Can you help me, please?	Kannst du / Können Sie mir bitte helfen?
How do you do this exercise?	Wie macht man diese Übung?
How do you spell …, please?	Wie schreibt man …, bitte?
Is this right? I'm not sure.	Ist das richtig? Ich bin mir nicht sicher.
Is it OK to …?	Ist es in Ordnung, wenn ich / wir …?
Is it true or false?	Ist das richtig oder falsch?
Sorry, I don't know. Ask …	Tut mir leid, das weiß ich nicht. Frag …
Sorry. Can you say that again, please?	Wie bitte? Können Sie das bitte wiederholen?
What does that mean?	Was bedeutet das?
What's for homework?	Was haben wir als Hausaufgabe auf?
What's that in English / German?	Was heißt das auf Englisch / Deutsch?

Vocabulary for instructions and activities

(Die mit * gekennzeichneten Begriffe werden im Fachlehrplan von mindestens einem Bundesland als Operatoren definiert. Die Verwendung der geforderten Operatoren in Green Line beginnt in Band 1 und wird Band für Band ausgebaut.)

Act (out) one of the scenes. / Act (out) the dialogues.	Spiele eine der Szenen. / Spiele die Dialoge.
Add more words / ideas.	Füge weitere Wörter / Ideen hinzu.
Ask your partner questions.	Stelle deinem Partner / deiner Partnerin Fragen.
Answer your partner's questions.	Beantworte die Fragen deines Partners / deiner Partnerin.
Check your partner's text.	Überprüfe den Text deines Partners / deiner Partnerin.
Choose a character / one of the situations / options.	Wähle eine Figur / eine der Situationen / Optionen.
Collect ideas.	Sammle Ideen.
*Compare English and German.	Vergleiche das Englische und Deutsche.
Complete the answers.	Vervollständige die Antworten.
Copy the grid / the mind map.	Schreibe die Tabelle / das Wörternetz ab.
Correct the wrong sentences.	Korrigiere die falschen Sätze.
*Describe what you see / how it makes you feel.	Beschreibe, was du siehst / wie du dich dabei fühlst.
Decide who writes which part.	Entscheidet, wer welchen Teil schreibt.

*Discuss different ideas.	Diskutiert verschiedene Ideen.
Divide your class up into two groups.	Teilt eure Klasse in zwei Gruppen auf.
Draw a picture.	Zeichne ein Bild.
Exchange your flyers / questions.	Tauscht eure Flyer / Fragen untereinander aus.
*Explain your answer. / Explain why.	Erkläre deine Antwort. / Erkläre warum.
Fill in your grid / the form.	Fülle deine Tabelle / das Formular aus.
Find the rule / the right word order.	Finde die Regel / die richtige Wortstellung.
Finish your brochure.	Stelle deine Broschüre fertig.
Form expert groups.	Bildet Expertengruppen.
Get organised.	Organisiert euch.
Give reasons. / Give examples / feedback.	Nenne Gründe. / Gib Beispiele / ein Feedback.
Go back to your home group.	Gehe zurück zu deiner ersten Gruppe.
Guess the new words.	Errate die neuen Wörter.
Imagine you're one of the people in the story.	Stelle dir vor, du bist eine der Personen in der Geschichte.
Improve your text / part of the report.	Verbessere deinen Text / Teil des Berichts.
Learn your text by heart.	Lerne deinen Text auswendig.
Listen to the sentences / the dialogue.	Höre dir die Sätze / den Dialog an.
Look at the picture / the examples.	Schau dir das Bild / die Beispiele an.
*Look up the words.	Schlage die Wörter nach.
Make a poster / a grid / a mind map / notes.	Fertige ein Poster / eine Tabelle / ein Wörternetz / Notizen an.
*Match the sentence parts.	Ordne die Satzteile einander zu.
Note down what is missing.	Notiere, was fehlt.
Plan the scenes.	Plane die Szenen.
Practise your scenes / the dialogues.	Übe deine Szenen / die Dialoge.
*Present the information from your text.	Präsentiere die Informationen aus deinem Text.
Put in the correct forms.	Setze die richtigen Formen ein.
Put the verbs in the right / correct form.	Bringe die Verben in die richtige Form.
Read your text aloud. / Read your text out loud.	Lies deinen Text laut vor.
Record your final report / dialogue.	Nehmt euren fertigen Bericht / Dialog auf.
Repeat the sentences / the dialogues.	Wiederhole die Sätze / die Dialoge.
*Report what the people say.	Berichte, was die Leute sagen.
Say the words / the sounds.	Sage die Wörter / die Laute.
Scan the text for details.	Suche den Text nach Details ab.
Share the information with your partner.	Teile die Informationen mit deinem Partner / deiner Partnerin.
Skim the text for the gist.	Überfliege den Text und finde die wichtigsten Aussagen.
*Sum up / Summarise what happens in the story.	Fasse zusammen, was in der Geschichte passiert.
Swap roles.	Tauscht die Rollen.
Take notes.	Mache dir Notizen.
Take turns.	Wechselt euch ab.
*Talk with / to your partner (about …).	Sprich mit deinem Partner / deiner Partnerin (über …).

***Tell** your partner about your experiences.	Erzähle deinem Partner / deiner Partnerin von deinen Erfahrungen.
Think – pair – share.	Nachdenken – Paare bilden – teilen / austauschen.
Think about different problems.	Denke über die verschiedenen Probleme nach.
Think of ideas for …	Überlege dir Ideen für …
***Translate** the words / sentences.	Übersetze die Wörter / Sätze.
Underline the words that change.	Unterstreiche die Wörter, die sich ändern.
Use the ideas / the vocabulary.	Verwende die Ideen / die Vokabeln.
Watch the film.	Sieh dir den Film an.
Work with a partner or in a group.	Arbeite mit einem Partner / einer Partnerin oder in einer Gruppe.
***Write** dialogues / a short text / a reply / a summary.	Schreibe Dialoge / einen kurzen Text / eine Antwort / eine Zusammenfassung.
Write about your friends.	Schreibe über deine Freunde.
Write down your ideas / key words.	Schreibe deine Ideen / Schlüsselwörter auf.

Useful words

activity – Aktivität	presentation – Präsentation; Vortrag
answer – Antwort	prompt card – Rollenkarte
class display – Ausstellung in der Klasse	puzzle – Rätsel; Puzzle
collocation – Wortverbindung	pros and cons – Vor- und Nachteile
description – Beschreibung	question – Frage
dialogue – Dialog	quiz – Quiz; Rätsel
dice – Würfel	quote – Zitat
draft – Entwurf; Konzept	report – Bericht
drawing – Zeichnung	revision – Wiederholung
example – Beispiel	rhyme – Reim
fact – Tatsache; Fakt	role play – Rollenspiel
folder – Ordner; Mappe	rule – Regel
game – Spiel	scene – Szene
grid – Gitter; Tabelle; Raster	signal word – Signalwort
heading – Überschrift	slogan – Slogan; Werbespruch
information – Information(en)	speech bubble – Sprechblase
key word – Schlüsselwort	story – Geschichte; Erzählung
list – Liste	task – Aufgabe
mind map – Wörternetz	theme – Thema
order – Reihenfolge	title – Titel; Überschrift
perspective – Perspektive	unit – Lektion; Kapitel
phrase – Redewendung; Ausdruck	useful phrases – nützliche Ausdrücke
picture story – Bildergeschichte	vocabulary – Vokabular; Wortschatz
point of view – Standpunkt; Ansicht	word bank – Wortsammlung

Grammar solutions

Unit 1

G1   You told us there was free wifi!

A message from Jack

Jack's mother: Jack sent me a message this afternoon. He said that **he'd had** a good trip and that **he'd arrived** safely. **He hadn't had** time to look around yet, so **he couldn't tell me** much, but he said that the hostel **was** clean and the people **were** very friendly. He said **he'd call** again later, but **he didn't know** when because **they were going** into town for dinner and **he wasn't sure** when **they'd be back**.

G2   Steve's blog

Eddie: Steve sent me a message from France last week. He said that the athletics event **had started the day before** and that **their** team **was** doing well. But it **was** very cold **there**. He said that if **he** ever **came back** to **that** place, **he'd bring** warmer clothes. **He wished he'd listened** to Ms W.

G3   He asked me what the purpose of my visit was

1. The man at passport control asked me **why I was** travelling alone.
2. He wanted to know **where I was from**.
3. He asked me **how long I planned** to stay.
4. He wanted to know **if I had** family in Bangladesh.
5. He asked **if I could speak** Bengali.
6. He wanted to know **if anybody was meeting me** at the airport.

G4   He told me to go into a side room

1. Rafiq's mum **asked him to say hello** to everyone from **them**.
2. She **told him to be careful** with his passport and **not to lose it.**
3. She **asked him to call her** as soon as **he got to** Dhaka.
4. She **told him to have fun** while **he was** there and **to take** lots of photos.

Unit 2

G5   Living here isn't bad

1. How about visiting a museum?
2. I don't really feel like going to a museum today.
3. OK, then, what would you suggest doing?
4. Mom keeps telling me about the spectacular views from Mt. Washington.
5. My mom loves going there too.
6. She never stops talking about the place.

G6   That's the worst thing to do!

1. I promise to be home before 6 p.m.
2. I didn't know what to say.
3. My parents don't want me to watch too much TV.
4. I didn't expect him to invite me to his party.
5. They always let her do what she wants.
6. Our football coach makes us train every day.
7. The best thing to do is say nothing at all.

G7   Gerund or infinitive: It depends on the meaning

Dear Diary,
Bad news! I got a mail from Matt today and it seems he can't stop **thinking** about Sophie. I'm sure Matt didn't mean **to hurt** me, but … When I told Madison, she said I should try **to forget** him. But how? M. thinks I should try **doing** yoga! She says she can remember **feeling** upset about something once, and it really helped her. But I'm not sure. I'm not really sure about anything at the moment: Should I go on **writing** to him? Should I tell him how I feel? I don't know. The only thing I know right now is that it's really late and I mustn't forget **to set** my alarm clock! Madison's mom is driving us to the mall outside Pittsburgh tomorrow. We want **to get** there early and it's two hours in the car, so that means **leaving** at 8 a.m.! Oh well, at least we can stop **to have** breakfast somewhere on the way.

Unit 3

G8   The boy who … / Diego, who …

1. Last year we visited **New York**, which is the largest city in the USA.
2. We stayed with **some friends** who live there.
3. They showed us **some amazing sights** which we would never have found on our own.
4. But they also took us to famous sights like **Rockefeller Center**, which was awesome too.
5. In Times Square we saw **the Naked Cowboy**, who is really only almost naked.
6. He is a **street performer** who has become one of New York's biggest tourist attractions.

G9   How long had they been doing that?

After Julia and Andrea from Germany **had been walking** around Manhattan all morning, they were very hungry. So they decided to go to Diego's Diner, which they **had read** about in the guidebook they **had bought** the day before. When they got there at 12:30, the diner was already very busy. Some of the people **had been waiting** to get their lunch for quite some time. The girls **had been learning** English since the age of ten, so they had no language problems. But when they tried to order, nobody seemed to notice them. Finally, after they **had been trying** to get a waiter's attention for about 15 minutes, a friendly Hispanic American came to their table and took their order.

Find more online:
8x6wn6

Irregular verbs

■ ■ ■ Grundform, *simple past* und *past participle* sind identisch
■ ● ● Grundform unterscheidet sich vom *simple past* und *past participle*
■ ● ■ Grundform und *past participle* sind identisch, nur das *simple past* hat eine andere Form
■ ● ▲ Grundform, *simple past* und *past participle* haben alle eine andere Form

■ Grundform	■ simple past	■ past participle	Deutsch
cost [kɒst]	cost [kɒst]	cost [kɒst]	kosten
cut [kʌt]	cut [kʌt]	cut [kʌt]	schneiden
hit [hɪt]	hit [hɪt]	hit [hɪt]	schlagen, treffen
hurt [hɜːt]	hurt [hɜːt]	hurt [hɜːt]	verletzen, sich weh tun
let [let]	let [let]	let [let]	lassen
put [pʊt]	put [pʊt]	put [pʊt]	legen, setzen, stellen
set up ['set ˌʌp]	set up ['set ˌʌp]	set up ['set ˌʌp]	erbauen, errichten
upset [ʌp'set]	upset [ʌp'set]	upset [ʌp'set]	aus der Fassung bringen

■ Grundform	● simple past	● past participle	Deutsch
bring [brɪŋ]	brought [brɔːt]	brought [brɔːt]	(mit)bringen
build [bɪld]	built [bɪlt]	built [bɪlt]	bauen
burn [bɜːn]	burnt [bɜːnt]	burnt [bɜːnt]	(ver)brennen
buy [baɪ]	bought [bɔːt]	bought [bɔːt]	kaufen
catch [kætʃ]	caught [kɔːt]	caught [kɔːt]	fangen; mitbekommen
dream [driːm]	dreamed [driːmd] / dreamt [dremt]	dreamed [driːmd] / dreamt [dremt]	träumen
feel [fiːl]	felt [felt]	felt [felt]	fühlen
find [faɪnd]	found [faʊnd]	found [faʊnd]	finden
get [get]	got [gɒt]	got [gɒt]	holen, bringen, bekommen; werden
hang [hæŋ]	hung [hʌŋ]	hung [hʌŋ]	hängen
have [hæv]	had [hæd]	had [hæd]	haben
hear [hɪə]	heard [hɜːd]	heard [hɜːd]	hören
hold [həʊld]	held [held]	held [held]	halten
keep [kiːp]	kept [kept]	kept [kept]	(auf)bewahren, behalten
lead [liːd]	led [led]	led [led]	(an)führen
learn [lɜːn]	learned [lɜːnd] / learnt [lɜːnt]	learned [lɜːnd] / learnt [lɜːnt]	lernen
leave [liːv]	left [left]	left [left]	(ver)lassen
lend [lend]	lent [lent]	lent [lent]	(ver)leihen
make [meɪk]	made [meɪd]	made [meɪd]	machen, tun
meet [miːt]	met [met]	met [met]	treffen
pay [peɪ]	paid [peɪd]	paid [peɪd]	(be)zahlen
read [riːd]	read [red]	read [red]	lesen
say [seɪ]	said [sed]	said [sed]	sagen
sell [sel]	sold [səʊld]	sold [səʊld]	verkaufen
send [send]	sent [sent]	sent [sent]	senden, verschicken
shoot [ʃuːt]	shot [ʃɒt]	shot [ʃɒt]	schießen (auf)
sit [sɪt]	sat [sæt]	sat [sæt]	sitzen

sleep [sli:p]	slept [slept]	slept [slept]	schlafen
smell [smel]	smelt [smelt]	smelt [smelt]	riechen, duften
spell [spel]	spelt [spelt]	spelt [spelt]	buchstabieren
spend [spend]	spent [spent]	spent [spent]	ausgeben, verbringen
spill [spɪl]	spilt [spɪlt]	spilt [spɪlt]	verschütten, auslaufen
stand (up) [stænd]	stood (up) [stʊd]	stood (up) [stʊd]	(auf)stehen
sting [stɪŋ]	stung [stʌŋ]	stung [stʌŋ]	stechen
tell [tel]	told [təʊld]	told [təʊld]	erzählen
think [θɪŋk]	thought [θɔ:t]	thought [θɔ:t]	(nach)denken, glauben
understand [ˌʌndəˈstænd]	understood [ˌʌndəˈstʊd]	understood [ˌʌndəˈstʊd]	verstehen
win [wɪn]	won [wʌn]	won [wʌn]	gewinnen, siegen

■ Grundform	● simple past	■ past participle	Deutsch
become [bɪˈkʌm]	became [bɪˈkeɪm]	become [bɪˈkʌm]	werden
come [kʌm]	came [keɪm]	come [kʌm]	kommen
run [rʌn]	ran [ræn]	run [rʌn]	laufen, rennen

■ Grundform	● simple past	▲ past participle	Deutsch
be [bi:]	was / were [wɒz / wɜ:]	been [bi:n]	sein
blow (out) [bləʊ]	blew [blu:]	blown [bləʊn]	(aus)blasen, (aus)pusten
break [breɪk]	broke [brəʊk]	broken [ˈbrəʊkn]	(zer)brechen, kaputt machen
choose [tʃu:z]	chose [tʃəʊz]	chosen [tʃəʊzn]	(aus)wählen
do [du:]	did [dɪd]	done [dʌn]	machen, tun
draw [drɔ:]	drew [dru:]	drawn [drɔ:n]	zeichnen
drink [drɪŋk]	drank [dræŋk]	drunk [drʌŋk]	trinken
drive [draɪv]	drove [drəʊv]	driven [ˈdrɪvn]	fahren
eat [i:t]	ate [et]	eaten [i:tn]	essen
fall [fɔ:l]	fell [fel]	fallen [ˈfɔ:lən]	fallen
fly [flaɪ]	flew [flu:]	flown [fləʊn]	fliegen
forget [fəˈget]	forgot [fəˈgɒt]	forgotten [fəˈgɒtn]	vergessen
give [gɪv]	gave [geɪv]	given [ˈgɪvn]	geben
go [gəʊ]	went [went]	gone [gɒn]	gehen, fahren
grow [grəʊ]	grew [gru:]	grown [grəʊn]	wachsen; anbauen
know [nəʊ]	knew [nju:]	known [nəʊn]	kennen, wissen
ring [rɪŋ]	rang [ræn]	rung [rʌŋ]	klingeln; anrufen
rise [raɪz]	rose [rəʊz]	risen [ˈrɪzn]	steigen, sich erheben
see [si:]	saw [sɔ:]	seen [si:n]	sehen
show [ʃəʊ]	showed [ʃəʊd]	shown [ʃəʊn]	zeigen
sing [sɪŋ]	sang [sæn]	sung [sʌŋ]	singen
sink [sɪŋk]	sank [sæŋk]	sunk [sʌŋk]	sinken, untergehen
speak [spi:k]	spoke [spəʊk]	spoken [ˈspəʊkn]	sprechen
swim [swɪm]	swam [swæm]	swum [swʌm]	schwimmen
take [teɪk]	took [tʊk]	taken [ˈteɪkn]	nehmen
throw [θrəʊ]	threw [θru:]	thrown [θrəʊn]	werfen
wake up [ˌweɪkˈʌp]	woke up [ˌwəʊkˈʌp]	woken up [ˌwəʊknˈʌp]	aufwachen; aufwecken
wear [weə]	wore [wɔ:]	worn [wɔ:n]	anhaben, tragen
write [raɪt]	wrote [rəʊt]	written [ˈrɪtn]	schreiben

The US school system

For most kids in the US, school starts at the age of 3–4 with pre-school (or nursery school), which can be compared to German *Kindergarten*. Different to Germany, kindergarten in the US comes after pre-school.

School systems differ around the US, but everywhere high school ends with the **high school diploma** after 12th grade. Then students can decide if they want to find a job or continue their education at college or university. A dual vocational training[1] like in Germany doesn't exist in the US.

State-run schools in the US are called **public schools**. The others are **private schools** mostly operated by religious institutions and organizations.

School takes up a lot of time

In America kids are at school all day. How early the day starts depends on how they get to school – with a school bus, by public or private transportation. Either the kids bring a bag lunch from home or eat a hot lunch in the school cafeteria. But even when classes are over in the afternoon, a lot of kids still don't go home because there are all kinds of activities going on. If you don't have sports practice for a school team, you might have a drama or chess club meeting. That means that many students don't get home until the evening.

Even on the weekend students spend a lot of time at school. Going to school sports events is a big social activity that involves a lot of different students, especially at the high school level. The school band plays at the game, the cheerleaders cheer, the dance team performs at half-time and the school newspaper photographer takes pictures.

High schools typically have formal dances several times a year. The most popular are the homecoming[2] dance after a football game and the prom[3] at the end of the school year.

Other school activities have more to do with the community. The students might organize a food or clothing drive to help poor families. Or

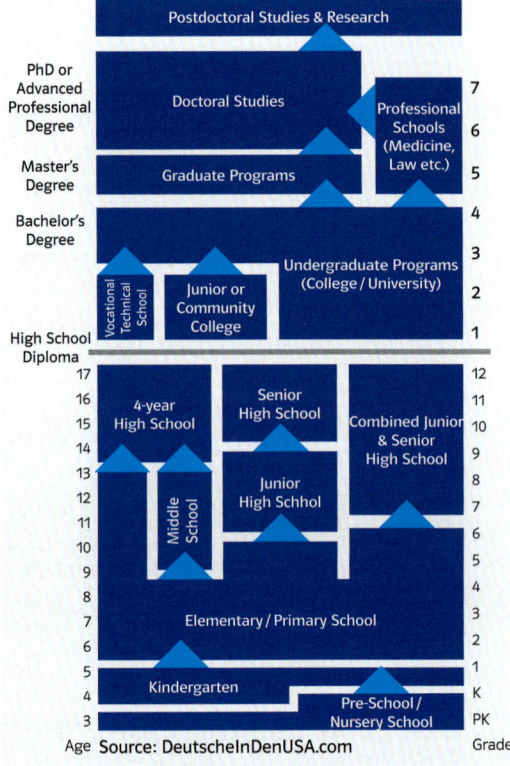

Age Source: DeutscheInDenUSA.com Grade

Surprising facts
- About 2 million students are home-schooled in America.
- Going to a private school can cost $50,000 a year.
- The largest high school in America has over 8,000 students.

they spend their weekend helping to build a playground in the neighborhood. Most of the students really do want to help, but they also know that participating in these activities will look good on their college applications[4]. Getting into a good college or university can be very competitive and kids start thinking about it at the beginning of high school already!

---

1 dual vocational training [duˈaːl voʊˈkeɪʃnl ˈtreɪnɪŋ] duale Berufsausbildung | **2 homecoming** [ˈhoʊmˌkʌmɪŋ] Ehemaligentreffen | **3 prom** [prɒm] *Ball am Ende des Schuljahres* | **4 application** [ˌæplɪˈkeɪʃn] Bewerbung

New York, New York

New York City, which was originally founded as a trading post in 1624, is the largest city in America with an estimated population of 8.6 million people (Berlin has about 3.5 million). In area, New York City is about half the size of Saarland.

The city is divided into five sections called **boroughs**[1]. The borough with the third-largest population is the smallest – **Manhattan**. This is home to the city's famous skyscrapers and three of the world's ten most-visited tourist attractions (Times Square, Central Park and the Grand Central Terminal). About 60 million tourists visit the city each year.

The least-populated borough and probably the most different compared to Manhattan is **Staten Island**. Most of the island is a residential area. It is connected to Brooklyn by a bridge and the free Staten Island Ferry.

The **Bronx** is home to the world's largest metro zoo and the New York Yankees professional baseball team. However, it's probably most well-known as the birthplace of rap and hip-hop culture. More than half of the population is Hispanic.

Queens is the largest borough in area and is considered the most ethnically diverse[3] urban area in the world. Almost 50 % of the residents are foreign-born and 50 % of New York City's Asian population lives here. Queens annually hosts the US Open tennis tournament at Flushing Meadows. Two of the world's busiest airports, John F. Kennedy and LaGuardia, are also located here.

The most populous borough is **Brooklyn**. There is wide cultural, social and ethnic diversity. The rapidly growing Chinese-American population has established[4] several Chinatowns. Brooklyn is also home to a strong independent art scene but also to many high-tech start-ups.

Surprising facts
- New York was originally called New Amsterdam.
- The name 'Manhattan' goes back to the Native American tribe that lived in the area, called the Mannahatta.
- Almost half of the city's residents over the age of five speak a language other than English.

New York's importance in the world

New York City is often called the cultural and financial center of the world. The city is home to the world's two largest stock exchanges[5], where global trading goes on continuously. The United Nations has been located in New York since soon after its creation in 1945. The world's perhaps most famous theater district is simply known by the street that hosts it – Broadway. This is the place to go for plays and musicals. Besides performing arts like the symphony and ballet, there are also important art museums in NY, like the Museum of Modern Art, or MoMA for short. New York City has a huge advertising industry too. It used to be concentrated on Madison Avenue, but has now spread out across the city.

---

1 borough ['bʌrə] Stadtteil | **2 residential** [ˌrezɪ'denʃl] Wohn- | **3 diverse** [daɪ'vɜːs] vielfältig | **4 to establish** [ɪ'stæblɪʃ] gründen | **5 stock exchange** ['stɒk ɪksˌtʃeɪndʒ] Börse

ALASKA
Denali▲
CANADA

CANADA

Seattle
Portland
WASHINGTON

OREGON

IDAHO

MONTANA

NORTH DAKOTA

M

WYOMING

SOUTH DAKOTA

NEBRASKA

San Francisco

NEVADA

UTAH

Denver

COLORADO

KANS

CALIFORNIA

HOLLYWOOD

Las Vegas

ARIZONA

Los Angeles

Pacific Ocean

San Diego

Phoenix

NEW MEXICO

OKLAHOM

TEXAS

HAWAII

MEXICO